POWER
&POLITICS
IN AMERICA
FOURTH
EDITION

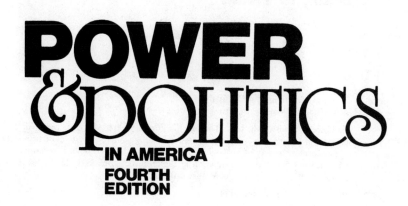

POWER & POLITICS IN AMERICA

FOURTH EDITION

LEONARD FREEDMAN
UNIVERSITY OF CALIFORNIA, LOS ANGELES

BROOKS/COLE PUBLISHING COMPANY
MONTEREY, CALIFORNIA

again, to Vivian

Brooks/Cole Publishing Company
A Division of Wadsworth, Inc.

© 1983 by Wadsworth, Inc., Belmont, California 94002. All rights reserved.
No part of this book may be reproduced, stored in a retrieval system, or transcribed,
in any form or by any means—electronic, mechanical, photocopying, recording, or otherwise—
without the prior written permission of the publisher, Brooks/Cole Publishing Company, Monterey,
California 93940, a division of Wadsworth, Inc.

Printed in the United States of America
10   9   8   7   6   5   4   3   2   1

Library of Congress Cataloging in Publication Data

Freedman, Leonard.
  Power and politics in America.

  Bibliography: p.
  Includes index.
  1. United States—Politics and government—
1945-   . I. Title.
JK274.F923 1982   320.973   82-12867
ISBN 0-534-01252-3

We wish to acknowledge the assistance of Pelican Publishing Company, Inc., in obtaining some of the
cartoons that appear in this book. They are taken from the *Best Editorial Cartoons of the Year* series,
1977, 1979, and 1980 editions. © Pelican Publishing Company, Inc.

Subject Editor: *Marquita Flemming*
Production Editor: *Marlene Thom*
Manuscript Editor: *Lois Oster*
Interior and Cover Design: *Katherine Minerva*
Illustrations: *John Foster*
Typesetting: *Typography Systems International, Dallas, Texas*

Power and Politics in America is cast in terms of controversy. It provides the reader with basic information about our system of government and politics and interprets this information from five sharply differing perspectives.

The framework is provided in chapter 1, which sets up a political spectrum. Along this spectrum five perspectives are identified. First, we define a centrist position, which sees the American system as, on the whole, a remarkably successful model of self-government. Flanking the centrists are liberal and conservative analysts, who argue that there are serious shortcomings in the way our system operates. At the poles of the spectrum are radicals of left and right who, from their respective vantage points, express still harsher, more fundamental dissatisfaction with our political system. The debate established among these five doctrines is pursued throughout the book.

In chapter 2 the context of the debate is the American constitutional system. The chapter begins with historical background: the making and subsequent evolution of the Constitution. This background is followed by five contemporary assessments of the work of the Founding Fathers.

In the four chapters that constitute part two of the book we look at the processes and instrumentalities of American politics—the electorate, parties, elections, and interest groups—and we debate some of the fundamental questions of power in a democracy: To what extent do the people at large affect the direction of public policy? How much involvement in politics do we need? What is the proper role of organized interests?

In part three we analyze the institutions of government: the presidency, Congress, the federal bureaucracies, the Supreme Court, and state and local governments. We explore the separation and division of powers and checks and balances and ask whether they are working today.

Part four applies everything we have dealt with up to that point to some of the overriding public policy issues of our time: the economy, minority rights, the environment and energy, and foreign policy. We examine not only the issues themselves but also the way in which the principal political and governmental institutions have approached these issues. Then we ask from various perspectives: How effective has the system been in dealing with these issues?

In the concluding chapter we sum up, reviewing the strengths and weaknesses of government and politics in America as weighed by each of the five perspectives in turn.

This way of looking at government and politics through rival interpretations has grown out of my own teaching in introductory courses. Why do I use this method? For one thing it reflects the real world of politics: democratic politics, especially the American brand, is made up in large part of conflicting ideas and interests. Then, too, this approach helps students shape their own interpretations out of the various alternatives presented. Although I hold strong beliefs of my own, I am much more interested in seeing students develop *their* capacities for independent critical reasoning than in having them adopt my positions.

However, like all organizing principles this method presents certain difficulties.

First, categorization is as dangerous as it is indispensable, and, at the close of chapter 1, I provide some warnings on the distortions that can result if my categories are used without great care and flexibility.

Then, it was not possible to give equal attention to all five perspectives in each chapter. This book, after all, is about the decision-making process, and the principal actors, the decision makers, have been mostly centrists. Again, I have drawn heavily on political science scholarship, and most of the scholarly writing in this field is by people who operate within a framework of centrism, liberal dissent, or (an increasing factor in the last few years) what is known as neoconservatism. Although the body of radical left writing has been expanding, proponents of the left tend to see economic institutions as more fundamental than governmental and political institutions; thus few of them have written in much detail about the latter. As for the radical right, the only scholarly sources are *about* the right and not *by* the right, so we cannot make more than a few basic points about it in this book. Nonetheless, in most chapters there will be at least some discussion of all five perspectives.

Another difficulty in our emphasis on conflicting interpretations is that it may imply that nothing matters but opinion. But this book is aimed at the development of informed opinion. For this reason the first part of each chapter provides an essential context of information. Then this information is interpreted in the context of varying perspectives. A concluding section attempts to sum up commonalities and divergencies among the perspectives, and suggests some prospects for the future.

A final difficulty is to provide all this information and all these interpretations on so many topics within the span of one book. So I must remind the reader that this text is intended only as an introduction aimed at opening up the workings of the American system in light of contemporary controversies. More exhaustive study will have to be undertaken on each of the subjects dealt with here if the reader is to arrive at more definitive answers to the very large questions I have raised. Accordingly, a Selected Bibliography is offered at the close of the book to help provide further dimensions and more precise formulations and distinctions.

CHANGES FROM THE THIRD (1978) EDITION

Although the general structure of the third edition has been retained, the present edition consitutes a major revision.

First, the main rationale for any new edition is the need to take account of recent research and the march of events. In this case, the required updating has had to be substantial, because developments since the last edition have compelled not only the substitution of new for old data, but also a rather fundamental rethinking and reshaping of most chapters.

The principal reason for these changes, of course, is the election of 1980. Ronald Reagan's victory, together with the election of a Republican majority in the senate, has produced a frontal challenge from the highest levels of the governmental structure to the assumptions and policies of nearly forty years of politics in America. Thus I have had to undertake a major rewriting of the chapters on parties, elections, and interest groups; of the institutional chapters, particularly those chapters on the presidency, Congress, the bureaucracies, and federal-state relations; and of all the public policy chapters, because the Reagan administration's programs dealing with the economy, the poor, blacks and other minorities, energy, the environment, and foreign and defense policies have departed in crucial respects from the programs of its Democratic and Republican predecessors.

Accompanying and reflecting these policy changes is the resurgence of conservative and neoconservative thought that has been taking place since the mid-1970s. One of the debates that recurs throughout this book concerns the extent to which the American electorate has swung toward conservatism, and whether the conservative gains of 1980 foretold a fundamental shift in American politics or were merely a transitory phenomenon. However debatable those questions may be, there is no denying the fact that the attention presently being paid to the ideas of conservative analysts and activists has not been seen in several decades.

An assessment of conservative ideas has been built into the structure of this book ever since its first edition as one of its three most significant perspectives. The fourth edition takes full account of the increased importance of this perspective in the political arena.

One other major change from the previous edition is a new chapter on the constitutional framework. We did not, of course, omit discussion of the U.S. Constitution from the previous editions, but the method we had adopted was to examine the relevant portions of the Constitution at appropriate points throughout the text. Several instructors have suggested that this approach has not given sufficient prominence to the historical context and underlying principles of American government, and I have responded accordingly with a new chapter 2.

In so doing I have been careful to avoid any suggestion that the debates at the Philadelphia convention could be fitted into the political spectrum set up in chapter 1. That spectrum applies to the contemporary political scene and cannot be transplanted two centuries back. However, I have used the spectrum to provide contemporary perspectives on the background and intent of the Framers, on the evolution of the Constitution, and on the viability of the principles of the Constitution today.

It is impossible to give credit to all of those teachers, colleagues, and friends who have been formative influences in the development of this book. The revision has been much affected by the comments of students who were assigned the third edition. It was greatly helped, too, by the suggestions of the following reviewers who provided invaluable assessments of the manuscript's strengths and weaknesses as well as specific comments that led to a number of major improvements: Alan L. Clem, University of South Dakota; Terry Curtis, Santa Rosa Junior College; Byron W. Daynes, De Paul University; Steven M. DeLue, University of Northern Florida; Larry Elowitz, Georgia College; John George, Central State University; Justin Green, Virginia Polytechnic Institute and State University; Bernard Hennessy, California State University, Hayward; Douglas Hobbs, University of California, Los Angeles; Robert Huckshorn, Florida Atlantic University; Loch

Johnson, University of Georgia; Kenneth J. Meier, University of Oklahoma; Michael D. Reagan, University of California, Riverside; Walter A. Rosenbaum, University of Florida; and Thomas G. Walker, Emory University.

Then there were the important contributions of Brooks/Cole editors, especially Marquita Flemming, Henry Staat, and Marlene Thom. Invaluable research assistance was provided by Peter Porehl, who also worked with me on the third edition.

The arduous task of manuscript typing was competently undertaken by Ms. Celia Herrera, Ms. Patricia Nicholas, and Ms. Clare Walker. Ms. Magdalen Suzuki supervised the various stages of preparing the manuscript for the editors with her invariable skill, dedication, and patience. To all of them, my grateful thanks.

Leonard Freedman

CONTENTS

part one: introduction 1

1 FIVE PERSPECTIVES ON THE AMERICAN SYSTEM 2

The Crux of the Debate: Political Power 2
A Political Spectrum 3
The Perspectives Introduced 4
The Basic Differences 7
Summary and Some Warnings 18
Notes and References 22

2 THE CONSTITUTIONAL FRAMEWORK 24

Before the Constitution 24
The Making of the Constitution 25
Basic Principles of the Constitution 28
The Evolution of the Constitution 30
The Constitution Today 32
Five Perspectives on the Constitution 33
Conclusion 39
Notes and References 40

part two: politics and the people 43

3 PUBLIC OPINION: WHO CARES ABOUT POLITICS? 44

What Influences Our Opinions? 44
How Do We Express Our Opinions? 53
The Big Question: How Much Interest Is There in Politics? 54
Five Perspectives on Public Opinion 64
Conclusion 69
Notes and References 70

ix

4   POLITICAL PARTIES: DO WE NEED THEM?   72

       Why Parties?—Their Functions in the Political System   72
       Why Two Parties?   74
       Distinguishing between the Parties   75
       Five Perspectives on Political Parties   86
       Conclusion   96
       Notes and References   98

5   ELECTIONS: MAJORITIES, MEDIA, AND MONEY   100

       Nominating Our Presidential Candidates   101
       General Election Strategies   111
       The Electoral College: Abolish or Reform It?   114
       Campaign Tactics   116
       Money and Elections   123
       Three Perspectives on Elections   128
       Conclusion   134
       Notes and References   135

6   INTEREST GROUPS AND THE PUBLIC INTEREST   138

       The Range of Interests   138
       Political Pressure   142
       Five Perspectives on Interest Groups   145
       Conclusion   154
       Notes and References   155

part three: the institutions of government   157

7   THE PRESIDENCY: TOO MUCH OR TOO LITTLE POWER?   158

       The Expansion of the Presidency   159
       Constraints on Presidential Power   162
       Presidents and Their Approaches to Power   164
       Proposals to Reform the Presidency   183
       Five Perspectives on the Presidency   185
       Conclusion   193
       Notes and References   194

8 THE CONGRESS: OBSTACLE COURSE OR BALANCE WHEEL? 196

The Roles of Congress   196
The Members of Congress   197
Congress and Its Constituencies   198
Power in Congress: Organization and Leadership   204
Congressional Procedures: How a Bill Becomes Law   212
Three Perspectives on Congress   215
Conclusion   226
Notes and References   226

9 THE FEDERAL BUREAUCRACY: A FOURTH BRANCH   228

The Dimensions of the Bureaucracy   228
The Range of Functions   231
Presidential and Congressional Supervision of the Federal Bureaucracy   234
Bureaucratic Automony   235
Five Perspectives on the Federal Bureaucracy   238
Conclusion   251
Notes and References   252

10 THE SUPREME COURT AND CONSTITUTIONAL RIGHTS   254

The Structure of the U.S. Court System   254
The Supreme Court and Judicial Review   255
The Court as an Instrument of the Political System   257
The Court as a Judicial Body   269
Five Perspectives on the Supreme Court   273
Conclusion   280
Notes and References   281

11 FEDERALISM: STATES AND CITIES   283

Characteristics of State and Local Governments   284
Sharing the Power   286
Contemporary Problems of State and Local Government   288
Five Perspectives on Federalism   299
Conclusion   307
Notes and References   307

part four: issues in public policy   309

12   ECONOMIC POLICY: SHARING THE WEALTH   310

What the System Produces   310
Problems Facing the American Economic System   311
The Tools of Government   316
The Economy, Poverty, and the Policy-Making Process   322
Five Perspectives on the Economy and Poverty   334
Conclusion   342
Notes and References   343

13   EQUAL PROTECTION? RACE, ETHNICITY, GENDER   346

The Populations of America   346
Blacks and the American Dilemma   347
Hispanics: A New Assertiveness   355
Other Disadvantaged Minorities   357
Women and the ERA   358
Disadvantaged Groups and the Policy-Making Process   358
Five Perspectives on Minority Rights   367
Conclusion   375
Notes and References   375

14   ENERGY AND THE ENVIRONMENT   378

How the Issues Evolved   378
The Clash of Issues: Environmentalism versus Energy   385
Energy and the Environment: The Policy-Making Process   386
Two Perspectives on Energy and the Environment   395
Conclusion   400
Notes and References   401

15   FOREIGN POLICY: A NEW ERA?   403

U.S. Foreign Policy: The Background   404
Containing Soviet Power   405
Other Dimensions of U.S. Foreign Policy   417
Foreign Affairs and the Policy-Making Process   419
Five Perspectives on Foreign Policy   429
Conclusion   442
Notes and References   443

16 POWER AND POLITICS: A REVIEW OF THE FIVE PERSPECTIVES 446

The Liberals   446
The Radical Left 448
The Conservatives   450
The Radical Right   451
The Centrists   453
Why Bother With Politics?   454
Notes and References   455

Appendix 1: The Constitution of the United States of America   456
Appendix 2: Presidents of the United States   471
Selected Bibliography   472
Index   481

POWER
&POLITICS
IN AMERICA
FOURTH
EDITION

PART one
INTRODUCTION

In this opening section we establish the framework for the debate that follows throughout the book.

In chapter 1 we introduce a political spectrum from left to right, and identify five alternative perspectives along that spectrum. Next we explain the distinguishing characteristics of each of those perspectives—their underlying values, their view of power in America, their proposals for change. Then we sound some cautionary notes about the use and misuse of ideological categories.

Chapter 2 provides a brief examination of the constitutional context within which all American political discussion must be placed. We draw attention to the fact that, although the emphasis in this book is on fairly recent experience, we cannot hope to understand contemporary events and problems without a strong sense of the country's past.

We touch upon the events leading up to the Constitutional Convention, then describe the compromises embodied in the Constitution. Next we explore the basic principles of the Constitution, the process by which those principles evolved, and the meaning of the Constitution today. Finally we apply to the Constitution five competing interpretations based on the alternative perspectives defined in chapter 1.

In this one short chapter we cannot, of course, dispose adequately of the great issues surrounding the Constitution of the United States. However, the reader must bear in mind that chapter 2 is merely a prologue to a debate pursued in different contexts in every one of the chapters that follows.

chapter one

FIVE PERSPECTIVES ON THE AMERICAN SYSTEM

This book deals with controversy, conflict, and the clash of ideas and interests, all of which are the essence of politics.

Many people wish this were not so. They yearn for agreement, consensus. They want politicians to stop quibbling and get on with the job of solving our problems. Not long ago, in fact, a number of American scholars suggested that we were within reach of this happy state of affairs in the United States, for we had acquired so much knowledge and technological competence that the old ideological debates were about to disappear.[1] They were wrong. Knowledge and technology have continued to advance at a headlong pace, but they have disposed of few problems and generated a host of new ones.

So controversy persists, and the unending debate over every aspect of American government and politics provides the framework of this book. We shall not try to resolve that debate here. I have my own views, of course. But the purpose of this book is not to provide a single, definitive answer to the questions we shall be considering; rather, it is to help each reader work toward his or her own conclusions after studying alternative positions on each aspect of our debate.

THE CRUX OF THE DEBATE: POLITICAL POWER

Basically the debate is about *power*—who should have it, and for what purposes should it be used. We shall be talking about *the power to make public policy through government and politics.* Since this statement is made up of key terms that will be used repeatedly in this book, we had better begin by defining them.

Power, for the purposes of this book, is defined as the capacity to play a significant part in the making of decisions. A closely related term is *influence,* which is the capacity to have an impact on the making of decisions.[2]

Public policy comprises the officially established goals on issues affecting the community as a whole—the economy, energy, education, national security, and so on.

Government consists of the institutions—executive, legislative, and judicial—that contain the official decision points for making public policy and putting it into effect.

Politics is the process through which a multitude of individuals and groups seek to affect the shaping of public policy.

At this stage these definitions may seem general and abstract. But we shall quickly discover that they describe matters that directly affect every one of us; our job prospects, the price of gas, the availability of educational and recreational facilities, sexual attitudes and practices, and what we eat, wear, and read are all subjects of fierce political disputes and hard-fought legislation.

Politics, of course, is not the only thing that matters. Trying to politicize everything is the hallmark of totalitarian systems, whereas one of the defining features of democracy is that it leaves to the individual a wide domain more or less free from the interference of government officials and politicians.

Even so, no area of our lives can be completely exempt from a general framework of laws shaped by the political process. So the subject matter of this book is wide ranging indeed. And the stakes we are dealing with are very high: the health of the economy, the quality of our lives, and perhaps the survival of the human race.

A POLITICAL SPECTRUM

The contemporary debate on power in America cannot be reduced to a simple pro-and-con formulation. Conflicting and strongly held views multiply in all directions. For the purposes of our debate we can set forth a spectrum of opinion from left to right. Then we can divide the spectrum into five broad perspectives that are varying ways of looking at and interpreting the political system and the policies produced by the system. (See figure 1-1.)

The first of these five perspectives is that of the centrists, who belong to the great American middle-of-the-road consensus. Flanking the centrists on either side are two smaller bands of opinion made up of people who challenge that consensus: the liberals and the conservatives. Toward the two poles of the spectrum are two still smaller groups—the radical left and the radical right—who are defined as radicals because their rejection of the middle-of-the-road position is much more deep rooted or fundamental than that of the liberals and conservatives.

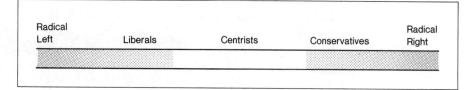

| Radical Left | Liberals | Centrists | Conservatives | Radical Right |

FIGURE 1-1. The Political Spectrum

Please take special note of two features of figure 1–1. First, each perspective is not a single point on the spectrum but a band of opinion within which there are wide divergencies. Second, the perspectives are not separated by high, un-scalable walls. They shade into each other, so that some of the people we shall be discussing bridge the categories. Moreover, most people do not fit neatly into a single category; on some issues they are centrist, on others liberal, conservative, or even radical.

Despite these qualifications (on which I shall expand at the end of this chapter) the spectrum describes in an approximate way the main divisions of opinion over government and politics in America today. Thus it gives us a useful point of departure for discussing the issues treated in this book.

THE PERSPECTIVES INTRODUCED

Let us take a brief look at some of the individuals, groups, and ideas associated with each perspective.

THE CENTRISTS

The centrist category comprises the largest body of opinion in the country. In this part of the political spectrum we find many political scientists, sociologists, economists, and historians. Most high school and many college texts on American history and government express a centrist perspective. The larger number of viewpoints expressed in the mass media are centrist, and most elected public officials are centrists.

This pervasiveness does not mean that centrists speak with a single voice. Large differences are found among them, ranging from the more conservative centrists, such as Gerald Ford, to more liberal centrists, such as Walter Mondale.

Just the same, all centrists tend to agree that the American political system is fundamentally sound. All of them will concede that it has its faults, and some frequently draw attention to shortcomings and failures and the need for change. Thus centrism is not a simple, stand-pat doctrine, defending the status quo in all circumstances. Still, centrists of all shades of opinion claim that, whatever its defects, the American political system serves the people at least as well as, and probably better than, any other system in the world today.

THE LIBERALS

To the left of the centrists on the spectrum we find a body of opinion that expresses a much deeper dissatisfaction with the American political system than is felt by even the most liberal centrists. The liberals do not agree that the system is working well. They see it riddled with inequities between rich and poor, powerful and powerless. They believe that it repeatedly fails to handle the problems facing the vast majority of people. They argue that major reforms are urgently needed.

Among these liberal critics are several political scientists, including James MacGregor Burns, some economists, notably John Kenneth Galbraith, political activists such as Ralph Nader, and such political leaders as former Senator George McGovern and Representative Ronald Dellums.

The Nation and *The Progressive* are magazines of liberal opinion, and the Americans for Democratic Action is one of the leading liberal organizations.

THE CONSERVATIVES

On the other side of the centrist band is a group of conservatives who argue that the American governmental system, as designed by the Framers, was brilliantly conceived and served the country well for almost a century and a half until it was undermined by the liberals' faith in an all-powerful federal government that has dominated official thinking since the New Deal of the 1930s.

The conservative group includes a considerable number of economists, among them Milton Friedman, who will be quoted frequently in this book. Then there are the political analysts and commentators who write for the magazine *The National Review,* including William Buckley and William Rusher. Conservative elected officials include Senators Barry Goldwater, Strom Thurmond, and Orrin Hatch.

Conservative organizations include the American Conservative Union, the Conservative Caucus, Young Americans for Freedom, and the National Conservative Political Action Committee. Among the conservative periodicals are *The National Review, Human Events, Policy Review, Modern Age, Conservative Digest,* and *Moral Majority Report.*

THE RADICAL LEFT

On the far left of the spectrum, beyond the liberals, we find a variety of *radical* groups, including the Communist Party, USA; the Communist Party (Marxist-Leninist); the Revolutionary Communist Party; and the Socialist Workers Party.

There are sharp, often bitter, differences separating these groups. In the 1960s, the Communist Party, USA, came under attack by the so-called "New Left," notably the Students for a Democratic Society (SDS). Beginning in 1960, SDS split into three factions, then disintegrated, and a further proliferation of tiny radical organizations came into existence, each devoting much of its energies to denouncing the others.

The disagreements among the groups of the left can be traced to a diversity of intellectual sources. The writings of Karl Marx are a prime source for most of them; but although the Communist Party, USA, draws heavily on the ideas of the Russian Revolution's Vladimir Ilich Lenin and Joseph Stalin, others look to Stalin's archrival Leon Trotsky, to China's Mao Tse-tung, to theorists of anarchism, or to the writings of philosopher Herbert Marcuse.[3]

Despite these differences there are some basic tenets on which all radical left groups agree. All of them argue that the American political system is controlled by monopoly capitalism, or big business, which is inherently unjust and repressive; that the liberals represent merely a minor variation of the centrists and conservatives; and that only root-and-branch, radical, and perhaps revolutionary changes can cure the sickness of the system.

Scholars of the left include the Marxist writer Paul Sweezy, Richard Flacks,

Todd Gitlin, and a group associated with the Center for Policy Studies, including Richard Barnet, Arthur Waskow, and Marcus Raskin. Radical left publications include the leading Marxist journal, *The Monthly Review,* and *Working Papers for a New Society.*

THE RADICAL RIGHT

At the opposite pole of the spectrum we find a cluster of groups, including extreme militant organizations such as the Nazis[4] and the Ku Klux Klan; organizations that draw upon religious as well as political doctrine, such as Billy James Hargis's Christian Crusade; and Robert Welch's John Birch Society, which publishes weekly and monthly magazines, including *American Opinion,* and a number of books sold through its bookstores.

The Nazis, whose inspiration is Nazi Germany and Hitler's *Mein Kampf,* have a tiny membership; but the Birch Society says it has about eighty thousand members. The various Klans[5] claim a membership running into hundreds of thousands, predominantly though by no means exclusively in the South; FBI estimates are much lower (about ten thousand), but membership has clearly been on the upswing lately.

Like the radical left groups, right-wing organizations are sharply divided on policies and tactics. Thus the Birch Society claims that, although it is opposed to the civil rights movement, it is not racist. The Nazis, however, are overtly and

COURTESY SCRAWLS-ATLANTA JOURNAL

virulently anti-Semitic and antiblack; and the driving force of the Klan since its origins in the Reconstruction era has been hostility to blacks, with resentment of Jews as a supporting motif. Whatever their differences, all radical groups unite behind one premise: that American government and politics are run by a small group of insiders who are leading us toward communism or a similar kind of dictatorship of the left.

THE BASIC DIFFERENCES

Having briefly defined each of the five perspectives we must explore further the differences among them. We shall look at their views on three types of questions:

1. Questions about *values:* how should people behave toward each other and what *ought* to be the standards of belief and behavior acceptable to the community?
2. Questions about *power:* who has power in America and who (if anyone) makes the key decisions on public policy?
3. Questions about *change:* how much, what kind, and by what means?

VALUES

At the heart of the disagreements among the perspectives is a conflict of values. Our values are our beliefs about what is good or bad conduct. They are statements of ideals to which we at least pay lip service, even though we fall far short of them in practice. For example, statements such as "human life is sacred," "government officials should be honest," and "private property is the essential condition of liberty" are all expressions of values. Given our present knowledge, we cannot prove or disprove any of them. Whole societies have existed for long periods on assumptions quite different from these. And within our own culture there is a great diversity of beliefs, intensely held and sometimes brilliantly argued, on these and other issues.

We can organize most of the value questions considered in this book around two concepts that have appeared persistently from the earliest political philosophers: *equality* and *liberty.*

Attitudes toward *equality*—of income, possessions, status, and power—constitute the most reliable litmus test of whether people stand right or left of center on the political spectrum. In general, as we move toward the left we find increasing support for the idea that justice cannot be achieved in the face of large inequalities; and as we move toward the right we find more emphasis on recognizing and rewarding differences in ability and effort.

However, when we turn our attention to *liberty,* we find that the task of differentiating among the various perspectives becomes much more complicated, for each of our perspectives claims deep and undying devotion to the principle that the individual should be free from government tyranny.

As soon as we go beyond these generalities, however, we find sharp differences on what constitutes government tyranny. Right of center the emphasis is on *economic liberty:* the freedom to do what we want with our money and property without government interference. Yet most thinkers on the right are very much in favor of strong government action to protect the social order against subversive, disruptive, or debased ideas or conduct.

Left of center, these attitudes are reversed. Liberty on the left tends to mean *civil liberty:* the protection of freedom of expression and personal behavior. But property rights are another matter, for there is enthusiastic endorsement on the left for government intervention in the economy and regulation of private business and property.

So, with some exceptions to be noted later, everyone favors strong government action in some areas, and whether this constitutes a denial of our liberties depends on which perspective we are talking about.

With these generalizations in mind we can proceed to examine in more detail the views of each of the five perspectives on the basic values of equality and liberty. Since the centrists' values tend to be middle-ground positions between the conflicting ideas on either side of them, we shall begin by examining the left-of-center positions, then the right-of-center positions, and then the centrists' beliefs.

The liberals.   Equality is a prime value of the liberals. They do not believe that a just society should tolerate the enormous disparities that exist in America between those at the top of the income scale and those at the bottom. They accept some differences of income, wealth, and status as inevitable and legitimate. But the large inequities that exist today mean that the needs of the poor are not attended to in the same way as the interests of the rich, for in politics money talks with a loud and clear voice. So liberals call for a major redistribution of the privileges now enjoyed by the well-to-do groups to the poor, blacks, Chicanos, Puerto Ricans, American Indians, and others who have been left behind in the struggle for success.

If this redistribution is to be accomplished, the key economic decisions cannot be left in the hands of great business corporations and wealthy individuals, for they will see to it that these decisions will protect their privileges. So government must play a leading role.

This intervention, the liberals concede, limits the liberties of some individuals. But unless these limits are imposed, liberty will be the exclusive prerogative of those who own most of the property, for they will dominate the economic life of the society and the freedom of the rest will be lost.

In any case, say the liberals, liberty should not be defined primarily in economic terms. We are free to the extent that we can say and write whatever we please, consort with anyone we want to, and control our personal lives and relationships as we see fit. Government should not interfere with these basic freedoms, which are clearly defined in the Bill of Rights, most particularly the First Amendment to the Constitution, unless the pursuit of our own liberties directly interferes with the personal liberties of others or immediately endangers the safety of the community as a whole.

The radical left.   Equality is the core value of the radical left, and they criticize the liberals for being willing to leave wide variations in income and property, and for failing to face up to the root cause of our present inequities. That root cause, they say, is the system of capitalism, which is based on private ownership of industry and agriculture. Capitalism thrives on inequality. It promotes competition, which sets people against each other in a struggle to gain more than the next person. It brings out the worst in people by encouraging greed for more and more goods. Moreover, it is a system of exploitation, in which members of the capitalist class make their profits and expand their property holdings from the efforts of the laboring masses. Capitalism must be abolished and replaced with socialism, a system in which, as Karl Marx put it, "the means of production, distribution, and exchange" are owned by the whole community. Under socialism, cooperation would eventually take the place of competition, and inequality would give way to a sharing of resources, so that everyone would have enough and no one would have too much.

Socialism, in the doctrines of the left, will bring not only social justice based on equality, but also true liberty to the masses of the people, unlike capitalism, which reserves freedom for the capitalist. But if liberty is a professed value of the left, achieving it confronts them with some awkward contradictions. To examine these contradictions we must distinguish between different strands on the left.

The Communist Party, USA, sees a strong central government as the mechanism for taking over power from the capitalists, and it urges government ownership of private businesses, especially the big ones. The enormous power this would vest in government is viewed as a temporary problem. Karl Marx predicted that in time socialism would produce so much abundance that there would be more than enough for everyone, which would mean that it would no longer be necessary to control people with laws. Government, including the entire machinery of bureaucracies, courts, and police forces, would "wither away" and for the first time in human history the individual would enjoy complete freedom.

This freedom is the eventual goal, the final stage of communism; however, Marx prescribed an interim stage of transitional "socialism," during which a "dictatorship of the proletariat" would guide the transition from capitalist institutions and attitudes. In the Soviet Union the dictatorship of the proletariat has lasted since 1917, government is still immensely powerful, and dissenting opinions are treated with great harshness.

Pro-Soviet Communists argue that this situation results from the fact that since its birth the Soviet Union has been surrounded by capitalist powers seeking its destruction, which has compelled it to maintain a strong central government and military establishment. This rationale does not satisfy other radical left groups, especially those that grew out of the student rebellion of the 1960s. These groups have no use for the Soviet Union's centralized bureaucratic structures, and they see no point in replacing the tyranny of great industrial corporations with the despotism of huge government agencies. They propose instead the creation of small-scale institutions, with control in the hands of communities or workers.

Yet even these antibureaucratic radical groups want to limit the dissemination of certain kinds of ideas. Tolerance, they argue, should not extend to such vicious ideas as racism, militarism, and other affronts to human dignity, and every effort must be made to ban them.

The conservatives.   Conservatives do not subscribe to the liberal belief in the importance of equality. On the contrary, as conservatives see it, people are intrinsically unequal. They are endowed from birth with differing qualities and abilities. These differences should be cherished, and diversity should be encouraged.

Among the qualities that people possess in differing degrees are effort, motivation, ambition, and thrift. The best device for encouraging the development of these virtues is competition. The social system should be constructed so that, if people compete successfully, they will be rewarded to the full extent merited by their performance.

The social system that embodies all these ideas is capitalism. The capitalist system is based on individual effort, enterprise, thrift, competition, and rewards for effective performance. It is the most successful economic system the world has ever seen, producing an abundance that socialist countries have dismally failed to achieve. And this abundance is not limited to the few, for particularly in America the great majority of the people have enjoyed a high and increasing standard of living.[6]

As for those who, because of physical disability or a lack of motivation, remain poor, a certain amount of government help may be needed to ensure that they do not go without the minimum requirements of food, clothing, and shelter. However, conservatives prefer private charity to government programs. In any case, they argue that the best way of providing enough to go around for everybody, including the poor, is to allow capitalism to generate ever more economic abundance.

And yet, say the conservatives, wherever capitalism exists, there are attempts to interfere with its functioning in the name of equality. This interference is misguided on two grounds. First, it is self-defeating. Differences in wealth and status (not to mention differences in natural abilities) cannot be extinguished without the ruthless use of massive power; and those who exercise this power, as in communist countries, become a self-perpetuating elite whose existence contradicts the very notion of equality.

Second, interfering with capitalism undermines liberty. From the conservatives' perspective, liberty is associated primarily with the right of the individual to acquire and use property and conduct business without hindrance from government. Thus capitalism, which is based on private property and the private ownership and operation of business, is inseparable from liberty, for it disperses decision making among a large number of individuals and groups, instead of concentrating it all in government.

Conservatives do not completely rule out any role for government in the economy. We need government to set up and referee the rules of the game; to help define and protect property rights; to resolve conflicts among the freedoms of different individuals; and to control the supply of money. But beyond these minimal functions of government, the cardinal principles underlying a free society are *economic individualism,* or free competition among private businesspeople, and *property rights,* or the ability to own and use without restraint a home, a business, and whatever else we can legally acquire with our money.

On the other hand, in the area of civil liberties, most conservatives are inclined to support more governmental intervention than are liberals. Conservatives argue that the freedoms contained in the Bill of Rights are viable only within a framework of order and stability. The latter are preserved by respect for tradition, patriotism, religion, and the family. They are undermined by communist subversion, the growing rejection of traditional ideas and beliefs, the spread of pornography, the abandonment of sexual taboos, and the vast increase in violent crime. Conservatives see a major role for government in formulating stronger laws and vigorously enforcing them to control these destructive elements.

The radical right.   There are contrasting strands within the radical right on the question of equality. Some, such as John Birch Society members, incline toward an extreme version of conservative thought, deeply antiegalitarian and strongly supportive of unlimited competition and rewards for superior performance. The other is "populist" in character; that is, it claims to speak for the people against established wealth and power. Right-wing populism has been particularly characteristic of the Ku Klux Klan and the right-wing fundamentalist religious groups. However, this populism is not truly egalitarian. Although it expresses resentment of the rich and wellborn, it is also directed downward against the demands of groups traditionally at the bottom of the status scale: the very poor, the blacks, and the ethnic minorities.

Whatever differences may exist among right-wing groups on the issue of equality, they do not differ very much on the question of liberty. Freedom is the right to develop our capacities; to own, buy, and sell property; to practice religion; and to live according to traditional standards of patriotism and morality. The enemies of these values—atheists, leftists, and other subversives—have been busily at work undermining the foundations of our system and destroying our liberties. So it is a contradiction in terms to tolerate the freedom to attack our freedoms and to advocate unpatriotic or "un-American" ideas.

The centrists.   In relation to both equality and liberty, centrist views reflect their location on the spectrum: the middle ground between left and right doctrines.

Thus centrists place their emphasis on *equality of opportunity,* which requires that no one be denied the chance to develop his or her full potential because of prejudice, discrimination, or lack of access to education. As the concept of equality of opportunity has expanded over the years, it has come to include equality before the law, equality of voting rights, and the equal right of all to a standard of living needed for survival and human dignity. Once these basic rights are provided, however, people should be able to use their opportunities to move ahead of others, so that equality of *opportunity* does not produce equality of *condition.*

With respect to economic liberty, centrists are for private enterprise, private ownership, and capitalism. Yet they believe that government should regulate business to prevent monopoly and other practices that hurt the consumer and the public at large. They favor laws that set minimum wages for workers and protect their right to organize into labor unions. They also feel that government has a crucial responsibility to intervene in the economy with budgetary, fiscal, and tax policies to keep the economy on an even keel.

Finally, in the area of civil liberties, centrists seek a judicious, moderate position between the demands of freedom on the one side and the need for order on the other. They regard the guarantees of the Bill of Rights as an indispensable part of our democracy. Yet the liberties of each of us are constantly coming into conflict with the liberties of others. Consequently we need a framework of law and government to settle individual and group conflicts. So government has a right to protect society and itself against disruption and violence. Centrists allow extensive scope for civil liberties, but they are more prepared to accept limits on those liberties than are liberals.

POWER: WHO RULES AMERICA?

So far, in discussing the values of equality and liberty, we have distinguished among the five perspectives on the basis of their underlying beliefs on how the world *ought* to be. Now we turn to their perceptions of reality, of how the world actually *is*. We consider their views on who has the power in America, and from each perspective we receive a different answer.

The closer we get to the center of the spectrum, the more likely we are to be told that power in America is widely distributed among a considerable number of people and institutions; the farther we move away from the center, the greater is the prospect of our hearing that we are ruled by a small elite group.

The centrists.   Although on this and all other topics in this book there are many differing positions within the centrist band, the most typical centrist view of the realities of the American system is that power is limited and diffused. To begin with, there is the framework of the Constitution that divides power between the national and state governments, and that divides power among the different branches of the federal government in a marvelously ingenious system of checks and balances.

The courts maintain the rule of law, that system by which everyone, including high government officials, is subject to carefully devised and impartially applied rules of conduct. A free press, television, and radio provide a constant stream of information to prevent government from conducting its affairs secretly and irresponsibly. Competition between two major political parties and a variety of small ones is a constant reminder to any administration that it must not wield power without concern for the wishes of the people.

Finally, the centrists are reassured of a balance of power by the fact that we have an enormous number of organized groups, representing small business and big business, organized labor, farmers, professionals, ethnic and racial minorities, and religious, civic, fraternal, and other causes. Some of these groups are more potent than others. Yet none of them, and no combination of them, is powerful enough to control the government, for they compete with each other, are watched over by the media, and are regulated by government. To complement the constitutional balance, then, we have a *group balance*.

So, through the separation and division of powers in the Constitution, the courts, the media, the parties, and the interplay of groups, centrists maintain that we have a system of *pluralism*, or many sources of power. The majority does not run things directly. Leaders (elites) in government and private organizations carry out most of the decision making. Still, the elected leaders may be replaced if they fail to carry out the majority's will on important issues. And this vulnerability of leaders, together with the dispersal of power to many locations, clearly establishes our claim to be a representative, constitutional democracy, a society in which the wishes of the majority are carried out by elected representatives according to orderly, generally accepted procedures.

The liberals. Unlike the centrists, the liberals perceive an *imbalance* of power in America. Certain groups, particularly business executives and those who possess large amounts of money and property, are overrepresented in the policy-making process and have a much greater impact on government decisions than other groups. The liberals also perceive an accumulation of power in recent years in the military, which results in absurdly inflated outlays on weapons.

The liberals concede that this disproportionate power is not completely unchecked and that some of the limits to which the centrists point are significant. Still, they are not sufficient, in the liberals' view, to prevent some people from obtaining a degree of power that contradicts the idea of democracy, or rule by the people.

One cause of this disproportionate power is the great inequity in the distribution of wealth in America. Another is the impact of the checks and balances that the Founding Fathers invented in order to set limits to power; instead they have provided people who have money and property with the opportunity to exercise undue power. Our decision-making machinery is so fragmented that well-organized and well-financed interest groups are able to maneuver among and infiltrate the decision points. The political importance of wealth is also demonstrated in large contributions to election campaigns, which put elected officeholders under an obligation to rich contributors.

So liberals favor changes in the system that would produce clearer lines of responsibility, make the decision makers less vulnerable to business and other special interests, and provide more responsiveness to underrepresented groups and to the people as a whole.

The radical left. The radical left perceives not merely an imbalance of power, but a concentration of power in the hands of a small stratum of the population, a *ruling class.* The top leadership of this class comprises the key decision makers in America—the ruling elite, the "power structure," or what sociologist C. Wright Mills called the "power elite."

At the center of this elite is big business, or corporate capitalism. To the radical left the most crucial kind of power is economic power, and the controllers of most economic power are the boards of directors and top executives of the largest industrial and financial corporations.

Working with these people are the top figures in the corporate law firms of Washington and New York; in opinion-molding institutions, especially the mass media and the universities; and in the federal government itself, in the presidency, the major cabinet departments and regulatory agencies, the FBI, and the military.

Although these various ruling elements do not constitute a completely integrated, single executive committee, they are linked in a number of ways. They are members of a white, affluent, upper social class. They move easily from one location of power to another. They belong to influential organizations: on economic issues, the Business Council and the Committee for Economic Development; on foreign affairs, the Council on Foreign Relations and the Trilateral Commission. And they subscribe to a common set of beliefs in capitalism and private property.

They do not agree on everything. Within the ruling elite there are liberal and conservative wings. But even the liberal wing accepts the values of private property and capitalism, subject to a certain amount of government guidance and protection, and they agree that our foreign policy should protect those values.

Thus our political parties, the media, educational institutions, and so on offer the people only a very narrow range of alternatives within the consensus established by the power elite. The real interests of the people are unrepresented, and the masses remain essentially powerless.

The conservatives. Conservatives, too, see excessive power in the hands of a small segment of the population. They believe that power has been skewed in the direction of an elite; but far from being a conservative, business-dominated elite, it is, according to the conservatives, a "liberal establishment."

The conservatives believe that tremendous power has gravitated to the institutions that produce information and ideas, with special reference to Harvard and other Ivy League universities; the major philanthropic foundations, especially Ford and Rockefeller; opinion-leading associations such as the Council on Foreign Relations; public policy research organizations such as the Brookings Institution; the television and radio networks; newspapers such as *The New York Times* and *The Washington Post;* and a number of periodicals, including *Harper's, Atlantic Monthly, The New Yorker,* and *Foreign Affairs.* According to William Buckley, these institutions harbor "the intellectual plutocrats of the nation, who have at their disposal vast cultural and financial resources."[7]

Then there is Wall Street. It may seem strange that conservatives, who champion the business system, should be critical of the great center of eastern finance and corporate law. But they complain that important elements in the New York financial community have betrayed the true interests of American business, for they have protected their interests abroad by having our government appease international communism instead of standing up to it.

Working with the knowledge industry and Wall Street have been the White House and the vast array of bureaucracies that are controlled by the president; and all too often the courts have issued rulings that reflect liberal establishment biases.

People drawn from the ranks of the liberal establishment have ruled America since the New Deal years of the 1930s. Consequently, limited government, as provided for by the Founding Fathers, has been undermined, and the separation of powers has fallen before the federal juggernaut. The only limits advocated by the establishment are the wrong kind: limits on the ability of the police to preserve

law and order and limits on the military budgets needed to halt the spread of
international communism.

According to conservatives, it is time to bring an end to the power that liberals
have exercised for half a century, which has brought us to our present position
of moral decline, economic deterioration, and international inferiority. In the
results of the 1980 presidential and congressional elections, conservatives saw the
possibility that the end of liberal establishment domination was at last in sight.

The radical right.   Ever since the Russian Revolution of 1917, the radical right
in America has warned that communism is spreading throughout the world and
conspiring to take over the United States. As time went on, the right became
increasingly convinced that the Communists and their socialist-cum-liberal allies
and dupes had won several vantage points of power in America and were steadily
increasing their hold on the system.

As Robert Welch of the John Birch Society put it in 1965, "The Communist
conspiratorial apparatus is now steadily closing in, with every conceivable pressure
and deception, on all remaining resistance to the establishment of its police state
over our own country."[8] The apparatus is gaining control of the media, the
universities and public school systems, and the philanthropic foundations.

It is even reaching for the presidency itself. In 1954 Welch wrote, "Dwight
Eisenhower is a dedicated, conscious agent of the Communist conspiracy."[9] This
claim was too much for many members of the John Birch Society, but the belief
remains widespread among the radical right that communism has taken over much
of the world, runs the United Nations, and is rapidly gaining ground in America
with the insidious help of its intellectual apologists.

Variations of this view have been put forward by radical right organizations,
including the John Birch Society. There is talk of a worldwide conspiracy called
the Illuminati. It has been proposed that the rulers of America may not all be
Communists as such, but rather a group of "insiders" who are out to establish
a collectivist dictatorship that, from the point of view of most Americans, will not
be very different from communism. These insiders, notably the Rockefellers and
their allies in government, eastern finance, the universities, and the media, aim
to divide up the world with the communist powers into spheres of influence in
which the ruling groups can preserve their privileges intact.

CHANGE

We have already discussed ideal values, or what principles should guide human
behavior, and power, or the reality of who runs America, from each of our five
perspectives. In each case we have found a gap between the ideal and the present
state of affairs. To bring what should be closer to what is, each perspective suggests
certain changes in our political system and advocates various methods to achieve
them.

The centrists.   Of all the perspectives, the centrists see the greatest degree of
concordance between what is and what ought to be. But it would be a mistake to

interpret the centrist position as an uncritical defense of the status quo.

It is true that centrists tend to defend the accomplishments of the American political system. Still, they recognize that along the way there have been blunders, failures, and even disasters, such as the Civil War and the Great Depression, which made clear the need for significant changes. Fortunately, our system, from its beginning, has included mechanisms to produce change. The Founding Fathers designed a Constitution of great flexibility, which has evolved to meet the political and economic stresses of each successive era. Change has been a permanent part of the American experience.

However, the key to the centrist approach is that change must come gradually, step by step. Rapid, sweeping changes put people under great psychic stress, raising the level of anxieties and endangering the fragile network of relationships that holds a complex society together. Moreover, changes undertaken faster than a step at a time, leaving insufficient opportunity to test the results of each move, usually make matters worse rather than better.

Within the system the means are readily available for producing incremental change through open discussion of the issues, free elections, and most particularly that process of negotiation and bargaining that produces *compromises*. Each compromise takes time to hammer out and usually represents no more than a moderate improvement over previous conditions. Yet the process has taken care of the grievances of one group after another throughout American history and can continue to do so as long as the system is not overloaded by unreasonable demands for immediate, sweeping changes.

The liberals.   Liberals find the centrists' approach to change complacent. They concede that the system has some real accomplishments to its credit. But they feel that, in large measure, the gains have resulted from the persistent criticism and pressure applied by liberals. Moreover, the achievements fall far short of what is needed.

All too often, government in America has not been effective. Its movement is so slow and erratic that we are unable to devise broad policies and long-range plans.

Liberals admit it takes time to produce changes. They accept the need for negotiation and compromise. They also believe that change must be accomplished within the framework of law and that revolutionary methods are both impracticable and undesirable. Still, liberals are much less inclined than the centrists to accept a slow pace of change, because they believe that we are confronted with a combination of social, economic, and ecological crises so intense as to pose threats to further progress and even to human survival. For liberals, it is imperative that we find ways to speed up the process of peaceful change.

The radical left.   The radicals of the left are more impatient with the liberals' attitude toward change than the liberals are with the centrists'. The system, say these radicals, is effective only in serving the interests of the ruling elite, who are leading us into economic and ecological disaster and the cataclysm of thermonuclear war. Thus, belief in the effectiveness of gradualism is absurdly wrong. We can no longer accept the kinds of changes that merely provide pacifiers to keep the system going. The game of compromise and expediency, which the centrists adore and the liberals are all too ready to accept, is worn out both morally and practically. We need radical change that will replace the present relationships of power with a new system based on humane values.

But how is this to be accomplished? The ruling elite has at its disposal an overwhelming machinery of official force. And the people are difficult to reach. Affluence and mass media manipulation have attached them to the system, and they have internalized its values. Their servitude is "voluntary"; they are not even aware that they are not free.[10]

A variety of strategies is proposed. A few small groups such as the "Weather Underground" have advocated terrorism and guerrilla warfare.[11] While rejecting this kind of calculated violence, many adopt the tactics of militant confrontation as a means of radicalizing workers, students, and intellectuals. Others go out to live among the poor to undertake community organization or take jobs in factories to try to convert the workers to socialism. Others establish new communities to demonstrate radically different ways of living.

Still others believe that, despite the far-reaching control exercised by the ruling elite, it is possible to use certain features of the system to educate the masses and turn them against the system. Thus, efforts are made to attract a broad base of support by engaging in pressure politics and election campaigns around such issues as nuclear energy and rent control.

These strategies are not mutually exclusive. Individuals and groups within the left may adopt combinations of these methods and shift from one to another as they seek to bring about a sweeping transformation of the system.

The conservatives. The changes sought by the conservatives are aimed at the restoration of the principles of the Founding Fathers, notably, limited government, respect for private property, and states' rights. They do not wish to turn the clock back and revert completely to the system as it was originally established, but they do believe that the purposes for which the Constitution was designed should be reasserted and restated in contemporary conservative terms.

To accomplish this reversion, conservatives propose procedures that the system itself provides. The only force to be used is legitimized force to restore law and order, aided by the removal of what conservatives regard as unreasonable restraints on the authority of the police.

In politics, conservatives use the traditional methods of education and advocacy, organized pressure, and the support of candidates sympathetic to their cause. Operating through the electoral process inevitably involves some degree of compromise. But because conservatives are seeking far-reaching changes, they support with particular enthusiasm candidates who take strong stands on the issues and call for more far-reaching changes than do most politicians. They believed they had found such candidates in Barry Goldwater in 1964 and Ronald Reagan in 1980.

The radical right. The radical right includes spokespersons for a number of conflicting approaches to the problem of change. Because they see the situation as desperate, drastic measures are called for to produce, in effect, a counter-revolution. A few of the most extreme groups have armed for violent insurrection (or, as they claim, for the defense of the Republic against violent insurrection from the left or imminent invasion by Communists from abroad). Others, such as the John Birch Society, oppose illegal tactics but maintain secrecy of membership, adopt authoritarian leadership, and use tactics of infiltration as ways of countering the methods that, they say, the conspiracy is using to take over America. However, the Birch Society and most other right-wing groups enter the electoral fray from time to time, giving strong support to very conservative candidates for various offices.

SUMMARY AND SOME WARNINGS

Table 1-1 sums up the differences among the five perspectives with respect to their views on the values of equality and liberty, the question of who has power in America, and the problem of how much change is needed and how it is to be brought about.

Having set up the categories and discussed the differences among them, we must recognize some dangers in the use and possible misuse of categorization in general and these categories in particular. Categories, after all, are artificial constructs that our minds impose on reality to make our experiences more comprehensible. Categories are, at best, rough approximations of reality, especially in our attempt to compress the entire range of American political opinion into just five categories. We should constantly remind ourselves of the following qualifications.

Each category represents a broad band of opinion.   Within each of the five categories there is conflict, often bitter.

A spectrum is a continuum.   Each position gradually shades into the next, and it is sometimes difficult to determine whether a particular individual or organization should be placed on the right edge of one perspective or the left edge of the adjacent perspective. For example:

- Michael Harrington, a leader of the Democratic Socialist Organizing Committee, is a Socialist; he therefore joins with the radical left in rejecting capitalism. Yet his strategies are moderate and gradualist, so that he has much in common with liberals such as John Kenneth Galbraith.
- Tom Hayden was one of the founders of the "New Left" Students for a Democratic Society, and he now leads the Campaign for Economic Democracy, which is dedicated to the radical task of bringing business corporations under democratic control. Nonetheless, he has sought the Democratic party's nomination for various political offices and is scorned by many of his former radical allies as a mere reformist liberal.

TABLE 1-1 The five perspectives: A summary

	Values			Power in America	Change
	Equality	Liberty			
		Civil	Economic		
Radical left	Full social and economic equality	Freedom of personal behavior, but ban on militarism, racism, etc.	Socialism (mostly marxism)	Ruling elite dominated by corporate capitalism	Radical/revolutionary
Liberals	Substantial redistribution of wealth, status, power	Freedom of expression and personal behavior	Severe limits on business, property rights	Imbalance favoring business, money, military	Faster
Centrists	Equality of opportunity; before the law; of voting rights; of the right to a basic standard of living	Balance: freedom and order	Mixed economy	Checks and balances Pluralism	Gradualism, compromise
Conservatives	Differentiation Rewards for ability and effort Competition	Freedom within framework of "law and order," tradition, anti-subversion, anti-permissiveness	Economic individualism, property rights Government only as rule setter and referee	Liberal establishment	Restoration
Radical right	Two strands: (1) strong emphasis on differentiation (2) populism	Loyalty Authority Control of dissent	Unrestricted private ownership	Small elite interwoven with international communism	Counter-revolution

- Irving Kristol, Norman Podhoretz, and Nathan Glazer are among a group of scholars (mostly former liberals) known as "neoconservatives," which means they could be placed on the conservative end of the centrist band or on the centrist side of the conservative band.
- The Moral Majority, led by the Rev. Jerry Falwell and other evangelical preachers, has supported a number of conservative candidates for office, including Ronald Reagan, and is often included in the conservative camp. However, some of the positions adopted by the Moral Majority, and the stridency with which it presents them, seem close to the fundamentalist religious wing of the radical right.

Most people do not fit into one category.   They may be liberals on questions of economic liberty (supporting massive intervention in the economy to attack unemployment), yet conservatives on matters of civil liberty (such as using government to attack pornography), or vice versa.

This refusal to be ideologically consistent is especially noticeable among political leaders, which does not necessarily mean that all politicians are completely un-principled. Some are, but others have strong convictions about the issues they deal with. However, as we shall see throughout this book, even highly principled politicians must deal not only with ideas and values but also with power. To be effective they must be elected; and once elected they must deal with the realities of officeholding, including the need to represent their constituents, who hold many differing views. In so doing, politicians are likely to fall into inconsistencies.

The only exception to this rule of political expediency will be members of minor political groups that have no immediate prospect of gaining any degree of power and thus can remain ideologically consistent. For example, the Libertarian party is completely consistent in its opposition to government intervention, whether it be in economic affairs or on questions of sexual behavior or marijuana smoking. The Libertarians have some strength on college campuses, and they attracted about 1 percent of the votes cast in the 1980 presidential campaign. But their principles have not yet been tested by the temptations that come with the proximity to power.[12]

Personality and politics often differ.   It is sometimes assumed that a person's political outlook closely reflects his or her personality and lifestyle; and there may be something in the generalizations that political liberals tend to be open and tolerant and conservatives more devoted to order and stability in their personal attitudes and behavior. Yet there are innumerable exceptions to these generali-zations: business people who are devoutly conservative in politics, yet adventurous and constantly innovative in their business lives; and university professors who support liberal proposals for far-reaching political and social change, yet resist any change within the structures of the universities.

Similar caution should be exercised in assuming that radical politics go with maladjusted personalities. Membership in Nazi organizations or in violent fringe groups on the far left suggests a prima facie case for some kind of character disorder. Some scholarly studies have associated right-wing politics with para-noia;[13] and the radical left behavior of militant students in the 1960s has been linked to "a self-hatred they try to escape from by fighting any establishment."[14]

On the other hand, a study of John Birch Society members suggests that its members are not suffering from any more psychological disturbances than most people;[15] and one psychiatrist has described the militant student leaders he talked to as sensitive, humane, and highly intelligent people, alienated from society not because they are neurotic but because society is maladjusted.[16]

Have all these qualifications, contradictions, and inconsistencies rendered our five categories meaningless? Of course not. All categories and labels distort reality to some extent and must be used with caution. But despite the popular distaste for using labels (and especially for having ourselves labeled), we cannot think, analyze, or approach an understanding of a problem without categories.

The five perspectives used in this book are quite widely used in political analysis and discussion. The division into left, right, and center, and the subdivisions into liberal, conservative, radical left, and radical right, provide a common-sense reflection of the principal controversies over politics in America. If handled with care, these categories will provide us with a useful framework for an introductory survey of American government and politics.[17]

Opinion is not enough.   An opinion is worth attending to only if it is based first on a solid understanding of the pertinent facts and second on a process of careful, cogent reasoning. And opinions of that quality are difficult to come by.

Getting at the facts is a complicated, often frustrating task. Five witnesses seeing the same accident will typically provide five different versions of what actually happened. The problem of observation is compounded when the facts in question are immensely complex; wide variations are found in investigations in the so-called "hard" sciences.[18] In the study of politics, the difficulty is complicated further by our habit of observing facts selectively through a screen of values. We tend to see what we want to see. From the five perspectives, we see different pictures of who actually has power in America, and we shall encounter the same problem of selective perception on issue after issue throughout this book.

This difficulty of getting agreement on the facts is discouraging enough. But, in addition to having a good grasp of the facts, we have to interpret them carefully through a process of critical reasoning. Again, our values tend to interfere with clear analysis, making us reluctant to follow the logic of an argument wherever it leads unless that is where we want to be led. Moreover, in political science our tools of analysis are still relatively crude. Many of the most significant political questions do not lend themselves to exact study, because we are dealing with human behavior with all its contradictions, absurdities, and imponderables, on the largest and most complex scale. The data available are often fragmentary, and rarely can we draw on controlled experiments or make accurate predictions.

However, we need not conclude that systematic study of politics is impossible. There are many facts on which everyone (or at least every scholar) agrees, no matter what his or her position on the spectrum. Moreover, the amount of pertinent data has been increasing rapidly in recent years, especially in such fields as public opinion, voting behavior, and legislative behavior.

Nor is controlled experimentation the only technique that qualifies as scientific method. The behavioral sciences are becoming more sophisticated in the development and use of analytical tools. Political scientists today are using case studies, survey research, intensive interviews, and statistical techniques. Familiarity with these techniques is not necessary to an understanding of this book. However, some of the results gathered by these means will be considered in various chapters.

The impossibility of completely excluding personal value judgments from political analysis does not mean that any interpretation is as good as any other. Passion and commitment are desirable qualities in the practice of politics. But in studying politics, feelings cannot replace intellectual rigor. Before we make final judgments, we must first seek out the pertinent data; second, set forth alternative interpretations of that data; third, select the most convincing alternative; then, and only then, make proposals for action.

NOTES AND REFERENCES

1. See, for example, Daniel Bell, *The End of Ideology: On the Exhaustion of Political Ideas in the Fifties* (New York: Free Press, 1960).
2. Power is not necessarily the same as *authority,* which is the legitimized right to wield power. Some people who have legal authority actually have very little power, whereas others exercise vast decision-making power even though no one has officially granted them the authority.
3. The Communist Party, USA, has looked to Lenin and Stalin as its inspiration and the Soviet Union as its model. The Communist Party (Marxist-Leninist) rejects the Soviet model in favor of Mao Tse-tung and the Chinese model. The Socialist Workers Party is bitterly anti-Soviet and anti-Stalinist, believing with Trotsky that communism cannot be built within single nations but must emerge from worldwide revolution.
4. Nazi organizations include the National Socialist Party of America, the National Socialist White People's Party, and the American Nazi Party.
5. The Klans do not consist of a single organization, but of several groups, each claiming to be the only true embodiment of their cause.
6. There is a school of conservatism in America that would take issue with some of this analysis. People such as Peter Viereck, Clinton Rossiter, and Walter Lippmann have not been devoted to individualistic capitalism and have criticized the individualist school as excessively materialistic. These "organic" conservatives have argued that society is not just the sum of separate, competing individuals, but a kind of organism that evolves and matures slowly out of the inherited and accumulated wisdom of the past, and that there is a public good over and above the conflicting claims of the separate, selfish interests. They argue, too, that America should not be run by business executives within a framework of business values, but by wise, responsible leaders expressing the lasting values of Western civilization. However, this variety of conservatism has been a more powerful force in Europe than in America, and here individualist conservatism has been the dominant strain.
7. William Buckley, "The Genteel Nightmare of Richard Rovere," *Harper's,* August 1962, pp. 51–55.
8. Robert Welch in *Bulletin of the John Birch Society,* July 1965, p. 4.
9. "The Conspirator," letter by Robert Welch circulated within the Birch Society.
10. Herbert Marcuse, *An Essay on Liberation* (Boston: Beacon Press, 1969), p. 6.
11. According to the FBI, members of the Weather Underground, the Black Liberation Army, and the May 19 Communist Action Organization, were involved in a bungled armored car robbery in October 1981, in which two police officers and a guard were killed.
12. Their 1980 candidate, Ed Clark, did move away from a Libertarian position by supporting the Equal Rights Amendment.
13. Richard Hofstadter, *The Paranoid Style in American Politics* (New York: Knopf, 1965).
14. Testimony by psychologist Bruno Bettelheim before the Senate Committee on Government Operations, Permanent Subcommittee on Investigations, *Hearings on Riots, Civil and Criminal Disorders,* 91st Congress, 1st Session, May 9, 13, and 14, 1969, Part 16, pp. 3069–3079.
15. See Ira S. Rother, "Social and Psychological Determinants of Radical Rightism," in *The American Right Wing: Readings in Political Behavior,* Robert A. Schoenberger, ed. (New York: Holt, Rinehart and Winston, 1969). J. Allen Broyles, in *The John Birch Society, Anatomy of a Protest* (Boston: Beacon Press, 1964), finds the organization's members to be generally intolerant, dogmatic, and authoritarian. However, he does not present psychological profiles as such.
16. Kenneth Keniston, *Young Radicals: Notes on Committed Youth* (New York: Harcourt, Brace & World, 1968), and *Youth and Dissent: The Rise of a New Opposition* (New

York: Harcourt Brace Jovanovich, 1971).

17. One additional objection to the spectrum used here should be mentioned. It is suggested that the spectrum should not be a straight line but a circle, for radical left and radical right are both extreme, dogmatic doctrines and basically minor variations of totalitarianism. In my view, while the radical extremes do have much in common, their views on the important value of equality are very different. So, while the straight-line spectrum is admittedly an oversimplification, a circular spectrum would be even more so. One way of dealing with this problem would be to have a separate spectrum for each issue; but this would provide an impossibly complex framework for an introductory text. (An alternative would be a three-dimensional spectrum, which would require a pop-up book.)

18. According to one study, "at least half the data reported in scientific journals are either wrong or else supported by so little evidence that readers can't tell how reliable they are." ("Scientific Data: 50 Percent Unusable?" *The Chronicle of Higher Education*, 24 February 1975, p. 1).

chapter two

THE CONSTITUTIONAL FRAMEWORK

To the list of perspectives presented in the first chapter, one more must be added: the perspective of time, of history. This sixth perspective is especially important for an understanding of American government, not only because, like all political systems, ours is profoundly influenced by the experience of the past, but also because we are still operating within an institutional framework established in 1787. The Constitution written in Philadelphia in that year has been amended, modified, and expanded in many ways. Yet its core concepts are very much alive in our contemporary political system.

So, before we launch into our study of today's political processes, institutions, and policies, we must briefly explore the background of constitutional ideas and practices deriving from the work of the Founding Fathers.

BEFORE THE CONSTITUTION

First came independence, the assertion in the eloquent phrases of the Declaration of Independence of separate nationhood. After the words came the revolutionary war.

It was not a particularly radical revolution. Much of the heritage of British ideas, laws, and customs remained firmly embedded in American thought and practice. Nor were the grievances of the revolutionaries those of brutally oppressed, desperate masses. Still, the war for independence was genuinely revolutionary in its rejection of the existing decision-making processes and in its insistence on replacing them with a very different model of self-government. Before the establishment of the new model, an interim structure was agreed on. In 1781 the

Articles of Confederation, linking together the thirteen states, were adopted and became the new framework of government when the war ended.

The Articles established a Congress with some of the authority typically associated with a central government, such as the power to declare war, make treaties, and coin and borrow money. However, the system suffered from grave limitations as the functioning government of a new nation confronted with immense problems and pressures. It was, after all, a *con*federation, which by definition is an association of essentially independent states in which a central government handles only matters delegated to it by the member states, and may not make laws that apply directly to individuals without further action by the states. In particular, the members of the Congress were regarded as delegates acting under strict instructions from their states. Each state had one vote, and no major legislation could be passed without the approval of nine of the thirteen states. There was no executive branch. Congress lacked the power to regulate commerce or impose tariffs. Also it had no independent taxing authority and was compelled to depend on voluntary assessments from the states.

Here, then, was a prescription for weak government, deeply divided within itself and plagued by confused and uncoordinated administration. Not surprisingly, Congress found itself chronically short of money, and the Confederation's financial credit collapsed. The states set up tariff barriers against each other. Debtors also issued their own paper money. Farmers who were in debt benefitted from this arrangement. Further, they obtained laws from some of the state legislatures impeding debt collection; and although Shays's Rebellion, an armed anticreditor revolt, was put down, it dramatized the inability of the central government to maintain a viable economic system.

Moreover, the conduct of foreign policy was bound to be severely inhibited by the absence of an executive branch and the existence of so much internal fragmentation and turmoil.

So the pressure built to do something about it, and in May 1787, fifty-five men representing twelve states met in Philadelphia at the request of Congress "for the sole purpose of revising the Articles of Confederation."

THE MAKING OF THE CONSTITUTION

It quickly became clear that the mandate from Congress would be exceeded. The governmental structure established under the Articles of Confederation was not merely revised; it was abandoned. These drastic changes were possible because of the stature and exceptional qualities of several of the delegates to the convention.

The historic reputation of such men as George Washington, James Madison, Benjamin Franklin, Alexander Hamilton, and Gouverneur Morris, and the brilliance of the discussions reported for posterity by Madison have endowed the Constitutional Convention with an almost mythical character. Yet we should not lose sight of the fact that the Constitution did not emerge full-blown from a totally dispassionate, elevated search for truth, but rather from the cut and thrust of

PAUL CONRAD, © 1975, LOS ANGELES TIMES. REPRINTED WITH PERMISSION.
Where have all the leaders gone?

hard-fought debates, each being resolved by compromise.

Two major proposals dominated the debates. First came the *Virginia Plan,* which called for a strong central government, with a two-house legislature empowered to veto state legislation and an executive and a judiciary chosen by the legislature. Opposed to this proposal was the *New Jersey Plan,* which called for revision of the Articles of Confederation rather than a new structure, with a somewhat strengthened one-house legislature, an executive elected by the Congress and lacking veto power, and a supreme court appointed by the executive.

After prolonged debate, a series of compromises was arrived at. The most important was the *Connecticut Compromise,* which settled the dispute over whether representation in Congress should be according to population (the Virginia Plan) or apportioned equally among the states (the New Jersey Plan) by using the population principle for the lower house and the state principle for the upper. Other compromises involved counting three-fifths of the slaves for representation in Congress and for direct taxes,[1] and assigning Congress power to regulate commerce but not to tax exports or interfere with the slave trade before 1808.[2]

RATIFICATION

The compromises, hammered out one at a time in the course of four months of intense discussion, did not bring the debate to an end. The new Constitution still had to be ratified by the states. The Articles of Confederation provided that they could not be amended without the approval of all thirteen state legislatures. The delegates to the Philadelphia convention ignored this constitutional requirement and declared that approval by elected conventions in any nine states would be sufficient for ratification of the new Constitution.

Even this compromise was not easy to achieve. The conflicts that had divided the framers of the Constitution now spread throughout the states, with the Federalists, the supporters of the new document, confronting strong opposition from the Antifederalists. Nonetheless, between December 1787 and June 1788 the Constitution had been endorsed by the necessary nine states. Virginia followed, after a debate in which James Madison led the federalist forces against the Antifederalists, led by Patrick Henry. Then came New York, where the advocates of the Constitution, led by Alexander Hamilton and aided by the publication of the masterly *Federalist* papers (written by Madison, Hamilton, and John Jay), prevailed at the state convention by a margin of only three votes. North Carolina entered in November 1789, Rhode Island in May 1790, and the old Confederation of thirteen states had become the United States of America.

ADDITION OF THE BILL OF RIGHTS

Although the Antifederalists were defeated, they were able to force an important concession from their opponents. Fearful of the power of the proposed federal government, they demanded a series of specific protections of individual rights to be written into the Constitution, and they extracted promises from the federalist forces in some of the state conventions to support the passage of appropriate amendments to the Constitution. The promises were kept, and by 1791 the Bill of Rights, constituting the first ten amendments to the Constitution, had been ratified.

BASIC PRINCIPLES OF THE CONSTITUTION

The compromises that made the passage of the Constitution possible reconciled contrasting concepts of government. First, the notion of government by the people at large was qualified by the idea of representative government. Second, agreement on the need to establish an effective national government was modified by a number of limitations designed to prevent the possibility of too much power being concentrated in any one location.

RULE BY THE PEOPLE—BUT INDIRECTLY

Independence had been won from the rule of the British, and no vestige of monarchy could be allowed in the new constitutional structure. Nor was there to be an inherited aristocracy: Article I, Section 9, banned any title of nobility.

Instead, government was to rest on the consent of the governed, and periodic elections by the people were specifically mandated. However, the power of the people speaking through the election process was limited in two ways. First, qualifications for voting were left to each of the state legislatures, and most states limited this right to male property owners.

Second, most of the delegates who framed the Constitution did not want to see too much decision-making authority in the hands of the people. Practically speaking, the size of the country and its population made it impossible for the entire citizenry to participate directly in the making of decisions. Consequently, the people would have to delegate authority to representatives, so *representative democracy* would have to prevail over the kind of *direct democracy* practiced by some of the city-states of classical Greece.

To the Founders this setup was not merely a practical necessity, but a matter of strong philosophic conviction. They believed that the tasks of government required men of exceptional intelligence, experience, temperament, and virtue. To find such men required, they believed, an elaborate winnowing process. Representative government was not enough; a very indirect version of representative government was called for.

A concession to the democratic principle was made in the provision that the House of Representatives was to be elected directly by all qualified voters. Senators, on the other hand, were to be chosen by the state legislatures. The president was to be selected by an electoral college made up of delegates from each state appointed by a process determined by the state legislatures. These electors, the majority of the Framers hoped, would be the kind of people who would not bow to the popular passions of the moment but would be equipped to select the candidate best qualified to undertake the high trust assigned by the Constitution.

Thus the ultimate source of political authority in the American constitutional system was to be the people, but they were to exercise that authority indirectly and only in the final analysis. Moreover, as we shall see in the next section, there were to be other limits on the power of the people built into the complex interrelationships between the various branches and levels of the governmental structure.

POWER AT THE CENTER—BUT RESTRAINED

The need to establish more power at the center brought the Founding Fathers together in Philadelphia. This need was the thrust of the Virginia Plan, and its proponents succeeded in replacing a loose association of autonomous states with a national government.

The Congress was given broad authority, including the power to tax, create money, regulate commerce, raise armies, and declare war, as well as to make "all Laws which shall be necessary and proper" for carrying out its other powers. In these matters national laws were to supersede state laws.

In cases of dispute over the meaning of the Constitution, or over national versus state laws, the final authority was placed in the hands of a national tribunal, the Supreme Court of the United States.

The Constitution also included what the Articles of Confederation lacked: an executive branch, headed by the president. Very little is said in the Constitution about the powers of the president. Still, the mere vesting of "The executive Power" in the president, who would appoint and preside over "the executive Departments," act as commander-in-chief, negotiate treaties, and make legislative proposals to Congress, guaranteed that there would be at least a degree of unified national action.

Although the Constitutional Convention created a national government, in an elaborate and ingenious manner that is the most distinctive feature of the American system it also placed bounds on the power of the national government.

Federalism.   To begin with, the Founding Fathers determined that power must be *divided* among the different levels of government, national and state. Confederation was to give way to federation—a system in which power was to be shared between national and state governments. The national government was to be supreme in certain areas, but the states were not to become mere administrative units of the central government. States' rights were assured in a number of ways.

First, as the Tenth Amendment made clear, a number of spheres of activity were to be reserved to the states. The states were also protected in their representation in the United States Senate: two to a state, irrespective of the size of the state. The electoral college, too, was the aggregation of electors selected state by state, with each state awarded a minimum of three delegates. Even in the House of Representatives, elected on the basis of population, there must be at least one representative from each state, no matter how small its population. The amendment procedure also reflected state interests, for it required action by three-quarters of all the state legislatures as well as two-thirds of both houses of Congress.

These protections were built into the Constitution primarily to prevent the smaller states from being submerged by the power of the larger states. However, the principle they embodied was not simply small against big states, but state against national power.

The separation of powers.   In addition to dividing power between national and state levels of government, the Framers built into the Constitution a principle known at the time as the "separation of powers"—actually the separation of institutions, legislative, executive, and judicial. Each of these branches was assigned its particular kinds of responsibilities and its own sources of election and tenure of office. The president was elected by the electoral college for a fixed term of four years. Senators were elected for six years, one-third every other year, by state legislatures. Representatives were elected by the people for only two years at a time from districts within the states. Thus each reported to a different constituency, had a different power base, and served for a different period from the others; and no member of either branch could be removed by action of the other (except through the process of impeachment).

As for the Supreme Court, although its members were appointed by the president with the consent of the Senate, their independence was assured by the fact that they served ("during good behavior") for life.

The checks and balances.   The separation of the three branches, although a central principle of the Constitution, was not complete. Superimposed on it was another principle: checks and balances, a complex system of relationships among the branches to prevent any one or combination of them from accumulating too much power.

The president could veto acts of Congress, but Congress could override the veto by a two-thirds vote in each house. The president was authorized to make senior appointments and negotiate treaties, but the concurrence of the Senate must be obtained. No law could go into effect unless it was passed by both houses of Congress.

Hence the system of separation of powers was also an intricate structure of shared powers, in which both legislative and executive branches must act before any new proposal was put into effect.

Protecting the individual.   The very existence of a written constitution as the basic law of the land, superior to all other laws, was itself intended as a protection of the individual against tyranny, for it exemplified the notion of the "rule of law," rather than of particular rulers.

In the Bill of Rights, the primacy of the individual was spelled out in specific terms. The Declaration of Independence had spoken of "inalienable rights" that were inherent in all people by virtue of their being human and that no government could take away. Through the first ten amendments these rights, including the freedom of speech, press, religion, and assembly, and the right to a fair trial, were not to be tampered with by government.

THE EVOLUTION OF THE CONSTITUTION

The making of the Constitution did not end in 1787, or with its ratification, or with the passage of the Bill of Rights. The Constitution has been in a continuing state of evolution since that time, undergoing adaptation, remolding, and reshaping.

This evolution was inevitable, because the Constitution was much too brief a document to cover all eventualities. Its brevity was no accident. Some issues were avoided because the Framers knew they could not be resolved at the convention and must be left for later resolution. But more significantly, the authors of the document knew that too much detail would tie the hands of later generations. So they dealt only with broad principles, leaving open the opportunity for interpreting those principles in the light of changing circumstances.

The evolution of the Constitution has come about through a variety of means.

Amendment.   Written into the Constitution are two specific processes of amendment. The first requires a two-thirds vote by both houses of Congress followed by approval by three-quarters of the state legislatures or special state conventions. The second involves the convening by Congress of a national convention at the request of two-thirds of the state legislatures. Only the first method has been used so far, though currently there is considerable support, especially among the radical right and some conservatives, for the convening of a constitutional convention.

Twenty-six amendments to the Constitution have been approved, among them the Bill of Rights; the Thirteenth, Fourteenth, and Fifteenth ("Civil War") Amendments, which ended slavery and forbade state interference with equal protection and due process; the Nineteenth Amendment, giving the right to vote to women; and the Twenty-sixth Amendment, extending the right to vote to every citizen at the age of 18.[3]

Statute.   Although laws passed by Congress do not have the same fundamental standing as the provisions of the Constitution itself, the Framers left Congress to fill in many of the details of the governmental structure. Thus Congress has set up the system of courts below the Supreme Court and acted to define the roles and functions of the executive departments and agencies. In recent years it has also established statutory limits on the president's freedom of action as commander-in-chief.

Presidential interpretation.   Neither the Constitution nor congressional statutes could possibly define all the circumstances in which policies are put into effect. So, as we shall see in chapter 7, the head of the executive branch will inevitably be engaged in a constant process of interpreting constitutional and statutory laws— and in so doing, remaking the laws.

Judicial interpretation.   Congress and the president may interpret the law, but the final authority on what the Constitution means is the Supreme Court of the United States. The justices of the Supreme Court have the power of "judicial review," the power to scrutinize acts of the legislative and executive branches and to nullify those acts if, in their view, they conflict with the letter or spirit of the Constitution.

Although the Constitution is clear on granting the Supreme Court power to invalidate state actions that conflict with national law, it does not specifically grant the judiciary the same authority over Congress and the president. Nor can we find in Madison's account of the debates at the constitutional convention an unequivocal intent to this effect. Still, most constitutional scholars believe that the preponderant opinion at the convention favored this key element in the system of checks and balances. In any case, we shall see in chapter 10 that with John Marshall's famous majority opinion in *Marbury* v. *Madison* (1803), judicial review became firmly established as part of our constitutional structure.

Political practice.   This framework of laws and interpretations has been supplemented by additional institutions and practices.

For example, the Constitution says nothing about political parties. But parties emerged here in rudimentary form during the ratification debates, with the Antifederalists opposing the Federalists, after which the party system evolved into a permanent feature of our system.

It was political experience, as well as statute, that defined the roles of the cabinet and its relationship to the president. Political practice and custom have also established the procedures under which Congress conducts its business, for the Constitution says nothing about the power of committee chairs, the seniority rule, or the filibuster.

However, if political practice has further defined and expanded some institutions, it has eroded others. For example, the Framers intended the electoral college to be a strong, independent, decision-making body. But with the rise of political parties, the meetings of the electors became a mere formality, ratifying a decision already made by the voters at large.

THE CONSTITUTION TODAY

The impact of these various changes has conflicted with the intent of the Framers in some important respects. For one thing, their preference for indirect representation has been rejected in the direct election of senators through the Seventeenth Amendment, the destruction of the electoral college's significance, and the introduction of the referendum and the initiative in state and local elections.

Further, even the proponents of the Virginia Plan at the Philadelphia convention would be astonished at the growth of national power since 1787. The status of the presidency has grown far beyond the expectations of the Framers as domestic and international crises have placed the initiative in the hands of the executive branch. The size and scope of the federal bureaucracies have expanded prodigiously since the 1930s. As for the states, their stature vis-à-vis the federal government has shrunk as the Supreme Court has extended the federal Constitution and statutes to cover more and more situations within the states, and as state governments have come to rely increasingly on money from Washington. Moreover, the mass media have tended to generate a common awareness of national problems and to create a single, homogenized culture overriding regional and local variations.

Nonetheless, the most essential elements of the original design, and of the compromises forced by the New Jersey Plan, are still very much with us. Although Congress has lost ground to the presidency, it still constitutes a formidable barrier to presidential power. The Supreme Court has not often ruled against Congress or the president, but it has done so enough times to remind the other two branches of its authority. Although the states have become increasingly dependent on federal largess, the roles of state and local governments have expanded greatly over the years.

Finally, the distrust of government power that permeated the debates in Philadelphia and in the state ratifying conventions has been a persistent strain in American political culture. Governments at all levels have grown, taken on more functions, become more powerful, all through the constitutionally established procedures. Yet, to a greater extent here than in most other countries, the prevailing attitude has been that governments and politicians are a necessary evil, to be regarded with suspicion and to be surrounded with bulwarks against the perpetual threat to liberty they represent.

FIVE PERSPECTIVES ON THE CONSTITUTION

The issues with which the Founding Fathers struggled stemmed ultimately from the same kind of considerations we discussed in chapter 1. They, too, talked about liberty and equality, power, and change.

However, it would be a gross misreading of history to place each of the men engaged in the debate over framing and ratifying the Constitution along our contemporary political spectrum, for today's definitions do not fit the political attitudes of the late eighteenth century. Hamilton, who distrusted the masses and admired business and commerce, might seem to us today to be a conservative. Yet, unlike today's conservatives, he was a passionate advocate of national power. Jefferson, on the other hand, is always included in any pantheon of liberal heroes. But he was an Antifederalist after 1793, and an opponent of shifting too much power to the central government. So the terms of the debate over institutions have changed drastically.

The following discussion is not a reconstruction of the arguments that took place among the protagonists at the Constitutional Convention, but rather the current debate over the Constitution among the five perspectives introduced in chapter 1.

THE CENTRISTS: THE CONSTITUTIONAL BALANCE

For centrists, the making and subsequent evolution of the Constitution is an extraordinarily impressive accomplishment. They admire the quality of the Founders themselves, the process by which the Constitution was shaped, and the balance and flexibility of their product.

They see the Framers as men of remarkable talent, whose explorations of the nature of government in the constitutional and state conventions and in *The Federalist* constitute one of the most brilliant examples of applied political theory ever undertaken.

One of the factors that led to the richness and practicality of the debates was the diversity of interests and values among the Framers. They represented big and small states, northern and southern, seaboard and inland, commercial and agricultural, and so on. Centrists concede that by no means were all interests represented in Philadelphia, for most of the delegates were educated, well-to-do men, and there were no poor farmhands or laborers (and, of course, no slaves).

However, centrists reject the conclusion of historians such as Charles Beard[4] that the Constitution was essentially a document reflecting the interests of an upper class, designed to protect property, and profoundly antidemocratic. Certainly, say the centrists, economic interests were a factor, and the Framers were concerned with protecting property against the kind of challenge represented by Shays's Rebellion. But it was not just property that was threatened. No society can survive if the whole structure of laws is challenged by armed insurrection.

As for the charge that the Framers were elitist and antidemocratic, centrists respond that, while the Framers did fear the abuse of majority power, they were also opposed to the abuse of power from *any* source. Their checks and balances were not designed primarily to protect the privileged against the masses, but to protect all the people against excessive power falling into the hands of any individual or faction. Besides, *in the context of the eighteenth century,* the Constitution and the Bill of Rights constituted a much more democratic framework than was to be found anywhere else in the world.

Furthermore, even if the allegations of economic motivations and antidemocratic intent were true, they "do not rob the Constitution of legitimacy nor destroy the importance of the political theory. For whatever the intent, the result stands independently."[5] No matter what the economic background of the Framers, they were statesmen with the capacity to rise above their personal interests and address the task of creating a new nation based on the principles of freedom and self-government.

Next, centrists admire the process by which the Constitution was shaped. Conflict was rife at the convention, and several times the delegates were deadlocked so seriously as to lead to threats of withdrawal by one or more groups. Yet each deadlock was broken, and the conflicts resolved, because of two factors. First, there was a framework of consensus on fundamentals: everyone agreed that something must be done to prevent a collapse into chaos and that the old tyranny from overseas must not be replaced with a new domestic tyranny. Second, at every crucial stage *compromises* were negotiated, brilliantly constructed solutions that provided a lasting framework of government for generations to come.[6]

The product of this intriguing process, say the centrists, superbly reflects the qualities of the men who wrote it: moderation, balance, and flexibility. The Constitution skillfully reconciles the competing forces with which all governmental systems must deal. There is the need to assign power and yet to restrain it, and no Constitution has ever balanced these contending needs so ingeniously. There is also the task of establishing a fundamental, enduring framework of law, yet allowing for change to accommodate the circumstances of each successive generation. In this respect, too, the Constitution has served us well, for the Framers built into their document the flexibility to allow for ordered change.

Centrists do not contend that the system originated by the Framers has always worked well. We have experienced the abuse of power and the underuse of power; and it took the Civil War to resolve one of the great questions with which the Framers had not been able to deal effectively. Nonetheless, no constitutional system anywhere seems to have worked any better, and the occasional failures of our system should not be allowed to obscure the fact that, under the Constitution, we have established the longest record of generally successful self-government of any nation in the world.

THE LIBERALS: A FRAMEWORK FOR DEADLOCK

There is much in the Constitution that liberals admire: the rule of law, the presidency, the Bill of Rights, the Civil War amendments. But liberals also express a great deal of dissatisfaction with the constitutional framework.

For one thing, they see it as a structure of the eighteenth century, created for a small, mostly agrarian, relatively homogeneous population, and therefore not likely to be well suited to the requirements of a huge, mostly urbanized, ethnically and racially diverse population two centuries later. Despite all the amendments and other changes, the central characteristics of the Constitution remain, and they are not characteristics that can handle the national and international stresses of the last part of the twentieth century.

In the context of 1787, no doubt, the creation of a national government, with powers going far beyond those provided by the Articles of Confederation, was a giant leap forward. But for today's needs those powers, even though greatly expanded since the Founding Fathers' time, are no longer sufficient. The overriding principle of this Constitution is the checking and limiting of power, with the result that it is now extremely difficult to get the different branches of government together to make decisions. Every so often there is a great burst of activity by the federal government, but mostly this phenomenon happens in response to some desperate crisis. We do not seem to be able to organize ourselves to prevent the crises from occurring. We suffer, says James MacGregor Burns, from "government by fits and starts . . . a statecraft that has not been able to supply the steady leadership and power necessary for the conduct of our affairs."[7] The basic reason for this discontinuity is the separation, division, and fragmentation of power built into the Constitution.

Those who suffer most from this profound tendency to inertia are the poor, the minorities, and the other less privileged segments of our population, for they are most in need of the decisive governmental action that our system discourages. Thus, whether or not the Framers of the Constitution were preoccupied with protecting property against the masses (and liberal analysts generally tend to emphasize the class interests and antidemocratic bias of the delegates to the convention), the results of their work have usually favored business and the affluent and have thwarted the wishes of the majority. Even the great advantage claimed for the system by the centrists that it protects against tyrannical abuses of power has failed to prevent periodic onslaughts on individual liberties. Examples include the anticommunist hysteria of the 1920s and 1950s; the internment of Japanese Americans after Pearl Harbor; and the Watergate affair. Moreover, the Vietnam War made it clear that, despite all the checks and balances, our leaders are still capable of plunging us into rash and terribly damaging foreign adventures.

But if we are to avoid the danger of tyrannical government, is there any alternative to the American constitutional model? Liberals believe there is. In fact, they argue, there are many examples

today of limited, democratic, self-governing systems quite unlike our own. Much more common than our system is the parliamentary model found, with variations, in Britain, Canada, West Germany, the Scandinavian countries, Israel, and elsewhere.

We shall have more to say about this kind of system in later chapters, but the point to be made at this stage is that in parliamentary governments there is *no separation of powers*. The people elect the legislature, the parliament. The party, or combination of parties, that constitutes a majority in the parliament selects the executive leaders, the government of the day. *Members of the government retain their seats in the parliament* and personally present their programs to that body.

Since the legislative and executive branches are interwoven, this legislature is much less likely than the American legislature to assert its independence, and much more likely to approve the proposals of the executive branch. The effectiveness of the executive branch is further enhanced by the fact that party discipline is usually much tighter than in the American Congress, so the members of the parties in the parliament are less prone to resist the proposals of the party leaders. But again we return to our question: With so much power in the hands of the executive, where are the restraints that distinguish democracy from dictatorship? Liberals insist that parliamentary systems impose a variety of limits on executive power. For one thing, government leaders, being members of parliament, are forced to debate their policies and submit to a daily barrage of questions on the floor of the parliament. Periodic elections must be held. In fact, if the government fails to hold its majority in the parliament, it is forced to resign; and if the legislature cannot agree on a new government from among its members, new elections must be held even though the full permissible term of the parliament has not expired.

Elections under parliamentary systems are fought mostly along party lines; and the existence of effective parties helps assure not only a strong government, but also a strong opposition, ready to take over whenever the government has lost the confidence of the electorate. Finally, in these other democratic countries, liberty is protected by free speech and press, a system of courts guaranteeing the rule of law, and (probably the most important of all prerequisites for democracy) the presence among the people and the politicians of attitudes, traditions, and practices favoring freedom, openness, and self-government rather than obedience to power and authority.

Thus, the liberals contend, it is possible to construct and sustain a democratic form of government, with all kinds of limits on its power, but without our rigid structure of separation of powers and elaborately contrived checks and balances.

Liberals realize there is no realistic possibility of importing the parliamentary system into this country. But they believe we can learn from the parliamentary experience and incorporate some of its advantages into our system. Two features in particular are recommended by liberals. First, we need more incisive and consistent presidential leadership and a greater willingness by Congress to give presidents a chance to carry out their programs. Second, liberals call for stronger, better organized political parties offering clearer alternatives to the electorate.

Through such changes, liberals contend, it would be possible to reach across the separation of powers and build into our system flexibility and strong leadership, while still retaining the limits on power and the democratic freedoms that are at the heart of the American tradition.

THE RADICAL LEFT: A CONSTITUTION FOR THE FEW

In the radical left interpretation, the Constitution grew out of a society dominated by a wealthy upper class. It was written by men representing that class, it reflected their interests, and it has served since then to perpetuate the privileges of the wealthy.

America in the late eighteenth century, say the historians of the radical left, was far from being an egalitarian society. Though there was no hereditary nobility, there were landed estates and colonial plantations, and on the eastern seaboard successful merchants acquired very large fortunes. On the other hand, a large proportion of the population cultivated tiny plots of land or worked for meager wages as farmhands, laborers, or domestic servants. About a third of the white male population did not have enough property to vote; and only a small fraction could meet the much steeper property-owning qualifications to run for office.

The Constitution, says Michael Parenti, "was framed by financially successful planters, merchants, lawyers, bankers, and creditors, many of them linked by kinship and marriage and by years of service in the Congress, the military, or diplomacy."[8] They were alarmed at the unrest and disorder resulting from the anger of poor farmers forced into debt by high prices and profiteering merchants. Shays's Rebellion reinforced their determination "that persons of birth and fortune should control the affairs of the nation and check the levelling impulses of that propertyless multitude which composed 'the majority faction.'"[9]

So it is hardly surprising that the document they wrote contained provision after provision to restrain the power of the majority, for that was the driving purpose of the entire structure of separation of powers, checks and balances, and indirect representation. It is true that the Constitution contained some concessions to the democratic principle, such as the direct election of the House of Representatives. But these concessions were necessary for securing ratification by the state conventions and for gaining the degree of popular support needed to ensure the survival of the new system, and they did not undermine the basic purpose of the Constitution, which was to protect the propertied against the propertyless.

The conflicts that split the convention did not involve fundamental principle—for there was an overwhelming consensus on the common class values of the delegates—but rather varying interests of different elements of the dominant class. Accordingly, merchants, manufacturers, and slave owners disagreed fiercely over ways of protecting their particular concerns. But the sections of the Constitution dealing with the federal government's power "to support commerce and protect property were decided upon after amiable deliberation and with remarkable dispatch considering their importance."[10]

This radical left analysis does not necessarily imply that the Founding Fathers were venal men who wrote the Constitution merely to serve their personal financial interests. No doubt, say the leftists, the Framers sincerely believed that they were inspired by the high purpose of creating an enduring structure for a new nation. But this high purpose was also compatible with their class interests. So what was at stake in Philadelphia was not so much immediate profits, but the question of "what kind of society would emerge from the revolution . . . and on what class the political center of gravity would come to rest."[11]

The final product of the work of the delegates to the convention was an elitist document, a framework to protect the concerns of the few against the many. They had little interest in individual rights; the Bill of Rights came later. Even with the Bill of Rights, the Constitution contained no mention of the fundamental human rights to food, housing, work, education, and medical care. It has taken prolonged struggle to get grudging and very limited recognition of those human rights; and this accomplishment has come despite rather than because of the body of fundamental law contained in the United States Constitution.

THE CONSERVATIVES: THE UNMAKING OF THE CONSTITUTION

Conservatives share with the centrists a profound admiration for the caliber of the Founding Fathers and the quality of the document they produced. Unlike the centrists, however, they do not believe the principles of the Constitution have survived essentially intact. On the contrary, those principles have been abrogated by the efforts of the liberals.

Certainly conservatives do not agree with the radicals of the left that the Framers were inspired by narrow class interests. The conservatives do not doubt that the Founders believed in property rights and were worried about the threat typified by Shays's Rebellion. But for conservatives there is nothing ignoble about a concern for property. As we saw in chapter 1, conservatives believe that ownership of property is a crucially important human right, providing the individual with a measure of liberty and privacy, as well as an incentive to achieve. In practice, conservatives point out, countries that deny the right to own property are totalitarian systems, the enemies of democracy.

Moreover, in defending property rights, the Framers were speaking for a value widely shared in their time. Most Americans wanted to own property, and more of them did than in any other country. Thus to favor property rights was not to express a single class interest but a core value of the society as a whole.

However, there was much more to the intent of the Framers than the preservation and advancement of property rights. They came to Philadelphia to try to find agreement on some basic principles of sound government. They succeeded, and two principles underlay all the rest.

The first principle was *limited government.* Conservatives do not contend that the Framers were anarchists. If they were they would have left well enough alone, for at the time the authority of the Continental Congress and the state governments was disintegrating. In fact, the delegates came to the convention to create an effective national government, equipped to maintain order at home and speak for the nation abroad.

However, as we have seen, they were determined not to allow any individual or group to use the power inherent in the new system for purposes dangerous to the community as a whole. They saw in human nature a tendency to selfishness and corruption, and that the temptations offered by governmental power could bring out the worst in human nature. So, through the separation of powers and checks and balances, they invented a system designed to serve the well-being of society and the rights of the individual.

The second principle was *shared government* between the national and state levels. The delegates represented the governments of states, and those states had jealously preserved their independence up to that point. There would have been no agreement at the Constitutional Convention, or at the state ratifying conventions, if the role of the states, especially the small states, had not been carefully protected. This protection was a practical political reality. But it also reflected another sound principle of government: the best government is that which is closest to the people and most fully represents the diverse values of each locality or region.

The rights of the states were written into the Constitution over and over again. Yet ratification might still not have been secured without the promise of the guarantee contained in the Tenth Amendment: "The powers not delegated to the United States by the Constitution, nor prohibited by it to the States, are reserved to the States respectively, or to the people."

To a very considerable extent, both of these principles of the Founding Fathers—limited government and shared government—have been discarded. The Framers would be astonished and dismayed at the prodigious growth of government, interfering with our right to run our business or use our property, and taking on functions that traditionally were performed by the family or by voluntary associations. The Framers would be equally shocked by the extent to which the federal government has bulldozed its way into the sphere of the states, reducing state governments to mere agents of its will or bypassing them completely.

These pernicious changes have been brought about by a number of factors: the enormous growth of the presidency (clearly not intended by the Framers, who assumed that Congress would be much more important than the president); the supine willingness of Congress from the 1930s onward to give the president what he wanted; the consequent massive growth of the federal budgets and bureaucracies; decision after decision of the Supreme Court approving the intrusion of the federal government into the economy and the states; and the climate of opinion created by the liberals in the media, the universities, and so on. The result, says conservative writer M. Stanton Evans, is that "while pretending to interpret and

adhere to the principles of the Founders, the proponents of centralized power have effectively turned the American Constitution inside out."[12]

In considering ways of undoing the damage that the liberals have wrought, a few conservatives have been attracted to the liberals' panacea of parliamentary government. That system, they believe, could provide the leadership needed for achieving conservative purposes and a party system that could present a true conservative alternative to the people.

For most conservatives, however, the business at hand is to rediscover the intent of the Framers and restore the principles on which they built the Constitution. This rediscovery means electing to office and appointing to the Supreme Court people who understand the Constitution. It also means supporting constitutional amendments on such subjects as federal spending and school prayers to bring under control the overextended power of the presidency and the gross misreadings of the Constitution by the Supreme Court.

THE RADICAL RIGHT: FIGHTING THE CONSPIRACY AGAINST THE CONSTITUTION

The radical right states the conservatives' criticisms in much more trenchant terms and offers some additional complaints about trends since the Constitution was written.

First, say the right-wing radicals, the letter and spirit of the Constitution are incompatible with the monstrous growth of central government in America. In the Constitution and the Bill of Rights "the total emphasis . . . is on telling the federal government *what it cannot do* to and for the people."[13] Clearly government should not be taking away our property rights in the autocratic way that has become the established pattern in this century. Nor was it anticipated that the federal government would usurp the rights of the states, which were built into the Constitution. "Modern 'liberalism,'" says Dan Smoot, "has abandoned American constitutional government and replaced it with democratic centralism, which, in *fundamental theory, is identical* with the democratic centralism of the Soviet Union."[14]

Then, say the radicals of the right, government may not interfere with the rights of individuals because they are, in the words of the Declaration of Independence, "inalienable rights." They are inalienable because all men have been "endowed by their Creator" with those rights. The Framers were profoundly religious men who believed they were doing the work of God, and, indeed, of Jesus Christ.[15] It is absurd, therefore, to suggest that the First Amendment's prohibition of an established religion or guarantee of freedom of worship was intended to deny any recognition by government of the existence of God or Jesus Christ.

Finally, leaders of the right insist, we are not a democracy but a republic, for that was the terminology of the Founding Fathers, and the entire constitutional structure of checks and balances and indirect representation testifies to their detestation of mob rule and their fear of factional or majority tyranny.

In all these respects, say the right-wingers, our domestic enemies of the Republic have conspired to destroy the Constitution. Our property is taken away by federal government regulations and confiscatory income taxes. The right of parents to have their children say a prayer, even a non-denominational one, at the start of the school day has been taken away by an arrogant, communist-inspired Supreme Court. The Framers' dislike of factions has been ignored in the growth of mass political parties, which undermine the principle of republican government—government that delegates authority to those best qualified to rule—and replace it with crude democratic appeals to the populace.

What can be done to restore the Framers' principles? The election of very conservative candidates can help a little but is not sufficient to stem the anticonstitutional conspiracy. Another method is to force a restating of the original constitutional doctrine by the passage of constitutional amendments. One such amendment would overrule the Supreme Court's ban on prayers in the public schools. The Liberty Amendment would require that the federal government "get out of private business," including the Tennessee Valley Authority, national forests, veterans' insurance, and Social Security. Cutting government back would facilitate the second part of the Liberty Amendment, the abolition of the federal income tax, thereby undoing the immense damage inflicted on the American system by the Sixteenth Amendment.

CONCLUSION

In several later chapters we shall be elaborating on the points made in these brief introductory perspectives on the Constitution. We shall encounter repeatedly a confusing aspect of all discussions of governmental institutions: that our attitudes toward particular institutions tend to change with the policies that come out of those institutions.

For example, liberals, who usually support presidential power and complain about congressional obstructionism, demanded that Congress oppose the presidential policies that got us into Vietnam, and during the Watergate controversy they cried out against the "Imperial Presidency." Conversely, conservatives, usually suspicious of the presidency, called on Congress to give President Reagan everything he asked for with dispatch. Radicals of the right, insisting that ours is a republic and not a democracy, nonetheless are ready in many states to go over the heads of legislatures and take their case directly to the people through a referendum or initiative.

These examples do not necessarily tell us that the advocates in question are being cynical or hypocritical. Instead they remind us that institutions are not ends in themselves, but means to achieve human purposes. Those purposes are related to the values we discussed in chapter 1. So if today the presidency is advancing the cause of high-income people, liberals will tend to look elsewhere (perhaps to the Congress) for support; but if tomorrow a chief executive favors the low-income groups, liberals are likely to applaud the institution of the presidency. The reverse may be true of conservatives. Ultimately, then, the real dividing lines will be over the policy issues discussed in Part IV of this book, rather than over the processes and institutions reviewed in Parts II and III.

Still, institutions are important, especially those that are built into a framework of fundamental law such as the Constitution of the United States. They enable us to bring order out of chaos and provide continuity in place of a succession of disconnected beginnings. Moreover, despite the inconsistencies in our attitudes toward institutions, over the long haul some institutions are more likely to serve the values of a given perspective than of another. We shall be illustrating this point in each of the chapters in the next two parts of this book.

NOTES AND REFERENCES

1. The northern states wanted slaves to count for taxes but not for congressional representatives, while the southern states wanted the reverse.
2. Southerners wanted no taxes on imports or interference with slavery.
3. ERA, the proposed Twenty-Seventh Amendment calling for equal rights for women, fell short of the required number of state endorsements despite a congressional extension to June 20, 1982.
4. Charles Beard, *An Economic Interpretation of the Constitution* (New York: Macmillan, 1931).
5. David G. Smith, *The Convention and the Constitution* (New York: St. Martin's Press, 1965), p. 23.
6. Calvin C. Jillson has argued that the debates at the convention were not between two fixed blocs—big versus small states, or North versus South—but rather between coalitions that changed from issue to issue. The result was that "at some point each state participated in the core of a winning coalition that secured their dearest aims. Thus, the delegates, almost to a man, departed the convention convinced that their constitutional glass was at least half full as opposed to half empty" ("Constitution-Making: Alignment and Realignment in the Federal Convention of 1787," *American Political Science Review,* September, 1981, p. 611).
7. James MacGregor Burns, *The Deadlock of Democracy* (Englewood Cliffs, N.J.: Spectrum, 1963), p. 2.
8. Michael Parenti, *Democracy for the Few,* 3rd ed. (New York: St. Martin's Press, 1980), p. 54.
9. Ibid., p. 55.
10. Ibid., p. 56.
11. Staughton Lynd, *Class Conflict, Slavery and the United States Constitution,* in Irwin Unger, ed., *Beyond Liberalism: The New Left Views American History* (Waltham, Mass.: Xerox College Publishing, 1971), p. 17.
12. M. Stanton Evans, *Clear and Present Dangers: A Conservative View of America's Government* (New York: Harcourt Brace Jovanovich, 1975), p. 49.
13. Dan Smoot, *The Invisible Government* (Dallas: The Dan Smoot Report, 1962), p. 108.

14. Ibid., p. 110. "Democratic centralism" in the Soviet Union is a system that encourages wide discussion and some criticism of many areas of governmental policy—particularly the implementation of policy—but retains the real decision-making control at the center. As Julian Towster puts it, the Soviet system provides "an upward stream of political intelligence, suggestion and accounting from the lower organs and a downward stream of laws, decrees, and instructions from the apex, or central organs." *Political Power in the U.S.S.R., 1917–1947* (New York: Oxford University Press, 1948), p. 207.
15. Writers from other perspectives have challenged this assumption, pointing out that some of the Founding Fathers were deists who did not accept the divinity of Jesus.

two

POLITICS AND THE PEOPLE

In Part Two we explore the broad context of American politics, the basic forces that contend with each other to influence the decisions of government officials.

We begin in chapter 3 with the electorate at large and discuss the relationship between public opinion and government. Then we assess the extent and quality of the electorate's participation in politics, finding that the majority of the people are still not very politically conscious, despite an increase in political awareness in recent years. So we ask: How serious a problem is it when only a minority are well informed and politically active?

In the next three chapters we look at the mechanisms through which individuals, groups, and the people at large express their political ideas and interests. Thus, in chapter 4 we study political parties and debate the implications of the general decline in support for the two major parties. Chapter 5 deals with elections and asks whether the electoral process provides significant choices of candidates and policies or whether elections are merely exercises in distortion and manipulation. Then in chapter 6 we describe the groups that organize the multiple interests of the people and analyze the effect of these special-interest groups on the political process; and we ask whether there is a reasonable balance among these groups or whether a few of them tower over the rest in their ability to influence political decisions.

In this section three key questions define the debate among the five perspectives: *Do the people at large rule? Can they? Should they?*

chapter three

PUBLIC OPINION:
WHO CARES ABOUT POLITICS?

Democracy, the dictionary tells us, is a political system in which power resides in all the people. But there are more than 230 million of us in America, so we cannot all exercise our power directly. A great many decisions have to be handled by relatively small numbers of leaders. Still, the democratic ideal requires that the leaders be responsive to the voice of the people, to what is commonly called "public opinion." Actually this phrase is misleading. We are not a single, undifferentiated mass of people holding a single opinion. We are made up of many "publics" holding a diversity of opinions.

In this chapter we shall begin by looking first at the factors that shape the opinions of these publics, then at the ways these opinions express themselves politically. Then we shall examine some disturbing data on the amount and distribution of political participation in America. This information will set the stage for a debate among our five perspectives on the extent to which the people at large are equipped to exercise political power.

WHAT INFLUENCES OUR OPINIONS?

We all like to consider ourselves self-determining thinkers, independent of the categories that bind other people. In fact, even if we assume that we retain an ultimate measure of free will, our ideas and behavior are powerfully influenced by a great range of factors when we make political decisions. Part of our response to politics springs from our deepest hopes and fears, our drives and impulses, our frustrations and aggressions—from that level of our personalities that is not fully subject to rational control. Then, too, our family background is an important factor in determining our personalities and our political values. People often reflect their parents' attitudes and political leanings, even though their lifestyles may be totally different.

At this stage, however, we shall not dwell on these aspects of individual behavior, for our concern must be with opinions in groups and in the mass. Let us begin by investigating the socioeconomic influences on our opinions.

THE SOCIOECONOMIC CONTEXT

Our political outlook is heavily influenced by a range of social and economic factors. So we shall provide some basic data about those factors, then explain the political implications of the data.

Income. The median annual family income of Americans in 1980 was close to $21,000, which means that half the families in the country earned more than this amount, the other half less. This figure establishes the United States as one of the most affluent countries in the world. Moreover, many people share in that affluence, for there is a large middle class. However, there are also considerable variations in income. The top 5 percent of income earners in 1978 received 15.6 percent of all money income, whereas the bottom 20 percent received only 5.2 percent of the total.

Occupation. The civilian work force in 1980 consisted of more than 104 million people. There have been four significant changes in the work force in recent years.

1. The proportion of jobs requiring substantial training and skills has increased greatly. More than a quarter of all jobs today are in professional, managerial, administrative, or technical categories, while nonfarm laborers make up less than 5 percent of the work force.

2. Producers of goods are increasingly giving way to providers of services—salespeople, secretaries, administrators, educators, entertainers, and so on. Over half of all jobs are in white-collar fields, only one-third in blue-collar occupations.

3. Not many people are left down on the farm. In 1900, 38 percent of the population was employed on farms. Now the proportion is down to barely 3 percent.

4. There has been a large increase in the number of gainfully employed women. Today close to half of all American women are in the labor market. (See table 3-6.)

Education. No country in the world matches the United States for the number of school years completed by its citizens or the proportion of the population in college. Of the 16–17 age group, almost 90 percent are still in school; and 1981 college enrollment was 12 million, including almost 40 percent of the 18–24 age group.

Geography. Americans are increasingly an urbanized people, with almost three-quarters of the population now living in metropolitan areas (communities of fifty thousand or more). Through the first half of the twentieth century, masses of people moved into the big cities of the Northeast and Midwest. Subsequently, however, large numbers (especially whites) have moved out of the cities into the surrounding suburbs.

However, since the mid-1970s there has been a trend away from metropolitan areas to smaller communities. The other major shift of population is a regional one: population growth has almost stopped in the Northeast (in New York State it actually declined by 4.2 percent between 1970 and 1980) and is occurring mostly in the West and in the South, reversing a long period of declining population in the southern states. (See table 3-1.)

TABLE 3–1 Population distribution by region (percent)

	1950	1970	1980	1990 (projection)
Northeast	26.1	24.1	22.6	21.7
North Central	29.4	27.8	26.6	25.9
South	31.2	30.9	32.5	33.3
West	13.3	17.1	18.3	19.0

Source: Statistical Abstract, 1981, U.S., Bureau of the Census.

The biggest growth is taking place in the sunbelt states at the expense of the frostbelt states, which has important consequences for the reapportionment of congressional seats and electoral college votes, as we shall see in later chapters.

Race and ethnicity.   The proportion of the population consisting of racial and ethnic minorities has been growing rapidly, partly because of higher birth rates (especially among Hispanics) and immigration from Latin America and Asia. (See table 3-2.)

TABLE 3–2 Distribution of population by racial and ethnic background, 1980 (percent)

Black	Hispanic	American Indian	Asian–American	White
11.7[a]	6.4[a]	0.6	1.5	78.8

[a] The Census Bureau later conceded that in the 1980 census blacks were undercounted by 5 percent, Hispanics by 4.4 percent.
Source: Statistical Abstract, 1981, U.S., Bureau of the Census.

On the whole, blacks, Hispanics, and American Indians experience lower incomes, higher unemployment, and less schooling than the majority. On the other hand, Jews, Japanese-Americans, and some of the Catholic nationality groups have moved to the top of the income ladder and have a well above average number of years of schooling.

Religion.   According to Gallup polls, a higher proportion of Americans say that religion is important in their lives than do most other people. As reported by the various religious bodies, U.S. church membership totals 134 million, of whom 74 million are Protestants, 50 million are Catholics, and 5.8 million are Jews; and Gallup surveys indicate that about 40 percent of people polled say they have attended church or synagogue in the past week.

However, the importance attached to religion has declined somewhat in recent years. In 1965, 71 percent of Gallup respondents rated religion as very important, 22 percent as fairly important. In 1978 the figures were as follows: very important, 53 percent; fairly important, 33 percent.

The political significance of religion has intensified lately with the emergence of organized Protestant pressure groups like the Moral Majority and the battles over abortion, gay rights, and prayer in public schools.

Age.   There have been important changes in the distribution of the population by age since 1950, as reported by the Census Bureau. The data contained in tables 3-3 and 3-4 and figure 3-1 point to the following future trends:

1. The elderly population of the United States will increase slowly through the 1980s and faster in the 1990s; by the year 2030 the elderly will probably

TABLE 3–3 Distribution of population by age (percent)

	1950	*1960*	*1970*	*1979*
Under 19	33.9	38.4	37.8	32.3
20–44	37.7	32.4	31.7	36.7
45–64	20.3	20.0	20.6	19.9
65 and over	8.1	9.2	9.9	11.2

Source: Statistical Abstract, 1980, U.S., Bureau of the Census.

TABLE 3–4 Median age of U.S. population

1950	*1960*	*1970*	*1979*
30.2	29.5	28.0	30.2

Source: Statistical Abstract, 1980, U.S., Bureau of the Census.

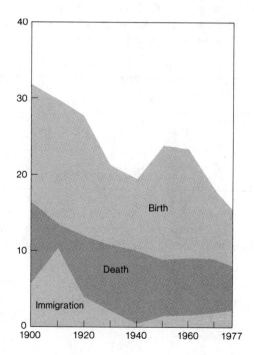

FIGURE 3–1. Birth, Death, and Immigration Rates, 1900–1977 (Per 1,000 Population)
Source: U. S., Department of Commerce, Bureau of the Census, Reflections of America: Commemorating the Statistical Abstract Centennial *(Washington, D.C.: Government Printing Office, 1980), p.146.*

constitute about 18 percent of the population. Even with later retirement this statistic will mean a higher proportion dependent on the working population, and a severe strain on Social Security and other retirement programs.

2. There will be a decline in the teenage and young adult population in the 1980s because of the decline in the birthrate in the 1960s and 1970s. However, there will be some increase again in the 1990s because of a slow upturn in the birthrate starting about 1978 and because of the large increase in the women of child-bearing age generated by the post–World War II baby boom. Thus, pre-schoolers will increase by 36 percent in the 1980s.

3. In 1980 there were 40 million people in the 20–29 age group. In the 1950s they placed heavy pressure on the school system and in the 1970s on the job market. This pressure is shifting to the housing market in the 1980s and will shift again to retirement programs in the next century.

Gender.   Women live longer than men (life expectancy of a girl born in 1980 is 81, of a boy, 72), so there are more widows than widowers and more women than men in the voting age population. (See table 3–5.)

TABLE 3–5 Males per 100 females, 1979

Total	Under 5	5–19	20–44	45–64	65 and over
95.0	104.7	103.9	98.4	92.2	68.4

Source: Statistical Abstract, 1980, U.S., Bureau of the Census.

As noted earlier, there has been a sharp increase in the number of women in the labor force. (See table 3-6). The employment of close to half of all married women is leading not only to higher family incomes but also to changing family patterns and probably to greater involvment in the political system. One of the issues leading to political action is the disparity between the median salaries of men and women ($15,070 for men and $8,814 for women in 1979).

TABLE 3–6 Percent of female population in the labor force

Year	All women	Single	Married	Married, husband present	Widowed/ divorced
1940	27.4	48.1	16.7	14.7	32.0
1950	31.4	50.5	24.8	23.8	36.0
1960	34.8	44.1	31.7	30.5	37.1
1970	42.6	53.0	41.4	40.8	36.2
1978	49.1	60.5	48.1	47.6	40.0

Source: Statistical Abstract, 1979, U.S., Bureau of the Census.

Family structure.   The rising rate of divorce (table 3-7), combined with the tendency toward later marriages and the greater longevity of women, is producing these results:

1. Smaller households: average size declined from 3.33 in 1960 to 2.78 in 1979.
2. More single person families: an increase of almost 50 percent in the 1970s.

3. A decline in the population of families headed by married couples from 80 percent in 1950 to a projected 50 percent by 1990.

TABLE 3-7 Marriages and divorce rates (per 1,000 population)

	1950	1960	1970	1979
Marriages	11.1	8.5	10.6	10.5
Divorces	2.6	2.2	3.5	5.3

Source: Statistical Abstract, 1980, U.S., Bureau of the Census.

Implications for political attitudes. What do these socioeconomic factors mean in terms of our political attitudes and opinions? Answering this question is an immensely complicated task. But it is possible, before we proceed to the complications, to make some very crude, approximate generalizations. Primarily, those segments of the population that feel least advantaged by the system, who have a sense of being "outgroups," are most likely to stress the need for more equality, and in that sense to be left of center on our political spectrum. Most often these people will be found at the lower end of the income scale and in the less skilled occupations. They are likely to have fewer years of schooling than the average. Many of them will be black or have Spanish surnames and will live in the inner cities. Others will be descendants of the later waves of immigration, who have a sense of grievance that those immigrants who got here first are the "established" groups who are reluctant to give the newer groups their place in the sun. Conversely, the more affluent, business and professional, college-educated strata of the population, living in the suburbs and descendants of the earlier settlers, tend to feel that they have the most to protect and thus to be less enthusiastic about egalitarian notions.

This simple scheme is useful as far as it goes. But, as we look at the strands of opinion more closely, we see that they move in all directions, producing extraordinarily complex patterns. Thus, some well-to-do, college-educated people— perhaps because of their personality structure, ideology, or family background— have a social conscience that impels them to advocate strong measures on behalf of the poor. At the other end of the scale, some of the poor have such racial or ethnic prejudice that they oppose policies that help the poor because they help the wrong poor.

As we look at the question of civil liberties, we are more likely to discover liberal or left-of-center attitudes among the affluent, college-educated segment of the population. For example, table 3-8 shows the responses to questions on whether an admitted Communist or homosexual should be allowed to teach in a college or university.

We come across further complexities when we examine the political attitudes of certain ethnic and religious groups. For example, many Catholics still feel that they are not fully accepted into the system, which they believe to be dominated by Protestants. This conviction inclines them to be left of center on a number of issues. Yet they are pulled in a different direction by their increasing affluence and also by the tenets of their church on issues like abortion and school prayers.

TABLE 3–8 Right to teach in college or university (percent agreeing)

Respondent by educational level	Communist	Homosexual
Less than high school graduate	28	33
High school graduate	40	55
Some college	52	68
College graduate	62	78
College graduate +	70	80

Source: National Opinion Research Center, combined responses for 1972–1974, 1976–1977, 1980 cited in *Public Opinion*, October/November 1980, p. 27.

Finally, there is the factor of age. Young people are on the whole more liberal, more disposed toward equality than their elders. Partly this is a matter of economics, for the young earn less and have much less property than older people. But even the young who are affluent tend to be more liberal than older people in the same economic bracket. As people grow older, they become more protective of what they have acquired, more resistant to social experimentation, and thus more conservative. But even this statement must be qualified, for people over 65, who tend to conservatism on many issues, are overwhelmingly in favor of such egalitarian policies as Social Security.

OTHER INFLUENCES ON PUBLIC OPINION

Political cues from opinion leaders.   There is more to the formation of political opinions than their association with social and economic conditions. Political opinions have to be articulated, and we receive help in articulating them from other people. Probably the most important source for our opinions is those individuals who form our network of personal relationships—parents, spouses, relatives, friends, and other acquaintances. They are closest to us, they tend to share our own socioeconomic background, we trust them more than other people, and thus they help to formulate and to reinforce our ideas and values.

Public and private schools, from kindergarten onward, provide another setting in which attitudes with significant political content are conveyed. Teachers, administrators, curriculum designers, and textbook authors play key roles in the process of *socialization,* or communicating to us the prevailing climate of social and political ideas. Then, too, we receive political cues from a variety of leaders, people who have attained some level of prominence or status and have developed relatively clearly stated opinions of which they try to convince us. They are leaders in politics and government, in private organizations, and in the institutions that disseminate information and ideas.

The role played by leaders of business, labor, professional, civic, and voluntary organizations in the formation of public opinion will be discussed in chapter 6. And the influence of elected and appointed governmental officials will be a major topic throughout this book. But influencing other people's views is only one of the many functions of these organizational and governmental leaders. Here we shall focus on that group of professionals whose prime functions are in the fields of information and opinion: people who work in the mass media, colleges and universities, research institutions, and philanthropic foundations.

Professional opinion makers. Television has become preeminent among the mass media as a source of political news. About two-thirds of the American people say they get most of their news from television, especially during great crises. The assassination of John F. Kennedy and the attempted assassination of Ronald Reagan were experienced largely through television. Television, through its coverage of the resistance to the civil rights movement in the South, gave that movement much of its impetus. The televising of the eruptions of violence in cities such as Watts and Detroit in the 1960s had a great impact on the public consciousness. The bloody battlefields of Vietnam, coming into American homes at the dinner hour night after night, helped turn public opinion against the war. And the televised Senate and House investigations and debates over the Watergate scandal were a principal means of establishing the climate of opinion that led to Richard Nixon's resignation from the presidency.

Presidential elections are fought increasingly in the arena of television. Even the traditional personal tours of the candidates are scheduled to get the best coverage on the local television stations. Vast amounts of money are poured into television commercials. And in 1960, 1976, and 1980, the televised debates between the major party candidates probably had a critical effect on the election results. Radio, a potent instrument of mass persuasion for political leaders in the 1930s and 1940s, has now fallen to a secondary role. However, the increasing number of all-news radio stations is an important source of information for people driving to and from work and for homemakers.

Thus, newspapers are no longer the public's prime source of political information and opinions. However, they can explore issues in depth, give the full background to a news story, and deal with problems that, though of crucial importance, are difficult for television to deal with visually. Not all newspapers do this. But those papers that do—*The New York Times, The Washington Post, Los Angeles Times, Chicago Tribune* and others—almost certainly contribute significantly to the shaping of public opinion. Nor is the impact of such newspapers solely on the general public. *The New York Times* and *The Washington Post* are read regularly in the White House and in Congress. Many political and organizational leaders, like the public at large, do not know what to think about a given subject until they have read columnists like David Broder or Joseph Kraft.

It is important to note, however, that television news and newspapers are not unrelated sources of information. The most likely watchers of the television network news programs are newspaper readers, and the day after a major story has appeared on television, newspaper circulation will generally rise, because many people want to know more about the story than they can glean from the usually superficial coverage given it on television.

Is there a particular bias in the presentation of news and opinions in the mass media? We shall have more to say on this question later in the chapter. For the moment we can indicate that some process of selection is inevitable in the presentation of news, because it is impossible to cover everything that happens, and the values and preconceptions of the individuals who decide what is important and what is not cannot be completely excluded from the selection process. In general, the majority of journalists are centrist to left of center, and the majority of publishers, whose editorial views are carried by their publications, are centrist to right of center.[1]

In addition to the mass media, an array of specialized journals speak to particular publics. Magazines with a primarily political emphasis offer analyses that cover the complete spectrum of opinion. In the center, *Time* and *Newsweek* have the largest circulations in this category (*Newsweek*, which is owned by *The Washington Post*, is rather more liberal than *Time*); *U.S. News and World Report* is more conservative. Opinion weeklies such as *The New Republic, Nation,* and *National Review* have much smaller circulations; and many organs of opinion on the far left and the far right speak to still smaller constituencies. Among the vast number of weekly and monthly publications that appeal to various tastes, hobbies, professional activities, and leisure-time pursuits, some give at least occasional attention to politics. Finally, a number of scholarly journals, especially those in political science and economics, bring the findings of recent research to bear on governmental affairs.

Another source of opinion in any society is the intellectuals, people whose primary interest is in philosophical, social, aesthetic, scientific, and political ideas. They work in a diversity of professions, but the bulk of them are found in colleges and universities, where they undertake the most characteristic functions of intellectuals: research, writing, and teaching. They influence opinion in the first place through their impact on their students and their peers. They reach the public at large through lectures, articles in the press and popular journals, and radio and television appearances. They also act as consultants to government and, as in the case of Henry Kissinger or Zbigniew Brzezinski, are even appointed to high official posts.

In general, college and university faculty members are considerably to the left of the public at large. However, there is no one pervasive ideology common to all academics. According to one study, 64 percent of the social scientists and 57 percent of the humanities professors call themselves "liberal" or "very liberal." The more distinguished universities with the largest number of research awards have more politically liberal faculties than do the less prestigious schools.[2] However, in business and engineering 60 percent of the professors describe themselves as "conservative" or "very conservative." The governing boards of universities and colleges are generally more conservative than their faculties, which has occasionally caused acute conflicts.

Three other kinds of agencies are concerned with the development of ideas. First, there are social science research centers, such as the Rand Corporation, the Brookings Institution, the Hoover Institution, the American Enterprise Institute, the Institute for Policy Studies, and others. Then there are organizations, such as the Council on Foreign Relations and the Committee for Economic Development, that help top-level business and professional people explore political and economic issues, and other organizations, such as the Foreign Policy Association, that are concerned with the education of the broader citizenry. Finally, several of the private philanthropic organizations, including the Ford and Rockefeller Foundations, have provided large amounts of money over the years to facilitate research into many areas of public policy. However, philanthropic foundations may jeopardize their tax-free standing if their grants are used for partisan political purposes.

The influence of events.   One other set of external forces acts on us to affect our political opinions: great events or major changes in the circumstances of our total society. Some of these are accidents or freak occurrences such as drastic changes in the climate, earthquakes, fires, floods, and assassinations. Other events—wars, oil embargoes, the collapse of foreign currencies—result from deep-rooted international problems. Technological advances such as television, atomic energy, and computers have an enormous impact on our lives and attitudes. So, too, do certain social forces, such as the movement for equal rights for women and the transformation of sexual attitudes and behavior.

Somehow a bewildered public, staggering from crisis to crisis, must confront all these pressures for change, absorb them into their value systems, and eventually react to them politically—deciding for or against the Equal Rights Amendment and the construction of nuclear energy plants, or judging government's perform-ance in dealing with international crises and natural calamities. To some extent, political, organizational, and other leaders of opinion can influence the reaction of the public to critical events and may even have an impact on the direction and pace of change. But of course they cannot fully control all these events, and, like the public at large, leaders find themselves groping for understanding, desperately trying to avoid being overwhelmed or bypassed by the surge of unpredicted, sometimes unpredictable, developments.

HOW DO WE EXPRESS OUR OPINIONS?

We have reviewed the various forces—socioeconomic factors, political leaders, professional opinion makers, and events—that go into creating political opinions. Now we shall reverse our approach and examine the ways in which publics try to make their opinions count.

Voting is the most common way in which people express their political opinions. Suffrage, or the right to vote, now includes all adult citizens, which was not the case at the beginning of the Republic, when only male property owners could vote. At the time, male property owners comprised a fairly high proportion of the people, because many of them were independent farmers. However, as more people became industrial workers, city dwellers, and tenants, property restrictions became discriminatory and pressures rose to do away with property and taxpaying qualifications for voting. By the middle of the nineteenth century, most of these restrictions were gone.

Three other major obstacles to universal suffrage remained in this country, but each was abolished after a long struggle. Although the right of black males to vote was guaranteed by the Fifteenth Amendment to the Constitution in 1870, not until Congress passed the Voting Rights Act of 1965 did this guarantee become effective for black people in the South. The right of women to vote was bitterly resisted until the passage of the Nineteenth Amendment to the Constitution in 1920. And the Twenty-sixth Amendment lowered the voting age to 18 in 1971.

Voting is not the only means by which people express themselves in political campaigns. They also attend political meetings and undertake a variety of tasks at campaign headquarters: stuffing envelopes, telephoning voters, writing speeches, and organizing motorcades and rallies. They put bumper stickers on their cars and contribute money to candidates and political parties. They go from door to door in precincts to present their candidate's case and to get out the vote on election day.

People are also active in organizations that take political stands. They write letters to their representatives and to the editors of newspapers. They talk to relatives, friends, and fellow workers. Where people's feelings are particularly strong and they are frustrated by the traditional channels of political communication, they engage in protest activities, such as marching, demonstrating, picketing, occupying buildings, obstructing traffic, and in extreme cases resorting to violence.

In addition to these various forms of active participation there is another, essentially passive, means by which the opinions of ordinary people find expression in politics: the public opinion polls. George Gallup's American Institute of Public Opinion and the Louis Harris survey are the best known of these polls. Further, national polls are conducted by the Yankelovich and Roper organizations, the television networks, Associated Press, and some major newspapers. Presidential and other major candidates retain their own pollsters, and there are several state-wide polls. There are also university-based organizations, such as the Center for Political Studies at the University of Michigan. All of them use a carefully devised *sampling* method for determining public views on a candidate or issue, which means that the people interviewed are taken to be representative of larger segments of the population. Gallup usually relies on a sample of about 1,500 interviews, Harris about 1,600.

How can such small numbers accurately represent the entire electorate? Pollsters claim that the sampling method has been shown to be valid through two tests. First, when the number of interviews is greatly increased, the results do not change much. Second, polls taken just before an election are measured against the actual election results. Questions about the accuracy of polls persist, as we shall see in chapter 5, but we can reasonably use poll results as indicating the general trends of opinion in the country. And most political leaders pay close, even hypnotized, attention to the polls. So, as a means of conveying the opinions of people in this country, opinion polls are potent tools.

THE BIG QUESTION: HOW MUCH INTEREST IS THERE IN POLITICS?

Several crucial questions arise from our discussion of what influences political opinions and how people express these opinions: How much do people care about politics in America? What proportion of the people have strong political opinions? How many take part in the political process? In general, we have found that, although the number who care and participate has increased in recent years, politics is still not a consuming passion of the majority of the American people, and a sizable minority have no interest at all.

KNOWLEDGE, INTEREST, AND IDEOLOGY

Not many Americans are well informed about politics. Polls indicate that little more than half of the electorate can name their member of Congress, and much smaller proportions can name the Speaker of the House, the Senate Majority Leader, and the Secretary of Defense. In September 1979 the Gallup organization asked a sample of the public about possible Republican candidates for the presidency in 1980. The question was: "Which of these men have you heard something about?" Among the responses were the following:

Candidate	Percentage
Gerald Ford	94
Ronald Reagan	91
John Connally	76
Robert Dole	60
Howard Baker	58
Alexander Haig	44
George Bush	38
Eliot Richardson	36
William Simon	31
John Anderson	22
Jack Kemp	18

DRAWING BY STEVENSON; © 1969. THE NEW YORKER MAGAZINE, INC.
"Undecided! Do you mean to tell me that despite the extraordinary and clearcut differences between the candidates and between their policies this year, you—an adult American—can't make up your mind?"

Several of these men, especially John Anderson, George Bush, and John Connally, became much better known when the election season got under way in 1980. But even by the fall of 1979 John Connally had a long-established reputation in American politics as the governor of Texas who had almost shared John Kennedy's fate in the Dallas motorcade in 1963, and then as President Nixon's secretary of the treasury; yet a quarter of the American public had apparently heard nothing about him. About two-fifths could not recall anything about Robert Dole, who had been Gerald Ford's running mate just three years before; about Alexander Haig, who had been the White House chief of staff in the last, highly publicized stages of the Nixon presidency; or about George Bush, who had been head of the CIA and ambassador to China, among other high offices. Only about a third knew anything about Eliot Richardson, who had held several top cabinet positions, or William Simon, President Ford's treasury secretary. Six percent knew nothing about Gerald Ford, and 9 percent could not place Ronald Reagan.

Much the same story applies to political issues. In September 1963, at the height of the great debate over the ratification of a nuclear test ban treaty, the Gallup poll found that 22 percent of the electorate had not heard of the issue. George Gallup found cause for reassurance in this. After all, 78 percent had heard of it, and 78 percent, said Gallup, was a high awareness figure as compared with what the public knew about other issues. Thus, even when politicians and the mass media develop a topic to the point of obsession, there will still be a quarter, even a third, of the adult population who have not the remotest idea that such a question has ever been raised. And of those people who have heard of the issue, a considerable proportion will have only the haziest notion of what it is about.

One reason for the widespread apathy and ignorance is that many of those people who do not know much about politics do not *want* to know much about politics. This fact becomes apparent every time a major political event is televised and preempts a popular program. When the Watergate hearings conducted by Senator Sam Erwin's committee were televised in 1973, they received good ratings; but 44 percent in a Gallup poll complained that the media were giving too much coverage to Watergate. Many angry viewers called local television stations to complain about not seeing their favorite programs.

Political leaders have learned to recognize the importance of not competing with popular television shows. For example, President Carter scheduled his 1978 State of the Union message for Thursday, January 19, rather than the date preferred by congressional leaders, Tuesday, January 24. The White House did not want to preempt prime time from the three ABC Tuesday night hit shows, "Laverne and Shirley," "Happy Days," and "Three's Company."

Another index of the level of public interest in politics is the style and substance of most election campaigns. Professionals who design the campaigns assume that a high proportion of the voters know little and care less about politics. So, as we shall see when we discuss elections in chapter 5, a large part of the budget of most candidates for high office goes into short television and radio commercials that inevitably oversimplify the issues and emphasize the candidates' personalities rather than public policy issues.

This evidence supports the conclusion of one of the major studies of the electorate, *The American Voter,* published in 1960. That conclusion was: "We have . . . an electorate almost wholly without detailed information about decision-making in government . . . almost completely unable to judge the rationality of government actions. . . ."[3] The authors of this study recognized that a segment of the population was well informed, followed politics very closely, and had some kind of ideological framework that helped them place candidates and issues on a liberal-conservative spectrum. But this "attentive public" constituted only a small minority. The greater part of the population was poorly informed and did not have any conceptual framework to help them assess the information they had. The majority, said *The American Voter,* were not able to think in ideological terms. They did not have any set of thoughtful, reasonably consistent political beliefs to which they could relate their impressions of events, candidates, and parties.

More recent studies show some improvement over this dismal assessment. According to a major work that appeared in 1976, *The Changing American Voter,*[4] the American electorate has become somewhat more politically aware and sophisticated since the 1950s. By the early 1970s considerably more people than in the earlier period thought in ideological or near-ideological terms about parties, candidates, and issues.

How do the authors account for this improvement? They point to two of the factors mentioned earlier in this chapter. The first factor is the increasing educational level of the electorate. Between 1956 and 1972 the proportion of the population that had been to college increased from under 20 percent to almost 30 percent. However, increased education is only part of the answer, because there has been discernible improvement among many who have not gone to college.

The other explanation is the impact of events and the nature of the times. The fifties were a relatively quiet period in American politics. There were few deeply disruptive issues. The majority were reasonably content with their government and the political system. Politics did not intrude very much into their lives.

But from the early 1960s there has been a succession of shattering events and issues. John F. Kennedy, Martin Luther King, Jr., and Robert Kennedy were assassinated, George Wallace was crippled in another assassination attempt, and Ronald Reagan was nearly killed by yet another gunman. The cities were torn by race riots and the campuses by student upheavals. We went through Vietnam and Watergate, inflation and recession, an oil embargo and huge increases in the price of gas, and the long ordeal of the hostages in Iran. Crisis has crowded crisis out of the headlines. All these events were driven into the consciousness of the public by an enormously potent medium that was only in its infancy in 1956— television. So the electorate was shocked into political awareness by a series of traumatic episodes.

Even so, it is important not to overstate the extent of the increase in the public's awareness and understanding of politics. In *The Changing American Voter* the average members of the electorate are not pictured as well informed citizens, constantly engaged in a process of cogent political analysis. The tests of ideological capacity used by the authors are not very stringent,[5] and many of those people who use terms such as *liberal, conservative,* and *socialist* do so in a very loose and vague fashion. Moreover, in a second edition that took into account the 1976 election, the authors showed that a good deal of the public's increased ideological perception had resulted from the polarization of parties and leaders that had taken place from 1960 to 1972, and that once ideological differences between candidates blurred again in 1976, the electorate, too, became less ideological in its judgment of candidates and issues.

As for the extent of interest in presidential elections, figure 3-2 suggests that the proportion of the electorate that is very interested increased between 1956 and 1980 and the proportion showing little interest declined; but the changes have not been large enough to be particularly encouraging.

In sum, although there has been a trend in the past twenty-five years toward greater political awareness, a majority of the American people are not particularly knowledgeable about or interested in political leaders, events, and issues, and large numbers of people hardly follow politics at all.

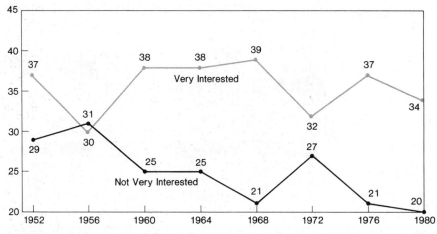

FIGURE 3–2. Proportion of Public Interested in Presidential Campaigns, 1956–1980 (Percentage)
Source: Norman H. Nie, Sidney Verba, and John R. Petrocik, The Changing American Voter *(Cambridge: Harvard University Press, 1979), p. 273; Bernard C. Hennessy,* Public Opinion, *4th ed. (Monterey, Calif.: Brooks/Cole, 1981), p. 14.*

PARTICIPATION

Our next concern is, What proportion of the American public participates in the political process? About a sixth of the population takes part in one way or another in political campaigns. Close to a quarter of the electorate claims to have done something at some time to help a candidate or party during an election. Slightly over a quarter say that they have written a public official to express an opinion. About one person in fifteen has written a letter to an editor.

The proportion participating in campaigns was higher in 1972 than in 1952, though somewhat below the peak level of 1960.[6] However, there has been a significant decline in voting participation since the early 1950s.

Thus, from the high point of 63.5 percent in 1960, turnout fell to 54.4 percent in 1976, and 53.9 percent in 1980. Since both Jimmy Carter and Ronald Reagan received about 51 percent of the total votes cast in 1976 and 1980, the proportion voting for them constituted little more than a quarter of the population of voting age. (See figure 3-3.)

In congressional elections the voting turnout is lower still. Especially in midterm years, when there is voting for Congress but not the president, voter turnout has been typically in the low- to mid-40 percent range.

These percentages are considerably lower than the voting percentages found in most other democracies. One major reason is that, in order to reduce the voting frauds that were commonplace during the nineteenth century, many states introduced procedures that required people to take specific steps to register. These procedures cut down on the fraud, but they also reduced the voting rolls, for many people forgot, did not bother, or could not get to a voting registrar's office, espe-

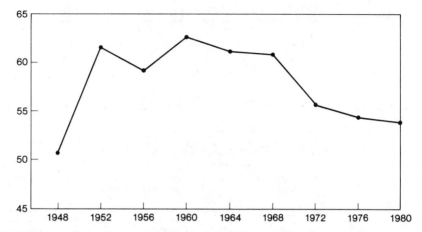

FIGURE 3–3. Voter Turnout for Presidential Elections (Percentage of Voting Age Population 1948–1980)

cially since registration had to be completed some time before an election when interest in politics is rarely high. By contrast, in most other democratic countries, automatic registration eliminates the requirement that citizens initiate steps to ensure that they are on the voting roll.[7]

According to one study, merely bringing the procedures of the more restrictive states into line with those prevailing in the states with the most open procedures (those that eliminated closing dates for registration, kept registration offices open to meet the convenience of working people, and permitted absentee registration for the sick, disabled, and absent) *would increase voting turnout by approximately 9.1 percent.*[8]

However, voter registration procedures cannot explain the *decline* in voting since the 1960s, for there has been a trend toward making registration easier. Several states have passed laws to simplify the registration process. The 1965 Voting Rights Act greatly increased the number of blacks who could register and vote in the South; and additional provisions of the act passed in 1975 helped Spanish-speaking and other minority people by requiring districts with 5 percent or more language-minority voters to print ballots and other election material in their languages. Moreover, in 1972 the Supreme Court established a maximum residence requirement of thirty days to qualify for voting in any election.[9] Yet the proportion of the electorate casting their ballots has continued to fall.

So far in this section we have examined the extent of political knowledge, conceptual ability, and participation in America. Now it is time to look at the distribution of political interest and involvement among the various segments of the public. In this context we find that the following are the most important variables.

Education.   The close relationship between educational level and political interest, knowledge, and participation can be clearly seen in the data drawn from 1972 election studies as shown in table 3-9.

TABLE 3–9 Relationship between education and political involvement in 1972

Years of education	Percentage who say they are very interested in politics	Percentage who are well informed about politics[a]	Percentage who voted
5–7	22	8	49
12	34	17	69
1–3 college	47	32	79
4 college	55	37	86
5 college +	75	59	91

[a]Respondents who knew at least five of the following six facts: number of terms president can serve; length of term for U.S. senator and U.S. representative; name of representative in Congress; majority party in Congress before election and after election.
Source: Raymond E. Wolfinger and Steven J. Rosenstone, *Who Votes?* (New Haven, Conn.: Yale University Press, 1980), p. 19.; and Center for Political Studies, 1972 National Election Study.

Income.   Income, which is fairly closely related to educational level, is another important determinant of political involvement, as shown in table 3-10.

TABLE 3–10 Income and turnout in 1972

	Under $2,000	$2,000–$7,499	$7,500–$9,999	$10,000–$14,999	$15,000–$24,000	$25,000+
Percent Voting	46	57	65	73	81	86

Source: Raymond E. Wolfinger and Steven J. Rosenstone, *Who Votes?* (New Haven, Conn.: Yale University Press, 1980), p. 21.

Occupation.   Occupation bears a close relationship to both education and income and is also a significant factor relating to voting turnout. Thus, in 1972, 86 percent of professional and technical people voted; 75 percent of clerks and salespeople; 64 percent of skilled workers; and 53 percent of semiskilled and unskilled workers.

So the people who are most likely to vote, follow politics, go to political meetings, and write letters to the editor are drawn disproportionately from the upper educational, income, and occupational groups. Of course, many lower-income, less educated people are deeply interested in politics and work very hard in campaigns. Labor unions, for example, draw considerable numbers of their members into active participation in elections. And there has been a dramatic increase in the amount of political activity by blacks since the early 1950s. By and large, however, poor people, those who have not graduated from high school, blacks,[10] Chicanos, and other disadvantaged groups are less likely than other segments of the population to follow politics closely, get involved in campaigns, or contribute money to candidates.

Age.   The next most important dividing line between the involved and the uninvolved is age. Clearly the older one gets, the more likely one is to vote, until physical infirmity and transportation problems begin to set limits on one's ability to participate.

Table 3-11 is based on the first year in which the effect of the Twenty-sixth

Amendment to the Constitution was felt. That amendment gave the vote to all from the age of 18—an additional 11 million people. There were also 14 million people between the ages of 21 and 24 in 1972 who had not been old enough to vote in 1968 (when the minimum voting age was still 21). Consequently, there were 25 million potential new voters in 1972. Yet their voting turnout was 15 percent below that of the population of a whole.

This statistic is consistent with the experience of other election years. The proportion of young people who vote and participate in politics has been considerably below the proportion of their elders.

TABLE 3–11 Turnout by age in 1972

	18–24	25–31	32–36	37–69	70–78	79+
Percent Voting	53	62	67	74	68	52

Source: Raymond E. Wolfinger and Steven J. Rosenstone, *Who Votes?* (New Haven, Conn.: Yale University Press, 1980), p.38.

In large measure the reasons are that most young people have not yet established their own families, settled into communities, placed children in the schools, and put down the kinds of social and economic roots that make people aware of their political environment. The young are also typically preoccupied with starting their careers, building personal relationships, and, in general, finding themselves, rather than worrying about national and international problems.

Among the young, however, college students are considerably more likely than members of the work force to think about politics and to vote; and some of the highest voting turnouts in the country are found in precincts around college campuses. Yet we should not exaggerate the extent of college students' devotion to politics. Even during the campus turmoil of the 1960s there was much less commitment to political action among the young than was commonly assumed. One study of students at Berkeley and Stanford published in 1968 found that a large majority of students were still "privatists" in their outlook, ranking their careers and future family life far beyond involvement in international, national, or civic affairs.[11] Since then observers of campus life report a weakening of political interest. For example, an annual survey of college freshmen showed that in 1981 only 39 percent of freshmen students rated "keeping up with political affairs" as an important objective, as compared with 51 percent in 1969.[12]

Gender. A less important variable is gender. Women are somewhat less likely to vote than men; but until the age of 40, the difference is very small, and it is only in their sixties that there is a marked falling away in the proportions of women voters.[13] The disparity may be somewhat larger, however, with respect to the relative proportions of men and women who pay close attention to politics. One indication of this disparity is that in the 1981 freshmen survey, the proportion of men students who listed keeping up with politics among their important objectives was 45 percent, as compared with 34 percent for women students.

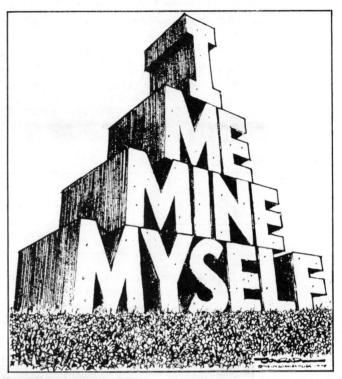

PAUL CONRAD, ©1975, LOS ANGELES TIMES, REPRINTED WITH PERMISSION.
Speaking of American cults. . . .

THE DECLINE OF TRUST IN GOVERNMENT

The data we have been reviewing contain a puzzle, an apparent contradiction. On the one hand, we have noted that educational levels and income have been rising and that these factors are associated with higher levels of political awareness and activity. On the other hand, the proportion of the population engaging in that most fundamental of all kinds of political activity—voting—has been going down.

A partial answer may be found in a factor we have just discussed: the addition to the electorate of a group with a low propensity to vote, the 18–20 age group. But this factor alone is not sufficient to explain the voting decline to less than 54 percent. A possible key to this riddle may be found in the abundant evidences of a general erosion of trust in government. Confidence in the leaders of major institutions of America has fallen sharply, as we see in table 3-12. Other surveys indicate sharp increases since the early 1960s in the proportions who agree that "you cannot trust the government to do what is right," "government is for the benefit of the few," or "public officials don't care much what people like me think." By the mid-1970s those sentiments expressed the views of close to two-thirds of the public.

Along with this erosion of confidence in government has gone a decline in the electorate's self-confidence. The University of Michigan Center for Political Studies' data show a large rise since 1960 in the proportion of the population that believes that political effort is futile. There has been a decline, in other words, in what social scientists refer to as *efficacy,* the sense that what we do makes a difference.

TABLE 3–12 Decline of confidence in primary American institutions

Question:
A. As far as people in charge of running _____ are concerned, would you say you have a great deal of confidence, only some confidence, or hardly any confidence at all in them?

	1966	1971	1973	1974	1975	1976	Feb. 1977	Nov. 1977	1978	1979	1980	1981
	Percentage of those expressing "a great deal" of confidence											
National, State and Local Government												
Executive branch, federal government	41	23	19	28	13	11	23	23	14	17	17	24
Congress	42	19	29	18	13	9	17	15	10	18	18	16
State government[a]	—	—	24	—	—	16	18	19	15	—	—	—
Local government[a]	—	—	28	—	—	19	18	21	19	—	—	—
Other Institutions												
Medicine	73	61	57	50	43	42	43	55	42	30	34	37
Higher education	61	37	44	40	36	31	37	41	41	33	36	34
Organized religion	41	27	36	32	32	24	29	34	34	20	22	22
The military	62	27	40	33	24	23	27	31	29	29	28	28
Major companies	55	27	29	21	19	16	20	23	22	18	16	16
The press	29	18	30	25	26	20	18	19	23	28	19	16
Organized labor	22	14	20	18	14	10	14	15	15	10	14	12
Average	47	28	34	29	24	21	25	28	26	23	23	23

[a]These institutions are not included in the averages since they are not asked about in every poll.
Source: Harris, Louis. *The Harris Survey.* New York: The Tribune Company Syndicate, Inc., October 22, 1981.

All the previous studies have shown that, not only in the United States but in a number of other countries, the better-educated, more affluent people tend to feel efficacious. They believe that political activity is worthwhile. In contrast, the poor tend to feel that no matter what they do they will continue to be ignored and discriminated against. This distinction has not yet been invalidated. As we have said, we still find more political activity, including more voting, as we go up the income and educational ladders. However, a significant number of well-educated, well-to-do people who are very interested in politics, very much aware of what is going on, and deeply concerned about the future have decided that voting is useless. Since political leaders and institutions are corrupt, remote, and unresponsive, why bother? So nonvoting is no longer merely a sign of apathy and ignorance. It is also the result of a positive decision to abstain on the part of a number of politically conscious citizens.

FIVE PERSPECTIVES ON PUBLIC OPINION

THE CENTRISTS: A FAVORABLE VIEW, NONETHELESS

Centrists can hardly take pleasure in the statistics showing a decline in voting, trust in government, and the sense of efficacy. These statistics are all indications of a troubled electorate and of some undesirable trends in American politics. Still, centrists insist that there is no cause for alarm. They persist in their belief that the data we have examined do not nullify their claim that we have a basically sound and responsive democracy in America.

First, they argue that even those people who do not have a detailed knowledge of a large number of specific events and issues still have a pretty good idea of how government policies affect their interests. If many people are not able to attach ideological labels to their thinking, they can still make effective judgments. In a general way they know what they want from government, and they have a sufficient understanding of what the candidates and the parties stand for.

Moreover, the voice of the majority is expressed in important ways, and it is listened to by the policy makers. Elections are still crucial events. Even the authors of *The American Voter* qualified their dismal conclusions by declaring: "It would be altogether wrong to suppose that the electoral process does not profoundly influence the course of government. Unquestionably it does. The decisions of the electorate play a role primarily in defining broad goals of governmental action or very generalized means of achieving such goals."[14]

Those same authors also point out that shifts in the tide of opinion *between* elections are closely followed by government. Those shifts are measured in many ways, but the public opinion poll is now firmly established as a powerful link between the mood of the public and the decisions of government leaders.

We should also note, say the centrists, that whatever deficiencies there may be in the dialogue between the mass of the people and the govern-

ment are remedied by the lively presence of that active minority, the attentive public. Even if we accept the lowest estimates of what proportion of the electorate should be placed in this category—perhaps a tenth or even less of the total—we are still talking about several million people who follow politics closely and worry about the state of the nation.

They have more influence than most of them realize. Since the majority do not have much detailed knowledge of political issues, they are likely to be influenced by others who are more knowledgeable. And since, as we have noted, the prime influences on our opinions are personal contacts, such as family, friends, acquaintances at work, and fellow members of organizations, those people we know who are better informed and more articulate than the average are likely to have a disproportionate impact on our political thinking. Then, too, the active minority is especially prone to write letters to members of Congress and to the newspapers, and decision makers in government are impressed with a few hundred, even a handful, of letters if they are thoughtfully expressed.

Moreover, public officials are forced to account for their policies not only to the general, politically interested citizenry. On every issue there is an abundance of organized groups whose leaders and staffs are specialists on that issue and who bring information and a diversity of opinion to the attention of government and the electorate. In addition the media, the journals of opinion, the universities, and other institutions contain a wealth of knowledge and insight into public affairs. Between government and the mass of the people is a stratum of interested, involved people who force government to explain and defend its policies publicly and who provide the general electorate with alternative sources of opinion.

The centrists also insist that it is by no means clear that the health of the system demands that a much greater number of people be more actively involved in the political process. Becoming an informed citizen today is an exacting and time-consuming undertaking. Issues and crises are all enormously complex. Even the experts, the scholars in the field of public issues, confess to wide areas of ignorance and are forced to specialize to preserve their authority in, at most, a few fields. The lay person cannot acquire more than a superficial knowledge across the range of public affairs.

If most people were to dedicate themselves to the effort to place their mark on public affairs, other pursuits of high importance to society would be neglected. The family, already much weakened as an institution, would suffer further. People would have no time to advance their careers. The arts and other leisure-time pursuits would not get the attention they deserve.

Lack of information results not only from apathy, but also from "the need not to find out."[15] One of the reasons that people do not want to know is that the news is too oppressive. There are many neurotic reasons for people's wanting to shelter themselves from the intrusions of public life. But in view of the multiplication of horrors contained in public issues in our era, the ability to screen out much of the suffering is a necessity of mental health; it may therefore not be a contribution to the good society to try to make everyone feel guilty for not paying more attention to issues that are likely to increase personal tensions. It is entirely natural and reasonable that many people are irritated when their favorite television programs are ousted in favor of coverage of a political controversy.

Finally, it is doubtful that a democratic society could stand the strain if everyone were stirred up about political issues and became intensely involved in them. Tempers would rise, antagonisms erupt, and conflicts grow unmanageable.

We are much better off with a specialization of functions between the mass of the people and the attentive public. On the one hand, the masses are given periodic choices of leaders and policies, and between times careful attention is paid to shifts in their attitudes and opinions. On the other hand, the attentive public takes care of political activity, of scrutinizing the conduct of government,

and of shaping and debating alternative public policies. This active minority tend to be better educated than the average, which is beneficial because education equips people to deal cogently with issues. And it is not an exclusive minority: anyone who has the motivation and energy can join its ranks.

The results of this system, despite the deficiences of knowledge of the majority of the people, are reasonably good. We are going through a period in which cynicism about politics and politicians is rife. However, some of this cynicism should be discounted as the normal attitude toward politicians found in all democratic societies. And, in recent years, it is a consequence of a series of unusual failures such as Vietnam and of scandals such as Watergate. If we can just manage to get through a few years without any more foreign disasters or gross abuses of power, we shall see the levels of confidence rise again to the levels that prevailed in the 1950s. If our system can provide reasonably competent, reasonably honest government, the electorate will not have to spend so much time worrying about politics, tension will be reduced, and a healthy relationship between government and the electorate will be restored.

THE DISSATISFIED LIBERALS

The liberals are not convinced by the centrists' arguments. They believe that the centrists are too ready to settle for a level of participation that is insufficient for a vital democracy. In a society that has lavished so much of its resources for so many years on education, liberals find the levels of popular involvement sadly disappointing. Nor do the liberals worry much about the dangers of increased political activity. They do not believe that a stepup in involvement and interest would necessarily increase tensions. On the contrary, political involvement is usually associated with a greater sense of efficacy, which is a positive, healthy feeling. And liberals do not accept the centrists' suggestion that greater participation would result in the neglect of other important aspects of American life. After all, the minority that are now actively engaged in politics also tend to be successful people in their careers and energetic devotees of the arts and various community causes. To the liberals, broader participation produces a more sophisticated citizenry, more competent to cope with the pressures that constant change imposes on our society and better equipped to force government to adopt alternatives to unsatisfactory policies.

More important still, wider participation means bringing into politics those segments of the population that are currently underrepresented in the system. The existing activists, the attentive public, consist predominately of the higher-income groups, an obviously unsatisfactory state of affairs for liberals, for whom equality is one of the core values. We shall not move far toward a reduction of the present inequalities of income and status as long as those people who suffer most from those inequalities are the least involved politically. Liberals urge measures that will encourage fuller participation by the groups who are presently uninvolved or underinvolved—the poor, blacks, Chicanos, the young, and women.

Here are some of the proposals made by liberals to improve the extent and quality of public involvement in the American system:

Make registration easier. Removing the obstacles that many states place in the way of registration would, according to the study by Wolfinger and Rosenstone, add about 9 percent to the voting turnout. Another substantial increase could be obtained if the United States followed the example of most other democracies and adopted a system of automatic, government-initiated registration.

Stop underestimating the intelligence of the people. Politicians and the mass media must emphasize issues instead of personalities and undertake the task of educating the electorate rather than distracting them with trivia and irrelevancies. A few politicians take this task seriously, but too many place themselves in the hands of campaign consultants and image creators. Some national television programs provide superb coverage of political events. But most television news is fragmentary and superficial, and local tel-

evision stations prefer "human interest" and crime stories read by newscasters chosen for their good looks and winsome personalities rather than their journalistic competence.

Undertake reforms of the political process. Among these reforms (which will be discussed at length in later chapters) are the following:

1. Restructuring the political parties to provide clearer choices to the electorate, thereby persuading people that elections make a difference and that voting is worthwhile.

2. Reducing the gross inequalities of income and wealth that give excessive power to business interests and undermine the sense of efficacy among the poor. If the poor today are not much involved in politics, it is the result not so much of apathy and ignorance but of a realistic recognition that their political participation is much less likely to be effective than participation by more affluent people.

THE RADICAL LEFT: POWER TO THE PEOPLE

The radical left slogan of the 1960s, "Power to the People!," captures their belief that the mass of the people should control their own destinies. In the left's doctrine, the people must bring to an end a system in which decisions are made for them by a small group of corporate rulers.

But the left's own analysis of power in America indicates that convincing the mass of the people of this necessity is a very difficult task indeed. As the left sees it, the corporate elite controls the institutions that communicate and interpret information, and this control gives them an enormous influence on public opinion.

Most of the top professional opinion makers are members in good standing of the power elite. The mass media are owned by the corporate rich. The metropolitan newspapers and the three major television networks are corporate enterprises. The leading magazines of opinion are owned by wealthy publishers. Although some diversity of opinion is allowed within the media, the political views of the owners and the pressures of the advertisers prevent the expression of any radical alternatives to capitalism.

The country's entire educational system is dedicated to the perpetuation of the established values. Public schools teach the virtues of the "free enterprise system." At the university level some young faculty members, especially in the social sciences, subscribe to radical left views. But their situations are generally precarious, especially if they participate actively in radical politics in the community.

Although many other faculty members think of themselves as politically liberal, they do nothing significant to challenge the prevailing policies of the ruling class. This passivity is not surprising since both liberal professors and their institutions are heavily dependent on federal research funds. An important part of this funding is for military-related purposes, the grants coming from the Pentagon and even, in some cases, from the CIA. Moreover, a number of faculty members act as consultants and advisors to government agencies. There has been a steady flow of personnel between universities and the federal government. So the notion that the universities are dedicated to independent critical reasoning and to challenging the conventional wisdom is a myth. They are part of the established system of ideas. It could hardly be otherwise when their ruling bodies, the boards of regents or trustees, are made up mostly of successful men in the fields of business, finance, and law.

The left also sees such organizations as the Council on Foreign Relations as instruments through which the corporate rich inject their ideology into foreign and domestic affairs. "Think tanks" such as the Rand Corporation and the Hudson Institute are always ready to serve corporate and militarist purposes, and the even more conservative Hoover Institution, American Enterprise Institute, and Heritage Foundation lavishly underwrite the research and publications of pliable scholars. The left has its own think tank, the Institute for Policy Studies. But this organization is pathetically underfinanced as compared with its centrist and conservative counterparts and is subject to investigation and accusations of subversion by reactionaries in the White House and Congress.

So it will not be easy to challenge the manipulative power of these men and their institutions. However, the left believes that the brainwashing of the people is beginning to lose some of its effectiveness because the failures and corruption of the men at the top have become too blatant. The task of the left is to alter the established values by persuading the people—especially blue-collar workers, the poor, minorities, and students—that the proper response to the present situation is not withdrawal and noninvolvement but militant action.

THE CONSERVATIVES: MANIPULATION BY THE LIBERAL ESTABLISHMENT

As we saw in chapter 1, conservatives believe that too much power in America is in the hands of a liberal establishment and that this establishment is able to exercise so much power largely through its ability to influence public opinion.

Conservatives perceive the mass media as heavily biased in favor of liberalism. The several conservative newspaper publishers in the country cannot prevail against the leftward slant of the majority of reporters and columnists. Moreover, no other newspapers can match the influence of the liberal *New York Times* and *Washington Post,* which are carefully read every morning by the top decision makers of the federal government. As for the television networks, conservatives believe that, under the guise of balanced objective news reporting, the top network newscasters present the news in a manner that persistently leans toward liberalism. Patrick Buchanan, a speechwriter for President Nixon who later became a newspaper columnist, put the conservatives' case against the network news staffs this way: "Simply stated it is that an incumbent elite, with an ideological slant unshared by the nation's majority, has acquired absolute control of the most powerful means of communication known to man. And that elite is using that media monopoly to discredit those with whom it disagrees, and to advance its own ideological objectives."[16]

The universities, too, are attacked by conservatives for pretending to pursue the ideal of objective scholarship while in fact teaching an overwhelmingly liberal line. As one conservative commentator put it: "Our colleges and universities have conformed themselves over the past two decades to the orthodoxy of secular liberalism."[17] Nor do the conservatives have any more use than the radical left for the Council on Foreign Relations and the Trilateral Commission, which they believe to be tools of eastern internationalists like David Rockefeller. Conservatives have also aimed their fire at the Brookings Institution, a policy research organization that has supplied Democratic administrations with many of their economic ideas and personnel. Conservatives take some encouragement from the growing stature of the Hoover Institution and the American Enterprise Institute, but they insist that the preponderance of professional social science research is still on the liberals' side.

The result of this dominance of the institutions of knowledge and ideas by the liberal establishment is an artificially imposed consensus behind bigger and bigger government at home and conciliation of our enemies abroad. Fortunately, the liberal establishment has not been able to indoctrinate the people completely. In the face of rampaging crime, for example, most people cry out for law and order despite the liberals' apparent concern only for the rights of criminals. And the transparent failure of New Deal liberal policies has at last produced a shift of opinion toward conservatism.

Still, in all too many areas the values of the liberal establishment have prevailed. They must be challenged, say the conservatives, by more active participation by the citizenry. In this sense, conservatives, like liberals, are calling for a reversal of the recent trends toward noninvolvement. However, the conservatives differ from the liberals in a very important respect. The liberals view the present registration laws as discriminating against the poor, the minorities, and the young, and they advocate postcard registration, for example, to remedy the situation. But conservatives see no reason to go this far. It is one thing to insist that people should not be prevented from voting by intimidation and by artificially contrived legal barriers. But it is not necessary to spoon-feed the electorate and remove any procedure that requires the slightest degree of initiative by the voter. Registration is not an onerous task. If people are too uninterested or too lazy to take even the small amount of time needed to register, why should we go to additional effort and expense to get their attention?

To the liberals' complaint that most of those people who do not register or participate are poor, conservatives respond that these people also happen to be the least educated, the least informed, and the least equipped to make careful, reasoned judgments on the issues. What is true of the poor also applies to the young. When they are settled, own property, and begin to worry about matters other than starting their careers and "finding" themselves, they are more likely to become involved and to vote. There is no need to force the pace; events should be allowed to run their natural course.

So conservatives are advocates of stepped-up participation but only by those segments of the population who have a sufficient financial stake in the community and enough education to play a meaningful role in political life. They argue that the majority of the population are homeowners, pay substantial taxes, and have at least some interest in and knowledge of political affairs. As for the rest, they should have equal opportunity to participate, but we should not bend the system out of shape in an attempt to coerce them into involvement.

THE RADICAL RIGHT AND THE "LEFT CONSPIRACY"

There are, as we have observed, two differing strands of thought on the radical right. One, of which the John Birch Society is the most prominent, is elitist. Robert Welch and other Birch Society members argue that America is supposed to be a republic, not a democracy—that is, a system based on rule by the best qualified rather than by the masses of the people. But we have gone from republic to democracy and in the process abandoned the precepts of the Constitution.

The other radical right strand is populist; it voices the dissatisfactions of considerable numbers of people of fairly low socioeconomic status who feel that the system has ignored them. In the 1960s, leaders such as George Wallace, the governor of Alabama, articulated these frustrations and stimulated intense political interest and involvement on the part of their followers.

Both the elitist and the populist factions of the radical right, however, are united in their hostility to the left-wing elites that conspire to control the country by controlling the minds of the people. There is an intense dislike of intellectuals, of what George Wallace used to call the "pointy-headed pseudo-intellectuals." Universities are perceived by the right as spawning grounds for vicious attacks on traditional values. The Ford and Rockefeller Foundations are criticized for using their tax-exempt status to give financial support to left-wing research and political activity. The command post of the communist or quasi-communist conspiracy is said by some right-wing commentators to be located in the headquarters of the Council on Foreign Relations. As Dan Smoot put it:

> I am convinced that the Council on Foreign Relations, together with a great number of other associated tax-exempt organizations, constitutes the invisible government which sets the major policies of the federal government; exercises controlling influence on governmental officials who implement the policies; and, through massive and skillful propaganda, influences Congress and the public to support the policies.
>
> I am convinced that the objective of this invisible government is to convert America into a socialist state and then make it a unit in a one-world socialist system.[18]

Other organizations believed by the radical right to be promoting one-world, anti-American ideas are the Committee for Economic Development and the Foreign Policy Association.

Carrying forth to the general public the doctrines of these powerful organizations are the television networks, most of the major newspapers, and several weekly and monthly journals of opinion. In their efforts to combat the thought control exercised by the left-wing "insiders," the radical right engages in several very active forms of politics. The populist right organizes rallies, which are sometimes large and enthusiastic, and buys time on television and radio, particularly in the South and Texas. The John Birch Society is deeply involved in small group meetings of its own members, in providing speakers for various groups, and in distributing its publications through the Birch Society bookstores. Like all radicals at both poles of the spectrum, people on the far right reject existing kinds of politics but are second to none in the intensity of their political activity.

CONCLUSION

It is difficult to find much comfort in the material we have covered in this chapter. Large numbers of people care little and do little about politics. A high proportion of these people are the poor and the minorities—those people who have most reason to be dissatisfied and most to gain from governmental action. The young are also among the uninvolved, yet it is their future that is being decided now by the policy makers. Although there has been some increase in political awareness and sophistication over the last twenty-five years, there are several reasons not to be delighted about this increase. First, the level of sophistication after all this improvement remains unimpressive. Next, it has been accomplished only partly by increased educational levels. Even more important, people have been shocked into political awareness by a series of crises, catastrophic events, and failures of government's performance. Finally, now that these people follow politics more closely than in the past, they do not like what they see, and more and more of them are refusing to vote.

It may well be that the centrists are right, that the erosion of trust and the decline in voting are temporary phenomena and that better and more honest performance by government can turn things around. But what if government, beset as it is by incredibly difficult problems, is not able to perform well enough to satisfy an increasingly critical populace? What if the voting proportions continue to fall, and the surveys on trust in government show a persisting decline? Will we at last fall below those levels of performance and confidence needed to sustain democratic institutions?

Of course, we do not know precisely where those minimal levels are or if we are in fact approaching them. For the moment, at least, only the radicals are convinced that we have already passed the point of no return. There is still a good deal of hope on the part of most political analysts that the worst will not happen. However, on the evidence of this chapter and of chapters to come, that hope must be expressed in cautious terms.

NOTES AND REFERENCES

1. On these matters, see Stephen Hess, *The Washington Reporters* (Washington, D.C.: The Brookings Institution, 1981).
2. Everett Carll Ladd, Jr., and Seymour Martin Lipset, *The Divided Academy* (New York: McGraw-Hill, 1975).
3. Angus Campbell, Philip E. Converse, Warren E. Miller, and Donald E. Stokes, *The American Voter* (New York: Wiley, 1960), p. 543. See also Bernard Berelson, Paul F. Lazarsfeld, and William N. McPhee, *Voting* (Chicago: University of Chicago Press, 1954).
4. Norman H. Nie, Sidney Verba, and John R. Petrocik, *The Changing American Voter* (Cambridge, Mass.: Harvard University Press, 1976, 1979).
5. In fact, some part of the improvement in ideological awareness from the 1956 to the 1972 study can be traced to the fact that the later work used somewhat less demanding criteria for what constitutes ideological awareness. See *The Changing American Voter,* 1979, p. 115.
6. See *The Changing American Voter,* 1979, p. 271.
7. In most democracies the government establishes voter lists by door-to-door canvassing or by mailing postcards to all residents.
8. Raymond E. Wolfinger and Steven J. Rosenstone, *Who Votes?* (New Haven, Conn.: Yale University Press, 1980), p. 73.
9. *Dunn* v. *Blumstein.*
10. However, upper-income blacks are at least as politically active as any group in the population.
11. Joseph Katz, Harold A. Korn, and associates, *No Time for Youth* (San Francisco: Jossey-Bass, 1968).
12. The survey is directed by Alexander Astin of the University of California at Los Angeles on behalf of the American Council on Education. In the 1979 survey, 63 percent of the respondents declared "being very well off financially" as one of their prime objectives.
13. Estimates of the difference in voting turnout between men and women vary from 10 percent (Lester W. Milbrath and M. L. Goel, *Political Participation,* 2nd ed., Chicago: Rand McNally, 1977, p.117) to 6 percent (Kirsten Amundsen, *A New Look at the*

Silenced Majority, Englewood Cliffs, N.J.: Prentice-Hall, 1977, p.124) to only 2 percent (Raymond E. Wolfinger and Steven J. Rosenstone, *Who Votes?,* New Haven, Conn.: Yale University Press, 1980, pp. 37–39). On the basis of 1972 data Wolfinger and Rosenstone find almost no difference in the rate of voting between men and women until the age of 40.

14. Campbell et al., *The American Voter,* p. 545.
15. Robert E. Lane and David O. Sears, *Public Opinion* (Englewood Cliffs, N.J.: Prentice-Hall, 1964), p. 65.
16. Patrick J. Buchanan, *The New Majority* (Philadelphia: Girard Bank, 1973), pp. 20-21.
17. Stephen J. Tonsor, "Alienation and Relevance," *The National Review,* 1 July 1969, p. 661.
18. Dan Smoot, *The Invisible Government* (Dallas, Tex.: The Dan Smoot Report, 1962), p. iv.

chapter four

POLITICAL PARTIES: DO WE NEED THEM?

In the last chapter we saw that there has been a general erosion of confidence in American governmental and political institutions. Surveys have indicated that, of all our institutions, none is distrusted as much as the political parties.

There is nothing new about this discovery. George Washington warned "in the most solemn manner against the baneful effects of the spirit of party . . ." and criticism of parties as divisive and corrupt has been a recurring motif throughout American political history. But we are in a particularly antiparty period today. There has been a sharp decline in the number of people willing to identify with a political party. By 1981 a full third of the electorate were calling themselves Independents; and of those voters who were still willing to describe themselves as Democrats or Republicans, a high proportion felt only a weak attachment to the party of their choice. From this and other evidence some political observers have concluded that we might be caught up in a "trend toward the gradual disappearance of the political party in the United States."[1]

In this chapter we shall examine the reasons for the decline of support for the parties and assess whether or not the predictions of their eventual demise are justified. We shall look first at the functions of political parties; then at the reasons for our having essentially a two-party system; and then at the nature of the differences between the parties and the forces that narrow the range of those differences. After that we shall provide five perspectives on the performance of the parties and on what, if anything, should be done to reform them.

WHY PARTIES?—THEIR FUNCTIONS IN THE POLITICAL SYSTEM

In view of Washington's warning against parties and the persistent hostility to political parties throughout our history, the question we must start with is not why they are in decline today, but how and why they got started in the first place and how they have survived so long.

Parties began in this country in pretty much the same way they begin everywhere. A group of people who agree on one or more public policy issues get together to try to persuade other people to accept their ideas. Then, in order to make their persuasion effective, they give themselves a label, a brand name, and they propose and try to elect candidates for public office under that label. The two essential concerns of any party are policy and power. There must be a program, and there must be an attempt to acquire the political power to put the program into effect by placing members of the party in government positions.

These elements came into play even while Washington was warning against the baneful effects of party. People who agreed with him that we needed a strong national government banded themselves together, called themselves the Federalists, and set about the task of ensuring that Washington's successor would agree with their view. A rival group, clustered around Jefferson, wanted a more decentralized system, came to be known as the Antifederalists, and organized to get people who agreed with them into the federal government. The Federalists and Antifederalists were very loose associations; but in a rudimentary form the key ingredients of party—programs and efforts to get people elected on those programs—were already there.

After that the parties slowly grew more structured and became an integral component of the American political system. They survived because they fulfilled a number of functions that, here as in all democratic countries, have been of great importance to the functioning of the system. What are these functions? They are of two kinds, the first pertaining to the electorate at large, the second to the institutions of government.

PARTIES AND THE ELECTORATE

The primary service that parties render to the public is to help them make *choices*. Parties organize alternative programs and candidates. Without the parties the electorate at large would be faced with a large number of individuals, each of them claiming to offer the best program and to be the best qualified to run the government. But in a country as large and varied as ours it would be well-nigh impossible for even the most politically aware members of the electorate to make intelligent choices; and, as we have seen, the majority are not especially attentive to politics. Parties act as intermediaries in the process of election by organizing behind the major issues and screening candidates for office. By putting their label on policy proposals and candidates, they make it possible for people to choose among the labels rather than among all the individual proposals and candidates.

PARTIES AND GOVERNMENT

In providing a systematic means for organizing alternative programs and candidates, parties fulfill functions of great importance to the operation of a democratic government. They help establish coherence and consistency within the executive branch, for presidents choose most of their cabinet members and other top officials from their own party. Parties encourage a degree of coherence within the legislature, too; if there were nothing to bind all the separate legislators together, it would be very difficult to get anything done. Parties also provide an important link between the executive and legislative branches, since presidents appeal to the leaders of their party in Congress for cooperation. The party establishes a bridge across the separation of powers.

Next, the party system provides one of the means by which the government is subjected to constant scrutiny and cross-examination. The opposition parties' purpose is to demonstrate that they are better qualified than the present government to exercise power and are ready to do so as soon as the electorate gives them the chance. Thus parties offer alternative governments, and they are instruments for arranging the orderly transfer of power from one set of policies and leaders to another.

Finally, parties are means of recruiting and preparing people for public office. Almost all top officeholders have used the machinery of party to attain their position. Even Jimmy Carter, the great outsider, who won his nomination in 1976 by battling the established forces within the Democratic party in the primaries, would have had no chance of winning the presidency if he had not carried the Democratic label in the general election.

WHY TWO PARTIES?

Ours is basically a two-party system. We have had an abundance of parties, including the Vegetarian, Prohibition, Populist, American, Libertarian, Communist, Socialist, Socialist Workers, and Citizens parties, and a few have made a strong showing in presidential elections. Theodore Roosevelt's Progressive party won enough votes in 1912 to take a victory away from the Republican party and throw the presidency to Democrat Woodrow Wilson. In 1968 George Wallace's American Independent Party gained close to 10 million votes. And in 1980 John Anderson, running as an Independent, attracted 5.5 million votes, or 7 percent of the total cast. Here and there in our history cities and even states have elected Socialist, Populist, or Farmer-Labor candidates.

Yet at all levels the prevailing rule has been for two parties to dominate. Only once has a new party ousted one of the two major parties: in the decade before the Civil War when the established Whig party (the party rivaling the Jacksonian Democrats) collapsed, and its place was taken by the newly created Republican party.

Outside the United States the two-party system is the exception rather than the rule. In most nondemocratic countries there is only one party, whose job is not to present alternatives to the people but rather to marshal opinion behind the government and to see to it that the government's policies are carried out. Democracies, on the other hand, all have more than one party, and most have several parties. France, Italy, West Germany, the Netherlands, Switzerland, the Scandinavian countries, and Israel all have at least three or four substantial parties and several others that cannot be ignored. Great Britain is among the few other democracies in the world in which two parties, until recently at least, have towered above the rest. But Britain is a much smaller, more homogeneous country than our own. How did such a huge, populous, diverse country as the United States develop with only two major parties?

One reason is habit. We started out that way, with the Federalists against the Antifederalists, who soon gave way to the Jeffersonian Republicans (or Democratic Republicans). After a period of complete dominance by the Jeffersonians, a new alignment formed in 1828, the Whigs against the Jacksonian Democrats (the inheritors of Jeffersonian Republicanism). With the disappearance of the Whigs we come to the rivalry that has lasted from 1860 until now: the Republicans (the "Grand Old Party," or GOP) versus the Democrats. Thus a pattern emerged at the outset. It fulfilled the functions of policy and power, which we described earlier, and so it survived; and once it had established its survival value, we grew attached to it, assumed that was the only way to do things, and were reluctant to break the habit.

The second reason for the dominance of two parties is that our electoral system makes it difficult for minor parties to gain a foothold. The principal problem they face is that we have single-member constituencies in federal elections. In congressional races we elect only one member for each district; and in most states whoever gets a *plurality* of the votes—that is, more votes than anyone else, even if that number is not a clear majority—is the winner. Similarly, in presidential elections, whichever candidate receives a plurality of a state's popular votes wins all that state's electoral college votes.

The consequence for minor parties is that even if they get 5 or 10 percent of the total number of votes cast in a national election, they can finish up with *no* seats in Congress (because they lack sufficient strength in each separate district to gain a plurality) and *no* states in a presidential race.[2]

With nothing tangible to show for their strenuous efforts in election campaigns, minor party activists become discouraged, and many voters who are attracted to a minor party's program fail to cast their ballots for its candidates because they feel that they are throwing their votes away.

DISTINGUISHING BETWEEN THE PARTIES

As we have seen, a primary function of parties is to present alternative policies to the public. In chapter 1 we set up a left-to-right political spectrum as a means of helping us to distinguish among alternative policies. This spectrum provides us with a convenient device for testing whether or not the two major parties in America, the Democrats and Republicans, are fulfilling the function of providing choices to the electorate. This breakdown along the spectrum requires that one of the parties represent a left-of-center, more or less liberal tendency; and the other, a right-of-center, more or less conservative tendency.

LIBERAL-CONSERVATIVE POLICY DIFFERENCES

Before we check to see if the parties actually offer such alternatives, let us remind ourselves of what these liberal and conservative tendencies mean in relation to stands on the issues. For this purpose we take five main policy areas—welfare programs for the poor, civil rights programs to help minority groups, federal intervention in the economy, civil liberties, and foreign policy—and see how the various perspectives respond to each issue.

With respect to *welfare* and *civil rights programs,* the strongest support for government programs is found in the liberal direction and the greatest resistance is found in the conservative direction. The same is true with respect to *government intervention in the economy.* Left of center we find approval for federal spending and government regulation of business, whereas right of center there is more concern for individual property rights and the unrestricted freedom of business. In the *civil liberties* area there is a much greater predisposition on the conservative than the liberal side of the spectrum to assert the claims of law and order and traditional values against dissent and change. In *foreign policy* the left-of-center, liberal inclination is for reduction of armaments, whereas the right-of-center conservative preference is for stronger military preparedness against communism.

By and large, the differences between the parties in these five policy areas are the ones most commonly used in discussions of contemporary American politics. When the Americans for Democratic Action rate the votes of members of Congress in terms of their degree of liberalism, they are looking for support of government welfare and civil rights programs, federal action to boost the economy and help the consumer, the protection of nonconformist ideas and behavior, and a lessening of the military emphasis in foreign affairs. On the other hand, when the Americans for Constitutional Action rate members of Congress by their degree of conservatism, their criteria are resistance to increased welfare spending and civil rights legislation, opposition to budget deficits, support of the rights of private property and business, protection for traditional values, and stronger military preparedness.

So we apply all this to our discussion of the two-party system and pose the question: Do the Democratic and Republican parties differ along liberal-conservative lines? Is one left of center and the other right of center? The answer is a highly qualified yes. Over the years the Democratic party has generally been more liberal than the Republican party with respect to its programs, its elected leaders, its active members, its group support, and its ideological appeal. However, a number of factors have operated to set limits to these party differences. So we shall now look at the respects that set the parties apart from each other, and then at the forces that impose constraints on their differences.

WAYS IN WHICH THE PARTIES DIFFER

Party platforms.   The content of the Democratic and Republican party platforms, drawn up every four years by their national conventions, usually provides significant liberal-conservative divergencies. These differences were especially evident in 1980, as we see from table 4-1. Although the differences indicated in this table are not completely polarized, clearly on these important areas of public policy the platforms of the two parties sent sharply contrasting messages to the electorate.

Elected leaders. Next there are differences in the policies of Democrats and Republicans when they are elected to office. Franklin Roosevelt, Truman, Kennedy, and Johnson were much more inclined to take vigorous governmental action on behalf of lower-income groups and blacks as well as to regulate business than were Eisenhower, Nixon, and Ford. Reagan's economic, social, and foreign policies included some dramatic departures from those of the Jimmy Carter era.

With respect to Congress, we shall see in chapter 8 that the Americans for Democratic Action find much more support for their liberal positions among Democratic senators and representatives than among Republicans.

TABLE 4–1 Excerpts from the 1980 party platforms

Issue	Republicans	Democrats
The economy	Reduce taxes (30% over 3 years), government spending, government regulation.	Make jobs the "highest domestic priority" ($12 billion federal program to create 800,000 jobs). Tax cuts for low- and middle-income groups as soon as not inflationary.
Energy	Emphasize production. End oil and gas price controls. Repeal oil company windfall profits tax. Revise "overly stringent Clean Air Act regulations." End 55 mph speed limit. More nuclear, including breeder, reactors.	Emphasize conservation. Massive program of residential conservation grants. More solar, less nuclear. Stop oil companies from buying coal and solar firms.
Health	Oppose "socialized medicine."	Support comprehensive national health insurance programs building on private sector.
Abortion	Support constitutional amendment to protect "the right to life for unborn children." Curb public funding for abortion, and appoint judges "who respect . . . the sanctity of innocent human life."	Oppose constitutional amendment and curbs on government funding of abortions for poor women.
Women's rights (ERA)	Leave ratification of Equal Rights Amendment to judgment of state legislatures.	Endorse ERA; pledge not to hold party meetings in states that have not ratified ERA and to deny support to candidates who do not support ERA.
Miscellaneous	Support restoration of voluntary school prayers. Condemn forced busing for school desegregation. Support capital punishment. Stop sale of drug paraphernalia.	Seek gun controls. Establish Martin Luther King's birthday as national holiday. Oppose discrimination against homosexuals.

Party activists. Active Republican party leaders are much more likely to be conservative than are active Democrats. Studies of delegates to the Democratic and Republican national conventions confirm what is obvious to the most casual viewer of these events on television: that the tone, the attitudes, and the policy views of Republican delegates are considerably more conservative than their Democratic counterparts.

Group support. In chapter 3 we saw that there is a relationship between socioeconomic background and political awareness and involvement. There is a parallel relationship between socioeconomic factors and partisan voting, as we see in table 4-2.

Although we must be cautious about drawing general conclusions from a single election (and the 1980 election was unusual in many respects), table 4-2 portrays fairly accurately some long-term relationships between the parties and various socioeconomic groupings. The lower down the income scale we go, the more Democratic voters we find, and vice versa for the Republicans. Similarly with respect to occupations, Democrats fare better among the lower-status positions.

TABLE 4–2 Social groups and the presidential vote, 1980

	Carter	Reagan	Anderson
Family Income			
Less than $10,000	50	41	6
$10,000–$14,999	47	42	8
15,000– 24,999	38	53	7
25,000– 50,000	32	58	8
Over $50,000	25	65	8
Occupation			
Professional or managerial	33	56	9
Clerical, sales, white collar	42	48	8
Blue collar	46	47	5
Unemployed	55	35	7
Agriculture	29	66	3
Education			
Less than high school	40	45	3
High school graduate	43	51	4
Some college	35	55	8
College graduate	35	51	11
Union membership			
Labor union household	47	44	7
No member in household in union	35	55	8
Community size			
Cities over 250,000	54	35	8
Suburbs and small cities	37	53	8
Rural and towns	39	54	5
Race			
Black	82	14	3
Hispanic	54	36	7
White	36	55	8
Religion			
Protestant	37	56	6
Catholic	40	51	7
Jewish	45	39	14
Age			
18–21	44	43	11
22–29	43	43	11
30–44	37	54	7
45–59	39	55	6
60+	40	54	4
Sex			
Female	45	46	7
Male	37	54	7

Source: CBS News/*New York Times* polls. The Election of 1980. Some rows do not equal 100 percent because of missing data.

And educationally the Republicans do better among the college educated, the Democrats among those people with less education (though college professors in the social sciences and humanities are more likely to be Democrats than Republicans). Democrats also do better in union families than in families without a union member, in big cities rather than in suburbs or small towns, among blacks and Hispanics than among whites, and among Jews more than among Protestants.

We encounter the same kind of distinction when we turn our attention from broad socioeconomic categories to organizations. Business organizations tend to support the Republican party and business executives to contribute to its campaigns. Labor unions have long been mainstays of the Democratic party, their money and manpower being vital elements in many Democratic campaigns. So, in very general terms, we can distinguish between the Democrats as the party of the working class and the "out groups," and the Republicans as the party of business and the more affluent and established elements.

These distinctions have been true of the two parties in considerable degree throughout most of their histories. For a while Abraham Lincoln's Republican party won the support of many working people and blacks, and Republican Theodore Roosevelt attacked big business; conversely, under Cleveland the Democrats gained a good deal of backing from business. But, more typically, thrice-defeated Democrat William Jennings Bryan gathered together poor farmers and laborers against eastern money and Democrat Woodrow Wilson spoke out against business power. Franklin Roosevelt and his New Deal programs in the 1930s solidified the lineup that we have described as differentiating between Democrats and Republicans. Roosevelt won the blacks over from the Republicans to the Democrats, secured the Jewish attachment to the Democrats by appointing Jews to high posts, and offered so many new social and economic programs to blue-collar workers that their gratitude to the Democrats lasted through generations. At the same time the groups antagonized by the New Deal became more firmly identified with the Republican party.

Ideology. In a general way the differences between the parties that we have described are recognized by the electorate, and, as table 4-3 shows, people who see themselves as liberals vote preponderantly for the Democrats, and the conservatives for the Republicans.

TABLE 4–3 Ideology and the presidential vote, 1980

	Carter	Reagan	Anderson
Liberals	57	27	11
Conservatives	23	71	4
Moderates	42	48	8

Source: CBS News/*New York Times* polls.

In sum, there are differences, which are perceived by a majority of the electorate, in the programs of the two parties, and these distinctions reflect the differences between the party activists, socioeconomic and interest groups, and bodies of ideological opinion lined up behind each of the two parties.

Yet the two parties are not poles apart. In fact, they are divided by differences of degree, not of kind, for a number of factors impose constraints on their actions and policies and force frustration on the ideological enthusiasts of each party.

FACTORS THAT REDUCE DIFFERENCES BETWEEN THE PARTIES

Among the forces that narrow the differences between Republicans and Democrats, some relate to the nature of the parties themselves, others to the American electorate, and others to our government structures.

The parties are loose coalitions.   In reducing the number of parties in America to only two, we have made it extremely difficult for either of them to be a cohesive, well-integrated organization with a sharply defined set of policies, for this country is enormous and very diverse. To build a national party with enough strength to win the support of a majority of the electorate requires welding a coalition including vastly different types of people in terms of class, race, ethnic group, religion, and region. A party that is identified too closely with one income group, one religion, or one region cannot hope to win a presidential election. Nor can a party win that appeals only to the strongly ideological liberals or conservatives, for there are not enough of them to elect a candidate.

As we see from figure 4-1, the Democratic and Republican parties have both recognized the need to construct broad coalitions, and both contain a great many differing elements, sometimes to the point of seeming incompatibility.

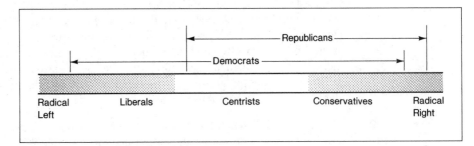

FIGURE 4-1. Alignment of Parties on the Political Spectrum

Thus the Republican party has included moderates like Thomas Dewey, Dwight Eisenhower, and Senator Charles Percy, conservatives like Senators Robert Taft, Barry Goldwater, and Jesse Helms, and even a few fairly liberal members, such as Senators Jacob Javits and Lowell Weicker. However, since the 1930s the GOP has been the smaller of the two parties: declared Democrats have outnumbered Republicans in this period by ratios ranging between 2 to 1 and 3 to 2. As the smaller party the Republicans have had fewer elements to bind together than the Democrats, and, particularly since 1964, the conservative wing has become dominant.

So the Democrats have constituted the most incongruous coalition, ranging across almost the entire spectrum from some very liberal members from the Northeast and the West to a number of archconservatives from the South.

The continued affiliation of so many southern conservatives with the more liberal of the two national parties stems from a tradition going back to the early stages of the development of the party system and reinforced by the Civil War and the Reconstruction era. During Reconstruction the Democrats spoke for the defeated South. Southerners were grateful and voted overwhelmingly for the Democrats. In fact, they voted almost exclusively for the Democrats, making the South practically a one-party region.

One-party politics proved to be very convenient for the white population of the South. It maintained white dominance by ensuring that there would be no alternative party that might be tempted to build its strength by going after black voters. Moreover, as long as there was little or no Republican competition, the same people could be reelected to Congress over and over again, thus building the seniority that brings the crucial committee chairmanships in both houses of Congress. So for southerners the Democratic party was built into their culture, commanding such strong loyalties that for a southerner to think of defecting to the Republicans was almost tantamount to rejecting one's birthright. As the late Senator James B. Allen put it when asked why, given his conservative views, he did not go over to the Republicans: "I guess my father would turn over in his grave if I became a Republican. He was a lifelong Democrat. I'm a lifelong Democrat. But that doesn't control how I stand on issues."[3]

Franklin Roosevelt was careful not to challenge these loyalties. In fact, he absorbed the South into his New Deal coalition, overlooking the racial prejudices of southerners in Congress to gain their votes for his economic program, which offered important benefits to the South as the poorest region of the country.

Eventually, however, the hold of the past over the mind of the South had to weaken. Industry moved to the South, and with it came some northern Republicans. The Democratic party became the civil rights party, and as it did so it began to lose favor with conservative white southerners. In 1952 about three-quarters of all southerners called themselves Democrats. By 1972 the proportion was down to less than half. It is true that only about a sixth were ready to declare themselves Republicans in 1972. But in presidential elections from 1952 onward, more and more of the southern white Democrats voted Republican, and in 1972 all of the South's electoral college votes went to the Republican presidential candidate. With Jimmy Carter of Georgia as the Democratic candidate in 1976 most of the South went back to the Democrats. But even then it was black southerners who gave Carter his margin, for the white South voted 52 percent for Ford over 46 percent for Carter. And in 1980 the white South went for Reagan over Carter by 60 percent to 35 percent.

There have been Republican advances at the congressional level, too, with four Republican gains in 1980 bringing their Senate total from the deep South to ten.

Still, the Democratic tradition among conservative southerners is by no means dead. As we shall see in chapter 8, President Reagan could still find a considerable number of supporters for his ideas among southern Democrats in both houses of Congress.

As long as one party includes among its members Representatives as liberal as New York's Benjamin Rosenthal and California's Ron Dellums and others as conservative as Mississippi's Jamie Whitten and Sonny Montgomery, it will be difficult for that party to present a clear, consistent set of programs to the nation. As Will Rogers, the popular humorist of the 1920s and 1930s, put it: "I'm not a member of any organized political party, I'm a Democrat."

The parties do not have strong, centralized organizations.   Until recently most studies of the big American political parties described them as highly decentralized confederations. It was said that we had no national parties, but only loosely associated collections of state and local parties, built up from the precinct and ward organizations or local clubs, through county and state central committees, to the national committees where there was very little power.

Now, however, it is suggested that the parties have been transforming themselves into truly national organizations, the Democrats by increasing the importance of the mass membership in the selection of presidential candidates, the Republicans by creating a strong party machine "built on techniques of business management and modern campaign technology."[4]

Despite these changes American parties are still not nearly as centralized as the parties of most other countries. There is little national committees can do to compel state and local organizations to follow the national party line, which greatly complicates the task of offering clear policy positions to the electorate, for on major issues many of the state and local organizations may be pulling in opposite directions from each other.

A further source of weakness in party organization is the lack of clear definition of party membership. In most other democratic countries party members *join* their party. They belong to a local branch of the party, and through that they are members of the national party. They pay dues, part of which go to the national headquarters; they are involved in the selection of candidates and in debates over policy; and they are bound by majority rule in their organization. But in the United States we have no agreement on what we mean by a Democrat or Republican. Sometimes we mean an active member of a party organization or club, sometimes someone who registers Democrat or Republican in order to vote in the party primary elections, and sometimes one who votes Democratic or Republican more or less consistently. The ambiguity of party policies is a reflection of the ambiguity of party membership.

Three other developments of recent years have undermined the strength of party organizations. The first development is the growing importance of television in elections. Candidates usually regard an appearance on a television news or interview show as a much more fruitful use of their time than speaking to the faithful at a local party meeting.

The second new threat to the importance of party organizations is public financing of presidential campaigns, which we will discuss in chapter 5. Party organizations have always been of great value to candidates in raising money for their election campaigns. Although parties still have a role under the new system, the federal exchequer has now taken over the larger part of their fund-raising role for presidential (though not congressional) races.

Finally, the growing importance of single-issue and ideological interest groups has sapped the vitality of the party machines, for many of these groups have been moving into the parties and taking on some of the key roles—organizing and financing campaigns and proposing candidates—that were traditionally the prerogative of the party's leadership structure.

The majority of the rank and file are moderates.   We have seen that parties are instruments for organizing and trying to win election campaigns, which means that they must study very closely the attitudes of the electorate. As they do so, they find reasons that compel them to soften the policies that party activists favor. Rank-and-file party voters are predominantly less militant than party activists. The mass of party voters are, generally speaking, less ideologically committed than the dedicated party workers and more inclined to subscribe to middle-of-the-road views. They are also less inclined to be consistent from one issue to another.

Although some studies indicate an increase in issue consistency over the years—that is, more people who are liberal or conservative in one or two areas of public policy are also liberal or conservative in other areas—a high proportion of the general public still harbors liberal and conservative attitudes side by side. Thus, many people who are liberal on questions of government spending to reduce unemployment are conservative on issues relating to race, pornography, or foreign policy and vice versa. And to the extent that people are ready to pull together their various attitudes under a single ideological label, the largest group prefers the "middle-of-the-road" designation to any other in most years.

Although there are wide variations among polls on the ideological labels chosen by the American electorate, from the 1970s most polls have shown that the self-declared liberals constitute about one-fifth of the electorate, the conservatives about one-third, and the moderates two-fifths or more.[5] Furthermore, many of those people who define themselves as conservatives or liberals prefer to qualify their labels with the word *moderate*.

If the attitudes of college freshmen give us a clue to the politics of the future, the preference for moderation is likely to continue. (See table 4-4.)

TABLE 4-4 Percentage ideological self-identification of freshman students (percentages rounded to the nearest whole number)

Year	Far left	Liberal	Middle of the road	Conservative	Far right
1970	3	38	42	16	1
1980	2	20	60	17	1
1981	2	18	60	20	1

Source: Annual fall surveys of students entering U.S. colleges and universities conducted by Alexander Astin on behalf of the American Council on Education. Responses number close to 200,000 each year.

It is not surprising that most politicians in most years prefer not to risk alienating large blocs of voters by taking strong ideological positions and choose instead to do everything possible to occupy the middle ground.

THE MAJORITY LACK DEEP PARTY LOYALTY

There have been times and places in American history when party loyalties ran very deep, but those loyalties are weakening. Thus, during the great waves of immigration, when masses of people poured off the boats into the cities of the East, unable to speak English, jobless, homeless, and often friendless, it was the city political "machine" that took them in hand, gave them food, helped them find a place to live and a job, asking only one thing in return—their support and their votes. Later the loyalties were sustained by the favors that the party machines performed for the people in their neighborhoods, giving them direct access to city hall. In time, however, personal favors gave way to regular welfare payments and services provided by large, impersonal bureaucracies; many of those voters who had grown up in the machine's orbit moved out into the suburbs, and the old loyalties weakened.

Then, too, the Democratic coalition that Franklin Roosevelt put together during the New Deal years is not as solid as it was. The combination of blue-collar workers, poor farmers, blacks, Jews, Catholics, Southerners, and intellectuals won Roosevelt reelection three times, and enough of it held together to elect Harry Truman in 1948. However, this coalition was forged by the Great Depression and its massive unemployment. As the grim memory of that period faded, so did the gratitude to the Democratic party for its efforts to revive the economy. And we have already noted that the South's historical attachment to the Democratic party is slowly weakening.

So today only about a quarter of the electorate consider themselves strong supporters of a political party. As we see from table 4-5, a further two-fifths declare a preference for one party or the other but have only a weak attachment to it; and the remainder, about a third of the electorate, call themselves Independents.

TABLE 4–5 Strength of party identification (percent)

	1960	1976
Strong Democrat	21	15
Weak Democrat	25	25
Independent Democrat	8	12
Independent	8	14
Independent Republican	7	10
Weak Republican	13	14
Strong Republican	14	9
Apoliticals: Don't know	4	1

Source: Center for Political Studies, cited in William J. Crotty and Gary C. Jacobson, *American Parties in Decline* (Boston: Little, Brown, 1980), p.28.

The result is that party is less important than it used to be in determining how people vote, and two other factors have become increasingly significant. The first factor is the personality and competence of the candidate: more and more voters prefer to vote for the person rather than the party.

The second factor of increasing importance is the voters' response to issues. According to *The Changing American Voter,* "the American public has been entering the electoral arena since 1964 with quite a different mental set than was the case in the late 1950s and early 1960s. They have become more concerned with issues and less tied to their parties."[6]

This emphasis on personal qualities and issues shows itself in a number of ways. There has been an increase in "ticket splitting"—voting for a Democrat for one office and a Republican for another. Moreover, many people switch parties from one election to the next. The most obvious evidence of these tendencies is the fact that, since 1952, Republicans have spent more years in the White House than Democrats. If voters divided strictly along party lines, the Republicans, who have consistently been greatly outnumbered by registered Democrats, would never have a chance of winning the presidency. Yet in 1952, 1956, 1972, and 1980 they not only won, they overwhelmed the Democratic candidate.

The party is by no means an irrelevant factor in voting. In congressional elections it remains the most important of all influences, and in most years before 1980 Congress was firmly in Democratic hands by roughly the same margins by which registered Democrats outnumbered registered Republicans in the country. Thus the "weak partisans" may defect from their party in presidential races, but they are still inclined to stay with their party in congressional races.

As for the Independents, two points must be stressed. First, the increase in the proportion of Independents is largely accounted for by new voters who have entered the electorate since the late 1960s. There has not been a massive abandoning of parties by former loyalists. Instead almost half the children of these loyalists have declined to accept their parents' affiliation, opting instead for independence. But an even more significant point for our purposes is that well over half these self-defined Independents are not completely liberated from party ties. As table 4-5 shows, they *lean* toward one party or the other, and more often than not they vote in the direction in which they are leaning.

So party is still very much alive in the minds and behavior of a high proportion of the electorate. But it has lost much of its potency. As party leaders and candidates look at the tendency of many voters to fluctuate between the parties and to split their tickets, they are likely to play down those aspects that set their party off sharply from the other. They know that people in the opposite camp can be won over to their side and that people in their own camp can be lost to the opposition. As for the Independents, some of these, perhaps an increasing number, are strongly ideological and may be looking for bolder policies than the parties have proposed until now. But a majority of the Independents, both the pure kind and the "leaners," are more likely to be found in the middle of the political spectrum. So, again, to attract their votes, most candidates avoid giving an impression of undue militancy or harshness on the issues.

Government weakens the parties.   Earlier we saw that parties are integral elements in democratic governments. Yet certain features of American government tend to weaken parties and undermine their ability to present clear policy alternatives to the people. First is the extraordinary power that the American system has vested in the presidency. A president needs his party's support to help him get elected, especially the first time. But even then a presidential candidate typically sets up a campaign organization separate from the party structure. And once he is elected, the party can do little if a president decides to pursue policies contrary to the promises of the platform. The national committee of his party is rarely among the president's inner circle of advisors.

As for Congress, party is an important factor in its decision-making process, but much less so than in the legislatures of other countries. Power in Congress is heavily concentrated in its committees and committee chairpersons. The party leadership in each house can make proposals and do its best to persuade the committees to accept a given policy. But it has few sanctions to enforce its will. And the separation of powers gives the Congress a good deal of independence from presidential will, even when (as is not always the case) the president and the majority in Congress are of the same party.

Finally, certain imperatives go with the exercise of power that detract from the willingness or ability of an officeholder at any level to carry out party platforms. Once the individual is elected, he or she must speak not only for the members of the party but for the entire constituency. And sometimes the officeholder discovers that, desirable though the party's platform may be, he or she cannot find the political support to put it through and so will be accused of reneging on the party's principles. This accusation will be leveled sooner or later at every elected official —liberal, conservative, and even radical. At some point the responsibilities that go with power must come into conflict with ideologies and subject them to compromise and dilution.

In summary, the differences between the parties are usually constrained because both parties are very broad coalitions, they are not tightly organized, the electorate still tends toward the center in elections, the majority of the people are not strongly partisan, and some of the elements in our governmental system weaken the ability of parties to control the policies of officeholders.

However, along the way we have observed that some changes are in progress, including a rightward trend in the Republican party and the gradual emergence of a two-party system in the South. So far these changes have not altered in any fundamental sense the workings of the party system in America. Whether they will and whether they *should* are subjects for debate among our five perspectives.

FIVE PERSPECTIVES ON POLITICAL PARTIES

THE LIBERALS: REALIGN AND RESTRUCTURE

As the liberals see it, much of the contemporary apathy and cynicism toward politics has resulted from the inadequate distinctions between the Democratic and Republican parties. Where the party programs do not offer real choices, and where government succeeds government without major changes in direction, the public at large is bound to see politics as a charade, a game of musical chairs, profitable for the participants but tedious and irrelevant for everyone else. Accordingly, the liberals propose that we reform our party system in two ways: ideological realignment and structural reorganization.

Realignment. If the people are ever to have a chance to choose true liberalism, rather than the mildly reformist centrism that has passed for liberalism until now, the parties must be realigned. One should become more liberal, the other more conservative. Actually, say the liberals, the Republican party does not have to change very much. It is already a predominantly conservative party, and if the few liberal Republicans would recognize that they belong in the Democratic party and act accordingly, the Republicans would have as much internal consistency as is needed.

The problem is with the Democrats. And to the liberals even this more substantial problem could be taken care of in large measure by one basic shift—the movement of conservative southerners out of the Democratic into the Republican party. This shift would remove the albatross around the liberal Democrats' necks.

The realignment proposed by the liberals would not constitute a total polarization of the parties, with only the liberals and some radicals of the left glaring across a great centrist no-man's land at the conservatives and some radicals of the right, as in figure 4-2. Rather, they are suggesting a moderate or limited realignment, in which the Democratic party would be composed of liberals

the more absurd contradictions within each party, especially within the Democratic party, would have been resolved, and the voters would have a reasonably clear choice between one party that consistently stood for fairly liberal policies and another that represented a considerably more conservative approach to government.

However, this liberal strategy seems to be very risky in two respects. First, how is a liberalized Democratic party to win presidential elections if southern conservatives leave the party? The liberals' answer is that the southern conservatives' votes would be replaced from other, more appropriate sources, particularly the following:

1. Blacks, Hispanics, and other minorities who are disproportionately poor. These groups already vote mostly Democratic but do not vote in large

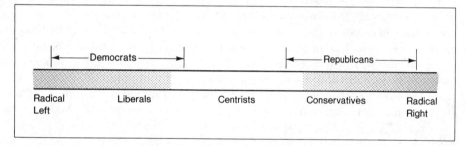

FIGURE 4–2. Polarized Realignment of Parties

joined by a few left radicals and a large body of centrists, and the Republican party would combine conservatives, some radical rightists, and centrists, as seen in figure 4-3. There would still be some overlapping in the appeal of the parties: both would be broad coalitions and both would have to go after the middle-of-the-road vote. But

enough numbers. Simplified registration procedures and voter drives would get more of them to the polls.

2. The young. Declared liberalism among college freshmen may be declining, and the youth vote in 1980 may have split about evenly between Carter and Reagan. Still, surveys indicate that

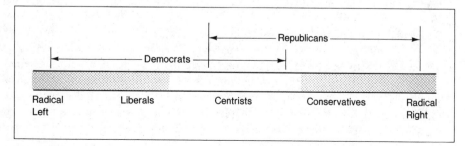

FIGURE 4–3. Limited Realignment of Parties

students tend to grow more liberal as they advance from their freshman through their senior years, and the most liberal voting records in the country are found in college-based precincts. Even the noncollege young are somewhat more liberal on a range of issues than their elders. Here again, the task is to get more of them to the polls by reform of registration procedures and intensive drives to encourage voting. The other problem is the high proportion of the young—over half of the age group—calling themselves Independents, which, say the liberals, results from cynicism about politics generated by the failure of the parties to stand for alternative policies. When the young see party politicians representing principle rather than expediency, they are much more likely to vote, and to vote liberal Democratic.

3. College-educated suburbanites. The income level and status of the people who live in the affluent suburbs would seem to put them in the conservative camp. But among this group there are many (liberals believe a rapidly increasing number) whose educational background and occupations as scientists, technicians, teachers, lawyers, administrators, and so on make them into a "new class." These people are ready, say the liberals, to respond to a party that puts the public interest before special interests, protects the environment before exploitative gain, and represents honest, rational government in place of conflicts of interest and obsolete procedures.

4. Women. By identifying the Democratic party strongly with women's liberation and the Equal Rights Amendment—ideas that are appealing especially to younger women—the Democratic party can become the party of the future among the more than half of the electorate that is female.

So the liberals see plenty of sources from which they can recruit replacements for the departing southern conservatives. However, they must also deal with a second problem: What makes liberals think that if the two parties presented a clear liberal-conservative choice, liberalism could win? As we saw earlier, conservatives have substan-

tially outnumbered liberals in ideological self-identification polls for some years now. There has been an unmistakable trend in the country against high taxes and against liberal causes like busing, affirmative action, and reduced military spending. And there was the sweeping victory of Ronald Reagan and the Republican capture of the Senate in the 1980 elections.

The liberals' response is that, while there has been a shift of opinion away from some of the causes they support, the change is much less dramatic than conservatives claim, and that it is a temporary shift that in no way diminishes their enthusiasm for a clearer liberal-conservative demarcation between the two parties.

To begin with, liberals question the significance of polls showing that more people call themselves conservative than liberal. When people use the word *conservative* they are often using it in the context of lifestyles and attitudes toward sex, marijuana, and other social and cultural questions rather than the traditional economic issues; and even on the lifestyle issues, the long-term trend sometimes moving in a conservative direction, sometimes toward liberalism, sometimes toward a confused combination of both.[8]

Liberals insist that the Reagan triumph in 1980 was much less a victory for conservatism than a rejection of Jimmy Carter's inept handling of the presidency.[9] Moreover, say the liberals, part of Carter's problem was precisely that he failed to represent properly the natural constituencies of the Democratic party—labor, minorities, the lower-income groups, and so on—and pursued budget-cutting policies that seemed to give credibility to Reagan's more far-reaching economic proposals. So 1980 did not provide the true liberal-conservative choice that liberals want to see.

If such a choice were provided, liberals concede is clearly in a liberal direction.[7] Moreover, as we shall see in later chapters, when we move away from vague questions about ideological self-definition to specific questions about particular issues, we find that attitudes among the electorate are highly complex, pulled between conflicting values,

© 1982 MARLETTE-CHARLOTTE OBSERVER

"It was horrible—I dreamed I was pregnant, unwed, and on food stamps, and they were busing me across town to an abortion clinic when we were hijacked by welfare cheats who forced me to sit in the nonsmoking section at an ERA rally."

that they would lose some of the time. But they believe they would win some of the time, too, whereas at present they lose *all* of the time. Even though Democratic presidents accept some liberal ideas, they put them into effect in such diluted form that they are ineffective and give liberalism a bad name. So the liberals would rather put up with strongly conservative administrations periodically, as long as liberals had a chance to show what they could do from time to time. At least the people would be able to see the alternatives clearly spelled out and put into practice. This system would be vastly preferable to the present minor variations in policy that submerge the possibilities for genuine reform of the American system.

Structural changes.   Realignment is not enough for the liberals. If the parties are to be effective, they must not only represent contrasting interests and policies but must also be able to hold together as organizations, providing enough strength in the party leadership to be able to speak with authority for the membership, yet giving the rank-and-file members an influential voice.

Thus the national party organizations should follow through on the party platforms and be given authority to discipline state and local units that refuse to abide by the national party positions or support the party's national candidates. Supporters of each party should be given a sense of active participation both locally and nationally. They should be asked to join a local party organization that is a unit within a national structure; membership dues should be charged by the local group, and a portion of these assigned to the national committees, which would then be in a better position than now to underwrite the campaigns of party nominees.

Along with these structural changes in the party organizations should come a stronger party role in Congress, whose committee chairmen should surrender much of their power to the congressional party leaders, who in turn would work closely with the national committee of the party.

So far the Democrats, despite some movement in the direction urged by the liberals, have not moved nearly far enough to quiet their criticisms. The resulting frustration felt by liberals periodically drives some of them into thinking about establishing a new, truly liberal party. This frustration was an impetus behind the formation of Henry Wallace's Progressive party in 1948, when liberals complained that Harry Truman's foreign policy was too belligerent. Eugene McCarthy offered himself as an Independent in 1976, alleging there was no real difference between Carter and Ford. And although John Anderson's Independent candidacy in 1980 was built on centrist ideas, a considerable number of liberals preferred him to Carter.

Still, for those liberals whose aim is to win the presidency rather than to register a protest, a realigned, reorganized Democratic party continues to be the principal objective.

THE CONSERVATIVES: MISSION ACCOMPLISHED?

Until 1980 conservatives were as dissatisfied with the party system as the liberals. They, too, believed that the people were not offered genuine alternatives and that the Republican and Democratic parties persistently sacrificed principle to expediency.

They had worked hard to persuade the Republican party to accept their doctrine. However, repeatedly from the 1940s the Republican party rebuffed the conservatives in selecting its presidential candidates, choosing liberal establishment spokesmen like Wendell Willkie in 1940, Thomas Dewey in 1948, and Dwight Eisenhower in 1952 and 1956 over authentic conservatives like Senator Robert Taft.

At last in 1964 Barry Goldwater, a real conservative, was nominated by the Republicans. Goldwater went down to a crushing defeat. But

from defeat came the conservatives' opportunity. The activists who had won Goldwater his nomination held on to key positions in the national party machinery and never relinquished control. Since then, no one who was not at least moderately conservative has been nominated for the presidency by the Republicans.

Conservatives were not delighted with the nomination of Richard Nixon in 1968, and they were strongly critical of some of his actions during his first term in the presidency. However, Nixon was not without conservative accomplishments, and after his landslide victory in 1972 there were signals from Nixon that, freed for the first time in his career from thoughts about reelection, he would launch a full-blooded conservative attack on the entrenched bureaucrats, judges, and media pundits who had for so long made liberalism the official American creed.

The conservatives' high hopes were, of course, dashed by Watergate. Gerald Ford restored some of his party's credibility, but the momentum of conservatism was gone.

In 1976 the conservatives tried to restore the momentum by pushing hard for the presidential nomination of one of the idols of their cause, Ronald Reagan. Reagan came to the Republican convention only a few votes behind the incumbent president. The outcome was to be determined by some still uncommitted delegates. The sentiment in the convention was clearly pro-Reagan. Yet the liberal minority, more intent on stopping the conservatives than beating the Democrats in November, filled the air with talk about Reagan's being too conservative for the electorate, suggesting that if he were nominated it would be 1964 all over again. But, said the conservatives, the two situations were not analogous. No Republican could have won in 1964. The polls showed a conservative tide in the country in 1976 that was not there in 1964. Moreover, Goldwater was not an effective candidate: Reagan, in sharp contrast, was a masterful campaigner and the most impressive exponent of the art of televised politics the medium had yet produced. Yet the old argument prevailed, Reagan fell short, and the Republicans lost in November.

So the conservatives argued among themselves. Should they continue to work within the Republican party? Should they form a new party? Or should they try to exert influence on both the Republican and Democratic parties?

The first of these proposals prevailed. Although there was conservative support for several Republican candidates for the presidency in 1980, the conservatives soon coalesced again around Ronald Reagan, this time helping him to an easy victory at the party's national convention.

Then came the triumph in November 1980. At last, said the conservatives, their time had come. The Democratic New Deal era was over. The opportunity had arrived to establish a long-term conservative Republican dominance of American politics. They supported this prognosis with a number of pieces of evidence.

The Reagan presidency. Reagan's victory over Carter by a large margin laid to rest the argument that a conservative could not win the presidency. Repeatedly over the years he had called on the Republicans to adopt conservatism as their creed and to hoist aloft "a banner of bold colors with no pale pastels."

Conservatives had some qualms about Reagan. In 1976 they had accused him of expediency because of his announcement that the moderate-to-liberal Senator Richard Schweiker would be his vice-presidential running mate if the Republicans nominated him for the presidency. They were critical of some of Reagan's appointments when he came to the White House. Then they complained that he did not move fast enough on issues like abortion and school prayer.

Still, his determined battle for budget and tax cuts and increases in military strength, and his appointment of a number of people detested by the liberals, were enthusiastically supported by conservatives. Now the cause of conservatism had at its disposal the power of the presidency, enhanced by Reagan's personal popularity and skill as a communicator. The task at hand was to ensure that he did not allow his undoubtedly conservative principles to be diluted by political opportunism.

The Republican Senate. Against the predictions of most of the experts, Republicans gained control of the Senate in 1981 for the first time since 1955. Nor was it a mere shift of party control. Some long-established champions of liberalism lost their Senate seats in 1980, and several of the new Republicans were staunch conservatives.

Although the Democrats retained their majority in the House of Representatives, their margin was reduced, and the shift after the election was clearly toward the right.

Population trends. The American people have been moving in large numbers away from the strongholds of liberalism, the frostbelt states of the Northeast, to more conservative regions, the sunbelt states of the South and West. Thus by 1978 slightly more than half of the population was located in the sunbelt region.

The 1980 census would therefore produce a reallocation of votes in the electoral college that elects the presidency, and of seats in the House of Representatives, that would almost certainly favor Republicans and conservatives.

Supreme Court appointments. With five members of the Supreme Court over 70 at the time of Reagan's accession to the White House, there was an excellent prospect that new appointments would help undo the liberal judicial revolution wrought by the court under Chief Justice Earl Warren. (See chapter 10.)

The Republican party. Since 1964 conservatives had been strongly entrenched in the Republican party's national organization. Although most polls indicated that even after the Reagan victory the Republicans remained the minority party in the country, they were beginning to make some real gains among the electorate,[10] and a successful Reagan administration would accelerate the party's improved standing.

Furthermore, the Republican party had overhauled its structure and become an extremely efficient mechanism. It was well managed, and it was financially sound (in contrast to the Democratic party, which was always struggling to pay off large debts inherited from the past election or even the election before the last).

Conservative organizations. Outside the Republican party the conservatives were now better organized than ever in the past. The National Conservative Political Action Committee spearheaded the attack on liberal senators in 1980. Richard Viguerie and his mass mailing organization raised large amounts of money for conservative candidates and causes. The Moral Majority focused attention on the moral decline inflicted on America by the liberals. And conservative foundations and think tanks like the Heritage Foundation, the Hoover Institution, and the American Enterprise Institute provided bases from which it has been possible to launch a counterattack against the dominance over opinion in America by the liberal establishment.

A conservative tide in public opinion. There has been a long-term shift in public opinion, say the conservatives, toward the right. Polls show that conservatives considerably outnumber liberals among the electorate. On the major issues of the time, the majority are thinking conservative: they are angry about inflation, high taxes, and government waste and corruption; they resent massive welfare programs, busing, and affirmative action; they are impatient with a court system unable or unwilling to deal effectively with criminals; they are frustrated with America's deteriorating position in the world; and they are ready to support increased military spending.

This growing conservative mood has undermined the sources of group support on which the liberals and the Democrats have traditionally depended. Many blue-collar workers, responsive to the conservatives' arguments on moral issues, busing, and foreign policy, voted for Reagan in 1980. Half of the young voted for him; and the liberals' decline on the campuses is clear in the freshman surveys. In 1980 a number of Jews departed from their long-time liberalism. Angered by the strident demands of minority group leaders and attracted by the conservatives' strong backing of Israel, many Jews were at last ready to recognize that they had much more in common with conservatives than with the liberal challengers to the system through which they had achieved so much. Finally, some of the intellectual stars who made liberalism seem the only doctrine an intelligent person could support moved over to conservatism or neoconservatism, thus providing sustenance for the notion that conservatism was not merely a selfish defense of monied interests but a set of significant ideas that must be taken seriously by thoughtful people.

So the conservatives believe that the 1980 election had a significance far transcending the irritation with Jimmy Carter's bungling or the effectiveness of Ronald Reagan as a communicator. They see it as a potential turning point, the staging ground for the great change toward conservatism first signalled by the election of 1968, then set back by Watergate, and finally established by the nomination and election of Ronald Reagan. With that election the conservatives confirmed their choice of the Republican party as their main political instrument, though they were also ready to help strengthen the conservative forces within the Democratic party.

However, conservatives are not convinced that 1980 completed their task. The deep-rooted tendencies within the American political system to blur the edge of principle and to fall back on compromise instead of pressing ahead to produce real change must be constantly resisted. Republican gains in the Senate must be consolidated and advanced in the House. The president must be kept up to the mark, his conservative instincts bolstered. Otherwise the golden opportunity to produce a permanent change in American political attitudes and behavior would be frittered away and might not return for another generation.

THE RADICALS: THE SEARCH FOR ALTERNATIVES

To a much greater extent even than the liberals and conservatives, radicals of left and right have perceived the two major parties as alike as Tweed-

BY PERMISSION OF THE *COLORADO SPRINGS SUN*

ledum and Tweedledee. To G. William Domhoff on the left there is only one major political party in the United States—the Property party, with two wings, Democratic and Republican.[11] And when Alabama Governor George Wallace headed the right-wing American Independent Party in the late 1960s, his rationale was that "there's not a dime's worth of difference" between the Republican and Democratic parties.

Given this view the natural inclination of radicals is to operate outside of the big parties in two ways. One is to operate through ideological pressure groups. The other way is to form separate parties to fight elections: on the left the Communist Party, USA, the Socialist Workers Party, the Peace and Freedom Party, and so on, and on the right the American Independent and American parties, and the extreme right-wing Nazi parties.

The great drawback of the separate party approach, of course, is that under the American electoral system nobody wins elections (except occasionally at the local level) but the big parties. Parties of the radical left have never managed to make much of a showing in national elections in America.[12] On the right there was a period in the late 1960s when George Wallace and the American Independent Party appeared to be on the verge of an effective challenge to the conventional wisdom about the ineffectuality of third parties. Wallace's oratorical skills and his attacks on the liberal intellectuals of the Northeast aroused the enthusiastic support of large numbers of whites in border and midwestern as well as southern states. Although there was no prospect of his winning the presidency, the polls indicated that he might win enough southern states to prevent either of the major candidates from getting a clear majority in the electoral college, thus throwing the election into the House of Representatives—where one or both of the candidates would have to deal with Wallace.

However, as election day approached, the inexorable logic of the electoral system took over. Expressing sympathy for Wallace's ideas as a protest against prevailing policies was one thing. To follow through with a vote that, from the point of view of electing a president, would be wasted, was another. Wallace's strength in the polls ebbed and fell below the point needed to force the decision into the House. In the next presidential race Wallace tried to move into contention for the Democratic party nomination for the presidency and showed considerable strength in some primaries until he was shot and seriously wounded in May 1972.[13] Subsequently no radical right party has been able to find a leader with the kind of popular appeal exercised by Wallace; and although there is still latent support for a populist right-wing party that appeals to resentments against both the poor and the rich, such a party cannot hope to capture electoral votes in the absence of a charismatic leader.[14]

But lesser-party politics are not a waste of time. Wallace's bid for the presidency influenced the thinking of both of the main parties. The Republicans in particular headed off his threat by incorporating some of his positions into their platform and their campaign strategy. Similarly, the Democrats in the 1930s borrowed some ideas from the Socialist party.

But to have a vague, indirect effect from outside cannot be very satisfying to activists who care as much about politics as the radicals of the left and right. They know that in elections the action, the power, is very much with the big parties. So the temptation is to dabble in major-party politics. The purists resist this temptation and are scornful of those who make the case for playing in the political big leagues. Still, Domhoff is among those on the left who argue for working in Democratic primaries. The differences between the Democrats and Republicans are narrow, he concedes. Both parties subscribe to the values of cap-

italism, private property, and imperialism. Still, the liberalism dominant in the Democratic party in some western and northern states contains the potential for expansion into more radical approaches; Ronald Reagan is even more dangerous than Jimmy Carter; and radicals must do whatever they can, wherever they can, to make their case until conditions ripen for a broad-ranging advance toward socialism.

Similarly, on the radical right one finds Birch Society members moving between the American Independent Party and the Republican party, and in the South others in the Birch Society who have become Democratic congressmen. And although there was deep distrust of Ronald Reagan by the radical right, who charged him with repeated opportunism, many rightists worked actively for his nomination and election in 1980.

THE CENTRISTS: IN DEFENSE OF THE PARTY SYSTEM

A number of scholars and commentators have developed rebuttals to these various attacks on the present two-party system.[15] They believe that its defects are far outweighed by its advantages.

Our major parties do provide alternatives. It is not true that the two-party system is merely a charade and that the choice between the Democrats and Republicans is meaningless.

At the very least, our two-party system provides for one of the essential conditions for democracy: a choice between the party of the "ins" and the party of the "outs." The party that forms the government is made constantly aware that, should it antagonize too many voters, another group is ready and able to take over in the next election.

But there are greater distinctions. As we have seen, there are important policy differences between the two parties. In the main, the Democratic party is to the left of center on the political spectrum, and the Republican party is to the right of center. The difference is perceived by the electorate, and in a general way it is reflected in the actions of Democratic and Republican administrations.

We do not need wider differences. Most of the time the differences between the actual policies of Democratic and Republican administrations are not wide, but this similarity is a profound virtue. The conflicts in beliefs and interests that divide Americans are numerous and deep. Tensions are part of our normal condition, and violence is all too likely to erupt at any time. Our two parties, because they are such large and diverse coalitions, are forced to emphasize compromise and conciliation as a condition of holding together.[16] In compromising they perform the vital function of building a degree of consensus among competing groups and reducing the amount of divisiveness that is so much a part of our culture. To sharpen the distinctions between the parties along liberal-conservative lines would promote not consensus but more conflict, which we do not need at this stage of our history.

The people do not want wider differences. Much is made by liberals and conservatives of the argument that people are rejecting politics because they do not see any difference between the parties. In fact, most people see the parties as stirring up conflict where none really exists, and one of the reasons for their dislike of partisan politics is the contentiousness and divisiveness of party politicians.

In the context of Vietnam and the other tensions of the sixties and early seventies, there appeared to be a trend toward the polarization of the electorate. But that trend was overstated by some analysts,[17] and by the mid-1970s the largest body of opinion was again where it usually is—in the moderate ranges of the spectrum.

In any case, the ultimate test comes when people cast their ballots. And, say the centrists, most of the voters who take strong, even extreme positions on issues will still not accept candidates they perceive to be outside the mainstream. This lesson was clear in 1964 and 1972.

Barry Goldwater in 1964 responded to criticisms that John Birchers and other right-wing extremists were among his chief supporters by declaring in his acceptance speech: "Extremism

in the defense of liberty is no vice." Then he made ambiguous statements about Social Security that alarmed pensioners, and he sounded bellicose on foreign policy. Lyndon Johnson occupied the great middle ground and trounced Goldwater by 43 million to 27 million votes.

In 1972 the Democrats moved outside the mainstream on the other side of the spectrum and nominated George McGovern. During the nomination campaign McGovern had called for a guaranteed annual income of $1,000 a person, the limiting of inheritances to $500,000, and a reduction in defense spending. At the Democratic national convention the nation watched as party regulars and moderate elements were overwhelmed, and in many cases excluded, by massed ranks of liberal ideologues. Once nominated, McGovern tried hard to soften his liberal image to win the support of party moderates; his failure is clear from the election result: Nixon 60.8 percent, McGovern 38 percent; Nixon 49 states, McGovern 1 state.

No doubt there were factors affecting the 1964 and 1972 results other than the candidates' stands on the issues. Neither Goldwater nor McGovern was believed by the majority to be competent enough to be president, and both conducted poor campaigns. Moreover, it is probable that no Republican could have beaten Lyndon Johnson in 1964, and that no Democrat could have prevailed against Richard Nixon in 1972.

Still, the extent of the Goldwater and McGovern defeats provides convincing evidence to centrists that for a major party to select a candidate who departs deliberately and aggressively from the mainstream is to court disaster at the polls.

But is this argument not contradicted by the sweeping victory of conservative Ronald Reagan over centrist Jimmy Carter? Centrists do not think so. Reagan had won the support of conservatives by appealing to them over the years with conservative rhetoric, and much of that rhetoric reflected Reagan's strongly held convictions. However, Reagan's victory was no mandate for unmitigated conservatism. Partly it resulted from

Carter's unpopularity: no president in polling history—not even Nixon at the depths of the Watergate scandal—had fallen so low in the polls. Yet Carter might have won had Reagan not gone to great pains to assure the people that, while he was indeed a conservative, he was a moderate, realistic one who would not destroy the programs to which they were strongly attached. Unlike Goldwater's defiant acceptance speech, Reagan's was a model of moderation and conciliation.

Subsequently he seized the opportunity provided by his televised debate with Carter to refute the charge that he was a conservative zealot, and his television commercials emphasized his record of pragmatic achievement while he was governor of California. The public was reassured. They were ready for a reasonable conservative, but not a Goldwater, and they believed they had found such a man in Reagan.

Centrists hoped that this perception would be sustained by his record in the presidency. But many of them were concerned that he might be carried away by the scale of his victory into a belief that he had received an unqualified conservative mandate. They feared that his tax reduction program was an imprudent experiment based on untested conservative dogma. They worried that he might adopt much of the social program of the Moral Majority. The true majority, the centrists believed, were uneasy about some of the excesses of the sexual revolution and the counterculture, but they did not want to repeal the moral changes of the twentieth century and re-

place them with an intolerant puritanism. If Reagan moved far in that direction the coalition he had put together in 1980 would come apart, the country would be torn with dissension, and the Republican party would be gravely damaged.

Centralization of parties is undesirable. One further aspect of the proposals of the liberal critics is sharply rejected by the centrists. The pressure to make our parties more centralized and disciplined seems to the centrists to be alien to the American tradition. It may be appropriate to Europe, but it will not work here. Local and state party organizations are not about to take orders from national committees, and legislative leaders will certainly not follow instructions given them by national party organizations.

How to restore respect for the party system. All that we need to restore the party system is a period of moderate policies competently executed. For in large part the declining support for the parties is merely one dimension of the general deterioration of trust in government that has resulted from the failings of government over the past decade and a half. An improvement in government performance will not make our parties popular; it is the fate of parties in democracy, especially American democracy, to be the butt of a great deal of abuse. Nonetheless, their condition will be healthy enough so that we need not engage in ill-conceived changes that are out of place in the American scheme of things.

CONCLUSION

Three major topics have surfaced repeatedly throughout this chapter: party realignment, the claims of conservative Republicans to have reshaped American politics for the foreseeable future, and the deteriorating position of parties in our political system.

WILL THE PARTIES REALIGN?

To some extent they already have. The Republican party now comes fairly close to satisfying the requirements of the "limited realignment" model shown in figure 4-3. The Democrats, we have suggested, continue to include some incongruous, even incompatible elements. But even there the range of opinions is not quite what it used to be. There are far fewer thoroughly reactionary southern Democrats in Congress than in the past, and even fewer hold those key committee chairmanships that used to make Democratic presidents come to them cap in hand.

Liberal-conservative realignment is still very slow and very limited. The continued presence in the Democratic party of a number of conservatives, and the loose, decentralized structure of the parties, make it extremely unlikely that the major American parties are close to attaining the degree of ideological cohesion found in many European parties.

Still, if the changes in our parties are not sufficient to satisfy the liberal realigners, they have already gone beyond the predictions that many centrists were making a few years ago.

IS CONSERVATIVE REPUBLICANISM THE WAVE OF THE FUTURE?

In the previous edition of this book, published in 1978, the question posed at this point in this chapter (a question widely discussed after the party's Watergate disaster and its subsequent election defeats) was: "Will the Republican party die?" The answer given was: "Probably not."

The 1980 election proved that the Republican party was very much alive. Indeed, many Republicans, especially the conservatives in the party, suggested that the real question had become: "Will the Democratic party die?" They were convinced that America was turning right and that the Republicans, if they continued on a conservative course, could dominate American politics more completely for the next twenty or more years than did the Democrats from 1932.

This prognosis is very plausible. There does appear to have been a conservative trend in the electorate. If the Reagan administration policies work reasonably well and if real progress is made toward bringing inflation under control, restoring buoyancy and productivity to the economy, and ensuring the nation's energy supplies while bolstering America's stature in the world, it would be difficult to prevent the Republicans from becoming the dominant party for many years.

However, as we shall see in our discussions of policy issues in the last section of this book, even a modest degree of success in these various areas will be hard to achieve. A major setback on any of these issues, or even some piece of misfortune quite unrelated to them, could blight the Republicans' prospects as severely as the Democrats were hurt by the disappointments of the Carter era.

We also cannot be certain that the conservative mood in the country is more than a temporary phenomenon. Conceivably the appetite for conservative policies could be quickly satiated by the Reagan program, forcing the pendulum to swing back toward more liberal programs.

Furthermore, the Democratic party is still the preferred party of considerably more people than is the Republican party. It has vast reserves of experience and adaptability built up since 1932. And a surge of liberal defiance to the Reagan administration's attacks on cherished Democratic programs of the past could bring renewed vitality to the Democratic party.

In sum, the great Republican tide that swept the party into control of the Senate and the White House in 1980 could be irreversible for another generation. But it would be as foolish to assert that this trend must inevitably continue as it would have been to insist in 1978 that the Republican party was sick beyond all hope of recovery.

IS THE AMERICAN PARTY SYSTEM ABOUT TO DISAPPEAR?

Probably not, but it may grow still weaker than it is now. Parties will not become extinct in America for the reasons suggested earlier: as long as people are free to organize anything, they will organize parties. However, it is growing increasingly difficult to contain all the political impulses of the American electorate within a stable two-party framework, even if this framework is realigned. So we may well see the emergence of either or both of the following trends.

First, there could be a proliferation of new parties. Given the nature of our electoral institutions, none of these is likely to grow strong enough to overtake the major parties. Taken together, however, they could be a source of increased confusion in elections.

Second, there could be an acceleration of the tendency for voters to attach themselves to candidates on the basis of personality and issues with little or no preference to party. This prospect led Walter Dean Burnham to the prediction cited at the beginning of this chapter, that political parties might disappear, leaving us with a volatile, unpredictable, unanchored electorate. We are not yet at that point, for, as we have seen, party is still an important factor in electoral decisions, and conceivably the parties have already hit the lowest point of their fortunes. But we had better suspend judgment on this question until we have taken a closer look at what happens in elections in the next chapter.

NOTES AND REFERENCES

1. Walter Dean Burnham, *Critical Elections and the Mainsprings of American Politics* (New York: Norton, 1970), p. 132.
2. An alternative system is *proportional representation*. Under this system (of which there are many variations) the electoral districts are large enough to return several members, and each party wins seats in proportion to the size of its vote in each district. Thus minor parties have a good chance of gaining at least a few seats, rather than being frozen out completely.
3. Interview with author, Washington, D.C., May 14, 1976.
4. Gerald Pomper, Ross K. Baker, Kathleen A. Frankovic, Charles E. Jacob, Wilson Carey McWilliams, and Henry A. Plotkin, *The Election of 1980* (Chatham, N.J.: Chatham House, 1981), p. 3. See also Cornelius Cotter and John Bibby, "Institutional Development of Parties and the Theory of Party Decline," *Political Science Quarterly*, Spring 1980, pp. 1–27.
5. The CBS/*New York Times* poll of voters as they left the polling booths in 1980 showed a split at 31 percent conservatives, 18 percent liberals, and 51 percent "moderates."
6. Norman H. Nie, Sidney Verba, and John R. Petrocik, *The Changing American Voter* (Cambridge, Mass.: Harvard University Press, 1979), p. 166.
7. According to a *Washington Post* survey, 56 percent of respondents saw changes in lifestyle (attitudes about divorce, coed dorms in college, men and women living together before marriage, and so on) as "a sign that Americans are becoming more tolerant,"

as against 37 percent who saw these changes as "a sign of increasing moral decay in America." Cited in *Public Opinion*, December–January 1980, p. 28.

8. On this question see Everett C. Ladd, *Wilson Quarterly*, Spring 1979, and "Realignment? No, Dealignment? Yes," *Public Opinion*, October–November 1980. Ladd himself does not fall into our liberal category but challenges the claims of conservatives that the 1980 election reflected a long-term shift toward conservatism among the American electorate.

9. See chapters 5 and 7 for more detailed discussion of this question.

10. See Adam Clymer and Kathleen Frankovic, "The Realities of Realignment," *Public Opinion*, June–July 1981, pp. 42–47.

11. See G. William Domhoff, *Fat Cats and Democrats: The Role of the Rich in the Party of the Common Man* (Englewood Cliffs, N.J.: Prentice-Hall, 1972).

12. The highest proportions of votes obtained by Socialist party candidates in presidential elections were by Eugene V. Debs (3 percent in 1904, 2.8 percent in 1908, 6 percent in 1912, and 3.5 percent in 1920) and Norman Thomas (2.2 percent in 1932). In 1948 leftist candidate Henry A. Wallace, running on the Progressive party ticket, received 2.4 percent of the vote.

13. By 1981 George Wallace was again expressing interest in running for state office, this time on the basis of more populist positions that were attracting support from some black civil rights leaders.

14. The American Independent party's standard-bearer in 1972 was John Birch Society member John Schmitz, who amassed something over a million votes nationwide. In 1976 the party split, and two rival right-wing parties mustered less than 0.5 percent of the total votes cast.

15. See, for example, Arthur N. Holcombe, *Our More Perfect Union* (Cambridge, Mass.: Harvard University Press, 1950); Herbert Agar, *The Price of Union*, 2nd ed. (Boston: Houghton Mifflin, 1966); Pendleton Herring, *The Politics of Democracy* (New York: Norton, 1940).

16. In multiparty systems each party tends to be more cohesive than our major parties. But since no one of them is likely to be strong enough to win an election by itself, two or more parties will have to enter into a coalition in order to have enough seats in the legislature to form a government. Each party in the coalition will then have to make compromises with the others to keep the alliance going. So the difference between the two systems is that in multiparty countries the compromises typically take place *among* the parties *after* an election, whereas in two-party countries the compromises are made *within* the parties *before* the election.

17. See Arthur H. Miller, "Political Issues and Trust in Government," *The American Political Science Review*, September 1974, p. 963; and Jack Citrin, "Comment: The Political Relevance of Trust in Government," ibid., pp. 973–988.

chapter five

ELECTIONS: MAJORITIES, MEDIA, AND MONEY

In the United States, the election process offers a choice of candidates for most public offices, awards each office to whoever gets the most votes, and thus builds the principle of majority rule into the governmental system. However, there is a great deal of debate on the extent to which our elections truly provide a choice and whether they register the authentic will of the majority. To set up the terms of that debate we shall discuss the various elements that go into nominating and electing candidates for office in America. Although we shall have something to say about elections at all levels, most of our examples will be drawn from presidential elections.

For a people who do not vote very much, we are called on to vote a great deal. A much larger number of public offices are contended for in elections in this country than in other countries. Every fourth November we elect a president, and at the same time we fill all the seats in the House of Representatives and one-third of the seats in the Senate. Two years later we go through the same process for the House and the Senate. Then, as we shall see in chapter 11, we are also called on to choose among candidates for a great array of state and local government jobs: governors and lieutenant governors, state senators and assemblymen, mayors and city council members, sheriffs and judges, commissioners and tax assessors, and more. In addition, we have laws that establish elections of state and local officials of political parties. And innumerable state and local issues are placed on the ballot to be disposed of by decision of the voters at large.

NOMINATING OUR PRESIDENTIAL CANDIDATES

PRIMARIES

We are not content with subjecting more offices to the election process than is the case elsewhere. We also bring the general public into the process of choosing—directly or indirectly—the candidates whom political parties put forward for election. In other democracies only the active, subscribing members of the parties are involved in deciding who their candidates will be. Here we have adopted the system of direct primaries, in which rank-and-file voters can participate. In most states each party's primary is "closed"—that is, reserved for those rank-and-file voters who register ahead of time with that party. Thus, in a state holding a closed primary, registered Republicans may vote for only Republican candidates. But there are some "open primary" states where this qualification is not imposed, and a voter can decide on the day of the primary in which party's primary he or she will participate. Primary elections are held for congressional and most partisan state offices, are official occasions paid for out of public funds, and are administered under legally authorized procedures in the same way as general elections.

Primaries have also become a major factor in nominating the parties' candidates for the presidency. Each party's presidential candidate is selected by a majority vote of the delegates to the party's national convention, which is held in July or August before the November election. The precise number of delegates needed to nominate a candidate varies from party to party and year to year; but both parties apportion delegates among the states mostly on the basis of population, with a bonus of additional delegates going to states that did well for the parties' candidates in the previous election. With the power to nominate a presidential candidate vested in these delegates, how they are chosen becomes a crucial question.

Historically, delegates were chosen at state conventions or committees—political assemblies to which delegates were elected from caucuses of the local party organizations. But in recent years more and more states have adopted presidential primaries as their means of selecting delegates to the national conventions, and the delegates' names have appeared on the voter's ballot along with various candidates for public office. The extent to which delegates are committed to supporting a particular candidate at the national convention varies according to the laws of the states. Some of the primaries bind the delegates to a candidate, whereas other states permit the delegates to express their individual preferences, leaving the delegates unpledged. However, the trend has been toward securing commitments to specific candidates based on the votes in the primaries of the party's rank and file.

John F. Kennedy was the first presidential candidate to depend heavily on the primaries to secure his nomination. As Theodore White tells it, Kennedy "clubbed the big city bosses into submission"[1] after winning some key victories in the early primaries. But Kennedy still needed those big city bosses, and his success did not establish conclusively that candidates must depend principally on primaries to gain the nomination. Thus, in 1964, Barry Goldwater won some primaries but lost others by big margins, and he received only 25 percent of the votes cast in the primaries he entered. But he won the nomination because in 1964 56 percent of the delegates to the national convention were picked at state conventions, and Goldwater was popular among the conservative Republican party leaders who were influential at those conventions. Then, in 1968, Vice-President Hubert Humphrey won the Democratic nomination without entering a single primary. Robert Kennedy's bid had been brought to a tragic end by an assassin's bullet; and since only fifteen states held presidential primaries in 1968, none of the other candidates had amassed enough delegates to prevent the established party leaders from choosing one of their own at the national convention.

By 1972, however, the number of states holding presidential primaries had been increased from fifteen to twenty-three, which was crucial to George Mc-Govern's success in mounting a liberal challenge to the candidates preferred by the Democratic party leadership. But even McGovern's victory was dependent to some extent on the efforts of his liberal supporters at state conventions, for he won only ten of the twenty-three primaries he entered, some by narrow margins.

The number of presidential primary states increased to thirty by 1976, and this increase was the essential factor in Jimmy Carter's nomination. He was very much the outsider challenging the established party leadership structures. But he won the opening primary in New Hampshire, and, although he suffered some important defeats later, he won enough primaries to ensure his nomination.

Even Gerald Ford, although an incumbent president, had to undergo a grueling ordeal in the 1976 primaries and only just came through. In a final bitter struggle to hold off a strong challenge from Ronald Reagan, the issue came down to ten states that were holding state conventions, and then to a quest for support, one person at a time, among the uncommitted delegates at the national convention. However, these late encounters should not distract us from the central fact of the Republican nominating process of 1976: the bulk of the delegates came from the primary process.

In 1980 presidential primaries were held in thirty seven states and territories, and three-quarters of the delegates to the national conventions were chosen in those primaries. As in 1976, the primary process confronted the incumbent president with a long and sometimes humiliating ordeal, during which Carter suffered defeats at the hands of Senator Edward Kennedy in several states. However, Carter won enough delegates to give him an insurmountable lead for the nomination.[2]

On the Republican side Ronald Reagan built on and greatly expanded the base of support he had established in the 1976 primaries. After coming in second to George Bush in the Iowa caucuses he reasserted his authority in the opening primary in New Hampshire; and although he was beaten by Bush in Connecticut, Pennsylvania, and Michigan, he won everywhere else, forced all his opponents to withdraw from the race, and went into the convention the overwhelming choice of his party as certified by the primary process.

The long ordeal of the nominating process. The extraordinary length of the presidential nominating process has come in for a good deal of criticism. The state caucuses and conventions begin in January in Iowa. The first primary is held in New Hampshire in March. But the final national convention does not take place until July or August.

This schedule places a disproportionate emphasis on small numbers of voters in the states that select their delegates early. In January 1976 Jimmy Carter won 2.7 percent of the 10 percent of Iowa's voters who participated in the state's caucuses. The media attention lavished on that 2.7 percent of Iowa's Democrats brought Carter out of political obscurity and established him as a viable candidate. The media are similarly fascinated by the New Hampshire primary results. Lyndon Johnson's prospects for renomination in 1968 were destroyed in New Hampshire even though he won the primary: the verdict was that he had not won by a big enough margin. McGovern, Ford, Carter, and Reagan all made much of their New Hampshire victories. Yet New Hampshire has less than 0.4 percent of the nation's population, and in 1980 it accounted for only 19 of the Democrats' 3,331 national convention delegates and 22 of the Republicans' 1,994.

Moreover, in 1980 most of the early primaries were in the East and South, with the result that the nominations of both parties were virtually locked up by the end of March before any state west of the Mississippi River had held a primary.

A second complaint about the length of the primary season is that it places a tremendous burden on the candidates, who must be in perpetual motion, flying from state to state, winding up the current primary while campaigning in the next and laying the groundwork for the ones after that. The process is confusing to the candidates and bewildering to the public.

Reform proposals. The growing dissatisfaction with the excessive length of the nominating procedure has produced a number of proposals for reform. One suggestion calls for carrying the logic of the primaries to its ultimate conclusion by establishing *national primaries*, with a runoff election between the two leading candidates if none receives more than 40 percent of the votes in the first round. A second proposal calls for *regional primaries*, perhaps one a month from March through July. A third measure consists of *compressing the nominating period*: the national parties would accept only those delegates to the national conventions chosen from their states during a three-month period from April through June.

In 1982 the Democratic Party decided on a modified version of this last proposal. All Democratic presidential primaries and caucuses in 1984 must be held during a 13-week period from March 13 to June 12, except for the Iowa precinct caucuses (to be scheduled no earlier than February 27) and the New Hampshire primary (scheduled for March 6).

THE NATIONAL CONVENTIONS

The character of the national conventions has been transformed by the growing use of presidential primaries. Earlier in our history the conventions were the setting for maneuvering by party leaders and decision making behind closed doors. Thus, in 1920, Harry Daugherty went to the Republican convention in Washington as a representative of the undistinguished claims of Senator Warren Gamaliel Harding. He explained his scenario to some reporters:

There will be no nomination on the early ballots. After the other candidates have failed, after they have gone their limit, the leaders, worn out and wishing to do the very best thing, will get together in some hotel room about 2:11 in the morning. Some fifteen men, bleary-eyed with lack of sleep, and perspiring profusely with the excessive heat, will sit down around a big table. I will be with them and present the name of Senator Harding. When that time comes, Harding will be selected, because he fits in perfectly with every need of the party and the nation.[3]

Events followed this program closely. There was a deadlock among the major candidates; at around two o'clock in the morning before the last day of the convention, a small group of men, after long discussion in the "smoke-filled room" of the convention hotel, wearily gave up on the possibility of nominating anyone but Harding. He was nominated the next day on the tenth ballot. As Harding put it: "We drew to a pair of deuces, and filled."

Nobody draws to a pair of deuces and wins a presidential nomination any more. Successful candidates have to arrive at the convention with a very strong hand. In fact, it has to be strong enough to overwhelm the opposition very quickly, for conventions now do not go to the 10 ballots required before Harding could get his majority (or the 103 ballots the Democrats took to nominate John Davis in 1924). Every Republican presidential nominee has won on the first ballot since 1948, and every Democratic nominee since 1956.

Sometimes there have been hard-fought struggles at the conventions to win on that first ballot. However, since Dwight Eisenhower narrowly defeated Robert Taft for the Republican nomination in 1952, there has been only one real cliffhanger—Gerald Ford's win over Ronald Reagan in 1976; and close though that contest was, there was little doubt by the time the convention began that Reagan had lost. Thus national conventions have become forums to ratify previously made decisions on the naming of presidential candidates.

However, conventions are still left with significant functions, and often dramatic struggles arise over those functions. There have been contests over delegates' *credentials*, as in the refusal of the Democratic national convention in 1972 to seat the delegation led by Mayor Daley of Chicago because it had not complied with a new rule requiring proper representation of women, young people, and minorities.

The party *platform* can also generate fireworks. Although Reagan lost in 1976 he was able to force through planks in the Republican platform that were implicitly critical of the Ford-Kissinger foreign policy. Similarly, although Carter's forces were clearly dominant at the 1980 Democratic convention, Senator Kennedy made an eloquent, impassioned speech that roused the liberals at the convention and forced acceptance of some of his economic proposals by voice vote.

Arguments over procedural *rules* can determine much larger issues. In 1976 the Reagan backers forced a showdown on the procedure by which vice-presidential nominees are selected. The proposal would have required Ford to follow Reagan's example and announce his selection for running mate before the vote on the presidential nominee. Any choice made by Ford might antagonize those delegates who preferred someone else and thus lose votes for his own candidacy. Not surprisingly, Ford opposed the suggestion, it was rejected, and its rejection foretold the final outcome of the Ford-Reagan struggle. In 1980 Kennedy, too, tried to use a rule change to improve his slim prospects at the Democratic convention. His backers, arguing that opinion in the country and the party had turned against Carter since his victories in the early primaries, proposed that all delegates be freed from the commitments made to particular candidates during the primaries. But the call for an "open convention" was inevitably resisted by Carter and easily defeated, after which Kennedy withdrew from the race.

Finally, the nominations for *vice-president* can cause conflicts. With the exception of 1956, when Democratic presidential nominee Adlai Stevenson let the convention choose his running mate,[4] conventions have endorsed the nominee's choice. However, in most cases the decision is made by the nominee during the convention after a great deal of pressure from competing forces in the party. Ford chose conservative Senator Robert Dole to placate the Reaganites in 1976, and Carter selected Senator Walter Mondale to please his party's liberals. In 1980 an otherwise predictable Republican convention came briefly alive with the possibility (an unlikely one in retrospect) that former President Gerald Ford would accept the second spot on a Reagan ticket.[5]

All these conflicts over credentials, platforms, vice-presidential running mates, and rules serve to focus public attention on politics. The long, noisy demonstrations for the candidates are of little interest to anyone not participating in them. And most of the speeches are full of predictable denunciations of the opposite party and repeated references to the party's own glorious achievements under past leaders. However, to the annoyance of party leaders, most of these speeches are interrupted or ignored by the television networks, which concentrate on trying to find out what is going on behind the scenes to resolve the conflicts facing the convention. Although some of these controversies are blown up beyond their true significance by the media, others are of great importance, and the media's instinct in concentrating on them rather than on the formal business of the conventions is sound.

Two kinds of criticism about the present state of the national conventions are heard today. The first is that the vital task of selecting the presidential nominee should not be taken away from the convention. Senator Kennedy's proposal in 1980 for an open convention had an obviously self-serving purpose, but many analysts of American politics believe that the call for a more significant role for the convention itself is sound. They suggest that the present process is defective in four respects:

1. It locks the party into a decision made in the early spring that cannot be changed no matter how circumstances have changed by the time the convention meets in the summer.

2. It places too much of a premium on the outsider—the ideologue like McGovern in 1972, or the novice like Carter in 1976. The Democratic party paid a high price for these nominations, with a crushing defeat in 1972 and an amateurish presidency under Jimmy Carter.

3. It does not allow the kind of thoughtful, deliberative process that is calculated to produce the candidate best equipped to hold a party together.

4. It undermines the party system, for it moves the central decision away from the convention, which is the most important of all party gatherings, to the pri-

maries, which are essentially devices for going over the heads of the party organizations.

Another kind of criticism of the condition of our national conventions is that, in the Democratic party in particular, experienced political leaders have been replaced as delegates by enthusiasts with no knowledge of party affairs or long-term interest in the well-being of the party.

The background for this development was the 1968 Democratic convention, which was disrupted by anti–Vietnam War demonstrations in the streets of Chicago. Liberals contended that the riots might not have occurred if representatives of the antiwar movement had been present in the convention rather than in the streets. In fact, they noted, eighteen states had sent delegations to the convention without a single person under 30, and blacks, Hispanics, and women were grossly underrepresented.

So a commission was appointed and drew up guidelines for the 1972 convention requiring all state delegations to include women, minorities, and the young "in reasonable proportion to their representation in the party as a whole in the state"; the guidelines also eliminated the automatic inclusion of top public and party officials. The result at the 1972 convention was the exclusion of many elected public officials and a huge increase in the number of women, minorities, and young people.

Complaints from the excluded groups forced a compromise for 1976 that brought back to the convention more of the traditional party leaders, but not enough to still the criticism.

Consequently the Democrats set up another commission, whose recommendations led to a decision by the party in 1982 to create a bloc of more than 500 delegates (nearly 15 percent of the total delegates in 1984) consisting of party leaders and elected officials, including up to two-thirds of the Democrats in Congress. Moreover, these party regulars were to be uncommitted, that is, allowed to support any candidate regardless of the results of primaries and conventions in their states.

CANDIDATES AND THEIR QUALIFICATIONS

With respect to both the election machinery and the selection of delegates, we have seen a trend toward making the nomination process less exclusive. To a limited extent this trend can also be seen in relation to the candidates themselves. What qualifications must a candidate have to be seriously considered as a presidential nominee? Here we must look at the candidate's personal origins and background, experience in public office, and character.

Personal origins and background. It used to be assumed that a presidential candidate should be a white male Protestant of North European extraction in his fifties. John Kennedy, a Catholic in his early forties, changed two of these requirements. And Barry Goldwater's ancestry was of East European extraction. However, Carter, Ford, and Reagan all fit the earlier profile. Polls indicate that fewer and fewer Americans say that they would not vote for a woman or black for president. Yet no woman or black has been seriously considered by a Democratic or Republican convention for the presidency or even the vice-presidency.

From the Civil War until 1976 it was assumed that a major party candidate must come from outside the South. Jimmy Carter demonstrated in 1976 that a southerner can indeed be acceptable to a national constituency. In fact, to the Democrats in 1976 the fact that Carter was a southerner was an asset, for it enabled them to win back a part of the country that had deserted them in recent presidential elections.

The educational requirements for a presidential candidacy have been growing more demanding. Generally speaking, delegates expect a viable candidate now to have a college education. In fact, since 1968 all the nominees but Reagan have gone on to graduate work—Nixon and Ford in law, McGovern in theology, Humphrey in political science, and Carter in engineering and physics.

It used to be thought that the proper age for a candidate was in the mid-fifties. However, John Kennedy was only 43 when nominated, and Ronald Reagan was 69.

Political experience. A candidate is expected to have substantial experience in public office. Since Dwight Eisenhower, who had held no elective office (though as leader of the Allied Forces in World War II he was deeply involved in public decision making with political leaders), all candidates for the presidency have had the experience of serving in an elective office.

What public offices are best suited for this purpose? In the past state governors were preferred, for a governorship provided executive experience. However, this requirement has changed. A governorship is still a good background, as the nominations of Carter and Reagan prove. But the examples of Goldwater, Humphrey, Nixon, and McGovern suggest that the United States Senate, which exposes its members to great national and international issues and also gives them excellent opportunity for exposure in the media, is a springboard to the presidency.

However, to win a presidential nomination the best kind of public experience is to be president already. Harry Truman said that any president who wanted the nomination of his party and did not get it was a damned fool. For a party to refuse to renominate its own president is to repudiate the performance of its own administration and to confess failure to the electorate. Still, incumbency can be a liability. Lyndon Johnson's identification with the Vietnam War became a grave political drawback and led to his decision not to seek his party's nomination again. And Gerald Ford, who had not himself been elected to the presidency, suffered from criticisms of his performance in the office.

Nonetheless, the fact that Ford managed to get his party's nomination, however narrowly, against such an effective campaigner as Ronald Reagan, is in part a tribute to the power of incumbency. As a political tactic, before some of the crucial state primaries in 1976 the White House would announce a federal grant or some other benefit to the state for which the candidates were contending. And during the last, close-fought struggle for the allegiance of the uncommitted delegates the president had the advantage. Obscure local party leaders would be deluged with calls and invitations from the rival camps. A luncheon with Ronald Reagan in person was an occasion to be long remembered. But it was not quite the same as an invitation to a banquet for a foreign dignitary at the White House and a personal chat with the president and his wife.

Jimmy Carter's bid for renomination in 1980 gives us another example of the liabilities and assets of incumbency. On the negative side there was the pervasive sense in the country that his presidency was a failure. A poll of Democrats in October 1979 indicated that 52 percent preferred that Carter not run again. The frustration over the Iranian hostage situation intensified the dissatisfaction and led many Democrats who supported him to fear that he could not win in November.

Nevertheless, incumbency proved to be Carter's decisive advantage in the race for the nomination. Like Ford and other presidents before him Carter won friends by his dispensation of federal largess and presidential status. Grants to Maine and New Hampshire increased as voters prepared to go to the polls. Carter telephoned delegates in the primaries, held presidential press conferences, and gave exclusive interviews with selected reporters covering the primaries.

But much more important, that same foreign policy that had done so much damage to his reputation could be used by him to rally the country at critical moments. In the light of the hostage crisis, said Carter, it would be inappropriate for him to spend much time politicking when his duty lay in the White House; so he could conduct a "rose garden" strategy, remaining presidentially at his post while his political opponents flailed away, demanding in vain that he come out and fight. Moreover, announcements of new initiatives to resolve the crisis were made just before the New Hampshire and Wisconsin primaries.

Following the Soviet invasion of Afghanistan, Carter responded by proposing a boycott of the forthcoming Moscow Olympic Games. That proposal was put forward the Sunday before the Iowa caucuses. And another stern warning on Afghanistan came two days before the Illinois primary.

Whether or not the timing was contrived, Carter's responses to world events clearly helped him during the nomination struggle. The impact of these events is demonstrated in table 5-1, which traces the rise and fall of Carter's standing vis-à-vis Kennedy during the struggle for the nomination. We see from these figures that the assessment of Carter was unfavorable in November 1979 and that coincident with the foreign policy crises it had risen impressively by January 1980 and held at high levels during the crucial period of the caucuses and early primaries. Approval for Carter had slipped by June, but by then it was too late to help Kennedy.

TABLE 5-1 Reputational index[a] of 1980 Democratic presidential candidates

	Nov. 1979	Jan. 1980	Feb.	March	April	June
Carter	0.50	0.75	0.84	0.80	0.75	0.64
Kennedy	.83	.73	.59	.64	.65	.60

[a] The reputational index is a composite giving equal weight to the degree to which a candidate is known and the relatively favorable impression people have of him.
Source: CBS News/*New York Times* polls, *The Election of 1980*, p. 11.

Carter had one other asset during this period—Kennedy's campaign. Soon after Kennedy announced his candidacy a televised interview with Roger Mudd, which had been taped in August, was released. Kennedy's performance was disastrous: he was hesitant, poorly briefed, and reduced almost to incoherence by a question about his great personal trauma—the death at Chappaquiddick in 1969 of a young woman in a car driven off a bridge by Kennedy, and his failure to report the accident until the next day. Later in the campaign Kennedy recovered his confidence, but he did little to demonstrate that he was an effective alternative to Carter until, his bid for the nomination ended, he drew a great ovation at the Democratic convention with a masterly speech.

However, given the developments in the world and Carter's response to them as president, it is doubtful that even a more impressive campaign by Kennedy could have overcome the advantages of incumbency.

Next to the presidency, the best prior experience for a presidential nomination is the vice-presidency, as is indicated by the examples of Richard Nixon and Hubert Humphrey. And the vice presidency was also the means of getting the top job in the cases of Harry Truman, Lyndon Johnson, and Gerald Ford. In some cases the vice-presidential nominees have been men of sufficient caliber to be considered prime presidential possibilities themselves, as was the case with Lyndon Johnson in 1960, Hubert Humphrey in 1968, Walter Mondale in 1976, and George Bush in 1980. In other cases, however, the main consideration has not been performance in public office, but rather the desire to balance the presidential ticket geographically and ideologically. This strategy caused the selection of William Miller, Barry Goldwater's running mate in 1964, and Spiro Agnew, Nixon's choice in 1972.

One other kind of experience is enormously important: service to the party. Gaining the support of delegates requires the cultivation of local party leaders and activists all around the country. Thus Barry Goldwater did well in the state conventions because from 1960 onward he had addressed fund-raising dinners that brought in large amounts of money for Republican candidates, and he had gotten to know state and local leaders personally.

Jimmy Carter, although unknown to the general public, was personally acquainted with large numbers of local political leaders well before the 1976 campaign started. He started his quest for the presidency in 1974 after his tenure as governor of Georgia was over. Working for local candidates wherever he went, he stayed at the homes of party activists. (There were about eight hundred of these hosts, and all were invited to a special White House reception the day after Carter was inaugurated in 1977.) Ronald Reagan, too, had travelled the country for years as a stellar attraction at Republican fund-raising functions.

In this respect Carter and Reagan had an important advantage over their rivals. The others still had to attend to their jobs in the Senate and the House. Carter and Reagan had been governors, but were so no longer. They were free to travel around the country, and both had enough money to do so (Carter from his peanut warehouse, Reagan from his radio program). So it may be that the best experience is *past* experience, with nothing to distract the candidate from active pursuit of the presidency.

Character. Although much has been written about the qualities of temperament and character needed to win a presidential nomination, we shall concentrate on three essential attributes. First, a candidate must have stamina. Thirty-seven primaries plus several state conventions impose enormous physical and emotional stress on a candidate. For many months, even years, he must be incessantly on the move, snatching sleep whenever he can, alternating snacks with monotonous political dinners, shaking hands, making speech after speech (or making the same speech over and over again), trying to project spontaneity, vitality, and individual concern at all hours of the day or night to people he has never met and knows little or nothing about. Physical endurance, then, the capacity to survive, is the first, indispensable requirement.

Second, under all this pressure a candidate must remain sufficiently cool and self-possessed to avoid blunders. Wherever he goes, he is bombarded with questions by the media, some sensible, some foolish. In dealing with these questions he knows that one serious mistake could end his candidacy. Thus, George Romney, the governor of Michigan, was widely assumed to be the front runner for the Republican nomination in 1964. But in a radio interview on a local station he explained his shift away from support of the Vietnam War by declaring that the first time he had gone to Vietnam he had been "brainwashed" by the military. The phrase was picked up by the national media and proved fatal to his candidacy. It destroyed the image he had created of a highly competent, aggressive executive and replaced it with the image of a vacillator who was easily brainwashed. Similarly, Maine Senator Edward Muskie was thought to be easily in the lead for the 1972 Democratic nomination. But during the New Hampshire primary television cameras caught him weeping publicly as he denounced a right-wing local newspaper that had printed a harsh criticism of his wife. His image of a cool, imperturbable leader was shattered, and his candidacy never recovered. Edward Kennedy's prospects, too, were severely damaged by his fumbling interview with Roger Mudd in 1980.

Some mistakes can be overcome. Carter, for example, told the *New York Daily News* during his primary campaign that he saw nothing wrong with communities of Polish, Czech, French-Canadian or black Americans trying to "maintain the ethnic purity of their neighborhoods." The "ethnic purity" phrase infuriated blacks, Jews, and liberals generally, and Carter made matters worse when, under pressure from the press to clarify his point, he said that, although opposed to housing discrimination, he would not use government power to promote "the intrusion of alien groups," or "black intrusion" into a neighborhood simply to bring about integration. Under a storm of protest, Carter apologized and survived, although the statements confirmed the liberals' distrust of him.

The final essential attribute of anyone who aspires to be a presidential nominee is ambition. He must want the nomination with an all-consuming passion. Walter Mondale was the liberals' favorite candidate for the presidency during 1974, but, after traveling around the country in search of campaign funds and supporters, he said in November of that year, "I did not have the overwhelming desire to be president that is essential for the kind of campaign that is required." He lacked the burning ambition to sustain him through the ordeal of the primary campaigns.

As one of his aides put it, he "didn't want to spend the next two years in Holiday Inns."

So, to gain a nomination, a candidate must be possessed by the certainty that this goal is what he wants in life above all else. And some of the time, at least, he must find it satisfying and stimulating rather than degrading. Otherwise, he will lose the zest that is essential to sustain his supporters as well as himself and to convince the voters that he above all others is best suited for the job.

GENERAL ELECTION STRATEGIES

Once nominated, a presidential candidate moves on to the final test in November— the general election. As the standard-bearer of a major party he will be guided by two main considerations. The first point is that to win an election he cannot rely only on the enthusiasts who carried his campaign for the nomination. He must build a broad enough coalition to gain the 40 million or more votes needed for victory. So he must bind up the wounds in his own party if the nomination campaign was strongly contested, and he must begin the process of reaching out to independents and those members of the opposition whose commitment to their party is weak.

But there is another important fact to bear in mind. People do not elect a president directly. The results of a presidential election are not determined until 538 electors in the *electoral college* have cast their ballots. The electoral college was part of the design of the Founding Fathers, who, cautious about the wisdom of people in the mass, preferred to have the president chosen by delegations from each state, the total number "equal to the whole number of senators and representatives to which the state may be entitled in the Congress." The Framers' assumption was that the delegates would vote on the basis of their independent judgments. In fact, as the two-party system evolved, electors cast their ballots mostly along party lines. Today voters in each state are presented a choice between lists or slates of electors selected by the state parties and pledged to the parties' candidates; and the slate that gets more popular votes than any other slate, no matter how small the margin, wins *all* the state's electoral votes. With this in mind the candidates set out to win 270 or more electoral college votes, a majority of the total 538 from the fifty states.

We can best understand candidate strategies for winning the necessary 270 votes by looking at the elections of 1976 and 1980.

THE 1976 ELECTION

The Carter electoral college strategy started with the South, which could be brought back to the Democratic camp by one of its native sons. The border states, those between North and South, were also generally Democratic in registration and might well ally themselves with their neighbor states to the South. The industrial states of the Northeast had large blocs of electoral votes and big-city populations of typically Democratic voters. If all the normally Democratic states of the South, the border region, and the Northeast went for Carter, he would gain

237 of his needed 270 electoral votes. Another 10 could be counted on from Walter Mondale's home state, Minnesota. Oregon and Hawaii, with 10 votes between them, were listed as probable Carter states. And either Ohio (25) or Texas (26) would take the total over 270. Although this left no margin of error, it also did not allow for hopeful prospects in California, Illinois, Indiana, and Wisconsin.

Ford on the other hand, needed to sweep the mountain states of the West (34 votes), the far West (61), the Midwest (98), and the traditionally Republican portions of New England (11), and to wrest 37 votes from Carter in the South and border states. These areas would give a total of 241. Ohio and Texas would put Ford over the top, and there was also the possibility of up to 28 votes in the East.

Of the two, the Ford strategy seemed much the more difficult. He started from a much smaller party base than Carter. The Ford electoral college plan was built on winning in a large number of states, several of which had small populations and few electoral votes. And most of the preelection forecasts in news magazines gave Carter a much bigger base of assured and probable states than Ford. Yet the Ford plan did not fall far short. Ford got almost 38.6 million popular votes (48 percent) to Carter's 40.3 million (51 percent). In the electoral college Carter prevailed by only 297 to 241. As the map in figure 5-1 indicates, Ford took the entire West except Hawaii, much of the Midwest, the hoped-for New England states, plus Connecticut, New Jersey, and Virginia. He fell short because Carter carried all but one southern state, most of the border states, just enough of the eastern industrial states, both Ohio and Texas, and Wisconsin as well as Minnesota. So close was the vote in several states that a switch of fewer than 8,000 votes in Ohio and Hawaii would have given Ford 270 votes in the electoral college; conversely, a total shift of 70,000 votes in eight other states would have made Carter's winning margin 337 to 201.

THE 1980 ELECTION

As they came out of the Democratic national convention the Carter strategists planned an electoral college strategy similar to that which had been so successful in 1976.

They would fight again to win the thirteen southern and border states, with their 145 electoral votes, and the traditionally Democratic Northeast, with its 99 votes. If all these states were captured, it would take only 26 more votes for victory, and there would certainly be 14 from Minnesota and Hawaii. The remaining 12 could be found among the 72 votes of Michigan, Ohio, Wisconsin, Oregon, and Washington.

Reagan took as his base the enormous expanse of the West, that great stretch of territory from Oklahoma to North Dakota and west to the Pacific Ocean that Ford had swept in 1976. This region would provide 131 electoral votes—almost halfway to the needed 270. Twenty-one votes should come from Iowa and Indiana, even though they had gone to Carter last time. Wisconsin had gone for Ford in 1976, and Ohio, Michigan, and Wisconsin were good prospects this time. If all these hopes were realized Reagan would need only 35 more electoral votes; and

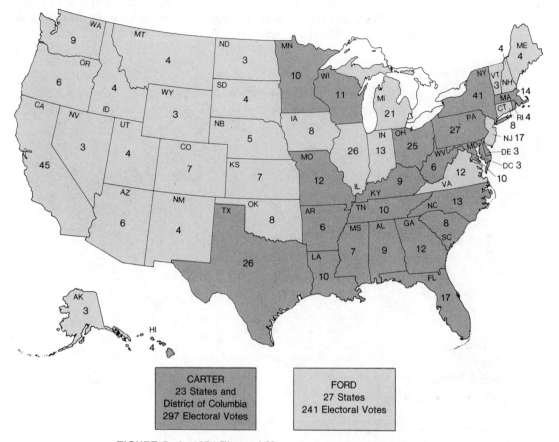

FIGURE 5–1. 1976 Electoral Vote

Texas' 26 votes, the Reagan strategists believed, were within their candidates' grasp. The rest of the South would not be conceded this time, and they saw a possible 71 votes in that region. Even the Northeast was not out of reach, for there were 48 votes in Pennsylvania, New Jersey, and New Hampshire that could be fought for. At the outset of their campaign, the Republicans could see a pool of about 350 electoral votes from which to draw the requisite 270.

This time Carter's strategy seemed the more difficult to accomplish, for he had won only narrowly in 1976, and his support in a number of states was much softer in 1980.

But even in their moments of deepest pessimism the Carter staff could not have foreseen the extent of the rout. As we see from figure 5-2 the Reagan planners' initial outside estimate of 350 electoral votes was exceeded by 139. Everything they had been confident about, plus everything they had included as possible but highly unlikely, came their way. Carter was left with 41 electoral votes from six states and the District of Columbia. Only one state from the South, his home base of Georgia, remained faithful to him.

John Anderson, the Independent, did not make as much difference as had been thought earlier, and his 7 percent was drawn from Republicans as well as Democrats. However, he inflicted more damage on Carter, who might have won at least New York and Massachusetts in the East were it not for Anderson.

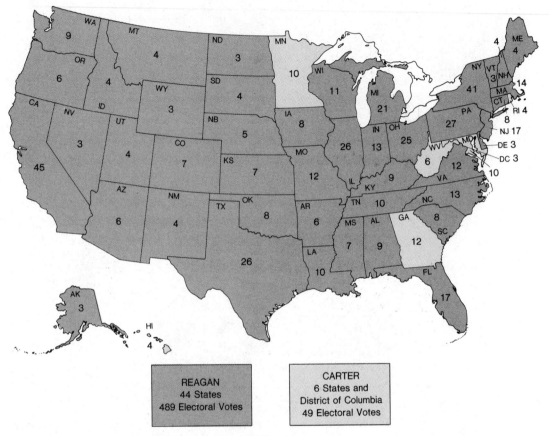

REAGAN	CARTER
44 States	6 States and
489 Electoral Votes	District of Columbia
	49 Electoral Votes

FIGURE 5-2. 1980 Electoral Vote

THE ELECTORAL COLLEGE: ABOLISH OR REFORM IT?

In most years there is a fairly wide disparity between the electoral college and popular votes. In 1972 McGovern got almost 40 percent of the popular vote, but was awarded only 17 electoral votes. In 1960 Kennedy beat Nixon by only 119,000 popular votes, but in the electoral college he prevailed by 303 to 209. And the 489–41 electoral vote in 1980 was hardly consistent with Reagan's 51–41 percent margin over Carter in the popular vote.

The reasons for these disparities between popular and electoral votes are of two kinds. First, the electoral college gives an advantage to the small states, since the Constitution assigns each state a minimum of three electoral college votes no matter how small its population. Far more significantly, another advantage goes to the most populous states, since tiny margins in the popular votes, by winning all of those states' large numbers of electoral votes, may more than offset large majorities for the opposition in smaller states, which have very few electoral votes. It is possible for a candidate to be elected after receiving fewer popular votes than his rival. This actually happened in 1824, 1867, and 1888, when Andrew Jackson, Samuel Tilden, and Grover Cleveland led in the popular balloting but were denied the presidency. Furthermore, Harry Truman's popular vote lead of over 2 million in 1948 could have gone for naught had there been a shift of thirty thousand votes in California, Illinois, and Ohio, states that awarded him large numbers of electoral votes.

A further problem with the electoral college is the procedure for breaking a deadlock should no candidate receive the required majority of 270 votes. In such a case the decision is thrown into the House of Representatives, where each state receives only one vote, and a majority of the states is required to elect a president, the House choosing from the three top electoral college presidential candidates.[6]

Only twice in our history, in 1800 and 1824, has the House been called on to settle the issue because no candidate won a majority of the electoral votes. However, the election campaign of 1968 was haunted by the possibility that it could happen again. The early opinion polls indicated a very strong showing by George Wallace, and it seemed possible that neither Nixon nor Humphrey would get a majority in the electoral college and that the Wallace delegations from the South would hold the balance of power in the House. As it happened, the Wallace vote declined by election day, and Nixon emerged with 301 electoral votes to Humphrey's 191 and Wallace's 46. Again, in 1980 John Anderson's strong showing in the early polls raised the possibility of the election's being thrown into the House. But Anderson's decline, and Reagan's upward surge, erased this possibility.

A third problem with the electoral college is that the requirement that an elector vote according to the instructions of the voters is not completely binding. Some states have passed laws to tie the electors' hands and there are very few examples of electors kicking over the traces. Nonetheless, in 1960 an Oklahoma Republican elector refused to vote the party line; in 1968 a North Carolina Republican bolted to George Wallace; and in 1972 a Virginia Republican decided that he had "reached the end of the line with the Nixon administration" and voted for the Libertarian party candidate.

This last problem is a minor one, but the first two—the possibility of a president's being elected even though he had fewer popular votes than another candidate, and the danger of the election's being thrown into the House of Representatives—have been the cause of great concern from time to time. The great Wallace scare of 1968, coming only two elections after the razor-thin margin of the 1960 Kennedy-Nixon race, brought to a head demands for a basic change in the system. In 1969 an overwhelming majority of the House of Representatives approved a constitutional amendment that would replace the electoral college with direct popular election of president and vice-president. The winner would be the candidate with the largest number of votes, so long as he secured no less than 40 percent of the total. If no candidate received 40 percent, there would be a runoff between the top two. A Harris survey had already revealed public approval for the abolition of the electoral college by 79 percent to 11. After some hesitation President Nixon came out in favor of the proposal.

However, the issue did not come to a vote in the Senate. Among the reasons was the fear that it would weaken the two-party system. Under direct elections a large number of candidates would probably enter the fray, hoping that there would be enough minor party votes to prevent anyone from getting the required 40 percent and thus providing all kinds of bargaining opportunities for the ensuing runoff. So the effort to eliminate the danger of minor party candidates such as George Wallace might actually lead to an increase in their number and influence. With the possible consequences uncertain and the immediate dangers removed, the pressure for abolition or reform of the electoral college dissipated.

CAMPAIGN TACTICS

Candidates for public office in America must get out and meet the people. They must be seen by as much of the public as possible, preferably with their wives and children; they must "press the flesh"—shake hands with thousands of voters; they must eat ethnic dishes, hold babies, and smile until their faces ache. Candidates for almost all offices must campaign this way, but most can concentrate on a single community, district, or state. Only the presidential and vice-presidential candidates have to try to make contact with the entire nation.

In the past the campaign train was the most effective means of doing this. In 1948 Harry Truman took his case to the people in a "whistle-stop" transcontinental train trip making speeches from the rear platform in large and small communities across the country. Now the jet plane, met at airports by a motorcade, has vastly increased the number of places a candidate can get to during a campaign.

Yet even with the jet there is a limit to the personal appearances a presidential or vice-presidential candidate can make between Labor Day, the traditional kickoff for the campaigns, and the first Tuesday after the first Monday in November, election day. In 1960 Richard Nixon made the mistake of promising to visit all fifty states during his campaign. The effort exhausted him, hurt his performance, and possibly cost him the election. So the focus has shifted away from showing the candidates to the people in the flesh to projecting them over the media. The radio was an essential campaign tool in the 1930s and 1940s. But since the 1950s television has predominated. Candidates still jet from city to city. Newspapers continue to play a vital role in their campaign coverage and advertisements. Radio, billboards, and direct mailings have their place. Volunteers in local campaign organizations are essential in making personal contacts and telephone calls, particularly during the last crucial effort to get voters to the polls on election day. But for the candidates, their staffs, and the public, television is the focal point of political campaigning today.

TELEVISION: THE FOCAL POINT OF CAMPAIGNING

Presidential candidates appear on television in various formats: news programs, spot announcements, longer commercials, telethons, and televised debates. An incumbent president has a considerable advantage over the challenger in the news format, since he and his administration can *make* news by proposing new programs or announcing dramatic developments in international affairs. Thus whatever slim hopes George McGovern might have cherished in the closing stages of the 1972 campaign were wiped out by Henry Kissinger's televised news conference just before the election declaring (prematurely) that "peace is at hand" in Vietnam.

Commercial spots were first used extensively in a presidential campaign in 1952. The Rosser Reeves advertising agency made a series of twenty-second television commercials. A typical spot had an announcer saying: "Mr. Eisenhower, what about the high cost of living?" The reply: "My wife, Mamie, worries about the same thing. I tell her it's our job to change that on November 4." "To think," said Eisenhower as they were putting on his makeup for one of these commercials, "an old soldier should come to this."

Adlai Stevenson, too, found this style of campaigning intensely distasteful. In his 1956 acceptance speech he told the Democratic party: "This idea that you can merchandise candidates for high office like breakfast cereal—that you can gather votes like box tops—is, I think, the ultimate indignity to the democratic process." Yet, in 1956, the Democratic National Committee prepared a publicity manual for candidates for office in which they offered advice on how to present issues on television. The central admonition was "Make it short and simple." Spot announcements, said the manual, should be in the form of a "simple slogan or message that is memorable and lends itself to repetition." All subsequent presidential campaigns, as well as a great many campaigns at the state level, have made heavy use of brief commercials as a means of conveying a candidate's position on the issues.

Toward the end of a campaign it is customary to supplement the commercials with longer presentations, for which candidates buy periods of half an hour on each of the networks. A typical show will consist of a documentary-style account of the candidate's life, shots of the candidate with his family, interviews with people from different backgrounds explaining why they will vote for the candidate, and some comments from the candidate on what he will bring to the presidency.

Finally, there are televised debates, which have become commonplace in races for the Senate and for the governorship in some states. The first set of televised debates for the presidency took place between Kennedy and Nixon in 1960. Kennedy's effectiveness in these encounters was almost certainly a major factor in his victory. Although televised debates took place between Robert Kennedy and Eugene McCarthy during the 1968 primaries, there were no further general election debates between presidential candidates until 1976, when Ford and Carter confronted each other on television three times. Polls and pundits generally gave a slight edge to Ford in the first debate and to Carter in the third debate. But the second in the series proved to be the most important, for there Ford made a major blunder. "There is no Soviet domination of Eastern Europe," he declared, and stubbornly refused to retract the statement for days afterwards, until at last he bowed to the storm of protest from people of East European extraction.[7]

The televised debates in 1980 were still more important in affecting the outcome. During the New Hampshire primary race Reagan destroyed George Bush's chances by graciously agreeing to allow several other Republican candidates to gate-crash what was to have been a one-on-one debate between Bush and Reagan, while Bush, on camera, obstinately argued that the others be kept out.[8]

Then in the fall campaign, after Carter had rejected a three-way debate including John Anderson, Reagan did well in a debate with Anderson alone. When at last a Carter-Reagan debate was arranged, Reagan seized the opportunity to challenge Carter's charges that his policies were outside the mainstream. The polls suggested that the debate might have contributed significantly to the size of Reagan's victory.

SELLING THE IMAGE: THE PERSONAL FACTOR

When we looked at political parties in the last chapter and at the election strategies of presidential candidates in this chapter, we emphasized party and issues as the basis for the voters' decisions on election day. But voters are also extremely interested in the personal characteristics of the candidates. Campaign managers are acutely aware of this fact, and they work assiduously to build up in the public mind a favorable image of their candidates and an unfavorable view of their opponents. The effort to produce favorable perceptions of a candidate was overwhelmingly successful in the case of Eisenhower. When he said, "I will go to Korea," he did not explain what he would do when he got there. But people trusted him to do what was necessary. They had faith in the man, in the image of authority, benevolence, and integrity that he radiated.

A principal purpose of the 1960 Kennedy campaign was to convey the picture of a man of great attractiveness, vitality, and drive. Television news coverage of his campaign helped accomplish this goal. But the Great Debates were especially important. The issue content of the debates was rather thin, but Kennedy projected a sense of excitement, whereas Nixon, part of the existing administration, was on the defensive. The contrast of styles and appearance was particularly apparent in the first debate, for Nixon was at a severe disadvantage through fatigue and a poor makeup job. (It is interesting to note that, for the majority of listeners on radio, Nixon won the debate, whereas the opposite verdict came from those people who watched on television.)

Again in 1968, a prime concern of organizers of the campaigns of both presidential candidates was to counteract unfavorable aspects of their candidates' images. Each candidate had his assets: Humphrey—open, outgoing, energetic, enthusiastic, knowledgeable; Nixon—competent, controlled, well-informed, experienced. Nonetheless, certain aspects of each candidate's personality made him vulnerable, and a considerable part of each campaign was devoted to warding off the efforts of the other side to exploit the areas of vulnerability.

Humphrey's advisers were hampered by his tendency to be overly talkative and impulsive. Nixon's problem was stated by Roger Ailes, a television executive producer who organized a series of live question-and-answer telethons for the candidate: "Let's face it, a lot of people think Nixon is dull. Think he is a bore . . . a funny-looking guy, . . . " a man who conveyed the impression that he had never had any other interest all his life but to work to become president. "That's why these shows are important. To make them forget all that."[9]

By 1972 the campaign managers' difficulty in formulating a suitable image for Nixon had vanished, for he was the incumbent president. Now he could be portrayed as the candidate of experience and proven competence— a man above the fray, attending to great affairs of state, building peace in the world—while his opponent indulged in partisan politics. And McGovern made it easy for them to draw the contrast, for his campaign was dogged from the outset by a series of blunders that conveyed to the voters the impression of indecision and incompetence.[10] Even with respect to trustworthiness, Nixon, whose career had been surrounded with an aura of slipperiness (captured in the nickname "Tricky Dick"), came out ahead of McGovern, a Methodist preacher, the representative of the "new politics" that was to replace the old, discredited, sleazy brand of politics.

Assessment of personal qualities was an important factor again in 1976. The Carter forces seized on the media's diligent reporting over a two-year period of Ford's proneness to slips of the tongue and to stumbling or banging his head when getting out of a jet or limousine. They presented Carter in contrast as a man of high intelligence, qualified by experience and intellect as a problem solver. The Carter campaign also placed great emphasis on Carter's claim to be a man of complete integrity, the outsider coming in to clean up the mess in Washington. Ford, they implied was a decent man, but his granting of a complete pardon to Nixon showed that he was part of the system that had to be cleaned up.

Yet Carter did not win the battle of personalities. His repeated claims to absolute integrity, his campaign promise that he would "never tell a lie, or make a misleading statement, or avoid a controversial issue," his message of love as against the divisiveness of the past, and his much discussed religious beliefs made him an irresistible target to the press. In the post-Watergate era nothing could be more pleasing to journalists than the opportunity to puncture an air of sanctimoniousness.[11]

In a preelection Gallup poll we find the responses of the voters to the candidates shown in table 5-2.

TABLE 5–2

Statements about candidates	Percentage for	
	Carter	Ford
He is a man I'm not sure I understand.	51	26
He may be promising more than he can deliver.	59	17
He leaves me with questions about the way he really feels about things.	54	30
He has a sound, stable personality.	30	52

Source: *Newsweek*, 1 November 1976, pp. 20–21.

By large margins, Ford, the alleged bumbler, also came out ahead of Carter, the problem solver, on questions relating to "good judgment in times of crisis" and "good leadership qualities and experience." Evidently, the sharp decline in Carter's margin in the polls from the beginning of the campaign to the end was at least partly attributable to the uneasiness that many people felt about his personal qualities.

As they went into the final 1980 campaign, however, the Carter strategists believed that they had the advantage in the contest of personal qualities. Of all the leading Republican candidates Reagan had been their preferred opponent. They believed that he could be portrayed as a conservative extremist. They planned to emphasize the widespread impression that Reagan was an intellectual lightweight, with inadequate understanding of the great issues of the time. And although it would be unwise to talk overtly about his age, it would not be unreasonable to question his energy level and to doubt whether his 9-to-5 working day as governor of California would be sufficient for the punishing demands of the presidency.

In the early days of the campaign, Reagan made a series of verbal blunders that seemed to play into Carter's hands.[12] Two-thirds of the public, according to an opinion poll, thought that Reagan "said too many things carelessly, without considering the consequences." And in response to the question: "Do you think that Jimmy Carter/Ronald Reagan understands the complicated problems a president has to deal with?" the answers were as shown in table 5-3.

TABLE 5–3 Understanding of problems facing the president, 1980 (percent)

	Carter		Reagan	
	Yes	No	Yes	No
Mid-September	68	27	48	44
Late September	68	29	62[a]	32
Mid-October	70	26	51	42

[a] The improvement in the public's assessment of Reagan's understanding of the issues followed Reagan's debate with Anderson. By mid-October (before the debate with Carter) Reagan's knowledgeability score had fallen again.
Source: CBS News/*New York Times* polls, *The Election of 1980*, p. 105.

Unfortunately for Carter, Reagan and his campaign settled down and there were few other gaffes. Reagan undertook a strenuous schedule, thereby undercutting the concerns about his age and energy. His years of media experience had made him a superb television communicator, which stood him in good stead in the culminating debate with Carter on television. Carter made no errors in the debate, clearly demonstrating his mastery of all the topics raised, and went on the attack in an effort to expose Reagan's conservatism and his lack of national experience and familiarity with the issues. But Reagan stood his ground, showed that he could remain relaxed under fire, appeared to know his material,[13] and reassured the public that he would not embark on rash foreign adventures or destroy Social Security. ("There you go again," he would protest amiably each time Carter cited one of Reagan's former, strongly conservative positions.)

THE POLLS: THEIR ACCURACY AND INFLUENCE

The use of political polls has become an important element in campaign tactics. When Gallup, Harris, or Roper—the three major polling organizations—indicates that a candidate is ahead, he will use that poll to argue that an irresistible momentum has been established in his favor. If the polls show him falling behind, he will cite the fact that Harry Truman won in 1948 against the evidence of all the polls, or he will hire a pollster to conduct his own private survey, from which data will be culled selectively to prove that the other polls are wrong.

Two major questions are constantly raised about the polls. First, how accurate are they? Second, how much influence do they have?

Since their unhappy experience in 1948, the major polling agencies have done fairly well with respect to their final preelection analyses (which they insist are not predictions, but merely readings of public attitudes on the day the poll was taken). In 1972 they were quite close to the mark.[14] In 1976 Gallup and Harris saw the outcome as a virtual tie; only the Roper Poll came close to Carter's 51–48 margin over Ford. Still, all were within the 3 percent margin of error in both directions that they admit their sampling method contains. However, their accuracy slipped in 1980, particularly in relation to the Reagan vote, as we see in table 5-4.

TABLE 5–4 Opinion polls and the 1980 presidential election result (percent)

	Carter	Reagan	Anderson	Others, Undecided
Gallup Poll[a]	44	47	8	1
ABC/Harris Survey	40	45	10	5
CBS/*New York Times*	43	44	8	5
Actual vote	41	51	7	1

[a] Undecideds allocated to candidates.

Final election results provide us with a clear test of the final pre–election day findings of the pollsters. However, we have no conclusive way of checking the results of surveys taken at other times. Consider, for example, figure 5-3, showing

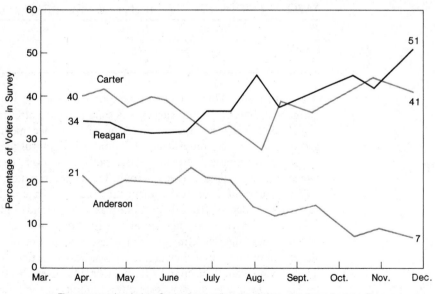

a. The surveys taken before September 1 reflect the choices of registered voters. The surveys taken after September 1 reflect the choices of likely voters. Late October results based on partial survey taken before the October 28 debate.

FIGURE 5–3. The 1980 Presidential Race in Gallup Polls[a]
Source: CBS News/*New York Times* polls, *The Election of 1980.*

voter preferences between the main presidential candidates from March through November 1980.

The fluctuations recorded by Gallup seem to square in a general way with the readings of election trends generally made by sophisticated political observers. Carter was ahead of Reagan during the spring because he was benefiting as President from the Iranian hostage and Afghanistan crises. By the summer Carter's popularity had slumped, and Reagan forged ahead, helped by the media coverage of his nomination at the Republican convention. Then Carter gained ground as attention shifted to the Democratic convention, and Reagan's errors as his campaign opened pulled Carter level with Reagan. Reagan did better for a while, but slipped as election day approached and uncertainties about Reagan persisted. Finally, the Reagan-Carter debates, and the intensifying dissatisfaction with Carter over the Iranian hostages, led to an apparent shift in the last few days to Reagan. So the poll findings seem to be consistent with a commonsense reading of the campaign year. Yet, with opinion in the country so volatile, and with so many people harboring strong reservations about all the candidates, we cannot be sure of the accuracy of any of the polls except the final, official vote count.

A further reason for doubts about the polls is that major discrepancies appear among them from time to time. In late 1975 Gallup and Harris conducted "trial heats"—Ford or Reagan against Humphrey—and came up with sharply differing results (table 5-5).

TABLE 5–5 "Trial heats" of potential presidential candidates, 1975 (percent)

Poll	Ford	Humphrey	Reagan	Humphrey
Gallup	51	39	50	42
Harris	41	52	43	50

It is true that Harris took his sampling just before Ford went on a visit to China and that the Gallup survey was conducted just after he got back. However, the Ford trip did not receive the kind of sustained media attention that had accompanied the Nixon visit in 1972, and it is doubtful that it could account for the sharp differences between the two polls. Moreover, Reagan did nothing between the two polls that could account for the discrepancy.

Whatever doubts may exist about the accuracy of the polls (and what we have said does not detract from their validity as at least crude indices of general trends in opinion), there is no question about the attention their findings command. It is sometimes suggested, in fact, that these readings of opinion actually become shapers of opinion, that they create a "bandwagon" effect that carries along with it voters who want to be on the winning side. However, this theory is not supported by Harry Truman's victory despite the findings of the polls, or by the extent to which both Hubert Humphrey and Gerald Ford closed the large gaps indicated by all the polls at the start of the 1968 and 1976 campaigns. Perhaps, then, the opposite of the "bandwagon" effect is true—that the polls create a groundswell of sympathy for the underdog. But in 1964 and 1972 the Johnson and Nixon landslides were indicated by the polls from start to finish. The polls are most influential on the conduct of the campaign itself. The candidates and their staffs are buoyed by a favorable poll and, in contrast, may come close to giving up if a poll shows them far behind. The polls are also critical factors in fund raising. Big contributors like to invest in a winner and do not want to throw their money away on a candidate who is doing poorly in the polls.[15]

MONEY AND ELECTIONS

Another crucial element in election campaigns is money. Once media advertising and polling became indispensable in campaigns, elections became enormously expensive. In a major city a thirty-second commercial in prime time costs well over $5,000. A spot commercial on a network can cost $20,000 and up, and a half hour of network time for a political program may run $100,000 or more, plus the production costs and the charge of the advertising agency that places the material. A one-page advertisement in a magazine like *Time* or *Newsweek* may range from $20,000 to $40,000. The cost of a statewide newsletter can now exceed $150,000.

So a race for the United States Senate for even a medium-sized state can hardly be conducted for less than several hundred thousand dollars. In fact, in 1970 Congressman Richard Ottinger of New York spent about $4.5 million in a losing effort to be elected senator. In 1976 eight candidates spent $1 million or more in running for the Senate, including John Heinz III, who spent $3 million of his family's catsup money and won, and Senator James Buckley of New York, who spent $2 million in his bid for reelection and lost. In 1978 eleven Senate campaigns cost $1 million or more: Senator John Tower won after spending over $3.5 million (against his opponent's $2 million), and the champion spender, Senator Jesse Helms, raised $6.7 million for his winning race.

Gubernatorial campaigns can be as expensive. Bill Clements spent $6 million to become the first Republican governor of Texas. Jerry Brown spent $4 million against his opponent's $3 million to be reelected governor of California. James Thompson spent $2.5 million to be reelected governor of Illinois against weak opposition.

As for the presidency, the cost of the campaigns is being brought under control by new campaign finance laws. Even so, outlays for primaries and the final election went up from about $100 million in 1968 to $160 million in 1976 to $250 million in 1980.

WHO CONTRIBUTES?

The cost of these large outlays has been covered from four main sources: organized interest groups, wealthy individuals, small contributors, and the federal government.

Organized interest groups.   Corporations have been forbidden since 1907, and labor unions since 1947, from making direct contributions to federal election campaigns. However, there were many ways of evading these restrictions.

Corporations can provide free services, such as office space, secretarial help, and public relations specialists, to campaigns, and they can buy tickets at fund-raising dinners and purchase advertising space in national convention books.

Labor unions similarly can provide free services and supply union officials and members to contribute to special funds like the AFL–CIO's committee on political education (COPE), which makes contributions to the campaigns of large numbers of candidates sympathetic to labor's causes or to key members of congressional committees dealing with matters of concern to the unions.

In 1974, the campaign finance reform law opened to corporations the possibility of forming *Political Action Committees* (PACs). They seized the opportunity with enthusiasm, and by 1980 the number of business PACs had passed 1100. Taken together with the PACs formed by trade associations and medical groups like the American Medical Association, business contributions were double the amounts available from labor.

Wealthy individuals. The rich have made enormous contributions to campaigns, especially presidential campaigns. W. Clement Stone, a Chicago insurance man worth $400 million, contributed nearly $7 million to Republican presidential campaigns between 1968 and 1972 in gifts and loans, including $2.8 million to the Nixon campaign in 1968 and over $2 million for the Nixon reelection drive in 1972. On the Democratic side Stewart Mott, of the General Motors family, gave $210,000 to Eugene McCarthy in 1968 and pledged $350,000 to George McGovern during the 1972 primaries. McGovern's campaign also received $320,000 from Max Palevsky, a Los Angeles businessman who has subsidized a number of liberal candidates and causes.

Wealthy candidates have also drawn on their own resources to finance their campaigns. The Kennedy money helped build the political careers of John, Robert, and Edward Kennedy. Rockefeller money has been spent lavishly to help elect and reelect Nelson Rockefeller in New York, Winthrop Rockefeller in Arkansas, and Jay Rockefeller in West Virginia. We have already listed John Heinz III and Bill Clements among the millionaires whose money has helped them move into high elective office. Others include Pennsylvania's Milton Shapp, Ohio's Howard Metzenbaum and Illinois' Charles Percy.

The role played by individual contributions to federal campaigns was significantly reduced by the 1974 reform law. However, the limits on contributions do not apply to candidates contributing to their own campaigns or to state offices.

Small contributors. For some candidates the accumulation of large numbers of small contributions has always been more important than a few large donations. George Wallace in 1968 received 750,000 contributions for his third-party bid. In 1972 George McGovern's primary campaign included a massive computerized effort to attract small donations that produced almost $4 million. But the master of computerized mass mailing solicitation for campaigns is Richard Viguerie, whose success in raising many millions of dollars for conservative causes and for candidates like Jesse Helms has made him a power in conservative circles.

The federal government.   With the 1974 campaign reform law federal funding became available for presidential primaries and general elections. The details of this reform need to be examined against the background of the law and the reasons for its passage.

REFORMING CAMPAIGN FINANCE

Legislation to limit the influence of private money in elections goes back to 1925 with the Corrupt Practices Act, which placed ceilings on spending for elections to both houses of Congress. The 1939 Hatch Act included a limit of $3 million a year for any political committee and of $5,000 a year for individual contributions.

However, ways of evading these restrictions were quickly found. For instance, several committees could be created, each of which could spend up to $3 million a year. Thus, Clement Stone's contributions to the Nixon campaign in 1972 were made in the form of seven hundred $3,000 checks made payable to such dummy organizations as Americans United for a Moral Society, Americans United for a Lawful Society, Americans United for Political Moderation, Responsible Leaders for a Balanced Society, Responsible Leaders for a Stable Society, and Responsible Leaders for Reform in Society. (This system also served Stone's personal income tax purposes, for the tax code allowed big donors to make huge contributions without paying gift tax by splitting their donations into multiple gifts of no more than $3,000 each.)

This situation existed until 1971, when the increase in the size and number of large contributions and the escalating costs of campaigns finally led Congress to pass new legislation. First, in the Revenue Act of 1971 political contributors could claim a tax credit for half of any contribution up to $12.50 ($25 on a joint return) or take a deduction for up to $50 ($100 on a joint return). Another provision allowed each taxpayer to earmark $1 of his or her taxes for a fund to subsidize presidential campaigns.

Second, the Federal Elections Campaign Act of 1971 set spending limits and required committees spending or receiving more than $1,000 in any year on behalf of federal candidates to report the names and addresses of all persons contibuting more than $100.

The 1971 legislation might have satisfied the reform impetus for some time had it not been for the astonishing revelations brought out by the Watergate investigation. Key figures in the Committee for the Reelection of the President (CRP or CREEP), together with two White House aides, had engaged in dubious financial transactions with respect to both fundraising and spending.

On the revenue side, the committee launched a drive to raise funds before April 7, 1972, thereby beating the disclosure requirements of the 1972 act. In the four weeks before the deadline over $11 million came in, some of it contributed illegally by business corporations after intense pressure from officials of CRP. Much of it was in cash which, with monies left over from the 1968 presidential primaries, was placed in safe deposit boxes in several cities and used subsequently for several purposes beyond the presidential campaign itself. There were the outlays for the men and materials involved in the Watergate burglaries and buggings. Then for the indicted men—for their legal defense, for support of their families, and, allegedly, for their silence—came parcels and briefcases of cash, surreptitiously passed along from messenger to messenger with code words and aliases reminiscent of a grade B spy movie.

Large sums were also provided to Donald Segretti and others for a campaign of "dirty tricks"—political sabotage aimed at various Democratic presidential aspirants during 1972. And $400,000 was allegedly sent into Alabama in 1970 in an abortive effort to thwart George Wallace's bid for the governorship.

Nor were Republicans the only ones guilty of receiving illegal campaign contributions. In the 1972 California primary Hubert Humphrey's campaign had received $300,000 from a Texas real estate speculator who was under investigation by several government agencies. And some of the businesses that illegally donated corporate funds to CRP had also donated to the Johnson campaign in 1964 and to the campaigns of a number of Democratic members of Congress.

The climate was receptive for an intensive lobbying effort by Common Cause and other groups determined to free campaigns from their dependence on large contributions, and a reform bill was passed despite the opposition of President Nixon and the Democratic leadership of the House.

THE FEDERAL ELECTION CAMPAIGN ACT OF 1974

The act contained four main provisions. First, it imposed limits on candidates' spending for presidential and congressional primary and general elections. Second, it set limits to the amounts that could be contributed to campaigns by individuals, by candidates and their families, and by organizations. Third, it authorized the funding of presidential campaigns from public funds (specifically the dollar that people could check off on their income tax form) for primaries, conventions, and general elections. Finally, it created a Federal Election Commission to supervise and monitor the other provisions of the act.

In January 1975 an appeal against the law's constitutionality was filed by a group ranging across the political spectrum from Senator James Buckley, the conservative periodical *Human Events,* Democratic Senator Eugene McCarthy of Minnesota, and the New York Civil Liberties Union. On January 30, 1976, as the candidates were already embarking on their quest for convention delegates, the Supreme Court handed down a complicated decision striking down some of the law's provisions and upholding others.

Two key sections were found unconstitutional: the spending limits and the structure of the Federal Election Commission.[16]

Striking down the structure of the Federal Election Commission caused some confusion and an interruption of federal funding in the primaries. However, Congress reconstituted the commission in a constitutionally acceptable form on May 21, 1976, and the disbursement of funds was resumed.[17]

The results of the 1974 act, the Supreme Court decision, and the 1976 amendments are given in table 5-6.

TABLE 5–6 Final provisions of the Federal Election Campaign Acts

Contribution limits per candidate			
	Primaries	General election	Total for all candidates
Individuals	$1,000	$1,000	$25,000 (plus $5,000 a year to a political action committee and $20,000 to a national committee of a party)
Organizations	$5,000	$5,000	No limit to the number of candidates
			No more than $100 in cash

Spending limits per candidate (presidential campaigns only)

Primaries	General election
$10 million	$20 million
	plus 20% for fund-raising costs
	plus 2¢ per voter by national party organization
	plus unlimited amounts in "independent expenditures" by individuals or committees who swear that the expenditures were not made in collusion with the candidate

Public financing per candidate (presidential campaigns only)

Primaries	General election
Matching funds from $100,000 up to $5 million for contributions of $250 or less; to qualify for minimum $100,000, candidate must obtain $5,000 from at least 20 states	$20 million for major party candidates; proportional amount for minor party candidates who received 5% or more of total vote in previous presidential election (or available retroactively if 5% obtained in current election)

Other provisions

Allows $2 million public financing per major party national convention.

Requires candidates to establish a single central campaign committee (no more multiple committees).

Permits business corporations and labor unions to maintain separate political funds. But company committees are generally limited to stockholders and executive and administrative personnel and families, and unions to union members and families.

Limits presidential candidates' personal or family contributions to own campaigns to $50,000 if public financing accepted.

Sets limits to speaking and writing honoraria that members of Congress and federal employees may receive.

Puts the administration and monitoring of the statute in the hands of a six-member Federal Election Commission empowered to administer regulations, seek court injunctions, and refer criminal cases to the Justice Department.

Provides for fines and jail sentences for substantial and deliberate violations of the law.

The 1976 and 1980 presidential campaigns were thus carried out under new financing arrangements. Spending on primaries and the final election campaigns was much less than would otherwise have been the case, especially in the fall 1980 election campaigns. Carter, Ford, and Reagan all spent close to the legal limit of about $25 million as compared with the 1972 totals of $61 million for Nixon and $30 million for McGovern when costs were considerably lower.

However, the 1976 and 1980 figures do not take account of some substantial expenditures allowed under two clauses of the 1974 act that did not receive much public attention at the time they were passed. The first allowed "independent expenditures" on behalf of a candidate as long as his campaign committee had nothing to do with it. Conservative groups formed such independent committees on behalf of Reagan in 1980. Their fund-raising ability fell short of their grandiose plans, but they were able to collect and spend almost $6 million on behalf of their candidate.[18] Of much more significance, as we have already noted, was the section allowing corporations to form Political Action Committees. In the 1978 federal campaigns PACs spent $35 million, as compared with less than $11 million contributed by the Democratic and Republican parties, and the figure for 1980 approached $55 to $60 million.

THREE PERSPECTIVES ON ELECTIONS

Here we concentrate on liberal, conservative, and centrist perspectives. Radicals enter campaigns, but their basic attitude on this subject has already been stated in the previous chapter: elections in America are mostly meaningless rituals, conducted by rival wings of a dominant elite, and thus failing to offer real alternatives to the people. Of course, radical left and right differ on the nature of the dominant elite. And on campaign finance, the radical left believes that the reforms backed by the liberals are a fruitless effort to limit the power of money in America, while the radical right rejects any limitation on the freedom of patriots to give their money to save the country from subversion. However, the more politically significant debate over our election processes is conducted by our other three perspectives.

THE LIBERALS: WE NEED
STILL MORE ELECTION REFORMS

Liberals make three basic criticisms of the electoral system in America. It does not help the people understand the issues or help them make choices on the basis of the issues. Second, it does not adequately express the clear will of the majority. Third, it is heavily influenced by private contributions of money.

Liberals contend that the issues are obscured and distorted in election campaigns. It is obvious that twenty-second television commercials cannot possibly present the issues properly. The whole emphasis of the modern election process is on packaging personalities. And since packaging is a highly intricate task, the conduct of campaigns is no longer in the hands of candidates and parties but instead is managed by media specialists and technicians. The mentality of these people was revealed in the statement of Roger Ailes, the producer of the Nixon telethons in 1968: "This is the beginning of a whole new concept. This is it. This is the way they'll be elected forevermore. The next guys will have to be performers."[19] So the medium is the message, and the ultimate expression of that reality was the election of Ronald Reagan, whose career as a movie and television actor made him a master of form rather than substance, of superficial rhetoric rather than depth of understanding.

Even presidential debates are not devices for clarifying the issues, but carefully rehearsed efforts to present the candidate's personality, presence of mind, and debating skills. We look for winners, and the winner is the person who comes across most attractively and avoids making mistakes. Thus Ford was said to have won the first of his debates with Carter because Carter seemed nervous at the beginning. And Ford lost the second debate because, in the heat of confrontation, he made a statement on Eastern Europe and the Soviet Union that obviously did not convey his real beliefs.

Moreover, the determined effort of candidates as they approach election day to avoid saying anything controversial produces a middle-of-the-road blurring of the issues. So, despite the majority's growing interest in the issues and readiness to be educated about them, our elections serve only to distract attention from the issues or to present them in distorted form.

The failure to clarify the issues makes it difficult to read the results of an election as a clear expression of the majority will, for the majority have not been asked to decide anything important. And in another respect, the majority will is not properly articulated. As we saw in chapter 3, almost half of the voting-age population does not go to the polls even in presidential elections. We speak of majority rule as an essential condition of democracy, yet our leaders are chosen only by minorities. Consequently, liberals strongly favor the reforms noted in chapter 3 to encourage more people to vote, such as simpler registration procedures and rigorous enforcement of the Voting Rights Act of 1965.

However, when we look at the mechanics of elections, we find the liberals, normally the champions of majorities and participation, caught in some apparent self-contradictions. First, primaries are efforts to involve the electorate at large in choosing nominees for election. It should follow that liberals would press for a change to national primaries, so that the voice of the majority can be expressed in the nomination process. In fact, most of them are unenthusiastic about this prospect.

The reason is that liberals are also advocates of stronger parties, and primaries, especially national primaries, tend to deprive parties of one of their most important roles: selecting candidates for public office.

Then again, the electoral college would seem, from a liberal's point of view, to be an absurd vestige of an eighteenth-century effort to place an impediment in the way of direct majority rule. Yet liberals have not pressed very hard for its abolition, for its existence pushes candidates into strategies that overemphasize the big industrial states, where liberals find their greatest strength.

With respect to money in elections, however, liberals have provided a strong impetus for reform. In their arguments that led to the passage of the 1971 and 1974 campaign finance acts, they declared that allowing wealthy individuals to buy personal influence in Washington through huge donations was a gross denial of the democratic spirit. They insisted that the big companies that, either illegally out of corporate funds or legally from the pockets of their executives, contributed heavily to campaigns were not doing it from pure altruism but because they wanted something in return: government contracts, tax advantages, or the prevention of legislation unfavorable to their businesses. The candidates who received those donations had to feel beholden to their contributors, and this fact more than any other led to the corruption of the political process.

On the whole the liberals were pleased with the 1974 reform act. Certainly there has been no repetition of the 1972 $2 million donation by Clement Stone.

However, liberals would like to modify or abolish two clauses in the law that they believe give a strong advantage to conservative and business groups. First, they see the provision allowing unrestricted spending on behalf of a candidate by "independent" committees as a flagrant breach of the principle of the law. They are skeptical about the possibility of enforcing the requirements that there be no collusion between the outside committee and the candidate's campaign organization. Second, liberals are gravely concerned with the approval given by the law to the establishment of corporate PACs. A principal aim of the liberals in pressing for the 1974 act was to reduce the influence of business in elections. Now that same act gave business a much greater freedom to intervene in elections than it had before.

In addition to this tightening of the law, liberals would like to see the concept of public financing extended to congressional campaigns. Its omission in 1974 was no simple oversight. The law was written by the incumbents, the people who hold the congressional seats. Incumbents generally have little difficulty raising funds, so they were not anxious to have the government take care of the fund-raising problems of their opponents. As the liberals see it, the only way to give challengers a chance and to free members of Congress of their servitude to the big contributors is to provide financing for congressional campaigns.

THE CONSERVATIVES: IMPROVE THE CAMPAIGNS, BUT DON'T TINKER WITH THE MACHINERY

Like the liberals, conservatives generally deplore the tone and style of contemporary election campaigns. They admire the high seriousness of the debates in which the men who founded the Republic engaged, and they believe that the vulgarity and superficiality of campaigns today are symptomatic of the general debasement of the quality of our national life. This debasement has resulted from our becoming a mass society in which politicians appeal to the lowest common denominator in a frantic effort to engage the attention of the least qualified members of the electorate. The media dominate the electoral process, and the liberal establishment, which controls the media, distracts the people with trivia and irrelevances rather than presenting them with the clear alternatives that would help them reject the establishment's ideas.

With respect to the machinery of elections, conservatives are disturbed by the trend toward placing all the decisions in the hands of the masses. They dislike proposals, for example, that would

©Engelhardt in *The St. Louis Post-Dispatch*/Reprinted by permission
"Now here's the cornerstone we want to replace."

abolish the electoral college. Although they do not ask for a return to the original intent of the Framers—that the college's electors make their own independent decisions on the choice of a president—they are not disposed to favor the complete abandonment of an institution that has been with us for so long. To do away with the electoral college, says the conservative analyst M. Stanton Evans, "would clearly diminish the authority of the states in the federal balance . . . and transform the presidency even more decisively into a 'national' plebiscitary executive."[20] The idea of the president as the product of a national "plebiscite," or the direct expression of the will of the mass electorate, is antithetical to the entire spirit of the Constitution, according to the conservatives. Conservatives are not opposed to making the system fairer than the present method of giving all the electoral votes of a state to the candidate who gets slightly more votes than any of his rivals. The reform they suggest is a "district" plan, whereby the electoral college and the role of the states would be preserved, but the electors would be chosen within congressional districts rather than statewide. This system would preserve the conservatives' principle of preferring local constituencies to the national, mass public.

Conservatives take issue with liberals over money in elections. They oppose the limits on contributions and spending and the idea of public financing. They argue that interfering with the right of individuals to give as much money as they want to a candidate is a clear denial of the freedom of expression guaranteed by the First Amendment. Although they were pleased with the Supreme Court's striking down of the spending limits in the 1974 act, they do not understand how

ART WOOD-COURTESY FARM BUREAU NEWS

the Court could then find that, while it is unconstitutional to limit expenditures, there is no constitutional barrier to controlling contributions.

Public financing of campaigns is another dreadful idea, say the conservatives. They do not see why the taxpayer should foot the bill for the monstrously wasteful folly that goes into political campaigns. Conservatives are concerned with the conflicts of interest and outright corruption that have resulted from the dependence of candidates on private contributions. Conservative spokespersons expressed outrage at the financial manipulations of the CRP. But their solution is not to tinker with the machinery or tamper with our constitutional rights. Instead we should attack the root cause of the problem: the growing entanglement of business in government. When businessmen allow themselves to become dependent on government contracts, seek special tax breaks, or submit to government regulations, it is difficult for them to avoid pressures from elected officials to contribute to campaign chests. So the most effective means of cleaning up politics is to get government out of business, for businessmen will then have no need and no inducement to make political contributions.

THE CENTRISTS: THE PEOPLE ARE NOT FOOLED

On the whole, the centrists argue, elections in America have served well enough to enable the people to make significant choices among candidates. They recognize that the mass media, especially television, have changed the style of elections and that there is a great deal of irrelevant nonsense in our campaigns today. But they demur from the complaints of the various critics in several aspects.

First, they doubt that all the defects of the process can be blamed on the media. Oversimplification and distortion of the issues have been present in all campaigns in recorded history. So has the emphasis on images and personalities. People with attractive, salable personalities have always been sought after as candidates. The difference is

simply that today the media require a special technique for projecting personality.

Moreover, the fact that the public has become very much concerned with the personal qualities of candidates is not an indication of the triviality of our political process. If we learned anything from the Johnson and Nixon presidencies it is that we had better look very closely at the character of our leaders as well as at their professed policies. And in the final analysis the people have been able to see through the advertising agencies' and media's images to the realities of character underneath. In the prolonged ordeal that constitutes a presidential campaign, a candidate is seen so many times, in so many contexts, that the majority of people, even those who are not particularly interested in the campaign, should be able to form fairly effective judgments about what kind of a person he actually is. Thus the impression of great vigor that John Kennedy conveyed in the 1960 campaign was not simply the consequence of successful mass media packaging. Kennedy had a genuine vitality that proved to be of great importance in his conduct of the presidency. Conversely, despite all the efforts of the image makers, television has pitilessly revealed the shortcomings of the men who have offered themselves for the presidency.

This statement is not contradicted by the fact that Richard Nixon was given an enormous majority in 1972. The people were not expressing strong approval of Nixon the man. In fact, his opinion poll ratings on various personal qualities were not very high. McGovern had behaved so ineptly that he was rated lower than Nixon.

Nor is it true that the emphasis on personal qualities and character has come at the expense of concern with issues. As we saw in chapters 3 and 4, the majority show considerable awareness of the issues. This awareness is applied to elections and results in choices based very largely on perceived differences between the candidates on the issues. Thus, in 1972, there was little to support the claim that media executive Roger Ailes had made in 1968: "The next guys will have to be performers." Neither Nixon nor McGovern was a charismatic personality or the embodiment of telegenic charm. Nixon won partly because McGovern's competence and trustworthiness were in question, but also because of the issues. On Vietnam, the economy, and other issues that the majority can understand clearly enough, despite all the campaign mumbo jumbo, Nixon was strongly preferred over McGovern.[21] In 1976 the issues were powerful factors in the minds of the electorate, for with respect to most personal traits the majority very much preferred Ford over Carter.

As for 1980, while Reagan's media skills undoubtedly contributed to his victory, the outcome resulted less from considerations of personality than from the electorate's trend toward conservatism and their view that Carter had performed poorly in the presidency.

On the machinery of elections the centrists are concerned about the multiplication of primaries and the declining role of the national conventions. They note that the claim for the primaries that they speak for the people as against the party politicians is weakened by the fact that voting turnout in primaries is typically less than half that of the final election, and that those who do vote tend to be more ideologically committed than the electorate as a whole.[22] Thus centrists are sympathetic toward proposals for rationalizing the primary schedule, increasing the proportion of experienced party leaders at the national conventions, and restoring the role of the conventions as deliberative and decision-making institutions. On the other hand, they question the argument of some critics that our election processes are not a true test of the qualities needed by a president. The election ordeal tests the candidates' stamina, organizational skills, diplomatic finesse, coolness under fire, and ability to attract the support of various segments of the public. Every one of these qualities is vital to effective performance in the White House.

With respect to money in elections centrists have serious reservations about the 1974 reforms.

First, they suggest that too much is made of the burden of campaign expenditures. In 1968 critics complained that $300 million was spent on elections. Yet in that same year Proctor and Gamble spent $270 million on advertising.

Centrists doubt that money is the dominant consideration in elections. For all his wealth, Nelson Rockefeller could not win the Republican nomination for the presidency; and, as the appointed vice-president, he could not even avoid the humiliation of being dropped from the Republican ticket in 1976 in favor of Robert Dole. In 1980 Republican John Connally was the only presidential candidate to reject public financing in the primaries. From private sources he raised and spent nearly $12 million—and gained one delegate. And although Democratic presidential candidates have usually been outspent by their rivals, Democrats have spent more years in the White House than Republicans since 1932.

Of course, it is helpful for a candidate to have plenty of money at the outset. But once a candidate can inspire enthusiasm, and especially if he seems to have a reasonable chance of success, the money will come. Moreover, to the extent that campaign contributions are made as financial investments, a skillful politician knows how to handle matters so that he takes the money but still goes his own way. In any case, wealthy people tend to donate to campaigns not to make more money but rather to have access to the prestige and the social opportunities that come from hobnobbing with presidents and other high officials.

Centrists recognize that the financial abuses connected with Watergate are intolerable. However, the most important reform of campaign financing, the requirement that sources of funds be fully disclosed, was accomplished by the 1971 legislation. The secret funds used in Watergate would not have been available had the 1971 act been in operation earlier. As it was, the CRP applied tremendous pressure on contributors to get their money in before the deadline for disclosure of sources went into effect. After disclosure, the only additional reform that was called for by the Watergate mess was to prevent large amounts of cash from coming into campaigns.

But centrists were highly dubious about the other elements that made up the 1974 law. They worried in particular about two things. First, there was the difficulty of challenging incumbents. Incumbents are overwhelmingly reelected to Congress. Of all members of Congress who run for reelection, 90 to 95 percent are successful. This success results from their newsletter mailing privileges, from the name recognition that their office brings, and from the fact that they have staffs on the public payroll who become campaigners for their reelection. It takes organization and media exposure to overcome such advantages, and it requires a great deal of money. The liberals are correct in stating that incumbents usually find it easier to raise money than do challengers. But the fact remains that some challengers can attract enough money to give the incumbents serious competition. Now their opportunity to do so is seriously impeded by the limitations on contributions imposed by the 1974 act. Fortunately, the Supreme Court struck down the limits on spending in congressional campaigns. However, although challengers can now spend as much as they raise, it is much more difficult than it used to be to raise money, and PACs give most of their money to incumbents.

The second major problem with the 1974 act, in the centrists' view, is that public financing of presidential campaigns and the consequent holding down of spending sharply reduce the opportunity of the candidates to get their messages across to the public. In 1976 and 1980 with the help of the free air time made available for the debates, the candidates were able to get a reasonable amount of exposure on television. But there are other aspects to a campaign than television, and in the last two elections much less money was available than in the past for local campaign organizations, for bumper stickers and campaign buttons, and for all those elements that lend color to a campaign and provide ways for volunteers to be actively engaged. Moreover, both camps were inhibited by having to constantly watch their expenditures to make sure that they did not exceed their permitted limits and make themselves vulnerable to prosecution.

Centrists oppose the liberals' proposal to extend public financing to congressional races. What is barely manageable in presidential elections would not be so if applied to hundreds of congressional elections. Policing so many elections would be an enormous task. And the difficulties in the way of unseating incumbents would become even greater than they are now, for public funding would never provide enough money to overcome the incumbents' natural advantages or to enable the rival candidates to do an adequate job of presenting the issues to the electorate. In the quest for an impossible degree of purity in politics we could cripple the electoral process and seriously detract from the people's opportunity to make effective choices.

CONCLUSION

In this chapter we have been discussing perhaps the most involved and complicated electoral system the world has ever seen. Somehow the procedures work, and vast numbers of public offices are filled on schedule. Yet the anomalies and complexities are so numerous that we are constantly considering proposals to reform the system.

Some of these proposals, like the abolition of the electoral college, are strongly supported in public opinion polls, debated periodically, and then shelved. In other cases we make changes, only to find that the changes have complicated the situation even more. Thus the increase in the number of primaries leaves candidates and public more harried than ever. If campaign finance reform has cleared up parts of the problem, it is difficult to understand the rational principles behind providing public funds for presidential but not congressional campaigns, and for limiting contributions but not expenditures (except in presidential campaigns).

People have been raising one question about presidential elections with increasing insistence and anxiety. For at least four elections in a row there has been a noticeable lack of enthusiasm about either of the major parties' nominees. Nixon, Humphrey, McGovern, Ford, Carter, Reagan—as candidates none has been admired by the majority. And a high proportion of the people voting for the victor in each case have expressed strong reservations about the personal qualities of the man they have made president. Why is it, people ask, that from all the extraordinary talent so abundantly available in America we cannot produce candidates who win not only the votes of the electorate but also their trust and esteem? From a population of less than 4 million in the 1780s America produced such marvelous leaders, but from more than 230 million people today we can find nobody who even remotely compares with those remarkable men.

It is important to set these harsh questions in context. For one thing, as historian Henry Steele Commager reminds us, two hundred years ago the top talent in America gravitated toward politics, for little else in those days required leadership on a large scale. Today many areas attract people of high caliber: business (which pays much more than politics at the top levels), science, law, medicine, and so on. Moreover, we have become so suspicious of politicians that many people of integrity and ability will not subject themselves to the abuse heaped on everyone who enters politics. In fact, our standards have become so high that we find fault with almost everything that political leaders say and do. So part of the problem may be that, in making unreasonable comparisons with the Founding Fathers and in establishing absurdly high standards, we cannot possibly find candidates who will measure up to our expectations.

Even if we have set up unreasonable expectations, few would maintain that our leaders have consistently been the best qualified among us. A substantial part of the reason may be our procedures for nominating and electing presidents, which effectively rule out some people who would be extraordinarily well qualified to be president. We have looked at the argument that there is no necessary contradiction between the qualities needed to *win* the presidency and the qualities needed to *be* a president, but that argument is clearly debatable. We may be in a better position to examine that issue when we have reviewed more fully the nature of the presidency, in chapter 7.

NOTES AND REFERENCES

1. Theodore H. White, *The Making of the President, 1960* (New York: Atheneum, 1961), p. 166.
2. Carter was helped by the fact that in 1980 all the Democratic primaries elected delegates by proportional representation, the system that allocates delegates according to the proportion of votes won by each candidate. Even though Kennedy won some big states in late primaries he had no chance of overtaking Carter, for Carter was always able to win a share of each state's delegates, thereby preventing any serious erosion of his big lead.

The Democrats had been moving toward proportional representation since 1972 but modified the principle in preparation for 1984 by allowing states to award an entire congressional district slate of delegates to a candidate winning only a plurality in the district. The Republicans, too, have shifted toward proportional representation, but in 1980 they left some states, including California, to operate under the old winner-take-all system.

3. Mark Sullivan, *Our Times: The United States 1900–1925,* vol. 6, *The Twenties* (New York: Scribner's, 1935), p. 37.

4. Tennessee Senator Estes Kefauver beat John Kennedy.

5. Ford let it be known that he would be interested if Reagan agreed to assign to him some crucial responsibilities never before delegated to a vice-president.

6. If the House is deadlocked, the Senate may proceed to elect a vice-president, who then becomes acting president until the House can agree on a president.

7. Evidently Ford was trying to argue that the spirit of independence among the peoples of Eastern Europe could never be crushed by the Soviet Union.

8. Reagan prevailed, and the others joined the debate.

9. Joe McGinniss, *The Selling of the President, 1968* (New York: Trident Press, 1969), p. 103.

10. The press uncovered the fact that McGovern's running mate, Senator Thomas Eagleton, had, some years earlier, received electric shock treatment for attacks of depression. At first McGovern supported him "1,000 percent," then wavered, then got Eagleton to withdraw even while assuring the press he was still behind Eagleton.

11. In an effort to dispel the impression that he was making a bid for sainthood, Carter gave an interview, published in *Playboy* magazine, on sex and morality, in which he explained that he did not believe in condemning sinners too easily. "Christ said, 'I tell you that anyone who looks on a woman with lust has in his heart already committed adultery.' I've looked on a lot of women with lust. I've committed adultery in my heart many times. . . . God forgives me for it. . . . But that doesn't mean that I condemn someone who not only looks on a woman with lust but who leaves his wife and shacks up with somebody out of wedlock" (*Playboy*, November 1976, p. 86). The article was released to television and the press in late September 1976.

12. Reagan expressed doubts about the theory of evolution, and he was forced to apologize for observing that Carter had opened his campaign in the birthplace of the Ku Klux Klan.

13. He had been thoroughly briefed in a grueling series of cross-examinations in which Carter's role was played by Representative David Stockman, who became Reagan's Director of the Office of Management and Budget.

14. The final vote was Nixon 61 percent, McGovern 38 percent. Gallup called it 59–36, Harris 59–35.

15. An additional issue on opinion polls is the practice of television networks declaring a winner in an election *before the polls have closed* on the basis of samplings of early voters as they leave the polling booth. This practice is especially a problem in a presidential election when (as was the case in 1980) networks declare the winner based on sampling on the East Coast, while the West Coast, with its time differential of three hours, still has several hours of voting time left. Apparently a considerable number of people on the West Coast decided not to bother to vote in consequence. This decision could not have affected the presidential outcome, but some Democratic candidates for Congress and other posts who lost by narrow margins contended they might have won but for the networks' declaration of Reagan's victory (compounded by a very early concession by Carter).

16. The commission was found to be in violation of the separation of powers, for some of its members were appointed by Congress, and the Court said that the legislative branch cannot make appointments to an executive body. However, the Court left intact the limits on contributions by individuals and organizations, public financing of campaigns,

and spending limits wherever a candidate accepts public funds for his or her campaign (which meant that the spending limits imposed by the 1974 law on congressional campaigns were invalidated, for the law did not include public financing for congressional races).

17. The Supreme Court had given the commission a grace period until March 22, but Congress could not agree on a new formula by then, so there was a hiatus of two months, which was very damaging to some of the candidates in the primaries. In its revised form the commission's members were all appointed by the president subject to Senate confirmation.

18. See *Common Cause Newsletter,* February 1981, p. 11.

19. *The Selling of the President, 1968*, p. 103.

20. M. Stanton Evans, *Clear and Present Dangers: A Conservative View of America's Government* (New York: Harcourt Brace Jovanovich, 1975), p. 67.

21. See Arthur H. Miller, Warren E. Miller, Alden S. Raine, and Thad A. Brown, "A Majority Party in Disarray: Policy Polarization in the 1972 Election," *The American Political Science Review* 70, no. 3 (September 1976): 753–778.

22. If true representation of the will of the party's rank and file were the object, then Reagan, for all his primary victories, might not have been nominated in 1980. A poll in March 1980 showed Ford leading Reagan as the choice of Republican voters by a margin of 52 percent to 27 percent.

chapter six

INTEREST GROUPS AND THE PUBLIC INTEREST

Thus far we have talked about public opinion, political parties, and elections—the various means by which government is connected with the will of the people. But we have noted that it is deceptive to describe the people as simply a great number of totally separate individuals. People congregate into groups, and we are all, in various ways, group members. At various stages in our lives, we all belong to the smallest group units, face-to-face primary groups: families, friendships, and work teams. We also fall into categories of sex, age, race, ethnic background, education, and so on that give us different kinds of group identification.

THE RANGE OF INTERESTS

Beyond these basic group linkages, America has an abundance of organizations—groups created to achieve specific ends. Although membership in organizations can sometimes be gained by inheritance, it normally requires an act of joining, and America is a nation of joiners. Three-quarters of the adult population are members of one or more organized groups. From almost any idea or interest, an organization springs forth, and in time that organization may spin off other organizations.

The principal concerns around which groups in America are organized are economic, social and political, and governmental.

ECONOMIC INTERESTS

Business.   A multiplicity of organizations speaks for business. At the national level the most prominent have been the Chamber of Commerce of the United States, with over eighty thousand members, and the National Association of Manufacturers (NAM), made up of thirteen thousand companies. Every field of economic activity encompasses many kinds of business, each brought together in trade associations. For example, in the field of housing there are national associations of realtors, builders, mortgage lenders, bankers, lumber manufacturers and dealers, building product suppliers, and apartment owners.

At the level of formulating policy, business leaders speak through such organizations as the Business Roundtable, consisting of presidents of 180 major corporations, and the Committee for Economic Development, which publishes studies of major issues in trade and economic policy.

Competition is a cardinal principle of the private business system. However, the extent of competition varies considerably from industry to industry, and in some fields there has been domination by one firm (monopoly) or a small number (oligopoly). Early in this century the Sherman and Clayton Antitrust Acts were passed to deal with this problem, and the Antitrust Division of the Department of Justice is charged with enforcing these laws.

Labor.   In 1935 the Wagner Labor Relations Act gave workers in most industries involved in interstate commerce the right to organize and bargain collectively, and since then labor union membership has grown from 3½ million in the mid-1930s to over 22 million today. Of these members, about 15 million are organized in the American Federation of Labor–Congress of Industrial Organizations (AFL–CIO), a federation of two former rivals. Independent of the AFL–CIO are the Teamsters Union, the United Mineworkers, and the United Electrical Workers.[1]

In recent years the growth of union membership has not kept pace with the increase in the work force. Unionists represented about 35 percent of the total number of employees in 1945, but by 1982 the proportion had fallen to about 24 percent. One reason for this decrease is that, with increased automation, the industries in which unions have been strongest, such as automobiles, steel, and mining, have needed fewer workers, whereas the labor force has been expanding in the service, computer, and other industries that have been difficult to unionize. Moreover, there has been a shift away from blue-collar and production line workers to white-collar, technical, and professional staffs. Only partially offsetting these unfavorable trends is the increasing unionization among teachers and government workers.

Then, too, the mandate given the unions by the Wagner Act of 1935 has been somewhat limited by laws passed since the 1940s. The Taft-Hartley Act of 1947 restricted their position in a number of ways, most significantly in outlawing the closed shop (a contract permitting the hiring only of union members) and allowing the union shop (which compels newly employed workers to join the union within a given period) only under certain conditions. Most obnoxious to the unions has been Section 14(b) of the act, which allowed states to outlaw the union shop and which was seized on by several states, especially in the South, to pass "right-to-work" laws. Subsequently the Landrum-Griffin Act of 1959 imposed restrictions on the internal workings of unions as a result of revelations of corruption and dictatorial rule in some of them.

Agriculture.   Agriculture is represented by a number of diverse organizations. Medium-sized to large enterprises have joined together in the American Farm Bureau Federation and the National Grange, as well as the American National Cattlemen's Association and other specialized groups. Speaking for small farmers and for farm workers are the National Farmers Organization, the National Farmers Union, and Cesar Chavez's United Farm Workers Union.

The current trends in agriculture are toward fewer people working and living on the land and toward larger farms. In 1925 there were about 6.5 million farms in America. By 1980 the figure was down to 2.3 million. Of those farms that remain, a fairly small number of big farming enterprises produce a high proportion of all agricultural output.

Since the Great Depression of the 1930s, which wiped out many small farms, agriculture has tended to look to the federal government for help. The government has been responsive, providing billions of dollars a year in subsidies to provide stable prices for the farmer and sometimes even paying farmers not to plant certain crops. However, federal aid to agriculture has been declining in recent years and constituted no more than about 6 percent of net farm income in 1980.

The Professions.   Each of the professions—doctors, lawyers, teachers, scientists, engineers, architects, and so on—has its national, state, and local organizations. Much of the work of these groups is concerned with the advancement of knowledge and improvement of practice in their respective professions. But they can also be viewed as economic interest groups. Some of the positions taken by the American Medical Association reflect the fact that most doctors' practices are organized, in effect, as small businesses. And the National Education Association, representing 1.8 million teachers, is not easy to distinguish from a labor union.

The Consumer.   Consumers constitute the broadest of all economic interests and are represented by an increasing number of organizations. There is a long tradition of consumer cooperative societies whose purpose is to sell food and other goods to members on a nonprofit basis. And since the 1960s the consumer perspective has had a potent spokesman in Ralph Nader, a lawyer who began with a solitary crusade on automobile safety and then institutionalized his activities through Public Citizen, Inc., and a number of centers specializing in the study of corporations, law firms, tax reform, auto safety, and Congress. These activities are financed by direct-mail campaigns, foundation grants, and Nader's lecture fees.

SOCIAL AND POLITICAL INTERESTS

Shared economic interests are by no means the only factors that bring people together in groups. Some organizations address the common problems of a particular demographic group, such as the elderly, women, blacks, Hispanics, Polish-, Italian-, or Irish-Americans. Others, like veterans' organizations, are built around a shared experience, an enthusiasm for a sport, a hobby, or an art, or a sense of being a victimized minority, like gays or overweight people. Fraternal and other social associations exist largely to help individuals make personal and business contacts. And the largest membership groups of all are the churches, with which over 40 percent of the population is affiliated, and which are themselves the focus of networks of organizations.

Although all these groups at one time or another are affected by politics and may become involved in some kind of political activity, the larger part of their time and energies is not directed toward politics. On the other hand, there has been a proliferation of organizations in recent years whose primary activity is in the political arena. These political interest groups are of two kinds.

The first kind is concerned with a *single interest,* or a small cluster of closely related interests. Thus organizations exist to fight for or against gun control, abortion, the Equal Rights Amendment, and the banning of pornographic books and movies.

The second kind of organization expresses a *broadly based ideology,* like the Moral Majority, the American Conservative Union, the Americans for Democratic Action, and the Campaign for Economic Democracy. Typically they take stands on a whole range of public issues. We consider these ideological organizations interest groups rather than political parties because, although they may propose, endorse, work for, and contribute financially to political candidates, they do not actually select candidates or officially run their election campaigns.

One step removed from these ideological organizations are such citizen action groups as Common Cause, founded in 1970 to press for reforms in the political process, and the League of Women Voters.

GOVERNMENT

Government is not merely a set of institutional structures. It is also a large aggregation of people, some elected, some appointed to the several levels of government in America. And they, too, form themselves into organizations to represent their institutional and personal interests. So there are national and state associations of mayors, boards of supervisors, governors, state legislators, judges, and other local and state officials.

The federal government, too, has produced its share of voluntary associations that represent federal employees, and within Congress there exist caucuses and clubs of blacks and women, liberals and conservatives, established insiders and freshmen representatives.

Table 6-1 gives some indication of the extraordinary range of organizations in America and their distribution among various categories.

THE EXTENT OF PARTICIPATION

The figures cited in table 6-1 are often used to reinforce the popular impression of a "nation of joiners," and indeed there is more widespread membership in voluntary associations in America than in most other countries.

However, impressive though these statistics are, they do not contradict the assertion made in chapter 3 that in America only a minority of the population is actively involved in the social, civic, and political work of our communities. Three-quarters of the population are members of at least one organization. But in a high proportion of cases that one organization is a church or labor union, in which membership for many is essentially passive. The true joiners—those who belong to three or more organizations—represent a much smaller proportion of the population, and the real activists are still a smaller proportion.

TABLE 6–1 National, nonprofit organizations

	Number	Percent
Trade, business, and commercial	3,175	20.7
Health and medical	1,474	9.6
Cultural	1,437	9.4
Public affairs	1,264	8.2
Scientific, engineering, and technical	1,080	7.0
Social welfare	1,061	6.9
Educational	1,008	6.6
Hobby and avocational	956	6.2
Religious	813	5.3
Agricultural and commodity exchanges	696	4.5
Legal, governmental, public administration, and military	571	3.7
Athletic and sports	519	3.4
Fraternal, foreign interest, nationality, and ethnic	436	2.8
Greek and non-Greek letter societies	319	2.1
Labor unions, associations, and federations	239	1.6
Veteran, hereditary, and patriotic	206	1.3
Chambers of Commerce	108	0.7
	15,362	100.0

Source: Denise S. Akey, ed., *Encyclopedia of Associations,* 16th ed. (Detroit: Gale Research Company, 1981).

POLITICAL PRESSURE

No public policy emerges from American government without some involvement by at least a few of the groups we have mentioned. Their representatives ("lobbyists") operate at all levels of government: national, state, and local. They follow the workings of legislatures and maintain close contact with executive agencies, from low-level bureaucrats to cabinet members and even the president. National interest groups retain lawyers in Washington to argue their cases in court. They try to influence the programs of political parties, and to inform, educate, and persuade the general public. And they educate their own members, for many people look to their organizations for guidance on what to think about politics and how to vote on candidates and issues.

TYPES OF POLITICAL PRESSURE

In their efforts to exert influence, organizations and their lobbyists employ three kinds of resources: *knowledge, money,* and *constituency* power.

Knowledge.   In making policy, government agencies and legislatures must draw on expertise wherever it exists. Interest groups possess a vast store of detailed, practical experience and are a prime source of expertise. Inevitably government bodies turn to these organizations for information on the content of proposed programs and for predictions on how those programs will affect the memberships represented by the organizations.

Money.   Money is one of the wellsprings of politics, and organizations are a principal source of political money. In earlier periods of American history bribery of public officials was commonplace. Even now, as we shall see in our discussion of Congress in chapter 8, periodic scandals reveal that bribes are still offered and accepted.

However, crude, illegal methods like bribery are much less common today than they used to be. Organizations have found a number of other ways to give funds to politicians. They provide lucrative speaking engagements and appointments to paid directorships of savings and loan associations. They retain law firms whose partners are members of legislatures, and, as we saw in chapter 5, they contribute funds to political campaigns—increasingly through the Political Action Committees that multiplied after the passage of the campaign reform legislation of 1974. (See table 6-2.)

TABLE 6–2 Growth of Political Action Committees

Year	Labor	Corporate	Miscellaneous	Total
1974	201	89	318	608
1976	224	433	489	1,146
1978	281	821	836	1,938
1980	276	1,127	984	2,387

Source: *Common Cause,* October 1980, p.13, based on reports of the Federal Election Commission.

Constituency power.   The power inherent in a particular group's membership must be reckoned with by government decision makers. A lobbyist's ability to bring the national leaders of his organization to Washington can exert a potent influence on Congress and on executive agencies. Moreover, most national organizations are made up of local units. Because members of Congress are generally very sensitive to opinion in their own districts, Washington lobbyists work hard at marshaling pressure from the folks back home. Whenever a decision point is approached in the legislative process, an organization's Washington staff can send the word around the country, and members of Congress in the areas affected may find themselves inundated with letters, telegrams, and phone calls from constituents.

There is a good deal of debate about the usefulness of this technique. Most legislators say that they refuse to be stampeded by a sudden barrage of messages that they know have been orchestrated by a lobbyist, because they are not genuine expressions of constituents' concerns but artificially engineered pressure campaigns.

Still, members of Congress have to be impressed by the ability of a national organization to produce an avalanche of comments from its members. Typically, a member of Congress will use the comments if they endorse his or her own position. If they do not, he or she will sometimes send out urgent pleas for mail from sympathizers. A deluge of letters and wires from a particular interest group, supplemented by individual contacts from influential group members in the district, may sway an undecided legislator to make a decision in their favor.

LOBBYING REFORMS

From time to time public concern builds that private organizations are exercising too much influence on public policy and that this influence is exerted through secret deals hidden from public scrutiny. In response to this concern, legislation has been passed to set limits on the influence of "pressure groups" and lobbyists and to open their activities to full public view. The most notable law addressing this problem is the 1946 Federal Regulation of Lobbying Act, which requires paid lobbyists, who are usually individual staff members of public relations or law firms, to register and file quarterly reports on all receipts and expenditures for lobbying purposes.

However, the reported figures fall far short of telling the full story of spending by lobbyists, for the 1946 act is full of loopholes. Although the Supreme Court sustained the constitutionality of the act in the *Harriss* case in 1954, it was held to apply only to groups and individuals who solicited, received, or collected money for the "principal purpose" of influencing legislation through direct contacts with members of Congress. Groups that spent their funds to influence legislation without hiring a lobbyist, as many of them did, or groups that could claim that their principal purpose was not legislative, as most of them could, were able to avoid disclosing the extent of their lobbying outlays. Moreover, the costs of indirect pressures on Congress through such methods as mass mailings from constituents were not covered by the act.

From the mid-1970s Congress began to give consideration to further reforms that would require fuller public disclosure by any organization spending substantial amounts of money to influence legislation. The organization would be called on to provide the names and salaries of its lobbyists and to list gifts and direct business ties to any federal official it tried to lobby. Both House and Senate passed such bills in 1976 but failed to agree on the details; the House passed another bill in 1978, but nothing emerged from the Senate; and reform advocates have been unsuccessful since then.

FIVE PERSPECTIVES ON INTEREST GROUPS

THE LIBERALS: GROUPS VERSUS DEMOCRACY

The way in which organized groups influence the American political process offends the liberals' concept of democracy in several ways: the disproportionate influence of business groups, the pressure tactics they use, and their neglect of the public interest.

The Business Bias. To the liberals business groups comprise the most formidable source of private power. They do not suggest that business is all-powerful, or that it represents a unified power bloc, and they concede that each firm is concerned with its own survival and profits, which can lead to intense rivalries with other firms. Nevertheless, they see in the business sector common interests that increasingly override the factors that make for competition.

First, the growth of monopolies has stifled competition. The antitrust laws have failed to prevent mergers of individual companies into industrial and financial giants. Today almost 60 percent of all the manufacturing assets of the country are owned by two hundred corporations, and over half the total deposits of money are held by the ten largest commercial banks. Moreover, the largest stockholders in some of the biggest manufacturing corporations—Ford, General Electric, and Mobil, for example—are banks and other financial institutions. The growth of "conglomerate" empires, such as Litton, which are able to absorb many firms from totally different fields into a single fiscal framework, results in a still further concentration of industrial resources. Nor does the trend toward concentrated business power stop at our coastline. Firms such as IBM, ITT, Ford, General Foods, and Singer are, in fact, huge "multinational corporations" that own plants and whole companies abroad.

Whatever mild constraints on business concentration existed in the past, say the liberals, have been abandoned by the Reagan administration,

PAUL CONRAD, © 1975, LOS ANGELES TIMES. REPRINTED WITH PERMISSION.

"I pledge allegiance to the flag of the country that gives me the best deal. . . ."

which has condoned a great wave of new mergers between huge corporations. The driving force behind these mergers, in the liberals' view, is not the optimization of efficiency and productivity, but rather the quest for power, security, and tax advantages.

In the liberals' view, the impact on politics of this concentrated business power is enormous and far exceeds that of any other combination of forces in influencing public policy. Liberals recognize that many groups, such as Common Cause, the Nader organizations, and labor, oppose business power and occasionally win significant victories over business. Yet the power of each of them is very limited.

Certainly they do not see labor as a match for business in the political arena. The strike, which is often pointed to as evidence of labor's great power, is sometimes effective in industrial confrontations, but it does not bring any political advantage with it; if anything, the unfavorable public reaction to strikes harms labor politically.

Unlike business leaders, labor officials have not been appointed to any of the top positions in the executive branch of government. Even the Secretary of Labor—not one of the central figures in any administration—has usually come from outside the ranks of labor. Men and women with a background in organized labor constitute only about 1 percent of the membership of Congress. Moreover, the weakness of the unions politically is starkly revealed by the passage of the Taft-Hartley Act of 1947 and the unions' subsequent failure to repeal its Section 14(b).

Although labor has been a major factor in the passage of most liberal legislation since the 1930s, organizations that cannot protect themselves from the passage of laws directly hostile to their own interests can hardly be regarded as sources of towering political strength.

Liberals admire Nader's efforts to protect the consumer but believe they do not go far to counterbalance the power of business. The notion that in the private enterprise system the consumer has the ultimate power is an illusion, say the liberals. Corporations limit consumer choice by monopoly and various kinds of collusion, deceive the consumer by manipulative advertising and deceptive packaging, defraud through short weight, poor workmanship, and overpricing, and endanger health and safety by recklessly selling faulty and insufficiently tested goods. The consumer interest is too diffuse to be effectively organized against these practices. We are all consumers, and when a category includes everybody it is difficult to give it the kind of meaning that can be translated into action.

Pressure politics. Business, say the liberals, is superbly equipped to translate its superior power into political action.

Two-thirds of the groups listed on the Lobby Index, the register of those organizations that admit to maintaining a legislative representative in Washington, represent business. The list does not include corporations like American Telephone & Telegraph, which supports about a dozen governmental relations employees in Washington yet has not registered a single lobbyist with Congress because it contends that the 1946 Federal Regulation of Lobbying Act does not apply to its activities.

The numerical preponderance of business lobbyists was attested to by Colorado Senator Gary Hart: "I hate to get on the plane for Denver. For three hours, the lobbyists just line up in the aisle to get a word with me." And most of the lobbyists, he said, are special pleaders for business.[2]

Not only do business lobbyists have the numerical superiority, say the liberals, but they command far and away the lion's share of the resources needed to sway public policy. They have the largest and best-paid staffs for the purpose of presenting information to government agencies and congressional committees, and command of information is one of the keys to power. Furthermore, only business and financial corporations can afford to have their interests represented by the celebrated Washington law firms whose partners have been in and out of key positions in government and have ready access to the top decision makers.

Then liberals contend that business has far more of that vital political resource, money, than does any other group, as is clear from the role played by business in contributing to political campaigns, a role that is rapidly expanding with the growth of business PACs.

Further, business groups are best equipped to provide members of Congress with lucrative speaking engagements at their national conferences, retain the services of the legislators' law firms, or provide them with stipends for serving on their boards of directors.

Business is also particularly skillful at organizing constituency power and at arranging for messages to be sent to Washington in such a way that the concerns of a small segment of the population are made to seem like the interests of the mass of the people. The U.S. Chamber of Commerce is adept at orchestrating pressure from local units in every sizable community in the country.

So are many of the national trade associations that represent particular industries. For example, the organizations that make up the housing industry have been successful in activating their local organizations—real estate boards, home builders, and savings and loan associations—to deluge members of Congress with letters, telegrams, and telephone calls. These messages are carefully timed to coincide with crucial stages in the progress of housing legislation, and their targets are key members of the committees dealing with the legislation. In addition, the associations arrange for personal contacts with committee members by close friends and large campaign contributors. The result has been the passage of laws providing federal guarantees of the loans that are essential to the building, buying, and selling of homes, and cutbacks in programs like public housing designed to help the poor.

Nor do the liberals rest their case on the lobbying successes of small and medium-sized businesses like those in the housing industry. They are even more concerned with the pressures applied by the great business corporations. In that realm of politics, people at the top talk to people at the top. For example, in 1970 the Antitrust Division of the Justice Department challenged the proposal of International Telephone & Telegraph to expand its conglomerate empire by taking over the Hartford Insurance Company, Canteen Corporation, and Grinnell Corporation. The Antitrust Division refused to accept ITT's offer to drop some of its other holdings if it were allowed to keep Hartford.

ITT then launched an intense pressure campaign, in which the corporation's president, Harold Geneen, and some of his vice-presidents met with Vice-President Spiro Agnew and top members of the cabinet and White House staff. Geneen also arranged for a partner in the New York banking concern that had put the merger together to meet with the assistant attorney-general as-

signed to handle the case and to make a presentation to the Antitrust staff. He warned the staff that if ITT had to dispose of Hartford there would be serious consequences for the stock market and for the country's international balance of payments.[3]

Six months after the head of the Antitrust Division had rejected ITT's offer he changed his mind. He attached conditions: ITT must give up Canteen, part of Grinnell, the home-building company Levitt, and Avis, the car rental firm, and must make a commitment not to acquire any other large companies without special approval from the government. But ITT's pressure campaign had achieved its purpose: gaining access to Hartford's cash flow of $1 billion a year in insurance premiums.

Reasserting the public interest. The liberals' dissatisfaction with the group process is not limited to their charges of an imbalance favoring business interests. They also complain that when organized groups get into politics they work for their narrow, selfish interests against the public interest.

Certainly, they allege, this charge is true of business, which puts profits before public responsibility. But the way business operates in politics is characteristic of the methods of most interest groups. Each fights for its own special concerns. The American Medical Association forgets the doctors' Hippocratic oath of service to patients and lobbies furiously against programs designed to help those people who cannot afford the escalating costs of medical care. The National Rifle Association, despite public opinion polls showing clear majorities in favor of gun controls, uses every kind of pressure tactic to intimidate Congress and prevent legislation that would set even minor limits to the availability of handguns. The gun lobby, in fact, is typical of the kind of group that has multiplied in the last few years: the single-issue lobby, uninterested in legislators' total records over the years and judging them exclusively by how they stand on one question.

Of course, any group, no matter how small, must have the right to express its ideas and interests to decision makers in government. But this freedom should not be used by self-interested minorities to impose their will on the majority through concentrated pressures and behind-the-scene deals.

How can this abuse be prevented? The liberals offer a number of proposals.

First, they would tighten the lobbying laws to force full disclosure of lobbyists' activities. They would also extend the reform of campaign financing and set some bounds on the proliferation of business PACs made possible by the 1974 campaign reform act.

Then, liberals have proposed attacking the biggest concentrations of economic power by splitting massive corporations like Standard Oil into smaller firms; creating competition in fields like energy production by establishing publicly owned corporations; enforcing antimonopoly laws more effectively; encouraging government agencies that are supposed to regulate business to do their jobs properly; ending government's underwriting of industry through tax advantages, tariffs, and subsidies; and placing representatives of workers and consumers on the boards of corporations.

The liberals also propose to offset the power of business and other powerful groups by building the influence of organizations that speak for broader but inadequately represented constituencies, such as consumers, women, and the poor.

Finally, as their sovereign remedy, they argue for the rebuilding and strengthening of the political parties, for parties speak for conceptions of the public interest as a whole, as against the narrower concerns of interest groups.

THE RADICAL LEFT: CORPORATIONS VERSUS THE PEOPLE

Much of the liberal critique of business is echoed by the radical left. However, once again the radicals complain that the liberals' analysis is timid and does not go to the heart of the matter. For the left, corporate capitalism is the central source of power in America, which holds true whether we are talking about private power or governmental power, since the distinctions between the two kinds of power are meaningless. The two form a seamless web. Decisions made in the privacy of the corporate board rooms become public policy.

There are no important rival sources of power in the system. Organized labor is puny by comparison. In any case, with few exceptions labor is part of the business system. Many unions participate in the management of vast pension funds, a considerable portion of which has been invested in stocks and land development projects. Some of the most prominent labor leaders subscribe to the values of capitalism and make belligerent foreign policy statements.

Middle-class organizations such as Common Cause and the Nader groups are no match for the corporations. The poor and the blacks, lacking money and the other resources needed to be effective, are able to muster only weak pressures.

The liberals' proposals for reform fall far short of what is needed. The regulation of lobbying, the strengthening of the two-party system, and so on do not get at the roots of the problem. Antimonopoly laws have been a dismal failure; in fact, they are counterproductive, for they create the illusion that effective action is being taken to check the power of the corporations. Nothing will do short of replacing the principle of private ownership and operation of economic resources with the ethic of cooperation and community.

Nationalization or government ownership is a traditional prescription of the left for the transfer of economic resources to the community. But, particularly since the 1960s, some groups on the left have suggested that this solution merely replaces one kind of servitude with another. Workers may be treated as harshly, and consumers as contemptuously, by government-employed bureaucrats as by capitalists. What is needed is democracy extended from the electoral constituency to the workplace, which calls for workers' control of economic enterprises.

Outside the work sphere it is necessary, say the

left-wing radicals, to spur the mass of the people into active participation in organizations. Today most organizations in America are controlled by small groups of activists, and these groups are drawn predominately from the affluent business and professional classes. To challenge their power new organizations need to be created that will be run not by the present cliques of self-perpetuating elites, but by the rank-and-file membership.

THE CONSERVATIVES: THE INVISIBLE HAND

The liberal left attack on business is flatly rejected by conservatives. From their perspective business is not the dominant power in the economy.

The relative unimportance of business monopoly. It is true that monopoly exists and that it is undesirable. But its extent has been vastly exaggerated. As Milton Friedman puts it, "The most important fact about enterprise monopoly is its relative unimportance from the point of view of the economy as a whole."[4] There are millions of separate businesses in America. Hundreds of thousands of companies are born, and a somewhat smaller number die, each year. Almost a fifth of the working population is self-employed.

In almost any industry that one can mention there are giant corporations and tiny firms side by side. IBM is far and away the biggest company in the computer field. But new firms, generated by the imagination and energy of inventive individuals, bring out new products and successfully capture a corner of the computer market.

To the extent that monopoly does exist in America, its greatest single cause is government intervention. Government regulation of industries is often nothing more than using public authority to "support and enforce cartel and monopoly arrangements among private producers."[5] Tariffs, special tax breaks, and subsidies of various kinds all enable inefficient industries to survive and grow, thus diminishing the impact of competition.

The conservatives will admit that the blame for this lack of competition cannot all be placed on government. Too many business leaders have turned to the government to protect them rather than take the painful steps necessary to enable them to prosper under the spur of competition. Some of these leaders regard themselves as conservatives and contribute to the campaigns of conservative candidates. In truth, any businessperson who seeks artificial aids from government is forsaking the true principles of conservatism, which are based on private initiative, not government handouts.

REPRINTED BY PERMISSION OF TRIBUNE COMPANY SYNDICATE, INC.

"Why does he keep tailgating me?"

Labor—the real monopoly. The truest monopolies in America are the great labor unions. They apply every kind of pressure available to them, including the force of law, to compel workers to join them. They control the labor force not just in individual firms but in whole industries. In fact, some unions, such as the Teamsters, reach across industrial lines and dominate wide segments of the economy.

Liberals complain that big businesses sometimes act in restraint of trade. But there is no restraint of trade that can compare with a strike, which can paralyze whole sectors of the economy or bring entire cities to a standstill. Yet labor is not covered by the antitrust laws, which are directed only at business corporations.

Organized labor's economic power has not even done very much for the workers. "The gains that strong unions win for their members," says Milton Friedman, "are primarily at the expense of other workers."[6] They have reduced employment opportunities for unorganized workers by pushing wages up to the point at which employers turn to machines rather than people. Strikes demonstrate the power of the union leaders, but even where they are "successful," strikes may cost the workers more in lost earnings than they gain by the eventual settlements.

The dominance of government. The single most important source of economic power in America today, however, is government. It not only interferes massively with the natural flow of market forces through taxation, budget deficits, and a never-ending barrage of rules and regulations; it also directly employs a substantial section of the work force. From the conservatives' viewpoint, business economic power is now greatly outweighed by government economic power.

Pressure politics. As they look at the tactics used by groups to achieve their political purposes, conservatives insist that every one of the devices used by business is also used by groups hostile to business. And, as conservatives read the record, the opposition has been more effective than business. Labor is an extraordinarily potent lobbying force. It uses its political funds to contribute heavily to campaigns. Unions also provide the manpower needed to get out the vote for their candidates.

The AFL–CIO maintains a staff of full-time lobbyists in Washington who are skillful in the arts of backroom lobbying. They have close relationships with the key congressional committees and subcommittees that deal with legislation of concern to labor. Furthermore, the AFL–CIO is well equipped to provide Congress with specialized information. Its lobbying team is backed by research groups in economics, Social Security, education, and so on, capable of producing fact sheets and position papers almost at a moment's notice.

As for grass-roots pressures, no group is better situated than labor for letting the lawmakers in Washington hear from the folks back home. It is not at all difficult for the heads of union locals to get their members to deluge Congress with letters and telegrams. And when the national lobby wants to reach a senator, they often arrange for a visit from the head of the AFL–CIO from the senator's own state.

The legislative product of all this power is regarded with dismay by conservatives. The enormous expansion of federal social welfare spending, and the crippling burden it has imposed on the economy, could not have been brought about, say the conservatives, without the support given the bureaucracies, the president, and the Congress by labor.

Nor are conservatives impressed with the argument that labor's failure to repeal the "right-to-work laws" of Section 14(b) of the Taft-Hartley Act is proof of its political weakness. After all, that clause does no more than allow states to sanction a nonunion shop. Business groups would like to see a federal law permitting the nonunion shop, so that unions everywhere will be deprived of the power to force workers to join unions against their will. But, under pressure from the labor lobby, inclusive right-to-work bills have never been given a hearing by Congress.[7]

The *education* lobby includes groups at every level of education demanding more and more federal money. Various organizations speak for elementary and high school teachers, administrators, governing boards, parents, and other constituencies involved in higher education. *All* of them want federal money. And all of them work hand in glove with the federal government. Indeed, in 1980 the education lobby's pressure achieved the creation of its own cabinet department (although this was scheduled to be dismantled under the Reagan administration).

Along with the professional educators, social workers, and others whose salaries and power grow as federal programs expand, a great many *"do-gooders"*—self-appointed protectors of the public welfare—join the pressures for more government spending. These groups include the social action committees of churches, women's organizations such as the League of Women Voters and the American Association of University Women, and others claiming to speak for minority groups, senior citizens, consumers, and the protection of the environment.

Most of these groups are masters of the arts of pressure politics. Notably successful have been Common Cause and the Ralph Nader organizations. They have made a close study of the vulnerable points in the system. They organize mass mailing campaigns to create the illusion of widespread support for their programs, and they know how to use television and other mass communications media to inflame public opinion against business.

Finally, the most potent of all sources of lobbying are the several agencies of the federal government. Every cabinet-level department has a congressional relations office, usually with a dozen or so staff members, and many of the bureaus and offices within the departments maintain a liaison staff with Capitol Hill, as do the federal regulatory agencies. Altogether the federal government supports several hundred staff members who devote all or a considerable part of their time to working with their political chiefs in lobbying Congress.

The White House itself includes an office headed by a presidential assistant in charge of congressional relations. No lobbyist in Washington can reach the key people in Congress as quickly as the top members of the White House staff and, of course, the president. No other lobby can compare with the resources of the executive branch of government in providing the expertise needed by congressional committees or in stimulating pressure from the grass roots in favor of programs from which they benefit.

So, in contrast with the liberals' picture of a system that produces results overwhelmingly favorable to business, the conservatives' view is that pressures from labor, education, "do-gooders," and government represent a combined power more than sufficient to outweigh the influence of business.

Business and the public interest. Liberal organizations claim that, unlike business groups, they speak for the public interest. Conservatives disagree on two grounds.

First, the leaders of liberal organizations do not necessarily speak for anybody but themselves.

Opinion polls and election results reveal that rank-and-file union members often disagree with the platforms and candidate endorsements issued by labor bosses. The liberal church groups that claim to articulate the political concerns of tens of millions of church members actually consist of small, unrepresentative social action committees. Common Cause is made up of a few hundred thousand affluent people, hardly a cross section of America. Ralph Nader's staffs consist mostly of young people, students and recent graduates, who constitute an elite far different in their tastes and beliefs from the great majority of Americans.

Second, conservatives object to the claim of these groups that only what they stand for can be defined as the "public good." In calling his organizations "Public Interest Centers," Nader is making an arrogant assertion. These liberals are identifying the public interest exclusively with liberalism and the attack on business. In fact, business can make a much better claim to represent the public interest than all the groups that have tried to copyright the idea with such titles as Common Cause, Public Citizen, and so on.

Conservatives agree with liberals that, to a considerable extent, the public interest is the interest of the consumer. But as they see it, Nader and others are attacking the system at its strongest point—its treatment of the consumer.

Consumers do have justifiable complaints. But any comparison with how consumers are treated in most other countries in the world must produce an assessment of the American business system as a brilliant success story. It has poured out an incredible abundance and variety of goods of generally high quality. Nowhere are the interests of the people better served.

Hence the conservatives argue that the proposals of the liberals and the radical left are the very opposite of what is needed. We should move in the direction of getting government out of business. We should even avoid pious pleas to business to fulfill its "social responsibility." In a free economy "there is one and only one social responsibility of business—to use its resources and engage in activities designed to increase its profit so long as it stays within the rules of the game, which is to say, engages in open and free competition, without deception or fraud."[8]

Of course, the framework of law must be there. The honest businessperson, as well as the public at large, must be protected against crooked practices. But other restraints, imposed or self-imposed, are undesirable. The best thing we can all do is pursue our own interests rather than pretend to be looking out for the good of others. Selfish though this policy may seem, the result will be for the benefit of all, so long as we are operating in a genuinely competitive economy. The competitive economy has a built-in genius first described by the father of the discipline of economics, Adam Smith, who concluded that a competitive market, though apparently chaotic, in fact was governed by a kind of natural law. Without benefit of government control, it was as though "an invisible hand" produced the good of the society as a whole out of the competing interests of individuals.

To conservatives, in other words, the public interest is served not by accepting the presumptuous claims of self-anointed leaders, but through the full, though fair, pursuit of private gain and by the competition between private economic interests.

THE RADICAL RIGHT: GROUPS VERSUS AMERICA

With the radical right we come to a still harsher indictment of those aspects of the system of interest groups criticized by the conservatives. Government intervention in the economy is equated with socialism, which is akin to communism. The growth of government has been brought about by pressures by labor unions and by organizations claiming to speak for minority races, churches, and the public interest—all of them, wittingly or unwittingly, serving the cause of the left-wing conspiracy.

Certain organizations still win the praise of the radical right for trying to preserve whatever is left of the American system. A number of patriotic groups, such as the American Legion and the Moral Majority, are heard from in the halls of Congress. And some business groups, fortunately, persist in opposing the spread of the welfare state and the takeover of the economy by government.

Like all groups that attack pressure politics as subversive of the common good, radical right organizations also use lobbying tactics when it serves their purposes. They pressure Congress to abolish the income tax and to reduce and eventually do away with the national debt. And various right-wing groups, including the John Birch Society, participate in the anti–gun control movement.

In a field such as gun control, the radical right feels that it has contributed effectively to saving America from subversive proposals. In general, however, the right wing believes that the system of pressure politics is dominated by groups aiming at the destruction of the American system.

THE CENTRISTS: PLURALISM AND THE GROUP BALANCE

To the centrists the group process is a key element in their explanation and defense of the American system. They see the existence of a large number of private groups as an essential guarantee of a free and open society. By fighting for their respective causes, groups contribute a great diversity of ideas, values, and interests, thus ensuring the availability of choices on which our democratic system thrives. They reject the criticisms we have discussed from the other positions on the spectrum, making the following counterarguments.

The group balance. Critics left of center declare that business and conservative groups dominate. Right of center the diagnosis is that labor and liberal groups are the most potent pressures. This disagreement provides clear evidence to the centrists that there is a rough balance of power between the competing forces. In any case, most centrists find it useful to talk about specific issues rather than about the group system as a whole. On specific issues sometimes business groups win, sometimes the antibusiness forces prevail, and sometimes the contending parties have to settle for a compromise.

Compromise, in fact, is the most common outcome of disagreements. Centrists can point to the very cases that liberals and conservatives use to make their respective arguments. In the field of housing, for example, the liberals complain that policy is determined by pressure from realtors, builders, and mortgage lenders. Yet on issues like public housing these groups have had to face strong opposition from labor, church and civic organizations, public housing officials, and federal agencies. The result is that, although there is much less public housing than its proponents wanted, the private housing groups' preference for none at all has been rejected.

In the ITT case, the corporation kept Hartford only at the price of having to get rid of several major, profitable companies.[9]

Similarly, the controversy over the closed shop shows that the rival estimates of labor's political influence are both wrong. Labor has proved itself sufficiently powerful to prevent any damaging federal laws relating to union affairs since the 1959 Landrum-Griffin Act. On the other hand, repeated efforts to get Congress to repeal Section 14(b) of the Taft-Hartley Act have failed.

Another source of restraint on the power of any one group is internal disunity. Business is certainly no monolith. The gasoline price increases that made such huge profits for the oil companies almost brought the automobile industry to its knees. On the labor side there are major unions outside the AFL–CIO, and within the federation there are wide differences of interest and of political ideology. As for the "education lobby," public school organizations generally resist the request of the Catholic schools for federal aid, teachers and administrators do not always see eye to eye, and student organizations sometimes take positions distinct from all other education groups.

Pressure politics.   In the public mind, terms such as *lobbying* and *pressure politics* have assumed covert, even sinister overtones. Two points should be made to correct the most common misconceptions. First, there is very little that is mysterious about lobbying. Anyone who takes the trouble to follow what is going on can discover which groups are applying pressure on which side of an issue. Of course, the precise details of each stage of discussion are not necessarily known im-

mediately to the public. But group politics is largely a process of quiet bargaining between competing organizations and public officials. It is impossible to conduct delicate negotiations in the full glare of publicity. In any case, few secrets are kept for very long in Washington. There are too many suspicious (and publicity-seeking) opposition groups, members of Congress, and investigative journalists to allow much to remain off the record indefinitely.

Undoubtedly there are still abuses. Some tightening of the lobbying disclosure laws might be desirable. Yet there are limits to how far regulation can be pushed without interfering with the First Amendment guarantee of free speech and the right of the people "to petition the Government for a redress of grievances." Moreover, on this issue of regulating lobbying, the more extreme proposals put forward by Common Cause in the name of good government have isolated it from other liberal organizations. The American Civil Liberties Union and a number of environmentalist groups have complained that the proposed requirements for registration and disclosure of all attempts to influence Congress would cost them an enormous outlay of time and money in filling out forms and would scare away some potential contributors.

Second, the power of lobbyists is vastly exaggerated in the liberal ideology and the popular imagination. Members of Congress are influenced, no doubt, by some lobbyists. But they are also affected by the climate of opinion in their constituencies and in the country, by the president, their party, their staffs, and other members of Congress, and by their own judgments, beliefs, and consciences.[10]

Defining the public interest.   No single group can define the public interest for everyone. All groups claim to be acting for the common good. Drug companies defend the large gap between their production costs and their price lists as being necessary to supply the research funds from which new, life-saving drugs can be generated. The National Rifle Association claims to be concerned not only with the rights of sportsmen but also with the defense of individual liberties and the implementation of the constitutional right to bear arms. The automobile industry contends that its profits are necessary not only to its shareholders but also to the health of the nation's economy. Business groups in general rest their case not on their right to make money but rather on the merits of the free enterprise system, which guarantees not only our prosperity but also our essential liberties. Labor unions speak not merely of wages and fringe benefits but of the need to stimulate the economy and to protect human rights.

The only resolution of this dilemma is to define the public interest as the result of group pressures. "What may be called public policy," says Earl Latham, "is actually the equilibrium reached in the group struggle at any given moment. . . ."[11] The same definition can serve for the public interest, which emerges out of the process of negotiation and mutual accommodation between groups that is characteristic of democracy.

The centrists are not taking quite the same position as the conservatives. They do not contend that government should play only a minimal role. Government has a major contribution to make in determining the public interest. But government has to be seen not as a source of ultimate and impartial wisdom, above the petty clamor of group pressures, but rather as a large number of institutions that are themselves very much a part of the group struggle, striving to inject their ideas along with the private groups.

So the centrists defend the group process against its critics and argue that it provides a vital supplement to the constitutional checks and balances by establishing an informal balance between a great number of power centers. It ensures, in other words, a pluralistic arrangement of power.

Groups represent the people. The other perspectives overlook another great virtue of our system of interest groups. The system provides an important means of representing the people. Public officials are elected to represent people geographically, where they live. But people are not only residents. They are workers, businesspeople, farmers, consumers, art lovers, collectors, believers in causes, and so on. And the organized groups to which so many of them belong speak for them so that these other aspects of their lives can be properly considered when public policy is made.

No doubt the representation is not perfect. Organizations, as the left complains, are run by the few. But this arrangement is not peculiar to American culture. Sociologist Robert Michels, after studying European Socialist parties in the early part of this century, concluded that an "iron law of oligarchy" operated, placing power in the hands of small minorities. But, as we noted in earlier chapters, centrists do not think that decision making by active minorities is necessarily harmful. And to the extent that it may be undesirable, we live, after all, in an imperfect world.

In sum, the system that we have serves our purposes well; for, in contradiction to the allegations of the critics, no group or combination of groups dominates the rest, lobbying tactics are mostly legitimate and are used effectively by all groups, and the prevailing balance produces a reasonable definition of the public interest.

CONCLUSION

We have reviewed in this chapter the range of interest groups in America, the purposes they serve, and the methods they use to influence political decisions. We have also examined five rival interpretations of how well the interest group system is working and the extent to which it represents a balance between contending forces.

Throughout this discussion the question has recurred: What is the public interest? We cannot hope to resolve it completely here. It has been a perennial subject of debate among political and legal philosophers. Does the public interest emerge, as though by an "invisible hand," from everyone's pursuit of personal interest? Or is it simply the point at which the interests of competing groups intersect at a given moment? Or is there a public interest over and above the sum of private interests?

American political practice favors the centrist argument that the public interest is a constantly changing notion emerging out of the interplay of the group process. Most American politicians fit into the centrist category and are not attracted by large, abstract conceptions of their role. Moreover, they spend a large part of their energies responding to and negotiating between a great diversity of organized pressures.

Yet practical politics is not conducted entirely without reference to the idea of a public interest. Even the most constituency-minded member of Congress will at least occasionally respond to appeals to the broad national interest. The most intensely dedicated organization leaders will, from time to time, put their loyalty second to their concept of themselves as citizens of the nation.

Two aspects make up the popular notion of the public interest: numbers (the larger constituency against the smaller) and time (concern with the future as against present gratification). Gradually, topic by topic, consensus develops on what constitutes the public good. Indisputably dangerous goods and drugs should be kept off the market. Debate may continue over the birth control pill but not over thalidomide (a drug prescribed as a sedative for pregnant women, which resulted in many babies' being born with terrible deformations). Children should not be allowed to work in mines. Cornices should not extrude from new buildings in earthquake country. The public interest on these matters has been settled and incorporated into law, even though, in each case, some private interests were hurt.

Today the effort to incorporate more areas into the public interest extends beyond questions of public health and safety to issues affecting the quality of life, particularly the protection of the consumer and the physical environment. As we shall see in later chapters, the issues in those fields become immensely complicated. The formulation we have suggested here—large numbers against small, the future against the present—will not always offer a sufficient guide to legislators trying to make policies protecting the public interest. Moreover, the balance between the majority and the minority cannot be determined only in terms of numbers but must also allow for the intensity of people's feelings. It is not surprising, therefore, that scholars cannot agree on the meaning of the public interest,[12] and some have even recommended that a notion so vague had better be abandoned altogether.

Yet in the practice of politics it cannot be abandoned. So we shall come back to the dilemma of the public interest in later chapters to see how it is dealt with in various contexts.

NOTES AND REFERENCES

1. The United Auto Workers left the AFL–CIO in 1968 but rejoined in 1981.
2. *Newsweek*, 6 November 1978, p. 48.

3. At one point President Nixon ordered Richard Kleindienst, the assistant attorney-general, to drop the case, but withdrew the order when Kleindienst threatened to resign. An additional element, which caused a public furor when it leaked to the press, was a secret pledge by Geneen to put up $400,000 toward the cost of holding the Republican convention in San Diego. (The money was to come from the Sheraton Hotel Corporation, an ITT subsidiary, with a view to making the San Diego Sheraton, then under construction, the Republican convention headquarters.) Since the Republicans decided to meet in Miami in 1972, Geneen's pledge was never redeemed.
4. Milton Friedman, *Capitalism and Freedom* (Chicago: University of Chicago Press, 1962), p. 12.
5. Ibid., p. 125.
6. Milton Friedman, *Free to Choose* (New York: Avon, 1980), p. 223.
7. The conservatives' proposals for limiting the power of labor include not only right-to-work legislation and bringing unions under the antimonopoly legislation, but also repeal of the Davis-Bacon Act. Passed in 1931, and considerably expanded by amendments since then, the Davis-Bacon Act decreed that workers on federal construction projects must be paid "not less than the prevailing rate of wages for work of a similar nature" in the area.
8. *Capitalism and Freedom*, p. 133.
9. ITT suffered an earlier setback in 1965 when it abandoned an effort to merge with ABC Television in the face of persistent opposition from the Justice Department.
10. See Lester W. Milbrath, *The Washington Lobbyists* (Chicago: Rand McNally, 1963).
11. Earl Latham, "The Group Basis of Politics: Notes for a Theory," *The American Political Science Review* 46, no. 2 (June 1952): 390.
12. See Carl J. Friedrich, ed., *The Public Interest* (New York: Atherton, 1962).

PART three

THE INSTITUTIONS OF GOVERNMENT

Now we turn from the forces that influence the decisions of government to the institutions in which the decisions are formally made. These institutions operate within a constitutional framework of checks and balances, which is designed to separate, divide, and share power among the three branches of government. In large measure this part of the book discusses whether the constitutional balance of power still holds or whether events have created an imbalance.

In chapter 7 we describe the enormous growth of the power vested in the White House, and we ask whether this growth has led to a dangerous concentration of power at the center, or whether this power is so surrounded by limits that it may still be insufficient to allow for effective leadership. In the discussion of Congress in chapter 8 we review its decline vis-à-vis the presidency, yet its continued status as perhaps the most powerful legislature in the world. Chapter 9 covers a more recent concentration of power, the federal bureaucracies, which now amount to virtually a fourth branch of government. We encounter the criticisms that have been heaped on the bureaucracies from all sides of the political spectrum, and we debate their validity. In chapter 10 we examine the powers and functions of the U.S. Supreme Court, exploring the tension between its judicial and its political roles. Finally, in chapter 11 we shift focus away from Washington to the states and the cities, assessing the federal principle of division of powers among the different levels of government—national, state, and local—and asking how much strength and vitality exists in the subnational units of government.

Throughout part three we return repeatedly to the debate among our five perspectives on the questions: *Is the system of checks and balances a good idea? Is it working today?*

chapter seven

THE PRESIDENCY: TOO MUCH OR TOO LITTLE POWER?

At the apex of political ambition in America stands the presidency. The office confers on its incumbent all the trappings of power and unparalleled status. It also offers a salary of $200,000; $50,000 in expenses and a pension of $69,300 a year; thirteen limousines, helicopters, and eighteen jet planes (two of which are designated as "Air Force One" whenever the president is aboard); a personal movie theater, tennis courts, and a bowling alley in the White House; a mountain retreat at Camp David; and a staff to take care of all travel and entertainment arrangements for the president and the president's immediate family.

However, a high price has to be paid for the power, prestige, and luxury. There is an immense burden of responsibility. There is the loss of almost all privacy. And there is constant danger. Despite the ever-present army of Secret Service bodyguards John Kennedy was assassinated, Gerald Ford was the target of two near-misses, and Ronald Reagan was shot and almost killed within three months of his accession to the presidency. Nor is there any final protection against determined assassins, other than the politically intolerable solution of preventing the president from going out in public.

Finally the president pays for these advantages by being the object of persistent criticism and abuse. The president's motives and policies are under constant attack, and the criteria for judging the conduct of the presidency keep changing. Sometimes the cry goes up that too much power has become concentrated in the White House and that we are heading toward a kind of elective monarchy or dictatorship; so the issue is to find ways of curbing the president's powers. But in other periods the general complaint is that the president is allowing things to drift and is not providing the leadership the country needs; then the big question is how to get the president to assert himself and overcome the innumerable constraints that surround the presidency.

To understand these changing attitudes toward the presidency we shall review first the great expansion in the president's responsibilities, and then the limits on the president's powers. Next we shall explore both the powers and the restraints in the context of the modern presidency, from Franklin Roosevelt through Ronald Reagan, and follow that with a listing of the different kinds of proposals that have been made to reform the institution. After that we shall look at the presidency through the eyes of our five perspectives.

THE EXPANSION OF THE PRESIDENCY

"The history of the presidency," says one of its leading scholars, "is a history of aggrandizement."[1] Indeed, the office has grown far beyond the limited range of functions prescribed in Article II of the Constitution. There the president is assigned the roles of chief executive officer and commander-in-chief of the armed services; given the power to make treaties and appoint senior officers of the government, subject to Senate approval; required to report periodically to the Congress on "the State of the Union" and to recommend legislation to them; and instructed to "take Care that the Laws be faithfully executed."

There is not much more than these instructions on the president's functions in the Constitution. But there is much more to be said after nearly two centuries of experience with the presidential office. Today the president has an extraordinary range of responsibilities.

To begin with, the office has symbolic functions. The president is our chief of state, the ceremonial leader of America in dealings with other countries. The presidency embodies the mystique of the American system and the continuity of the nation.

The young child's first perception of government is typically centered on the president. The horror that swept the nation after the assassination of John F. Kennedy was elicited not only by his personal popularity, but also by the fact that the president, the symbolic leader, had been killed. Even when Warren Harding, an inept leader who was surrounded by corruption, died in office, there was a deep and widespread sense of personal loss in the country.

But the president is, of course, much more than the symbolic leader. He is the head of the government, the top policy maker.

As chief diplomat he is the principal shaper of foreign policy. The armed services and our entire machinery of diplomacy report to him as commander-in-chief. He is expected to preserve the security of the nation, maintain the peace, or, failing that, win the war. Since the atom bomb was dropped on Hiroshima in 1945, the president's role in foreign and defense policy has become a matter of life and death not merely for large numbers of individuals but also for whole nations, possibly the entire world. The president has many others to help make decisions, but only the president is followed everywhere by a military aide carrying a suitcase, the so-called "football," with the coded instructions that could unleash a thermonuclear war.

In domestic affairs the president, more than anyone else, is expected to maintain harmony among socioeconomic groups and among races, protect the environment, and prevent a recurrence of the Great Depression of the 1930s. The president must work for high economic growth and low unemployment and still keep prices from rising too rapidly.

To carry out these responsibilities the president exercises leadership in many directions. He influences public opinion by speaking to the people at large about his policies, and nobody can match his opportunities for reaching the public. Not even the biggest entertainment or sports stars are as regularly in the news, and the president is usually on the front page and the evening network news.

The president also legislates. The Constitution speaks only of the president's suggesting ideas to Congress, but not much major legislation gets through Congress unless the White House proposes it and works hard for its enactment.

Next, the president is the head of his political party, so he is actively engaged in partisan politics.

Finally, the president is chief executive, which means that he must direct a vast machinery of government to help him shape and carry out his legislative program, determine and control the federal budget, and administer foreign policy.

THE MACHINERY OF THE EXECUTIVE BRANCH

As the responsibilities of the president have grown, so has the size of the presidential staffs. As we shall see in chapter 9, there were almost 2.9 million civilian federal employees in 1981, spread over a vast panoply of institutions. Among these institutions are the cabinet departments and the many administrative and regulatory agencies that will be discussed more fully in chapter 9.

The vice-president.   The next highest ranking officer in the executive branch is the vice-president, who sits in the cabinet and the National Security Council, is nominally the president of the Senate, and is given a variety of executive, political, and ceremonial assignments. Until recently, despite the assurances of each incoming president that the vice-president would take on functions of vast significance, vice-presidents were rarely given anything important to do, and energetic, experienced men like Hubert Humphrey and Nelson Rockefeller found their time in the office frustrating and sometimes even humiliating.

However, Walter Mondale was given a number of valuable policy and political assignments by Jimmy Carter, as was George Bush by President Reagan. Even so, no president allows the vice-president or the presidential staff to build up an independent base of power that might undermine the president's own authority.[2] So the one overriding function of the vice-president is still what it has always been: to understudy the president. Any vice-president had better take this role seriously, because of the thirty-six men elected to the presidency, eight have died or been killed in office, others have escaped death narrowly, and one has resigned the office. In this century Theodore Roosevelt, Calvin Coolidge, Harry Truman, Lyndon Johnson, and Gerald Ford rose to the presidency following the death or resignation of a president.

The executive office.   Central to the carrying out of the president's purposes are the people he appoints to the Executive Office of the President. This office includes several agencies, the number varying with the changing needs of each president. Among the most important of the Executive Office agencies have been the following:

1. The National Security Council, which was established by Congress in 1947 to help the president pull together the foreign policy planning of the Departments of State and Defense and the Central Intelligence Agency.

2. The Office of Management and Budget, which was established by President Nixon in 1970 and which rides herd on the sprawling bureaucracies of the federal government. The OMB absorbed the Bureau of the Budget, set up by Congress in 1921 to act as the president's instrument for shaping the federal budget out of the proposals of hundreds of agencies and for scrutinizing the performance of those agencies.

3. The Council of Economic Advisers, which was brought into being under the terms of the Employment Act of 1946 and which declared as public policy the maintenance of a high level of employment and a flourishing and stable economy. The council consists of three people with substantial standing in the field of economics.

In recent years the Executive Office has also included councils and offices on environmental quality, energy, telecommunications policy, wage and price controls, international economic policy, and drug abuse.

The White House staff.   Closest of all to the president within the Executive Office is the White House staff. They provide informal channels of information and ideas, undertake political negotiations, carry out liaisons with Congress, help write the president's speeches, handle press relations, and monitor appointments. The senior staff members (some of them with top Executive Office positions) have a great deal of authority. Such men as Theodore Sorenson during the Kennedy administration, Bill Moyers during the Johnson years, and Hamilton Jordan under Carter were White House staff members whose advice was sought daily by the president.

In foreign policy the president's assistant for National Security Affairs has, in some cases, superseded the secretary of state as the president's chief adviser on foreign affairs. This situation was true with McGeorge Bundy under both Kennedy and Johnson, and with Bundy's successor in the Johnson era, W. W. Rostow. In the same job Henry Kissinger was Nixon's top foreign affairs aide even before he became secretary of state; once appointed secretary of state he continued to hold the White House staff post until he reluctantly gave it up during the Ford presidency.

The power of the White House staff was especially great during Richard Nixon's presidency. John Ehrlichman and H. R. Haldeman were the two top "assistants to the president." Ehrlichman was responsible for supervising domestic affairs machinery, including several cabinet departments. Haldeman was the

White House chief of staff, in charge of the president's appointment list. He was present at most of the president's meetings and was responsible for following through on decisions reached at those meetings. The shock waves set off when Watergate toppled these two aides from power were a measure of the authority that they exercised.

The special advantage of the White House staff is that they are close to the president physically and see him regularly. (Indeed, status in the White House is determined to a large extent by how close one's office is to the president's office.) There is also a special kind of power that accrues to a presidential aide who can telephone a senator or corporation president and have the operator say, "White House calling!"

The members of the immediate White House staff are not the only people the president listens to. A few senior cabinet members in each administration exert great influence. So, reputedly, did Carter's wife Rosalynn, who sometimes sat in on cabinet meetings and acted as a sounding board for her husband's ideas. Moreover, every president has one or more close confidants (called "cronies" by the president's critics) with whom the president can talk freely and without fear of breach of confidence. Sometimes these close associates may undertake crucially important assignments for the president, as did Colonel House for Woodrow Wilson and Harry Hopkins for Franklin Roosevelt.

CONSTRAINTS ON PRESIDENTIAL POWER

With such a vast expansion of their functions and staff resources, presidents should feel enormously powerful. But in fact, many of them have complained that on all sides they are hedged in by constraints. Some of these constraints are built into the Constitution; others result from political realities.

Congress.   With its traditional, ingrained jealousy of presidential authority (as we shall see in chapter 8), Congress creates continual constraints on the president's power.

The court system.   Harry Truman discovered the power of the courts when, confronted by a steel strike that stopped production during the Korean War, he ordered a takeover of the steel industry by the federal government. The workers resumed production, but the Supreme Court found the president's act unconstitutional,[3] the industry went back to its owners, and the workers resumed the strike.[4]

The doctrine of federalism.   The constitutional separation of powers between the states and the federal government reserves some powers to the states that are therefore not available to the president.

National elections.   This constraint has been weakened by the Twenty-second Amendment to the Constitution, ratified in 1951, which prevents a president's running for more than two terms. Even so, presidents want to have their own party win the next election rather than face the knowledge that they have been repudiated by the people.

Public opinion polls.   Between elections, too, presidents nervously watch their ratings in the public opinion polls. The wide fluctuations experienced by all presidents are revealed by the results (shown in table 7-1) of surveys on the percentages of people who felt that the president was doing a good job. Generally speaking, presidents have hit their high points at the beginning of their administrations. But they have seen their popularity and influence plummet after severe setbacks to their policies. Thus Truman hit his low point in the polls because of Korea. For Johnson the damage was done by Vietnam; for Nixon, Watergate; for Ford, his pardoning of Nixon; for Carter, his failure to secure the release of the American hostages in Iran.

TABLE 7-1 Gallup surveys: Popular approval of presidents (percent)

President	High	Low
Roosevelt	84	54
Truman	87	23
Eisenhower	79	49
Kennedy	83	57
Johnson	80	39
Nixon	68	24
Ford	71	37
Carter	71	21

The administration.   Although the president is leader of his party, American political parties are too loose and undisciplined to be reliable instruments of the president's will. Members of his own party in Congress often refuse to go along with his legislative programs, and his problems are compounded when Congress is in the hands of the opposition party, as happened for all or part of the terms of Truman, Eisenhower, Nixon, and Ford. The cabinet, although it is selected by the president to carry out his programs, can also include people of independent will who may not see things the president's way and thus limit his power. This situation is even more true of some members of the permanent bureaucracies of the departments and agencies of the federal government. Harry Truman made the point when Eisenhower, a long-time general, was about to take over the presidency: "He'll sit here, and he'll say, 'Do this! Do that!' *And nothing will happen.*"

Foreign powers.   A further limitation on presidential power is that all of America's money, technology, prestige, and military force do not necessarily prevail in other parts of the world. The closest of allies, even those countries dependent on our support for their survival, can prove to be infuriatingly balky. No president can harbor any longer what the British scholar D.W. Brogan called "the illusion of American omnipotence."

The changing world.   Both at home and abroad, great social forces are in motion, and science and technology unleash sweeping transformations of our world—all with hardly a bow to the power of the presidency. So, if people outside the White House view the presidency as a center of awesome power, presidents tend to see themselves as surrounded by a myriad of constraints on their freedom of action.

PRESIDENTS AND THEIR APPROACHES TO POWER

The extent to which presidential power has expanded has varied with the incumbents. The administrations of Grant, Tyler, Taylor, Fillmore, Pierce, Buchanan, Harding, and Coolidge were not associated with great accomplishments or the restless accumulation of power. In some cases these men were simply out of their depth or content to accept the constraints of the presidency as proper to the role assigned by the Founding Fathers. As President William Howard Taft saw it, the Constitution does not give the president many functions, and the president would be exceeding his authority if he tried to exercise powers that were not clearly indicated by the words of the Constitution or by appropriate statutes passed by Congress.

But other presidents took a much broader view of their responsibilities. The presidents after Washington whom children hear about from grade school on— Jefferson, Jackson, and Lincoln—were leaders whose actions could not be explained by a strict construction of the language of the Constitution. Both Jefferson in making the Louisiana Purchase, and Lincoln in committing the national government to action against the South, acted first and consulted Congress later, thereby demonstrating the far-reaching power to take initiatives inherent in their role as chief executive.

Early in the twentieth century Theodore Roosevelt provided a rationale for such vigorous exercises of presidential power. The Constitution, in his view, was deliberately written in general terms to provide the flexibility needed for growth of the office. Thus Section 3 of Article II instructed the president to take "such Measures as he shall judge necessary and expedient," and to "take Care that the Laws be faithfully executed." This wording gives the president plenty of scope; and it was the president's duty, said Roosevelt, "to do anything that the needs of the Nation demanded unless such action was forbidden by the Constitution or by the laws." If he did not act in this way, he would find himself overwhelmed by the countless potential limits on presidential power and would fail to carry out his constitutional responsibilities.

In the debate over the powers of the modern presidency, Theodore Roosevelt's interpretation has prevailed. Franklin Roosevelt, Truman, Kennedy, Johnson, and Nixon, each in his own way, saw the need to reach out for power and overcome the constraints in order to respond to the needs of his time. However, the growth of the office has not been steady. With the election of Eisenhower after Truman, and the succession of Ford after Nixon, the nation turned to leaders who slowed down the pace of presidential action. The world had changed too much for Eisenhower and Ford to go back to Taft's doctrine of the limited presidency. But each represented at least a pause, a modest shift away from Theodore Roosevelt's concept of the aggressive presidency. So, as we turn to a brief analysis of presidencies since the 1930s, we see periods of *expanding power*, each followed by shorter intervals of *consolidation*.

FRANKLIN ROOSEVELT, 1933–1945

We date the history of the modern presidency from the administrations of Franklin Roosevelt not simply because he had an expansive view of his responsibilities. In this century Woodrow Wilson as well as Theodore Roosevelt took an energetic view of presidential responsibilities and fought to provide strong leadership in domestic and foreign affairs. But during the successive administrations of Franklin Roosevelt the scope of the federal government and the power of the presidency itself took a quantum jump that could never be fully retraced.

DRAWING BY PETER ARNO; © 1936, 1964. THE NEW YORKER MAGAZINE, INC.
"Come along. We're going to the Trans-Lux to hiss Roosevelt."

This enormous change was made possible by a crisis more serious than any that had afflicted the country since the Civil War: the collapse of the economy, known as the "Great Depression." Roosevelt was elected to do what his predecessor Herbert Hoover had not been able to accomplish: to rescue the drowning economy. He had no program at the outset, so he and his associates improvised a grab bag of bold and unprecedented programs known as the "New Deal." Industry, banking, and agriculture were brought under federal regulation and were given subsidies. New rules were established for the operation of the stock market. The right of labor unions to organize was protected. Large numbers of jobs were created by special government projects. Money and services were provided to the poor. To administer all these services, government agencies proliferated. To pay for the programs, the federal government spent far more than it took in and large budget deficits were incurred.

Of course, so many changes could not be brought about without opposition. To overcome this disagreement, Roosevelt could not simply issue commands. He had to use the most important power of the presidency: what Richard Neustadt has called "the power to persuade." And Roosevelt was a superb persuader both in face-to-face discussions and with the public at large. Using speeches, informal press conferences, and, most effective of all, "fireside chats" over the radio, he was able to project his ideas and his personality with charismatic impact on the public at large.

He was not always successful. Some of his early programs for industry and agriculture were administrative monstrosities that had to be abandoned or completely overhauled. He never really solved the unemployment problem until the time came to prepare for World War II. Still, the New Deal brought the federal government deeply and irreversibly into the economy.

America's entry into World War II in 1941 brought the centralized planning that accompanies all major wars and vested even greater power in the national government. That war placed Roosevelt in the one presidential role he had not fully played until then: commander-in-chief of the armed services. For almost thirteen years, through Roosevelt's more than three terms in the White House, the people came to identify the institution of the presidency with the ideas, character, and personality of Franklin Roosevelt; and Roosevelt projected the presidency into the consciousness of the nation with an impact that was to have a lasting effect on the nature of the institution.

HARRY TRUMAN, 1945–1953

Truman came to the presidency on the death of Roosevelt less than a year after Roosevelt's reelection for a fourth term. He could not hope to match the charismatic leadership style of his predecessor, and at first he was somewhat overawed by his enormous responsibilities. Nonetheless, he quickly concluded that some major decisions had to be made, that only the president could make them, and that "the buck stops here," in the Oval Office of the White House. So he did not shrink from the need to exercise power and developed a brisk self-confidence in making big decisions without much agonizing.

Thus he gave the order to drop the atomic bombs on Hiroshima and Nagasaki to force a quick end to the war against Japan—a decision that changed the character of foreign policy as profoundly as the New Deal had changed domestic policy. He played a major role in shaping the Marshall Plan, a program of billions of dollars in aid to help rebuild war-shattered Western Europe. Although the constitutional authority to declare war is vested in Congress, Truman led the nation into a war in Korea, getting congressional approval *after* he had acted. In the course of that war he fired (after a good deal of vacillation) a magnetically popular military leader, General Douglas MacArthur, thereby protecting the principle, essential to a democracy, of civilian supremacy over the military. In the domestic field he worked hard for his "Fair Deal," a series of programs in housing, health, and education that were intended to be the next wave of social reform after the New Deal.

Unfortunately for Truman the electorate was growing tired of so many years of activism by government at home and abroad. Although Truman managed to win reelection in 1948 against apparently overwhelming odds, he won acceptance for only a few of his Fair Deal proposals. And as the Korean War dragged on with no victory in sight and tens of thousands of American troops killed, Truman's popularity dropped to abysmally low levels. He had lost his ability to lead. The potency of the presidency was gone.

DWIGHT EISENHOWER, 1953–1961

The election of Eisenhower reflected the end of an era of social change and wars. The mood of the people seemed to favor a pause, a time for consolidation, a reluctance to respond to challenges from vigorous presidential leadership.

Eisenhower fitted the mood of the time perfectly. Although he had none of the eloquence or the vivid, almost theatrical style of a Franklin Roosevelt, vast numbers of people found his sincerity, warmth, and geniality immensely appealing, and few presidents have matched his personal popularity. Yet he did not use this popularity to muster support for bold new programs. A moderate conservative, he believed in slowing the pace of change.

His style of leadership reflected this approach. He delegated more authority than had Roosevelt or Truman. He vested extensive authority in Sherman Adams, the assistant to the president, while upgrading the importance of the cabinet and the National Security Council and establishing greater formality in their procedures.

This approach led many contemporary critics to dismiss Eisenhower as a do-nothing president who left all the decisions to others and spent most of his time on the golf course. Subsequently historians and political scientists have shown that Eisenhower was an active, hard-working president who had a clear perception of his responsibilities. In foreign affairs he took the initiative that ended the Korean War. He overruled the majority of his advisers who wanted him to send military support to the French during their last stand in Indochina. And after the death of his hard-lining secretary of state, John Foster Dulles, Eisenhower tried to soften the bitterly anti-Soviet tone of U.S. foreign policy by bringing Soviet premier Nikita Khrushchev to this country for a visit. In domestic affairs the federal highway and Social Security programs were expanded during Eisenhower's years in the White House; despite delays and obvious reluctance he made the decision to send National Guard troops to Little Rock, Arkansas, to enforce the Supreme Court's decision on school desegregation; and (although he was much criticized for not dealing with the problem more directly and forcefully) he played a key role in isolating and eventually crushing the power of the right-wing extremist, Senator Joseph McCarthy.

Clearly Eisenhower was not a Grant, a Harding, or a Coolidge. Just the same, Eisenhower's view of the powers of the presidency was somewhat more restrained than the views of his immediate predecessors. His perspective did not diminish his personal popularity. Yet by the end of Eisenhower's second term in office there was a widespread sense that we had consolidated long enough. The economy was in the doldrums, unemployment was high, and the Soviet Union dealt a blow to U.S. prestige and self-respect when it beat us at our own technological game by being the first to put a satellite ("Sputnik") into orbit around the earth.

JOHN KENNEDY, 1961–1963

John Kennedy built his 1960 presidential campaign around this sense of restlessness in the country. The nation, he argued, had lost its momentum. It was time to get things moving again across the "New Frontier." We needed a president who would challenge events, not merely respond to them, and who would provide bold, imaginative leadership. The narrowness of his election victory limited his ability to produce on his promises, but he set about the task of revitalizing national policies at home and abroad with immense enthusiasm.

He presented new legislative programs in such fields as education, health care, housing, and space exploration. When Congress did not act fast enough on his proposals, the president used televised press conferences to build up support for his positions. When the U.S. Steel Company raised its prices after Kennedy had negotiated with industry and labor to keep the prices down, he forced the company to cancel the increase by using all the persuasive powers of his office. In foreign affairs he got off to a miserable beginning with a bungled effort to bring about Castro's downfall by landing a small force of Cuban refugees at the Bay of Pigs, but this failure was followed by a strong and effective handling of the Cuban missile crisis. Subsequently, he initiated efforts to reduce the tensions between the Soviet Union and the United States, including the signing of a treaty between the two nations to ban the testing of nuclear weapons in the atmosphere.

Kennedy's perception of the purposes of the presidency was reflected in the way he organized the office. He was much less inclined to delegate authority than Eisenhower. He did not wait for issues to work their way through various departments, reaching his desk only in their last, refined state. He wanted to know not merely the eventual alternatives but the information and reasoning that went into shaping these alternatives. To get at this information he did not care much about the proper channels but would get in touch directly with anyone who might shed some light on an issue, even though this person might be a middle-level member of an agency. He was impatient with the cabinet and the other institutions that comprise the formal machinery of government, and he created whatever institutions he needed, sometimes on an ad hoc basis. His brother Robert and his chief White House assistant, Theodore Sorenson, were his closest confidants, but neither was given a chief of staff role.

This organizational style served him well in the Cuban missile crisis, but sometimes it created uncertainties and confusion. Still, Kennedy's methods reflected his personality, his view that the governmental machinery ought to be forced out of its tendency to inertia, and his expansive view of the responsibilities vested in the presidency. And Kennedy did succeed in capturing the public imagination. People were captivated by his vitality, his wit, his lucidity, and his mastery of information. His wife, Jacqueline, was on the cover of women's magazines week after week. The Kennedy children became public favorites. The large Kennedy clan and their friends became the center of a revitalized Washington and New York social life. The media spoke of a new "Camelot," conveying a promise of an exciting, more colorful, more fulfilled life for America. The source of this promise was the energy generated by the White House.

When the president was struck down by an assassin's bullet in Dallas on November 22, 1963, the sense of loss in the nation seemed irreparable.

LYNDON JOHNSON, 1963–1969

Lyndon Johnson, whose television style lacked force and conviction and who was not an appealing personality to the public, could not match the youthful attractiveness of Kennedy. Nonetheless, where Kennedy brought zest to the tasks of presidential leadership, Johnson applied himself with compulsive energy. "Presidents," he said, "deal with power." Johnson sought it and dealt with it. This philosophy was clear from his decision-making structures. He called cabinet meetings, but they were little more than evangelical assemblies in which cabinet members and their staffs were exhorted to work ever more effectively for the president's programs. The National Security Council was consulted periodically, but Johnson worked primarily through small groups of advisers. For foreign policy he looked to the secretaries of state and defense and his White House national security aide. On domestic affairs his confidants were members of the White House staff.

But always at the center of the decision-making process was Lyndon Johnson himself—restless, constantly inquiring, talking, working, subjecting senators, congressmen, governors, party leaders, journalists, and others to the "Johnson treatment." This treatment consisted of an overwhelming array of techniques, including flattery, cajolery, humility, and threats, as well as appeals to conscience and party, all directed toward getting his legislation through Congress and receiving favorable treatment in the press.

The results in domestic policy were prodigious. The years 1964 and 1965 saw a dazzling succession of presidential triumphs in Congress in the fields of civil rights, housing, health, education, and poverty—all building blocks in the construction of the "Great Society." Nothing like it had happened since the New Deal years.

Reelected in 1964 with a huge majority, Lyndon Johnson seemed unassailable, and, as the Great Society legislation poured out of Congress at Johnson's instigation, the presidency appeared to be the key to the creation of a better life for the great majority of Americans. But then came Vietnam, which dealt an even more savage blow to Johnson's popularity and prestige than Korea had inflicted on Truman.

Johnson inherited the Vietnam problem from his predecessors, particularly Kennedy, who had sent South Vietnam large quantities of arms and growing numbers of so-called military "advisers."

After his reelection in 1964 Johnson decided to expand our intervention. He sent substantial numbers of troops with air support, then more, and more again. These actions looked very much like war, and the Constitution says that the president cannot declare war without congressional approval. So Johnson refused to call it a war. It was merely a military intervention. In any case he claimed that he had already received congressional sanction for his actions. In August 1964, North Vietnamese PT boats twice attacked American destroyers in the Gulf of Tonkin, off Vietnam. It was never really clear who had started the fighting. But when a president tells the Congress that American servicemen have been the victims of unprovoked aggression, Congress finds it difficult not to give him what he wants. So Congress passed a joint resolution—known as the Tonkin Gulf resolution—authorizing him to "take all necessary measures to stop aggression in Southeast Asia." This resolution, said the administration later, was the "functional equivalent" of a declaration of war.

Now it seemed that presidential power had reached its zenith. In both domestic and foreign affairs the presidency had achieved a clear dominance over all other aspects of the system. Few kings or emperors in the past, said some commentators, could match the power of the American president. We had produced, said Arthur Schlesinger, Jr., "the imperial Presidency."

But, of course, Vietnam did not prove to be the final proof of the aggrandizement of presidential power. On the contrary, it broke the power and the reputation of Lyndon Johnson. Each escalation only produced a counterescalation. No matter how much money, manpower, and ingenuity the United States threw into the war, the promised "light at the end of the tunnel" remained as distant as ever.

The president found himself attacked persistently and ferociously in the Senate. His hold on mass opinion declined, at first gradually, then with a rush; even though his ratings improved briefly after each escalation (and after each peace overture we made), he discovered that a president can only control public opinion over the long run if his policy works. But Vietnam did not respond to the Johnson treatment. His frustration became intense. "Power?" he said bitterly. "The only power I've got is nuclear and I can't use that."

At last, faced with the ultimate testing ground of presidential power, a presidential election campaign, he gave up. On March 31, 1968, he announced his decision to change course on Vietnam and not to run for another term in office.

RICHARD NIXON, 1969–1974

Once again a pause was indicated. It was time to assimilate the enormous quantity of social legislation passed during the Johnson administration, to scale down our overseas involvements, and to deemphasize the power of the presidency. So the general expectation was that just as Eisenhower had cooled things down after the New Deal, the Fair Deal, and Korea, so Richard Nixon would follow the New Frontier, the Great Society, and Vietnam with a period of restraint.

Indeed, very little emerged during Nixon's first hundred days in office, the traditional "honeymoon period," which a new president is expected to exploit fully before his popularity begins to slip. Some commentators began making comparisons with the Eisenhower era.

It soon became clear, however, that the Eisenhower analogy was inappropriate. It did not square with some of the things Nixon had said about the presidency during the 1968 campaign. "The days of a passive Presidency," he argued, "belong to a simpler past. . . . The next President must take an activist view of his office. He must activate the nation's values, define its goals, and marshal its will. . . . The President's chief function is to lead, not to administer." This tone belonged not to William Howard Taft, but to Theodore Roosevelt.

Nixon's methods of organizing his administration reflected his view that he could not depend on many allies outside his own immediate orbit. Congress was in the hands of the opposition party. The bureaucracies and their programs had grown mostly during the terms of his Democratic predecessors, and it was difficult to bring them into line behind new policies.

In his view the media were controlled by the liberal establishment. He used television and radio to explain his policies to the people, but mostly in the form of addresses that did not allow for cross-examination. He held fewer press conferences than his predecessors. He saw his administration as a beleaguered group of carefully chosen men who would ensure him of the advice and support he could not get from anywhere else. So he gave unprecedented power to the top members of his White House staff, particularly to assistants to the president, H. R. Haldeman and John Ehrlichman, who were dubbed by a hostile press "the palace guard."

The long-run purposes espoused by Nixon and his administration were to reduce the massive involvements of the American federal government in solving the problems of the world in general and the American system in particular. His strategies for achieving these purposes were built on the vigorous display of presidential power.

Thus in foreign policy he and his secretary of state, Henry Kissinger, finally ended the involvement of U.S. troops in the Vietnam War. Moreover, by making a historic visit to the People's Republic of China, then going on to the Soviet Union, they instituted the policy of détente, the reduction of tensions with the communist powers. At the same time, Nixon was determined that his actions not be read as an indication of weakness. Thus he took four years to accomplish the withdrawal from Vietnam and, along the way, ordered the invasion of Cambodia and Laos, the mining of North Vietnamese harbors, and massive bombing of

North Vietnam. These attacks provoked bitter criticism in Congress and upheavals on college campuses. But Nixon refused to be deterred from his resolve.

In domestic affairs, Nixon's basic purpose was to halt the expansion of the role of the federal government in economic and social affairs. This aim did not mean the dismantling of all the programs introduced since the New Deal. In some respects, indeed, Nixon sought to achieve bold social reforms, as in his unsuccessful effort to replace the existing welfare programs with a Family Assistance Plan (see chapter 12). He also presided over enormous federal spending programs, which involved a series of large budgetary deficits. And, in his attempts to get inflation under control, he twice imposed federal government controls over wages and prices. Nonetheless, during his first term of office he fought to hold down some of the spending plans of the Democratic Congress that he believed would ruin the economy.

Once reelected for his second term, Nixon made it clear that he intended to go over to the offensive. In an interview given to the *Washington Star-News* in November 1972, Nixon declared that it was time to bring to an end the philosophy of the social welfare programs of the 1960s, the philosophy of "throwing money at problems."

He took the enormous majority by which he won the 1972 election to be a mandate for his policies. His triumph, however, was short-lived. He was able to do little about his policies in his second term, which was cut short by his resignation. The basic reason for his downfall was that, although his avowed policies called for lessening the role of the federal government, he did not connect this reduction with a reduction of the power of the presidency. On the contrary, he and the men he chose to work with him built their power enormously and abused it. Their abuse of power came to be symbolized by the word *Watergate*; and just as Johnson's authority was destroyed by Vietnam, so was Nixon's by Watergate.

On the evening of June 17, 1972, five men were arrested for breaking into the headquarters of the Democratic National Committee (DNC) in the Watergate office and apartment building in Washington, apparently to place a bug in the telephone of DNC chairperson Lawrence O'Brien. Among the five was the director of security for the Committee to Reelect the President, James McCord. Another carried an address book containing the name and White House address of an E. Howard Hunt.

In response to inquiries the president's press secretary dismissed the break-in as "a third-rate burglary." As the story unfolded piece by agonizing piece over a period of over two years, there was much more to it than that. It was a small part of a much larger pattern of action by top officials that was to force the first resignation ever of a president of the United States. The major elements in the story were as follows.

1. The Watergate break-in was planned by leading members of the administration and of the Committee to Reelect the President. These members included Attorney General, later CRP director, John Mitchell; Jeb Magruder, who became CRP director after Mitchell resigned; and Charles Colson, a top aide to

Nixon and Haldeman. Heading up the break-in itself were CRP counsel G. Gordon Liddy and E. Howard Hunt, both of whom were former CIA men who had carried out various assignments for the White House as members of a Special Investigations Unit, known as "the plumbers" because their purpose was to stop national security leaks.

2. The break-in was one incident among several aimed at opponents of the Nixon administration. These incidents included the burglarizing, at John Ehrlichman's direction, of a psychiatrist's office in a fruitless effort to find the medical records of Daniel Ellsberg, who was accused of leaking Defense Department documents to the press;[5] phone tappings and illegal breaking and entering by the FBI; the compiling of an "enemies list" (people targeted for harassment by the Internal Revenue Service and other federal agencies); and a series of election "dirty tricks" during the 1972 campaign by Donald Segretti and others under White House direction.[6]

3. The president personally participated in an illegal "cover-up" of the Watergate break-in. Nixon insisted that he had known nothing about the White House involvement in the break-in until the counsel to the president, John Dean, revealed some of the story to him in March 1973, nine months after the break-in. From the beginning, Nixon insisted, he had told everyone in his administration to tell the truth to FBI agents investigating the affair. Some conversations and documents would have to be withheld for reasons of national security and the separation of powers; they were protected by the doctrine of "executive privilege," which, he claimed, gives the president the right to keep confidential communications within his official family. Nonetheless he was determined, he said, to get at the truth and make it known to the public.

There was widespread skepticism that he wanted the truth known. Criticism of the White House widened and deepened. *The Washington Post*, whose reporters Robert Woodward and Carl Bernstein had first exposed the links between the burglars, the CRP, and the White House,[7] stepped up its investigations, as did other newspapers and news magazines. Federal district court judge John Sirica, who had been dissatisfied with the prosecution's lack of zeal in trying to establish the White House link during the Watergate break-in trial, imposed harsh sentences on the defendants, offering to soften their sentences if they told what they knew. This offer produced a confession by John McCord, the CRP security man, that perjury had been committed at the trial, and a federal grand jury investigation of Watergate under Sirica's direction was ordered.

The mounting pressure forced the resignations on April 30, 1973 of Ehrlichman, Haldeman, Dean, and Attorney General Richard Kleindienst. Still the president insisted that, even if his top aides had been involved and had tried to cover up, he had known nothing about it.

But then John Dean told a televised Senate hearing, chaired by Sam Ervin of North Carolina, that he believed the president had known about the complicity of the White House in the Watergate burglary at an early stage and that the president had probably engaged in the cover-up with his aides. It was Dean's word against the president's until a White House staff member told the Senate committee that, ever since 1970, Nixon had taped most of his conversations and phone calls at the White House and at the presidential retreat, Camp David.

From that time the story was one of Nixon's desperate efforts, under the claim of executive privilege, to prevent the content of the tapes from becoming known. In the course of these efforts he fired Archibald Cox, the special prosecutor for Watergate-related crimes whom Congress had forced him to appoint, because Cox had gone to court to seek enforcement of a subpoena for several of the tapes.[8]

However, John Sirica's grand jury got some of the tapes from the president's lawyers (one containing a suspicious gap of 18½ minutes); the new special prosecutor, Leon Jaworski, issued subpoenas for more; and under intense pressure from Congress and the media, Nixon produced and made public transcripts of some of the tapes. Although they were heavily edited, they gave clear indications that Nixon had talked with Haldeman, Ehrlichman, Dean, and others about how the White House staff should commit perjury and how to arrange for payments and promises of pardons to keep the Watergate burglars from revealing what they knew about the involvement of the higher-ups.

This evidence was enough to start the House Judiciary Committee on the road to *impeachment*, that constitutional process for the removal of a president from office for "treason, bribery, and other high crimes or misdemeanors." The process involves a vote by the House Judiciary Committee to recommend articles of impeachment, their approval by a majority of the House, a trial by the Senate, and conviction by a two-thirds vote of the Senate.

After an extensive staff study during the spring of 1974 the Judiciary Committee conducted a televised debate on the various charges, grouped under five articles of impeachment. Nixon's defenders claimed that by "high crimes and misdemeanors" the Founding Fathers were referring only to criminal conduct, which had not been proven against the president. Nixon's opponents replied that when the Founders used the word *misdemeanors* they had in mind not its modern meaning of illegal offenses short of felony, but gross abuses of the public trust even when they were not palpably criminal.

Following a televised debate the accusers prevailed on three articles of impeachment: Article I, dealing with the "obstruction of justice" represented by the president's involvement in the cover-up; Article II, covering the president's alleged "abuses of power" (setting up the plumbers' unit and misusing the IRS, FBI, and other agencies); and Article III, covering Nixon's refusal to honor a Judiciary Committee subpoena for some of the tapes.[9]

However, there was no need for the process of impeachment to go on to the Senate. Special Prosecutor Jaworski's subpoena produced a unanimous Supreme Court decision in July 1974 requiring Nixon to produce more tapes.[10] One of them dated back to June 23, 1972, six days after the Watergate break-in, and it included a conversation between the president and Haldeman in which they agreed to try to get the deputy CIA director to tell the acting FBI director not to pursue the Watergate investigation because it had national security ramifications. Here was the "smoking gun," the final proof that the president had lied repeatedly to Congress, to the press, and to the public on television when he insisted he had known nothing about the Watergate affair until nine months after it happened and had tried aggressively to get the truth out. On August 8, 1974, Richard Nixon avoided the prospect of becoming the first president of the United States to be removed from office by impeachment, by becoming the first president of the United States to resign his office.

During 1974 Mitchell, Haldeman, Ehrlichman, Dean, Magruder, Colson, and Nixon's former appointments secretary, Dwight Chapin, were tried and convicted on charges related to the Watergate cover-up and other activities, and all served jail sentences.

Nor were these men the only members of the Nixon administration to suffer disgrace. In October 1973, Vice-President Spiro Agnew was accused of taking bribes from Maryland businesspeople in return for government contracts, payments that had started when he was in state politics and had continued while he was in the White House. He avoided a trial by pleading "no contest," essentially a plea that implies guilt on some charges but eliminates the process of presenting and proving these charges. He was fined and put on probation for income tax evasion, and several other charges against him were dropped on condition that he resign from the vice-presidency. Nixon then nominated Gerald Ford to fill the vacancy under the terms of the Twenty-fifth Amendment to the Constitution, which provides for the president to nominate a new vice-president subject to confirmation by the Senate. The nominee received the Senate's endorsement. Less than a year later Ford was president of the United States.

GERALD FORD, 1974–1977

Gerald Ford saw his presidency as having two basic functions. The first was to restore the integrity of the office by putting a stop to the abuses to which it had been subjected and ending the practices of deceit, guile, and secretiveness. His second purpose was to continue the general direction of Nixon's policies of reducing the role of the federal government in economic affairs and combining military and diplomatic strength with a lowering of tensions in international affairs.

Ford was well suited to perform both these functions. His open, unpretentious manner contrasted sharply with the deviousness of Nixon and Johnson. Nor did he isolate himself as Nixon had done. He maintained a large White House staff and there were power struggles within it and between the staff and cabinet members, but none of his top assistants had the power or the personal style of H.R. Haldeman. He also moved to put an end to the illegal actions of the CIA and the FBI and to restore their tarnished reputations.

However, Ford's image of integrity was somewhat damaged by his granting Richard Nixon a "full, free and absolute pardon . . . for all offenses against the United States which he . . . has committed or may have committed during his tenure as President." There were accusations that a "deal" had been worked out, that the pardon was set up earlier as Nixon's condition for agreeing to resign. Ford denied this charge, insisting that his only motive was to get an ugly episode in our national life behind us once and for all.

As for his policies, Ford's views were close to Nixon's in both national and domestic affairs. Although he presided over the expenditure of vast sums of money and accepted huge budgetary deficits, he followed Nixon's example in fighting Congress's desire to spend even more, and he vetoed a total of fifty-six bills. In foreign affairs he supported Henry Kissinger's continuation of the policy of détente. At the same time Ford pushed for higher spending on defense, and he took strong action against a communist country in May 1975 when he dispatched marines to recapture the American merchant ship *Mayaguez*, which had been seized by Cambodia.

Although Ford won a good deal of public approval for his style and his policies, the overwhelming support that greeted him when he began his presidency eroded before long. The granting of a pardon for Nixon was extremely unpopular. Then came a growing sense in the country that he lacked the competence and decisiveness needed in a president. A considerable part of his difficulty was that Congress was in the hands of the opposition party. So he had to make his arguments not through his own initiatives but through the use of his negative power, the veto; and even there Congress overrode his vetoes eleven times. Finally, the Ford administration was roundly criticized for not being able to bring unemployment down below 7.5 percent.

So Ford encountered increasing political difficulties, some of them within his own party. Although his nominee for vice-president, Nelson Rockefeller, was confirmed by the Senate after an intensive and embarrassing investigation of the Rockefeller family finances, Ford did not have the sway in the Republican party to keep Rockefeller on his ticket in his 1976 reelection bid. And he was barely able to ward off Ronald Reagan's challenge for the Republican nomination. At last, when he sought the endorsement of the national constituency in November 1976, he could not convince the people that what he stood for was what the country needed for the next four years.

JIMMY CARTER, 1977–1981

Jimmy Carter's diagnosis of what the country needed from its president included two main points.

First, it would be necessary to complete the work of Gerald Ford in demystifying the presidency, doing away with its imperial trappings, making it a more open, accessible presidency. He began this change of image by walking down Pennsylvania Avenue in his inaugural parade instead of riding in the presidential limousine; wearing a sweater instead of a formal business suit in his first televised address from the White House; cutting the number of cars and chauffeurs available to the White House staff; selling the presidential yacht; participating in "town hall" meetings in small communities and fielding questions phoned in from people around the country on live television and radio programs; and keeping a fluid, open staff structure in the White House to avoid the danger of his being cut off from the country by a "palace guard."

The second part of Carter's approach to the presidency was to provide vigorous, positive leadership in place of Ford's "government by veto." Carter warned in his inaugural address that government could not accomplish everything, that "even our great nation has its recognized limits, and that we can neither answer all questions nor solve all problems." Nonetheless, he offered an ambitious agenda: cutting inflation and unemployment, reforming the tax system, reducing our dependence on foreign oil, reorganizing the federal government, providing a broad program of health insurance, giving more aid to the cities, bringing the arms race under control, *and* achieving a balanced budget by 1980.

Carter's accomplishments with this agenda were limited. In foreign policy, the efforts of several presidents culminated in the signing and Senate approval of a treaty that, over a period of years, will turn the Panama Canal over to Panama. Carter's personal diplomacy at Camp David brought Begin and Sadat to agreement on an Israeli-Egypt peace treaty. In domestic affairs Carter established a Department of Energy, sought and finally got congressional action on major energy legislation, and succeeded in reducing America's dependence on oil imports.

Yet these successes were not enough to avoid a crushing sense on the part of the public that Carter was not an effective president. The Camp David agreement was scorned by the other Arab states, and the Middle East continued to be a troubled area. The Organization of Petroleum Exporting Countries (OPEC) imposed huge price increases, then raised them again in defiance of the feeble protests of the United States and other importing nations. The Panama Canal treaty was approved in the Senate by the narrowest of margins. The second stage of the Strategic Arms Limitations Talks (SALT II) with the Soviets was signed by the Carter administration but stalled in the Senate, with no prospect in sight of its being approved. The Iranian hostage crisis brought a temporary boost to Carter's standing; but an attempt to free the hostages by military action failed ignominiously, and they were not freed until the day Carter turned over the presidency to Reagan, much too late to prevent the issue's doing dreadful damage to Carter's reputation.

On the domestic front, inflation and unemployment increased during the last part of his term in office. The hopes of balancing the budget never came close to realization. The energy bills that emerged from Congress had taken years to get through and were very different from Carter's original proposals. The promised reforms of welfare programs, consumer laws, and labor legislation were not acted on by Congress.

The sense grew in the country that the Carter White House was not providing the energizing force that his programs called for and that his presidency was weak. The very unpretentiousness and openness of which he had made so much at the beginning of his tenure, and which had been well received at the time, now seemed to contribute to the sense of disorganization and lack of assurance that emanated from the presidency.

In the summer of 1979 Carter made a desperate effort to persuade the people that he was not a weak president. He called leaders from all walks of life to a series of meetings at Camp David to get their advice on what needed to be done. He told the public on television that the people had lost their faith in the future of the country and that something must be done to restore their confidence in themselves and their institutions. Then he conferred with his staff and issued a

COURTESY ARKANSAS GAZETTE

statement that they had resolved to "do better" in their task of leading the nation. To this end the White House staff was reorganized, a tighter structure imposed, and his top aide, Hamilton Jordan, took on the functions, although not the title, of chief of staff.

But it was too little and too late to change the perception of Carter as an unsuccessful, somewhat inept president, which was a principal cause of his defeat in the 1980 election.

Carter's defenders argued that this judgment was cruelly unfair. They doubted that even a Franklin Roosevelt, a John Kennedy, or a Lyndon Johnson would have done very much better given the difficulties that had confronted Carter. Congress, they pointed out, had been even more obstreperous than in the past; after Vietnam and Watergate its members were determined to reassert themselves and would have been almost unmanageable for any president. Although previous presidents had had to deal with complex problems, never before had the issues seemed so intractable, so resistant to the skills of the experts, so unresponsive to the power of America. Furthermore, although the public looked to the president for strong leadership, there was no mood in the country to support major innovations. Roosevelt was given a blank check by the people to get the country out of the Great Depression. Lyndon Johnson's legislative successes came, partly at least, as a tribute to a president struck down at the height of his popularity. No such circumstances helped Jimmy Carter. Instead he came to office while the post-Watergate suspicion of presidential power still lingered and when the media had entered an era in which journalistic reputations were made by the systematic destruction of the reputation of political leaders.

Although there was considerable merit in these arguments, they could not overcome the prevailing judgment that Carter had contributed to his problems and had made the worst of an admittedly difficult situation. Several reasons for his failure were suggested:

1. He lacked experience of national politics, did not know his way around Washington, and handled his relationships with congressional leaders clumsily.

2. His personal qualities were not well suited to his responsibilities. Although he was highly intelligent, knowledgeable, a fast study, and a dedicated, tireless worker, there was a rigidity and narrowness to his intellectual style, an insistence on neat, rational solutions, and an impatience with loose ends and unresolved problems.

3. He was uncomfortable with the process of bargaining and negotiation that is the essence of the political process, especially in dealing with congressional leaders. His political touch was unsure. He lacked a sense of timing, and he suffered from a kind of political tone-deafness that had led to his "ethnic purity" remark during the 1976 nomination campaign and then to the whimsical comment during a state visit to Mexico that he had suffered from "Montezuma's revenge" during a previous visit to that country.

4. Although his speeches were clear and well constructed and his press conference answers were lucid and literate, he was rarely eloquent. His style had none of the charisma, the special quality of vitality, that prevents the public from growing bored with a president's frequent messages to them.

5. The White House staff reflected his own shortcomings. Had he chosen a staff who complemented his own qualities and made up for his deficiencies of experience and personality, he might have done much better. But several of the key positions went to trusted aides from his days as governor of Georgia, and they, too, lacked Washington experience and tended to treat leaders of Congress as relics from a discredited past.

6. Even in terms of the high moral tone that Carter had promised to bring to Washington he had problems with the people around him. His long-time close friend, Office of Management and Budget Director Bert Lance, resigned after a congressional investigation of his practices as a banker in Georgia revealed some questionable financial dealings.[11] Hamilton Jordan was the target of some unfavorable publicity for his behavior in Washington bars. The president's brother Billy caused him almost perpetual embarrassment by his stream of outrageous statements, his alcoholism, his sponsorship of a new (unsuccessful) brand of "Billy" beer, and his receipt of large unsecured loans from the unsavory government of Libya.

Some of these problems were just bad luck: presidents often have trouble with their relatives and friends. But Carter's critics charged that he brought much of the trouble on himself by failing to draw on wide enough ranges of experience in the appointment of his White House staff.

Thus Carter's many admirable personal qualities were submerged beneath his shortcomings and those of his associates, and his achievements were lost in the attention paid to his failures. Later assessments by historians may well upgrade his standing, but he left the office of the presidency without glory and amidst the general verdict that his presidency had been a failure.

RONALD REAGAN, 1981–

Ronald Reagan brought to the White House a paradoxical presidency. Both organizationally and ideologically he seemed to incline toward the tradition of a limited presidency. When asked which twentieth-century presidents he most admired, his answer was: Dwight Eisenhower and Calvin Coolidge. Now Eisenhower, as we have seen, was by no means the slothful president that some of his contemporaries accused him of being, but Coolidge was reputed to have slept ten to twelve hours a night while in the White House and to have had a nap most afternoons. When friends asked him how he remained so untroubled, he said: "By avoiding the big problems."

Reagan, of course, does not believe he can avoid the big problems and does not sleep as long as Coolidge. But neither does he subscribe to the view that the president must work around the clock at a frenzied pace, as did Kennedy, Johnson, Nixon, and Carter. He prefers an approach taken from private industry. "Show me an executive who works long, overtime hours," he has said, "and I'll show you a bad executive." So he believes in delegating responsibility to the White House staff and to cabinet members and committees, keeping for himself only the final decisions on major questions and the setting of the framework of policy.

Furthermore, Reagan's ideological convictions seem to lead in the direction of a presidency of limited powers, because he believes in a *government* of limited powers. Calvin Coolidge proclaimed in the 1920s that "the business of America is business," and for many years Reagan has put forward a similar doctrine. Government, he argues, has become so bloated that it has stifled the creativity and productive capacity of the business system. So the federal government must be curtailed by cutting federal budgets, taxes, and regulations.

This concept brings us to the paradoxes built into the Reagan presidency. For one thing, government has become so large that to bring us back to limited government and thus a limited presidency must first require the unremitting efforts of a very powerful presidency indeed. In fact, rolling back the responsibilities of government to the limits of Coolidge's time is no longer possible and is not part of Reagan's expectations. But even the kind of scaling down intended by Reagan, which goes well beyond the more cautious, consolidating plans of Eisenhower, Nixon, and Ford, must contend with the strong attachment of the electorate to a multitude of governmental activities, the powerfully entrenched interests depending on those activities, and a Congress sensitively attuned to those interests. An easy-going, relaxed kind of presidency can have little chance against such sources of opposition.

Furthermore, Reagan does not take a limited view of America's responsibilities in the world. In the 1920s conservatives took an essentially isolationist view of international affairs. Today conservatives like Reagan believe that without the determined use of American power the Soviet Union will take over the world. The post-Vietnam reluctance to become militarily involved anywhere in the world must be abandoned. A large increase is needed in defense outlays, which involves a large growth in that portion of the federal budget.

So, despite the greater degree of delegation of authority in the Reagan administration than in the administrations of his predecessors, and despite Reagan's refusal to spend his energies on long hours of administrative detail, the early stages of his presidency were marked by the very strong application of presidential power. In particular Reagan made impressive use of the following key presidential prerogatives:

1. Theodore Roosevelt had called the presidency a "bully pulpit," and so it was to Reagan, who applied his skills as a mass communicator through well-crafted, well-delivered speeches.

2. He cultivated the leaders of Congress, including the leaders of the Democratic House of Representatives, showing them the respect that Carter had failed to demonstrate but also challenging them directly when he felt they were obstructing his proposals.

3. He chose an experienced White House staff, headed by Edwin Meese, counselor to the president with cabinet rank, who sat in on most of the president's meetings; James Baker, the White House chief of staff; Michael Deaver, deputy chief of staff; and, from the time he became the president's national security adviser, William Clark. Meese, Deaver, and Clark were long-term associates of the president from his California years. But Baker, who had managed Ford's election campaign in 1976 and George Bush's nomination drive in 1980, was one of several Reagan staff members with extensive national and Washington experience. Because of them, Reagan's lack of experience on the national scene was less of a handicap than it had been for Carter.

4. He used his Executive Office staff to bring pressure to bear throughout his administration to ensure support for his policies. During the first year of his administration a particularly potent role was played by David Stockman, director of the Office of Management and Budget, in forcing draconian cuts on reluctant cabinet members and departmental bureaucrats.

5. The president used his power of appointment to build an administration compatible with his views. All of his top appointees were at least moderately conservative, such as the secretaries of state and defense, and others, including the secretaries of interior and energy, were very conservative. Most of the second- and third-level appointees also fell within the range of moderate to extremely conservative political views.

6. The president's authority as chief executive was applied firmly (his critics said harshly) in his firing of air traffic controllers who went on strike in 1981. Strikes by federal employees are illegal, but other presidents have negotiated and reached agreements with striking federal staffs, notably postal workers. Thus the air traffic controllers' union was stunned when, despite the fact that the great majority of its members joined the strike, the president refused to negotiate, gave orders for the controllers to be fired, and refused to allow them to be rehired despite the consequent reductions in commercial air traffic.

In the early going these methods and tactics, combined with Reagan's affable, appealing personality, made for a very effective presidency indeed. Undaunted by the existence of a Democratic majority in the House of Representatives, he won congressional approval of sweeping spending and tax cuts and of a major boost in defense spending. In the face of widespread predictions that his efforts would fail, the president succeeded in getting Senate approval for the sale of AWACS (airborne warning and control system) to Saudi Arabia largely by personal persuasion of Senate members, one by one and in small groups.

The opinion polls showed Reagan standing quite high in the public's favor. Although there was some early slippage in his ratings, they moved up sharply in the aftermath of his near-assassination and the coolness and good humor he displayed in his brush with death.[12]

Despite these initial successes, questions about the Reagan presidency continued to be raised in the following respects:

1. *The president's delegation of authority.* His administrative system seemed to work well at the outset, and the effectiveness of the government did not falter seriously even while he was in the hospital after the assassination attempt.[13] However, before the first year of the Reagan presidency was over, criticism of the administrative styles of Ed Meese,[14] David Stockman,[15] and other White House aides was being heard, and reports were mounting of bitter disagreements within his administration over both domestic and foreign policy. Critics asked whether these developments were symptoms of a lack of control from the top, and they suggested that a nine-to-five president, who insisted on making only the ultimate decisions, would finish up making none.

2. *The challenge from Congress.* In the next chapter we shall discuss the difficulties that even the most popular president has in getting Congress to go along with his plans once the honeymoon period has worn off. By his second year Reagan was finding that he was not to become an exception to this rule. Congressional resistance, especially to his economic proposals, stiffened, and there was little prospect that his programs would be passed into law without significant modifications.

3. *The problem of sustaining public support.* Though Reagan continued to demonstrate an impressive ability to rally public support for his programs through televised appeals, his rating in the polls began to decline substantially by the fall of 1981 and slumped further as the economy deteriorated during the spring of 1982.

4. *The danger of policy failure.* Ultimately, Reagan's standing with the public, and later his ratings by historians, would depend on the extent to which his policies worked. If his policies brought down inflation, unemployment, and taxes, and if America's standing in the world were strengthened without bringing war closer, then the Reagan presidency would be judged a very successful and a very powerful one. But there has not been a fully effective presidency in many years, and with recession and rising unemployment from the latter part of 1981 and the prospect of enormous budgetary deficits for years to come, the skeptics were reinforced in their belief that a successful American presidency has now become well-nigh impossible.

PROPOSALS TO REFORM THE PRESIDENCY

The account we have given of how presidents from Franklin Roosevelt onward have exercised their authority suggests that, although the presidency is our governmental system's prime source of energy, it has not provided that energy at a steady pace, with reasonable variations. Rather it has lurched between overheating the system, subjecting it to almost intolerable strains, and relapsing into a pace so slow that the needed energy is no longer applied. A number of proposals have therefore been offered to reform the institution: borrowing from the parliamentary system, restructuring the presidency, and screening personal qualities.

BORROWING FROM THE PARLIAMENTARY SYSTEM

There are proposals to adopt certain elements of the parliamentary, or cabinet, system of government. As we saw in chapter 2, this system is not based on the separation of powers and thus avoids the danger of stalemate between the executive and legislative branches. Yet, its protagonists argue, the fact that the executive leaders remain within the legislative branch increases their accountability to the legislature and reduces the possibility of their cutting themselves off in the kinds of defensive isolation that led to the Watergate abuses.

Whatever the merits of this proposition, there is no prospect that our constitutional separation of powers will be abandoned. However, various proposals have been made that draw on features common to parliamentary systems.

A constitutional amendment has been proposed that would follow the parliamentary model by separating the offices of chief of state and head of government. The proponents of this amendment suggest that we have vested too much of the aura of monarchy in the presidency by making the president not only our governmental and political leader but also the embodiment of the myths, rituals, and traditions of the nation as a whole. By assigning the ceremonial functions to a separate chief of state, we would not only relieve our governmental leader of a number of time-consuming burdens but also remove the danger that a president might come to see himself as more than the temporary incumbent of an institution of representative government.

Another adaptation from the parliamentary system would be the establishment of regular question periods in Congress, when the president and members of the cabinet would be compelled to answer for their policies in detail. Currently, the only devices for forcing the president to account for his policies are the State of the Union and other major addresses to Congress, appearances by administration officials (but not the president) before congressional hearings, and press conferences, which are convened only at the president's pleasure and are fairly easily manipulated by a skillful president.

RESTRUCTURING THE PRESIDENCY

Another set of proposals accepts the separation-of-powers model but aims at improving the efficiency of the presidential office and removing any dangerous tendencies it might contain.

Some of these proposals are directed at the White House staff. It has been suggested that the appointment of people to positions of such great importance should be subject to Senate approval, as is the case with cabinet members and other high administration officials. There have also been proposals to streamline the White House staff, thereby keeping it as an instrument of the purposes of the president rather than an expanding bureaucracy with its own agendas.[16]

The role of the cabinet has also been the subject of a number of reform proposals. In the aftermath of Watergate and of Nixon's "palace guard," it was common to urge that the president shift power from the White House staff to the cabinet, and it has become a ritual for incoming presidents to swear to make their cabinets collegial forums in which all major administrative policies will be hammered out. Before Reagan, little ever came of this plan, because most cabinet heads were generally preoccupied with running the affairs of their separate departments. In the Reagan administration, however, cabinet members were brought into consideration of issues that reached beyond their own jurisdictions by being assigned to cabinet committees, each dealing with a broad policy area. Yet even under Reagan the major policy decisions emerged from consultations between the president, his top White House advisers, and perhaps one or two cabinet members, rather than the cabinet.

One more proposal for constraining presidential power is to limit the president to a single six-year term. This proposal would extend the logic of the Twenty-second Amendment, which allows a president no more than two terms, thus denying time to establish one individual's power too thoroughly.

SCREENING PERSONAL QUALITIES

The proposals we have examined for institutional change come slowly at best, says political scientist James Barber,[17] and in the meantime we should put more emphasis on selecting people for the presidency who are free from the personality defects that lead to abuses of power on the one hand or an inability to exercise authority on the other.

Barber uses two criteria for testing candidates' qualifications for the presidency. The first is their view of presidential leadership, ranging from *active* to *passive*. The second is their basic personality structure, ranging from *positive* to *negative*.

In Barber's view the two Roosevelts, Truman, Kennedy, Ford, and Carter were active-positive types: confident, flexible, attacking the nation's problems with energy and zest. Eisenhower was a passive-positive type, a secure, well-adjusted personality who, however, did not enjoy the political hurly-burly and did not seek to use presidential power aggressively. Before Reagan's election he, too, was seen by Barber as likely to be a passive-positive president, because he was "a booster, an optimist, a conveyor of hopefulness . . . (yet) passive in the sense that he has a long record of saving his energies, of not working too hard."[18]

Both Johnson and Nixon were the worst possible combination: active-negative types, combining an assertive view of presidential power with a conviction that people did not like or accept them personally.

So we should set up mechanisms, says Barber, for selecting out the potential active-negative types before they get their party's nomination. Candidates should be screened by a panel of experts drawn from psychology and psychiatry, political science, journalism, and other appropriate fields. The panel would have no power beyond presenting its findings to the public. It would not presume to make the final selection and would almost certainly not arrive at unanimous conclusions. But it could reasonably hope to issue effective warnings against those people whose personality structures render them profoundly unfit to be president.

FIVE PERSPECTIVES ON THE PRESIDENCY

THE LIBERALS

Historically, the liberals have been the great champions of presidential power. The presidency seemed the most likely institution for achieving far-reaching economic and social change. This was the one office elected by the people as a whole and equipped with the authority to move decisively.

Liberals, as devout believers in the free society, might have worried about the potential threat to our liberties in the enormous growth of presidential responsibilities, but they dismissed such fears as alarmist. After all, there were those restraints on presidential power mentioned earlier, limits imposed by the Constitution, political practice, and so on. Wherever the president looked, there were limits on this power. Those presidents who worked vigorously to use their "power to persuade" were successful; those presidents who had not were failing to carry out their responsibilities under the Constitution. This liberal fondness for the presidency was shaken for a while by the Johnson and Nixon administrations.

For his first two years in the presidency Lyndon Johnson surprised and delighted the liberals. They had known him as a southerner with a background as a power broker in the Senate and with a scornful attitude toward liberal reformers. They were enthusiastic when he used all the powers of his office to produce the flood of Great Society legislation.

This early assessment was soon revised. Increasingly liberals turned against Johnson, finding his treatment of the press and his staff overbearing and boorish, his style devious and manipulative, and his ethical standards dubious.

Yet, if Johnson's problems had been solely matters of style and personality, most liberals might have found excuses for him, as they did during his first year or so in office. Their response was changed by Johnson's foreign policy, especially in Southeast Asia. As the Vietnam War escalated, so did the liberals' bitterness, and they began to use language that in the past had belonged to conservatives.

The president's power, they proclaimed, had grown dangerously, and with a passive Congress passing the Tonkin Gulf resolution, discussed earlier, there were no apparent checks on that power. Previously they had been impatient with the checks and balances of the constitutional system. Now they began to ask: What have we done? Are these actions the fruits of the philosophy we have expounded? How do we control the Frankenstein's monster we have created? So the repudiation of the Lyndon Johnson policies had forced a reappraisal of the liberal view of the presidency itself.

The Nixon presidency forced the liberals to intensify their reappraisal. In Watergate they found confirmation of all the charges they had made against Nixon since he had first appeared on the political scene. They had always found Nixon ruthless, unprincipled, and neurotic. So they were not surprised when he and the people around him endorsed wiretapping, breaking and entering, an enemies list, misuse of election funds, and cover-ups of these activities, followed by persistent lying about the activities and the cover-ups.

But if the liberals were not surprised, they had to be dismayed by the ways in which the presidential powers they had admired had now been used, in the name of national security, to put the president and his men above the proprieties, above accountability, and above the law.

Fortunately the worst did not happen. The danger of a police state was checked. Those individuals who had ruthlessly abused power were indicted and sent to prison—all but the chief perpetrator, the president himself.

However, the liberals saw these convictions as no cause for complacency. America had been lucky. If the burglars had not been bunglers, if they had not taped a door open in such a way as to lead to its discovery by a security guard, they might not have been caught. Or, if the federal judge in the break-in case had not been John Sirica, the tough and persistent search for the truth might not have been made. Or, if the *Washington Post* had assigned its regular political writers to the case, rather than two young men eager to make their reputations and able to work around the clock, the story might not have been so diligently pursued. Or, if Nixon had not had his conversations taped, there would not have been enough hard evidence to ensure his ouster. Or, if he had ordered the tapes destroyed as soon as their existence came to light, claiming the needs of national security, he could probably have ridden out the storm. The country was saved, then, by accidents and miscalculations. Furthermore, the corruption of presidential power had not started with Nixon. We had had two presidents in a row acting furtively and deviously, treating their opponents as conspirators, and inflicting terrible damage on the political system.

So the liberals joined the post-Watergate discussion about ways of limiting the powers of the presidency. But their flirtation with proposals that would weaken the office did not last long after the downfall of Nixon. With Gerald Ford in the White House the liberals were again complaining that the president, instead of applying the powers of his office to advance beneficial legislation, was acting as a mere obstructionist, a wielder of vetoes over the initiatives of Congress.

Still, liberals could hardly expect otherwise of a rather conservative Republican president. Jimmy Carter aroused their deeper resentment. This president, unlike Ford, had large majorities of his own party in control of both houses of Congress. Yet he was unable to use the wide-ranging powers of the presidency to place on the statute books any of the programs that liberals were promoting. It is true that he offered to Congress several items that had languished for years on the liberals' list: a consumer protection agency, labor law reform, and diluted programs of welfare reform and health insurance. But Carter lacked the ability, and perhaps the conviction, needed to put these programs through Congress. In fact, in his timidity and his obsession with a balanced budget he had increasingly turned against his party's natural labor, minority, and liberal constituencies. He was a failure as president, said the liberals, because he did not understand the presidency or how to put its power to work on behalf of the people.

As a result it was left to Ronald Reagan to demonstrate the uses of presidential power. James Barber might define Reagan as a "passive-positive" president, but it turned out that Reagan had an instinct for the ways the presidency could be used to produce change. It was change in the wrong direction for the liberals, but they hoped the next Democratic president would learn from Reagan's experience and use some of his techniques to accomplish a different kind of change.

Still, if the liberals do not want the next Democrat in the White House to be another Jimmy Carter, neither do they want him to be a Lyndon Johnson. How are both extremes to be avoided?

The liberals' answer is not to weaken the presidency. Their preferred solution is to borrow at least some of the features of the parliamentary system. The liberals have always been fascinated by the way the British and Canadian models assign enough power to generate fast and effective action, yet provide the constraints necessary to a democracy.

But even without that kind of constitutional shift the liberals believe it is possible to have a strong presidency that is not a threat to our liberties if we undertake the reforms discussed earlier in this book: revitalizing the two-party system, so that the president sees himself as the leader of a responsible party, not as an autonomous, uncontrolled center of power; reforming the nomination system, so that the presidency is less likely to fall into the hands of a naive, inexperienced outsider like Carter; encouraging the development of an informed and active electorate; imposing more effective controls on special interests; and reducing the power of money in politics. These reforms, say the liberals, are the real checks on presidential power, the best assurances of an open presidency, and the only real guarantees against future Vietnams and Watergates.

THE CONSERVATIVES

Historically, the conservative view of the presidency favored a strictly limited role for the office. A president's constituency, they pointed out, is the mass national electorate, so he is much too likely to respond to demands to limit property rights and interfere with business. Hence the traditional cry of conservatives has been to check the power of the president by bolstering the authority of Congress and by keeping more of the action at the state and local level rather than in Washington, the president's domain. They have also preferred the restrained leadership style and orderly structure of an Eisenhower to the more aggressive and freewheeling approach of a Kennedy or a Johnson.

However, this conservative affinity for a modest presidency ran up against the difficulty we have already noted in our discussion of the paradox of the Reagan presidency: since Franklin Roosevelt's time the federal government's intervention in the economy has been so extensive that it will require sustained, herculean efforts to restore the situation to a level acceptable to conservatives. This goal cannot be accomplished without a period of vigorous presidential leadership.

As we saw in chapter 4, conservatives believe that the turnabout might have begun after Richard Nixon's landslide reelection in 1972. Indeed, it was his stated intention to inaugurate a new era in American politics. Unfortunately, Nixon threw away his golden opportunity in the Watergate disaster.

Conservatives do not accept all the liberal criticisms of Nixon. They supported his Cambodian intervention and complained only that he did not follow it up aggressively enough. They were impressed by Nixon's reminder that, when he set up the special machinery that led to Watergate, he was acting to deal with serious problems of domestic and international security. In a statement made on May 23, 1973, Nixon warned the nation:

> In the spring and summer of 1970, another security problem reached critical proportions. In March a wave of bombing and explosions struck college campuses and cities. There were 400 bomb threats in one 24-hour period in New York City. Rioting and violence on college campuses reached a new peak after the Cambodian operation and the tragedies at Kent State and Jackson State. The 1969–70 school year brought nearly 1800 campus demonstrations and nearly 250 cases of arson on campus. Many colleges closed. Gun battles between guerrilla-style groups and police were taking place. Some of the disruptive activities were receiving foreign support.

Further, the illegal break-in of the psychiatrist's office should be seen in light of the fact that Daniel Ellsberg, whose file was the object of the search, had illegally removed a massive, secret study of the history of decision making in the Vietnam War. This action, said the president, had breached the confidentiality of our entire defense system and jeopardized delicate negotiations on a number of fronts.

Furthermore, the conservatives argued, Watergate was nothing new. Nixon differed from previous presidents not in that he sanctioned illegal acts but in that he was caught.

During the Kennedy administration the FBI, acting on orders from the White House, had bugged the telephones of civil rights leader Martin Luther King and collected a dossier on his sex life—in order, it was said, to check on the possibility of his being mixed up with subversive, left-wing elements. Also during the Kennedy era the CIA had prepared assassination plots against Cuban Premier Fidel Castro and other foreign leaders. There was documentation of White House phone calls between President Kennedy and Judith Exner, with whom the president was apparently having an affair. In itself this situation might not have been viewed as much worse than imprudent. But Exner had also been the mistress of a leader of organized crime, with whom she was still in touch, and she had played a part in one of the abortive efforts to kill Castro in which the CIA had worked with leaders of the syndicate. (See chapter 15.)

As for Lyndon Johnson, he had enjoyed salacious tidbits about the sex lives of various politicians fed to him by FBI Director J. Edgar Hoover from the agency's files, and there was speculation that Johnson had also used the Internal Revenue Service to harass his political opponents. So the problem of the corruption of presidential power did not begin with Nixon or even with Johnson.

Just the same, conservatives had their own bitter criticisms of Nixon. For one thing, even if his instincts were conservative he had always been an opportunist ready to impose wage and price controls or sell out Taiwan in favor of communist China if these moves were to his political advantage. It was natural that he would surround himself with pragmatic technicians like Haldeman and Ehrlichman, who put power before principle and public relations before politics.

Then, said the conservatives, Nixon's personality was unsuited to leadership under pressure. His belief that he was surrounded by enemies had a foundation in fact. Entrenched in Congress, in the federal bureaucracies, and in the media were legions of people hostile to his programs. But a leader must be able to deal with hostility, and temperamentally Nixon was unable to do so. Increasingly he trusted none but his palace guard, lying not only to the people at large but even to some of his most devoted supporters. Questioned closely by conservatives in Congress as to whether he was holding anything back, he repeatedly reassured them he was not, right up to the surrender of the "smoking gun" tape. As revelation followed revelation, his supporters' credibility-was damaged almost as much as his own because he made them look like fools. This situation did great harm to the cause of conservatism.

Finally, he was a bungler. Entangled by incompetents, he lacked the ability to extricate himself. Had he, at the outset, admitted White House involvement in the Watergate break-in, denied personal knowledge, and fired a few staff members, he would have suffered only a minor setback. Or, had he ordered the tapes destroyed, there would have been a great furor but he would have survived. He lacked the judgment to see that, once the cover-up was started and as long as the tapes existed, executive privilege could not finally protect him. Thus Richard Nixon threw away his opportunity to undo the damage caused by forty years of liberalism.

Gerald Ford was not the man to restore the hopes of the conservatives. Although he possessed solid, midwestern, Republican credentials, he was a politician of the old school. His choice of Nelson Rockefeller as his vice-president made clear his dependence on the eastern establishment; he lacked a clear understanding of conservative doctrine; and, although he was an amiable enough man, he did not have the force of personality to overcome the legacy of Watergate and a Democratic Congress.

With Ronald Reagan in the White House the conservatives saw their prospects born again. They were far from complacent. They were unhappy that he had selected George Bush as his running mate. They did not like his appointment of Bush's man, James Baker, as a key White House aide, or of Alexander Haig, a former associate of Kissinger, as secretary of state, or of a number of other people whose conservative credentials were in question. Most conservatives were also deeply concerned about the huge budget deficits that Reagan was accepting. Further, they worried that he would allow his policies to be diluted in the face of the inevitable resistances from Congress, the bureaucracies, and organized interests. Still, no president since the 1920s had been as sympathetic to the conservatives' views as Ronald Reagan, and they urged him on to wield the power of his office ever more aggressively.

The ultimate purpose of this aggressive use of power, in their view, was to reduce the scope of the federal government and thus scale down the presidency from the inflated stature derived from the Franklin Roosevelt era. But to reach that goal it would first be necessary to take on the vigor and mass appeal that Roosevelt had brought to the office.

THE RADICAL LEFT

Radical groups on both left and right see the president as little more than a servant of a small group of men who rule America. In the eyes of the left, the liberals' dismay at the abuses of presidential power is absurd. The left has never accepted the position that their purposes can be achieved by an expanding presidency. For one thing, it is inconceivable to them that an institution so remote from the control of the people, operating through vast bureaucracies that render popular participation in executive decisions impossible, can serve the interests of the people. Nixon's isolated decision making was the ultimate expression of the extent to which power has been removed from the people at large.

Second, the presidency to them is but one element in a ruling elite and can only produce the policies the ruling elite want. They note that the men appointed by presidents to key positions of power fit perfectly the characteristics set forth in power elite theory. Eisenhower's secretary of defense was Charles Wilson of General Motors, and Johnson's was Robert McNamara of Ford. A succession of investment bankers occupied the post of secretary of the treasury. H.R. Haldeman and several other members of the White House staff came from big advertising and public relations agencies, a very appropriate background for Nixon's purposes. The top foreign policy jobs in the State Department and the White House went to corporate lawyers (John Foster Dulles and William Rogers), foundation and Harvard or M.I.T. men (McGeorge Bundy, Walt Rostow, and Henry Kissinger), a general, Alexander Haig, and a business executive (George Shultz, president of the giant Bechtel corporation, who succeeded Haig and joined another former Bechtel executive, defense secretary Caspar Weinberger.)

Moreover, since World War II a succession of presidents had called on certain types of men from outside their administrations for advice and help in times of crisis, and these men were typically members of the ruling elite. A perfect example was the ever-present corporate lawyer John McCloy. At the time of the 1962 Cuban missile crisis the *New York Times* reported: "In Frankfort John J. McCloy was about to go into a big private business conference when he got a call from President Kennedy. He told the waiting businessmen, 'Sorry, boys, I hate to drop names, but the President needs me.' He took the next plane home."[19] Once home, he sat at Adlai Stevenson's elbow at the United Nations while crucial negotiations were conducted.

McCloy served both Democratic and Republican presidents. Other advisers changed with the party of the administration, but the changes were never very significant. Donald Kendall, chairman of the board of Pepsi-Cola, was a Nixon confidant; Nixon had gotten to know him when Pepsi had been one of the clients of the corporate law firm that Nixon joined while awaiting his second run for the presidency. Under Jimmy Carter Pepsi-Cola was out and Coca-Cola was in, because Atlanta is the Coca-Cola headquarters, and J. Paul Astin, the company's board chairman, acted as an unofficial emissary abroad for the Carter administration.

With the exception of Kennedy, no president from Harry Truman on came from a typical ruling elite, upper-class background; on the contrary,

their origins were quite humble. But this fact does not in itself destroy the left's analysis of the presidency. The power elite, says the radical left, knows how to co-opt able people from lesser classes and make them into members of the ruling class. Thus Eisenhower loved to consort with businessmen. So did Nixon, whose political career was launched with the help of a special fund subscribed to by realtors, manufacturers, and oil and gas interests;[20] whose partnership in a New York law firm enabled him to live in a luxurious Fifth Avenue apartment and join exclusive clubs; and whose closest friends during his presidency, Bebe Rebozo and Robert Abplanalp, were wealthy men who helped Nixon purchase the Western White House in San Clemente.

Ronald Reagan had been surrounded throughout his political life by a coterie of wealthy businessmen, mostly from California. Once in the White House his continued affiliation with them was made blatantly clear by their actually being assigned space in the Executive Office Building adjoining the White House, which they gave up when Reagan's staff decided their presence was becoming an embarrassment. Undaunted, some of them formed a new group dedicated to raising $50,000 apiece from major corporations to finance a nationwide fund-raising affair to build support for Reagan's programs. Again the top White House staff put a stop to their efforts when word spread that the pressure they were applying to business firms was reminiscent of the heavy-handed fund raising by CRP in 1972.

If the devotion of Reagan and Nixon to businessmen and business values took particularly crude forms, it was not, in the eyes of the left, fundamentally different from the support of the business system by Democratic presidents. Roosevelt's New Deal interfered with business. Truman vented his spleen on the monied interests. Kennedy raged against U.S. Steel when it raised its prices despite a promise to him. Carter made political capital out of attacks on the big oil companies. But in the final analysis Democrats in the White House posed no threat to capitalism. On the contrary, from the New Deal on, the kind of government intervention they championed was the necessary condition for the survival of capitalism. Some capitalists might fight the measures that were saving their system, but the corporate chiefs of the ruling elite knew better.

THE RADICAL RIGHT

To the radical right, the presidency is an office that is almost bound to serve undesirable ends. "Those who control the President indirectly gain control of the whole country," said one right-wing author.[21] Woodrow Wilson was controlled by Colonel House, who worked with Wall Street to get us into World War I and bankroll the Bolshevik Revolution of 1917. Nelson Rockefeller controlled Richard Nixon. He was then chosen by Ford as his vice-president and was successful in placing his men in key positions on Ford's White House staff. Although conservatives forced Rockefeller off the 1976 Republican ticket, he continued to be a dominant force behind the scenes until his death in 1979.

Foreign policy under Nixon and Ford was in the hands of Henry Kissinger, who was a Rockefeller man *and* a Harvard man, the most undesirable combination possible from the perspective of the right.

The proof of the dominance of the Rockefellers and the Kissingers was in the policies themselves. Nixon openly admitted that he was a Keynesian, a disciple of the British economist John Maynard Keynes, who was the prophet of deficit spending, the socialist New Deal, and the welfare state. Under Nixon the national debt rose, inflation ran rampant, and the dollar depreciated abroad.

What was happening in America was merely part of the preparation for a world federation. As Robert Welch explained it in a John Birch Society newsletter in 1971, Nixon (who had publicly criticized the society for several years) was using the presidency as a stepping-stone to becoming ruler of the world. He could only accomplish this goal with the approval and even the support of the communist powers. Welch came to this conclusion as a result of Nixon's announced trip to China,

his monetary policy, and his appointments of "left-wingers" to his administration.

With Jimmy Carter the policy of handing America over to our enemies continued at an even faster pace, which was hardly surprising, because Carter, Vice-President Walter Mondale, Treasury Secretary Michael Blumenthal, and other members of the administration had all been members of the Trilateral Commission, established and funded by David Rockefeller of Chase Manhattan Bank to ensure his dominance of the economic policies of the United States, Western Europe, and Japan. The executive director of the commission was Carter's national security aide, Zbigniew Brzezinski. So Nelson Rockefeller's man, Kissinger, had given way to David Rockefeller's protégé, Brzezinski.

Clearly it has made little difference whether the White House is occupied by Republicans or Democrats. The left-wing establishment has continued its rule.

Could this situation be changed by Ronald Reagan? Some members of the radical right hoped that it might and worked for his election. But there were grave doubts on the right that anyone who had come to the highest office by the usual political mechanisms, and who must try to get his programs approved through those mechanisms, could prevail against the powerful forces that controlled America for so long.

THE CENTRISTS

Centrist scholars have been among the great admirers of the presidency. They have seen the growth of the responsibilities and powers of the office as a demonstration of the flexibility of the constitutional system established by the Founding Fathers, allowing every generation to deal with contemporary problems without destroying the original framework.

During the Johnson and Nixon presidencies, however, centrists grew uncomfortable. Although they were attached to the presidency as an institution, they believed in a balance between the different branches of government. For a while it seemed that the enlargement of presidential power was throwing the system out of balance.

The mounting evidence of improper and illegal conduct in the Nixon presidency was acutely unsettling to the centrists. The precedents in the Kennedy and Johnson periods were distressing, too, but they provided no justification for the Nixon abuses, which were far more systematic and pervasive than the abuses of his predecessors.

The fate of the two presidents who had gone beyond reasonable bounds in their use of presidential power was immensely reassuring. Vietnam, which had driven Lyndon Johnson to mishandle power, destroyed his power. The inability to overcome the resistance of a small country, and opposition in the Congress and in the country, clearly demonstrated the limits on presidential power and forced his withdrawal from politics.

As for Watergate, nothing could show more plainly that the plan of the Founding Fathers was as effective and relevant as ever. The Congress, the courts, the free press, and public opinion all came into play to check the undoubted excesses of presidential power.

Liberals argued that the outcome was in large part the result of luck. But to centrists it was the system itself that had prevailed. The president and the men around him had overreached themselves in so many directions that somewhere along the line it was inevitable that a judge, a reporter, or a congressional committee would sound the alarm. Without the lucky breaks, it might have taken a little longer. But in the American system there are too many people in too many places with a vested interest in challenging the White House to allow power to get completely out of hand.

Centrists were not satisfied with Carter's conduct of the presidency. Although they gave him more credit for his achievements than did the liberals and conservatives, they found Carter's inability to lead the public and Congress a fatal flaw. But the flaw, they believed, was primarily in Carter himself, not in the system. Under the American system no president can or should be completely dominant. Yet unless the president knows how to apply the arts of leadership the essential balance of the system will be upset, and the other tendencies of the constitutional structure will produce drift and inertia.

It was left to Ronald Reagan to give a convincing demonstration in the first year of his presidency of the leadership potential of his office and to provide a healthy corrective to the hesitancy of the Carter era. Though centrists had strong reservations about some of Reagan's policies, especially in the economic sphere, they could look to Congress to set limits to the damage that might be caused if the president's policies were put into effect without modification.

The imperatives of office. Centrists do not accept the accusations from the radicals of left and right that the presidency is merely a captive of outside groups. No matter who has helped a president with campaign money and other kinds of support, he has to answer to two imperatives. The first imperative is the electorate, and there is no group or business that can offer a president a greater reward than reelection to the presidency. So presidents repeatedly disappoint influential supporters by acting expediently—that is, in response to the wishes of the people at large.

The second imperative is the institution of the presidency itself. No matter what their class, background, or socioeconomic affiliations, presidents become deeply aware of the history and obligations of the office. They think of presidents who came before them, and they want to measure up to the best of them. They are concerned with the verdict of history.

The need for a strong presidency. Some reforms are needed within the presidency, say the centrists, to make the White House a more efficiently organized center for getting the nation's business done. But we do not need to incorporate any of the elements of the parliamentary system into our own. Within our existing constitutional structure we can provide for strong presidential leadership that ensures that crucial decisions will be made in a timely fashion.

But it is not only a strong presidency that the

times require. We also need a strong Congress, a strong Supreme Court, and a strong system of state and local governments, as well as a potent public opinion, press, and interest group system. We must maintain the kind of balance that emerges not from weakness on all sides, but from the interplay of strong forces, sometimes cooperating, sometimes competing with each other.

CONCLUSION

We have seen in this chapter that until the mid-1960s the office of the presidency had become enveloped in a mystique that carried it beyond human scope. It was not only the courtiers in the White House who invested their presidents with the mysteries and rights of monarchs. The scholars who wrote the college textbooks extolled the presidency in exalted terms. Theodore White, who wrote chronicles of each presidential election from 1960 to 1972, described Kennedy and Nixon as if they had become mythic figures in some great poetic drama.

The Johnson and Nixon experiences produced a period of debunking the presidency. It was time, said presidential scholar Thomas Cronin, to deflate our rhetoric and see the presidency for what it is: a human institution, occupied by fallible men. Great responsibility has gravitated there, but the power of the office is not unlimited. It is absurd to burden this single office with all the hopes and aspirations of the entire society.[22]

It is now clear, however, that despite the deflation and debunking that have occurred, the presidency will remain an institution of substantial power no matter who occupies the office. For one thing, there is little prospect that we will separate the functions of chief of state and head of government. The president will continue to be our ceremonial leader, and the media will continue to lavish attention on every move of the president and the president's family, as though they were a kind of royal family. This situation occurred even with the unpretentious Jerry Ford. When Jimmy Carter chose to walk the inaugural parade route with his family rather than ride in the presidential limousine, the media went into paroxysms of delight, as though he were a king who was deigning to walk. Ronald Reagan and his wife, Nancy, restored the emphasis on the ceremonial and symbolic aspects of the office and of the White House.

The governmental and political responsibilities of the president cannot help but confer on that individual great power. Some presidents, like the Roosevelts, Kennedy, and Johnson, will exercise their authority with enthusiasm and work constantly to overcome the constraints that confront them. Others, like Eisenhower, will adopt a more subdued role. But no incumbent of the White House can any longer escape the reality that the presidency is easily the most potent source of power in American government.

Vietnam and Watergate are constant reminders to us of the dangers inherent in this concentration of power at the center. Perhaps the fact that we have experienced Vietnam and Watergate will serve to protect us against any more such abuses of presidential power. However, the evidence discussed in this chapter provides us with no firm assurance on this point.

NOTES AND REFERENCES

1. Edward S. Corwin, *The President: Office and Powers*, 3rd ed. (New York: New York University Press, 1948), p. 38.
2. For this reason alone, the negotiations between Ford and Reagan at the Republican convention in 1980, which would have made Ford a vice-president with unprecedented delegated authority, could not succeed.
3. *Youngstown Sheet and Tube Co.* v. *Sawyer* (1952). Truman had acted under his inherent power as chief executive and commander-in-chief, but the Court held that the president did not have power to seize private property without congressional authorization. However, in *United States* v. *Curtis-Wright Export Corp.* (1936), the Court had upheld the validity of a joint resolution of Congress that had delegated broad powers to President Roosevelt to ban arms shipments to foreign belligerents. Rarely, in fact, has the Court interfered with a president's actions in foreign affairs. Thus in 1981 the Supreme Court upheld President Carter's agreement with the government of Iran, which led to the release of the American hostages, even though the agreement affected the holdings of a number of American banks and companies.
4. As we shall see in chapter 10, some of President Franklin Roosevelt's key New Deal legislation was vetoed by the Supreme Court, and he was able to proceed with his program only after a bitter confrontation with the Court.
5. These documents were published by *The New York Times*, and later in book form, as the "Pentagon papers." See Neil Sheehan, Hedrick Smith, E. W. Kenworthy, and Fox Butterfield, *The Pentagon Papers* (New York: Bantam Books, 1971).
6. In July 1970 the president had given his approval to the "Huston plan" (named after its chairperson, Tom Huston) for extensive domestic intelligence operations, including breaking and entering premises without warrants. The plan was drawn up by a committee representing the FBI, the CIA, the Defense Intelligence Unit, and the National Security Agency, and it was aborted only by the disapproval of FBI Director J. Edgar Hoover, who saw in the plan a threat to the authority of his agency. However, the thinking that went into the Huston plan found expression in the formation of the plumbers' unit.
7. See Carl Bernstein and Bob Woodward, *All the President's Men* (New York: Warner Books, 1975).
8. Nixon ordered Cox to stop the court action. Cox refused. Nixon ordered Attorney General Elliot Richardson to fire Cox. Richardson resigned rather than do so. Assistant Attorney General William Ruckelshaus supported Richardson's position and was fired. So Nixon had to turn to the third-ranking man in the Justice Department to get the job done. These events occurred on Saturday, October 20, 1973, and were dubbed the "Saturday night massacre."
9. The first two articles passed by large margins, with several Republicans joining the Democrats in voting against the president. Two other articles, one charging the president with invading Cambodia illegally, the other with tax evasion (Nixon's tax accountant had altered the dates on a contribution of Nixon's vice-presidential papers to the National Archives to make them eligible for a huge tax deduction), were defeated.
10. *United States* v. *Nixon* (1974).
11. Lance was later indicted on charges of banking malpractice but was eventually acquitted.
12. Reagan's approval rating in various polls reached almost 70 percent in May, 1981, but slipped to the mid-fifties by the fall of 1981, and into the upper forties by the spring of 1982. These levels were generally slightly below those for Jimmy Carter during the first part of his presidency, and well below the levels for presidents Kennedy and Johnson.
13. However, there was a highly publicized conflict over who was in charge immediately after the shooting. Secretary of State Haig appeared on television to explain that he was in charge in the White House until the vice-president got back into town, a claim that was strongly resented by the top White House staff and by Secretary of Defense Weinberger.

14. Meese was criticized on two counts. First, it was said that he had taken on too much of the president's authority, a charge given wide currency in 1981 when he allowed several hours to elapse before awakening the president to tell him that U.S. planes had shot down two Libyan fighter planes off the coast of Libya. Second, he was criticized for being away from the White House too much of the time on speaking tours.

15. Stockman touched off a furor when a series of interviews he gave led to an extremely revealing article on his views on the Reagan economic program in the *Atlantic* (December 1981, pp. 27–54). The article quoted Stockman as knowing that some of the budgetary figures used by the administration were pure guesswork and as having little faith in the projections of some of the "supply side" economists who were advising the president. (See chapter 12.) The article cost Stockman much of his credibility in dealing with Congress and with cabinet secretaries.

16. See Don Price and Rocco Siciliano, "A Presidency for the 80s," November 1980, report submitted to the Reagan transition team.

17. James David Barber, *The Presidential Character: Predicting Performance in the White House*, 2nd ed. (Englewood Cliffs, N.J.: Prentice-Hall, 1977).

18. James David Barber, "Carter and Reagan: Clues to Their Character," *U.S. News and World Report*, 27 October 1980, p. 30. "Reagan," said Barber, "is a little bit frightened by power and likes to delegate it. If you delegate to the right people, that's fine, but if you don't delegate to the right people, that's not so fine."

19. *New York Times*, 3 November 1962.

20. The uncovering of the Dana Smith fund would have cost Nixon his spot on the Eisenhower ticket in 1952 but for his brilliantly contrived plea on television, famous for its references to his little dog Checkers and his wife's "Republican cloth coat."

21. Gary Allen, *None Dare Call It Conspiracy* (Rossmoor, Calif.: Concord Press, 1971), p. 34.

22. Thomas E. Cronin, *The State of the Presidency*, 2nd ed. (Boston: Little, Brown, 1975).

chapter eight

THE CONGRESS: OBSTACLE COURSE OR BALANCE WHEEL?

o most of the Founding Fathers, Congress was to be the preeminent institution under their new Constitution. They would be surprised, and probably distressed, at the extent to which the balance of power has tilted over the years toward the White House.

Nonetheless, their plan has not been entirely overruled. Congress is still very much a force to be reckoned with by any president. In fact, the Congress of the United States may well be the most powerful legislature in the world today.

THE ROLES OF CONGRESS

Consider the array of congressional functions and responsibilities:

1. *Legislation*. The Constitution, in Article I, declares Congress to be the law-making, or legislative, branch of government, with the power to make laws, establish and maintain armed forces, raise and spend money, and control commerce between the states, as well as anything else "necessary and proper" to carrying out its other powers.

2. *Representation*. Congress speaks for the people in the districts and the states, and also in relation to the organizations to which they belong. In their representative capacity, members of Congress must not only take account of constituency views in how they vote in Congress, but must also provide a variety of services to constituents in their dealings with the federal government.

3. *Financing government*. The president, the federal bureaucracies, and to an increasing extent state and local governments must await the actions of Congress in raising money and in appropriating funds for particular programs and projects. With a federal budget approaching three-quarters of a trillion dollars in 1982, Congress' power of the purse is a formidable power indeed.

4. *Administrative oversight.* Congress follows up its enactment of general laws with a continuous process of overseeing the implementation of the laws by federal agencies. It performs this function by a variety of means, including special oversight hearings conducted by its various committees and periodic review of the granting of funds to the agencies.

5. *Informing the public.* Congress provides a national forum for educating the electorate on the issues facing the nation. It performs this function on the floor and in committees by its debates, which are covered in the press and, in the case of the House since 1979, on television. Congressional committee hearings, sometimes televised in prime time, present an array of expert witnesses on the issues, sometimes fiercely cross-examined by committee members. Moreover, Congress has opened up to public awareness a whole range of problems through special investigating committees[1] such as committees on organized crime (Senator Estes Kefauver of Tennessee), communism (Senator Joseph McCarthy of Wisconsin), malnutrition (Senator George McGovern of South Dakota), Watergate (Senator Sam Ervin of North Carolina), and the CIA (Senator Frank Church of Idaho).

6. *Checking and balancing power.* Under the constitutional structure Congress is assigned a crucial role in preventing too much power from becoming concentrated in any one location. Particularly, congressional power provides a balance wheel to control presidential power. The president must obtain the approval of the Senate for top appointments and for any treaties entered into with other countries. No money may be spent without specific congressional appropriation. The president may veto a congressional bill, but that veto can be overridden by a two-thirds vote of both houses of Congress.[2]

Of course, the checks and balances were not directed only at controlling the power of the executive. The potential for excessive legislative power was also feared by the Framers, and so they divided Congress within itself, requiring that the laws be ratified by two separate chambers and that each of these chambers have different terms of office and different constituencies.

Taken together these functions and responsibilities provide Congress with a formidable degree of authority. Whether this system is good or bad is a question for debate among our perspectives. But before we reach the debate we must set forth the major characteristics of the institution: its members, its constituencies, its organizational and leadership structure, and its procedures.

THE MEMBERS OF CONGRESS

As is clear from table 8-1, Congress is made up of people from a great diversity of professional, business, religious, racial, and ethnic backgrounds. This diversity is greater in the House than in the Senate, and it has increased over the years: the proportion of lawyers is lower than it used to be, the number of minorities and women has grown, and the influx of young members, especially since the mid-1970s, has changed the perception of Congress as an old man's institution.

Even so, table 8-1 also tells us that the membership of Congress is far from being a precise cross section of the American electorate. The typical member of Congress is a white, male, Protestant lawyer or businessman, in his early fifties.

TABLE 8-1 Profile of the 97th Congress (1981–1982)

House		Senate	
Party			
Democrats	243	Republicans	53
Republicans	192	Democrats	46
		Independent	1
Sex			
Men	416	Men	98
Women	19	Women	2
Religion			
Protestants	270	Protestants	72
Roman Catholics	118	Roman Catholics	16
Jews	27	Jews	6
Others	20	Others	6
Profession			
Lawyers	186	Lawyers	57
Businesspeople	117	Businesspeople	23
Educators	42	Educators	5
Public officials	29	Farmers, ranchers	5
Farmers, ranchers	20	Journalists	2
Journalists	16	Astronauts	2
Congressional aides	8	Pro athlete	1
Dentists, doctors	3	Veterinarian	1
Clergymen	3	Airline pilot	1
Others	11	Navy admiral	1
		Judge	1
		Public official	1
Race			
Caucasians	410	Caucasians	97
Blacks	17	Orientals	3
Hispanics	5		
Orientals	2		
Polynesian	1		
Age (median)			
	52.4		54.1

CONGRESS AND ITS CONSTITUENCIES

One of Congress' jobs is to represent the people, which it does in relation to two kinds of constituencies: geographic and organized interests.

GEOGRAPHIC CONSTITUENCIES

As we have noted, the Framers of the Constitution decided on a two-house legislature as an element in their structure of checks and balances. All legislation would have to pass through both chambers, and each was to be elected for a different term by different constituencies.

FROM *THE HERBLOCK GALLERY* (SIMON & SCHUSTER, 1968)
"Tell the peasants we find their appeals amusing."

The House of Representatives.   The House, reelected every two years, was to be the popularly elected chamber—in fact, it was the only institution in the original design whose members would be directly elected by the people.

Implicit in this system was the democratic principle of equal representation for each voter. Only in recent years, however, has this principle been fully applied, because in the past there were gross inequities in the populations of congressional districts. The boundary lines between districts are determined by state legislatures and redrawn after the census every ten years; and the rurally dominated legislatures often ignored the surge of population away from the small towns and farms toward the cities, continuing to give small numbers of rural people the same representation in Congress as large numbers of urban and suburban dwellers. Gradually, however, the big population centers gained ground in Congress, and their position improved still further in 1964 with the Supreme Court's decision in *Wesberry* v. *Sanders* that wide disparities in populations of congressional districts were unconstitutional. Subsequently the states redrew their boundary lines under persistent prodding from the Supreme Court, and since the 1960s there has been a decline in congressional representation of predominately rural areas and a corresponding increase in the representation of suburban districts.

Equality of population, of course, does not mean equality of size, because the less populated rural districts are necessarily spread over larger areas than the urban districts. Moreover, as long as redistricting is decided by vote of state legislatures, it is not possible to eliminate completely the practice of *gerrymandering*—the process by which congressional boundary lines are manipulated to protect the seats of incumbents or to gain an advantage for the majority party in the legislature.

One further respect in which the principle of equal representation in the House is abridged is the constitutional requirement that each state be guaranteed a minimum of one representative. Alaska, Delaware, Nevada, Vermont, and Wyoming each have only one member in the House.

The distribution of the 435 House seats in effect from January 1983 is indicated in figure 8-1.

The Senate.   Senators serve for six years (one-third being elected every two years). Each state elects two senators, regardless of the size of its population. In 1980 Alaska's two senators represented a population of about 400,000, whereas California's senators represented over 23 million.

Because there are over four times as many representatives as senators, and because members of the House must stand for election every two years, they believe they are closer to the people than the senators. On the other hand, senators can point out that, since the passage of the Seventeenth Amendment in 1913, they, too, report to the people directly, rather than through state legislatures; and they argue that they speak for large, diverse areas including cities, suburbs, and farms, whereas each representative typically speaks for a much more limited constituency.

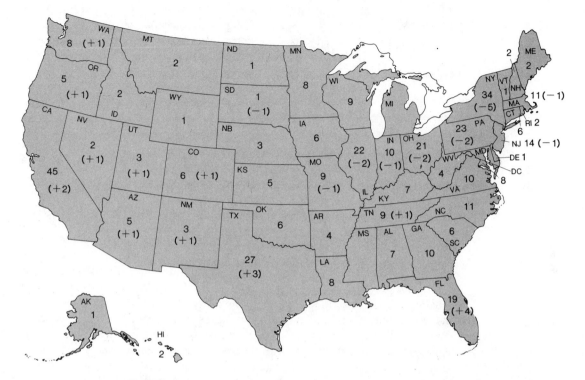

FIGURE 8–1.   Membership in the House of Representatives by States after 1980 Census (with gains and losses from previous allocations)
Source: U.S. Bureau of the Census, Statistical Abstract of the United States *(Washington D.C.: Government Printing Office, 1981).*

Localism.   Separating the constituencies of House and Senate makes for important differences in the ways in which representatives and senators see their roles. Even more important in the constitutional scheme, however, is the difference between the constituencies of the two houses of Congress on the one hand, and of the president on the other.

The president (with only the intervention of the electoral college) is elected by the nation as a whole. But because members of Congress are given their offices by districts or states, their political roots are deeply embedded in the communities. Much of the money for their campaigns, their organizational strength—in short, their power bases—is in their home districts, so they are particularly sensitive to the expressed needs and concerns of the people back home.

Consequently, senators and representatives frequently take on the role of helping constituents in their dealings with the bureaucracies of the federal government (a function that, in Scandinavian countries, is handled by a special official, the "ombudsman"). In a broader context the member of Congress is expected to speak for the economic and social well-being of the areas he or she represents. This difference of interests will often create conflict between Congress and the White House. A president may appeal to Congress on grounds of party or national interest, and the president has some powerful resources to back up this appeal. But in the final analysis the member of Congress must build a case for reelection in his or her district or state rather than on the national scene.

ORGANIZED INTEREST CONSTITUENCIES

Voters turn to their members of Congress to represent them not only in the context of their community or state but also of their work lives, leisure-time pursuits, and ethnic, religious, and ideological concerns.

All of these interests, as we saw in chapter 6, are the focus of organized group activity, and representatives and senators must deal with the leaders, the lobbyists, and sometimes the mass membership of interest groups. Many of these groups speak for local interests, and the member of Congress does not dare ignore people who speak for local industrial, commercial, agricultural and other enterprises, because these groups are the source of the community's jobs and income.

But not only local interests are taken up by Congress. Representatives and senators from Michigan, for example, voice the concerns of the whole automobile industry. Members from California and Texas may be rivals in the struggle for defense and aerospace contracts, but they may combine forces when the issue is the size of the *total* defense and aerospace budgets. Business, labor, agriculture, abortion, or gun control organizations can all find members in both houses of Congress who speak for their positions nationally as well as locally.

Ethics.　Representation by legislators of a multiplicity of organized interests is an inevitable, and in itself desirable, facet of a democratic system. However, some interest groups are willing, even eager, to spend large amounts of money to advance their purposes. Members of both houses earn $60,700 a year, which is well above the national average but much less than the income of most of the business and professional leaders with whom the legislators deal. Consequently, many members are interested in supplementing their incomes in various ways.

Some of these ways have been illegal or at least grossly unethical. There have been cases of small-scale personal corruption: placing friends or relatives on the payroll, extorting kickbacks from employees, and padding expense accounts. Over the years there have been several indictments and convictions of members for such activities.[3]

More serious are those practices that involve the efforts of organized interests to influence members of Congress and their staffs. As we observed in chapter 6, campaign contributions are one of the means by which interest groups try to bring their claims to the attention of legislators, and these contributions have sometimes been diverted by members of Congress and their staffs for their personal purposes. Thus Bobby Baker, a protégé of Lyndon Johnson, built a fortune of $2 million while secretary to the Senate majority leader, and he went to jail for holding on to some of the funds contributed to the Democratic Senatorial Committee by savings and loan associations. In 1967 Senator Thomas Dodd of Connecticut was censured by the Senate for taking monies from campaign fund-raising dinners and using them for private purposes. In 1979 Senator Herman Talmadge of Georgia was denounced[4] by the Senate for falsifying campaign finance reports and office expense claims.

Campaign contributions, along with personal gifts, were involved in the scandal that came to light in 1976 over the activities of Tongsun Park, a South Korean businessman apparently acting on behalf of a branch of the South Korean government. Park donated considerable sums of money and expensive gifts to several members of the House and threw lavish parties attended by members of Congress. Among the recipients of his hospitality and donations were some high congressional leaders, including Speaker "Tip" O'Neill and two successive Democratic whips. Subsequently three California congressmen were reprimanded by the House ethics committee for receiving gifts ranging from $1,000 to $3,000, failing to disclose the gifts, and lying when questioned about them.

More damaging still to Congress' reputation was the indictment in 1980 of six members of the House and one senator in the "Abscam" affair, a "sting" organized by the FBI. Agents of the FBI, posing as representatives of Arab interests, offered bribes to the legislators in return for various favors. The meetings were videotaped and then produced in court: they were also played on network television for extended periods. Most of the accused members were convicted. Among them was Representative Michael Myers of Pennsylvania, who was expelled from the

REPRINTED BY PERMISSION OF TRIBUNE COMPANY SYNDICATE, INC.
"I hope you realize, sir, that if you were a member of the House of Representatives you'd be censured for this!"

House—the first member to be ejected in 119 years (and the first ever for a crime other than treason). Similarly the Senate Ethics Committee recommended the expulsion of Senator Harrison Williams of New Jersey after his conviction in the Abscam case; he resigned when it became clear that he would otherwise be expelled.

Apart from these obvious cases of betraying the public trust, there is the more subtle problem presented by conflicts of interest. Can legislators deal objectively with proposed legislation when they retain their associations with law or business firms, or when they have financial investments in a field affected by the legislation?

Official reports on the outside interests of members of the House indicate that the problem is widespread. A considerable number have an interest, usually stock ownership, in banks, savings and loan associations, and finance companies. Among them are members of the House Banking and Currency Committee and the Ways and Means Committee, which pass on legislation affecting the taxes paid by financial institutions. Others, including Armed Services Committee members, have holdings in defense companies. Several have interests in real estate, and a considerable number are lawyers still receiving income from their legal practices.

Reforms.   In an effort to deal with these problems Congress has established codes of conduct for members and employees of both houses.[5] The principal remedy adopted is *disclosure*. All members are required to report any substantial business interests or sources of outside income. In the case of the House these reports are made public. For senators, however, the most significant data merely have to be placed on file with the Congress and can be opened to the public only in case of investigation of charges of unethical conduct.

The codes imposed limits on outside earnings from speaking engagements, articles, and other sources (although the Senate in 1979 voted to postpone this requirement until 1983, and in 1981 the House doubled the limit to 30 percent of the annual salary). In addition, gifts from lobbyists were restricted to $100 a year, limits were placed on the use of the free-mailing privilege for constituency newsletters, and controls were tightened on office and foreign travel expenses.

As we shall see later in this chapter, these restrictions were regarded by some critics of Congress as insufficient to deal with the problem. Within Congress, however, many members felt that the restrictions imposed an unreasonable burden on those legislators who do not enjoy inherited wealth and must seek a reasonable supplementation of their congressional salaries. In a growing number of cases members of the House declared themselves to be so disenchanted with the mistrust and hostility toward Congress engendered by the misbehavior of a small minority of its members that they gave up their congressional careers and returned to the private sector.

POWER IN CONGRESS: ORGANIZATION AND LEADERSHIP

The dispersal of power that permeates the American constitutional system is supplemented by a further fragmentation *within* each house of Congress. As a result, nowhere in our governmental structure is it more difficult to discover who has the responsibility for making decisions than in the Congress.

Power in Congress is distributed in several directions, which often rival each other. The political party, the congressional committees, and the committee chairpersons determine the power bases in both houses.

POLITICAL PARTY: ITS IMPORTANCE AND ITS LIMITATIONS

In most national legislatures the political party is a principal means of providing leadership, especially in parliamentary systems. Under those systems the executive branch of the government is not elected directly by the people but by the legislature from among the members of the party or combination of parties that constitute a majority in the legislature. The chosen members of the executive branch continue to constitute the government only so long as their party or parties in the legislature continue to support them.

The power of party is much less in the United States, but it is not insignificant. Party plays an important role in the organization and leadership of Congress. Almost all members of Congress run for office under one of the two main party labels, and they stay with their party affiliation faithfully during the first votes of every new session of the House and Senate, which determine which party will hold the official leadership positions.[6]

As figure 8-2 illustrates, the top positions in both House and Senate include the leaders of the majority and minority parties, as well as the parties' whips, whose job it is to provide liaison between party leadership and rank and file and also to achieve as much party unity in voting as possible.

On the House side, however, there is also the position of Speaker, who is the leader of the majority party, official spokesperson for the House, and next in line to the presidency after the vice-president. Thus the majority leader in the House is its second-ranking officer.

In the Senate, on the other hand, the majority leader is the top-ranking party official, even though he or she is ceremonially outranked by the vice-president of

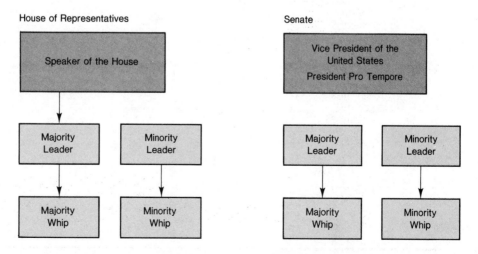

FIGURE 8–2.   Leadership Structure of the Congress

the United States, who sometimes presides over the sessions of the Senate, and the President Pro Tempore,[7] who is the main presiding officer in the vice-president's absence.

Party considerations also prevail in the selection of the chairpersons of the several committees that, as we shall see, do a large part of the work of both houses of Congress.

As table 8-2 shows, from 1932 through 1980 the Democrats were the majority party in both houses in every year except 1947–1948 and 1953–1954, so usually the Democrats held all the top positions. As a result of the 1980 election, however, the leadership positions in the Senate in the 97th Congress[8] were held by Republicans, and Democrats continued to hold a majority in the House.

Also contributing to the party spirit in Congress are the various groups and committees that bring together party members in each house. At the broadest level there are the party conferences (the Democrats in the House call their conference the "caucus"), consisting of all members of the party. Each conference has a steering committee, but the real party strategy organs and agents of the conference are the policy committees.[9]

Within each party, too, there are factional groups—informal associations of members who are to the left or the right of the prevailing consensus within their

TABLE 8–2 Party distribution of House and Senate, 1932–1982

No. of Congress	Years	Senate			House		
		Democrats	Republicans	Other	Democrats	Republicans	Other
73	1933–1934	60	35	1	310	117	5
74	1935–1936	69	25	2	310	103	10
75	1937–1938	76	16	4	331	89	13
76	1939–1940	69	23	4	261	164	4
77	1941–1942	66	28	2	268	162	5
78	1943–1944	57	38	1	222	208	5
79	1945–1946	56	38	1	242	190	2
80	1947–1948	45	51		188	245	1
81	1949–1950	54	42		263	171	1
82	1951–1952	49	47		234	199	1
83	1953–1954	47	48	1	211	221	1
84	1955–1956	48	47	1	232	203	
85	1957–1958	49	47		233	200	
86	1959–1960	64	34		283	153	
87	1961–1962	65	35		263	174	
88	1963–1964	67	33		258	177	
89	1965–1966	68	32		295	140	
90	1967–1968	64	36		248	187	
91	1969–1970	57	43		244	191	
92	1971–1972	54	44	2	255	180	
93	1973–1974	56	42	2	244	191	
94	1975–1976	61	37	2	291	144	
95	1977–1978	61	38	1	250	145	
96	1979–1980	58	41	1	276	159	
97	1981–1982	46	53	1	243	192	

party in Congress. The most potent of these associations is the Democratic Study Group in the House, which includes most of the Democrats' more liberal members along with some of their moderates.

The result of all this party machinery, and of the fact that our parties, after all, do stand for something, is that more often than not members vote with a majority of their party. Typically in recent years, about two-thirds to three-quarters of members of Congress have voted with their party leaders whenever an issue clearly separated Democrats from Republicans, with a slightly higher degree of unity in the House than in the Senate and with Republicans holding together somewhat more than Democrats.

But if this information suggests a degree of party cohesion, it also reveals a much higher incidence of crossing party lines than is true in the legislatures of most other democratic countries. Elsewhere it is most unusual to find from a quarter to a third of the members of a party voting against the proposals of their party leadership.

The main reasons for this relative weakness of party structure in the Congress are to be found in points discussed earlier. First is the importance of the local constituency to the members of Congress. If the member believes that the party leader's position is contrary to the wishes of a vital segment of opinion back home, the member may well decide to refuse to go along with the leadership.

Second, parties are weak in the Congress because they are such loosely knit, heterogeneous coalitions; this is particularly true of the Democrats. As we saw in chapter 4, the Democratic party is a most unlikely combination of conservatives and liberals. It is not surprising that Democratic conservatives should have repeatedly kicked over their party's traces—some of them 60 percent of the time, a few even 70 percent—yet have continued to call themselves Democrats.

On very rare occasions, punishment has been inflicted on members who came out flagrantly against their own party. In 1965 two Democratic representatives, one from Mississippi, the other from South Carolina, were deprived of their seniority for openly supporting Barry Goldwater in the previous year's presidential election.

But this case is most exceptional, and there have been no sanctions against Democrats who voted with the Republicans within Congress. Thus there has been nothing to restrain the regular appearance in congressional voting of a *conservative coalition*, in which a majority of conservative Democrats have joined forces with most of the Republicans.

The effectiveness of this cross-party coalition has waxed and waned over the years. But it surfaced repeatedly to thwart Jimmy Carter's legislative program. And it took on a special significance in 1981 when it was instrumental in passing Ronald Reagan's spending and tax proposals.

The Democrats in the House in 1981 outnumbered the Republicans by 51. However, a number of them, ranging from a hard core of 29 up to as many as 63 on some issues, banded together in an informal group called the Conservative Democratic Forum, or the "boll weevils,"[10] the name given a bloc of southern Democrats who exercised great power in Congress in the years after World War II. Actually the boll weevils in 1981 were not all southerners; they were drawn from fifteen states, and the majority of southern Democrats stayed with the leadership of their party on most votes. Still, preponderantly they came from the South, and although they were much smaller in number than their namesakes of three decades ago, they held a pivotal role in the decisions on Reagan's economic proposals in 1981.

The key to their effectiveness was the high degree of cohesion on the Republican side. The Republicans were not without their waverers—about two dozen moderate Republicans, mostly from the Northeast and Midwest and dubbed the "gypsy moths."[11] They harbored grave doubts about some of the Reagan cuts, but most of them resolved their doubts in favor of the president.

Consequently, when 29 of the boll weevils (24 of them southerners) voted for the president's budget cut proposals, the president won by 217 to 210. On the administrations's tax cut legislation only 1 Republican deserted the party, and with 48 Democrats moving the other way the administration prevailed by 238 to 195.

COMMITTEES

Legislatures, like all large decision-making bodies, must do some of their work in committees. National assemblies are too big to handle details expeditiously. Moreover, committees serve the purpose of dividing up their members so they can specialize in one or more of a vast multitude of complex problems.

However, in Congress the committees take on roles and powers considerably exceeding the powers of most other legislatures as a consequence of the weakness of other sources of leadership, particularly party leadership. So the permanent, or standing, committees of Congress have taken on a large part of the work of both houses, but especially of the House, the larger and more formally structured of the two chambers. The committees have become, in effect, small legislatures in their own right, considering whether or not proposed measures should even be discussed, holding public hearings on their merits, debating them, assigning them spending levels, amending them in minute detail, sometimes even replacing them with their own very different ideas.

The power of the committees is not absolute, for their recommendations may be overruled or modified by the majority of the House or Senate or challenged by other committees. Still, in most cases recommendations emerging from a committee with a clear majority carry great weight in their own house, and few major measures are passed in the teeth of opposition by a standing committee.

Committees of the two houses in the 97th Congress are shown in table 8-3.

There is a hierarchy of power among the standing committees. In the House, members particularly value positions on Appropriations (which determines how much money will be provided for each federal program approved), Ways and Means (which raises the money), and Rules (which guides the flow of business through the House). In the Senate the committees on Appropriations, Finance, Budget (which pulls together the spending and taxing sides of the Senate's work), and Foreign Relations are the most prestigious groups. However, even less im-

TABLE 8–3 House and Senate committees, 97th Congress, 1981–1982

House of Representatives

Agriculture	Interstate and Foreign Commerce
Appropriations	Judiciary
Armed Services	Merchant Marine and Fisheries
Banking, Finance, and Urban Affairs	Post Office and Civil Service
Budget	Public Works and Transportation
District of Columbia	Rules
Education and Labor	Science and Technology
Foreign Affairs	Small Business
Government Operations	Standards of Official Conduct
House Administration	Veterans' Affairs
Interior/Insular Affairs	Ways and Means

Senate

Agriculture, Nutrition, and Forestry	Environment and Public Works
Appropriations	Finance
Armed Services	Foreign Relations
Banking, Housing, and Urban Affairs	Government Affairs
Budget	Judiciary
Commerce, Science, and Transportation	Labor and Human Resources
Energy and Natural Resources	Rules and Administration
	Veterans' Affairs

portant committees such as Agriculture, Public Works, and Interior may provide valuable opportunities for bringing benefits to constituents or for gaining national publicity by holding televised hearings on issues of public concern.

The pressure to specialize has led Congress to go even further in splitting up decision-making responsibilities, because most of the standing committees are divided into subcommittees. Thus, the 97th Congress' 37 standing committees (22 in the House, 15 in the Senate) were supplemented by 356 subcommittees, some of which had a good deal of responsibility and status.

A further problem with the committee structure both in the House and the Senate is in overlapping and competing jurisdictions. Several committees claim that they have total or at least partial jurisdiction in such fields as energy, transportation, health, and research and development. In 1973 a select committee of the House under the chairmanship of Richard Bolling of Missouri undertook a study of this problem. After two years and an expenditure of $1.5 million, the Bolling committee brought in proposals for a substantial reorganization of committee assignments and responsibilities. However, almost all the recommendations were rejected by leaders of the House Democrats, who did not want their various committees to lose any of their power. The Senate, on the other hand, has put through a modest reorganization of its committee system involving a reduction in the number of committees and a limit on the number of committees and subcommittees on which each senator may serve.

There has been one important improvement in the committee structure of both houses: the establishment in 1974 of the Budget Committees charged with the task of bringing expenditures into line with revenues. Previously the committees responsible for deciding how much money should be spent on various programs operated independently of the committees deciding how to raise the money to pay for those programs. Now the Budget Committees set an upper limit for total federal expenditures early in the year, relating this ceiling to the tax programs needed to produce the agreed-on expenditures. Then they review the spending recommendations coming out of the spending committees in the course of the year and apply pressure to ensure that the total of these recommendations does not exceed the budgeted expenditure ceiling.

STAFFS

No discussion of congressional membership and committees is complete without mention of the professional staffs they appoint to help them do their work. So complex has this work become that both houses of Congress have expanded their staffs considerably. Representatives are limited to eighteen full-time and four part-time aides, although some have additional staff members hired with personal funds or outside contributions. Senatorial staffs are still larger, some of the committees employing two hundred or more people. Altogether Senate and House staff workers increased from about seven thousand in 1960 to over eighteen thousand in 1980. At the professional level these staffs include specialists in the legal

JIM BERRY
c NEA

"Look! One of the senators is briefing his staff."

and procedural matters involved in drafting legislation and others who work on the technical substance of policy issues. In some cases they build up such a body of expertise in a particular field that they become important participants who not only provide data and analysis on issues, but actually conduct negotiations that lead to the shaping of legislation.

COMMITTEE CHAIRPERSONS

For many years the power of committees was almost synonymous with the power of their chairpersons. The chair, if sufficiently determined and adept, could usually be the decisive voice on such pivotal matters as selecting and assigning committee staff, appointing subcommittee chairpersons, allocating funds, and deciding whether and when committee hearings should be held and votes taken. In extreme cases (and there were more than a few such cases) the chair used these powers arbitrarily and despotically, ignoring the wishes of the majority of the committee.

This power was reduced by reforms that began in the early 1970s. In the House, Democrats weakened the power of committee chairpersons over subcommittees, giving the subcommittees their own budgets, staffs, and areas of jurisdiction; they barred legislators from chairing more than one committee or subcommittee, thus giving junior members a chance to chair a subcommittee; and they forced the election of chairpersons by the party caucus. Further, meetings of congressional committees were opened to the public except when a committee specifically voted to close them on a particular day. The House Democrats, prodded by the Democratic Study Group, also took steps to increase the influence of the caucus, so that committee chairs would take account of the sentiment of the entire party membership in the House, not only their own and the committees' preferences.

On the Senate side, there has been a similar trend toward a reduction of the power of the committee chairs, although (the Senate being a less structured body than the House) this reform has come about in a less formal manner than on the House side.

SENIORITY

In 1910 the House revolted against the power of the Speaker, "Uncle" Joe Cannon, and stripped him of the power to decide who would chair House committees. After that time both House and Senate resorted to the practice of promotion through seniority. Seniority operates through the process of political survival. A member is appointed to a committee and, if reelected to Congress, remains on that committee until other committee members who were there longer die, retire, or move to other committees. At that point the surviving member takes over the chair if he or she is of the majority party in the Congress, or becomes the ranking minority member on the committee.

It is important to bear in mind that the seniority principle only counts toward leadership once a member is on a committee, and it does not determine which committee a member gets on in the first place. Moreover, seniority applies only to the committees themselves, not to the party leadership positions: Speaker of the House, the majority and minority leaders, and the party whips. Still, the committees are important centers of congressional power, and committees were pretty much the domain of whoever was in the chair until change came in the 1970s.

First the Republicans in the House made the minority leadership in each committee subject to election by all Republicans on the committee. Then the Democrats required that the selection of chairpersons be decided by secret ballot of the entire caucus. As a result three committee chairs in their seventies and eighties were removed from their positions in 1975. The ranks of the older, prestigious committee chairs were further diminished when two of them resigned in the midst of highly publicized sexual scandals: Wilbur Mills of Arkansas, whose authority for many years as chair of the Ways and Means Committee sometimes seemed to outrank the president's,[12] and Wayne Hays of Ohio, whose chairmanship of the House Administration Committee had given him intimidating authority over House members' office, staff, expense, and travel allocations.[13]

But it is not only procedural changes and sexual scandals that have weakened the stranglehold on the congressional system by elderly committee chairpersons. The average age of members of Congress has been declining, and large numbers of younger people have been entering the two houses, impatient to play a part in policy making without being compelled to wait for twenty years or so. Moreover, there has been a decline in the seniority acquired by southern members. Southerners who were returned in election after election with little opposition held half the important committee and subcommittee chairmanships in the House in 1964. Subsequently, more northern Democrats were repeatedly reelected, and with the retirement of some of the southerners and the increasing competitiveness of seats in the South, the accumulated seniority began to move northward.

CONGRESSIONAL PROCEDURES: HOW A BILL BECOMES LAW

In most parliamentary systems legislation is introduced by the executive branch, and the legislature is expected to examine, debate, and sometimes amend it. However, the final form is usually not fundamentally different from the original proposal, and the process is not a lengthy one. In the U.S. Congress, however, a proposed bill must pass through many stages and be subjected to intensive and prolonged scrutiny; and it stands a high risk of being either killed or altered beyond recognition. Following is a description of the procedure by which a bill becomes law.

THE HOUSE OF REPRESENTATIVES

A bill is first introduced in one or both houses. Assuming in this case that it begins in the House, the Speaker refers it to a standing committee, or, where appropriate, to multiple committees. From there the bill will usually be referred to a subcommittee for preliminary discussion and hearings, except where the majority party members on the committee vote to keep it in the full committee.

The hearings themselves may prove to be a substitute for action and may conclude that more study is needed. However, if the subcommittee decides that action is called for, its members proceed to a "mark up" session in which, line by line, the bill is drafted, debated, rewritten, and amended. The final version then goes to the full committee, which debates the bill again, often considering further amendments; the bill is then put to a vote. If the vote is favorable the bill will be reported to the full chamber accompanied by a report explaining its action, and often by a minority report from dissenting members.

Before it can reach the House floor, however, the bill must traverse yet another House committee. Of the twenty thousand or so bills and resolutions introduced into Congress each session, something over one thousand are approved by the standing committees. Most of these bills do not raise large issues and proceed routinely to the floor of the House for action. Still, there are enough bills of substance emerging from the standing committees to require that priorities be assigned. Priorities are the job of the Rules Committee. Almost no legislation proceeds to the floor of the House without procedural instructions assigned by Rules.

Deciding when a bill will be presented for a vote and the terms on which the bill will be debated places a great potential for power in the Rules Committee. For years this potential was exploited to the full by Judge Howard Smith of Virginia. Chairing a committee that then consisted of twelve members, he could often find five others—a conservative southern Democrat and four Republicans—to join him in opposing legislation he disapproved of. Without a majority no bill could advance. Sometimes when it appeared that he could not keep all his allies in line, he would avoid a vote by going home.

This situation has changed considerably. The power of the chair has been reduced; Judge Smith has gone; and the committee, whose membership has been enlarged, now includes a number of moderates and liberals. So the Rules Committee is no longer a graveyard for large numbers of bills. Even so, the standing committees of the House cannot ignore the power of the Rules Committee. There are still times when a bill that emerges from a standing committee with a strong endorsement is stalled by lack of support in Rules, and the Rules Committee is very much involved in controlling the procedures by which business is conducted on the floor of the House.

Once on the floor of the House the bill will be further debated under a "closed rule," which requires that the bill be voted up or down without amendment, or an "open rule," which allows amendment. Commonly further amendment takes place, and sometimes there is even complete rejection of a bill proposed by a standing committee.

THE SENATE

If the bill succeeds in passing the House, action must still be taken in the Senate and its network of committees. The standing committees of the Senate often hold extensive hearings that in considerable measure duplicate the committees of the House.

The Senate has no counterpart of the House Rules Committee, so the scheduling of bills coming to the floor from the committees has fallen into the hands of the majority leadership. Once on the floor a bill is not encumbered with the tight rules and procedures governing floor debate in the House. In fact, the Senate still allows the *filibuster*, a tactic that takes advantage of the Senate's rules permitting unlimited debate and allowing a flow of oratory that can be ended only if its participants drop from exhaustion or if *cloture* is voted. Cloture, the closing of debate, used to require the support of two-thirds of the members present and voting, which for many years was very difficult to secure. Consequently, the Senate tolerated a solo, continuous oration of 15½ hours by Huey Long of Louisiana, another of 22 hours by Wayne Morse of Oregon in 1953, and yet another (the record) of over 24 hours by Strom Thurmond of South Carolina in 1957. Other filibusters, conducted by relays of Senators, went on much longer and succeeded in killing many civil rights bills by preventing the Senate from doing any other business until their proponents agreed to drop the bills.

However, the filibuster was finally broken on the two most important civil rights bills ever considered: the Civil Rights Act of 1964 and the Voting Rights Act of 1965. Subsequently, the number needed to apply cloture was reduced to 60; and once 60 members had voted to halt discussion, all debate had to stop within 100 hours.

CONFERENCE COMMITTEES

When a bill passes the Senate, it may differ from the product that emerges from the House. If the House is unwilling to accept the Senate's version, as is typically the case on important measures, a conference committee is convened, usually consisting of three to twenty "managers" appointed by the presiding officers of the two chambers.

Occasionally, the differences between the two chambers cannot be reconciled, and a bill that has survived the rigors of the two houses separately dies in the conference. In other cases agreement is reached only after sections in dispute have been referred to both the House and the Senate for further instructions. When the conference committee manages to arrive at an acceptable compromise, a conference report is drawn up and submitted to both houses for approval on a take-it-or-leave-it basis, because further amendment is not allowed. If approval is obtained, the bill goes to the president for signature. However, under his constitutional authority the president may *veto* the bill by sending it back with his objections to the house that initiated it. If Congress is to prevail, it must override the veto by a two-thirds vote in both houses. A bill can become law without the president's signature if he neither signs nor vetoes it within ten weekdays after it reaches him. On the other hand, if Congress adjourns within those ten weekdays, the president can kill the bill by taking no action, thereby exercising the *pocket veto*.

APPROPRIATIONS

Even if the president signs a bill, the matter does not necessarily end there. Most legislation has little meaning unless funds are provided to implement it. The process just described, although usually specifying the expenditure of funds, merely provides congressional *authorization* to spend the money once it is provided. The money cannot be provided until Congress has gone through the state of *appropriation*, which will normally originate in the House and will be initiated in each chamber by the Appropriations Committees.

Often this step is a mere formality. But sometimes it is the occasion for further discussion and debate, conducted first in the Appropriations Committees and then on the House and Senate floors. The result more often than not is that the amount of money in the appropriations bill is less than the amount authorized in the bill establishing the program.

Figure 8-3 gives us a summary of the procedures we have just described for passing a bill.

THREE PERSPECTIVES ON CONGRESS

For the purpose of this chapter we shall limit ourselves to an examination of only three perspectives: liberal, centrist, and conservative. There is little radical writing specifically on the subject of Congress as an institution, and the radical positions are easily derived from the material provided in earlier chapters.

THE LIBERALS: OBSTACLE COURSE FOR LIBERAL PROGRAMS

Most of the time liberals have found Congress to be extremely reluctant to put their proposals into effect. This situation occurs in Congress, liberals argue, because of the nature of its membership, its excessive preoccupation with local interests, and defects of leadership, organization, and procedures.

Membership.   As liberals look at the socioeconomic makeup of the Congress they do not find much cause for encouragement. According to table 8-1, in the 97th Congress of 1981–1982 almost 27 percent of the representatives and 23 percent of the senators came from a business background. Lawyers constituted nearly 43 percent of the

House membership and 57 percent of the Senate, and lawyers do much, if not most, of their work for business. A further 5 percent in each House were farmers or ranchers, occupational groups that usually tend toward conservative views.

There was not a single labor union official (a notable difference from the legislatures of most other democratic countries) and no blue-collar workers. Women, blacks, and Hispanics were all grossly underrepresented in both Houses. Thus there was only a minimal presence in the 97th Congress of some of the key groups in the population that provide the liberals with their sources of support.

Although the 97th Congress was more conservative than most, its socioeconomic composition was little different from the 96th Congress. In fact, the only real change in the makeup of members of Congress in recent years is that the average age has declined. The Senate has long been a rich man's club: at least nineteen of its members in the 96th Congress were millionaires, and there were another forty or so millionaires in the House.

Moreover, Congress for all too many of its members is seen as an opportunity to make more

Most bills begin as similar proposals in both houses . . .

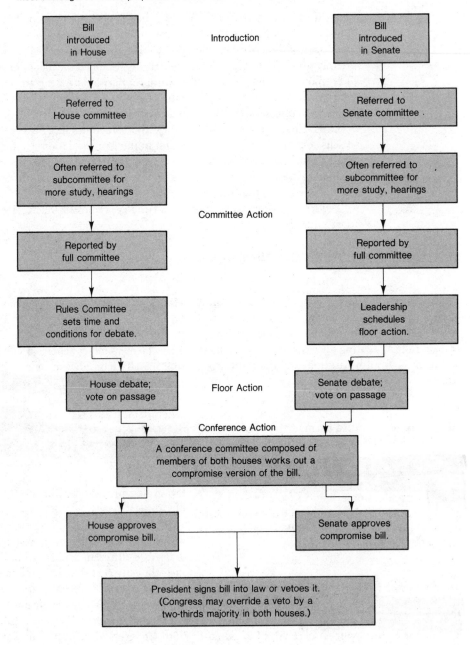

FIGURE 8-3.   How a Bill Becomes Law

money. Liberals are angered not only by the gross cases of corruption revealed in the Abscam affair and other scandals, but by the more widespread and persistent financial conflicts of interest involved when members of Congress refuse to disqualify themselves from acting or voting on issues in which they have a personal financial stake. The reforms requiring disclosure are a small step in the right direction, but they do not prevent members from acting from self-interest. Liberals also note that limitations on outside earnings do not apply to investment income from such sources as stocks and bonds; the Senate has postponed the application of these limits to its own members, and the House has doubled the limits on additional earnings.

A further factor biasing the behavior of members of Congress toward business interests is the desire of many to be given lucrative jobs when they leave Congress. The hiring of former legislators as lobbyists by Washington-based special interest groups, particularly businesses and corporate law firms, has become a common practice. Over a third of the ninety-two senators and House members who retired or were beaten in 1980 stayed in Washington as employees of such organizations, usually at much higher salaries than they had earned in public service.

So the liberals express strong doubts that the majority of members of Congress, with their affluent backgrounds, their tendency to advance personal interests through their congressional positions, and the glittering prospects of lucrative careers after Congress, are likely to worry about the problems of the less advantaged members of our society.

Localism. Before the Supreme Court's reapportionment decision a common complaint of liberals was that Congress overrepresented small towns and rural areas, so that the interests of the impoverished residents of the inner cities were neglected. With this rural bias more or less corrected, liberals have moved to a more generalized criticism about the overrepresentation of local interests to the neglect of the larger national interest.

Liberals insist that they are very much concerned about local affairs, that they want to see much greater involvement of people at the local level, and that members of Congress should be active representatives of individual constituents who are having problems dealing with the federal bureaucracies. Yet the main solutions advocated by liberals to public policy issues are national in scope. They want federal aid to education, national health insurance, and federalization of welfare programs.

Members of Congress, liberals allege, are too preoccupied with state and local matters to take the larger, national view. Members from California and Texas devote their energies to fighting for space and defense contracts. Representatives from sheep and cattle states argue for import quotas on meat. Michigan members resist smog and safety controls on automobiles. And senators and representatives from every state wage war against the growth of the federal budget but demand more spending for their own states and districts.

Defects of leadership, organization, and procedures. In the liberals' view the conservative, probusiness bias of Congress is reinforced by its patterns of leadership, its organizational structure, and its procedures. Although they approve of the changes that have taken place with respect to seniority, the filibuster, and so on, liberals persist in their belief that the way Congress operates places extraordinary difficulties in the path of liberal programs.

To begin with, there is the diffusion of leadership resulting from the lack of party cohesion. As we saw in chapter 4, liberals are advocates of strong, responsible parties, so the casual approach to party discipline found in both houses of Congress is bound to arouse their displeasure.

They might not be quite so unhappy if the crossing of party lines occurred purely in relation to the individual needs of each constituency. In fact cross-party voting is not entirely haphazard. A pattern has emerged with some frequency, the ideological pattern of a conservative coalition that reached its first zenith during the heyday of the southern committee chairmen, and again in the 97th Congress in 1981.

This pattern means that a mere Democratic majority, even a large one, is not sufficient to pass liberal legislation, because included among the Democrats are 40 to 50 members whose conservative leanings lead them to vote frequently with the majority of Republicans. On the other side, a much smaller number of Republicans are sometimes found in the same voting lobby as a majority of Democrats. For this reason, for example, President Kennedy was unable to get very much legislation through Congress even though the Democratic margin in the House when he was elected was 89. Lyndon Johnson in 1965 had a Democratic majority in the House of 145, which was enough to get him most of what he wanted. But when the 1966 election reduced the Democratic margin in the House to 61, Johnson's domestic program was in trouble again.[14] As we saw in the last chapter, most of Jimmy Carter's more liberal legislation failed to get through Congress even though the Democrats controlled the House by 288 to 147 in his first two years, and by 276 to 159 during his last two years.

Apparently the liberals cannot hope for much favorable action from Congress unless the Democrats control both houses by overwhelming margins and there is also an energetic and politically adept Democrat in the White House. Unless these conditions exist, liberals contend that their proposals cannot overcome the built-in inertia of the congressional system. Despite the reforms that have been made, that system is still characterized by diffused leadership and endlessly complicated procedures. And it is a system, the liberals contend, that serves particularly well the purposes of organized interest groups and associations, which can present a unified front to the fragmented system of congressional power and play one power center off another. The mysterious, subterranean windings of bills through Congress also provide repeated opportunities for skilled lobbyists to inject their ideas at various stages and to work out quiet, unpublicized understandings with friendly legislators. The congressional system offers no

advantages for the kinds of social legislation favored by the liberals. On the contrary, Congress becomes a hazardous obstacle course, and the process of getting programs that the people want through the two houses of Congress can take years, even decades.

Among the examples cited by liberals to support this argument are the following:

1. *Health insurance.* President Harry Truman proposed the idea of compulsory national insurance in 1945. Not until 1958 did the House Ways and Means Committee get around to holding hearings on a bill that would provide benefits only to people over 65. Even then the proposal was watered down by the committee because of intense lobbying by the American Medical Association, the opposition of Ways and Means Committee chair Wilbur Mills, and the generally conservative leanings of the members of the committee. ("We don't want any screwballs," said one committee member, "and since I've been a member we haven't had any screwballs. These men are pretty carefully selected, you know, so we won't get any screwballs.")[15]

As pressure mounted in the country for a health insurance program, Mills combined forces with Senator Robert Kerr to produce a limited program of federal support for state programs. Then the landslide victory of Lyndon Johnson and the Democrats in 1964 gave the supporters of further action a clear majority on Ways and Means. Mills faced the inevitable and provided the leadership to enact Medicare, national medical insurance for the elderly.

Liberals were pleased but unimpressed. It had taken twenty years, they said, for Congress to respond to what the polls had repeatedly shown to be the will of the majority. Moreover, the result was a much more limited program than existed in every other industrialized country, none of which restricted their coverage to the elderly.[16]

2. *Federal aid to education.* Harry Truman presented this idea to Congress in 1945. Here again, said the liberals, the proposal received persistent support in the polls, yet fell afoul of one

legislative technicality after another until it was approved in 1965 within the rubric of Lyndon Johnson's War on Poverty.

3. *Public housing.* Truman's proposal to expand government-owned housing for the poor actually passed through Congress in 1949, a mere four years after he had proposed it. Yet subsequently private housing groups persuaded congressional committees to reduce the appropriations for the program, with the result that the target of 810,000 units in six years was not reached for twenty years.

4. *Gun control.* The National Rifle Association (NRA) has spearheaded a coalition of gun owners, manufacturers, and distributors, together with conservative organizations, to oppose the registration of firearms or control of their sales. The coalition has been successful in beating back repeated efforts to pass legislation, even after the assassinations of President Kennedy, Martin Luther King, and Robert Kennedy, the shooting of George Wallace in 1972, two abortive efforts to shoot President Ford, and the near-fatal shooting of President Reagan. The typical sequence was an avalanche of mail demanding gun controls after a shooting; the movement of legislation in Congress in response to the demands; then, after the first wave of indignation had passed, the dwindling of procontrol letters; a counterattack by the NRA, with mail pouring in against the proposed legislation; then the abandonment of the legislation or its passage in greatly diluted form.

So liberals complain that getting their proposals through Congress is a herculean labor requiring years, even decades; and in the end they may achieve only a small portion of their goal or nothing at all.

It is primarily liberal legislation that is thwarted by the congressional obstacle course, say the liberals. They point to the speed with which Ronald Reagan's drastic spending and tax cuts were rushed through Congress in 1981. Congress prides itself on being a deliberative body, an institution that subjects every proposal to the most careful and thorough scrutiny. Yet when it approved the budget in 1981, most members had not seen a final version of the document, and for some time afterwards key committee members were still trying to decide exactly what they had voted on.

Still, the general outlines of the legislation were clear enough. The economic program passed by Congress in 1981 was an extremely conservative one. Even if the Democratic leadership in the House had managed to substitute their own proposals for Reagan's the results would not have been more favorably received by liberals. The Democrats' tax bill was slightly more skewed toward the lower- and middle-income groups than the administration's, but it included at least as many special advantages for business groups and the rich as Reagan's plan. In fact, in the final battle for votes, both sides were engaged in a frantic bidding war to win the support of undecided members by offering special windfalls to local and other special interest groups.

So, the liberals claim, Congress has not been even-handed in subjecting proposed legislation to long, rigorous scrutiny. This treatment has been applied over and over again to legislation proposed by moderately liberal presidents. But in 1981, with a determined conservative in the White House, the congressional barriers to speedy action were swept aside.

The liberals conceded that this complete subservience of Congress did not continue into 1982, and that Congress reasserted itself, forcing the president to accept modifications to his program. But the struggle which ensued over the budget in 1982 between president and Congress, between the two houses of Congress, and between factions within each house demonstrated again to the liberals the inability of the congressional system to produce effective decisions and policies. The most likely outcome to liberal observers was a weak compromise, skewed in the conservatives' direction, and unlikely to address the deep problems of the economy.

Reforms.   Congress, in this analysis, is not likely to become a stronghold for liberal causes. Senate committees in the 97th Congress in the hands of arch-conservatives such as Jesse Helms (Agriculture, Nutrition, and Forestry), Jake Garn (Banking, Housing, and Urban Affairs), Strom Thurmond (Judiciary), Orrin Hatch (Labor and Human Resources), and John Tower (Armed Services) would give short shrift to liberal ideas. Even with much more liberal chairpersons in the 96th Congress like Edward Kennedy, Claiborne Pell, Alan Cranston, and Frank Church, the Senate produced little to gladden the hearts of the liberals. As for the House, the fact that it remained in Democratic hands in the 97th Congress was not likely to mean much given its record during the Carter years.

Still, the liberals are not ready to give up on Congress. For one thing, its investigative powers might still be used to expose the abuses of business, other special interest groups, and the military. During the 1940s and 1950s the House Un-American Activities Committee and the inquisitions of Senator Joseph McCarthy provoked a liberal campaign against the powers of Congress. But with that era gone, and the Un-American Activities Committee abolished, liberals changed their view as congressional committees launched investigations into Vietnam and Cambodia, the CIA, the big oil companies, and Watergate.

Moreover, liberals believe that with the right kind of reforms and with substantial Democratic majorities again, Congress could still prove to be a responsive and responsible institution that could deliver important programs whenever a more liberal president takes over the White House. The key reforms they propose are the following:

1. *Abolish seniority and the filibuster.* The reforms of the past decade are only timid steps in the desired direction. Although a few elderly or scandal-ridden chairpersons have been removed, the top jobs still go to the people who have been there the longest. In a democratic institution, ability, not age and length of service, should determine who is selected for leadership. Similarly the filibuster is an inappropriate impediment to majority rule. Even though liberal causes have sometimes benefited from the use of the filibuster against

conservative proposals, the general view of liberals is that legislatures can find plenty of other ways to ensure that its minorities are heard from.

2. *Reorganize the committee structure of the House.* Years after the Bolling committee issued its report, the problems it identified are still there, and the proposals it made are still valid.

3. *Strengthen the conflict of interest laws.* Disclosure is not enough. Members should be forbidden to serve on committees that have jurisdiction over matters in which they have a personal financial interest, or at least they should be compelled to disqualify themselves from involvement in such matters.

4. *Reform election finance laws.* Public financing should be provided for congressional finances, and limits should be placed on how much money political action committees can raise and spend on congressional campaigns.

5. *Strengthen the party system.* It must be strengthened both with respect to Congress' internal workings and to Congress' relationship to the presidency. Only by this means can the individual member be provided with a framework that protects the legislator from the pressures of organized lobbyists, and only by this means can Congress be brought to work with the president on national problems instead of being totally occupied with narrow, parochial concerns.

Liberals are not proposing that Congress become a mere appendage of the presidency. Congress should serve as the nation's great forum for debating the major policy issues of the time. It should review presidential proposals with great care and subject them to an intensive process of discussion and amendment. It should engage in a continuous review of executive branch actions to expose failures of administration and abuses of presidential and bureaucratic power.

These roles are all enormously important, say the liberals, and Congress ought to reorganize itself to perform them more effectively. But the core function of Congress is to legislate on the large public policy issues. To this end, it must develop more effective mechanisms for cooperation with the presidency—and not only when the president is as conservative as Ronald Reagan.

THE CENTRISTS

For most centrist analysts, Congress is their favorite governmental institution. They concede that it is far from perfect, and they have endorsed the reforms of the 1970s. However, the only additional reforms they favor are essentially technical and managerial in nature, and they reject strenuously most of the liberal critique we have just presented. In particular, they do not agree with the charges that, by its composition, Congress overwhelmingly represents conservative and business interests; that it ignores the national interest in favor of provincial concerns; and that the way it organizes its affairs has made it almost incapable of producing anything worthwhile.

The membership.   The liberals' complaint that the makeup of Congress gives it a deep-seated bias toward conservatism is not well-founded. About a quarter of the members of the 97th Congress came out of business. But not all businesspeople are conservative, nor do they represent, as we noted in chapter 6, a single, monolithic interest. Then, easily the largest single group in each house is composed of lawyers (which is almost always true of legislatures), and lawyers spread across the entire political spectrum. We also saw in table 8-1 that the House in 1981–1982 contained forty-two educators, twenty-nine public officials, sixteen journalists, and eight congressional aides, and these occupations are all likely to contain moderates and liberals as well as conservatives.

Of course, Congress is not a precise cross section of the population. Legislators are not expected to be average people, but representatives with leadership qualities. Most of them are college graduates, which takes Congress well above the national educational average. Moreover, it is hardly surprising that, before becoming members of Congress, some of them should already have proven their abilities in other fields and that these other fields should include business and the law.

Centrists also challenge the liberals' assertion that members of Congress are typically so caught up in the business system and its values, so intent on making money during and after their congressional careers, that the institution is deeply tainted with corruption and conflicts of interest. Centrists cannot deny that such examples as the Bobby Baker, Tongsun Park, and Abscam cases put Congress into disrepute. But they see these cases as exceptions, and they believe that to read too much into them is unjust and does grave damage to the credibility of our entire system.

Centrists also recognize that the cost of elections may confront a candidate with ethical problems, but they doubt that the problems are as serious as the liberals allege. Members of Congress are only as beholden to their financial contributors as they choose to be. A skillful politician knows how to get money from people on both sides of an issue, because each side is afraid that not to contribute will give an advantage to the other side. Once funds have come in from both sides, the officeholder is obligated to neither side and is free to vote the way he or she wants. Whatever disadvantages the present system entails are outweighed by the dangers of the system proposed by the liberals of federal funding for congressional races.

Centrists contend that conflicts of interests stemming from legislators' outside earnings have always been exaggerated. The new ethics codes, although well intentioned, may have gone too far. After all, the majority of legislators' political careers are insecure. Why should a person who is chosen to represent a constituency for two years and may then not have the appointment renewed sever all contact with alternative careers? Cutting off all such avenues when a person runs for office gives the advantage to people who are independently wealthy or assured of a job with a big organization on their return. Most members of Congress have not allowed their outside affiliations to influence their voting in Congress. It is difficult to prove this claim, because only the abuses fill the columns of journalists who make their livings by innuendo and by alleging guilt by association. But those scholars who have studied Congress most closely, say the centrists, do not accept the muckrakers' view of the institution as deeply corrupt.

Localism.   Centrists dispute the liberals' contention that Congress is excessively concerned with provincial matters to the neglect of the national interest. Certainly, say the centrists, the members are sensitive to local community concerns, and so they should be. Local interests are being overwhelmed by mass communications, giant industry and labor, and big government. A prime function of a national legislature in a country as large as the United States is to protect the local constituency, to speak for diversity against standardization.

There is also nothing wrong, say centrists, with legislators' spending a good deal of their time as ombudsmen, dealing with the concerns of individual constituents and local communities. This role does not prevent members of Congress from attending to national and international issues. Nor, in dealing with those larger issues, are they necessarily limited by the views of their constituents, partly because they may not be able to determine the views of their constituents and partly because most of the time their constituents know very little about what positions their members of Congress are taking. As long as they are careful to voice the wishes of their constituents on matters of local concern, members of Congress may often vote their own consciences (or their party line) on major policy questions.

Leadership, organization, and procedures. The liberals complain that Congress' diffusion of leadership, elaborate organization, and endless procedures prevent its being effective—that is to say, effective in producing programs that the liberals favor.

The way Congress operates does put obstacles in the way of new proposals. But Congress is charged by the Constitution with acting as a check on presidential power, and it would be ignoring its obligations if it did not subject every proposal

coming from the White House to the most meticulous scrutiny. Moreover, because legislation often has an enormous impact on large numbers of people, it is essential that each interest likely to be affected by a piece of proposed legislation be given every opportunity to express its reaction.

It is wise to require that any proposal for change win the approval of standing committees, usually after extensive hearings designed to ensure that the relevant information is brought forth and all points of view are heard. It is essential that full provision be made for debate on the floor, that both chambers be fully involved, and that differences between the two be reconciled in conference committees. Moreover, with hundreds of billions of dollars involved it makes sense to have to submit every proposal to the Appropriations Committees. Clearly the Founding Fathers intended that Congress should be a deliberative body and should make haste slowly. Congress' structures and procedures, although always subject to modification, are within the spirit of the Constitution.

The filibuster, although it is not specifically established by the Constitution, is also within that spirit. The Framers were acutely sensitive to the need to protect minorities against majority tyranny. The filibuster serves that end by holding up action until the concerns of the minority have been attended to. For years the filibuster served the purposes of southern segregationists and acquired the onus of that association. But it has stopped serving those purposes since the filibusters against civil rights bills were broken in 1964 and 1965.

Today liberals, too, resort to the filibuster. Liberal senators filibustered in September 1971 to force extended debate on the draft and on an amendment to end the Vietnam War. The Senate voted cloture, and Senator Alan Cranston, formerly an advocate of efforts to make it easier to shut off a filibuster, was annoyed. "When our dislike of filibusters," he said, "becomes more important than our distrust of the draft or our revulsion with Vietnam, it's time we took another look at the filibuster. I look upon the filibuster as a means, not an end. When it can be used to good purpose, I support it. When it is used against ends that I favor, I shall oppose it."[17] Conversely, many conservatives have voted for cloture. Cloture is no longer difficult to accomplish because the votes needed for this purpose have been reduced to sixty. So the filibuster remains as a protection for minority rights but not as a constant threat to the orderly conduct of Senate business.

In any case, centrists do not argue that Congress is there merely to veto proposals for action. It is a legislature, and it does legislate. Its procedures have evolved over a long period of time to enable a large body of people to handle its tasks as effectively as possible. The structure of committees and subcommittees was not developed to provide bastions of power for a few obstinate old men but to provide specialized institutions that could examine an enormous number of proposals with some degree of understanding and sophistication.

Even the principle of seniority, so deplored by the liberals, expedites action, because with any other principle of selection a considerable part of each session (which lasts only two years) would be lost in bitter struggles over the leadership positions. Moreover, seniority brings other advantages. Long years of service have made the people who become chairpersons masters of specialized subjects and highly skilled at scrutinizing legislative proposals and reviewing executive performance. The seniority principle does not mean that today's chairpersons are all in their dotage. The increasing rate of turnover of the membership of Congress has led to a number of important committees' being chaired by people in their fifties. The liberals' assumption that seniority produces mostly conservative chairpersons has been less and less true since the grip of the southern segregationists was broken. Even in the Republican Senate of the 97th Congress the committee chairs included moderates like Charles Percy (Foreign Relations), Charles Mathias (Rules and Administration), and Mark Hatfield (Appropriations), along with the conservatives listed earlier.

In any case, the proof of the argument that Congress is a productive institution is found in its output. A large number of important statutes emerge from Congress every year. Although few years match the frenetic pace of Lyndon Johnson's Great Society programs of 1964 and 1965, the normal pace is impressive enough.

Furthermore, in the aggregate the product of Congress' work has certainly not been as profoundly conservative and probusiness as the liberals claim. The enormous growth of the welfare state, the huge expenditures on programs designed to help the poor, and the laws protecting the consumer and the environment could not have been brought about without the dedicated efforts of Congress after Congress, under Republican as well as Democratic presidents.

Of course, not everything the liberals propose is accepted by Congress, and it does not move as fast as they would like. But Congress is not inefficient or uninterested in sound legislation, as we see if we look again at some of the examples given by the liberals to make their case that Congress' procedures are essentially exercises in procrastination. Implicit in this case is the assumption that Congress, working with selfish, special interests, has repeatedly thwarted the will of the people on a clearly established public interest. But this charge is not borne out by the example of federal aid to education. It is true that polls showed that a clear majority of the electorate supported the idea in principle. But the large percentages in favor began to break up when people were asked whether they favored federal aid to parochial schools and whether they were ready to support higher taxes to pay for the federal aid.[18] Even the most representative legislatures have to go beyond generalities to deal with specific conflicts, and, in doing so, they do not find it easy to register the majority will precisely.

The fact that Wilbur Mills and his colleagues on the Ways and Means Committee did not push a radical health insurance program through as soon as it was proposed does not mean that they were reactionaries, determined at all costs to prevent change. In fact, they were prudent, highly competent legislators who would initiate action when, and only when, it was clear that this legislation was what the majority in the country and in Congress wanted. For some years the existence of that majority remained questionable. But once the undeniable majority for Medicare was established, Mills took charge of the situation, told the American Medical Association representative to stop making speeches to his committee attacking "socialized medicine," and secured the passage of a bill that was even more liberal than the Johnson administration's proposal.

Other proposals have been introduced into Congress to carry the principle of national health insurance still further. But if we are still short of the British National Health Service, it is because we are not sure that this system would be popular or workable in America.

Of course the centrists are not arguing that Congress is always prudent, always produces sound legislation, and always reflects the majority will. There are periods in which the two houses become embroiled in petty bickering and get very little done. At other times the action happens so fast that it leaves no opportunity for thoughtful deliberation, as for example was the case in 1964–1965, when under Lyndon Johnson's relentless pressure an excessive number of programs poured out of Congress. It happened again in 1981 when the budget cuts were rushed through with insufficient concern for the human consequences.

Yet, over the long haul, the legislative record of Congress has been good. If 1964–1965 brought too much of a good thing, those years also brought some legislation that was overdue. The 1981 cuts represented another extreme, a reaction against the bloated expansion of the federal government and its programs. The budget cuts hardly constituted what the liberals called the repeal of the New Deal, because the federal budget *after* the cuts still amounted to more than $700 billion. Congress' actions in 1981 consisted of not much more than a crudely executed trimming of the Great Society programs of the 1960s, which fair-minded people agreed needed to be pruned. Any further cuts should be imposed with more care and compassion, and centrists believed that in this respect Congress would provide the necessary con-

straints on overzealous proposals by the administration. Moreover, centrists welcomed the congressional resistance that emerged in 1982 to the huge deficits contained in the administration's budgetary proposals, resistance that included some of the "boll weevils" on whom Reagan had depended for his successes in 1981.

Centrists expressed concern about the proposal of some conservatives in the Senate to move beyond the economic area into socioreligious issues like abortion, school prayers, and so on. Centrists were divided among themselves on such issues, but they feared that if Congress took strong action on these issues the fragile consensus on which the social order rests would be torn apart.

So centrists placed their hopes for preventing such measures on the innumerable barriers that reside in the structure and procedures of Congress; and their hopes were realized in 1982 when liberal senators filibustered successfully against conservative efforts to overrule the Supreme Court on abortion and school prayers.

Reforms.   Centrists look for those reforms of Congress that would enable it to carry out in full its responsibilities as a balance wheel of the Constitution. They recognize that the balance is not the same as the plan originally prescribed, and that today a great deal of the legislative initiative is in the president's hands.

Just the same, they insist that Congress still has a central role. Indeed, many of the programs for which presidents have claimed credit have been adopted by the White House after long study by committees of Congress. Centrists want to see Congress become even more important, so they advocate the kind of reforms that would help Congress to propose long-range public policy of its own, thereby lessening the president's dependence on the federal bureaucracies; to scrutinize more rigorously the legislative programs coming from the administration; and to do a more thorough and extensive job in overseeing the legislation of administrative agencies.

To these ends centrists would like to see Congress take further steps toward more rational management, including reorganization of the House committee structure and the enhancement of Congress' ability to gather and interpret information through computerization and the appointment of more research staff.

But, the centrists insist, we do not need drastic departures in the leadership structure of the Congress. Seniority, having been made accountable, should be preserved. So should the modified filibuster. And at all costs we should avoid the liberals' prescription to replace traditional procedures and leadership styles with centralized party organization. Persuasive guidance from party leaders in Congress is appropriate. Tight party discipline, backed by the power to expel a dissenter from the party, has no place in the American scheme of things.

THE CONSERVATIVES

In considerable measure conservatives agree with the centrists' rebuttal of the liberals' criticism of Congress, so we need not repeat those rebuttals under the conservatives' analysis. Still, the conservative appraisal of Congress also has some special features of its own.

Traditionally, conservatives have much preferred Congress to the presidency. Congress is a representative body in a fuller sense than the presidency. Thus Willmoore Kendall spoke of the presidency as an institution responding to the national mass electorate, "a *plebiscitary* political system, capable of carrying through *popular mandates*," whereas Congress represented the electorate in all its complexity and diversity. Against the liberalizing dynamic of the presidency, Congress was an institution that could serve conservative purposes by supporting the reduction of government spending, strong measures against internal subversion, large military forces, and vigorous nationalism.[19]

But then disenchantment set in for the conservatives. The federal budget began to increase by enormous amounts each year, with Congress sometimes outbidding the president in its enthusiasm for more spending and its tolerance for huge deficits. This situation was not surprising, said the conservatives, because Congress was unlikely to care very much about protecting the country from unnecessary federal spending when its members' appetite for feeding at the public trough was growing so voraciously. They voted themselves large salaries, generous retirement programs, and other fringe benefits. They obtained excessive travel expenses to and from their districts, frivolous overseas junkets, and free mailing privileges. They built oversized staffs that enlarged their career opportunities by pushing for bigger federal budgets and programs that would require more supervision by Congress and thus result in more power for themselves.

Conservatives also became discouraged by the weakening of the factors that had given Congress its conservative bias: the disproportionate influence of rural, small-town areas and the South, and the filibuster, seniority, and the power of the Rules Committee. And there were the efforts to make Congress more modern and efficient. For modernness and efficiency, said the conservative analyst James Burnham, look to "Hitler's Reichstag and the Kremlin's Supreme Soviet. . . ."[20]

However, by the late 1970s conservatives again began to see hope for Congress. The resistance to growing federal spending in the country began to be reflected in the voting behavior of the two houses. A sample of the freshmen lawmakers entering the 96th Congress in 1979 showed that only 11.4 percent rated themselves as liberal or moderate liberal, 34.1 percent as moderate, and 54.5 percent as conservative or moderate conservative.[21]

The 97th Congress was even more promising for conservatives. A 1981 survey indicated that 78 percent of the freshmen saw themselves as conservative or moderate conservative, with only 7 percent in the liberal to moderate liberal camp.[22] Then, of course, there was the Republican triumph in the 1980 elections to the Senate, with the defeat of some leading liberals and the accession to the top committee positions of several stellar conservatives. Conservatives were delighted with a Senate that gave so much power to Strom

Thurmond, Orrin Hatch, John Tower, Jake Garn, and Jesse Helms (whose influence as a national leader of the "New Right" went far beyond his chairmanship of the Agriculture Committee). With moderates like Howard Baker as Majority Leader and Charles Percy as Foreign Relations chair, there was still room for improvement, but still, the National Conservative Political Action Committee and other conservative organizations had done extremely well in electing so many conservatives to Congress in 1980. With further efforts in subsequent elections Congress would become an even more securely conservative bastion than it used to be.

The task at hand was to continue the work of reducing the federal budget that had been so well begun in 1981, and then to press forward into areas of social policy, such as abortion and school prayers, using legislation and, where necessary, constitutional amendments proposed by Congress to undo the havoc brought by the Supreme Court on our structure of moral values.

These goals would require a period of forceful action by the Congress. Then Congress could get back to its traditional pace and traditional roles: making laws carefully and slowly, keeping in check the power of the presidency and the bureaucracies, providing the resources needed to protect our national security, and preserving the traditional values of America.

CONCLUSION

Congress is not well regarded by the American people. In an era in which all of our institutions are given poor ratings in opinion surveys, Congress ranks among the lowest. In 1979, when Jimmy Carter's performance was given only a 19 percent good or excellent rating in an Associated Press/NBC poll, the comparable figure for Congress was 13 percent, with 47 percent saying that Congress' work was "only fair" and 36 percent describing it as poor.

Among the reasons commonly cited for this dismal assessment are the various scandals involving members of Congress (the 1979 poll was taken in the midst of the Abscam affair). But there is also widespread dissatisfaction with Congress' legislative performance, especially its alternations between interminable squabbling and subservience to the presidential will. In both directions Congress is widely perceived among the American electorate to be a weak, ineffectual body.

The perception abroad tends to be rather different. The ability of Congress to thwart a president's will and the delays and drastic modifications imposed on both domestic and international proposals of the executive branch are regarded abroad with awe, incredulity, and exasperation.

Perhaps this view from abroad is overstated. The United States is not a complete exception to the rule that an era of perpetual crises must be an age of executives rather than of legislatures. And yet, among the world's legislatures, there is none quite as potent or quite as remarkable as the Congress of the United States.

NOTES AND REFERENCES

1. Although the Constitution does not specifically say that Congress can conduct investigations, the Supreme Court has found that investigations are a natural corollary of Congress' legislative authority, because they help Congress gather the information needed to make the laws. The investigative power carries with it the power to subpoena

witnesses and compel them, under threat of imprisonment for contempt of Congress, to testify under oath (unless they take the Fifth Amendment). However, in recent years the Supreme Court has set some limits to Congress' power to punish, insisting that Congress not "expose for the sake of exposure" and that it relate its questions to its legislative purposes.

2. In recent years the president has been confronted by an increasing number of laws providing Congress with a one-house veto. This legislative veto allows Congress, by a simple majority vote in either House or Senate, to block an action by a federal agency without any further legislation. This kind of veto was being reviewed by the federal courts in 1982.

3. For example, in 1979 Representative Charles Diggs of Michigan was sentenced to jail for inflating the salaries of staff members and then accepting kickbacks from them.

4. The word *denounced* is regarded as less severe than the word *censured,* and Talmadge took it as "a personal victory" that he had not been censured.

5. The new codes of ethics were drawn up by special committees in the House and Senate in 1977 and codified into law in 1978.

6. In the House the only leadership position determined on the floor is that of Speaker. However, the other positions are party choices, too, settled in the majority party caucus.

7. The President Pro Tempore is usually the member of the majority party with the longest consecutive service in the Senate.

8. The number of a Congress is advanced every two years after each congressional election.

9. The Democrats in the House have a combined Steering and Policy Committee, which is responsible for making committee assignments and for working with party leaders to set legislative priorities.

10. The boll weevil is an insect that bores into cotton bolls and ruins whole fields of the crop.

11. The striped-wing gypsy moth devours forest foliage in the Midwest and Northeast.

12. Mills ran into trouble in 1974 when his alcoholism led him into erratic behavior, including public escapades with a burlesque dancer known as "Fanne Fox, the Argentine Firecracker." Mills gave up the Ways and Means chairmanship under pressure from House leaders.

13. Hays resigned his chairmanship in 1976 after being accused by a former staff member, Elizabeth Ray, of having put her on his payroll in exchange for sexual services rendered to him and others designated by him.

14. Of course, by 1966 Johnson was more involved with Vietnam than with domestic programs. But even without Vietnam the congressional arithmetic would have created problems for him.

15. John F. Manley, "The House Committee on Ways and Means: Conflict Management in a Congressional Committee," *American Political Science Review* 59, no. 4 (December 1965): 934.

16. Theodore R. Marmor, "The Congress: Medicare Politics and Policy," in Allan P. Sindler, ed., *American Political Institutions and Public Policy* (Boston: Little, Brown, 1969), p. 15.

17. Alan Cranston, "A Liberal's View: Why We Need the Filibuster," *Los Angeles Times,* 10 October 1971.

18. See Frank Munger and Richard Fenno, Jr., *National Politics and Federal Aid to Education* (Syracuse, N.Y.: Syracuse University Press, 1962), pp. 93–94.

19. Willmoore Kendall, *The Conservative Affirmation* (Chicago: Henry Regnery, 1963), pp. 22–24.

20. James Burnham, *Congress and the American Tradition* (Chicago: Henry Regnery Company, 1959), p. 266.

21. *U.S. News and World Report,* 22 January 1979, p. 31.

22. *U.S. News and World Report,* 16 March 1981, p. 50.

chapter nine

THE FEDERAL BUREAUCRACY: A FOURTH BRANCH

As Ronald Reagan saw it, his great election victory in 1980 gave him a mandate to cut down to size the huge institutions in Washington that employ large numbers of federal employees.

This purpose placed him squarely in the tradition of American conservatives. Yet, in recent years, the attack on the federal bureaucracy has not been the exclusive prerogative of conservatives and the far right. From the mid-1960s federal agencies have been the target of pungent criticism from the radical left. And in the mid-1970s Jimmy Carter and a number of other politicians of the center joined the assault on the bureaucracy and made it a prime political issue.

It was easy to join the assault on the bureaucracy because of a growing resentment of the federal government among the public at large. A Gallup survey in June 1978 indicated that 84 percent of those people polled felt that the federal government was spending too much; and another poll showed 76 percent agreeing with the assertion that "the government in Washington is getting too powerful for the good of the country and the individual person."[1]

THE DIMENSIONS OF THE BUREAUCRACY

In 1800 the federal government employed about five thousand people, and the total budget was under $6 million. By 1980 the number of civilian employees had risen to almost 2.9 million, and the budget was over $650 billion. (See tables 9-1 and 9-2.)

The staffs of the federal government work for a number of organizations: the White House, the cabinet departments, a variety of more or less independent agencies, and government corporations.

TABLE 9-1 Federal civilian employment, 1940–1980 (in thousands)

1940	1,128
1945	3,375
1950	2,117
1955	2,378
1960	2,421
1965	2,588
1970	2,881
1975	2,890
1980	2,899

Source: U.S., Department of Commerce, Bureau of the Census.

TABLE 9-2 Federal expenditures, 1901–1980 (in millions of dollars)

1901	525
1910	694
1920	6,358
1930	3,320
1940	9,456
1950	42,597
1960	92,223
1970	196,588
1980	658,800

Source: U.S., Office of Management and Budget.

THE EXECUTIVE OFFICE OF THE PRESIDENT

Immediately serving the president is the White House staff, the president's top advisers and staff members and their subordinates, consisting in recent years of some three hundred to five hundred people.

This core group is part of the larger Executive Office of the President, the size of which has varied over the years according to the councils and offices that each president has decided to include, but which has lately employed around four thousand to five thousand people. Key agencies in the Executive Office include the Office of Management and Budget, the National Security Council, and the Council of Economic Advisers.

THE CABINET

The cabinet departments have also changed in recent years through the consolidation of old functions and the addition of new. Jimmy Carter created a Department of Energy and broke up the Department of Health, Education, and Welfare into two departments: Health and Human Services, and Education. Neither of these developments pleased Ronald Reagan, who proposed the abolition of both the Energy and Education departments. Still, Reagan began his administration with the thirteen cabinet departments left by Carter: State, Defense, Treasury, Justice, Labor, Commerce, Agriculture, Interior, Transportation, Housing and Urban Development, Energy, Health and Human Services, and Education.

By far the largest of all the federal staffs is the staff of the Department of Defense, which employed almost a million civilians in 1981. Then came the Departments of Health and Human Services (160,000), Treasury (131,000), Agriculture (122,000), and Transportation (71,000).

Heading each cabinet department is the secretary (the attorney general in the case of the Justice Department), who is appointed by the president, subject to confirmation by the Senate. The secretary reports directly to the president (although some presidents, notably Richard Nixon, have used their White House staff as intermediaries between them and their cabinet chiefs). The secretaries' top aides hold the title of undersecretary or deputy secretary, and there are assistant secretaries at the next level. (The structure of the Department of Defense is more elaborate, because the secretaries of the Army, Navy, and Air Force report to the secretary of defense, not to the president.)

Within the departments there are various bureaus, offices, services, and administrations. For example, the Justice Department includes the FBI, the Immigration and Naturalization Service, and the Drug Enforcement Administration; the Department of Commerce houses the Bureau of the Census, the Maritime Administration, and the Office of Minority Business Enterprise; and, as figure 9-1 shows, within the Department of Health and Human Services are the Public Health Service, the Social Security Administration, and the Health Care Financing Administration.

THE INDEPENDENT AGENCIES

Next there are a number of "independent" agencies, so called because they are not directly under the supervision of a cabinet department nor part of the Executive Office of the President. The extent to which they are independent of direct control by the president, however, varies considerably, as we shall indicate when considering each category of independent agency.

Regulatory agencies. These agencies include the Federal Communications Commission and the National Labor Relations Board. Their jobs are to regulate the practices of business, labor, and other private economic organizations in accordance with principles established by federal legislation. The commissioners of these agencies are appointed by the president, subject to Senate approval, but are provided by law with a good deal of autonomy: their appointments are for fixed terms, and the president cannot fire them as he can a member of the cabinet or White House staff. Each agency is run by three or more commissioners with overlapping terms of office, and in some cases Congress has established the requirement that their membership be bipartisan to keep the agencies free of political bias.

Administrative or executive agencies. These agencies are directly involved in operating or supervising governmental programs, unlike the regulatory agencies, which intervene in the affairs of private businesses without trying to run them directly. Agencies in this category include the National Aeronautics and Space Administration (NASA) and the Veterans Administration (which employs about a quarter of a million people).

Government corporations. Government corporations own and directly operate major services to the public. For example, the Tennessee Valley Authority, created in the 1930s, provides hydroelectric power, irrigation, and flood control, and the U.S. Postal Service has a near-monopoly of mail delivery. Although these corporations are public agencies owned by the government, they have a good deal more flexibility than cabinet departments and are not subject to the detailed administrative and financial controls that the White House and the Congress impose on the departments.

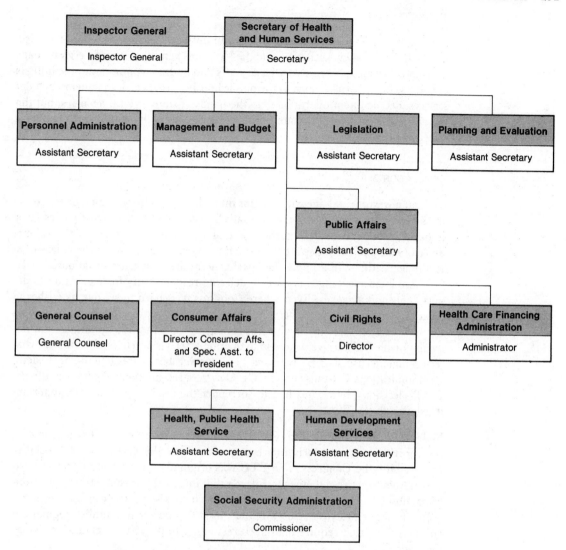

FIGURE 9–1.   Department of Health and Human Services, 1981
Source: U.S. Government Manual, 1981–1982.

THE RANGE OF FUNCTIONS

The functions of these various federal governmental agencies cover almost every kind of responsibility of modern government, including administering and implementing programs, drawing up specific rules or legislation, adjudicating or settling disputes, and enforcing legislation.

ADMINISTRATION

In various degrees many federal agencies administer programs. The Postal Service, the Tennessee Valley Authority, and the Veterans Administration directly manage enormous enterprises, with very large staffs and budgets running into the billions of dollars. In other cases, such as the public housing program or the unemployment services, detailed administration is in the hands of state or local agencies, but the federal agency retains ultimate administrative control by establishing national policies and guidelines.

LEGISLATION

Federal governmental agencies are not limited to the administration or execution of the laws. In many cases, they actually legislate. When Congress passes laws, it usually couches them in rather general terms, leaving it up to the cabinet departments and the independent regulatory agencies to draw up the rules—that is, the legislation—that apply the laws' generalities to specific situations.

There is no escaping this need to delegate responsibility for legislation to departments and agencies. Even where Congress tries hard to set out its wishes in detail, it cannot anticipate every eventuality. For example, Congress simply does not have time to become involved in setting up the specific regulations that determine who will receive a license to operate a television channel or under what terms that license will be renewed. This power has to be left to the Federal Communications Commission (FCC). Congress retains the right to overrule the FCC's decisions, but it has had to surrender the authority to initiate important legislation to the FCC.

Federal Trade Commission (FTC). The work of the Federal Trade Commission provides a particularly interesting example of the delegation of legislative responsibility by Congress. The FTC was originally established to protect businesses from practices by other businesses that impeded fair competition, but Congress subsequently gave the FTC broad authority to also protect consumers against unfair business practices. The FTC has used this power to establish regulations on advertising that require manufacturers either to prove their claims or change their ads.

When Norelco claimed that its product shaved "up to 50 percent faster"; when General Electric declared that its air conditioners reproduced the "clean freshness of clear, cool mountain air"; when Smith, Kline and French told people that "a summer cold is a different animal" requiring a different medication from a winter cold, the FTC demanded that they prove it. Although the FTC did not challenge Profile Bread's assertion that it contained fewer calories per slice the commission pointed out that this claim was true only because Profile's slices were thinner, and it required future advertising to make this point clear. Similarly, Lysol's claim that it "kills germs on environmental surfaces" was true enough. But, said the FTC, this claim meant very little because communicable diseases are transmitted by airborne germs.

The FTC also issued guidelines governing the use of celebrities in advertising. Unless they actually used the product, the FTC would challenge the ads as an unfair trade practice. So former baseball stars Whitey Ford and Mickey Mantle could not endorse Lite Beer on television commercials unless they also drank it offscreen. (However, an ad that showed quarterback Joe Namath wearing panty-hose could be considered "fanciful" under the guidelines, so he did not have to wear them regularly.)

The FTC's authority over false and misleading advertising was also used to limit cigarette advertising. In 1955 the FTC issued guidelines banning claims that cigarettes were good for you. (Kool cigarettes offered "extra protection" in the winter months, and Julep cigarettes were touted as a remedy for coughs.) The FTC took action on a 1964 report of a Surgeon General's Advisory Commission on Smoking and Health. The agency began a series of steps that led eventually to the inclusion of a health warning on all cigarette packages and advertisements, and to the banning of all cigarette commercials from television and radio.

Food and Drug Administration (FDA).   This agency provides further examples of the vigorous use of legislative power by administrative agencies. Using the authority that Congress gave it to protect the consumer against harmful foods and drugs, it has ordered many drugs off the market or insisted that they be sold by prescription only. Acting under the so-called Delaney Amendment to the food and drug laws, requiring that any additive shown to cause cancer in animals must be banned, the FDA forbade makers of dietetic drinks or foods from using cyclamates, a synthetic sugar substitute. Then in 1977 an order was issued to limit the sale of saccharin on the same grounds. Furthermore, FDA regulations now require that labels on food products must identify nutrients, vitamins, and fat and cho-lesterol content.

ADJUDICATION

In addition to administering and legislating, some federal agencies adjudicate—that is, they settle conflicts between contending parties much as courts do.

Over the years Congress has passed a flood of legislation aimed at regulating and controlling business, labor, agricultural, and professional groups. Laws of that kind inevitably give rise to disputes, sometimes between the affected groups and government, sometimes among the groups themselves. These disputes have become so frequent and complex that the regular courts of law have neither the time nor the expertise to handle them. Consequently, federal regulatory agencies have been assigned a judicial, or quasi-judicial, function. In some cases this func-tion has led to their establishing hearing procedures that, although not as formal as the courts themselves, are nonetheless rigorous and quite elaborate.

The National Labor Relations Board (NLRB) is a good example of a federal agency that spends much of its time adjudicating disputes. Congress has passed laws forbidding unfair labor practices, and in a general way the legislation in-dicates the criteria for what constitutes an unfair practice. But whether or not management or labor has acted unfairly will depend on the very specific circumstances of a labor dispute, and this dispute will often be settled by the NLRB after full-scale hearings between the parties to the conflict.

ENFORCEMENT

Yet another responsibility of federal agencies is enforcement. Although most of the law enforcement activity in the country is carried out at the state and local levels, many federal statutes include provisions for criminal penalties. For example, penalties were included in federal laws dealing with kidnapping, forgery, unauthorized wiretapping or electronic bugging, income tax evasion, violating the election finance code of 1974, or engaging in consumer fraud in any business that crosses state lines. Several agencies employ staffs to investigate, apprehend, and prosecute persons suspected of breaking such laws, most notably the FBI and U.S. attorneys in the Department of Justice, and the enforcement officers of the Treasury Department.

Sometimes all these functions—administration, legislation, adjudication, and enforcement—are exercised by the same agency. For example, the Interstate Commerce Commission *legislates* when it makes rules regulating the rates charged by railroads and trucks; it *adjudicates* when it sits as a tribunal to determine if its regulations have been violated; it enters the realm of *enforcement* when it investigates complaints and initiates proceedings against alleged violators.

So the constitutional principle of the separation of powers does not seem to set bounds to the work of the federal agencies. In this respect, they are not unique. As we have seen, the president is also a legislator, and congressional investigations sometimes take on the aura usually associated with the judiciary. Still, the federal agencies are even less bound by the separation of powers than any of the traditional three branches of government.

Taken together, federal government agencies spend vast sums of money, employ very large staffs, and make great numbers of decisions, some of enormous significance to the lives and fortunes of millions of people.

PRESIDENTIAL AND CONGRESSIONAL SUPERVISION OF THE FEDERAL BUREAUCRACY

Nominally, the federal agencies are subordinate to the executive and legislative branches, and the president and Congress have a number of specific devices available to them to assert their power over the bureaucracy.

PRESIDENTIAL INFLUENCE

The president can place the stamp of his policies on the bureaucracy by appointing people to the top positions. Most of these positions are filled by members of the president's own party, and special efforts are made to find people whose views are compatible with the president's views for the upper-level appointments.

Presidents also have ways of checking on the work of the departments and agencies. In the Executive Office the president has advisers who can give detailed information on economic, national security, and many other problems, so that the president does not have to rely only on the information submitted by the various departments and agencies.

Next, the budget proposals of every department have to be cleared through the Office of Management and Budget (OMB) in the Executive Office of the President.

Finally, presidents themselves, through their previous legislative or administrative experience, usually develop specialized knowledge in a number of fields and can have a powerful impact whenever they decide to concentrate their efforts in any of these fields.

CONGRESSIONAL INFLUENCE

The bureaucracies must also reckon with Congress. In chapter 8 we saw that one of the legislator's functions is to intervene with the bureaucracies on behalf of constituents. But representatives do not go cap in hand to beg for favors. After all, most members of the bureaucracy maintain a healthy respect for the wishes of Congress because a department's requests for funds and proposals for legislation must be scrutinized by congressional committees and subcommittees whose staff and senior members will probably have acquired close knowledge of the department's activities and a special insight into the agency's patterns of spending. Another check on federal bureaucracies is the reports to the Congress by the head of its General Accounting Office, the U.S. comptroller general, which frequently point out the failures in existing programs, thereby giving Congress a warning signal against approving similar proposals for the future. Congress can also investigate government programs through its Government Operations committees or any of its standing committees or special investigation subcommittees.

Finally, Congress has established precise rules governing the procedures of the regulatory agencies, and increasingly in recent years it has built into its laws a kind of "legislative veto," under which an agency's regulations can be modified or annulled or, in some cases, prevented from being issued.

Congress intervened to delay and dilute the Federal Trade Commission's efforts to regulate cigarette advertising. Further, Congress delayed the proposed Food and Drug Administration's ban on saccharin in 1977 pending further research, even though the ban was imposed under the requirements of Congress' own Delaney Amendment.

BUREAUCRATIC AUTONOMY

In many ways, then, the federal bureaucracies are directed, supervised, checked on, and sometimes harassed by the president and Congress. Yet it would not be correct to see them as merely instruments of the elected branches of government. Each bureaucracy has a life and a will of its own, and it is difficult, sometimes impossible, to bring it completely under control.

The president, as we have seen, appoints most of the top policy makers. But these people comprise only about two thousand out of almost 2.9 million federal civilian employees. Most of the rest are protected by Civil Service rules, which were designed to cut down on the corruption in government commonly associated with a *spoils system*, a system under which appointments go to political allies, friends, or relatives. Civil Service also increases the attractiveness of federal careers by providing security of employment.

As for the independent regulatory agencies, the president's control is even more limited than over the regular cabinet departments because the commissioners who run the agencies serve long, staggered terms and the president's right to remove them has been severely restricted by Congress.

The fact that the agencies are staffed mostly with people making a lifetime career in the bureaucracy means that each agency develops its own continuing identity and long-range purposes, which are not easy to change. The president's appointees fill the top positions, but they do not reach far down into the administration hierarchy. The existing staff have to be persuaded to accept proposals for change.

SPECIALIZED INFORMATION

However, the staff may be able to show that newly proposed ideas cannot work. The staff members, after all, have built up years of experience and practical knowledge. They can draw immediately on a staggering array of data of which a new director at the top is relatively ignorant. They can command the kind of technical and scientific competence that is increasingly necessary in making effective decisions and that is not usually part of the preparation of presidents (other than Herbert Hoover and Jimmy Carter, who were trained as engineers) or most of their top advisers.

Even though presidents have been trying to offset the bureaucracies' informational advantage by building up their personal staffs of technical advisers in the White House and the Executive Office, and although Congress, too, has steadily improved its facilities for gathering data, these staffs cannot possibly keep up with everything for which they are responsible. With over one thousand federal programs to supervise the informational resources of president and Congress must be spread so thin that most programs can receive only occasional and perfunctory review.

INERTIA

Even when an incoming administration is determined to produce major changes and refuses to accept the bureaucracy's expert arguments as to why the changes will not work, new policies may be slow in coming. Although the secretary can pass the word down the line that this policy is what the president wants and that the matter is urgent and must be given top priority, the response from the permanent staff may be one of inertia, an unwillingness to move and to accept change: "We're working on it, Mr. Secretary. We're moving as fast as we can. But these things take time. A great many people will be affected by the change, and they have to be consulted. There are statutes and legal problems and congressional sensitivities to take into account. It may cost more money than is available." And so on.

Only persistent, energetic pressure from the top can overcome this kind of resistance. And at the top all too many responsibilities and pressures divert attention from the issue at hand.

CONSTITUENCIES

Bureaucracies do not operate in a vacuum. Over the years they build their own constituencies around the country. Agencies develop close ties with big and small businesses, professional groups, labor unions, farmers, veterans, minority groups, and consumer organizations. Thus the Federal Housing Administration works with home builders' organizations, the Department of Agriculture with farmers, and the Air Force with the aerospace industry and the Air Force Association. As a result the agencies can muster outside support for their policies, which may or may not coincide with the policies of president and Congress.

MANEUVERING BETWEEN PRESIDENT AND CONGRESS

Federal agencies can also advance their programs by playing the executive and legislative branches off against each other. Any high departmental official who knows his or her job will try to establish close relationships with key congressional committee and subcommittee chairpersons. The president expects those relationships to be used for his own ends, and he demands that his appointed officials present and defend his policies before Congress; federal agencies can thus be among the most effective lobbies for a president's programs.

But it may not always be so. Suppose the official is a general who is appearing before Congress to explain the administration's position that a new weapons system should be cut from the budget. He loyally presents the policy of the president and the secretary of defense. But then a member of the Armed Services Committee (who may possibly have discussed this plan ahead of time with the general) presses him hard on whether or not he really agrees with the policy. By some turn of phrase or intonation he may then let slip the possibility that he harbors doubts about the wisdom of that policy. This insinuation would hardly present his civilian chiefs with sufficient grounds for punishing him. But the doubts the general has raised may well have damaged the chances that the president will have his way.

Thus the federal bureaucracies, by protecting their programs with specialized knowledge and inertia, by cultivating organized constituencies, and by maneuvering between Congress and president, have become much more than an instrument of presidential and congressional power. They have become a power in their own right—in a sense, a fourth branch of government. Power on this scale, with large numbers of people in vast institutions and impressive financial resources, will attract many critics. We shall review their arguments from various points on the spectrum, concentrating on the conservatives' strong criticisms and the liberals' defense of the bureaucracy.

FIVE PERSPECTIVES ON THE FEDERAL BUREAUCRACY

THE CONSERVATIVES: THE THREAT TO LIBERTY

To the conservatives the greatest menace to the American constitutional system is the enormous growth of government. To them it is potentially the death knell of our freedoms, taking us at an ever faster pace toward state socialism.

Concentrated power: people and money. The sheer size of the resources—both in personnel and in money—accumulated in government represents a concentration of power of staggering dimensions. In addition to the nearly 2.9 million civilians who work for the federal government (plus 2.1 million in the military services), state and local governments employ over 13 million people. Thus there are about 16 million civilians who work for government in America, which is close to one-sixth of the total civilian work force. Then, too, there are several million on welfare, and millions more who work on research grants funded by the federal government, get farm or other federal subsidies, or receive help from Washington in the form of reduced interest rates or guarantees of loans, as in the housing industry.

When so many people are dependent, directly or indirectly, on the public exchequer, it becomes increasingly difficult to avoid governmental control of our entire society. The danger is reinforced by the fact that the expansion of governmental employment has been far exceeded by the growth of governmental spending. In the twenty-five years from Truman to Nixon the federal budget went up tenfold, from $30 billion to $300 billion, then doubled again by the end of the Carter presidency.

This rate of increase in federal spending has far exceeded the rates of inflation and of population growth. In addition, state and local government spending and employment have been increasing at a reckless pace.

In part this rise is because of the proliferation of programs providing financial help to almost every imaginable constituency. The rest results from the growth of the governmental payrolls. Of all the groups that benefit from larger government budgets, none can compare with the employees of government.

Until recently a career in government was regarded as secure but relatively low paid. The protection of civil service was accepted as a justification for rather modest salaries. But now, as the demand for government services has grown and government employees have banded together in militant unions, there has been strong upward pressure on salaries. With generous pension plans, vacations, and sick leaves, most government employees today are clearly doing better than workers in private industry.

Big government limits individual freedom. This colossus of government interferes with our lives and liberties in many ways. First, big government imposes an intolerable tax burden. When so much of our money is taken in taxes, we are denied the right to make our own choices on how to spend it.

Second, when government bureaucrats make decisions on our behalf, they assume that they know better than we do what is good for us. This assumption underlies the banning of cigarette advertising on television and radio. Even if a relationship between cigarettes and cancer has been proven (and there is still some question as to whether the statistics conclusively prove a causal relationship), it does not follow that government should interfere with the right of citizens to make their own decisions.

The Food and Drug Administration (FDA) is another agency determined to protect us from ourselves, especially since stringent new guidelines for the agency were adopted in 1962. It banned cyclamates as a sugar substitute when research showed that rats who were fed massive doses of the chemical sometimes developed cancer. But if rats are fed massive doses of anything—far beyond the dosage likely to be ingested over several years by people—some ill effects will show up. When later research threw doubt on the earlier results, the FDA was unmoved. In fact, it proceeded to take action against saccharin. Who will protect obese people from the FDA?

Conservatives now question whether the FDA should exist. The agency has approved far fewer drugs than it used to before 1962, and it has taken longer to give its approval. Admittedly, these delays have kept some dangerous drugs off the market. But by slowing down the rate of innovation, the tougher standards have also prevented or delayed the appearance of drugs that might have saved lives or alleviated ailments. As figure 9-2 shows, we have enmeshed the pharmaceutical industry in far more red tape than is the case in most other countries, with the result that Americans who can afford it travel to Europe to buy drugs and receive treatment unavailable here.

FIGURE 9–2 Months[a] needed to approve new drugs

Great Britain	5
Switzerland	12
Canada	16
Norway	17
U.S.	23
Sweden	28

[a] Figures are average from time fourteen important new drugs were submitted for government approval until permitted to be sold.

Source: U.S., General Accounting Office, 1981.

MIKE PETERS, DAYTON DAILY NEWS, DAYTON, OHIO.
"Remember the good old days when we only had to smoke a few cigarettes and eat saccharin?"

We are being forced, say the conservatives, into a national hypochondria. Hidden dangers lurk in every commodity. Whatever was once wholesome and life-giving is now a deadly poison. Undoubtedly there is a degree of danger in everything we do or use. But when we try to eliminate all risk from our lives we pay a terrible price in the surrender of our liberties.

Third, big government has all but deprived businesspeople of the freedom to run their firms in the interest of themselves, their stockholders, and their customers. Owners and managers are no longer free to make their own decisions but must operate within policies, set by government and monitored by armies of bureaucrats, on occupational safety and health, labor relations, environmental protection, motor vehicle safety, "affirmative action" on the hiring and promotion of minorities and women, antitrust requirements, and so on. (See figure 9-3.) With so much of the decision-making process referred to Washington, the most important merit of the capitalist system—that it decentralizes and diffuses power—has been seriously eroded.

Bureaucratic waste and incompetence. Our national bureaucracies, say the conservatives, are appallingly wasteful and incompetent. The very word *bureaucracy* is synonymous for conservatives with rigidity, extreme caution, confusion, duplication, evasion of responsibility, and lack of sensitivity and imagination. Without the lash of competition or the lure of profits, and protected by Civil Service security, federal bureaucracies lack the incentives that inspire private business to perform well. It is no wonder that, when government agencies are called on to manage large enterprises such as the Postal Service, their performance is pathetically inferior to the performance of private business.

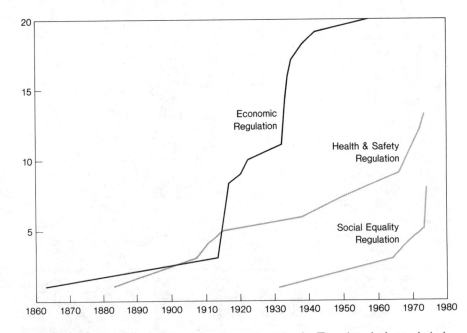

FIGURE 9–3. Creation of Federal Regulatory Agencies, by Type (graphed cumulatively over time)
Source: Advisory Commission on Intergovernmental Relations, "The Federal Role in the Federal System: The Dynamics of Growth," Washington, D.C., August 1981, p.77.

In place of effective decisions and sound policies the bureaucrats issue vast quantities of minutely detailed regulations. One of these regulations, for example, prescribed when paper clips should be used on food stamp files and when the files should be stapled. Altogether, by 1980 there were 180 federal agencies engaged in this process of issuing regulations to business. The listing of these regulations in the Federal Register ran to 87,000 pages.

Complying with the regulations required businesses to complete each year billions of pages of forms, applications, and reports; and sorting and filing this mountain of paper provided jobs for over 200,000 federal employees.

Obscurity in written communication is another persistent problem in the federal bureaucracy. Lyndon Johnson's secretary of labor, Willard Wirtz, was often baffled by the memos sent to him:

> Most sentences are long. Three or four ideas are loaded in to increase the odds that one will be impressive and that if another is wrong it will get lost. Paragraphs are built like sandwiches, the meat in the middle. . . . The Department's effectiveness would be doubled if its prose were cut in half, if those who initialled documents read them, and if those who signed them wrote some of them. In none of this is the Department of Labor in any way exceptional.[2]

Another cause of massive waste is the duplication and overlapping of effort that results from the great size and diversity of the federal establishment. It presents an intolerably unwieldy mass that cannot possibly be properly supervised and coordinated.

Resources are given to the bureaucracies not on the basis of rational allocation but as a result of presidential fiat and constituency pressures. And, once a program is established, it is extraordinarily difficult to put an end to it. "Of all our institutions," says Peter Drucker, *"business is the only one that society will permit to disappear."*[3] Government agencies and programs, by contrast, survive long after they have outlived their usefulness. For example, during World War II, school districts that received a sudden influx of defense workers or service personnel were designated as "impacted areas" and were given federal aid. In the 1970s hundreds of millions of dollars a year were still going from Washington to impacted areas, although many had become high-income communities.

Not only do federal agencies survive; most of them expand. Once a program has been started, there are always impressive reasons for its growth. Government agencies can show with great conviction and plausibility why they ought to have more money and staff. However small the first appropriation for a program may be, the camel's nose is under the tent and soon the rest of the beast will follow.

A new department, a new bureau within a department, or a new office within a bureau becomes a pressure group for its own enlargement. To be effective it must build a large staff. It must also develop outside constituencies: farmers for the Department of Agriculture, hospital administrators and social workers for the Department of Health and Human Services, and so on. It nourishes those constituencies with grants and subsidies of all kinds. Conservatives enjoy citing Democratic Senator William Proxmire's "Golden Fleece Awards," given to recognize federal grants for mind-boggling research projects, such as $84,000 to find out why people fall in love and $120,000 to determine how smoking marijuana affects the sexual arousal of male college students.

Among the leading recipients of this federal largess are academics; and conservatives take particular objection to the many grants going to social scientists. Such grants, they contend, are a waste of money at best, and at worst they subsidize the kind of research that produces still more government interference in our lives.

Corruption. When such huge amounts of money are at stake, fraud and corruption on a large scale become inevitable. Billions of dollars in taxpayers' money have been misappropriated through fraud in welfare programs, kickbacks in defense projects, and payoffs to government inspectors charged with checking on performance under various kinds of federal contracts. A huge bribery and kickback scandal rocked the General Services Administration (GSA), the federal government's purchasing and housekeeping agency, in the late 1970s. Some 140 GSA staff members and others were convicted on charges including systematically stealing from GSA supply stores, conspiring with contractors to pay millions of dollars for work that was never performed, and receiving bribes including cash, sailboats, jewelry, and trips to the Bahamas to fix the bidding on competitive contracts or to inflate the price paid to contractors.

Damage to business and the economy. Not only is government inefficient in itself, it is the cause of inefficiency in others. The cost of regulations is not only that incurred by federal agencies. A Presidential Task Force on Regulatory Relief appointed by President Reagan reported in 1981 that "the budgetary costs of these excessive regulations were passed on to individuals in the form of higher taxes, while regulatory compliance costs by businesses added billions of dollars per year to the price of goods and services Americans bought." And the administration estimated that its efforts to review, postpone, or modify its first list of targeted regulations would show a one-time saving of up to $18 billion, followed by annual savings of as much as $6 billion.

Nor would these savings be for government and big business alone. According to a 1980 study by the Small Business Administration, the nation's ten million small business firms were forced to spend about $10 billion a year in producing over 300 million reports filed with 103 federal agencies; and another $2.7 billion in costs was forced on small businesses by the reporting requirements of state and local governments.

Another kind of damage inflicted by government on business, say the conservatives, was noted in our discussion of interest groups in chapter 6. In this perspective, when government protects business with subsidies, tariff barriers, and special tax breaks, it undermines the efficiency of the economy by cushioning the impact of competition, thus enabling incompetent businesspeople to survive and even flourish.

Incentives are further weakened, say the conservatives, by the large bite that taxes take out of personal income. Finally, huge federal budgets and deficits year after year are, in the conservatives' analysis, the principal cause of inflation. And, they argue, nothing is more demoralizing and harmful to the economy than inflation.

The conservatives' proposals for reform. To deal with these problems conservatives have proposed the following reforms:

First, we should sharply reduce federal spending and staffs. Government is needed only to perform certain essential functions, notably protecting the public health and safety, preserving the national security from external threats, regulating the supply of money, and enforcing private contracts. Beyond these basic tasks we should reduce and eventually do away with massive giveaway programs that serve only to provide funds for professional researchers, make business inefficient, and justify the existence of the bureaucracies.

Second, we should curtail federal regulation of business. Regulations have proliferated in such areas as worker safety and environmental protection that take no account whatsoever of cost. Although safety on the job and a healthy environment are certainly important values, they cannot be pursued so far as to eliminate all other values, such as reasonable prices, productivity, and timely delivery, not to mention freedom from bureaucratic domination.

As for the protection of the consumer, conservatives would eliminate all government interference with business except for laws to protect against gross fraud. As James Kilpatrick puts it: "I hold to this simple proposition: that the government has no business passing laws to prevent a man from making a durned fool of himself—so long as his conduct harms no one else."[4] Thus we should cut down the regulatory powers of the Federal Trade Commission and curtail or abolish the Food and Drug Administration.

Certainly we should resist the proposal sponsored by liberals to create a consumer protection agency that would ride herd on other federal regulatory agencies. This example is typical of the poverty of liberal thought. Confronted with the shortcomings of federal agencies, their remedy is to create yet another federal agency. The trend should be in the opposite direction. Thus conservatives support "sunset laws," under which every new program must be reevaluated at regular intervals and abolished unless it is clearly serving a useful purpose.

Third, we should adopt businesslike practices in the operation of the federal government by bringing more businesspeople into government and freeing them to use the methods they have applied so successfully in industry. We should also undertake a determined new effort to reorganize and simplify the federal bureaucracies. There have been a number of attempts to accomplish reorganization in the past, following various studies, of which the most notable was the Hoover Commission on Organization of the Executive Branch in 1949. Although the various reorganizations have produced some savings, they have not succeeded in overcoming the enormous waste and duplication in the federal government. The reason is that they have dealt with reorganization in the context of massively overgrown government. Reorganization can only be effective when it accompanies a reduction of the federal government that brings it down to manageable proportions.

Fourth, we should decentralize. As many functions as possible should be moved from the federal government to other management units. Some services would be run more efficiently by private industry or subjected to competition by private companies. For example, government should abandon its monopoly of first-class mail, allowing private companies to enter the field and provide the type of healthy competition that is now limited to parcel delivery and to second- and third-class mail. In other cases responsibility should be shifted to state and local governments. Although such a shift does not necessarily remove the taint of socialism from governmental activities, at least it lessens the huge, inefficient concentration of power in Washington.

Conservatives were delighted that President Reagan adopted all these proposals from the earliest days of his administration. Reductions in federal spending and taxes were the first order of business. Next in the order of priorities was a reduction of federal regulations, and a top-level committee under the chairmanship of Vice-President Bush pointed the way to the elimination of vast numbers of burdensome and expensive rules. Many of the last-minute regulations imposed by the outgoing Carter Administration in several fields of commerce, industry, and agriculture were frozen by the new president. Thirty-four air pollution and safety regulations were eliminated or relaxed with the intent of saving the automobile industry $1.3 billion. Proposed regulations for bilingual education that would have cost about $1 billion over five years were scrapped. The new head of the Occupational Safety and Health Administration (OSHA) declared that his agency would issue no new rules unless there was a demonstrated and significant risk to workers and if the cost of the changes was worth the benefits. Proposed rules governing the exposure of workers to cotton dust would be reviewed, and the Reagan administration's preference would clearly be for protective masks for workers rather than the expensive workplace engineering changes favored by the Carter administration.

But conservatives worried that the antiregulatory momentum of the Reagan White House and of his appointees to federal agencies might be slowed down in time by the fierce resistances of the bureaucrats whose jobs depended on the federal programs and the organized constituencies who were sustained by those programs. Federal money, federal protection, and federal regulation have become so deeply embedded in our economic system that the businesspeople who cry out against government interference still turn to government to provide a cushion against risk.

Only sustained pressure by conservatives on the administration could protect it, they believed, from entering into so many compromises with opponents in Congress, in the federal agencies, and even in the private sector, that the bureaucrats would once again emerge as a pervasive, dominant element in the American system. To provide permanent protection against this possibility, some conservatives have proposed a constitutional amendment that would set a ceiling on federal spending. An amendment to mandate a balanced budget would not be sufficient to satisfy these conservatives, because it does not protect against establishing a balance at increasing levels of spending supported by increasing levels of taxation. So we need constitutional protection against the pressures from all sides for expanded services and expanded outlays in order to guarantee the freedoms intended by the Founding Fathers.

THE RADICAL RIGHT: THE BUREAUCRATIC CONSPIRACY

The conservatives are angry with the growth of the federal bureaucracies, but the radical right is enraged. Conservatives see the expansion of the welfare state as leading eventually toward socialism; the radicals see the danger as going deeper and farther: "There are many stages of welfarism, socialism, and collectivism in general, but communism is the ultimate state of them all, and they all lead inevitably in that direction."[5]

Moreover, conservatives see the trend toward socialism as being accomplished by people who, although often well-meaning, do not understand that their policies are leading us toward the end of our freedoms. The radical right, on the other hand, believes that the advance toward socialism-communism is a carefully planned operation, conducted by people who know exactly what they are doing. These conspirators include elected leaders who have brainwashed the people into choosing them. But they also include large numbers of career officials, bureaucrats who, year after year, are working away at building their power and subverting American institutions.

These bureaucrats, some of them Communists, others close allies of the Communists, are heavily entrenched in the State Department and have been largely instrumental in controlling the policies that have allowed Soviet imperialism to extend its sway over so much of the world. Others are found in the civilian staff of the Defense Department, where they hamstring and overrule the military. Others control our monetary policies from their positions on the Federal Reserve Board. Still other agents of the conspiracy are in key posts in monstrously large agencies such as the Departments of Health and Human Services and Housing and Urban Development, which direct tens of billions of dollars taken from ordinary taxpayers into the pockets of social workers, university researchers, and community troublemakers; or they are in the Federal Trade Commission and the Food and Drug Administration, which are used as bases for the constant harassment of businesspeople.

These bureaucrats are able to exercise their power almost without restraint. They have devised a Civil Service system that makes it wellnigh impossible to get rid of them. Their command of information and their ability to build their own constituencies to support them makes it difficult for their political chiefs to resist their proposals. In any case, the possibility of resistance from the top rarely arises, because most of our political leaders agree with the programs that the bureaucrats devise and administer.

Thus, in the radical right analysis, our gigantic bureaucracies represent one more, particularly pernicious, dimension of the ruling elite that is engaged in a carefully planned operation to destroy the American system.

THE RADICAL LEFT: DECENTRALIZATION AND PARTICIPATION

In the classical Marxist-Leninist analysis, government is essentially the instrument of the ruling class of monopoly capitalists. Even so, it can be tactically useful to join other groups in forcing concessions out of the capitalists in the form of federal government programs such as public housing and other programs for the poor. Moreover, Communists look to the central government as the machinery through which they must achieve their revolution, and which will persist until, in the ultimate communist society, it withers away.

As we noted earlier, however, there are other strands of thought on the radical left, particularly anarchism, that view central government with profound suspicion. Variations of this position became a prominent aspect of American left-wing thought during the 1960s, particularly among groups based on university campuses. To these groups bureaucracy was the enemy—bureaucracy as the expression of remote, impersonal institutions that reduce the people to a state of helplessness. And among those institutions are federal government agencies.

The left has changed a good deal since the 1960s. There is less emphasis than before on the cry from the "counterculture" for creative, spontaneous expression in place of rationality, organization, and planning. But the hostility to big government bureaucracies is still there, and two alternatives are proposed: decentralization of government and active participation by the people.

Decentralization. The left's approach to decentralization is quite different from the conservatives'. The left certainly does not want to see government programs handed over to private business. The corporations themselves are run by great, impersonal bureaucracies, which are even less concerned with the interests of the people than are the government bureaucracies.

As for state and local governments, the left perceives them to be controlled generally by the same kind of forces who are in control in Washington. However, in the 1970s left radicals began to run for state and local offices. For one thing, they had a better chance of winning there, and they did, in fact, have some successes, as we shall see when we discuss state and local government in chapter 11. Furthermore, the local scene is precisely the

context in which the left wants to demonstrate its ideas. Its major concern is to bring the decision-making process down to the neighborhood and the workplace. There people can get a sense of accomplishment; because they are dealing with problems on a human scale, they can see the impact of their actions, and they can thereby overcome their feelings of helplessness and dependency on faceless institutions.

Participation. Decentralization of policy making will give people a chance for active participation. Without this participation there is no meaning to democracy. As things now stand, the federal government discourages the involvement of people in the decisions that directly affect their lives. Only in the "maximum feasible participation" clause of the 1964–1965 War on Poverty legislation, which required representation of the poor on the boards that ran the community antipoverty programs, was this idea given official approval. And, as we shall see in chapter 12, governmental officials were furious when the mandated participation of the poor led to challenges to existing power structures.

THE CENTRISTS: JOINING THE ATTACK

From the 1970s the onslaught on the federal government, which had started with the conservatives and the radical right and had been joined by the new left, found reinforcements among the centrists. Although some centrist politicians, such as Hubert Humphrey, continued unabated in their support of bigger government, others, such as Jimmy Carter, expressed doubts that government could solve all our problems. In fact, in his quest for the 1976 Democratic presidential nomination, Carter took as a central issue "the horrible, bloated, confused, overlapping, wasteful, insensitive, unmanageable, bureaucratic mess in Washington."

Subsequently the majority of Democratic politicians joined in the criticism of excessive government spending, taxes, and regulations; and even the opposition to the 1981 Reagan budget proposals in the House of Representatives was built around countermeasures that would have cut deeply into many of the federal programs created and nurtured by a succession of Democratic administrations.

However, the centrist doctrine and temperament does not extend to the unbridled enthusiasm for the dismantling of federal programs and functions found among conservatives. Centrists generally believe that the federal government has become too big, unwieldy, inefficient, and wasteful, but they still believe that government has vital roles to play in protecting the consumer, the worker, and the environment; in preventing the economy from staggering between uncontrolled boom and catastrophic slump; in assuring the poor, the elderly, and the disabled of a reasonable living standard; and in providing a range of services to the community as a whole that it is not economical for the private sector to offer.

To centrists the Reagan regime may provide a healthy shakeout of overgrown, sometimes superfluous programs, but centrists do not want to see government reduced so far as to be unable to make its proper contribution in the public-private balance that is needed for the health of the American system.

THE LIBERALS: DEFENDING BIG GOVERNMENT

The liberals have been shaken by the attacks on the federal government and bureaucracy. They recognize, in James MacGregor Burns' words, that "no part of our system has appeared to sink so swiftly in popular esteem as the executive branch in recent years."[6] They concede that the criticisms cannot be dismissed out of hand, and they have themselves expressed unhappiness with certain features of the federal bureaucracies.

However, as we review the major points of the critics through the liberals' eyes, we shall see that, although they have given some ground, the liberals still look to the federal government and the bureaucracies to help put their programs into effect.

Liberty and the growth of government. Liberals worry much more than they used to about the threats to freedom represented by the growth of government. The Watergate revelations brought home the dangers that could result if the president gained complete control of the bureaucracy. Had Nixon succeeded in placing his own people in all the key positions in bureaucracy, it would have been very difficult indeed to limit his power.

Thus the liberals were strong supporters of the Freedom of Information Act, passed in 1966 and strengthened in 1974, because it opened up the processes of government by requiring that, with certain exceptions, all records of federal agencies be made available for public scrutiny on request.[7] And there were protests from liberals when the Reagan administration moved to impose more restrictions on the extent of information made available under the act.

Liberals' suspicion of federal bureaucracies stems from their concern with civil or personal liberty. If a federal agency, such as the FBI or the CIA, attacks civil liberty, liberals will attack that part of the bureaucracy. But the great expansion of the federal bureaucracy, after all, has resulted from economic policies. Liberals, we have seen, are tough-minded when it comes to the liberties of business. Liberals are enthusiastic supporters of government intervention in economic and business decisions. In their view, this kind of government intervention increases rather than diminishes freedom.

First, without federal interference to reduce gross inequalities, freedom would be the monopoly of the affluent. People at the bottom of the income scale would lack that minimal degree of security without which the concept of freedom is meaningless. Devoid of resources we have no ability to make choices; without choices there is no liberty.

Second, without the power of big government, who would set limits to the power of the massive business corporations?

Also, say the liberals, the growth of the federal government has been exaggerated. To begin with, the number of federal employees has not grown very much in recent years. The increase in civilian employees was from 2.1 million in 1950 to nearly 2.9 million in 1980, less proportionately than the growth of population. The big jump was in state and local employment. But this increase does not represent a concentration of power in Washington. On the contrary, it represents a trend toward decentralization with which conservatives ought to be pleased.

Although the federal budget and the federal payroll have grown at a rapid rate, part of the budgetary increase is attributable to inflation and the growth of population. Moreover, the conservatives' complaint that the tax burden to support the increase in government spending has become intolerable should be set in perspective. In most other industrialized, democratic countries taxes represent a higher proportion of total output of goods and services than in the United States, as shown in table 9-3.

TABLE 9–3 Tax revenue as a percentage of Gross National Product, 1979

	1960	1979
Sweden	25.5	52.9
Netherlands	30.1	47.2
Norway	31.2	46.7
Denmark	25.4	45.0
Austria	30.5	41.2
France	33.0	41.0
West Germany	31.3	37.2
Great Britain	28.5	33.8
Italy	34.4	32.7
Switzerland	21.2	31.5
United States	26.6	31.3
Canada	24.2	31.2
Australia	23.5	28.8[a]
Japan	18.2	24.1[a]
Spain	16.0	22.8

[a]Figures are for 1978.
Source: Organization for Economic Cooperation and Development. Estimates for France and Spain, 1960. (Published 1980.)

Similarly, to the conservatives' charge that the expansion of federal activities represents a mad rush toward socialism, liberals reply that we have accepted a much smaller dose of socialism here than in almost any other industrialized country in the world.

The governments of most other economically advanced, democratic countries have nationalized their railroads and airlines, their postal services, and their coal, gas, and electric industries. They own and operate at least one television and radio network and build a great deal of public housing.

In the United States federal ownership and operation is much more limited. We have the Postal Service, the Tennessee Valley Authority (a public water and power-generating corporation that works closely with farmers and private business), and a relatively small public housing program (administered by local housing authorities). Then, through the Corporation for Public Broadcasting, we funnel federal money to meet part of the costs of the seriously underfunded public television and radio networks. In addition, at the state and local levels there are extensive programs of public education and several municipally owned gas, electric, and transportation services. But all these programs taken together constitute a much smaller segment of public ownership and operation than is found elsewhere.

Even if we follow the trend of several Western European socialist parties and define socialism not in terms of nationalization but of the expansion of welfare services, we have been very timid in America. We do have a major Social Security program, which provides for unemployment and retirement benefits and some medical care for the aged. But in the field of health insurance we still lack the comprehensive program of national health insurance that is standard fare in almost all other advanced economies.

We do have an enormous amount of government underwriting of private enterprises. The American way is not to take over an industry but to subsidize it, give it government contracts, or protect it with tariffs or special tax advantages. Our system provides socialism for the rich and private enterprise for the poor.

Government regulation of business. The American way is not only to subsidize private business but also to control it through government regulatory agencies that are supposed to protect the public interest. Liberals have generally supported the notion of regulation of business so long as the public interest is, in fact, protected. The trouble is that, all too often, federal regulating agencies have served the purposes of industry rather than of the public.

Typically, a regulatory agency is created against a background of public protest against abuses of private power, such as monopolistic practices and exploitation of the consumer by business. After a period of crusading zeal, the agency tends to become established and routinized, and the spotlight moves on to other issues. Then comes a stage at which the business or other leaders who are the objects of regulation begin to work closely and sympathetically with the regulating agency. This stage is usually associated with movements of personnel between government and industry. A governmental agency looking for expertise in a given industrial field quite naturally hires people from that industry. Thus many Food and Drug Administration officials once worked for drug and chemical companies.

From Democratic and Republican administrations alike, officials leaving high positions in cabinet departments, the White House staff, and regulatory agencies are appointed to top positions in business—typically in companies that are regulated by government or are potentially the target of government antitrust suits, or that do much of their business with federal agencies. And many of the lawyers who argue cases on behalf of private companies before regulatory agencies like the Federal Power Commission once worked for those agencies.

Up to a point, then, liberals agree with the conservative critics of government regulation as a means of providing undesirable protection to industry. Indeed, a number of liberals in Congress joined conservatives in a successful effort to get the Civil Aeronautics Board to allow airlines to compete with each other by cutting fares, and there was further liberal pressure to force the deregulation of the trucking industry.

However, liberals are against only the kind of regulation that puts government on the side of industry in gouging the consumer. What liberals want to see generally is not less regulation, but more effective regulation, especially in the area of public health and safety.

Liberals reject the conservatives' argument against government control of cigarette advertising. To James Kilpatrick's proposal that a person should be allowed to make a fool of himself so long as his conduct harms no one else, liberals contend that the harm from cigarette smoking is not only to the smoker. It irritates and in some cases damages the health of the nonsmoker. And the cost of treating lung cancer is born by government-supported research and hospitals and by all the subscribers to health insurance programs.

So the liberals were pleased when the Federal Trade Commission, after years of timidity and caution, finally began to take its responsibilities seriously and moved against the cigarette companies, then against the misleading advertising practices of a number of other industries. Liberals also applauded the efforts of the Food and Drug Administration to protect the consumer against what they saw as the premature and excessive claims of the drug companies for their new products. As a result, some beneficial drugs may not get onto the market as soon as they might. But it should be remembered that the requirements for careful testing date from 1962, when FDA action prevented the use in the United States of thalidomide, a drug prescribed as a sedative for pregnant women, which had caused thousands of babies in West Germany, England, and Japan to be born horribly deformed.

Liberals also approve of the efforts of the U.S. Consumer Product Safety Commission to force manufacturers to eliminate hazards to children in toys, sleepwear, household drugs, and caustics. For example, beginning in 1973 the federal government required that aspirin bottles include safety caps to make it difficult for small children to open them. This device may be annoying to adults, but the number of children who died from aspirin poisoning dropped from 46 in 1972 to 17 in 1975, and in the same period the number of children made ill by aspirin fell from over 8,000 to under 5,000.

Regarding the protection of workers from hazards on the job, in 1978 the Occupational Safety and Health Administration (OSHA) issued a regulation limiting the amount of cotton dust in textile mills. The agency estimated that out of a total of 500,000 production workers in the cotton industry, close to 84,000 had contracted brown lung (byssinosis), a respiratory disease caused by cotton dust, and that as many as 35,000 employed and retired workers had been permanently disabled by the disease. The Reagan administration proposed that the OSHA regulation be interpreted in the context of "cost-benefit" analysis to determine the most "cost-effective" solution to the problem. When the issue came before the Supreme Court the justices found that Congress, in passing the Occupational Safety and Health Act of 1970, had not required government regulations to consider the costs to industry of complying with standards on toxic substances.[8] However, the administration persisted in its preference for cheaper alternatives to engineering controls at the workplace, such as respirators. According to Ralph Nader and others, respirators, besides being uncomfortable for workers, do not provide anything close to the protection that can be achieved by engineering changes designed to cut down the amount of cotton dust.

This heartless attitude of the Reagan administration, say the liberals, puts profits before health and ignores the cost to society and to the employer of a high incidence of worker disablement. It is all part of a rush to demolish the protections, painfully erected over decades, to civilize the industrial process and force employers to recognize that they have a responsibility not only to their shareholders but also to their employees and to the entire community.

The question of inefficiency. To liberals the conservatives' charge that the federal government is massively incompetent is a gross overstatement. They draw attention to the many remarkable achievements of federal agencies.

For example, in 1967, with less than a year to make the arrangements, the Social Security Administration enrolled 19 million people in Medicare and set up machinery in fifty states to pay hospital and doctor bills, all with a minimum of dislocation. The greatest organizational achievement of the 1960s, the landing on the moon, although it involved many private companies, was ultimately the accomplishment of a government institution, the National Aeronautics and Space Administration.

As for the charge of government incompetence and impersonality in dealing with individuals, a University of Michigan national survey of people served by employment, workmen's compensation, welfare, and social security programs indicated that only two in ten thought the administrators were inefficient, and the great majority said their problems were handled quickly and efficiently.[9]

Liberals do not deny that, despite these contributions, there is a good deal of inefficiency and waste in the federal bureaucracy. But they contend that the reasons are not to be found in any natural mediocrity of government employees or the welfare state. Instead they point to the following factors:

1. To prevent mistakes, and especially to avoid the misuse and misappropriation of public funds, Congress writes into most of its laws stringent rules and elaborate reporting requirements. Most of the bureaucratic paperwork is imposed not by the agencies' appetite for routines but by the restrictions imposed by the 535-person board of directors that Congress comprises.

2. Many of the problems that government agencies are asked to deal with are intrinsically more difficult and complex than the problems that most other institutions must manage. These problems, after all, have been thrust on government because no one else has been able to cope with them. They include the great social issues, which

DOONESBURY   **by Garry Trudeau**

arouse the most intense pressures and resistances from many parties. They do not respond easily to simple notions of managerial efficiency. And the Postal Service has run deficits because it deliberately provides some uneconomical services, such as maintaining services in rural communities where the costs are inevitably high.

3. Inefficiency is not unique to government. In every kind of human activity a large part of the time and energy expended is wasted. Corporations are certainly not exempt from this rule, and big business suffers from much the same problems as big government. Like government, big business must employ huge bureaucracies—staffs that work within a framework of standardized procedures. Big business, too, is capable of massive failures, such as the vast numbers of automobiles recalled after sale for dangerous defects, Detroit's persistent obsession until the end of the 1970s with large automobiles, and the huge cost overruns of defense companies.

Moreover, such mistakes are made by people who are paid well enough to do better. Fifteen corporate leaders each earned $1 million or more in 1980, with a median income among top executives surveyed of approximately $330,000.[10] By contrast, the highest federal government salary, the president's, is $200,000. The top White House aides received $60,000 in 1981. Senior civil servants could earn no more than $50,000, which

has accounted for a "brain drain" from federal employment, with many of the most able public servants leaving to accept private industry offers of much higher salaries and freedom from the stigma attached to government employment.

4. Liberals rebut the argument that businesses, unlike government agencies,[11] go under when they are not performing. This statement, say the liberals, is true only of small business. Once a company reaches a certain size, it stays alive no matter how many disasters its incompetence creates. Too many banks have lent it money, and too many legislators worry about the loss of jobs and income in their district to allow it to go bankrupt. This situation occurred when Chrysler Corporation teetered on the brink of bankruptcy in 1980. The Carter administration and Congress approved $2 billion in loan guarantees to prevent Chrysler from going under, and presidential candidate Ronald Reagan told unemployed auto workers in Michigan that he supported the guarantees.

The liberals' proposals for reform.   Liberals persist in their belief that there is still room to expand the roles of the federal government. They want it to do more to keep the economy healthy and reduce unemployment. They call for increased spending in most areas except defense, and although such increases might exert some inflationary pressure they doubt that government spending is the prime cause of inflation. Liberals put much of the blame instead on price fixing by business corporations. They also want government to bear down harder in its efforts to regulate business, for instance by creating a consumer protection agency to take cases to court and represent the consumer in public hearings of the other federal regulatory agencies.

These changes are likely to produce still bigger bureaucracies, and liberals do not deny that, with government growing ever larger, something must be done to improve its performance. So they propose various kinds of reforms.

1. They join conservatives in supporting the principle of "sunset laws," through which all new programs would be subjected to periodic review to determine whether or not they should survive.

2. Liberals urge that more must be done to protect the public against conflicts of interest in the executive branch. They welcomed the code of ethics for policy-level officials introduced by the Carter administration. This code required disclosure of assets and income, divestiture of interests that might conflict with official responsibilities, and an understanding that, after leaving the government, officials would not intervene for two years in any matter in which they had been involved while in government.[12] Liberals were also

pleased with the 1976 "Sunshine Act," compelling most regulatory agencies to hold their meetings in public and thus cutting down on quietly arranged understandings between federal agencies and industry. But more needs to be done, say the liberals, to ensure that federal officials pursue the public interest rather than their personal interest.

3. Liberal political scientists such as James MacGregor Burns present the need for reorganization of the federal agencies to bring them more clearly under the authority and direction of the president.[13] As long as the agencies can go their separate ways, supported by their special constituencies, the public as a whole will not be properly served by its government. They must be more effectively coordinated and brought within the framework of purposes established by the one public official elected by all the people, the president. Of course, liberals are likely to argue this case with lessened enthusiasm when the president is a conservative like Reagan, bent on using his authority to cut down the size and power of the federal agencies. But, as we saw in our earlier chapter on the presidency, liberals still view that office as the most cohesive, responsive, and effective part of government, and over the long haul they believe their purposes are most likely to be served by a strong presidency administering a strong, well-coordinated executive branch.

CONCLUSION

At the beginning of this chapter we cited opinion polls showing widespread public resentment of federal power and spending. Yet the evidence of the polls does not all point in the same direction.

We noted that 84 percent believed in 1978 that the federal government was spending too much money. However, another survey in 1978 found 57 percent wanting more money spent on "improving and protecting the nation's health," as against only 7 percent who felt too much was being spent; and 54 percent thought not enough was being spent on "improving the nation's education," compared with 11 percent who thought too much was already being spent.[14]

Moreover, although 76 percent in 1978 thought that the government in Washington was getting too powerful, 52 percent of those people surveyed by Gallup in that year favored bringing back wage and price controls, as against 37 percent opposed; and support for wage and price controls had risen to 57 percent by 1979.

A *CBS/New York Times* poll in January 1978 showed that 58 percent agreed with the statement that "the government has gone too far in regulating business and interfering with the free enterprise system," with 31 percent disagreeing. Yet a Harris survey in August 1978 showed 26 percent calling for more government regulation of business and 31 percent wanting the current level to be maintained, with only 32 percent wanting less regulation.

To some extent these differences reflect problems of public opinion polling: a few months separating two surveys can produce a shift in opinion, and a subtle difference in the wording of questions can evoke contradictory answers. It is also likely, however, that the seemingly conflicting evidence from these surveys reflects a deep-seated ambivalence about government on the part of the public. Although there is a genuine dissatisfaction with the great expansion of government, the enthusiasm for cutting government usually applies to the services government provides to *others*, rather than to the indispensable services that government is providing to *us*.

Hence, liberals are on strong ground when they contend that government serves too many vital purposes and is too attractive a mechanism for too many constituencies for the conservatives to have it all their own way in dismantling the structures of government that evolved since the New Deal. In time liberals may find some solid ground under their feet in resisting the Reagan administration's onslaught on federal programs and spending, and the pendulum could begin to swing back.

Still, for the foreseeable future it is unlikely that expanding government will be as popular as it was during Roosevelt's New Deal or Johnson's Great Society. Huge federal bureaucracies may be necessary, but they will continue to be resented. The problem is not so much the impersonality of federal bureaucrats or the alleged inefficiency of their organizational structures. The problem is the cost. And although the cost may be quite reasonable in relation to the services provided and in comparison with government outlays in other countries, Americans will persist in objecting to high taxes and in believing that there is less virtue in the spending of money by government than by business or the individual consumer.

So, although the conservatives may find that even a conservative presidency cannot do away with as much government as they would like to see demolished, hostile attitudes toward the federal bureaucracies will continue to be widespread among the population and will keep the liberals on the defensive in their efforts to use government to achieve their ends.

NOTES AND REFERENCES

1. Survey by Center for Political Studies of the Institute for Social Research, University of Michigan, cited in *Public Opinion*, December–January 1980, p. 20.
2. U.S. Department of Labor, *56th Annual Report: Fiscal Year 1968* (Washington, D.C.: Government Printing Office), p. 7.
3. Peter Drucker, *Age of Discontinuity* (New York: Harper & Row, 1969), p. 221.
4. James Kilpatrick, *Los Angeles Times*, 7 December 1975.

5. Robert Welch, *The Blue Book of the John Birch Society* (Belmont, Mass.: John Birch Society, 1961), p. 142.

6. James MacGregor Burns, *Uncommon Sense* (New York: Harper & Row, 1972), p. 126.

7. Those people requesting the information must pay for the costs of reproducing the material. Exceptions to the requirements of public accessibility include income tax records, personnel records, criminal investigation files, interoffice memos, letters used in the decision-making process by executive agencies, and national defense and foreign policy documents, although the latter exceptions are subject to court review.

8. *American Textile Manufacturers Institute* v. *Marshall* (1981).

9. Robert L. Kahn, Barbara A. Gutek, Eugenia Barton, and Daniel Katz, "Americans Love Their Bureaucrats," *Psychology Today*, June 1975, pp. 66–71.

10. See *U.S. News and World Report*, 18 May 1981, p. 81.

11. Some government agencies were abolished even before the Reagan administration, including the Subversive Activities Control Board in 1972, the Renegotiation Board in 1977, and several minor agencies in 1978.

12. Previously this requirement had been for one year only.

13. See Burns, *Uncommon Sense*, pp. 126–127.

14. National Opinion Research Center, General Social Survey, 1978, cited in *Public Opinion*, December–January 1980, p.21.

chapter ten

THE SUPREME COURT AND CONSTITUTIONAL RIGHTS

Alexander Hamilton, in *The Federalist*, said the judicial branch would be "beyond comparison the weakest of the three departments" in the new federal government. It would have "no influence over either the sword or the purse, no direction either of the strength or of the wealth of the society." Hamilton was right only up to a point. The judiciary has not had much influence over "the sword" in the sense that determining foreign and military policy has been pretty much in the hands of the presidency. But during some periods the courts have been heavily involved in questions of economic policy. And, especially in recent years, the judiciary has been a major participant in decisions concerning the rights of individuals under the Constitution.

So, in areas of great importance to many people, the courts have exercised significant power, and where there is power there will be controversy. In this chapter, after briefly describing the structure of the system of courts in the United States, we shall show how the use of judicial power has varied from one period to another according to changing conceptions of the purpose of the highest court in the land, the Supreme Court of the United States. Then we shall set forth the contrasting views of our five perspectives on the proper role of the courts, particularly in the area of constitutional rights, and on whether the courts have used their power wisely or abused it.

THE STRUCTURE OF THE U.S. COURT SYSTEM

Article III, Section 1, of the U.S. Constitution declares that: "The judicial Power of the United States, shall be vested in one Supreme Court, and in such inferior Courts as the Congress may from time to time ordain and establish" (see Appendix 1). Congress has proceeded to establish the federal court system through the

Judiciary Act of 1789 and subsequent legislation. As figure 10-1 indicates, most federal cases begin in U.S. district courts and may be appealed to a U.S. Circuit Court of Appeals, and from there to the U.S. Supreme Court. Today there are ninety-seven district courts and eleven circuit courts of appeal.

In addition, each of the states has established its own court system, starting with city, county, and state trial courts, then moving up to courts of appeal, and finally to a state supreme court. Anyone accused of violating a state law may appeal to the federal courts,[1] but only after the case has been heard in the state courts and only when it can be shown that an issue in the case has implications for the federal Constitution or a federal statute.[2] In simplified form, figure 10-1 shows us the various stages that most cases must traverse before coming to the U.S. Supreme Court.[3]

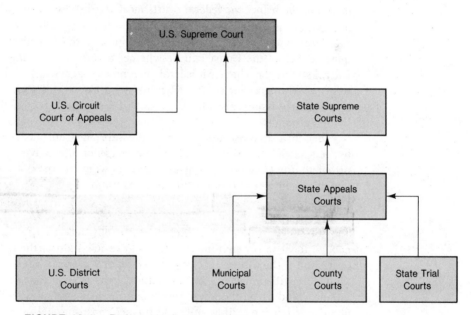

FIGURE 10-1.   Paths to the Supreme Court

THE SUPREME COURT AND JUDICIAL REVIEW

Most of the discussion in this chapter will focus on the U.S. Supreme Court, where the great constitutional issues are determined. The Supreme Court has the last word on what the Constitution means, despite the fact that the Constitution does not explicitly give the Court this authority. Although it is reasonably clear that the Framers intended the Supreme Court to be able to declare state legislation unconstitutional, the authority to strike down acts of Congress can only be inferred from general provisions of the Constitution.

Indeed, if the Court in its early years had not had a strong chief justice, it might never have attained its powerful stature. But John Marshall was a very strong chief justice, and his Court's decision in *Marbury* v. *Madison* (1803), finding a section of the Judiciary Act of 1789 unconstitutional, established the principle that congressional statutes could be ruled invalid by the Supreme Court. The Court, in other words, had gained the power of *judicial review*, which is the power to examine federal as well as state legislation and declare it null and void if it conflicts with the Court's interpretation of the U.S. Constitution.

In our preoccupation here with the Supreme Court and its constitutional authority, we should not lose sight of some important facts about the judicial system in America. First, only a tiny proportion of all cases that are tried in the United States ever reach the Supreme Court. The vast majority are settled in local and state courts, mostly at the lowest levels of the judicial hierarchy; and of those cases that do come before the federal courts most are disposed of in the district courts.

Next, of the three to four thousand cases that come before the Supreme Court each year, most do not involve interpretation of the Constitution. Instead, the question before the Court will be whether a state or local law conflicts with a federal statute, or whether a federal government agency has acted contrary to the terms of a congressional law. Moreover, the Court will usually deal with the constitutional issues raised by a case only if it cannot dispose of the case on more limited grounds.

When it raises constitutional issues, the Supreme Court does so only in relation to the specific case before it. The Court does not offer advisory opinions to the president, the Congress, or anyone else who wants to know whether a proposed law or action would conform to the Constitution. The Supreme Court will not act until the proposal has been acted on and until somebody brings a suit against another party, is dissatisfied with the decision of the lower courts, and appeals to the Supreme Court. Then, if the Supreme Court feels that this case is important enough for it to review (and it declines to review most of the cases that are sent to it), and if the case cannot be resolved on any grounds but constitutional ones, the Court will provide an interpretation of the Constitution. But that interpretation is binding on the lower courts only in very similar situations; and plenty of room is left for further suits and further constitutional interpretations where the circumstances vary to a sufficient degree from the case in question. These last considerations reflect the fact that the Court controls its own docket. It hears only those cases it wishes to hear.

Despite these qualifications, the Supreme Court's responsibility to declare whether or not federal and state laws and executive actions are constitutional makes it an extremely powerful institution. And because it is reviewing public policies made by political bodies—the presidency, Congress, and state and local executives and legislatures—its role cannot help being a part of the public policy-making process and thus having direct political implications.

The Supreme Court, then, is part of our political system. Yet it is more than just another political institution. It is also a court, a judicial body, which makes it act differently in some very significant ways from legislative and executive bodies. The central theme of this chapter is the tension between the political and the judicial characteristics of the Supreme Court. We shall look first at the political context of the Court's work, then at the judicial considerations.

THE COURT AS AN INSTRUMENT OF THE POLITICAL SYSTEM

The nine members of the Supreme Court are not elected but are appointed for life by the president with the concurrence of two-thirds of the Senate; therefore they are not as influenced by every shift in the political wind as are the members of the elected branches of government. Still, the Court is made up of people who are products of their time and who are not totally oblivious to what is going on in the political world. Periodically the Court has changed the tenor of its decisions as the political environment has altered.

In the modern era there have been three major changes of direction by the Supreme Court: the first in the 1930s, in the struggle over the New Deal; the second, under Chief Justice Earl Warren in the 1950s and 1960s; and the third in the 1970s under Chief Justice Warren Burger.

THE COURT AND THE NEW DEAL

Through a large part of America's history the Supreme Court protected the individual's right to do whatever that individual wanted with money, property, or business without governmental interference. Thus in 1905 the Court struck down as a deprivation of liberty without due process a New York state law limiting employment in bakeries to ten hours a day and sixty hours a week.[4] In 1926 the Court found that Congress had denied due process in setting a minimum wage for the District of Columbia.[5] So it was not surprising that when Franklin Roosevelt gained overwhelming congressional approval for proposals to impose detailed regulations of manufacturing, industry, and agriculture, the Supreme Court found the legislation unacceptable. In seven cases in 1935 and 1936, much of the early New Deal legislation was struck down. The statutes, said the Court majority, represented an unconstitutional invasion of the power of the states by the federal government, an unconstitutional delegation of power to the president by the Congress, or a denial of the constitutional protection of due process of law. Angrily, the president, labor, and liberal groups attacked this usurpation of power by "nine old men," appointed for life by Republican presidents in the 1920s. "The Court," said the president, "has been acting not as a judicial body, but as a policy-making body"; and its policies were oriented toward preserving entrenched propertied interests.

But then, from 1937, the Court backed away from its confrontation with the president and Congress. In that year the Wagner Labor Relations Act of 1935 was reviewed by the Court. The same Court that had voted by margins of five to four and six to three against the earlier New Deal legislation now found in favor of the Wagner Act by a five to four margin. The difference was that Chief Justice Hughes and Justice Owen Roberts voted against Roosevelt's programs in 1935 and 1936 and for them in 1937.

Two events had intervened. The first, in 1936, was a massive victory at the polls for Franklin Roosevelt and for the Democratic party in Congress, enabling the president to claim a clear mandate for his policies. The second was a request by President Roosevelt in 1937 for authority to add one justice for each member who reached the age of 70, had served ten years, and refused to retire within six months, subject to a maximum Court membership of fifteen.[6] The purpose of this proposal was either to force some of the elderly judges who were opposing Roosevelt's programs to retire or to add enough sympathetic new members to the Court to outvote the old guard. The Senate vetoed this plan to "pack" the Court. Nonetheless, the Court could not ignore this reminder that it was vulnerable to attack from other branches of government.

Hughes and Roberts denied that these events had anything to do with their verdicts in the 1937 case. The circumstances, they insisted, were different from the facts of the earlier cases. Yet fundamentally the same issue—the right of the federal government to interfere with business—was involved. After that, in Roosevelt's and subsequent administrations, the Court supported with few exceptions the steady enlargement of the role of the federal government in economic affairs.

But the relationship between government and the individual is not limited only to economic issues, and courts must deal with a great range of questions concerning the rights and liberties of individuals and groups. These rights became the subject of the next great change in direction of the Supreme Court, which took place under Chief Justice Earl Warren in the 1950s and 1960s.

THE WARREN COURT

From the time that Earl Warren became chief justice in 1953, the Supreme Court, at first slowly and then with increasing momentum, handed down a series of decisions in the areas of the First Amendment freedoms of speech, assembly, press, and religion; the rights of the accused in criminal cases; the reapportionment of legislatures; and the rights of racial minorities. The thrust of these various decisions was to favor the rights of individuals and minorities against the power of government. The Constitution, and especially the Bill of Rights, said the Warren Court, guaranteed certain liberties to the people, and these liberties could not be taken away by *any* level of government. So, by a process of "incorporation," the rights afforded by the U.S. Constitution must be assured not only against the federal government but also against the actions of state and local governments.

First Amendment rights. The First Amendment to the U.S. Constitution, a crucial component in the Bill of Rights, declares: "Congress shall make no law respecting an establishment of religion, or prohibiting the free exercise thereof; or abridging the freedom of speech, or of the press; or the right of the people peaceably to assemble, and to petition the Government for a redress of grievances." But these statements are subject to interpretation. The question the Warren Court, like every U.S. Supreme Court, had to consider was: What is the proper balance between these First Amendment freedoms and the needs of society for order and stability? Generally speaking, the Warren Court reversed the trend of earlier

Courts, which had tended to emphasize the need for order as the necessary condition for individual liberties.

Free speech and the Communist party. A classic statement of the right of government to impose limits on free speech was made in 1919 by Justice Oliver Wendell Holmes, Jr.: "The most stringent protection of free speech would not protect a man in falsely shouting fire in a theater and causing a panic. . . . The question in every case is whether the words are used in such circumstances and are of such a nature as to create a clear and present danger that they will bring about the substantive evils that Congress has a right to prevent."[7] An even broader limitation on the right of free speech was contained in a 1925 case in which the Supreme Court found that speech could be banned if it represented a "dangerous tendency."[8]

In the post–World War II period in the United States, the great test of these doctrines was the extent to which the Communist party was to be allowed to organize and speak freely. Hostility to the Soviet Union ran high during this era, and the prevailing sentiment in Congress and the country was that the Communist party of the United States and its advocacy of the Soviet system constituted not only a "dangerous tendency" but also a "clear and present danger" to the survival of the American system. In this context the Supreme Court, under the leadership of Chief Justice Fred Vinson, considered the appeal of eleven leaders of the Communist party against their conviction under the 1940 Smith Act, which had made it illegal to advocate "overthrowing or destroying any government in the United States by force or violence." In *Dennis* v. *United States* (1951) the Court upheld the convictions and the constitutionality of the Smith Act. Subsequently, during the era of anticommunist investigations by Senator Joseph McCarthy and the House Un-American Activities Committee, the Vinson Court rejected appeals against the congressional committee's tactics. The Court also upheld the right of state governments to require "loyalty oaths" from public employees—sworn declarations that they would uphold the Constitution of the United States and of their own states and that they were not members of the Communist party. Only two members of the Vinson Court, Justices Hugo Black and William O. Douglas, consistently argued against these positions, protesting that the Bill of Rights was being abandoned.

In this climate President Eisenhower appointed Earl Warren chief justice in 1953. In a number of key free-speech cases Warren sided with Justices Black and Douglas, and their position gradually became the majority view on the Court. New rulings relating to the Smith Act limited its applicability so severely that it became virtually unenforceable. The Court also overturned legislation denying passports to Communists and excluding them from jobs in defense industries or from leadership positions in labor unions; and it threw out a number of contempt of Congress convictions on the grounds that the procedures of congressional investigating committees were unfair and arbitrary.

Free speech and obscenity. The Warren Court never gave quite the same protection to obscenity or pornography that it provided to political expression.

However, it proceeded from a rather restrictive view on the issue to a position that gave fairly broad protection against sexual censorship.

Thus in two 1957 cases, *Roth* v. *United States* and *Alberts* v. *California*, the Warren Court upheld federal and state statutes banning the dissemination of obscene materials.

However, in *Memoirs* v. *Massachusetts* (1966) the Supreme Court established criteria that made indictments for publication and dissemination of indecent material extremely difficult. The case dealt with the banning of a new edition of *Fanny Hill*, a detailed account of the sexual adventures of a country girl in the big city, written in 1749. The Court produced some new guidelines. Now for a work to be found obscene it must be established that "(a) the dominant theme of the material taken as a whole appeals to a prurient interest in sex; (b) the material is patently offensive because it affronts contemporary community standards relating to the description or representation of sexual matters; and (c) the material is utterly without redeeming social value."

When literary critics testified that *Fanny Hill* had literary significance, the Court found that the book had "redeeming social value" and could not be banned.[9]

Prayer in the public schools. In the 1940s the Supreme Court had handed down decisions building what Justice Black called "a wall of separation between Church and State." These decisions were an interpretation of the First Amendment's declaration that: "Congress shall make no law respecting an establishment of religion, or prohibiting the free exercise thereof." Accordingly the Court had found in *McCollum* v. *Board of Education* (1948) that a school board could not provide religious instruction during regular school hours.[10] In 1962, in the case of *Engel* v. *Vitale*, the Court went a step further. A daily school prayer could not be required even if it were entirely nondenominational. In *Abington Township School District* v. *Schempp* (1963) the Court declared that public schools may not open with a Bible reading or a prayer. Thus the Court insisted that school prayers constituted an "establishment of religion"—the creation of an official form of worship because the power of the state was used to compel attendance at religious worship, in defiance of the Constitution.

Rights of the accused. The Warren Court did not limit its concern for the rights of the individual to those rights covered under the First Amendment. It gave a great deal of attention to the rights of the accused in criminal cases. In *Mallory* v. *United States* (1957) the Supreme Court, under its authority to supervise the lower federal courts, declared that confessions obtained during any "unnecessary delay" in bringing an accused person before a magistrate were not admissible. In *Gideon* v. *Wainwright* (1963) and *Escobedo* v. *Illinois* (1964) the Court extended the constitutional right to be represented by counsel, *Gideon* requiring free counsel for indigent persons in criminal cases, *Escobedo* establishing the right to counsel when a police interrogation moves from "the exploratory to the accusatory stage." In *Miranda* v. *Arizona* (1966) Chief Justice Warren declared that a suspect "must be warned prior to any questioning that he has the right to remain silent, that anything he says can be used against him in a court of law, that he has the right to the presence of an attorney, and that if he cannot afford an attorney, one will be appointed for him prior to any questioning if he so desires."

Thus the Warren Court was making clear its insistence on scrupulous attention to constitutional guarantees of the right to counsel and of protection against self-incrimination, and the general requirement established by the Fifth Amendment, and extended to the states by the Fourteenth Amendment, that no person may be "deprived of life, liberty or property without due process of law." Accordingly, the Court rejected police lineup tactics it found to be deliberately biased, and it set stringent limits to the types of searches police can conduct without a warrant.

The Warren Court did not always decide against the wishes of law enforcement authorities. The right of police to frisk citizens on the street without probable cause for arrest was upheld, and electronic eavesdropping was sustained as long as a warrant was obtained.

On the whole, however, the Warren Court expanded the protection provided by the Constitution to people accused of crimes. In particular, the Court extended an "exclusionary rule," according to which any evidence obtained without scrupulous attention to the constitutional rights of the accused must be excluded from the accused's trial.

Reapportionment. A further provision of the Fourteenth Amendment led the Warren Court into another field of great political importance: legislative reapportionment. Previous Supreme Courts had refused to accept suits that complained that the boundaries between legislative districts were deliberately drawn in such a way that some districts had much greater populations than others. This practice, said the plaintiffs, conflicted with the Fourteenth Amendment's instruction that no state shall "deny to any person within its jurisdiction the equal protection of the laws"; if people are unequally represented, they are unlikely to get equal protection. However, the courts had repeatedly said that this question was a political matter to be decided by legislatures, not by the judiciary. But in *Baker* v. *Carr* (1962) and *Reynolds* v. *Sims* (1964) the Warren Court moved boldly into the reapportionment issue. Legislatures must stop justifying wide disparities in the populations of districts on extraneous grounds such as the need to protect the interests of rural areas. "Legislators," said Chief Justice Warren in *Reynolds* v. *Sims*, "represent people, not trees or acres. Legislators are elected by voters, not farms or cities or economic interests." Boundaries must be drawn to contain equal numbers of voters. "One man, one vote" was the principle to follow, or there could be no "equal protection of the laws."

Desegregation. The "equal protection" clause was applied by the Warren Court in yet one more policy field of surpassing importance: the segregation of the races. In *Plessy* v. *Ferguson* (1896) the Supreme Court had found that separate railroad facilities for white and black people were constitutional as long as the accommodations were of equal quality. In 1954, this decision was overruled in its application to public schools in the case of *Brown* v. *Board of Education of Topeka, Kansas*. Black children did not have the equal protection of the laws as provided for by the Fourteenth Amendment, said the Warren Court, if the laws forbade them to go to the same schools as white children. In subsequent decisions the Court applied this principle to all public facilities. By definition, separate could not be equal, because implicit in laws requiring segregation of the races was the assumption that one race was inferior to the other.

Why the Warren Court was different from its predecessors.   The key factor in producing these departures from the past was the change in the Court's membership that began with Eisenhower's appointment of Earl Warren as chief justice and William Brennan as associate justice. Together with Hugo Black and William Douglas they had to pick up only one more vote to gain a majority for a more liberal approach to the rights of individuals. With Lyndon Johnson's appointment of Arthur Goldberg, this majority was assured; and when Goldberg resigned from the Court to become ambassador to the United Nations, Johnson replaced him with the fairly liberal Abe Fortas. Then Thurgood Marshall, the first black justice, was appointed, which strengthened the liberally oriented bloc further. Against this group the more conservative members dwindled in number. In the last years of the Warren Court they included only Tom Clark (until he was replaced by Thurgood Marshall) and John Marshall Harlan, with Potter Stewart and Byron White joining sometimes with the more liberal group, sometimes with the more conservative members.

The attack on the Warren Court.   Now the Warren Court was subjected to bitter criticism. A movement was launched, led in Congress by Senator Everett Dirksen of Illinois, to repeal the Court's school prayers and reapportionment decisions either by a statute removing these issues from the Court's jurisdiction or by a constitutional amendment. A Harris survey in November 1966 indicated that, although almost two-thirds of those people polled agreed with the Warren Court's antisegregation rulings and three-quarters supported the reapportionment decisions, two-thirds disagreed with the Court's disallowing confessions without counsel, 70 percent were opposed to the outlawing of prayers in the classroom, and there was an even division on the question of letting Communists have passports.

These critical reactions might eventually have influenced the Warren Court to be somewhat more cautious in its decisions. But no major alteration was likely as long as the membership stayed as it was. Lyndon Johnson saw this fact clearly when, in 1968, Earl Warren announced his intention to retire. Johnson jumped at the chance to appoint a new chief justice before he left the White House, and he nominated Justice Abe Fortas, who was already a member of the Court. However, Fortas faced strong opposition in the Senate, and his position became untenable when some revelations about his financial affairs suggested conflicts of interest. Fortas protested his innocence but at last withdrew his name from nomination.

Now the way was open for a new president to appoint the chief justice. In his 1968 campaign for the presidency, Richard Nixon made it clear that he would take care to avoid appointing people to the Court who would continue the direction charted by Earl Warren and his colleagues. This policy was confirmed by his first appointment, that of Warren Burger, a Republican from the U.S. Court of Appeals, as chief justice of the United States.

THE BURGER COURT

Soon after the appointment of Burger there was another vacancy on the Court. The press had uncovered additional indiscretions in Fortas's finances, and, although Fortas insisted he had done nothing wrong, he resigned from the Court.

Nixon ran into difficulties in replacing him; the Senate rejected his nominations first of federal district court Judge Clement Haynsworth of South Carolina and then of federal court of appeals Judge Harrold Carswell of Florida. In May 1970, however, the Senate accepted the appointment of Judge Harry Blackmun of Minnesota.

Now the Court headed by Chief Justice Burger began to moderate its liberal tendencies somewhat, particularly in the field of criminal law. However, the holdovers from the Warren days were still able to muster a majority on a number of issues, with Burger, frequently joined by Blackmun, in vigorous dissent.

In September 1971 Justices Hugo Black and John Marshall Harlan resigned because of ill health. In their places Nixon proposed and the Senate accepted Lewis Powell of Virginia and William Rehnquist of Arizona, the assistant attorney general under John Mitchell. Both were known to be conservative in their leanings, particularly Rehnquist, who had been a strong supporter of Barry Goldwater in his 1964 bid for the presidency.

These justices were the last of the Nixon appointees. However, when Justice William O. Douglas, the unreconstructed liberal on the Court, retired because of ill health in 1975, President Ford appointed Judge John Paul Stevens from the U.S. Court of Appeals in Chicago. Now only four justices remained from the Warren Court—Marshall, Brennan, White, and Stewart; and only Marshall and Brennan had been more or less consistently on the side of the majority that had forged the liberal direction of the Warren years.

However, the Warren decisions were not to be totally repudiated. The picture, in fact, was a very mixed one. In some fields the Burger Court kept to the course charted by the Warren Court. In other areas the Warren Court's positions were modified but by no means abandoned. And even on those issues on which there was a clear departure from the earlier Court, some vestiges of the previous doctrines persisted.

Reapportionment.   In the years following *Baker* v. *Carr* and *Sims* v. *Reynolds* legislatures had been reapportioned, and that fact could not be changed. However, the Burger court did make some relatively minor qualifications to the "one man, one vote" rule, as in their upholding of an election system for an Arizona water district, in which property owners cast votes in proportion to the amount of land they owned.[11]

Abortion.   The Burger court handed down some bold decisions on the fiercely controversial subject of abortion. In *Roe* v. *Wade* (1973) Justice Blackmun read the majority decision that states could forbid abortions only during the last three months of pregnancy, that they could do so only to protect the mother's health in the second three months, and that they could not forbid it at all during the first three months. Blackmun based his decision primarily on the right of privacy. No such right is mentioned in the Constitution, but the notion has evolved in Court decisions over the years as a combination of First Amendment freedoms, Fifth and Fourteenth Amendment due process, and Ninth Amendment rights "retained by the people."

Subsequently the Court struck down a state requirement for approval of an abortion by a husband or parent.[12] But this decision was qualified in 1981 by a decision that states may require a doctor to inform a minor's parents before performing an abortion on her. And in another case the Court ruled that neither the Constitution nor the federal Medicaid law required the government to provide free abortions for indigents if the abortions were not medically necessary.[13]

Sex discrimination.   The Burger Court ventured further into the field of the rights of women than had previous Courts. Some of its decisions came down in support of these rights. The Court found that the exclusion of women from juries deprived defendants of their right to a fair trial, that women cannot be forced to make higher pension contributions than men, even though they tend to live longer and collect more in benefits, and that under the 1964 Civil Rights law women could bring sex discrimination lawsuits even though they were working in jobs that were held only by women.[14]

On the other hand, the Burger Court rejected the claim of women's organizations that veterans' preference for federal jobs discriminates unconstitutionally against women because most veterans are men. The Court also allowed employers to deny sick pay for pregnancy and childbirth (although it did not allow employers to withhold the accumulation of job seniority during maternity leave).

Further confusion was sown by the Burger Court when on the one hand it found that men must be treated equally with women (widowers must be given the same survivors' benefits under Social Security as widows; alimony laws should be written on the basis on need, not sex; and men in Oklahoma should not have to wait until they were 21 to buy beer, although women could buy it when they were 18), yet it decided that Congress could force men, but not women, to register for the draft.

The rights of gays.   The Burger Court declined to review a conviction under a state statute outlawing sodomy. But it also left standing a state court decision striking down a university rule forbidding the use of campus facilities to gay organizations.

Race.   The Nixon administration appealed to the Court under Chief Justice Burger to give the South more time to carry out the *Brown* v. *Board of Education* mandate for school desegregation. But the Court insisted that the South had had more than enough time and ordered immediate compliance. The Court then proceeded to uphold lower courts' decisions requiring desegregation not only in the South but also in some northern cities, even though this process sometimes involved the hotly contested device of school busing.

However, as we shall see in our discussion of the racial issue in chapter 13, the

Burger Court gradually began to qualify the extent to which desegregation was required, moving toward a doctrine under which desegregation would be ordered by the Courts only where segregation had been deliberately contrived by governmental bodies.

As we shall also see in chapter 13, the Burger Court provided an elaborately qualified approval of the principle of affirmative action (government requirements for special treatment to redress past discrimination against minorities and women).

Free speech and press.   In the area of the First Amendment freedoms, the Burger Court handed down some decisions that strongly sustained the liberties of speech, assembly, and press. In 1972 the Court overturned the banning of a chapter of the left-wing Students for a Democratic Society from a college campus. In 1973 it struck down the conviction of a man for wearing an American flag patch on the seat of his pants. And in a landmark case it repudiated the efforts of the Nixon administration to prevent the publication of the "Pentagon papers," which Daniel Ellsberg had leaked to *The New York Times*.

However, in other cases the Burger Court sided with government against the claims of individuals to speak their minds. The Court agreed in 1972 that the State Department did not have to give a visa to a Belgian scholar who was a member of the Communist party so that he could speak at American University. In 1981 the Court upheld the State Department's revocation of the passport of Philip Agee, an ex-CIA agent who was attacking his former agency and who had been invited to participate in a war-crimes trial of the fifty-two Americans held hostage in Iran. There were also several decisions that made the press unhappy, including one upholding a surprise search of a newspaper office by police so long as they had a properly issued warrant.

Obscenity.   In the area of obscenity the Burger Court provided a much narrower reading of the First Amendment freedoms than the Warren Court had undertaken in the *Fanny Hill* case. In *Miller* v. *California* (1973) the Burger Court upheld the conviction of a California bookseller who had mailed unsolicited advertising brochures for such books as *Sex Orgies Illustrated*. The court went back to the earlier *Roth* doctrine that obscenity is not protected by the First Amendment. Then it went on to provide new guidelines for what constituted obscenity or pornography. They were: "(a) whether the average person, applying contemporary community standards, would find that the work, taken as a whole, appeals to the prurient interest; (b) whether the work depicts or describes in a patently offensive way, sexual conduct specifically defined by the applicable state law; and (c) whether the work, taken as a whole, lacks serious literary, artistic, political, or scientific value."

Chief Justice Burger elaborated on what the Court meant under guideline (b). It included "patently offensive representations or descriptions of ultimate sexual acts, normal or perverted, actual or simulated," and "patently offensive representations or descriptions of masturbation, excretory functions and lewd exhibitions of the genitals." Guideline (c) replaced the "utterly without redeeming social value" test and insisted that the First Amendment could not apply without a clear showing of "serious literary, artistic, political, or scientific value."

Now, said Burger, it was a matter for local communities to take whatever action they saw fit, so long as it stayed within the new guidelines. No one, he said, would suffer under these rules except hardcore "pornographers." This promise was kept in subsequent cases, when Chattanooga was told that it could not ban the rock musical *Hair*, and an Albany, Georgia, jury was overruled when it held the movie *Carnal Knowledge* obscene. As Rehnquist made clear in the *Carnal Knowledge* case, the Court would not "uphold an obscenity conviction based upon a defendant's depiction of a woman with a bare midriff." Even nudity was not sufficient grounds for censorship; not even the simulation of the sex act, so long as it was not actually conducted in full view and in graphic detail. Nor, said the Court, could juries consider the impact on children as part of "contemporary community standards."

Still, pornography, as the Court defined it, could now be banned by a community.[15]

Rights of the accused.   It is in the area of the rights of the accused in criminal cases that the Burger Court has made its most significant departures from the Warren years. Here again, the change has not been total. The Burger Court has not scrapped the constitutional rights of individuals to a fair trial and to protection from arbitrary government action. Thus government wiretaps of six hundred people used in sixty cases were invalidated because Attorney General John Mitchell had not followed the letter of the law, which required that the orders must be signed by himself or by a specific assistant attorney general.

The Court found that no person may be sentenced to jail, even for a day, without representation by a lawyer or unless the right to be represented has been specifically waived (upholding the "due process" clauses of the Fifth and Fourteenth Amendments, and the Sixth Amendment's guarantee of the "Assistance of Counsel"). It also ruled that the police cannot search a person simply because he or she happens to be at a location being searched; or search a person's home without a warrant even though the police believe that a suspect, for whom they have a warrant, might be found there.

But plenty of other Burger Court decisions made it clear that the majority felt the balance had swung too far in the direction of the rights of the accused and against the security of society. Thus the Court has found that a police officer arresting a motorist can conduct as complete a search of the suspect as necessary, even without a warrant; and that the right of indigents to free legal counsel does not continue to apply if they want to appeal their cases to higher courts.

Although the Burger Court did not overturn the *Miranda* rule setting limits on the use of confessions in trials, the rule was modified in a number of cases. For example, testimony by a witness whose name was learned by police during the illegal questioning of a suspect did not have to be thrown out; police were given permission to resume an interrogation after a suspect had exercised the right to remain silent as long as they stopped if the suspect renewed the protests; police officers need not read the precise words of the "*Miranda* warning" before questioning suspects so long as they clearly convey their rights to the suspects; and suspects must be advised of their constitutional rights only if they are taken into custody, not if they go voluntarily to a police station and confess under questioning.

In 1972 the Supreme Court, by a majority of five to four, invalidated the death penalty as then administered by the states.[16] But two members of the majority indicated that their decision was based on the argument that capital punishment was meted out randomly and unpredictably. This explanation suggested that, if state legislatures passed new laws setting forth clear standards for judges and juries, or defining capital crimes more precisely, the death penalty might still be found constitutional in some future cases. Subsequently, many states and the federal government wrote new statutes designed to meet the Supreme Court's standard by making the application of capital punishment less capricious. Some states, for example, made death mandatory for certain specific crimes, such as murder by an already convicted killer, and the federal government declared that murder during an air hijacking was a capital offense.

In July 1976 the Supreme Court found, by seven to two, that some of these new laws were constitutional.[17] "There is no question," said Justice Potter Stewart for the majority, "that death as punishment is unique in its severity and irrevocability. But . . . it is an extreme sanction suitable to the most extreme crimes." But the decision was qualified when the Court found the mandatory death penalties in two other states unconstitutional because they took away the discretion of judges and juries to reduce the penalty despite mitigating circumstances. And in 1977 the Court declared that it was unconstitutional to impose the death penalty for rape.[18] "Rape is without doubt deserving of serious punishment," said Justice Byron White, "but in terms of moral depravity and of the injury to the person and the public, it does not compare with murder."

Hence the Court was still setting stringent limits to the states' authority to sentence people to death, and there would be grounds to continue to appeal the sentences of many of the several hundred prisoners who had already been waiting for months or years on death row. However, in January 1977 a convicted murderer, Gary Gilmore, who had long been pleading to be put to death by a firing squad, was granted his request in a Utah prison. He was the first person to be executed in the United States since 1967. Others followed, but with long intervals separating each execution, because the ambiguities of the Supreme Court's decisions left room for elaborate reviews and appeals. As the appeals process ran its course, however, eventually there would be a sharp increase in the rate of executions.

By 1976 the Burger Court had moved to the view that concern for the rights of the accused must be balanced and sometimes outweighed by the need to protect society. As Burger saw it, the Warren Court's exclusionary rule, excluding from a trial any evidence seized illegally, had been applied so rigidly that it had become an intolerable handicap for law enforcement. In relaxing restrictions on searches and seizures, expanding the power of arrest, and accepting more confessions, the Burger Court gave the police more leeway and served notice that only flagrant misconduct by law enforcement agencies would result in the overturning of a conviction. The impact of all these changes can be measured by the declining proportion of cases won by the American Civil Liberties Union (ACLU), a liberal organization that fights, mostly in the courts, for the unqualified upholding of the Bill of Rights. In 1968–1969, the last of the Warren years, the ACLU won 90 percent of the cases in which it supported the appellant before the Supreme Court. By 1974–1975 the proportion had fallen below 50 percent, and increasingly the ACLU shifted its emphasis from the federal to the state courts.

The Burger Court in the Reagan era.　The dissatisfaction of the ACLU with the Burger Court did not, we have noted, mean that the Court had become un-equivocally conservative. In fact, in 1981 a common criticism of the Court by legal authorities was that it lacked any consistent direction and that it was drifting and creating confusion about the meaning of the law.

Yet the prospect appeared that the indeterminate nature of the Burger Court during the Nixon, Ford, and Carter years was merely a stage on the way to a more complete reversal of the doctrines of the Warren Court. And once again this prospect was based on changes in the personnel of the Court. In June 1981 Justice Potter Stewart who was 66 years old, announced his intention to retire. Five other members of the Court—Burger, Brennan, Marshall, Powell, and Blackmun—were 72 or older, and the health of Blackmun, Marshall, and Brennan was questionable. It appeared, therefore, that President Reagan would be able to make anywhere between one and six appointments to the Supreme Court.

In making those appointments, said Reagan, he would look for people who would "interpret the law" rather than "enact new law by judicial fiat."[19] Judge Sandra Day O'Connor, of the Arizona Court of Appeals, met that criterion, he believed, and the Senate endorsed her appointment unanimously despite the qualms of a few of the Senate's arch-conservatives.

Stewart in his later years on the Court had often sided with the conservative group. However, O'Connor in her first term joined Burger and Rehnquist more frequently than had Stewart, and the departure of Brennan or Marshall or both would open the way for a further rightward shift on the Court.

Further conservative pressure on the Court came in the form of proposals to introduce constitutional amendments that would repeal some of the decisions that conservatives found obnoxious; and this tactic was recommended by President Reagan in May 1982, when he called for a constitutional amendment to permit voluntary prayers in public schools. However, the amendment process is a lengthy and tortuous one, rarely successful in the absence of a broad national consensus; so conservatives turned to another possibility in 1981.

The Constitution gives the Court its appellate jurisdiction "with such exceptions and under such regulations as the Congress shall make." So a number of conservative members of the House and Senate claimed that this "exceptions clause" gives Congress the authority to remove from the Court's jurisdiction whole areas of public policy, such as abortion, school desegregation, or school prayers. In the past Congress had used this jurisdictional authority to deal only with minor housekeeping and administrative questions, such as the minimum dollar amount that would justify bringing a case to the federal courts.[20] But now the conservatives were ready to try all the legal devices available to them in an effort to reverse decisions made by the Burger as well as the Warren Courts.

Thus we see a number of factors leading to a political interpretation of Supreme Court decision making:

1. There is an apparent relationship between the shifting tides of public opinion and the trend of court judgments.

2. In making their nominations for membership on the Supreme Court, presidents have generally looked for people who share their own political philosophy. A similar consideration generally applies to the appointment of federal judges, because overwhelmingly presidents appoint people of their own party to the bench.

3. There is an important relationship between judges' philosophical beliefs and their decisions on the Court. Justices often ask their law clerks to provide them with past legal decisions that will provide legal backing for decisions they have arrived at on the basis of their intuitive sense of right and wrong.

4. Factions, or blocs, emerge periodically on the Court that consistently vote together on important issues, with a basically liberal group of justices opposed to a basically conservative bloc, and with some other justices sometimes tipping the balance on the liberal side, sometimes on the conservative side. For example, in the 1974–1975 term of the Burger Court, Douglas, Marshall, and Brennan tended to vote together as a liberal bloc, and Rehnquist and Burger were commonly on the conservative side of the issues, often joined by Blackmun and Powell. White and Stewart hovered around the middle of the road, perhaps slightly to right of center but sometimes siding with the liberal group.

5. As Woodward and Armstrong show in their account of the Burger Court, *The Brethren*,[21] there is a constant process of negotiation and bargaining between the justices as individuals and as factions. Understandings are arrived at and compromises struck in a manner reminiscent of the political process.

So we may well ask the following question: If a principal criterion for selecting justices of the Supreme Court is their political affiliation; if their decisions fit into a pattern based on their political and ideological outlook; and if they split into voting blocs that can be identified on our political spectrum, isn't the Court just another political institution, exercising political power according to political criteria? The answer is that, although the Supreme Court is a part of our political system, it is also a distinctly judicial body whose procedures and decision-making criteria are characteristic of a court.

THE COURT AS A JUDICIAL BODY

PROCEDURES

In a number of ways the Supreme Court functions very differently from the other branches of government, as its procedures clearly illustrate. The Court does its own work. Its staff is limited to nine justices and their law clerks (recent law school graduates who do much of the justices' research and some of the drafting of opinions). The justices do not delegate any of their work to committees or task forces. All nine are involved in every case, unless any disqualify themselves for having been associated with one of the parties to a case.

Because there are no committees, there are no separate bastions of power within the Court. The chief justice, as chairperson of the Court conferences, does have some advantages, because the chief justice can formulate the issues and determine how long debate will continue. Whenever the chief justice is on the side of the majority he can also decide who will write the opinion (so any justice who offends the chief justice may be assigned to write nothing but cases of little importance and massive technical complexity). How great these advantages are depends on the chief justice and the other members of the Court. But the chief justice's power is never as great as that of a chairperson over a congressional committee, or that of a president over the presidential staff and cabinet.

Of course, as we have indicated, the Court cannot conduct its business without a certain amount of bargaining and seeking of compromises. Wherever decisions are made, in large or small groups, in public or private institutions, people must learn to make their adjustments to other people's feelings and ideas, so the political process will come into play. In the case of the Supreme Court Woodward and Armstrong suggest that this process is very much at work. Some of their anecdotes, in fact, convey such a sense of maneuvering, calculation, and logrolling among the justices as to cast a long shadow over the Court's reputation for propriety. Although there have been challenges to the accuracy of *The Brethren*,[22] other close observers of the Court over the years have known that many crucial decisions are arrived at after a period of hard bargaining among the justices. Even so, the structure and mode of operation on the Court are very different from the legislative process.

One of the differences is the secrecy in which the Court arrives at its decisions. *The Brethren* aroused such an outcry because it exposed to the glare of publicity a process that previously had never received such treatment. Moreover, the book consisted of reconstruction well after the event. (The authors were at pains to point out that they were avoiding any cases that had not been settled some time before.) Yet detailed accounts of how the president and Congress made decisions only yesterday—or are making them at the moment—are the common fare of daily columnists and network news reporters. Occasionally members of the Court make public speeches in which they make their views on the issues known. By and large, however, the Court differs from our other governmental institutions in that it does not seek, and even studiously avoids, the glare of publicity.

All these factors help protect the Court from the immediate pressures of the political world outside. Although it cannot be isolated from the society of which it is a part, it can preserve through its procedures a greater degree of autonomy, free of the demands of specific groups and interests, than can the legislative and executive branches. Faced with the confidentiality of the justices' conferences, pressure groups lack the knowledge they need as to when and how to apply pressure. Although individual judges have their own acquaintances and contacts and frequently go out into the world, the Court is generally not accessible to Washington lobbyists who might try to work on the justices and arrange for pressure from the folks back home. Of course, organized groups often turn to the courts to protect their interests when other branches of government are not giving them what they want.[23] However, because the justices have lifetime tenure, they are immune to direct constituency pressures.

JUDICIAL CRITERIA

Facts and logic.   The Court's differences from other governmental agencies are not limited to matters of procedure. Its criteria for testing issues are by no means identical with the criteria of legislative and executive agencies. The Court is very much concerned with the facts of a case. Of course, so is Congress, which accumulates data massively, but in the legislative process facts tend to be mutilated under the bombardment of competing statements and special pleading. Although the Supreme Court, like any other human institution, cannot claim complete objectivity in its identification and selection of facts, it may still be true that, as Justice Jackson claimed, "most contentions of law are won or lost on the facts."

Logic is another powerful consideration. As they interrogate the attorneys who appear before them to argue cases, the justices will often pursue the logic of an argument even though it leads them in a direction contrary to their own preconceptions; rarely is this procedure paralleled in congressional committee hearings.

Professional opinion.   The justices are sensitive to professional opinion, especially as it is expressed in the law journals, which assess the performance of justices not only in relation to the validity of their conclusions but also the legal quality of the opinions they deliver. This concern helps to explain the large number of *concurring opinions*, which support the majority view but provide different or additional reasons. It is not enough for the writers of these opinions to cast their vote. They must offer their own special legal reasoning to show

ART WOOD-COURTESY U.S. INDEPENDENT TELEPHONE ASSN.
A difference of opinion!

exactly the grounds on which they base their decision and how their reasoning differs even from the justices whose votes they are supporting. The same procedure occurs with minority opinions, and sometimes there are several dissenting opinions in a single case.

Precedent. A fundamental principle of Anglo-American law is *stare decisis*: to stand by what has been decided. The assumption is that the courts will generally follow what they have said in the past, and the justices are careful to quote precedents extensively in their decisions and to avoid overruling precedents casually.

Judicial restraint. Both the Warren and Burger Courts have struck down as unconstitutional all or part of a number of congressional statutes. But typically the Court looks for other grounds—the ambiguity of a statute, its incompatibility with another statute, or the failure of the executive branch to comply with a statute—rather than the question of constitutionality itself. The Court has felt much freer to reject state and local laws, and actions by local law enforcement authorities, on grounds of their incompatibility with the federal Constitution or with federal statutes. Even there, however, it has tried to avoid handing down rulings that could cause administrative chaos, such as making a criminal law ruling retroactive, which could result in the release of thousands of prisoners convicted under earlier rulings.

The Constitution. "We must never forget," said Chief Justice John Marshall, "that it is a Constitution we are expounding." The Court has adopted this doctrine and established itself as *the* authoritative interpreter of the Founding Fathers' document. Congress and the president also see themselves as defenders and interpreters of the Constitution, but at times, under the spur of events, they override protests that their proposals may be unconstitutional with the answer that, if that be so, the courts will take care of it.

THE DIFFICULTY OF PREDICTING DECISIONS

The result of these important differences in procedure and criteria between the Supreme Court and the other branches of government is that, although the Court is very much a part of the political system, many of its decisions cannot be predicted simply by projecting each justice's partisan and ideological leanings. Innumerable cases prove this point. In *Wallace* v. *Ohio* (1968) the Court found, six to three, that Ohio had no right to keep George Wallace off the presidential ballot. Among the majority were men who were obviously hostile to George Wallace's politics—Douglas, Black, Brennan, Fortas, and Thurgood Marshall, a black man.

The Burger Court, too, provides us with many illustrations of this unpredictability. As we have noted, the appointment of four justices by President Nixon did indeed stem the liberal judicial tide established in the Earl Warren era. Moreover, there were perceptible patterns of voting, with three holdovers from the earlier court—Douglas, Brennan, and Marshall—tending to take liberal positions, while the Nixon appointees—Burger, Rehnquist, Blackmun, and Powell—were more likely to be found on the conservative side of the issues.

However, as we also noted earlier, these patterns broke down in a number of cases, particularly on the conservative side. Certainly *Roe* v. *Wade*, the case striking down antiabortion laws, does not fit into the main conservative strand of thinking in the country. The majority opinion was written by Justice Blackmun, and he became the target of vitriolic attacks by antiabortion organizations. On other issues, too, Blackmun could not be fitted neatly into the conservative classification; and as time went on Blackmun, who had grown up in the same area as Burger, was less and less likely to be dubbed Burger's "Minnesota twin." Powell's decisions, too, were difficult to predict, and he was often found with the centrist group (later joined by Stevens) that became the controlling force on the Burger Court in a number of cases. Even the conservative Burger, not wanting to find himself in the minority in too many cases, would sometimes join with the center-liberal combination in the final decision.

In *United States* v. *Nixon* (1974) the Burger Court gave us the ultimate illustration of the danger of oversimplified classifications of the justices based on partisan and ideological affiliation. In that case the Supreme Court told the president that he must comply with the special prosecutor's subpoena of the Watergate tapes. The vote was eight to zero.[24] Thus Burger, Blackmun, and Powell decided against the man who had put them on the Supreme Court and joined with the others in the verdict that sealed Richard Nixon's fate.

Nor was Nixon the only president to be surprised and disappointed by the decisions of people he had appointed to the Court. Dwight Eisenhower called his appointment of Earl Warren "the biggest damn fool mistake I ever made."

These examples do not invalidate the analysis presented earlier in which we saw that the justices' basic philosophical preconceptions show through in their decisions and that certain general patterns of voting emerge within each Court. Indeed, this way of looking at the Court is likely to become even more applicable as further appointments are made to the Court by President Reagan. But it is essential not to lose sight of the other considerations that enter into the thinking of most, if not all, of the justices and that stem from the fact that the Supreme Court is a legal, judicial body and thus different in important respects from the other branches of government.

FIVE PERSPECTIVES ON THE SUPREME COURT

THE CONSERVATIVES: AGAINST JUDICIAL ACTIVISM

Generally speaking, conservatives have judged the Supreme Court's decisions according to whether or not the decisions agreed with the conservative political positions of the moment.

When the Court struck down New Deal legislation, conservatives applauded its decisions.

They lauded the Vinson Court's refusal to save Communist party leaders from jail. They were outraged by the Warren Court's judgments in such fields as communist activities, congressional investigations, school prayers, criminal justice, and federal-state relations.

Richard Nixon won conservative plaudits by

his criticisms of the courts in his 1968 presidential campaign for going too far "in weakening the peace forces against the criminal forces in this country"; and conservatives were pleased by the movement in the Burger Court away from the Warren Court's positions in the fields of criminal law and obscenity. Yet they were perplexed and disappointed by the decision upholding the right to abortions, and by the Burger Court's upholding mandatory school desegregation, even when desegregation involved busing, with only limited qualifications. So they urged President Reagan to appoint people to the Supreme Court so clearly conservative in their views that the damage brought by the Warren Court would be completely undone, and they objected to the appointment of Sandra Day O'Connor because her known views, although rather conservative, were not sufficiently so to satisfy them.

These pronouncements were the predictable assessments of the Court's decisions by most conservative politicians and activists. Some conservative analysts, however, have provided a more fundamental critique of the institutional role of the Supreme Court than the extent to which it satisfies ephemeral political needs. The laws of men, they argue, must operate within the constraints of a higher law based on fundamental principles of man and God. Our Constitution represents the attempt of the Founding Fathers to capture in an approximate way the principles of that higher law. If the executive or legislative branches of government breach the principles of the Constitution, they must be held to account. The body that exercises this restraint over the elected representatives of the people and prevents their exercising uncontrolled power is the Supreme Court. The Court is an essential element in the principle of checks and balances. Perhaps more than any other part of the system, in fact, it is the guardian of the constitutional structure.

But suppose that, instead of acting as a protector of the Constitution, it assumes an unhealthy degree of power itself? This situation occurred with the Court under Earl Warren. Whenever the Warren Court concluded that the elected representatives of the people were not acting with sufficient vigor, it sprang into action itself, usurping the role of the legislature on reapportionment, abortion, and school desegregation.

A strict construction of the Constitution. What, then, is the proper role of the Supreme Court? It should construe the Constitution strictly, say conservatives. Although the Constitution is brief, the spirit of the Constitution is clear. It calls for limited government. The Framers did not want the powers of government to be expanded by great leaps, and the Courts should not read anything into the document that is not there in order to justify more and more government.

All parts of the Constitution should be given equal importance. Some justices, including the liberals' idol, William O. Douglas, have argued that the Bill of Rights is more fundamental than the rest and that the First Amendment must be given a preferred position. To conservatives, there is nothing in the language of the Constitution that gives some rights preference over others. In fact, as we saw in chapter 1, conservatives believe that property rights are as essential as any other kind of rights. Certainly the First Amendment freedoms must be protected. But liberals fail to make the necessary distinction between liberty and license. Moreover, the protection of all liberties and all rights is dependent on the preservation of a fundamental framework of order, and in their obsession with the rights of criminals liberal judges are bringing us close to the point at which the whole framework of law and order is in danger of collapsing.

Judicial restraint. The Court should exercise great restraint in reviewing the claims of the federal government to override the decisions of state governments and their local subdivisions. Yet the Supreme Court, and especially the Warren Court, has persistently ignored the language of the Tenth Amendment, which reserves to the states or to the people those powers not delegated to the federal government.

Conservatives were pleased to note that Chief

Justice Burger was anxious to avoid having his Court usurp the functions of the states. Repeatedly he warned against the tendency to move cases out of the states into the federal courts. He warned that the burden on the federal court system was becoming intolerable. In the course of these warnings he sounded another note that fell pleasingly on conservative ears; not only the federal courts, but also the state systems, were being overloaded. Suddenly everyone was demanding rights, and almost everyone was litigating, turning to the courts to handle conflicts that used to be resolved by private bargaining or through political bodies. Blacks and women, in particular, were flooding the courts with demands for equal access to jobs, higher education, and every other kind of opportunity; and this litigation was generating an avalanche of legal counterattacks by white males. The overreliance on courts of law, said the conservatives, was the inevitable result of the impossible expectations raised by the liberals' rhetoric and the Warren Court's encouragement of unreasonable claims.

Precedent. Because conservatives believe in preserving the values of the past, it is natural that they should have great respect for precedent. The Warren Court, they insist, was all too ready to abandon the rulings of previous courts to make way for its own preferences. Inevitably, over a long period of time, some earlier cases may come to be overruled. But these cases should be the exceptions. Where precedents are easily ignored, there can be no stable body of law. And without legal stability, there can be no rule of law.

Appointments to the Court. The Conservatives want to see on the Supreme Court people who will construe the Constitution strictly, respect the acts of state governments, and value precedent. Such people are of substantial legal training and judicious temperament, preferably people with substantial judicial experience. Yet only about a quarter of the justices have had really extensive judicial careers. Conservatives would like to see this proportion raised.

Conservatives recognize that their prescription for the Court may, from time to time, have to be adjusted. Given the rampant activism of the Warren Court, it may be necessary for a time to be activist in the opposite direction. Thus some of the Warren precedents may need to be overturned in order to repair the damage they have inflicted on the constitutional system.

In general, however, conservatives declare themselves to be opposed to judicial activism. We have more than enough legislatures in this country already. We do not need the Supreme Court to legislate for us. Certainly we do not need it as our supreme legislature.

THE LIBERALS: MOSTLY FOR JUDICIAL ACTIVISM

To the extent that the conservatives detested the Warren Court, the liberals loved it. Here and there a decision of the Court might not please them, but on the whole they found it the one institution of American government whose product they could endorse with enthusiasm. They applauded the decisions on reapportionment, racial desegregation, free speech, and obscenity.

In criminal law they have been principally concerned to see that police power is not abused, and they would rather see a guilty person go free than take a chance on an innocent person's being wrongfully convicted. They share Earl Warren's indignation when, in explaining the *Miranda* decision, he quoted from several police manuals on interrogation. One of these manuals suggested that questioning take place in a police station, where "the investigator possesses all the advantages," rather than in the suspect's home. The same manual advised the questioner to "interrogate without relent, leaving the subject no prospect of surcease." Various methods were suggested to encourage a confession, including the mention of other related crimes and a lineup with coached witnesses, in the hope that "the subject will become desperate and confess to the offense under investigation in order to escape from the false accusations."

So liberals were unhappy with the extent to which the Burger Court weakened the Warren Court's positions, but they were as pleased as the conservatives were disappointed by the Burger Court's upholding the constitutionality of abortion.

Yet, as we have already observed, the conservatives' perspective on the Court is not argued solely in terms of its product. They also present an analysis of the Court as an institution in the American governmental structure. They ask that the Court adopt a strict construction of the Constitution, use restraint in dealing with the states, and venerate precedent. And they believe that the Court should consist of people of judicious temperament and judicial experience. What is the liberals' response to these positions?

A flexible interpretation of the Constitution. In most areas liberals favor a more flexible interpretation of the Constitution than do the conservatives. Because the document is brief, it must be cast in general terms, and generality breeds ambiguity.

It is absurd to suggest that the Warren Court went far beyond the Constitution in its decisions on the right of the accused to counsel. The Fourteenth Amendment says that no state shall "deprive any person of life, liberty, or property, without due process of law." The Sixth Amendment says that an accused person shall have the right to "have the Assistance of Counsel for his defense," and for some time the Supreme Court has found that this procedure is a necessary part of "due process." But the Constitution does not tell us when the right to counsel begins and under what conditions. So in *Escobedo* and *Miranda* the Warren Court said that the right is meaningless unless it begins early in the investigative process, and that, if the accused cannot afford an attorney, the Court will appoint one free. This right does not appear in the language of the Sixth Amendment. But can there be due process without these protections?

Similarly, the Constitution makes no specific mention of abortion, school segregation, or por-nography. But when individuals and groups bring these grievances to the courts, the Supreme Court has no alternative but to search the language of the Constitution to see what guidance it can find in the general principles of the document that can apply to the issues of our contemporary world. Moreover, the intent of the Framers must be construed in a twentieth-century context.

Liberals, however, take a much less flexible view of the First Amendment freedoms. The rights of freedom of speech, press, and assembly must be "preferred rights," because without them all other rights lose their protection. They may not be absolute—they can be limited by laws concerning libel and slander, for example—but they should generally be given a preferred status over such protections as property rights.

Precedents cannot always rule. Liberals do not deny that judges should treat precedents seriously. However, they are not as reluctant as conservatives to depart from past rulings. In fact, the Court has overruled its own prior decisions more than one hundred times in its history. And Justices Felix Frankfurter and John Marshall Harlan, who were among the Court's principal advocates of judicial restraint and adherence to precedent, have both participated in the overturning of precedents.

Frankfurter joined in the unanimous decision on *Brown* v. *Board of Education* (1954), which in essence reversed the finding of *Plessy* v. *Ferguson* (1896) that separate could be equal. And in *Gideon* v. *Wainwright* (1963), which established the right to counsel for indigents in criminal cases, Harlan supported the overruling of *Betts* v. *Brady* (1942), which had rejected this interpretation of the Constitution.[25]

Justices need not have judicial experience. Liberals are not overly impressed with the argument that the people appointed to the Supreme Court should be experienced judges. Some of the greatest, most "judicial" members of the Supreme Court have not come from the lower courts. The first great chief justice, John Marshall, did not.

Nor did Chief Justices Taney, Hughes, and Stone, or such eminent associate justices as Louis Brandeis and Felix Frankfurter.

Liberals are unconvinced that coming from a lower court increases the likelihood that a Supreme Court justice will be free from political preconceptions. Politics plays an important role in appointment to the lower courts. When Warren Burger was selected as chief justice, Nixon was mindful of the fact that Burger had been instrumental at the 1952 Republican convention in delivering the Minnesota vote to Eisenhower and that Burger was appointed by Eisenhower first as an assistant attorney general, then to the U.S. Court of Appeals in Washington.

Politics is very much a factor, then, in getting onto and moving up the judicial ladder, and liberals believe this process to be inevitable. However, they are concerned about the criteria for appointments to the Supreme Court, but their complaint is that the Court is unrepresentative of the population. Mostly the justices have come from the upper-middle or upper class and have been predominately white Anglo-Saxon Protestants. Thurgood Marshall, appointed in 1967, was the first black on the Court. Not until 1981 was there a woman on the Court. It is time, say the liberals, to make the Court, which deals in great issues of public policy that affect the future of the entire population, more representative of that population.

The liberals' dilemma.   The Supreme Court consists of nine mostly elderly, mostly well-to-do, mostly white men. They have lifetime appointments. They have the power to render null and void the decisions of legislative and executive bodies duly elected by the majority will of the people.

Considering these facts, how can the liberals, devout advocates of majority will, offer an elaborate structure of reasoning why the decisions of these unelected men and woman should outweigh the acts of the representative branches of government? If they support majority rule, how do they deal with the fact that in the 1940s and 1950s the majority did not believe that Communists had the right to propagate their ideas? Or that in the 1960s the majority were much more concerned with the rights of the victim than with the rights of the accused and were strongly against the Supreme Court's ban on school prayers?

The liberals' response to these questions is that democracy is concerned not only with majority rule but also with individual and minority rights. If the majority is allowed to make its own mistakes in the area of free expression, those mistakes may involve the suppression of rights. If dissenting opinions are suppressed, an essential condition of democracy—the free play of ideas through which alternative policies are presented—may disappear. Of course, it would be better if elected executives and legislatures did their job of preserving and advancing our rights and freedoms. But on school desegregation, reapportionment, and other issues the president, Congress, and state governments had failed to act. There has been a gaping void, and the Supreme Court had to move into the void.

Although the liberals make this case, they are not entirely comfortable with it. At least some liberal scholars, including James MacGregor Burns, doubt that they should rely on the Supreme Court to do their work for them in any area except the freedoms guaranteed in the Bill of Rights. On such issues as school desegregation and reapportionment they worry about the liberals' having looked to the Warren Court to bail them out rather than getting action from the executive and legislative branches of government. Judicial activism in the hands of the Warren Court produced highly desirable results for the liberals, but judicial activism can be a two-edged sword. The Warren Court has established the precedent of having the Court intervene vigorously in many issues. What will the liberals, who applauded the Warren Court's activism so enthusiastically in the 1960s, have to say if a later, much more conservative Supreme Court decides to intervene vigorously on the conservative side in social, economic, and sexual issues? No doubt the liberals will set up a great outcry, as they did in the 1930s. But their opponents will be able to turn against them the arguments for activism that the liberals used so passionately in the 1960s.

This reasoning took on particular force with the election of Ronald Reagan and the likelihood of his being able to appoint two or more members to the Court. So liberals had to conclude that, even if the Court in the 1980s did not undo much of the work of the 1960s, it would not continue to deliver for them what they were unable to achieve through the other branches of the federal government.

THE RADICAL RIGHT: HOW THE SUPREME COURT HAS SUBVERTED AMERICAN VALUES

The far right has found little to enthuse about in the decisions of the Supreme Court since 1936. The brief effort by the Court to stop the New Deal's advance to socialism was abandoned in 1937. For a while in the late forties and early fifties the Court took a stand against communism, but the Warren Court put an end to that. The entire Warren era was a disaster from the radical right's perspective. In their view the Warren Court was working not merely for a domestic but for a foreign dictatorship, and as long as Earl Warren was allowed to continue to issue his arbitrary decisions there could be no hope for the return of the rule of law in America.[26]

The Birch Society launched a campaign to "Impeach Earl Warren" that included the sale of large billboard posters and packages of pamphlets by Robert Welch and Mississippi Senator James Eastland. Others who joined in the demand for Warren's impeachment included the right-wing radio and television commentator Dan Smoot and the fundamentalist preacher Billy James Hargis, who was particularly incensed by the school prayers decisions and called for the impeachment of every member of the Supreme Court who had voted with Warren on this issue.[27]

The passing from the scene of Earl Warren did little to mollify the radical right. The Burger Court's decisions in the criminal law area took some of the steam out of the widespread hostility that the Warren Court had aroused, which made it harder for the right to find allies on the "law and order" and "support your local police" movement. But they could work with local groups that, although not part of the radical right, were enraged by Supreme Court decisions on prayer, abortion, and school desegregation. And they could fight for constitutional amendments that would overturn those decisions.

THE RADICAL LEFT: THE MYTH OF EQUALITY UNDER THE LAW

For the radical left the Supreme Court is the apex of a rule of law designed to protect the interests of the ruling elite. Leftists see equality before the law as a myth. Law enforcement is applied overwhelmingly against the poor, minorities, and political activists. White-collar criminals who subvert the law by swindling the masses and manipulating huge amounts of money through a variety of crooked schemes are usually untouched by the criminal law. On the rare occasions when they are brought to trial, white-collar defendants are treated gently, in contrast with the poor, who are treated like faceless rabble.[28]

LOU ERICKSON-COURTESY ATLANTA JOURNAL

"Gentlemen of the board, something must be done to stop this awful crime in the streets."

Although the Warren Court made an effort to restrain the methods by which the police harass blacks, the young, and political dissidents and trick them into convicting themselves, the police have learned how to go through the motions, protect themselves technically, and still employ brutal tactics. And the Burger Court has steadily eroded even the thin protections demanded by the Warren majority.

But even the left admits that courts can sometimes produce justice for the oppressed. Juries acquitted the "Chicago Seven"—leaders of the left accused of conspiracy to incite riots at the Democratic National Convention of 1968—and twenty-one Black Panthers accused of acts of violence against the police in 1971. These acquittals were achieved by a new generation of lawyers, dedicated to service to the people rather than to business corporations, and by juries of ordinary people who refused to accept the manipulations and distortions of the ruling elite and its agencies of repression.

THE CENTRISTS: SOUND JUDGMENT AND GOOD CRAFTSMANSHIP

Here again, centrists look for a balance among the institutions of government and a middle ground between the liberal and conservative positions.

As they review the recent history of the Supreme Court, centrists find that the Court in the 1930s was too stubborn in its rejection of New Deal legislation (although some of that legislation had to be abandoned as unworkable). On the other hand, they are offended that Franklin Roosevelt tried to "pack" the Court.

The centrist verdict is that the Warren Court was altogether too adventurous. Many of its decisions were necessary, but it moved on too many fronts at once and made itself vulnerable to attack from several directions. This aggressiveness damaged not only the reputation of the Supreme Court but also respect for the law itself.

So, whatever the merits of particular decisions of the Burger Court, in the centrist perspective it has served the necessary function of swinging the pendulum back toward the center. This has been especially important in the area of criminal trials, for in a period of rising crime rates it is important that the courts be as sensitive to the needs of society and of victims as to the rights of the accused. There may be a danger that the pendulum will swing too far, but, in time, this action is likely to produce motion in the opposite direction.

Centrists strongly object to some of the current proposals put forward by conservatives to undermine the role of the Court by removing its jurisdiction over major areas of public policy. This tampering is on the same order as Roosevelt's court-packing plan. True conservatives, say the centrists, should have no part of any scheme that endangers the entire constitutional structure of checks and balances.

Unfortunately, say the centrists, some of the Court's decisions have invited this kind of attack. Although the Court should not allow itself to be governed by opinion polls, neither should it set too great a distance between the trend of its decisions and the long-range climate of opinion in the country. It should neither fall too far behind the mood of the people as in the 1930s, nor get too far ahead of it as in the 1960s. Otherwise, instead of being a force for stability and moderation—the traditional role of the law—it becomes a source of tension and hostility.

In addition to sensible political judgment by the justices, the centrists look for good craftsmanship in their decisions. The public at large may look only at the outcome of a decision, but lawyers study the reasoning behind an opinion. If that reasoning is sound and well-crafted, lawyers, even if they disagree with the conclusions, respect it. And lawyers, being influential people, may in time win broad public respect for the opinion. Generally speaking, the best and most enduring decisions are based on sound logic and a thorough grasp of the techniques of the law.

CONCLUSION

In this chapter we have reviewed the two dimensions of the Supreme Court's work: the political and the judicial. The Court, we have seen, is no metaphysical abstraction detached from the ways of the world. It is a human institution, and the individuals who are its members cannot separate their actions completely from the way they perceive the world. As Judge Jerome Frank pointed out: "Much harm is done by the myth that, merely by putting on a black robe and taking the oath of office as a judge, a man ceases to be human and strips himself of all predilections, becomes a passionless thinking machine."[29] It is often said that ours is a government of laws, not men. Yet the laws must be interpreted by men, and those men cannot be completely insulated from the currents of political opinion that have shaped their own experience and that move in the society at large.

Moreover, the Supreme Court has responsibilities that go beyond the merely legal. It is charged with the task of testing the actions of other branches and levels of government against the Constitution, so it cannot help engaging in policy making. Even if it refuses to overturn acts of Congress and state legislatures, it thereby affirms their constitutionality and thus participates in the making of policy. Doing nothing, in this case, is doing a great deal. So the battle surrounding the Court today, as it has always been, is how it exercises its power in broad fields of public policy.

At the same time, the Supreme Court is also a judicial body, a legal institution. We saw in our discussions of the presidency, Congress, and the bureaucracies that, although these branches of government are all deeply engaged in the political process, each of them has particular institutional characteristics that powerfully affect the way it operates. This fact is even more true with the Supreme Court, which must attach great weight to the Constitution, the acts of executives and legislatures, and precedent. Further, the procedures of the Supreme Court are very different from the procedures of the other branches of government.

These judicial considerations make it difficult to predict how each justice will vote on a given issue, and these same considerations cause conservatives and liberals alike to be caught up in self-contradictions. Conservatives, who believe in strict construction of the Constitution, respect for state legislatures, and deference to precedent, sometimes call for decisions that stretch the wording of the Constitution to the utmost, overturn state government actions, and overrule precedents. But the liberals' inconsistencies are greater still. Although they are believers in majority rule, on some issues they are unwilling to abide by the majority will and turn to the most unrepresentative body in the federal government to protect them from the majority.

I do not mean to suggest that conservatives and liberals are cynically playing with symbols and using whatever arguments come to hand to serve their purposes. The point is simply that, try though they will to address themselves to the debate over institutions, they cannot lose sight of the fact that institutions are not ends in themselves, but human creations to serve human purposes.

NOTES AND REFERENCES

1. Technically an appeal from a state to a federal court may be brought only to the Supreme Court. The lower federal courts may take jurisdiction of a state case only by removal or by writ of *habeas corpus*.
2. Most of the cases coming to the U.S. Supreme Court do so as a result of a writ of *certiorari*—an order issued by the Supreme Court calling for the records of a case to be sent up for review.
3. In addition to the *appellate* jurisdiction of the Supreme Court (its authority to take cases on appeal from lower courts), the Court has *original* jurisdiction (the authority to receive a case directly without its going through the lower courts) where the parties to the case are states. Moreover, when the Supreme Court decides that a matter is of great public importance it can bypass the appeals courts and take a case directly.
4. *Lochner* v. *New York.*
5. *Adkins* v. *Children's Hospital.*
6. Roosevelt's court-packing proposal also included the addition of two new seats to the Supreme Court.
7. *Schenck* v. *United States* (1919).
8. *Gitlow* v. *New York* (1925).
9. On the other hand, in *Ginzburg* v. *United States*, handed down in 1966 at the same time as the *Fanny Hill* case, the Warren Court sustained a five-year prison sentence for publisher Ralph Ginzburg for sending obscene materials through the mails. Justice William Brennan delivered a Court opinion that used as a test the intent of the purveyor. Ginzburg's publications, said Brennan, were "originated or sold as stock in trade of the sordid business of pandering." Ginzburg had deliberately represented the publications as "erotically arousing," which "stimulated the reader to accept them as prurient." Among the evidence on which Brennan based his conclusion was that Ginzburg had tried to get mailing privileges (which would place the name of the town on the envelopes) for one of his publications from Intercourse, Pa.; rejected there, he settled for Middlesex, N.Y.
10. On the other hand, in 1947 the Court had found in *Everson* v. *Board of Education* that New Jersey's granting state subsidies for bus fares for parochial as well as public school children did not breach the separation of church and state. In 1980 the Court, in a five to four decision, decided that New York state was not in violation of the First Amendment's ban on the establishment of religion when it reimbursed church-related schools for the cost of administering certain standardized tests or for reporting data required by the state (*Committee for Public Education and Religious Liberty* v. *Regan*).
11. *Ball* v. *James* (1981). The Court was split five to four, the dissenters complaining that the principle accepted here was "one acre, one vote."
12. *Planned Parenthood of Central Missouri* v. *Danforth* (1976).
13. *Beal* v. *Doe* (1977); *Maher* v. *Roe* (1977); *Poelker* v. *Doe* (1977).
14. *County of Washington* v. *Gunther* (1981). This decision involved a suit brought by former women patrons employed in the women's section of a jail who complained they were paid much less than the male corrections officers. The decision went beyond the principle of equal pay for equal work, because the women worked in a separate part of the jail. However, it was a limited decision that did not finally resolve the complex question of "comparative worth" of jobs held predominately or exclusively by women as against jobs held overwhelmingly by men.
15. In *Cooper* v. *Mitchell Brothers* (1981), the Supreme Court ruled that the U.S. Constitution did not require local officials to prove "beyond a reasonable doubt" that movies they want to ban from their communities are obscene. And in *New York* v. *Ferber* (1982) the Court unanimously decided that states may ban child pornography whether or not it is legally obscene.

16. *Furman* v. *Georgia* (1972); *Jackson* v. *Georgia* (1972); *Branch* v. *Texas* (1972).

17. *Gregg* v. *Georgia* (1976); *Proffitt* v. *Florida* (1976); *Jurek* v. *Texas* (1976).

18. *Coker* v. *Georgia* (1977).

19. Attorney General William French Smith, in an address to the Federal Legal Council on October 29, 1981, said: "We believe that the groundswell of conservatism, evidenced by the 1980 election, makes this an especially appropriate time to urge upon the courts more principled bases that would diminish judicial activism. The very arbitrariness with which some rights have been discerned and preferred, while others have not, reveals a process of subjective judicial policy-making as opposed to reasoned legal interpretation." Smith objected to court rulings that established judicial control over school boards, prison systems, and public housing.

20. The exception was a law passed in 1868 stripping the Supreme Court of jurisdiction over *habeas corpus* cases in order to prevent the release from jail of a Mississippi newspaper editor who had criticized the northern generals sent to oversee Reconstruction. Subsequently the Supreme Court upheld the law.

21. Bob Woodward and Scott Armstrong, *The Brethren: Inside the Supreme Court* (New York: Simon & Schuster, 1979).

22. See, for example, Anthony Lewis, "Supreme Court Confidential," *New York Review of Books,* 7 February 1980, pp. 3–8. Lewis checked one of the allegations in *The Brethren* with the law clerks who were apparently its source, and all denied categorically that the alleged episode had occurred. Other critics have pointed out that Woodward and Armstrong's refusal to divulge their sources, in line with their journalists' code of professional privilege, makes it well-nigh impossible to check the accuracy of many of their anecdotes. In reply the authors have insisted that all their statements were checked with more than one source, and that their sources included bona fide written documents, as well as interviews with several law clerks and some of the justices.

23. Clement E. Vose, "Litigation as a Form of Pressure Group Activity," *Annals of the American Academy of Political and Social Science* 319 (September 1958): 20–31.

24. Rehnquist disqualified himself because he had served as assistant attorney general under a Watergate defendant, Attorney General John Mitchell.

25. The overturning of *Betts* came in stages. In cases after *Betts* the Court decided that indigents must be offered free counsel in capital cases and in complicated cases. *Gideon* provided a further expansion of exceptions to *Betts* which had already been made.

26. See Robert A. Rosenstone, *Protest from the Right* (Beverly Hills: The Glencoe Press, 1968), p. 9.

27. Pamphlet, "Six Men against God," 1965, quoted in Benjamin R. Epstein and Arnold Forster, *The Radical Right* (New York: Vintage Books, 1967), p. 22.

28. See Robert Lefcourt, "Law against the People," from *Law against the People: Essays to Demystify Law, Order and the Courts* (New York: Random House, 1971).

29. Jerome Frank, *Law and the Modern Mind,* 6th ed. (New York: Coward, McCann & Geoghegan, 1949), p. xx.

chapter eleven

FEDERALISM: STATES AND CITIES

lthough most of this book is concerned with our national government, it would be a grave mistake to identify government in America with Washington, D.C. Certainly this notion would be abhorrent to the representatives of the thirteen states who assembled in Philadelphia in 1787. They had no intention of establishing a unitary system, with dominant power vested in the central government. Even the acceptance of a *federal* structure, which divided authority between national and state governments, came only after fierce debate and over the grave reservations of many delegates at the convention.

Today the elaborate structure of federalism that the Founders created has taken on new dimensions of complexity. In addition to the fifty states we have tens of thousands of subdivisions of state government: counties, municipalities, townships, and school districts, as well as a proliferation of special districts for such matters as water supply, fire protection, smog control, and public transportation.

In this chapter we shall describe the main characteristics of these eighty thousand units of government (table 11-1) and explore the relationships between these

TABLE 11–1 State and local units of government and employees, 1977

	Units	Employees (approx.)
States	50	3,700,000
Counties	3,042	1,800,000
Municipalities	18,862	2,550,000
Towns and townships	16,822	400,000
School districts	15,174	4,200,000
Special districts	25,962	445,000
Totals	79,912	13,095,000

Source: Advisory Commission on Intergovernmental Relations and U.S., Bureau of the Census, 1979.

units and the federal government. Then we shall examine some contemporary problems of state and local government, and with this background, present five perspectives on the federal system.

CHARACTERISTICS OF STATE AND LOCAL GOVERNMENTS

THE STATES

There are a number of similarities between the governments of the various states and the federal government. Each state has a written constitution. And each state has adopted the principle of separation of powers. There is an executive branch headed by a governor; state legislatures, all of which have two houses except Nebraska, which has only one house; and a hierarchy of courts, beginning with local police courts and moving up through courts of appeal to a supreme court.

However, there are also important differences between state and federal governments. To begin with, the state constitutions are much longer than the U.S. Constitution. Although a constitution is supposed to be the underlying or fundamental law, many of the state constitutions have become cluttered with immense masses of technical detail. Moreover, constitutions tend to grow longer in several of the western states because, in addition to the most common method for amending state constitutions—a two-thirds vote of the state legislature followed by a vote of the general electorate—provision has been made for amendment through the *initiative*. This procedure allows a proposal to be placed on the ballot by securing a sufficient number of voters' signatures on petitions even if the state legislature has not voted on the matter.

Then there are significant differences between the power of state and federal executives. Whatever we have said about the frustrations of presidents is even more true of governors. For one thing, they are held accountable for many problems, such as the increase in unemployment and in welfare costs, that can only be handled at the national level. Then in most states a number of members of the executive branch—for example, the lieutenant governor, the attorney general, the secretary of state, the state treasurer, the superintendent of education—are elected separately from the governor and thus have their independent bases of power, which effectively limits the power of the governor. Most governors, however, wield a weapon that the president lacks: the *item veto*, the authority to trim items from the budget proposed by the legislature rather than take or leave the whole thing.

The state legislatures differ from Congress in a number of important respects. For the most part, their members serve part time, and in all but a few of the largest states the legislators are paid far too little for them to consider their legislative office their principal occupation. Salaries are increasing, however, and the larger number of state legislatures now hold annual sessions rather than the former practice of meeting every other year. Unlike the U.S. Congress, in which the lower chamber represents the widely varying populations of the fifty states, both chambers of each state legislature draw their members from districts having roughly equal populations (although state senators are drawn from fewer and larger districts than are the representatives of the lower house). This arrangement is the result of the U.S. Supreme Court's reapportionment decisions, *Baker* v. *Carr* (1962) and *Reynolds* v. *Sims* (1964).

As is the case at the national level, state courts may strike down any state law that conflicts with the state's constitution. However, whereas the U.S. Supreme Court has the final word on the interpretation of the U.S. Constitution (unless the Constitution is amended), state and local court decisions may be appealed to the federal courts, *as long as there is a federal issue involved.*

And a notable difference between state and federal judges is that the latter are appointed for life, whereas most local and state judges have to face the judgment of the electorate from time to time. A high proportion become judges in the first place by running for election. In other cases they are appointed by the governor after nomination by a nonpartisan commission and then have to stand for election after they have served their first term.

THE LOCALITIES

Governments in the communities vary more widely even than state governments. Most of the larger cities—those cities with a half million or more population—and about half the smaller cities have a mayor and a city council, usually elected independently from each other. However, the relative strength of mayor and council varies enormously. In some cities, especially in the West, departments of city government may be headed by commissions, whose members are appointed by the mayor and ratified by the council but who may have a good deal of independence from both. These commissions deal with special fields such as airports, harbors, and fire and police services. Almost half of the middle-sized cities have adopted a council-manager form of government, in which the elected council hires a professional city manager to run the city government subject to general policy direction by the council.

The counties usually include less densely populated areas than the cities, although population growth in some formerly rural areas has made some counties, such as Los Angeles, very populous indeed. Counties are usually run by elected boards of commissioners or supervisors, and there are a number of other elective offices such as sheriff, county prosecutor or district attorney, and county coroner. The smallest units of American government are towns, townships, and small urban places typically called villages.[1]

Cutting across various units of local government are the special districts, set up to deal with problems or services that reach across governmental boundaries and that need a tax base broader than a single government unit. In some cases the boards running these special districts are directly elected, as is true of most school boards. In other cases, where the problems are particularly complex, as with rapid transit or smog control, the members are usually appointed by the elected leaders of the communities participating in the special district.

ELECTIONS AND POLITICAL PARTIES

Elections to these various units of state and local government are by the same franchise that prevails in federal elections—anyone from age 18 who registers to vote. In some parts of the country the voters have the power to do more than elect representatives. New England has its tradition of the town meeting, in which local issues are settled by vote of the entire citizenry, although interest in the town meetings has fallen off considerably. A number of states in the West use the referendum and the initiative, which enable voters to decide issues directly through the ballot box.

In state elections, political parties are still important devices for nominating and electing candidates, but at the local level parties are a less important factor than statewide, and their significance is diminishing fast. Political bosses are a dying breed, as we saw in chapter 4. In fact, the crudities and corruption of the political machines of the eastern cities started a reaction against parties in local government that began in the early part of this century and persists to this day. The reaction has been especially strong in the West, where most cities require that the election of the mayor, the city council representatives, and other office-holders be at least nominally nonpartisan.[2]

SHARING THE POWER

This multitude of state and local governments touches the lives of ordinary citizens in more ways even than the federal government. They are charged with the responsibility of protecting the people's safety, health, morals, and general welfare. They regulate and administer schools and colleges; provide police and fire protection; run transportation systems; build and maintain roads and parks; supply water, electricity, and gas, or regulate those agencies that do; help the poor with money and social and health services; control the use of land by zoning and other methods; establish laws on marriage and divorce; and levy taxes to pay for all these functions and a myriad of other services.

THE FEDERAL ROLE

At the same time the federal government's actions have an impact on the lives of citizens in their states and communities, and the respective roles of the different levels of government must therefore constantly be redefined. Some tasks, such as making foreign policy, are assigned exclusively by the U.S. Constitution to the federal government. The Fourteenth Amendment to the U.S. Constitution instructs the states to provide the individual due process and the equal protection of the laws. As we saw in chapter 10, the U.S. Supreme Court has extended the guarantees of the Bill of Rights to protection against state and local government as well as federal action. Further, the Supreme Court has construed the constitutional authority given to Congress to regulate commerce between the states, to allow the federal government to regulate businesses that are locally based but that send a portion of their product across state lines or provide a service to interstate travelers.

Then, too, the federal government has been drawn more and more into state and local affairs by virtue of its financial contributions. Federal "grants-in-aid" to states and communities—funds to support programs in education, health, welfare, transportation, and many other fields—amounted to about $3 billion in 1955. By 1981 they had passed $90 billion—28 percent of the total income of state and local governments. (See figure 11-1.) The federal aid spent in 1981 was allocated to almost 500 different programs that were governed by 1,260 federal rules and regulations.

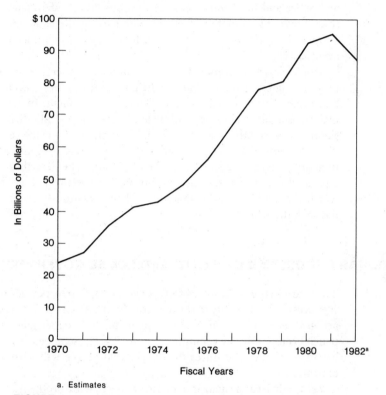

FIGURE 11–1.   Federal Grants to States and Localities, 1970–1982
Source: Advisory Commission on Intergovernmental Relations.

Thus the federal government is heavily involved in shaping decision making at the state and local level. In programs such as the state employment services, in fact, federal rules are so detailed that the state officials who administer the programs are left with little discretion and must stick to the rules or face the denial of unemployment checks and the virtual elimination of their staff. Even in such fields as education, which would appear to be among the powers that the Constitution reserves to the states, local districts have to abide by federal guidelines if they want to receive the federal aid that most of them regard as indispensable.

THE LOCAL IMPETUS

Although the role of the federal government in the affairs of states and communities is substantial, there is still a strong local impetus in the American system. As we saw in chapter 9, the expansion of the federal government since the 1930s has not resulted in a reduction in the scale of state and local government activity. Instead, the demand for public services has increased so prodigiously that it has produced a vast expansion of the role of government at *all* levels. Total state and local expenditures increased from less than $50 million in 1959 to about $400 billion in 1981. State and local outlays for education, health services, highways, welfare, and police and fire protection are still much greater than federal expenditures in those areas. The number of people employed at the state and local levels—over 13 million in 1980—was more than four times the number working for federal agencies.

Moreover, the example of the state employment services, which are dominated by Washington, is not typical of state and local programs, even of those programs that receive financial help from the federal government. In some of them decision making is a joint endeavor, with federal, state, and local officials all participating significantly. In others, the local people dominate. Thus the respective roles of the different units of government vary from program to program and are interwoven in many patterns. Federalism in America cannot be described in terms of clearly separated strata of responsibility, but is better expressed as "a marblecake"[3] in which the state and local ingredients lend essential elements of substance and flavor to the whole.

CONTEMPORARY PROBLEMS OF STATE AND LOCAL GOVERNMENT

There are many advantages to this system of shared powers we call *federalism*. It expresses the diversity of the country and the people while providing for national action where it is needed. It offers opportunities to experiment with programs and policies community by community, state by state, long before a national consensus has taken shape. It reduces the danger that power will become excessively concentrated.

Yet the federal system in America is beset with problems. Chief among these problems are citizen apathy, jurisdictional conflicts, corrupt officials, and a chronic shortage of funds.

VOTER APATHY

In chapter 3 we saw that a smaller proportion of people bother to vote in our national elections than is the case in most other industrialized countries. But it is sometimes argued that this fact is true because what happens in Washington is remote from the interests of most people in their daily lives. It ought to follow, then, that the closer we get to home the more people are likely to be involved in government and politics. The unhappy fact is that as we move from national government to state and then to local government we tend to find smaller and smaller proportions of the people going to the polls. For presidential elections we get voting turnouts in the 50 percent range, and for Congress somewhat less than this. But races for a governorship or a state legislature often attract less than 40 percent of the potential electorate (unless candidates for president appear on the same ballot). And in some local elections less than 20 percent cast their votes.

JURISDICTIONAL CONFLICTS

Both the states and the localities encounter difficulties because their geographical areas of jurisdiction are often inappropriate to the social and human needs they are intended to serve. The state boundaries were drawn long ago. They may have corresponded initially to the major groupings of population, but populations have shifted, whereas boundaries have not. Moreover, there are many problems that refuse to stop conveniently at the state line. There is a good deal of cooperation between the states, and in the form of *interstate compacts* this cooperation has been formalized to deal with such concerns as water pollution, flood control, port operations, recreation and parks, and conservation. However, members of interstate compact commissions are appointed by state governors, feel their first loyalty to their respective states, and can embark on new activities only if they are unanimously agreed on. So interstate cooperation continues to face severe limitations, which gives us another reason for the massive intrusion of the federal government into state affairs.

In the communities the problem of governmental boundaries is even more acute. The large majority of local units are far too small to be able to deal effectively with many contemporary problems. Over half of the nearly 40,000 territorial governments—counties, municipalities, townships, towns—contain populations of under 1,000; less than 10 percent have more than 10,000 inhabitants; less than 1 percent have over 100,000.

There are also complicated and confusing layers of government. The metropolitan area around New York City includes almost 1,500 distinct political entities. And within Los Angeles County, a solid metropolitan area (which is part of a metropolitan region), there are more than 500 units of government: cities, school districts, and a variety of special districts and taxing jurisdictions.

The resulting system has been criticized for fragmenting responsibility, confusing the voter, and preventing the economies of scale. Accordingly, there have been proposals for the consolidation of governmental units, especially in the metropolitan areas, into regional governments corresponding to large concentrations of population, industry, and resources. There has been some movement in this direction. Dade County, Florida, and the Twin Cities Metropolitan Council in Minnesota are federated systems that assign areawide functions to the upper tier of government and local functions to units closer to home. There have also been some city-county consolidations, including consolidations of Nashville with Davidson County, Tennessee; Indianapolis with Marion County, Indiana; and Lexington with Fayette County, Kentucky. Portland, Oregon, and twenty-six neighboring jurisdictions have combined in another model known as "Metro," which handles functions such as waste disposal, running the zoo, and maintaining air and water quality for its constituent units. And there has been so much school district consolidation that the number of local government units in America has actually declined by 75,000 since 1942. Even so, fragmentation of service and responsibility continues to be one of the major problems of our system of local government.

CORRUPTION OF PUBLIC OFFICIALS

In the chapters on interest groups and Congress we looked at breaches of integrity ranging from conflicts of interest to outright bribery. We encounter the same problems in state and local units of government. At the state level matters have improved since the period during the nineteenth century when railroads would "buy" entire state legislatures. Nonetheless, flagrantly corrupt behavior by state politicians has persisted in a number of states. For example, when Spiro Agnew resigned the vice-presidency in 1973, he admitted that, while he was governor of Maryland, he had accepted payments from contractors who wanted business from the state; he had used some of the money for private purposes; and he had not paid taxes on the income. He explained: "My acceptance of contributions was part of a long-established pattern of political fund raising in the state."[4] Apparently the pattern persisted, because in 1977 Maryland governor Marvin Mandel was convicted of mail fraud and racketeering to help friends with legislation favorable to a racetrack they owned. Similar practices have surfaced from time to time in Illinois, New Jersey, and other states involving the legislatures and even, in a few cases, members of state supreme courts. Many other states have gone through periodic scandals because legislatures have received payoffs from lobbyists, or because state officials have connived with business interests to give them favorable tax treatment.

Examples of dubious practices are found in profusion at the local level. But here again matters are not as bad as they used to be. The old political party machines in the big cities were lubricated by graft. George Washington Plunkett, the boss of the New York City political organization known as "Tammany Hall," saw nothing wrong with this practice as long as it was "honest" as against "dishonest" graft. Honest graft provided a profit to the politician but no loss to the public, because the issue was which among equally competent and equally priced companies or banks would handle the city's business. Dishonest graft involved paying a politician for an arrangement that cost the city more than it should spend.

Today there is not much left of the party machines, the indulgent attitude toward "honest graft" is gone, and the prevailing ethos calls for honesty and efficiency in government rather than the system of personal favors on which the old machines flourished. Even so, in many cities, large and small, elected and appointed officials have been convicted of receiving money for awarding a city contract or for supporting legislation favoring a particular business. In some instances the pattern of graft has extended into the very agencies that are mandated to enforce the laws—the police departments—and communities have been wracked periodically with scandals indicating that a high proportion of the police are taking bribes.

Why are conflicts of interest and unqualified corruption even more serious problems at the state and local levels than in the federal government? The answer is to be found in a combination of low pay, high expenses, and strong temptation. Running for office costs money, sometimes a great deal of money. And the people who hold local offices are called on to make decisions that may make the difference between large profits and bankruptcy for private interests.

This system opens the way for a number of possible scenarios. For example, the owner of a new enterprise that needs governmental approval, such as a racetrack, approaches a legislator and offers to set aside some stock in the enterprise—to be held anonymously for the official and issued at a price much lower than it will be worth when sold to the public. Or a member of a city council or zoning board approves a land development and is given an opportunity to buy into the development on highly advantageous terms—that is, if the public official is not already a part of the business.

Then, too, because public officials generally cannot afford to give up their regular profession or business, and because all but a few state legislators and local councils have very small staffs, the expertise of the members must be used to the full. The result is that banking committees are made up mostly of bankers, insurance committees of insurance agents, agricultural committees of farmers, and so on. As a result, legislators must sometimes pass judgment on matters in which they or their companies have a direct interest—and commonly they do not disqualify themselves because of their special interest.

The consequence of all these arrangements is that in many states and communities, giving public officials a piece of the action has become part of the normal cost of doing business. Some businesspeople resent this fact and wish they could operate differently, but they feel compelled to go along with the prevailing practice. Others feel no compunction and have refined the art of corrupting government as their means of getting ahead of the competition. Within the latter group are organized criminal elements that use government to provide an entree into legitimate businesses in which funds obtained through illegal activities can be invested. Newark, New Jersey, is one of the cities that has attracted the interest of organized crime. In 1970 a former mayor of the city was convicted of extortion and conspiring to extort money from an engineering firm doing business with the city while he was mayor, and two of the men convicted with him were reputed to be leaders of a crime syndicate.

This is not to say that all or most of the decisions made by state and local governments are tainted. Vast numbers of contracts are awarded by scrupulously conducted competitive bidding; elaborate procedures are established for the auditing of public funds; and rules and regulations to guard against improper expenditures are often so rigorous that they promote inefficiency and long delays. And the fact that legislators take campaign contributions from lobbyists does not necessarily mean they will accept those lobbyists' advice.

Moreover, the national revulsion against Watergate has produced a wave of reform in state government, and since 1972 close to half the states have passed new laws requiring lobbyists to disclose their activities and their contributions.

THE FISCAL SQUEEZE

Sources of local and state government income for 1980 are indicated in table 11-2. By the early 1980s some of the major items in this list of revenue sources had become so vulnerable that many state and local governments faced the prospect of being unable to deliver the services for which they were responsible. The major difficulties were resistance to local property taxes, federal aid to the states, and the condition of the economy.

Resistance to local property taxes. As table 11-2 indicates, more than a quarter of local government revenues in 1980 came from the property tax, much of which is levied on private residences. The property tax has been the target of three kinds of criticism. First, it is a "regressive" tax: it tends to cost low- and middle-income people a higher proportion of their incomes than upper-income people. Second, it causes inequality not only between individuals but also between localities; for example, school systems, which are funded in large part by property taxes, are much better endowed in rich than in poor communities. Third, rapidly rising property values in some parts of the country have pushed property taxes so high that many people, especially the elderly, have been forced to sell their homes.

TABLE 11-2 Sources of local and state government income (percent)

Local revenues		State revenues	
State government	31.6	Sales taxes	25.8
Property taxes	26.6	Federal government	22.1
Federal government	8.8	Income taxes	18.1
Utility revenues	7.9	Insurance trust funds	14.3
Other taxes	7.7	Other sources	13.0
Other sources	17.4	Other taxes	6.7

Source: Reprinted from *U.S. News and World Report,* 11 May, 1981, p. 46. Copyright 1982, U.S. News and World Report, Inc.

This last objection has proved to be immensely potent politically. California voters showed their strong feelings on this subject when, in 1978, they passed by a 2 to 1 margin "Proposition 13," an amendment of the state constitution requiring a massive rollback in the level of residential and business property taxes. In 1980 Massachusetts voters followed suit with "Proposition 2½," which required cities and towns to reduce real estate property taxes to no more than 2.5 percent of value.

Few other states went quite as far, and California in 1980 rejected another ballot measure that would have forced a slash in state income taxes. Still, resistance to higher state and local taxes, and hostility to prevailing levels of property taxes, have placed sharp limits on the ability of local governments to meet their financial obligations.

Consequently the communities have been turning increasingly to the state governments to help them out; and the 1980 figures show that state governments have met more than 31 percent of local governments' expenses. But their ability to sustain this level, let alone to increase it, has been threatened in turn by their dependence on the federal government and on the state of the economy.

Federal aid to the states.   By 1980 well over one-fifth of state governments' income was coming to them via Washington, and the federal government also provided local governments with almost 9 percent of their revenues.

The money came in three forms. First, there was an array of categorical grants, limited to very specific areas and subject to close regulation from Washington. Second, block grants covered much broader subject areas, such as crime control or education, and were less subject to federal regulation. Third, in 1972 Congress accepted President Nixon's proposal to provide funds to the states and localities in the form of revenue sharing:[5] distributing a proportion of federal tax revenues with very few strings attached.[6] One-third of the revenue-sharing money went to the states, two-thirds to cities, counties, and townships.

As we have seen, the combination of these three kinds of grants became a rapidly increasing source of funds for states and communities. However, from 1980 it became clear that the rate of growth would not continue and that the federal government would not be willing to solve the fiscal dilemmas of the sub-national levels of government.

In 1980 Congress balked when the time came to extend revenue sharing. Congress had never been particularly enthusiastic about the program, for it imposed on Congress the onus of raising the money through taxes, yet it gave the credit for providing the funds to state and local politicians. Moreover, in the 1970s several of the states had benefited from the general prosperity of the economy and were in strong fiscal positions, yet they were receiving revenue-sharing funds from a federal government whose budget was perennially in deficit. After prolonged debate, Congress responded to the intensive lobbying of state and local officials and reauthorized revenue sharing for three more years. However, the states came out of the struggle in much worse shape than the local governments, because the states' portion of revenue sharing could only be obtained if they gave up an equal sum from categorical grants, and their share was subject to year-by-year appropriation by Congress.

The states' problems were further compounded by the plans of the Reagan administration. President Reagan proposed a "new federalism,"[7] whose purpose was to reverse the trend of moving responsibility and power from the states to the federal government. First he moved to consolidate a large number of categorical grants for health, energy, and social service projects into a few block grants, under which states and localities would have wide discretion on how to spend the money.

Then, in 1982 Reagan proposed to return close to $40 billion in federal programs to state and local governments to be financed by the income from some federal excise taxes, a process that was to be accomplished over a ten-year period to avoid disruption. Included in the Reagan plan would be an administrative and financial swap, the federal government taking over Medicaid (the state supplement to Medicare), and the states assuming all responsibility for the Aid to Families with Dependent Children program. (Initially Reagan proposed shifting responsibility for food stamps to the states, but this idea was dropped.)

© 1982 AUTH-PHILADELPHIA INQUIRER

The proposed reduction of federal control and monitoring was a direct response to the bitter complaints of many state and local officials that they were being submerged in federal red tape and subordinated to centralized control. However, they were asked to pay a high price for their enlarged responsibilities. The Reagan administration's budget cuts meant severe reductions in aid to the states and cities. In particular, the consolidation of categorical into block grants was to carry with it a funding cutback of close to 25 percent.

The condition of the economy.   For a time in the 1970s, we have noted, a number of states did very well out of an expanding economy, and tax receipts flowed into bulging state coffers.[8] However, this phenomenon was temporary. From the late 1970s rising unemployment and the emergence of a flat, near-recessionary economy slowed receipts from income and sales taxes at the same time that property tax increases were being halted or even rolled back. States were finding it increasingly difficult to keep up with the rising costs resulting from inflation.

So it was unrealistic of the localities to look to the states to bail them out of their financial troubles. In the meantime there was no letup in the demand for state and local government services. Even amidst the apparent antigovernment fervor generated in California by Proposition 13, polls indicated that the majority did not want to see cutbacks in any government service except welfare. And two years after the passage of the proposition, a California Field Poll showed that, although most of those people who had voted for it were glad they had done so, more than 80 percent of those voters questioned opposed cuts for schools and community colleges, health programs for the elderly and poor, mental health programs, and payments of money to the old and the poor. Apparently the voters believed that reductions in costs could be achieved without cuts in programs by eliminating waste and inefficiency.[9]

Yet it became increasingly clear that, with the restrictions imposed on state and local income by property tax resistances, federal cuts, and a sluggish economy, it would not be possible to support all the demands for government services. Pension costs for police officers, fire fighters, and other government workers were escalating at a frightening pace. High rates of unemployment sent welfare and social service outlays soaring. The problems of the inner cities imposed heavy expenditures on all levels of government. Something had to give.

By the early 1980s states and cities across the country had begun to cut down on a wide range of services previously taken for granted by the citizenry. Library hours were cut back and small branches closed. Museums, hitherto free, imposed admission charges. Maintenance of highways, public buildings, and parks was reduced. Hospital and clinic services to the poor declined. Large numbers of government employees were laid off. And in some places even those most sacrosanct of public services, the police and fire departments, were allowed to fall below full strength.

TROUBLE IN METROPOLIS

All the problems we have been discussing have come together in their most intense form in the nation's great metropolitan centers. The concentration of millions of people in a relatively small space has produced air and noise pollution, massive traffic tie-ups, overloaded recreational facilities, and a long catalog of urban ailments.

But the urban problem is not just a matter of numbers and congestion. As the twentieth century progressed a growing proportion of people migrating to the cities were blacks, coming from the poorest areas of the country in the rural South, looking for the jobs, opportunities, and services their own communities lacked. Later came waves of immigrants from Mexico and other Latin American countries and then refugees from the wars and upheavals of Southeast Asia; and most of them came to the cities.

In the cities, either by choice or through discrimination, they lived predominately with others of their own race or national background, so the cities became more and more segregated ethnically. The blacks and Hispanics were concentrated mostly in the oldest and poorest parts of the cities, where housing was overcrowded and deteriorating and job openings few and poorly paid. Moreover, as is commonly the case in poverty areas, crime, including violent crime, was much more prevalent than in other areas of the cities. By 1980, in fact, the crime rate in many American cities had reached epidemic proportions, as shown in table 11-3.

TABLE 11–3 Crime rates[a] for selected American cities (per 100,000 population)

	Murder		Rape		Robbery	
	1972	1980	1972	1980	1972	1980
Chicago	21.3	29.1	45.9	42.8	705.9	550.4
Detroit	40.6	46.1	55.2	110.1	1159.2	1126.4
Houston	22.5	41.2	36.9	68.6	390.8	717.7
Los Angeles	17.3	34.6	76.2	96.2	491.9	870.7
Miami	22.6	70.1	28.7	100.0	740.8	1995.6
Washington, D.C.	32.4	31.5	94.5	57.5	1025.6	1400.1
New York	21.4	25.8	41.5	52.9	991.2	1433.2
San Francisco	11.4	16.6	71.0	112.6	642.8	1116.6

[a]Accurate figures on crime rates are notoriously difficult to obtain. Local law enforcement agencies use different criteria for collecting and reporting their statistics, and varying political circumstances may encourage either exaggerated or understated figures on the extent of crime. However, we may reasonably assume that the FBI figures in this table present a fairly reliable indication of the generally upward trend of most types of crime in most cities in the 1970s, as well as the considerable variations from city to city.
Source: FBI reports.

Confronted by rising crime rates, poor housing, congestion, unsatisfactory schools, and a general decline of community amenities, upper- and middle-class people found life in the cities unattractive. Moreover, the demand for single family housing led people to look increasingly to the cheaper land available outside the cities.

So the growth of city populations slowed down, and in the 1970s the cities actually suffered a net decline in population of 0.6 percent. Table 11-4 presents data on some of the more dramatic population losses during the decade.

The bulk of those people moving out of the central cities went to the suburbs, and during the 1970s suburban populations increased by over 17 percent, or about 14.5 million people.[10] However, the 1970s also saw a growing trend toward the small towns, a dramatic change from the long-established expansion of metropolitan areas at the expense of smaller communities. In the 1970s nonmetropolitan areas increased their population by 15.5 percent as compared with a growth of 10 percent in the metropolitan areas.[11] The longer-term trends are illustrated in figure 11-2.

TABLE 11–4 Population declines for selected central cities, 1979–1980 (figures rounded to nearest 1,000)

	Decline since 1970	1980 Population
Boston	562,000	78,000
Chicago	3,000,000	383,000
Cleveland	573,000	178,000
Detroit	1,197,000	317,000
Minneapolis–St. Paul	638,000	105,000
New York	7,035,000	860,000
Philadelphia	1,681,000	269,000
Pittsburgh	424,000	96,000
St. Louis	451,000	171,000

Source: U.S., Bureau of the Census.

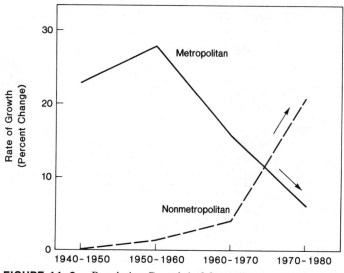

FIGURE 11–2. Population Growth in Metropolitan and Nonmetropolitan Areas
Source: U.S., Bureau of the Census.

Since the 1950s there has been a further shift in historic patterns in the form of movement away from the Northeast and Midwest and toward the sunbelt states of the Southeast, Southwest, and West,[12] where the warm climates and expanding economies lured the resources and populations that had built the great urban centers of the North.

Of those people who remained behind in the central cities, a disproportionate number were very low-income people whose needs and problems placed heavy demands on city services—welfare, health, law enforcement, and so on—but who were not able to contribute much to the tax rolls that paid for those services.

Many of the citizens who could afford to pay had moved out to separately incorporated cities in the suburbs, or neighboring small towns, so that even if they continued to work in the cities they paid their property taxes elsewhere.

The consequence of this combination of circumstances was a further deterioration of the city centers, the spread of slums, the decline of investment in transportation and other services, an increase in crime and delinquency, and the emergence of a serious possibility that major American cities could go bankrupt.

The financial plight of the northern cities. In 1975 New York City came to the very edge of having to declare itself bankrupt. The city's expenses were enormous because it provided welfare payments and an array of services to a large population of poor people—blacks, Puerto Ricans, and others; it offered a free university education on an open admissions basis; and its employee salaries and pension benefits were among the highest in the nation. Yet its revenues were depleted by the exodus of affluent families and business concerns from the city. So for years the city ran budgetary deficits that were covered by short-term loans from whoever would lend the city money: banks, purchasers of bonds, even labor unions representing teachers and other city employees. This repeated borrowing, combined with the longer-term loans issued by the city for its construction projects, finally undermined the city's credit. New York could not borrow any more money, and for several months in 1975 the only question seemed to be exactly when the city would default on its obligations and declare bankruptcy.

This grim prospect was avoided through the reluctant help of the federal government, agreement by the state to back new ten-year bonds to replace $1 billion worth of city bonds that had come due, cooperation by the banks, purchase by the unions of more of the city's bonds, major cuts in the budget, a reduction in the number of city employees, the charging of tuition by the city university, and the imposition of new taxes. Slowly New York regained its fiscal health and balanced its budget, and by 1981 it was able to sell its own bonds again.

But although New York managed to survive, it was by no means clear that some other cities would do as well. Detroit, its problems compounded by the severe slump in the auto industry, staved off catastrophe in 1981 by getting its residents to approve a sharp increase in income tax. Even so the city faced deficit budgets, inability to borrow on the bond market, and draconian budget cuts. Boston, standing to lose 70 percent of its income because of the property tax reduction approved in Proposition 2½, had to cope with a school system that had run out of funds and a housing authority that was in receivership. Buffalo, Newark, and St. Louis were among the other cities facing serious financial problems. Even Los Angeles, a generally well-managed city located in an area of high-technology industry, feared for its future because of the very high pension costs of its police and fire departments.

Some hopeful signs.   In the long run the apparently desperate conditions of some of our major cities may take a turn for the better. The great immigration from the most deprived regions of the country to the northern cities has almost run its course. And the 1980s may well see another reversal of population trends: a shift back to the central cities from the suburbs by middle-income people. For one thing, the escalating prices of houses and apartments in the suburbs are making the central cities the only areas close to people's jobs with affordable housing. For another, American families are smaller than they used to be, and there are more people living alone. For singles, or for couples with no children or only one child, the spaciousness of life in the suburbs can be less important than the diversity, entertainment, and other facilities that the city provides. Finally, rising costs of transportation make suburbs far removed from workplaces uneconomical. Already in some cities a slow but discernible shift back to the central metropolis is taking place, and "gentrification"—the rehabilitation of dilapidated areas by affluent purchasers—is well advanced, sometimes assisted by federal and state programs of urban renewal and redevelopment.

New York's ability to overcome apparently impossible odds and to restore its solvency has been a source of encouragement to cities with similar problems. Cleveland worked with the banks and the unions to produce a fiscal package that, together with an income tax increase and budget cuts, put the city back on the road to fiscal health. Philadelphia, despite a dwindling manufacturing base, declining population, and inner city decay, held down its work force and wage levels and managed to keep its budget in the black. Elsewhere a previously open-handed approach to employee wages and pension benefits, and to the provision of city services, has given way to a much more cautious approach to spending.

Even the loss of population from the metropolitan centers may have its redeeming qualities. Congestion is reduced, and we no longer hear the once fashionable predictions by urbanologists that by the year 2000 half the total population of the country would be concentrated in three unbroken built-up areas: "Bos-Wash" (Boston to Washington), "Chi-Pitts" (Chicago to Pittsburgh), and "San-San" (San Francisco to San Diego). That appalling prospect now seems much less likely, and the fears that the present metropolitan crisis would assume nightmarish proportions beyond all hope of solution have receded accordingly.

Just the same, the hopeful indications for the future offer little immediate comfort to the troubled cities of the North. The fiscal situation of some of them still borders on the desperate. To the extent that they succeed in restoring solvency the cost in the deterioration of city services to their populations may be almost intolerably high. Nor, as we have indicated, can they look to the states to do very much for them; and their former benefactor, the federal government, has become a much less generous source of support. So, at least for the near future, most of the big cities of America face a troubled time indeed.

FIVE PERSPECTIVES ON FEDERALISM

THE LIBERALS: THE FAILURE OF GOVERNMENTS

Over the years liberals have shown a general preference for federal as against state and local action. For one thing they believe that the types of programs they advocate—economic planning, national health insurance, welfare reform—can only be undertaken effectively on a national scale. Anything less must make for administrative fragmentation, excessive costs, and wide inequities from one area to another.

Second, they argue that the federal government was forced to take on more responsibilities because the states were too complacent, apathetic, and incompetent to act themselves. Liberals have been persistent critics of those deficiencies of state and local government described earlier—the archaic structures and procedures of state governments, the maze of local jurisdictions, the widespread corruption, and the failure to raise the funds to pay for needed services. And liberals believe that in considerable degree these shortcomings are the result of a failure of political will.

Governmental structures, say the liberals, are made by people and can be changed by people—if they want to urgently enough. The difficulty of producing sufficient revenues from local taxpayers is only partly a consequence of the large amounts siphoned off by the federal Internal Revenue Service. It is not indisputably true that state and local taxes cannot be increased significantly. Tax levels in the United States are still not as high as they are in some other industrialized countries. And it is absurd for the wealthier states, whose per capita income far exceeds the income of any other part of the world, to cry poverty.

Although state and local government activity and spending have been increasing rapidly, there is a dearth of sound, long-range planning. State and local agencies, even more than the federal government, demonstrate the American governmental tendency to react to crises rather than to anticipate and prevent them. This syndrome is especially apparent in the cities. But the attack on the terrible and mutually reinforcing ailments that plague the cities is feeble. True, there are dazzling cultural complexes going up in some communities. Skylines are dramatically transformed by towering edifices. Some dilapidated areas are cleared by urban renewal and redevelopment plans. Yet the plight of the cities grows deeper, and the leaders of the cities' political life grow more helpless in the enveloping morass.

The central reason for this deterioration—more important than the structural and fiscal deficiencies of metropolitan government—is the fact that the desperate condition of the cities has not generated a sense of crisis for the majority of the people who live in the metropolitan areas. Why? Because very large numbers of people, including those people who are the prime leaders of political and social opinion, do not live in the inner city but in the suburbs. There is no total sanctuary from the cities' problems even in the suburbs, but the intensity is usually diminished as one moves away from the central city. Crime is everywhere, but the crimes of violence are mostly on the other side of town. Poor people and black people are more or less excluded from middle-class communities, and their children go to different schools than do the children of the suburban whites.

Consequently, there is no great dynamic for change among the great numbers of urban dwellers who live outside the inner cities. The suburban middle classes are provoked into involvement only when something threatens to change the "character of the neighborhood": a zoning variance, a proposed park or highway, or a new housing development (especially a development that might include low-income people and thus racial and ethnic minorities).

To a degree, this liberal dissatisfaction with the performance of state and local government has been modified in the last few years. A number of states have been improving their governmental structures and taking steps to combat corruption. Liberals are pleased that in some cases states and localities have moved ahead of the federal government in protecting the environment, legalizing abortion, asserting the rights of homosexuals, and so on.

Yet, on balance, the liberals' judgment is that the states and localities have failed to undertake imaginative social experimentation. On the contrary, conservatives have long used the slogan "states' rights" to preserve racial segregation in the South and business privileges everywhere against pressures for change from the federal government. If some states led the way in legitimizing abortion, others spearheaded the attack on the Supreme Court's decision upholding the right of abortion. The most pernicious examples of censorship and persecution of unpopular views are to be found in local communities. And the climate of opinion that gave Reagan his opportunity to slash government programs received its initial credibility from California's Proposition 13 and Massachusetts' Proposition 2½. Generally speaking, liberals have seen the states as supporting narrow, provincial attitudes against the forces of progress.

Liberals offer a number of remedies for the inadequate performance of the states and communities. First they advocate a revival of the two-party system in local politics. They do not propose that we go back to the old party machines, because essentially these machines ran one-party systems. But in place of the nonpartisan politics of the West, they advocate two-party competition as the best means of presenting clear alternatives and securing broader participation, because voter turnout is highest in those states where the two parties are both strong.

Second, they urge the consolidation of jurisdictions, leading toward metropolitan, county, and even regional governments in place of the present chaos of overlapping and fragmented governing bodies.

With respect to the fiscal problems of state and local governments, liberals urge stepped-up federal aid and more vigorous and equitable efforts by state and local units to raise money themselves.

Liberals believe that it is a gross dereliction of the federal government's responsibilities to cut back on aid to the cities. The enormous burdens cities have had to carry have not been primarily of their own making, but are the result of great national forces, such as the influx of immigrants, mostly poor, from the American South, Puerto Rico, Europe, Cuba, Mexico, and Southeast Asia. To ask that, out of their diminishing revenues, the cities bear the cost of the hardest cases in our society, those people left behind after the exodus from the central urban areas, is unreasonable and unconscionable.

As for the distribution of federal funds, liberals were never enthusiastic about revenue sharing, because they saw the urgent need for help's being concentrated in the big central cities, whereas much of the revenue-sharing money went to the states and to smaller communities. In the argument between categorical and block grants, liberals could see merit in the objections to the red tape that accompanied the categorical funds, yet they did not regard all the strings as harmful. Sometimes federal conditions for accepting grants can be the means by which local officials are forced to face up to the shortcomings of their governmental structures and practices. For example, local governments have been organizing regional planning associations because federal agencies have refused funding for various urban programs unless they demonstrate their ability to cooperate across their boundary lines.

Moreover, block grants typically go to the states, and liberals question whether many of the state governments have the expertise to administer the grants effectively or the ability to withstand the political pressures from less needy communities to get an inappropriate share of the money.

But the most important question for liberals is not so much the machinery for distributing the funds as the total amount available. The crucial defect of the Reagan "new federalism," as the liberals saw it, was that it was federalism that sharply reduced the federal government's contribution to the states and cities.

So the liberals call for precisely the opposite strategy than the Reagan administration's. In addition to increases in grants-in-aid in areas such as education, health, transportation, and housing, liberals advocate the federalizing, in whole or in part, of some services now provided by states and communities. In particular, they would like to see the welfare programs replaced by a national guaranteed minimum income. (See chapter 12.) Liberals objected to the Reagan proposal to shift the welfare program to the states in exchange for Medicaid because they feared that in several states the poor would get short shrift at the hands of state legislatures.

However, liberals are not asking that the federal government do the whole job. They suggest that state and local governments could do much more than they are now doing to expand revenues from their own populations. Most states could raise their income taxes. Alaska, Connecticut, Florida, Nevada, New Hampshire, South Dakota, Tennessee, Texas, Washington, and Wyoming levy no income tax at all. For a married couple with two dependents and an adjusted gross income of $25,000, state income tax in Louisiana was $68 in 1980, in New Mexico $130, and in Mississippi $307, whereas it was $1,382 in Minnesota, $1,145 in the District of Columbia, and $1,055 in New York. Much more could be raised, too, from corporation, liquor, cigarette, and gambling taxes. And more of the huge profits made by land and property speculators, which result in large part from the increase in values created by the community as a whole, should be diverted to the local exchequers.

THE RADICAL LEFT: MORE POWER ELITES

As we saw in our discussion of the federal bureaucracies, the traditional communist left focuses on the need for highly centralized power until the revolution has been accomplished and power is in the hands of the masses. The more common view on the American left today, however, favors the greatest possible degree of decentralization to the smallest possible unit of government. However, this plan does not mean shifting power to the existing structures of state and local government. To the left, these structures are as repressive as the federal government because they replicate, many times over, the national power elite.

Thus, as the left sees it, Anaconda, the great copper-producing corporation, dominates the economic life of Montana; Delaware is controlled by the duPonts;[13] and Texas is under the thumb of the big oil producing corporations. In those states where no single business interest is all-powerful, public policy is nonetheless shaped in the interests of business firms through their capacity to lobby legislatures, work closely with regulatory agencies, finance election campaigns, and own and control the media.

As for the cities, C. Wright Mills, Floyd Hunter,[14] and others have argued that an upper social class, a monied aristocracy, is very much in evidence, and that business and financial leaders drawn from that class make most of the key policy decisions for the community.

This fact does not mean that these top leaders make every local decision. Although they live in local communities and their corporate headquarters are located there, their interests are national and multinational. The only kind of local decisions they are really concerned with are related to securing the best possible tax situation for their corporations and the maximum services from state and local government for the least possible outlay.

High on their list of necessary services is protection for their personal and corporate property by the courts and law enforcement agencies. "The law" says Michael Parenti, "leans consistently in the direction of business,"[15] and this statement is no less true of state than of federal courts. Indeed, the repressive nature of the system takes even more visible form at the local than at the national level, because it is at the local level that the police operate and that their bias against the minorities, the young, and the nonconformists in favor of established, propertied interests is most blatantly displayed.

In response to these problems, the left sees no hope in the liberals' proposals. Increased federal aid will be used in the future, as it has been in the past, to reinforce the position of the present power structures.

Instead, says the left, we must take action at the grass-roots level. Power must go to the people, which means that the people must be brought together in groups small enough to make partic-ipation possible for everyone. The answer is community control, exercised through the smallest units of the community, the neighborhoods.

Some steps have already been taken to build popular participation to challenge the existing order. Poor people have been organized in some areas to fight for improved health facilities and to resist the process of "gentrification," which forces the poor out of their own neighborhoods to make way for higher-income people. In other cases the poor have been joined by middle-class people who have been radicalized in struggles for rent control. In some cities, such as Berkeley and Santa Monica, California, candidates of the left have been elected to local office.

The left recognizes that it faces a long, slow, uphill battle. But leftists believe that they must begin among people in their neighborhoods and build upward from there, if the present remote, depersonalized institutions are to be replaced by a society built on the principle of community.

THE CONSERVATIVES: FEDERALISM AND LIMITED GOVERNMENT

Support of state and local governments as against the federal government is an essential part of the conservatives' creed. There are four reasons for this belief:

1. The power of state and local governments sets limits to the power of the central government. The division of powers between the national and state governments was an essential element in the Founding Fathers' plan to prevent dangerous concentrations of authority anywhere in the governmental system.

2. The federal system encourages diversity, the varying expressions of regional and local interests and cultures, as against the kind of bureaucratized uniformity the federal government tries to impose nationwide. Consequently, conservatives have no use for proposals to rationalize local services by incorporating them into larger, regional units of government.

3. Conservatives find the most support for their values in local communities, where private property is most solidly established in the form of home

ownership. Nothing contributes more effectively to conservative attitudes than ownership of a home, as was demonstrated in California with the passage of Proposition 13. The local community also provides the focal point for church, ethnic identity, and family, and along with these concepts go the values that protect against the peddlers of pornography and other debauchers of our traditions. Liberals scorn these attitudes as narrow, provincial, and unsophisticated, but to conservatives they are the core values of Western civilization.

4. State and local governments cannot be as reckless in spending the taxpayers' money as is the federal government because, unlike the federal government, they cannot print money to cover their deficits; and so they must balance their budgets.

However, conservatives fear that the virtues inherent in the states and localities are being overwhelmed by federal money and power. There has been the enormous expansion of the role of the presidency. Congress has abused its law-making authority to reach deep into the prerogatives reserved to the states by the Tenth Amendment to the Constitution. Education, housing, social services, fire prevention, and law enforcement were once handled exclusively at the local and state levels. Now all these areas are the subjects of innumerable federal statutes.

Sometimes, as with requirements for the handicapped and with drinking water standards, Congress has told the states what to do but has not provided any money to help defray the cost of enormously expensive new programs.

Having passed its laws, Congress hands over the detailed rule making and enforcement to armies of federal bureaucrats who know little about the needs of local communities. Yet they are able to harass and intimidate state and local officials into acquiescence in programs that are often profoundly repugnant to the people of the communities.

Far from protecting the people from these federal usurpations, the courts have encouraged the process. Instead of respecting its mandate to uphold the Constitution, the Supreme Court has "incorporated" federal power into the sphere of the states. And it has interpreted the interstate commerce clause to allow federal regulation of every kind of business activity, even where businesses are involved in only the most indirect and occasional activity across state lines.

Consequently, conservatives applauded when, in 1969, President Nixon called for a redistribution of power between the federal government and the states: "After a third of a century of power flowing from the people and the states to Washington, it is time for a new Federalism in which power, funds, and responsibility will flow from Washington to the states and the people."

Yet the conservatives' response to Nixon's revenue-sharing plan was lukewarm. They conceded that it was superior to categorical grants because it placed the authority to spend money closer to the people from whom it came, and it reduced the power of the swollen bureaucracies in Washington. But what conservatives look for is not a mere reshuffling of government authority to spend tax money but a sharp reduction of government spending and taxing. Yet during the past forty years or so, state and local government spending has increased at an even faster rate than federal spending, and most of the increase in government employment has taken place at the subnational level.

So it was Ronald Reagan's new federalism that impressed conservatives rather than Richard Nixon's. Reagan proposed not merely a shift of responsibility from the federal to state and local governments, which would reduce the amount of centralized bureaucratic control, but also a substantial cutting back of financial aid to the states and localities. This plan would leave more money where it should be—in the pockets of ordinary people.

In response to the liberals' plea that much more federal money is needed to help deal with the problems of the cities, conservatives do not deny that our urban communities contain serious problems. But they doubt that these problems constitute the desperate crisis the liberals love to talk about. The conditions of the poor generally, and the blacks specifically, are not as bad as the liberals claim. Although racial prejudice and discrimination are not to be condoned, segregation is in large measure a result of self-selection. Many poor people find a sense of community in a slum neighborhood. Nor is it true that the ghettoes consist mostly of slums. They contain a wide variety of living standards, some of them very attractive and most of them improving. The problem is that regardless of how much conditions improve, they cannot keep up with the reckless increase in expectations encouraged by the liberals.

Furthermore, when we shift our gaze from the ghettoes, we find that for most urban dwellers life is far from intolerable. In fact, says Edward C. Banfield: "By any conceivable measure of material welfare the present generation of urban Americans is, on the whole, better off than any other large group of people has ever been anywhere. What is more, there is every reason to expect that the general level of comfort and convenience will continue to rise at an even more rapid rate through the foreseeable future."[16]

So it is entirely understandable if the suburbs fail to become galvanized into action by proposals to change the character of their communities. People who find the quality of their lives satisfying will usually resist having change imposed on them. This fact is true even in the ghettoes, where there is growing resistance to the kind of urban renewal programs that, in the name of progress, move people out of the communities they know and have become attached to.[17]

So we should stop experimenting with the kind of programs—urban renewal, public housing, antipoverty projects—that arouse expectations that cannot be fulfilled and encourage militant demands for change. We should respect the patterns of suburban and ghetto life. We should allow the workings of the economic system to continue the process of raising the standard of living for most of the people.

As for the soaring crime rates in our cities, we must respond by giving the police and the courts the authority they need to act firmly.[18] This action is necessary not, as the left suggests, merely to protect business and property, although if this protection is not provided the entire community suffers. But as long as ordinary people, blacks as well as whites, fear to walk in the streets of their own neighborhoods, the very fabric of our civilization is threatened. The remedy, say the conservatives, is providing more effective law enforcement, not lavishing vast amounts of federal money on the cities for an array of programs that have nothing to do with crime.

It is time, say the conservatives, for the cities to stop looking to Washington to solve the problems that they have brought on themselves. New York City was an object lesson in this respect. One city administration after another tried to win votes by giving more money to municipal unions, minority groups, and others. The deficits resulting from this plundering of the taxpayer were hidden year after year by financial sleight of hand, until at last there was no more room for manipulation and bankruptcy loomed.

Then the cry went up to have the federal government save the city. Conservatives objected. New York, said Milton Friedman, should have been left to default on its obligations, then forced by bankruptcy proceedings to undertake the needed reforms. Every other proposal "founders on the very fallacy that has brought New York to its present condition—the belief that it is desirable to do good with someone else's money—in this case, that of the taxpayers outside New York."[19] For a time it seemed that President Ford would listen to this advice, but then he bowed to pressure and agreed to some federal help to straighten out the city's affairs.

Now, just as the conservatives warned, other cities in trouble want the same kind of federal help that was given to New York. They would be well advised, say the conservatives, to stop looking at the federal component in the New York rescue operation and concentrate on the self-help actions that were the heart of the solution: the end of profligate spending and the acceptance at last of fiscal responsibility. This advice may seem a harsh message to be delivering to a city like Detroit, faced with the problems associated with the declining automobile industry. But those problems must be dealt with by the people of Detroit and of Michigan working with the auto companies. If Washington tries to save them there will be no end to the demands on the federal exchequer by communities facing economic difficulties.

However, President Reagan suggested that there might be circumstances in which the federal government could intervene in the cities. Because federal tax and other policies had contributed heavily to the flight of business from some cities, Washington might reasonably develop some programs that would reverse the process. But this help, said Reagan, should not take the form of federal subsidies, but rather of tax incentives: rundown inner city areas might be designated as "urban enterprise zones," in which businesses would be encouraged to locate by the waiving of federal, state, and local taxes, and the granting of freedom from a number of federal rules and regulations.

It is this kind of program, which involves government only in undoing the damage caused by previous government policies, that conservatives favor. It brings into play the elements of our society that conservatives value: local rather than federal agencies, private enterprise rather than government intervention.

THE RADICAL RIGHT

As we saw in chapter 9 in discussing the federal bureaucracy, the radical right has been passionately opposed to the expansion of the federal government, seeing in it the all-but-final transformation of the United States into a left-wing dictatorship. Yet even at the state and local levels they see the same trends toward socialism. New York City is only the most vicious example of the combination of ruinous government action and the collapse of traditional values associated with big city life. Other major eastern cities are on the same course of trying to do for people what they should be doing for themselves, and they are leading the way to socialism by a spineless surrender

to the demands of big labor, minorities, the media, and the intellectual establishment.

Only in the South, the Southwest, parts of the West, and smaller communities in the Midwest is there still hope of building pockets of resistance. There the right can lead campaigns against the selection of subversive or obscene textbooks by state and local boards of education; against pornographic movies, performances, and books; against the fluoridation of water; and so on.

There, too, the battle against high taxes can be waged most effectively. To the radical right, this battle is the most crucial of all. Revenue sharing is not the answer, because it involves simply a reshuffling of confiscatory taxation. Instead the right has supported a variety of propositions on the ballots in various states to freeze state spending, limit employment in state government, require a majority of all registered voters for any state or local action that would lead to an increase in taxes, limit the tax rate by constitutional mandate, and reject federal aid.

The radical right, too, knows that its struggle is uphill, because control of the system by the federal government, working as the agent of the Rockefellers and other "insiders," is already far advanced. But successes in local communities here and there can be used as bridgeheads from which the counterattack can be launched.

THE CENTRISTS

Like the liberals, centrists express concern about the multiplication of jurisdictions, the confusion of decision-making responsibility, the inefficiency and corruption found in many units of state and local government, and the fiscal dilemma of the subnational governments. Still, their prognosis of state and city government is much less gloomy than the outlook of the liberals.

As centrists see it, the shortcomings of state and local governments do not prevent them from performing quite well in a number of respects. They provide a vast array of excellent public services. The special districts may be confusing to voters, but they supply clean water, prevent floods, and develop parklands, usually with a high degree of efficiency. State governments have funded fine systems of higher education, developed impressive water and highway systems, and given local governments indispensable financial help. Moreover, they are improving their structures and performance. State legislatures have become more representative since the Supreme Court's reapportionment decisions. They are modernizing their constitutions and increasing their expertise by hiring skilled staffs and consultants; and similar trends are operating in the cities. These facts disprove the liberals' argument that the shift from categorical to block grants is unwise because the state governments are not competent enough to handle the money effectively without close federal supervision.

On the other hand centrists worried about the extent of the cuts in federal aid that President Reagan proposed. They recognized the need to break the pattern of ever-increasing dependency by state and local governments on Washington. They agreed that cities had to be brought to see the dangers of the New York experience. But the change in policy should be accomplished prudently and carefully. Moreover, the intensity of the problems faced by some northern and midwestern cities was so great that a reasonable level of financial help from Washington would continue to be necessary for some years to come.

In time federal aid might become less necessary. Improvement in the national economy would bring more money into the coffers of state and local governments. A declining birthrate could lead to a reduction in spending on schools. The return to the central cities by growing numbers of young, middle-class people could revitalize those areas. But these proposals are long-term factors. In the meantime the federal government should not turn its back on the cities, although it should be much more careful with its subsidies than the liberals want it to be.

The centrists' approach to the financial problems of the cities is consistent with their approach to federalism in general. They are ardent admirers of the Founding Fathers' ingenious distribution of power geographically so that there is an appropriate role for each level of government.

On the one hand, there is sufficient authority at the center to ensure that the nation holds together and that certain basic standards of justice and living conditions are provided to individual citizens no matter where they reside. On the other hand, there are levels of government closer to home to which individuals can relate more directly than to the federal structures in Washington. And, say the centrists, these subnational governments have been an important source of initiative and experimentation in our system. Liberals may complain that state innovations have included measures like Proposition 13. Conservatives dislike proabortion laws at the state level. But in both cases, centrists note, state action anticipated moves by the federal government through the legislative, executive, or judicial branches. We may or may not approve of such measures, but they are demonstrations that the states do carry out their role as laboratories in which to try out ideas that may, in time, command nationwide support.

To the radical left's argument that the constitutional division of powers is a myth because local versions of the ruling elite are found throughout the country, centrists insist that this statement is generally not true. In the second half of the nineteenth century some state governments may have been almost totally controlled by railroad and other business interests, but no state government in America today, the centrists contend, can be accurately described as a mere appendage of one or more business corporations. And although there are examples of business and financial interests having a potent impact on policy making in some cities, most communities, according to Scott Greer, are ruled "not by a sinister power elite behind the arras, but by the men who (hold) formal political office and power."[20] Conceivably if the business and financial leaders of the cities made up their minds to run their communities they would be able to do so. But because their policies are nationally rather than locally determined, because they live in the suburbs rather than the cities, and because they do not want to attract community hostility by the heavy-handed exercise of influence, they have rarely chosen to transform their potential power into actual control. [21]

So the centrist analysts contend that the patterns of power below the federal level are enormously varied, and generally come closer to the pluralistic than the ruling elite model.

CONCLUSION

As we have noted, predictions about the viability of state and local government in America are subject to rapid change. In the 1960s city after city was torn with racial riots, and the general prognosis was that the metropolitan areas were about to become unlivable war zones. Then things settled down, and more cheerful scenarios for the future became commonplace. Next, some of the big cities began to struggle with severe financial difficulties, and the worst fears seemed to be confirmed by the seemingly hopeless condition of New York City in 1975. But the worst did not happen in New York. And, as the states benefited from the expansion of the economy, they appeared for a while to be so prosperous as to be able to take over some of the federal government's role in helping the cities. In turn, these hopes faded with the weakening of the economy and the intensifying resistance to state and local taxes.

Consequently, it would be foolhardy to try to offer firm projections about the future of states and cities in America. Perhaps their present difficult situation will become desperate. It is also possible, however, that the more hopeful signs discussed earlier in the chapter will take hold fairly quickly.

However, it is difficult to be optimistic about two problems. The first is the perilous financial condition of at least a few of the major cities of the North and the Midwest. They have avoided bankruptcy until now by last-minute crisis actions. But it is far from clear that without the federal help that is unlikely to come they have any more scope for raising taxes and cutting services when most of their populations consist of low-income minorities.

The second problem, closely related to the first, is the plight of the disadvantaged minorities in the inner cities. None of the cities involved in the riots of the 1960s erupted again in the 1970s. But there was an ugly outbreak in Miami in 1980, and the orgy of looting that took place during a power blackout in New York in 1977 was a reminder of how fragile is the maintenance of ordered relationships in our big cities. We shall return to this troubling issue in chapter 13.

NOTES AND REFERENCES

1. Towns are the major units of government in New England. Towns are also found in New York, Pennsylvania, and some other Middle Atlantic states but are much less important there than the counties. West of the Appalachians a town (often called a "township") is a six-square-mile parcel of land surveyed by order of the Northwest Ordinance and subsequent land laws. In some cases these towns or townships are

organized units of government, but others are merely designations for surveying and identification of property deeds. Villages are small clusters of dwellings and commercial properties that are incorporated under state laws and provide some services, elect some officials, and usually possess a limited taxing power.

2. However, parties are still an important element in county government.

3. See Morton Grodzins, "The Federal System," in *Goals for Americans: Report of the President's Commission on National Goals* (Englewood Cliffs, N.J.: Prentice-Hall, 1960).

4. Statement by Spiro T. Agnew, October 10, 1973.

5. Revenue sharing first came to public attention in the early 1960s as a result of proposals by Walter Heller, chairman of the Council of Economic Advisors under President Kennedy. But nothing happened until Nixon picked up the idea as part of his declared strategy for shifting power from Washington to the states.

6. The only major condition of revenue sharing was that the funds not be spent in ways that discriminated against minorities and women.

7. President Nixon had used the same phrase, "new federalism," for his policy, so Reagan's was actually a newer, or a new, new federalism.

8. In California, the full effects of Proposition 13 were not felt for about three years after the measure passed in 1978 because a large state surplus cushioned the impact. With the surplus exhausted by 1981, the consequences of the proposition at last became apparent to the public.

9. In 1980, when the California electorate feared that a proposed income tax cut initiative *would* damage the programs, the proposal was voted down.

10. In only five of the largest metropolitan areas did the suburbs lose population during the 1970s: Boston, Buffalo, New York, Newark, and St. Louis.

11. In 1980 the population of the metropolitan areas was 165 million; the population of nonmetropolitan areas was 61 million.

12. In contrast to the declines in the northern cities, the population of Phoenix increased by 31 percent between 1970 and 1980, Houston 29 percent, San Diego 25 percent, and San Antonio 20 percent.

13. See John Gunther, *Inside USA* (New York: Harper & Row, 1951), p. 678.

14. Floyd Hunter, *Community Power Structure* (Chapel Hill, N.C.: University of North Carolina Press, 1953).

15. Michael Parenti, *Democracy for the Few* (New York: St. Martin's Press, 1980), p. 123.

16. Edward C. Banfield, *The Unheavenly City* (Boston: Little, Brown, 1970), pp. 3–4.

17. See Martin Anderson, *The Federal Bulldozer: A Critical Analysis of Urban Renewal* (Cambridge, Mass.: The MIT Press, 1965).

18. See Banfield, *The Unheavenly City*, pp. 245–246.

19. *Newsweek*, 17 November 1975, p. 90.

20. Scott Greer, "The Shaky Future of Local Government," *Psychology Today*, August 1968, p. 66.

21. Edward C. Banfield, *Political Influence* (New York: The Free Press, 1961).

four

ISSUES IN PUBLIC POLICY

In this final part of the book we turn our attention to some major issues in public policy: the economy in chapter 12, minority rights in chapter 13, energy and the environment in chapter 14, and foreign policy in chapter 15. In each case we shall be interested in more than just the nature and causes of the problems. Because this text is about the American political system and not about sociology, economics, or technology, we are concerned primarily with the *politics* of the issues and the ways in which they are handled by our policy makers and political institutions.

Thus this final section pulls together the material dealing with the political processes and institutions covered in parts two and three and examines these processes and institutions in action, in the operational setting of contemporary issues. Each of the four chapters on public policy is divided into three sections. First, we provide historical, descriptive, and analytical background on the issue and some proposals for resolving it. Second, we describe how the relevant institutions of politics and government have tried to deal with the issue. Finally, each chapter presents a five-perspective debate on the most important of all questions considered in this book: *Can the American political system deal effectively with the great issues facing the people today?*

chapter twelve

ECONOMIC POLICY: SHARING THE WEALTH

By what principles should the goods and services produced by the economy be distributed among the population? All societies must confront this central question. As we examine in this chapter its application to the American system, we shall focus on one particular aspect of the problem: Can we abolish poverty in America?

In order to understand this issue, we cannot concentrate on public policy only as it relates to the poor. We have to review the entire context of economic policy, because without looking at the size and growth of economic output as a whole we cannot know how much is available for distribution among the population, including the poor.

So our procedure will be first to discuss the product and expansion of the American economy, then to review the range of problems afflicting the economy today, and then to describe the devices used by the federal government to deal with those problems. Next we shall examine the roles of the various aspects of the governmental and political system that have been involved in shaping economic policy in general and poverty programs in particular. With this background we shall be ready to proceed to our five-perspective debate.

WHAT THE SYSTEM PRODUCES

The output of the American system has been prodigious. In 1982 the Gross National Product (GNP)—the total value of all goods, services, and investments generated in a year—passed $3 trillion. As table 12-1 indicates, by 1980 the *real* GNP (that is, the total adjusted for inflation) had almost tripled since 1950, doubled since 1960, and increased by about a third since 1970. This record of growth is impressive, far outstripping the increase in population during that period. It translates into a staggering supply of homes, automobiles, television

TABLE 12-1 Gross National Product (in billions, rounded to nearest 100 million)

	1950	1955	1960	1965	1970	1975	1980
Gross National Product (GNP)	290	400	510	690	980	1,500	2,600
GNP in Constant (1972) Dollars	530	650	740	930	1,070	1,200	1,480

Source: U.S., Department of Commerce, Bureau of Economic Analysis.

sets, computers, college educations, hospitals, highways, nuclear missiles, hamburgers, and an array of other goods and services.

This rising level of output produced a high and rising standard of living for the majority of the American people. By 1980 the median family income was approximately $21,000, which means that half of America's families earned over $21,000, and the other half earned less than $21,000.

Thus the American economic machine has generated a vast, rising output that has provided a high standard of living for the bulk of the population. However, this success story is by no means unblemished, and in recent years the economy has been faced with a number of problems of increasing seriousness.

PROBLEMS FACING THE AMERICAN ECONOMIC SYSTEM

LOSS OF OUR COMPETITIVE EDGE

Even though our GNP has been expanding, over the past decade our economy has been growing at a slower rate than the economies of a number of other countries, including Japan, West Germany, and France. Although our standard of living was once far above the standard of living of any other country, with the possible exception of Sweden, our material affluence is now at least equaled, perhaps surpassed, by West Germany, Switzerland, and Denmark, as well as Sweden. Moreover, Japan, West Germany, and others are now able to produce automobiles, television sets, and other high-technology mass-produced articles of a higher quality than our own products, and sell them in the United States at a lower price than our products.

Moreover, the explanation that other nations can charge less because they pay their workers lower wages no longer holds, because wage rates in Germany and Japan have been rising rapidly. Instead, the principal reason for our higher costs appears to be a decline in the annual rate of productivity growth in the United States from 3.3 percent in the period from 1948 to 1965 to 2.3 percent from 1965 to 1973, and to only 1.2 percent from 1973 to 1978. Although output per worker is still higher in the United States than in any other nation, the gap has been closing rapidly, as figure 12-1 makes clear.[1]

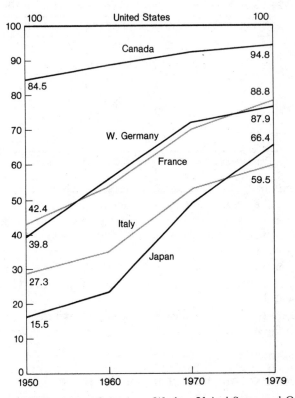

FIGURE 12-1. Output per Worker, United States and Other Nations (U.S. = 100)
Source: U.S., Department of Labor, Bureau of Labor Statistics.

Various explanations have been given for our downward trend: we save less and invest less proportionately than many other industrialized countries; there has been a shift in employment toward office jobs and service industries, all of which have to be sustained by a diminishing number of production-line workers; people want to take more of their increased standard of living in leisure time rather than in material goods; and so on. But whatever the explanation, the trend is clear, and it is a subject of growing concern to policy makers.

UNEMPLOYMENT

In the depths of the Great Depression in 1932, 23.6 percent of the civilian labor force were unemployed, and not until the United States entered World War II did the figure fall below 14 percent. We have not approached such a level of unemployment since that time. From 1946 through 1969 the annual percentage ranged between 3.0 percent and 6.8 percent, mostly hovering around 5 percent. Since 1969, however, the trend has been upward, as shown in table 12-2. By December 1981, in fact, the jobless rate had reached 8.9 percent, and it rose still further to 9.8 percent in July 1982—the highest in forty years.

INFLATION

In the 1950s and 1960s prices paid by consumers typically rose at a rate of 1 to 1.5 percent a year. But in the 1970s the inflation rate moved up sharply, never falling below 3.3 percent, and reaching a high of 13.5 percent in 1980.[2] In 1981 it began to move down, and the decline accelerated in 1982; but there seemed little prospect of its falling to the low, stable levels that prevailed before the 1970s. (See figure 12-2.)

TABLE 12–2 Unemployment rates, 1969–1980
(annual average percent of labor force)

1969	3.5
1970	4.9
1971	5.9
1972	5.6
1973	4.9
1974	5.6
1975	8.5
1976	7.7
1977	7.0
1978	6.0
1979	5.8
1980	7.4
1981	7.6

Source: U.S., Department of Labor, Bureau of Labor Statistics.

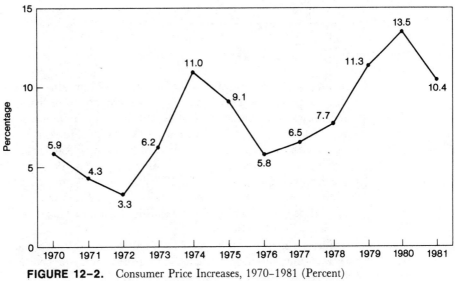

FIGURE 12–2. Consumer Price Increases, 1970–1981 (Percent)
Source: U.S., Department of Labor.

The high inflation rate creates an impression of economic improvement that may, in fact, be nonexistent. In 1980 the median family income of $21,020 represented an increase of 7.3 percent over the previous year, but because the inflation rate for 1980 was 13.5 percent, the actual buying power of the typical family *fell* by 5.5 percent.

One further unhappy fact about inflation in the 1970s was that it coincided with high rates of unemployment. Previously there had been an inverse relationship between the two evils: when unemployment fell, the rate of inflation tended to go up, and vice versa, and government could adopt policies based on a choice between them. That choice is much less clear now, as we see from the 1980 figures of 13.5 percent inflation and 7.4 percent unemployment. We suffer much of the time from *stagflation*—the unhappy combination of a stagnant economy (which generates high unemployment) and unhealthy levels of inflation.

THE PERSISTENCE OF POVERTY

Despite our high median income, the distribution of income in America is far from even. As we see from table 12-3, the top 5 percent family income group earned over 15 percent of all income in 1978, and the bottom 20 percent family income group brought in a little more than 5 percent of the total income.

TABLE 12-3 Distribution of aggregate money income, 1981 (by each fifth and top 5 percent of families)

Top 5 percent	15.3
Highest fifth	41.6
Fourth fifth	24.3
Middle fifth	17.5
Second fifth	11.6
Lowest fifth	5.1

Source: U.S., Department of Commerce, Bureau of the Census.

Among that lowest fifth of the income groups are the very poor. In 1980, 29.3 million people, or 13 percent of the population, were living below the official, federally defined poverty line of $8,414 for an urban family of four. This statistic represented great progress since the 1930s, when Franklin Roosevelt could speak of "one-third of a nation—ill-housed, ill-clad, ill-nourished," or from the 22 percent of the population still classified as poor in 1960. But most of the gains were made before the end of the 1960s. In the 1970s the figure hovered obstinately in the 11 to 12 percent range, then rose to 13 percent in 1980 (an increase of 3.2 million people over the previous year), and continued to rise into 1982. (See figure 12-3.)

These statistics include people from almost every kind of background and from every ethnic, racial, and religious group. However, the poor are most likely to be found among the following categories:

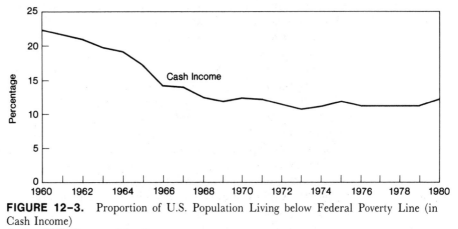

FIGURE 12–3. Proportion of U.S. Population Living below Federal Poverty Line (in Cash Income)
Source: U.S., Bureau of the Census.

1. Minorities. Minorities constitute almost 40 percent of all the poor. Blacks, Latinos, and American Indians are represented far more than proportionately among the poor.
2. The elderly. About 13 percent of the total number of people below the poverty line are elderly. Many people over 65 did not earn enough money during their working lives to save much, or they had their savings wiped out by an illness and live on a small pension.
3. The young. Over 40 percent of the total of the poor are young. These people include the children of poor families and teenage high school dropouts without jobs or marketable skills.
4. Families headed by women. These families constitute about 50 percent of the poor. One-third of all families with no father in the home are below the poverty line, as compared with only 6 percent of two-parent families.
5. The South. Over 40 percent of the poor live in the South. Despite the improving economic conditions of most of the South, states like Mississippi, Alabama, and South Carolina are still much less industrialized than the rest of the country and contain large numbers of families below the poverty line (especially, but by no means exclusively, blacks).[3]

Poverty is also found concentrated in the inner cities, which are heavily occupied by the low-income minorities; in areas like the Appalachians, where the local industry has died; and among small tenant farmers and migrant agricultural workers.

Thus among the people *most* likely to be poor are elderly black people living in Mississippi, divorced mothers of large families in a central city of the North, or migrant Chicano farm workers. *Least* likely to be poor are middle-aged, white suburban families who are Jewish, Catholic, or Episcopalian.

The poor suffer from many disabilities apart from their lack of money. They are below the national average in years of schooling. They are more likely than the average to be out of work, to live in squalid housing, to be in poor health, and to be the perpetrators—and the victims—of crimes of violence. Some sociologists and anthropologists have viewed these various deficiencies as part of a vicious cycle of poverty: poor people are likely to get poor schooling, which leads to unemployment, which breeds poor health and antisocial attitudes, which reinforce the likelihood of remaining poor. This cycle of poverty, say these scholars, reflects a *culture of poverty*, a way of life that is found not only in this country but wherever there are significant numbers of people who are the inheritors of several generations of poverty. People who grow up in this culture have a strong feeling of fatalism, dependence, and inferiority.[4]

Other sociologists disagree. Although they recognize that poverty can be severely damaging to the belief in self, they doubt that there is a universally recognizable poverty culture or that the attitudes of the poor are very different from the majority's. In this view it is only the *circumstances* that are different, and the behavior of the poor could be changed quickly by dramatic changes in the social environment.[5]

Still, if there is disagreement about the existence of a deep-rooted poverty culture, there is little question but that millions of people in America live today in conditions of poverty; that a great many of the poor have developed a sense of defeat and low self-esteem; and that the various disabilities of life below the poverty line feed on and reinforce each other.

THE TOOLS OF GOVERNMENT

Until the 1930s the federal government played a very limited role in directing the economy and providing help to the poor. The economy was largely an arena left to the decisions of private businessmen. The poor were left to the efforts of local government, private charity, and big city political bosses, who offered food and jobs to the immigrants arriving from Europe in exchange for their votes.

This situation was changed by the stock market crash of 1929, the subsequent collapse of the economy, and the massive unemployment and poverty that characterized the Great Depression. From that time on the federal government has involved itself actively in the efforts to maintain a growing and stable economy and redistribute income in favor of the disadvantaged. The principal devices it has drawn on follow.

MONETARY POLICY

The federal government prints the currency, and it can put more money or less money into the economy by a variety of methods. It can also influence the supply of credit by raising and lowering the interest rate. Thus, if the economy is slipping the federal government may try to pick it up by injecting more money into the economy and by lowering the interest rate to encourage businesses to borrow and invest; it can reverse its course when the economy seems to be moving ahead so fast as to be generating inflation.

FISCAL POLICY

Fiscal policy includes two broad elements: public spending and taxes. Until the 1930s the government used common sense to deal with economic slumps. Because times were bad and government revenue was falling, the federal budget was cut to keep the budget in balance. But common sense was not necessarily economic sense. Cutting the budget took money out of the economy and depressed still further the level of business activity and the number of jobs. So, as unemployment reached almost a quarter of the work force in the 1930s, the administration of Franklin Roosevelt began to adopt the principles put forward by the British economist John Maynard Keynes. The Keynesian theory said that, as the economy turned down, government should compensate for the decline in private investment by increasing its own spending. So, as part of the Roosevelt New Deal, the federal government launched a number of programs designed to stimulate business and create jobs, and it deliberately ran deficits in the budget—that is, it spent more money than it raised in taxes and other sources of revenue. The deficits were covered by printing more money and increasing the national debt—the money the government owes to private lenders.

From that time Keynesian principles prevailed until the arrival of the Reagan administration. Federal spending has increased at a rapid rate, from less than $10 billion in 1940 to $196 billion in 1970, and then by great leaps to over $400 billion in 1977 and more than $700 billion in 1982. The distribution of federal expenditures is illustrated in figure 12-4.

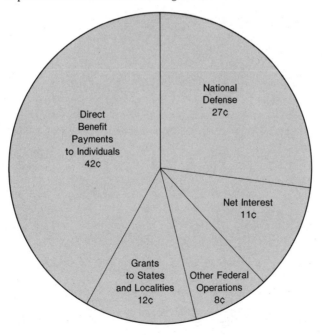

FIGURE 12–4. Where the Federal Budget Dollar Goes, 1982
Source: U.S., Office of Management and Budget.

In most years the increases in federal spending have not been sufficiently offset by rising revenues. So, as figure 12-5 indicates, in most of the years from 1954 through 1980, there were deficits in the federal budget. The result of these cu-

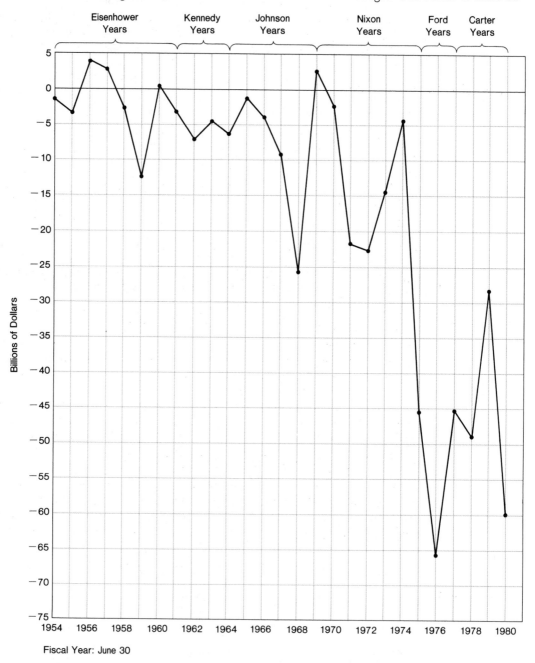

Fiscal Year: June 30

FIGURE 12–5. Federal Budget Deficits, 1954–1981
Source: U.S., Office of Management and Budget.

mulative deficits was that by late 1981 the national debt had reached a trillion dollars and required interest payments of more than $100 billion a year.

Taxes.   The principal sources of tax revenue by the federal government are income taxes from individuals and corporations; social insurance taxes to finance Social Security and other insurance programs; excise (sales) taxes on tobacco, liquor, gasoline, air travel, and so on; and customs duties. (See figure 12-6.)

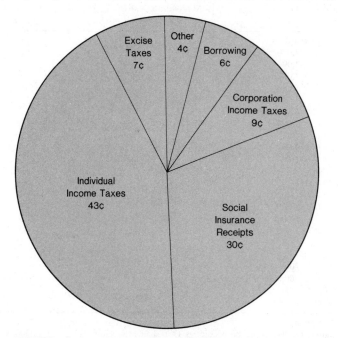

FIGURE 12–6.   Where the Federal Budget Dollar Comes From, 1982
Source: U.S., Office of Management and Budget.

The tax system has two purposes: to pay for the enormous range of programs in which the federal government is involved and to redistribute income and wealth from richer to poorer people. In this second respect the income tax is particularly important, because it is specifically intended to be a "progressive tax"—that is, not merely does it take more from upper-income than from lower-income people, but it takes *proportionately* more. Thus, until the Reagan administration's tax cuts started in 1981, federal income tax rates were 50 percent on wages and salaries and 70 percent on unearned income, whereas the percentages were smaller on smaller incomes, and nothing at all was taken from the lowest incomes.

In fact, even before the Reagan tax cuts, the income tax was considerably less progressive than a reading of the tax tables would suggest. The reason is that the tax laws allow a variety of deductions from gross income. Middle-income people claim some of these deductions—on property taxes and ortgage interest, for example—but the rich gain most from writeoffs of business losses and the use of "tax shelters" in the form of investments—which shelter or remove much of their income from tax liability—in such fields as real estate developments, oil, cattle, movies, and tax-free municipal bonds. Thus, there is an important distinction to be made between the official tax rates and the actual proportion of income paid by people in different income brackets, as shown in table 12-4.

TABLE 12-4 Actual taxes paid as compared to nominal tax rate

Total income (dollars)	Nominal tax (as percent of total income)	Actual tax paid (as percent of total income)
Under 1,000	14.2	a
1,000–2,000	15.1	a
2,000–3,000	16.2	1.4
3,000–4,000	17.0	3.4
4,000–5,000	17.8	5.0
5,000–6,000	18.6	6.3
6,000–7,000	19.3	7.2
7,000–8,000	20.0	7.9
8,000–9,000	20.8	8.6
9,000–10,000	21.6	9.3
10,000–15,000	23.9	10.3
15,000–20,000	28.0	12.4
20,000–25,000	32.0	14.2
25,000–50,000	38.4	17.4
50,000–100,000	49.0	25.2
100,000–150,000	57.0	29.6
150,000–200,000	60.6	30.2
200,000–500,000	63.8	30.4
500,000–1,000,000	66.9	30.7
1,000,000 and over	67.5	31.4

[a]Less than 0.05.
Source: Derived from the Brookings 1970 Tax File (sample of about 95,000 returns). Rates and other provisions are those in effect in 1973. Cited in Richard Goode, *The Individual Income Tax*, rev. ed. (Washington, D.C.: The Brookings Institution, 1976), p. 309.

Government regulation. As we saw in our discussion of the federal bureaucracies in chapter 9, the federal government has developed a large number of regulatory programs designed to intervene in the economy. These programs had such goals as the prevention of a recurrence of the great stock market crash of 1929, the provision of safe working conditions, and the protection of the consumer against unfair and deceptive business practices and advertising.

Social welfare programs. The Great Depression threatened the well-being not only of the lowest income group but of the great majority of the people. This threat created a political environment in which the federal government could develop programs to protect the working population against loss of income caused by unemployment, disablement, or retirement. Unemployment insurance, funded by a payroll tax and administered by the states under federal supervision, provided payments for limited periods of time to workers laid off from their jobs.

Still more important was Social Security, financed by compulsory payroll assessments on employers and workers and on the self-employed, to provide old-age pensions and payments to disabled workers. This program became the core to which other benefits were attached, notably Medicare, which pays part of the medical costs of retired people.

By the 1970s Social Security was running into financial difficulties. As the proportion of older people in the population grew, a rapidly increasing burden was placed on those people still in the work force to generate the funds needed to support the retired. In 1950 there were approximately sixteen workers paying Social Security taxes for every person receiving benefits. By 1960 the ratio was down to 5 to 1; by 1970, 3.5 to 1; by 1980, 3 to 1; and by the year 2035 it is estimated that there will be only two people paying into the system for every recipient of its benefits. The result is that, of the three Social Security trust funds—retirement pensions, disability benefits, and Medicare payments—the first two were paying out more than they took in by 1980 despite large increases in Social Security taxes, and the balances were declining so rapidly that they were heading for huge deficits by 1984.

Programs for the poor.   The poor benefited from many of the government activities already mentioned—efforts to expand the economy and combat unemployment, Social Security and Medicare, and so on. But the New Deal also included a number of programs specifically directed toward people at the lowest end of the income scale. These programs were expanded by later administrations, particularly by Lyndon Johnson under the rubric of the "War on Poverty." The main categories of assistance to the poor were the following:

1. Job creation and job training. The New Deal's Works Projects Administration (WPA) pioneered the way for a variety of subsequent efforts to provide job and training opportunities, including the Johnson administration's Job Corps, which trained young men and women for work in conservation camps and residential centers, and the 1973 Comprehensive Employment and Training Act (CETA), most of the funds for which went to state and local governments to provide opportunities for the unemployed and the unskilled.

2. Housing. The New Deal programs included public housing apartments for very low-income people under a program of federal subsidies to specially created local housing authorities. The Housing Act of 1949 provided for 810,000 additional units of this low-rent public housing. Variations on this program were developed in the 1960s, including the rehabilitation of run-down housing. And the War on Poverty included the Model Cities program, which undertook a coordinated effort to upgrade the blighted areas of a number of urban communities.

3. Education. When federal aid to education was finally approved in 1965, it came in under the rubric of the "War on Poverty," and special attention was paid under the program to the needs of the schools in the poverty areas of the cities. Head Start, a program for preschool children in low-income areas, was launched in an effort to overcome the educational and cultural disadvantages associated with a poverty background. Financial aid programs were provided for low-income

students in colleges and universities, together with work-study opportunities, which provided employers with federal money for offering part-time jobs to students.

4. Welfare. The New Deal introduced the notion of providing federal grants to the states to help them provide support to needy people. These grant programs have grown under successive administrations and were given a major new impetus by the War on Poverty. They include the following:

a. Aid to Families With Dependent Children (AFDC), which dates from 1935, grew rapidly even as the proportion below the poverty line fell during the 1960s. This growth occurred because of the migration of poor people, mostly blacks, from the rural South to the northern inner cities, and because of the large increase in the number of families headed by women.

b. Supplemental Security Income was started in 1974 to provide federal funds for blind and disabled people and for the elderly.

c. The food-stamp program is a program begun in 1961 to provide the poor with stamps redeemable at markets as part payment for food purchases.

d. Medicaid is a federally funded program administered by the states to provide medical care for indigent elderly people not covered by Medicare.

Each of these programs has expanded at a rapid rate, as is made clear by figure 12-7.

5. Community action. The Johnson administration's 1964 Economic Opportunity Act introduced an innovative approach to the problem of poverty, the Community Action Programs (CAP), under the Office of Economic Opportunity. Instead of merely giving financial and other benefits to low-income people, CAP invited the "maximum feasible participation" of the poor in decisions affecting a wide range of community problems. The basic assumption of CAP was that poor people are afflicted by a sense of helplessness, of being passive objects of decisions that other people make for them. To increase their belief in themselves, CAP set out to give the poor a chance to participate actively in the decision-making process at the community level. Policy boards were set up in the communities to make decisions on the spending of federal poverty funds, and representatives of the poor were given a major voice on these boards.

THE ECONOMY, POVERTY, AND THE POLICY-MAKING PROCESS

The issues involved in the production and distribution of wealth in America provide an excellent context in which to apply many of the concepts developed earlier in this book, particularly those concepts related to the presidency, Congress, the federal bureaucracies, interest groups, and public opinion.

THE PRESIDENCY

Our analyses in the chapters on parties and the presidency appear to lead us to two conclusions: first, that strong federal government intervention in the economy

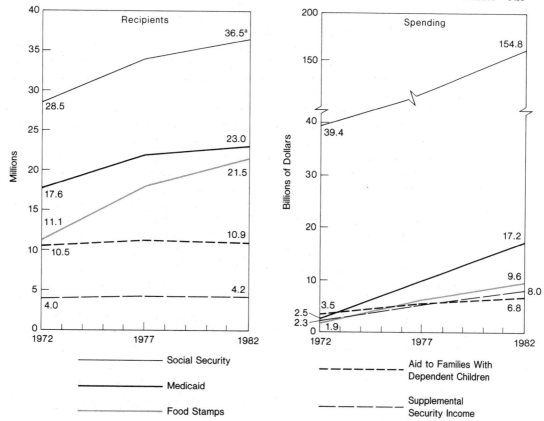

a. Actual number of recipients is lower because some receive both federal civilian and military pensions.

Note: Figures for 1982 are estimates and assume adoption of spending cuts proposed by President Reagan.

FIGURE 12-7.   Growth of Federally Supported Programs for the Poor

Source: U.S., Depts. of Agriculture, Health and Human Services and Labor, and Office of Management and Budget.

and on behalf of the poor would require energetic presidential leadership; and, second, that this intervention would be more likely to occur under Democratic than under Republican presidents.

The second statement has not invariably been true. Twice Nixon, faced with inflationary surges resulting first from Vietnam spending, then from the 1973 Arab oil embargo, turned to wage and price controls instead of the traditional Republican remedy of drastic cuts in federal spending.[6] Moreover, Nixon proposed to replace AFDC with a Family Assistance Program (FAP). This program would have provided a federal foundation "under the income of every American family with dependent children that cannot care for itself"; it would require work or job training for all able-bodied recipients of aid except mothers of preschool children (and day-care centers would be provided to encourage these mothers to take a job); and it would contain an incentive to work because, unlike AFDC, FAP allowed people to keep half their earnings and still receive benefits until their income reached the limit of almost $4,000.

Conversely, on the Democratic side, Carter, particularly toward the end of his presidency, took positions that opened him up to the charge of deserting his party's principles. He began with proposals that seemed to be in the classical Democratic mold. By the end of 1979, he declared, unemployment must be brought down to between 5 and 5.5 percent; inequities in the tax system must be removed; and the existing welfare programs should be replaced with a new cash assistance program called the "Program for Better Jobs and Income," which was essentially a somewhat more generous version of Nixon's Family Assistance Program. However, Carter emphasized that this program, as well as any proposal for national health insurance, must be phased in slowly and carefully so as not to conflict with two other goals: a balanced federal budget by 1981 and a reduced rate of inflation to between 4 and 4.5 percent by 1979.

As we saw in earlier chapters, Carter got little of his program through Congress. AFDC remained largely unreformed. Moreover, with inflation getting out of hand and the prospect of a balanced budget fast receding, Carter would not consider wage-price controls and called instead for cuts in federal programs, including a number of programs directed toward the poor and minorities.

Despite these exceptions, there has generally been a discernible difference of emphasis between Democratic and Republican presidents in their economic and social welfare policies. Certainly no Republican president would have been likely to undertake the sweeping intrusions into the economy launched by Franklin Roosevelt or the wide-ranging, expensive battery of programs that constituted Lyndon Johnson's War on Poverty.

The Reagan administration.   Conversely, the drastic reversal of previous policies embarked on by Ronald Reagan would not have been politically possible for any Democratic president.[7] Indeed, no Republican president had tried anything like it—not Eisenhower, Nixon,[8] or Ford.

As we saw in earlier chapters, Reagan was undertaking not merely to slow the pace of economic and social change but to reverse its direction. This goal meant major cutbacks in many of the programs that came out of the New Deal and the Great Society, sharp reductions in income taxes, and the attack on federal regulations described in chapter 9.

Spending cuts.   The spending reductions that Reagan pushed through Congress in 1981 cut $35 billion from the previously proposed 1982 budget, and because defense spending went up substantially, programs designed to help low-income groups had to sustain a large share of the reductions. The federal government, Reagan insisted, would continue to provide a "safety net" for the "truly needy." Social Security would have to be reexamined and probably reformed, but its integrity would be protected. But several other programs had grown far beyond their original purposes, had become wasteful and riddled with corruption, and would have to be brought under control or even, in some cases, abolished.

Consequently the fiscal 1982 federal budget contained a number of sharp cuts in social services. These included reductions in food stamps (about a million people were cut from the rolls), school lunches, Aid to Families with Dependent Children, the Comprehensive Employment and Training Act (CETA) programs, unemployment benefits, low-income housing, college student grants and loans, and Medicaid and other state health programs.

Other programs cut in the fiscal 1982 budget included highways, mass transit, energy research and development, aid for schools "impacted" by U.S. installations, farm and dairy price supports, the Small Business Administration, and arts and humanities programs.

Tax cuts. In 1981 Congress also approved Reagan's request for substantial reductions in individual and corporate income taxes. Individuals were granted a 25 percent cut in income taxes spread over three years. Investors received reductions in the maximum tax range and in capital gains tax. Various provisions were designed to cut the taxes paid by business concerns.[9]

However, these tax reductions appeared to jeopardize another of Reagan's declared aims: the reduction and eventual elimination of budget deficits. The problem was further compounded by sharply increased military spending, the slowing down of tax receipts caused by a sluggish economy, and outlays on benefits paid to the increasing numbers of unemployed workers. So critics charged that the Reagan administration's policies were contradictory and self-defeating.

The initial response of the Reagan administration to these pessimistic analyses was that they were false because they were based on the old Keynesian economic notions of "demand management," instead of the new kind of "supply-side" economics.[10] Under the Keynesian doctrine, which had been followed by previous, especially Democratic, administrations, the big question for the federal government was how much money to put into people's hands. If business was bad and unemployment high, taxes were cut and federal spending increased. These actions would put more money into the economy, which would create more consumer demand, which would stimulate companies to expand their output. Then, if the economy boomed too fast and inflation started to become a threat, taxes could be raised and federal spending cut.

However, the old system was not working. Inflation had reached intolerable levels; unemployment was high; and federal deficits were enormous. So a new approach was called for, based on providing *incentives* to increase production. This approach, like the Keynesian policy, involved cutting tax rates. But the supply-siders emphasized cutting corporate taxes and income taxes at the middle and upper levels. These cuts would enable companies to retain and invest more profits; they would stimulate a higher rate of individual savings, which would be available for investment in new and expanded businesses; and they would encourage people to work harder, because they would not have to give up most of their increased income to the tax collector. By placing the emphasis on incentives to business and individuals, productivity and output would increase; more goods and services would be sold; and, despite reduced tax rates, the total tax revenues to government would, within two or three years, actually increase.

A further stimulus to business, said the Reagan administration, would be provided by a general reduction of the government rules and regulations that undermine incentives. And along with the cuts in taxes would go cuts in government spending. Thus, after a year or two of continued large federal deficits, the size of the deficits would come down rapidly until, within three to four years, the budget could be brought into balance.

By the time the president presented his annual budget to Congress in February 1982, however, it was clear that the budget could not be balanced on this schedule. Administration forecasts (which were later revised upward) projected deficits of close to $100 billion in 1982, declining to about $70 billion by 1985. Much higher deficits were predicted by the Congressional Budget Office.

There was disagreement among economists on whether deficits on this scale are necessarily disastrous. But there was little doubt that in the money markets the deficits were regarded as pernicious. Financial institutions believed that large budget deficits forced up interest rates by causing the government to borrow more and more, thus bidding up the price of money. In fact, interest rates in the spring of 1982 remained at obstinately high levels (16 percent or more) with crippling consequences for the housing and automobile industries.

As we shall see, some members of the Reagan administration began to call for a change in direction, and argued for slowing down the tax reductions and cutting back the increases in defense spending. The president was reluctant to change course. To back down now would be to provoke comparisons with the hesitations and retreats of the Carter presidency. Moreover, Reagan was convinced that his program could still work. Already the inflation rate had gone down dramatically. Given enough time the supply-side approach—providing incentives to business and investors—would reinvigorate the economy, reduce unemployment, and bring general prosperity.

But with unemployment reaching 9.8 percent in July 1982, with a continued bleak outlook for business, and with elections approaching in November, Congress insisted on bringing down the deficits. Reagan held fast to his general strategy of the three-year, 25 percent income tax cut along with substantially increased defense spending. But reluctantly he conceded the necessity of reducing the prospective deficits, and he threw his weight behind a proposal for tax increases, mostly directed at business and the wealthy, amounting to $98 billion over three years, along with further reductions in federal spending. (He also gave his support to a congressional proposal for a constitutional amendment to mandate the balancing of future budgets, but Congress rejected this in 1982.)

The president was still a key figure in the process. No budget plan could pass in the teeth of his opposition. But if 1981 had seen an impressive demonstration of presidential power in economic affairs, 1982 brought evidence of limits on that power—limits imposed by the nature of our constitutional system and by implacable economic forces.

CONGRESS

As we saw in chapter 8, major liberal legislation in the economic and social areas requires not only leadership from Democratic presidents but also very large Democratic majorities in both houses of Congress. These conditions were satisfied in Franklin Roosevelt's first two terms and in the first two years of Lyndon Johnson's presidency.

With Kennedy and Truman the presidential will was present, but the large congressional majorities were lacking, so their records of programs on behalf of lower-income groups were limited. Conversely, there were substantial Democratic margins in Congress in Eisenhower's second term and during the Nixon and Ford presidencies, but without the kind of pressure that Roosevelt and Johnson exerted the congressional leadership was not able to produce much innovative social legislation. In fact, under Louisiana Democratic Senator Russell Long, the Senate Finance Committee was able to kill Nixon's Family Assistance Plan, as well as any tax reform that went beyond minor adjustments.

The Carter presidency taught us that, even if the conditions we have described are met, and large Democratic majorities in the two houses are combined with a Democrat in the White House, nothing much may happen to help the poor. Carter tried—perhaps not hard enough—but by this time Congress was even more worried about inflation and high taxes than was the president.

In his first year Reagan demonstrated what a determined president could move through Congress, even though his party had a majority in only one of the two houses. He was able to accomplish what he did because his course was in a very different direction from the course charted by his predecessors. And Congress, reading the changed will of the electorate, set about the task of slashing many of the programs that previous congresses had constructed over the years on behalf of the lower-income segment of the population.

Still, as we have noted, it is not in the nature of Congress as an institution to be perpetually subservient to the president. Even in his first, triumphant legislative year Reagan, confronted by intense congressional opposition, backed away from a proposal to cut out the minimum Social Security benefits for some of its recipients. By the second year (a congressional election year) the legislators were hearing from unhappy industrialists, bankers, and unemployed workers.

The barrage of criticism troubled Republicans as well as Democrats. But if there was a consensus on the need for changes in the president's program, there was no agreement on what exactly should be done about it. The Republican leadership found itself at odds not only with the Democratic leadership, but also with Republican supply-siders opposed to the Reagan-backed $98 billion tax increase. The Democratic leaders again had difficulty dealing with the "boll weevils" and with the party's liberal faction. Committee chairs staked out rival positions. And a further source of dissension resulted from the control of the Senate by one party and the House by another.

Thus the long-drawn-out confusion surrounding the making of the 1982 budget provided one more illustration not only of Congress' power to frustrate a president, but also of the diffusion of power within the congressional system.

ADVISERS AND BUREAUCRATS

The planning and implementation of economic and social policies involve several members of the White House staff and the Executive Office of the President, and a number of federal departments and agencies.

In the first year of the Reagan administration the people principally involved in economic affairs were the following:

- David Stockman, director of the Office of Management and Budget, which is charged with reviewing all executive department budgets (and, in Stockman's case, cutting most of them).
- Murray Weidenbaum, chair of the Council of Economic Advisers, the three-person group of economists created by the Employment Act of 1946 to keep the economy moving at a healthy pace.
- Martin Anderson, White House staff member responsible for advising on economic policy.
- Donald Regan, secretary of the treasury and chair of the cabinet Council on Economic Affairs, which included Vice-President George Bush, cabinet officers particularly concerned with economic matters, and other top economic officials.
- Malcolm Baldridge, secretary of commerce and chair of a cabinet advisory group on trade.
- Paul Volcker, chair of the Federal Reserve Board, the nation's central bank responsible for determining monetary policy through a variety of intricate mechanisms for influencing the supply of credit and the rate of interest.

President Reagan also drew on the economic advice of his secretaries of transportation, labor, and agriculture and his White House trade representative. From outside his official staff he consulted periodically with former members of the Eisenhower, Nixon, and Ford administrations, then in banking, business, or higher education, such as Alan Greenspan, George Shultz, Paul McCracken, and Walter Wriston.

In the area of social welfare the president's policy advisers included his White House staff members, Meese, Baker, Stockman, and Anderson, and the secretaries of Health and Human Services and Housing and Urban Development.

Because the president appoints most of these people himself they are likely to reflect his own economic and social views. However, we are discussing here fields in which the stakes are very high, in which there are clamorous demands among powerful conflicting interests, and in which there is no consensus among the experts. Inevitably there will be discord periodically among the president's advisers. All agreed on the need for major spending and tax cuts from the levels prevailing under previous administrations, but beyond that consensus there were significant disagreements. Some favored the monetary policies of Milton Friedman, who argued that steady, but restrained, expansion of the supply of money was the key to economic well-being and the control of inflation. Others favored the innovative supply-side prescription of economist Arthur Laffer. Others preferred a more orthodox mix of economic techniques.

More specifically, David Stockman was skeptical of the claims of the supply-siders. He worried about the dangers of high budget deficits, and he wanted increased excise taxes introduced in 1982, along with a scaling down of the defense increases. Treasury Secretary Regan, on the other hand, opposed any excise tax increases because he feared that they would weaken the stimulating effect of the income tax reductions and make it more difficult to break out of the economic recession of 1981–1982.

Regan also fought on another front—this time against the tight money policies of the Federal Reserve Board (FRB). In January 1982, Regan publicly criticized the FRB for following an "erratic" monetary policy that, he claimed, helped trigger the recession, expand the budget deficit, and drive up interest rates. In reply, Volcker insisted that it was the administration's projected budget deficits that were forcing up interest rates,[11] and indicated that tight monetary restraint would continue until inflation was brought under control. (With inflation slowing by fall, 1982, the FRB engineered a decline in interest rates.)

Actually, there was nothing new about conflict between a president's administration and the FRB. The man Nixon appointed as FRB chair in 1970 and reappointed in 1974, the highly respected Arthur Burns, took public issue with the economic policies first of Nixon, then of Carter, complaining that both were flirting dangerously with inflation. What makes such independence possible is that members of the board serve for fourteen-year terms, and their chairperson is selected from among them for four years at a time—and not necessarily by the incumbent president. (Volcker, a conservative banker, was appointed by Carter.) Neither the members nor their chair can be fired by the president just because he dislikes their policies. All that he and his colleagues can do when they disagree with the FRB is to reason with them, and, in case of continued disagreement, take their case to the public.

As we noted in chapter 9, the lesser members of the bureaucracies can be another source of frustration to presidents by dragging their feet in carrying out his policies, especially when those policies are designed to blaze trails with which the bureaucrats are unfamiliar. For this reason Lyndon Johnson, looking for new ways to attack the poverty problem, decided to bypass the existing channels and set up the Office of Economic Opportunity (OEO). This office, which included the Job Corps, work-study programs, and the Community Action Program, reported directly to the White House, and in the local communities it was not required to operate through the old-line federal departments.

Nixon and Ford did not find the work of OEO much to their taste. Community Action, with its principle of maximum feasible participation of the poor, had stirred up militant protests and demonstrations in some communities and enraged some mayors and governors.[12] So, one by one OEO's functions were spun off to other departments.

INTEREST GROUPS

Economic policy is the focus of more extensive and persistent interest group pressures than any other area of public policy.

Business. As we saw in chapter 6, business fought for many years against the enlargement of the welfare state. Its representatives in Washington protested the coming of the income tax, deficit spending, Social Security, Medicare, and federally funded public housing.

However, since the Great Depression many business leaders have accepted—even encouraged—a great deal of government intervention in the economy. For one thing, the federal government became a force for stability, evening out the tendency of the economy to lurch from prosperity to massive bankruptcies and unemployment. For another, government could take much of the risk out of business by subsidies, loan guarantees, tariffs, and so on.

Business corporations even came to see some merit in certain kinds of antipoverty programs. The National Association of Manufacturers and corporations like Xerox and Standard Oil of New Jersey came out in favor of Nixon's Family Assistance Plan.

The Reagan administration's policies attracted a great deal of public support from business, especially the reduction of corporate taxes and government regulations. Even so, there was considerable anguish among segments of industry hurt by the high interest rates of 1981–1982, and there was much anxiety in many corporate boardrooms that the administration's bold departures from long-established economic and social patterns might destabilize the economy.

Labor unions, public interest groups, and education and urban lobbies. Forthright opposition to the Reagan proposals to cut back government programs has come from a loose coalition of groups that has consistently supported the expansion of the welfare state. First, and most important among these groups, are the labor unions. Then there are the public interest groups, such as Common Cause, the Ralph Nader organizations, and a number of liberal church social action groups. Next is the education lobby, particularly the National Education Association, which helped secure the enormous increase in federal funding for schools and which lobbied fiercely against the Reagan administration's plans to reverse the process. Usually, too, the urban lobby (the National League of Cities and the U.S. Conference of Mayors) is found on this side of the interest group lineup, as are social work professionals.

The elderly. There are also the organizations representing the elderly, articulating the concerns of an increasing proportion of the population. There are a number of national and state associations in this field, and politicians have become closely attuned to the interests of their older constituents. Consequently Congress was reluctant to act on Reagan administration proposals to trim, even modestly, Social Security benefits.

The poor. Then there are the poor themselves. Until recent years they had not been able to do much in an organized way to improve their lot. Their position in the economic system was weak; possessing few marketable skills, they filled menial positions or none. Their pay was low, their jobs in many cases threatened by new technologies. Efforts to organize them into labor unions were sporadic and successful only in a few limited situations. And powerlessness in the economy was matched by powerlessness in the political arena. Political involvement and potency are, as we noted in chapter 3, associated primarily with affluence and education. The poor tend to be apathetic, uninformed, and noninvolved. Most politicians view them as an inadequate and unreliable resource because they are hard to get to the polls, they are not active in campaigns, and, by definition, they are not a source of campaign funds.

Still, despite the general principle set forth in chapter 6 that the poor are weakly represented in the interest group system, some organizations speak directly for large numbers of poor people, and their potency has increased rapidly. We have mentioned the elderly, a considerable proportion of whom are numbered among the poor.

Then, the increased importance politically of blacks and other disadvantaged minorities has been a factor in helping build the various services for lower-income groups ever since the 1960s. Democratic administrations feared that, if the moderate civil rights leaders were not given something to show for their efforts, they might be pushed aside by more militant contenders for leadership.

Finally, the antipoverty programs themselves generated new elements in the coalition fighting for expanded social welfare programs. Most important among these elements was the National Welfare Rights Organization (NWRO), an organization of welfare recipients. NWRO has taken the position that people on welfare have rights and that they must fight in an organized, aggressive way for those rights. Hence, when NWRO decided that Nixon's Family Assistance Plan was grossly inadequate, they contributed to its defeat.

PUBLIC OPINION

As we saw in chapter 3, attitudes of the general electorate toward public policy issues tend to be volatile, and today's burning issue may be tomorrow's forgotten fad. However, figure 12-8 shows us that, with some fluctuations, the economy has

Question: What do you think is the most important issue facing the country today?

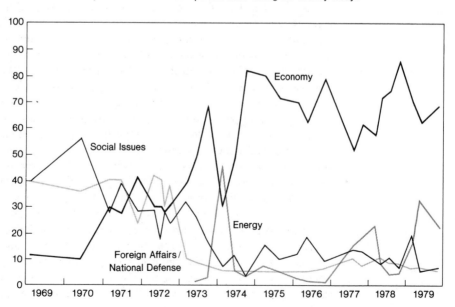

FIGURE 12–8. Public Opinion and the Economic Issue (Percent)
Source: Gallup Surveys, published in Public Opinion, *December–January 1980, p. 40.*

been the top issue on people's minds since 1973. To earlier generations the economic issue was primarily related to unemployment and stagnant business conditions. The memory of the Great Depression persisted for decades as a formative influence on political attitudes, and the prevailing opinions called for the federal government to sustain strong growth and keep unemployment down.

These attitudes are still an important element in public opinion. But as time has passed the Depression of the 1930s has exercised a diminishing hold on the public consciousness, and the driving force behind the high concern with the economic issue revealed in figure 12-8 has been double-digit inflation.[13]

Whom does the public blame for inflation? In 1959 labor was held to be the chief culprit. Since 1968, although labor has still been held more responsible than business, government has been seen as the principal cause of rising prices. (See table 12-5.)

TABLE 12-5 Who is most responsible for inflation? (percent)

	Government	Business	Labor	No opinion
1959	14	15	41	30
1968	46	12	26	16
1978	51	13	20	16

Source: Gallup Surveys.

What do people think should be done about inflation? First, there is strong support for government-imposed controls on wages and prices. In 1974, when President Nixon removed the wage-price controls that he had introduced, 50 percent of those people polled by Gallup favored a return to controls, with 39 percent opposed. By 1979 the margin in favor of restoring the controls was 57 percent to 31 percent.

Second, there is strong support for a constitutional amendment requiring a balanced federal budget each year. Gallup and other surveys have consistently indicated approval for this proposal by about 80 percent of the people queried.

However, when people are asked which programs should be cut to make the balanced budget possible, we come up against the phenomenon noted in earlier chapters: the only program that a majority are ready to see cut is welfare.

This latter point reflects another important aspect of public attitudes on economic and social issues: the resentment toward the poor. This antipathy is not unqualified: most people believe that government should see to it that poor people do not lack the necessities of life, and both Johnson's War on Poverty and Nixon's Family Assistance Plan received broad approval in the polls.

However, contrasting with this attitude is another view, often held by the same people who support many government programs to help the poor. The traditional American position is that people ought not to get something for nothing. This emphasis on self-reliance became less central as the farmer gave way to the urbanite, and it was severely shaken by the Great Depression. Still, the belief persists that we are more worthy if we contribute to the economy and work for a living, and that dependence for survival on the support of the community makes us morally inferior. Accordingly, to large numbers of people the poor are a shiftless lot—lazy, apathetic, much given to antisocial behavior, including crime—with no one to blame for their misfortune but themselves.

Generally speaking, the affluent have been the least prone to these unsympathetic attitudes. Hostility to the poor in recent years has been more commonly found among those people who are little more than just above the poverty line. Typically they lived separately from the very poor, but not far removed. And they did not want their communities to be invaded by the poor, because this intrusion, they thought, would lead to a decline in their property values, deterioration of the standards of the neighborhood schools, and disruption of the public order.

One other dimension to the resentment of the poor was racial prejudice, for many of the people on welfare were black. But the resentment was also felt against poor whites. After all, many working-class and lower-middle-class whites had established only a precarious foothold on success. They were having great difficulty in sustaining what they regarded as a reasonable standard of living. They had to make payments on their mortgages and put some money aside because they wanted to give their children a better start in life than they had had themselves. Higher taxes to underwrite people who for lack of will or effort or morality (for this image was held by the majority) were perpetual failures inevitably aroused resentments.

So there were two competing pulls within majority attitudes toward the poor— the one benign and charitable, the other grudging and resentful. Which of them dominated varied with the circumstances of the time. During the Great Depression a majority were poor, related to someone poor, or afraid of imminently becoming poor. So poverty was no stigma but a socially produced calamity. But later, when the majority had been able to take advantage of the opportunities opened to them by the system, they tended to assume that those people who had not been able to "make it" had something wrong with them as individuals, some defect of will or character that made them unwilling to work for a living.

The poor should not be left to starve. The majority still maintained that government must do something about them. And the majority's benevolence could be especially expansive in the case of the War on Poverty, for the declaration of this war closely followed a federal income tax cut of $11.5 billion.

But these circumstances changed quickly. Inflation, fueled by the Vietnam War, began to impose severe strains on the economy. More and more claims were made on the federal budget, and some of them had to be rejected. Expenditures on antipoverty programs were going up. Then there was the frustrating fact that, despite all the money that was being spent on so many antipoverty programs, the number of people on welfare in several states and cities was actually increasing. The Aid to Families with Dependent Children program became the most rapidly growing part of relief outlays. And, although there was general support for the view that government must help children, there was also growing resentment at what was felt to be irresponsible behavior by the parents—behavior that placed a heavy tax burden on the rest of the population.

Throughout these events, ironically, the fundamental political problem of the poor in the post–World War II era has been the fact that their numbers have been reduced to a minority, a decreasing minority, of the population. This very accomplishment has made the position of the poor weak, tending to isolate them from the rest of the society. Prospects for programs helpful to the poor have improved when these programs have also offered benefits to much broader segments of the population, which was true of Social Security, for example, and of Medicare. But support for programs that are seen by the majority to be designed specifically and exclusively for the poor—public housing, the War on Poverty— has generally been lukewarm at best.

FIVE PERSPECTIVES ON THE ECONOMY AND POVERTY

THE CONSERVATIVES: PROGRESS THROUGH INCENTIVES

As we have noted in previous chapters, the key to the conservative approach to economic affairs is the need to provide incentives to stimulate output and thus increase economic growth. The most important incentives, as conservatives see it, are the lure of profits and the spur of competition.

However, since the 1930s incentives have been taken away through high taxes and government regulation. Moreover, the enormous expansion of government and the increase in the money supply to pay for that expansion have been the principal causes of the most harmful of all economic diseases—inflation.

Inflation is the great threat to economic growth, stability, and justice. It unfairly penalizes people on fixed incomes, notably the elderly. It pushes up the cost of government. It unleashes an ever-upward wage-price spiral that, at some point, leads businesspeople to lose confidence in the economy's stability and cut back on inventories and new orders. This pattern leads to a recession, which involves high rates of unemployment. Thus the conservatives argue that their concern with inflation is not a heartless disregard of the suffering caused by unemployment but a necessary condition of preventing unemployment.

In any case, say the conservatives, by the 1970s we had sluggish growth, unemployment, and inflation at the same time. The much-admired

Keynesian techniques for government regulation of the economy were obviously not working. As they failed to restrain prices, the public, misled by the false teaching of the liberals, called for wage and price controls.

To conservatives, wage and price controls are abhorrent on two grounds. First, they represent the grossest interference with people's freedom, and they take us a long way down the road to serfdom. Second, the conservatives insist, controls do not work. As soon as the media carry reports that controls are being considered, businesspeople push up their prices before the controls are imposed. Then, when the controls are introduced, black markets spring up to circumvent them. And as soon as the controls are taken off, the pent-up pressures of inflation burst forth to make up for lost time, because nothing has happened in the meantime to remove inflation's underlying causes.

The conservatives call for a totally different set of concepts to deal with our economic ailments, and on the whole, they see these concepts embodied in the program presented by the Reagan administration. There are, as we have noted, divisions within the conservative camp on the specific programs adopted by the administration. Monetarists disagree on important points with the supply-side analysts,[14] and the supply-siders are also criticized by those conservatives who believe that first priority must be given to bringing budgetary deficits under control. However, there is a conservative consensus behind the three principles of the Reagan administration's economic policy: less government spending, lower taxes, and reduced government regulation.

This prescription for economic growth, as we noted, starts from the assumption that people will try harder and risk more if they are given material incentives to do so. As a result, some will rise well above the average and some will fall below, so that inequality must be accepted and even applauded. However, says Milton Friedman, it is simply not true that capitalism "is a system under which the rich exploit the poor. Wherever the free market has been permitted to operate, . . . the ordinary man has been able to attain levels of living never dreamed of before. Nowhere is the gap between rich and poor wider . . . than in those societies that do not permit the free market to operate."[15]

These results occur, says Friedman, in feudal and caste-ridden societies; and they are no less true in totalitarian countries like the Soviet Union, where most of the power goes to a small self-perpetuating elite, and with it material privileges far beyond the reach of ordinary citizens.

Certainly in the United States there are some very rich people. But their wealth is necessary both as an incentive to themselves and others and as a source of investment. Moreover, the mass of the people live extraordinarily well by the standards of any other society in history.

This fortunate state of affairs does not quite include everybody. The poor are still with us. But, say the conservatives, they are not with us to the degree suggested by the official statistics. Figure 12-3 indicated an inability of our system to bring the proportion living below the poverty line to less than 12 percent of the population, but these statistics are misleading for two reasons. First, many of the poor do not report their full income because to do so would cost them benefits under various government welfare programs. Second, low-income people are eligible for food stamps, housing subsidies, medical care, and other services that are the equivalent of income. If these noncash benefits are taken into account, the proportion of people

living in poverty in America in 1979 was little more than 3 percent rather than the 12 percent identified by the Census Bureau.[16]

Conservatives do not conclude from this data that government should do nothing about the poor. However, in their view the federal government has been doing all the wrong things. It has created programs like AFDC and food stamps, which reinforce a dependence on the governmental handout. Moreover, some of the programs have been riddled with corruption. Billions of dollars a year are lost through cheating by welfare recipients, dishonest doctors making fraudulent claims under Medicaid, and parents underestimating their incomes to qualify their children for free or reduced-price school lunches. As for food stamps, they have become a second currency, used in the purchase of almost any commodity, including liquor and guns, and extensively counterfeited.

Given the nature and size of these programs corruption is inevitable; and given the constituencies served by the programs and the bureaucracies they employ, they have a built-in drive for expansion. As we saw in figure 12-7, the number of people receiving food stamps doubled in a decade, and the program's cost went up almost 500 percent; the cost of AFDC went up nearly 100 percent, Medicaid almost 700 percent. We could not go on this way, and the Reagan administration did the right thing in calling a halt to their runaway expansion and in cutting back on their cost.

Instead of these programs, conservatives want to see more of the burden assumed by the family and by private charity; government's role should be limited to the hard core of people who, because of physical or mental disability, or the lack of any competence to handle a job, are simply not able to fend for themselves. Welfare programs should be reformed to achieve the removal from benefits of all but the truly needy, the establishment of a benefit structure that does not take away the incentive to work, the elimination of fraud, improved administrative efficiency, and a shift of more responsibility from the federal government to state and local governments and to private institutions.[17]

SIMPSON IN "TULSA TRIBUNE"

"Uh, doctor . . . how long are we going to continue collecting medicaid for Mr. Grimsley, here?"

In addition to welfare reform, conservatives would remove the barriers to the creation of job opportunities that have been erected by federal legislation. The minimum wage should be lowered or abolished; by imposing an artificial minimum, government forces some employers of unskilled labor out of business or makes them substitute machines for people. Then, too, the ease with which people can qualify for unemployment benefits, the size of the benefits, and the extension of the period for which they are given have encouraged a considerable number of people to go on the unemployment rolls rather than look for work.

Finally, conservatives believe that the ultimate solution for poverty in America is to follow their prescription for economic growth. By providing the incentives to invest and work harder we can restore the vitality of the private enterprise system and thereby create an even more abundant society than we have enjoyed hitherto. This abundance will not be distributed equally, and any attempt to make it do so will be self-destructive, because it will take away the incentives that are the dynamic element in the system. But the opportunity will be there for anyone who makes the effort to enjoy a high and rising standard of living. For those people who cannot, society has an obligation to provide a sufficiency. For those people who can but will not, society has no such obligation.

THE RADICAL RIGHT: STOP THE RUSH TO SOCIALISM

To the radical right, America's economic policies since the 1930s have been essentially indistinguishable from socialism. Keynesianism, the product of an effete British intellectual, is a set of techniques for the socialist takeover. It has been adopted by American intellectuals and their institutional bases in the universities, the Brookings Institution, the Ford and Rockefeller Foundations, and the Committee for Economic Development. They drew up the blueprints for the New Deal and the Great Society, and they drafted the plans for disruption and riot that went by the name of the Community Action Program.

The partners of these socialist intellectuals were the great armies of bureaucrats their scheme brought into being, who then became an irresistible force for their self-perpetuation and self-aggrandizement.

Between them they created enormous constituencies of noncontributors to society, shiftless people who would rather get on welfare than work or who demand that government support their illegitimate children rather than provide a stable family upbringing themselves. In their turn these recipients of lavish public philanthropy organize to force government to give bigger and bigger grants to more and more people, all at the expense of the overburdened taxpayer.

Behind all these groups is a small group of very rich insiders: the Rockefellers, Fords, Kennedys, and so on. But why should the rich be working for socialism? It is because "socialism is not a share-the-wealth program, but in reality a method to *consolidate* and *control* the wealth."[18] This fact is true in the Soviet Union, which is not an egalitarian society but a highly stratified system in which a few at the top live very well. In this country, the rich design programs that hand out money to the poor at the expense not of themselves but of the great majority of the country, including businesspeople who are not part of the club of superrich insiders.

Poverty, the extent of which is vastly exaggerated by the intellectuals, the media, and the other opinion molders of the country, should be dealt with by private charity and by strictly administered state and local action. The problems of the poor should not be used as a rationale for moving the country faster and faster toward socialism.

Instead, government spending should be slashed, budget deficits ended, and the income tax abolished by repeal of the Sixteenth Amendment.

THE LIBERALS: INEQUALITY IN AMERICA

To the liberals the policies promoted by the conservatives, and adopted in large part by the Reagan administration, are both unworkable and morally wrong.

They are unworkable, the liberals contend, for two reasons. First, the combination of reduced domestic spending and high interest rates was producing a depressed economy, with high unemployment and large numbers of business bankruptcies. Second, the reduction in inflation, which was the administration's only accomplishment in 1982, is likely to be only temporary. Over the long run the military buildup could well have the same kind of impact on inflation as did the spending on the Vietnam War. That spending, without any countermanding tax increase to siphon off the money that it poured into the economy, started the upward spiral of prices that has never been halted. Now we are about to spend further vast sums on military affairs, and far from imposing a tax increase to pay for it, we are actually cutting taxes.

Still, the pragmatic question is not the most important aspect of the liberal critique of Reaganite economics. After all, the first phase of the tax cut in 1981 came at a time when the economy was moving so slowly as to be close to a recession; and Democratic administrations, following Keynesian principles, had been known to cut taxes to stimulate the economy.

The real complaint of the liberals was that the conservatives were pursuing a policy that was morally reprehensible. It was wrong on two counts, both related to the liberals' belief in a more egalitarian society.

First, the tax reductions advocated by conservatives and accepted by the Reagan administration were heavily biased in favor of the upper-income groups and business corporations. The very poor, of course, benefited not at all because they paid

© 1981 AUTH-PHILADELPHIA INQUIRER

little or no income tax. But because the percentage reduction in taxes was the same for all who paid taxes, those taxpayers who paid the highest rates gained the most. This change is precisely opposite from the kind of change in the tax structure that liberals advocated. For years they had been arguing for tax reform, by which they meant closing down the tax shelters and eliminating the loopholes opened in the law by the armies of accountants and lawyers retained by the rich to make a mockery of the progressive aspect of the income tax. The reformers had been able to make some minor changes during the Carter years, but despite the conservatives' complaints that the income, inheritance, and capital gains taxes were taking away all incentives to earn more, somehow the rich survived. And some are very rich indeed: a few are billionaires; at least 50 families are worth $100 million or more; some hundreds of families own around $10 million; and close to 600,000 are in the millionaire class.[19] Almost a quarter of the wealth of the country—real estate, stocks, bonds, cash, and so on—is concentrated in the hands of 1 percent of the population.[20]

Yet the conservatives claimed that the tax system was unfair to the upper-income groups, and the Reagan administration responded by changes in the income and inheritance taxes that would increase still further the concentration of wealth.

The rationale for this arrangement was that the wealthy would put their increased funds to work in productive investment, and that eventually, as David Stockman explained in his all-too-candid utterances reported in the *Atlantic* in December 1981, the benefits would "trickle down" to the poor.[21] But that process had usually provided only crumbs for the poor. Even that much should not be anticipated in this situation, said the liberals, because the extra money would most likely be used by corporations to buy other corporations, and by individuals to purchase more luxuries or to engage in nonproductive financial manipulations.

It was not only the Reagan administration's tax program that the liberals believed to be unfair and discriminatory. They found the spending cuts reprehensible, because here again the lowest-income groups bore the brunt of the reductions. The diet of the poor, their already inadequate hospital care, and their children's opportunity to go to college all suffered severely at the hands of the conservatives in the White House and in Congress. Yet the Pentagon's budget was planned to go up by 7 percent or more a year *after inflation*.

In justifying these reductions conservatives argue that the extent of poverty is greatly overstated by the official figures and that much federal money is wasted on people who are not really needy. To this argument the liberals reply that the 12 to 13 percent figure used by federal agencies in assessing the proportion living below the poverty line is, in fact, an underestimate. The poverty level for an urban family of four in 1980 was set at $8,414. Yet each year the U.S. Department of Labor issues an estimate of living costs for high, intermediate, and low standards of living for an urban family of four. In 1980 its figure for the *low* standard was $14,044. A poverty line set at 60 percent of the department's lowest category was not, in the liberals' interpretation, overly generous.

It is true, the liberals say, that poverty in America has been significantly reduced since the 1950s. But most of those gains were made in the 1960s as a result of the vigorous efforts of the federal government. Those gains did not continue into the 1970s. The proportion living in poverty remained at about 12 percent; it went up to 13 percent in 1980; and the Reagan policies would add millions to the numbers below the poverty line.

The liberals do not contend that the poverty programs have been without fault. But the cases of fraud and waste have been greatly exaggerated by conservatives and by sensational media coverage. We do not need the conservatives' heartless slashing of federal aid to the poor, but rather we need an expanded effort based on the principles of a guaranteed annual income, an expanded array of other federal programs for lower-income people, full employment, and controls when inflation becomes excessive.

A guaranteed annual income.[22] In a country of such abundance we should be able to provide to all of our people a minimum standard below which no one should be allowed to fall. The fact is that we already accept this idea in principle. But, because we are afraid to recognize it as a basic right, we surround it with bureaucratic restrictions and paperwork that are enormously expensive, that infuriate and humiliate the recipients, and that invite evasion and cheating. Benefits under the programs vary enormously from state to state, and they impose a burden on state and local budgets that makes the programs—and the poor—the target of widespread hostility. What is needed is a federal program that will cut through all the red tape and offer an assured subsistence level for all those people who, for whatever reasons, are simply unable to provide adequately for themselves.

An expanded array of other federal programs for lower-income people. Even with a guaranteed minimum income, the cost of certain commodities, particularly medical care and housing, has become so great that people with low or even moderate incomes cannot possibly afford them without some government help. Medicare helps the elderly, but the health problems of younger people can only be attended to through a comprehensive national health program. And the public housing program is too limited and too sterile. Without a much greater involvement of the federal government in the housing field, we shall see a serious deterioration in our stock of housing, because the cost of construction and credit is so high that in many communities nobody can afford to buy a home unless he or she is in the upper-middle-income group.

Full employment.   At the center of the liberals' economic proposals is a policy of full employment. A number of surveys indicate that most of the poor want to work as long as the job pays them a reasonable wage. Some—the aged, the incapacitated, large families headed by the mother alone—cannot work, so they need the guaranteed income and other government assistance. Some who can work do not want to, but these people constitute a small minority, probably no larger than the shiftless element found at any economic level. If there are plenty of jobs and training programs to develop the necessary skills, there will be a strong demand for workers, just as during World War II, when there were hardly any unemployed.

Yet since the 1970s unemployment has ranged most of the time between 7 and 9 percent; and these figures do not take account of the people—mostly married women and teenagers—who have given up any hope of getting a job and so have withdrawn from the labor market. Liberals recognize that full employment does not mean that 100 percent of the work force should have jobs, because there will always be some people between jobs, and there will be shifts in the economy that will cause temporary dislocation. But liberals contend that, given a vigorous economy, there need be no more than about 4 percent out of work at any given time, which means that we must pursue monetary policies that do not choke off the supply of money needed by an expanding economy; fiscal policies that provide the needed infusion of government spending whenever the economy lags; and a program of federal, state, and local jobs that makes government the "employer of last resort" when the private sector fails to put people to work.

Controls when inflation becomes excessive.
Liberals are generally more tolerant of a certain amount of inflation than are conservatives, be-cause they fear that the traditional methods for combating inflation are likely to cause a further rise in unemployment. Still, they recognize that the pace of price increases since 1973 has been excessive; and although they do not agree with conservatives that inflation is caused primarily by government spending and deficits,[23] they concede that the major increases in government spending that they advocate could cause further upward pressure on prices.

To combat inflation, liberals propose three kinds of action. First, the tax loopholes that favor the rich should be closed, thereby bringing in more revenue. Second, the defense budget should be reduced by tens of billions of dollars. Third, the ability of giant business corporations to raise prices at will must be attacked. The free enterprise doctrine is based on the notion of prices being set by open competition between a large number of firms. In fact, in many fields a few corporations have become so dominant that they are no longer subject to competitive market forces. Even when business falls off they raise their prices. What we are faced with in those cases is not a competitive price structure but "administered" prices imposed on us by administrative decision of the managers of the corporations.

To some extent this problem can be dealt with by much more vigorous enforcement of the antitrust laws. But this way involves slow and cumbersome procedures; the surest way for government to deal with inflation of more than 10 percent a year is to impose controls on prices and wages. And if these controls are to be effective, they cannot be adopted as a stopgap interlude, but must be a long-term policy sustained until the underlying pressures for rapidly rising prices have been dissipated.

This approach may seem draconian, say the liberals, but if a conservative president like Nixon was ready to adopt controls as a temporary expedient, liberals should not flinch at the prospect of a more thoroughgoing strategy for dealing with inflation—a strategy that simply replaces price controls by the corporations with price controls by the public.

THE RADICAL LEFT: RULE BY THE RICH

However strong the liberals' attack on the prevailing economic policies, they are still denounced by the left for their failure to see that no fundamental redistribution can come about within the existing framework.

Certainly some concessions have been made by the ruling group. The moderate wing of the power elite are capable of "reacting to pressure from below and granting some degree of satisfaction to the unhappy," says G. William Domhoff.[24] But they make these concessions to provide a safety valve for what might otherwise be dangerous discontent, and the concessions do not challenge the privileges of the rulers or narrow the range of inequality.

In fact, the liberals, by persisting in their fight for reform measures, prevent the people from seeing the basic realities and inequalities of the system. Gradualism does not lead us toward a just society; it moves us farther away from it. By moving a proportion of the population out of acute poverty into a slightly more tolerable condition, gradualist reform lessens the hostility needed to create a revolution.

Of all the antipoverty proposals considered in this chapter, only one is perceived by the left as containing acceptable values. The idea in CAP that the poor must be helped to organize themselves to develop a sense of power and meaning, to free themselves from the inferiority to which they have been assigned, and to challenge existing bastions of power is very much in line with the strategies advocated by the radical left.

However, in the left's perspective CAP was doomed to failure. Beyond a point, government would not allow structures created by itself to challenge its own authority. Once the administration realized that it had unleashed forces that could be dangerously abrasive, it was inevitable that it would quickly rein in those forces.

At the heart of the matter is the fact that we are controlled by a ruling class that is ready to make some concessions from time to time but never to relinquish its power or to change its cherished values. As Michael Parenti puts it: "By its very nature, the capitalist system is compelled to exploit the resources and labor of society for the purpose of maximizing profits. It is this operational imperative of the system which creates the imbalances of the investment, the neglect of social needs, the privation, wastage and general oppression and inequality which bring misery to so many."[25]

So it is a contradiction in terms to expect capitalism to abolish poverty. As long as the acquisitive, competitive ethic that is fostered by corporate capitalism remains, it is inevitable that the poor will be derided and scorned by the rest of society. Only when the corporations become servants of the community, rather than of large shareholders, will they be turned away from frivolous and even dangerous purposes toward the task of ending poverty. Only when we care less about success and ambition and more about building a community in which everyone is accorded dignity and respect can the curse of poverty be lifted.

THE CENTRISTS: THE GREAT AMERICAN MIDDLE CLASS

Until recently, whenever centrists looked at the American record on the production and distribution of wealth, they saw a remarkable success story. "Something has happened in the United States in recent years," said Ben Wattenberg in 1976, "that has never happened before anywhere: The massive majority of the population is now in the middle class."[26]

This situation had come about in the first place because of the impressive growth of the economy. Business, labor, and agriculture were the prime movers in this achievement, but government had played an essential role. Economic growth in America was the product of the partnership between the public and private sectors.

Then, too, the United States had achieved a remarkable degree of economic stability. We had acquired the economic tools to ensure that the Great Depression would never happen again. There would be unemployment, and in a dynamic economy the liberals' goal of only 4 percent unemployment was too ambitious, but 5 or 6 percent was certainly within the realm of possibility.

Finally, through a combination of private sector efforts and government programs, poverty had been reduced to a small minority of the population. Although the problem was still greater than the conservatives were prepared to admit, the system had worked well in reducing the proportion below the poverty line to 12 or 13 percent. (In fact, when food stamps and other benefits are taken into account, the true poverty figure is less than 13 percent.) Moreover, by the standards of most of the people of the world, the poor in America enjoyed an enviable standard of living: so much so that great numbers continued to pour illegally across our southern borders to participate in the fruits of our economy.

Doubts began to mar this roseate view of the American economic system from the mid-1970s. The slowing of economic growth and the decline in productivity; the erosion of our competitiveness with imported manufactures; the years of double-digit inflation—all caused centrists to be a little less certain about the American economy's becoming the first in the world to produce true abundance and to offer unlimited opportunities to all its citizens.

Even so, centrists today insist that the predictions of economic disaster heard on all sides are without foundation, and that the remedies need not be nearly as drastic as either the liberals or conservatives propose.

Thus the Reagan administration was right to slow down the growth of federal spending and to set limits to antipoverty programs that sometimes lavished money on people well beyond the poverty range. However, the Reagan cuts went too far, too fast.

Centrists were still more concerned about Reagan's three-year, 25 percent reduction in income tax rates at a time when inflation was still high and bigger federal budget deficits were in prospect. This policy appeared to them to be an imprudent gamble based on ideological rigidity rather than on sound economic analysis.

At the same time, centrists reject the liberals' proposals for further large increases in federal spending and for wage-price controls as a means of restraining inflation. These policies seem to centrists to be irrelevant, based on the same kind of ideological inflexibility that afflicts the conservatives.

In fact, the long-term economic outlook is not necessarily bleak. The enormous increases in oil prices of the 1970s are unlikely to be repeated in the 1980s, which will remove one of the major sources of economic instability. Further improvement can be obtained if government, working with business and labor, provides a modest amount of stimulation through monetary and fiscal policies.

As for the distribution of the resulting increases in output, due attention should be paid to the needs of the poor. But there must also be concern for the interests of the middle class. We must reject proposals that ignore those interests in favor of the poor (as is true of the liberals' ideas) or of the rich (as is the case with some of the Reagan administration's policies). Such proposals make for bad public policy. They are also likely to be politically suicidal, because the group they neglect happens to be the majority of the American electorate.

CONCLUSION

The subject of the American economy has habitually defied the predictions of the experts, because in this field the tools of policy making are still clumsy and error-prone.

For three decades or so the Keynesians held sway, and indeed we enjoyed a period of economic growth with only mild fluctuations instead of the wide swings from prosperity to depression that used to be the pattern. This stability created the near-certainty that we now had available the techniques required to ensure steady and permanent growth. All that was needed now was "fine-tuning"— delicate adjustments in one direction or the other to keep unemployment and inflation within bounds.

But the experts' sophisticated techniques could not handle the inflationary forces unleashed by Vietnam, exploding oil prices, and a variety of other factors. With unemployment also holding at levels previously considered politically intolerable, the prestige of the Keynesian school fell into decline.

Then came the turn of the "classical" school of economics, which taught the virtues of private enterprise and the market system. However, believers in this school are burdened by the fact that, apart from the Civil War, the greatest disaster ever suffered by the American system—the Great Depression—came out of an era of almost untrammeled private enterprise. Moreover, even within this school there are disagreements, including concern by some about the timing of the Reagan administration's tax cuts.

This skepticism will be out of favor—and the Republican party will dominate the next decade of American politics—if during the Reagan years we experience a revitalized economy, stable prices, and progress toward a balanced budget. Yet even then the state of our knowledge is such that we shall not be sure how much of the success is due to the Reagan policies and how much to world forces little influenced by our actions.

On the more specific subject of poverty in America we again encounter wide differences based partly on ideology, partly on uncertainty about the facts. We know that poverty has been substantially reduced since the 1950s. But there is disagreement on why this happened and on how much poverty remains. The only thing that is clear is that enough poverty persists to be a cause of tension and instability in the social order. This fact becomes especially apparent when we relate it to the subject of our next chapter: the condition of disadvantaged minorities in America.

NOTES AND REFERENCES

1. However, the United States was not alone in facing a decline in the rate of productivity increase. According to the Joint Economic Committee of Congress, in Japan the annual productivity gains from 1960 to 1973 were 10.3 percent, but from 1973 to 1979 the rate was down to 6.9 percent. In the same period Sweden's annual productivity gain declined from 6.7 to 2.4 percent, France's from 5.8 to 4.8 percent, and Britain's from 4.0 to 0.5 percent. The decline in West Germany was much less: from 5.5 to 5.3 percent.
2. These figures are based on the Consumer Price Index, prepared by the Department of Labor from a theoretical market basket of goods and services purchased by urban wage earners. The items are changed periodically to reflect shifts in consumer patterns and tastes, but the index is still criticized as being insufficiently sensitive to these shifts.
3. Totals for these categories are more than 100 percent because some people, such as black southern families headed by women, or young unemployed Latinos, fit into two or more categories.

4. See, for example, Oscar Lewis, *La Vida* (New York: Random House, 1966).

5. See, for example, Leonard Goodwin, *Do the Poor Want to Work?* (Washington, D.C.: The Brookings Institution, 1973).

6. Nixon believed he had lost to Kennedy in 1960 because Eisenhower had allowed a recession to develop, and Nixon was determined not to let that happen again.

7. Jimmy Carter had been accused by liberals of trying to accomplish this aim. But he subsequently became a strong critic of Reagan's approach, contending that its cuts in programs for the poor went much too far.

8. As we noted in the chapter on the presidency, however, had it not been for Watergate Nixon, in his second term, might have moved in the direction later followed by Reagan.

9. In 1982, the second year of the income tax cut, a family of four with $20,000 in taxable income saved $228; a family with $40,000 saved $639; a family with $100,000 saved $2,137. For investors, the top tax rate on unearned income was cut from 70 to 50 percent, and the maximum tax rate on capital gains (profits from the sale of assets such as stocks and bonds and real estate) was lowered from 28 to 20 percent. New depreciation rules, faster tax writeoffs, the exchange of tax credits, and reductions in corporate tax rates for small corporations would produce a large reduction in corporate taxes. Other 1982 tax changes included reductions in inheritance taxes; Individual Retirement Accounts enabling individuals to save $2,000 a year, deductible from income tax, with interest tax-free until retirement, even if they are already covered by retirement programs at their places of work; and a change in taxes paid by married couples to correct an inequity favoring two single people with the same total income as a married couple. Also approved was a plan to follow the 25 percent income tax cut with tax *indexing*, a system of adjusting the income tax tables to prevent people from being moved into higher tax brackets simply because their earnings had been pushed upward by inflation.

10. Among the principal proponents of supply-side economics were University of Southern California economist Arthur Laffer and Congressman Jack Kemp.

11. The case for this position is that the government, in order to finance the deficit, must either create new money, which is likely to be inflationary, or borrow in the credit market; if it borrows the huge amounts required to cover the deficits, the government will be competing with other borrowers for limited amounts of funds, which will force up the interest rates.

12. Community Action was the brainchild of a task force appointed by President Johnson and chaired by President Kennedy's Peace Corps director, Sargent Shriver. Shriver drew on the advice not only of the regular departments of the federal government, but also of people from business, city government, the universities, local welfare agencies, the Ford Foundation, and two writers of the left, Michael Harrington, a Socialist, and Paul Jacobs, a radical writer and editor. The Economic Opportunity Act, which grew out of their deliberations, created local poverty agencies that bypassed the existing structures of local and state government, much to the distress of a number of elected political leaders. It seems clear that the plan to go outside and around the conventional political structures was not really understood by President Johnson, who was surprised at the vehemence of the opposition provoked by the Community Action agencies.

13. However, by early 1982 polls suggested that a rising proportion of the public was beginning to worry more about unemployment than about inflation.

14. In response to criticisms mounting by late 1981 that their remedies were not working, supply-side theorists made three points:

   a. The criticism was premature; their prescription had not had enough time to work.
   b. If it failed it was because it had been applied too slowly. A large one-time tax reduction would have jolted the economy out of its doldrums. The three-year phased reduction, starting with only a 5 percent cut, had merely offset Social Security tax increases and the tax boost that inflation foisted on people in the absence of indexing.
   c. One other element needed to be added: a return to the gold standard.

15. Milton Friedman, *Free to Choose* (New York: Avon, 1981), p. 137.

16. See Morton Parglin, "Transfers in Kind: Their Impact on Poverty, 1959–1975," paper presented at the Hoover Institution Conference on Income Redistribution, October 1977, p. 14; and *Newsweek*, 23 March 1981, p. 24.

17. See Martin Anderson, "Welfare Reform," in Peter Duignan and Alvin Rabushka (eds.), *The United States in the 1980s* (Stanford, Calif.: Hoover Institution Press, 1980), pp. 170–177. Earlier Milton Friedman had proposed a "negative income tax," which would establish a minimum level of income and use the Internal Revenue Service mechanism to provide anyone whose income fell below that level the amount needed to bring them up to the prescribed minimum. This plan was designed to replace existing programs for the poor, and the premise was that poverty is simply a lack of income, so the cure is to put money into the pockets of the poor to get them into the market economy. However, few other conservatives bought the idea, because it sounded too much like the liberals' prescription for a guaranteed minimum income.

18. Gary Allen, *None Dare Call It Conspiracy* (Rossmoor, Calif.: Concord Press, 1971), pp. 32–33.

19. See *Newsweek*, 2 August 1976, pp. 56–59, and *U.S. News and World Report*, September 22, 1980, p. 12.

20. See James D. Smith and Stephen D. Franklin, "The Concentration of Personal Wealth, 1922–1969," *American Economic Review* 64, no. 2 (1974); James D. Smith, unpublished estimates, The Urban Institute, Washington, D.C., and the Pennsylvania State University; and U.S. Congress, House Committee on the Budget, *Data on Distribution of Wealth in the United States.*

21. As Stockman explained it, the across-the-board tax cut was essentially a "Trojan horse," because unless the middle classes had been included it would have been politically impossible to provide the tax relief where the administration believed it would do the most economic good—among the upper-income groups and the corporations. William Greider, "The Education of David Stockman," *Atlantic*, December 1981, p. 46.

22. See Robert Theobald, *Beyond Despair*, rev. ed. (Cabin John, Md.: Seven Locks Press, 1981).

23. Liberals point out that other countries with larger deficits than our own have had lower rates of inflation. In 1977–1979, total government deficits in the United States were less than 1 percent of GNP; the equivalent figure in West Germany was over 3 percent and in Japan over 6 percent—yet inflation rates in both those countries were well below our own. See Walter Heller, "Economic Policy for Inflation," in *Reflections of America* (Washington, D.C.: U.S., Department of Commerce, Bureau of the Census, 1980), p. 86. Similarly liberals argue that the other great ogre of the conservatives, the national debt, has grown in the aggregate but has declined as a proportion of GNP from 50 percent in 1959 to little more than 30 percent in 1982.

24. G. William Domhoff, *The Higher Circles: The Governing Class in America* (New York: Vintage Books, 1970), p. 250.

25. Michael Parenti, *Democracy for the Few* (New York: St. Martin's Press, 1980), p. 33.

26. Ben J. Wattenberg, *The Real America: A Surprising Examination of the State of the Union* (New York: Capricorn Books, 1976), p. 51.

chapter thirteen

EQUAL PROTECTION? RACE, ETHNICITY, GENDER

The most widely used metaphor to depict the making of the American nation out of many national backgrounds is that of the "melting pot." This phrase implies that, through universally available education and access to unprecedented opportunities, each immigrant group in turn was "Americanized" into a common set of beliefs, attitudes, and loyalties, as well as a common language.

Some critics have challenged this notion, contending that America remains a profoundly diverse country culturally, and that a number of ethnic groups, especially those from Eastern and Southern Europe, have retained powerful loyalties to their separate ethnic customs and values.[1]

Whether or not the melting pot idea applies to the white ethnic groups, there can be no debate about the fact that certain minorities have not yet been fully absorbed into the mainstream of opportunity and, on the average, do not enjoy the same levels of income or educational and occupational attainment as do the majority. Among these groups the most disadvantaged are blacks, people of Spanish origin,[2] and American Indians. Many of the recent arrivals from various parts of Asia suffer from considerable deprivation, but, generally speaking, Asian-Americans have tended to move up the educational, economic, and occupational ladders quite rapidly.

THE POPULATIONS OF AMERICA

As table 13-1 shows, population gains among these minorities since 1970 have been much greater than among the white majority. Asians and American Indians have grown faster than any other group, but blacks and Hispanics constitute easily the largest minority groups in America. In 1980 blacks officially constituted 11.7 percent of the total population, Hispanics 6.4 percent. The distribution of blacks and Hispanics by state and city is indicated in table 13-2.

TABLE 13–1 Population growth for majority and minority groups, 1970–1980

	1970 (millions)	1980 (millions)	Percent increase
Whites	177.7	188.3	6
Blacks	22.6	26.5[b]	17
Spanish origin[a]	9.1	14.6[b]	61
American Indian, Eskimo, and Aleut	.8	1.4	71
Asian and Pacific Islanders	1.5	3.5	128

[a]Fifty-six percent of the Spanish origin group defined themselves as "white," the remainder as "other." So 56 percent of those people of Spanish origin are also included in the total for whites.

[b]Census Bureau estimates of black and Hispanic populations have been challenged as undercounts because of the difficulties in conducting the census in inner city areas. Hispanic leaders, in particular, have contended that the undercount of undocumented aliens from Latin American countries is so great that people of Spanish origin are already close to outnumbering blacks.

The Census Bureau has conceded that in 1980 blacks were undercounted by 5 percent and Hispanics by 4.4 percent. But the bureau claims that its coverage in 1980 was much improved over 1970, so some part of the increase in minority populations is attributable to the improvement in techniques. The bureau does not agree with the Hispanic leaders' projections and insists that, if present trends continue, Hispanics will not outnumber blacks before the year 2057.

Source: U.S., Bureau of the Census, 1981.

Because blacks still constitute the largest of our disadvantaged minorities, their problems will be the principal focus of this chapter. However, we shall also discuss other minorities, particularly Hispanics; and because some federal government programs designed to overcome the disadvantages of minorities have been extended to a majority group—women—we shall include consideration of the occupational and other disabilities that have been imposed on women.

BLACKS AND THE AMERICAN DILEMMA

It is impossible to understand the relationship between blacks and whites in America today without an awareness of its long, troubled history. It began in the sixteenth century when blacks were brought here as slaves from Africa, chained and packed together in such dreadful conditions that great numbers of them died on the voyage over. Once here they were sold and bartered and became the work force for the plantation economy of the South. Recently some economic historians have suggested that the life of the slaves, although harsh, was not as bad as most accounts have suggested, and was better in many respects than the conditions under which many factory workers lived in the North.[3] Other historians have bitterly disputed these findings, both on methodological and factual grounds. But no one questions the central core of the problem: whatever their living conditions, black people were slaves. Apparently, the wording of the Declaration of Independence, that "All men are created equal," did not apply to blacks, because they were property rather than people under the law.

This denial of the blacks' humanity worried more and more people as the nineteenth century progressed, and a move for the abolition of slavery slowly

TABLE 13-2 Distribution of black and Hispanic populations, 1980

	Black		Spanish origin	
	1980 black population	Percentage of total	1980 Hispanic population	Percentage of total
States				
Alabama	995,623	25.6	33,100	0.9
Alaska	13,619	3.4	9,497	2.4
Arizona	75,034	2.8	440,915	16.2
Arkansas	373,192	16.3	17,873	0.8
California	1,819,282	7.7	4,543,770	19.2
Colorado	101,702	3.5	339,300	11.7
Connecticut	217,433	7.0	124,499	4.0
Delaware	95,971	16.1	9,671	1.6
Florida	1,342,478	13.8	857,898	8.8
Georgia	1,465,457	26.8	61,261	1.1
Hawaii	17,352	1.8	71,479	7.4
Idaho	2,716	0.3	36,615	3.9
Illinois	1,675,229	14.7	635,525	5.6
Indiana	414,732	7.6	87,020	1.6
Iowa	41,700	1.4	25,536	0.9
Kansas	126,127	5.3	63,333	2.7
Kentucky	259,490	7.1	27,403	0.7
Louisiana	1,237,263	29.4	99,105	2.4
Maine	3,128	0.3	5,005	0.4
Maryland	958,050	22.7	64,740	1.5
Massachusetts	221,279	3.9	141,043	2.5
Michigan	1,198,710	12.9	162,388	1.8
Minnesota	53,342	1.3	32,124	0.8
Mississippi	887,206	35.2	24,731	1.0
Missouri	514,274	10.5	51,667	1.1
Montana	1,786	0.2	9,974	1.3
Nebraska	48,389	3.1	28,020	1.8
Nevada	50,791	6.4	53,786	6.7
New Hampshire	3,990	0.4	5,587	0.6
New Jersey	924,786	12.6	491,867	6.7
New Mexico	24,042	1.8	476,089	36.6
New York	2,401,842	13.7	1,659,245	9.5
N. Carolina	1,316,050	22.4	56,607	1.0
N. Dakota	2,568	0.4	3,903	0.6
Ohio	1,076,734	10.0	119,880	1.1
Oklahoma	204,658	6.8	57,413	1.9
Oregon	37,059	1.4	65,833	2.5
Pennsylvania	1,047,609	8.8	154,004	1.3
Rhode Island	27,584	2.9	19,707	2.1
S. Carolina	948,146	30.4	33,414	1.1
S. Dakota	2,144	0.3	4,028	0.6
Tennessee	725,949	15.8	34,081	0.7
Texas	1,710,250	12.0	2,985,643	21.0
Utah	9,225	0.6	60,302	4.1
Vermont	1,135	0.2	3,304	0.6
Virginia	1,008,311	18.9	79,873	1.5
Washington	105,544	2.6	119,986	2.9
West Virginia	65,051	3.3	12,707	0.7
Wisconsin	182,593	3.9	62,981	1.3
Wyoming	3,364	0.7	24,499	5.2
U.S. total (including Washington, D.C.)	26,488,218	11.7	14,605,883	6.4

TABLE 13-2 Distribution of black and Hispanic populations, 1980 (continued)

	Black		Spanish origin	
	1980 black population	Percentage of total	1980 Hispanic population	Percentage of total
30 Largest Cities				
New York City........	1,784,124	25.2	1,405,957	19.9
Chicago..............	1,197,000	39.8	422,061	14.0
Los Angeles	505,208	17.0	815,989	27.5
Philadelphia	638,878	37.8	63,570	3.8
Houston	440,257	27.6	281,224	17.6
Detroit	758,939	63.1	28,970	2.4
Dallas	265,594	29.4	111,082	12.3
San Diego...........	77,700	8.9	130,610	14.9
Baltimore	431,151	54.8	7,641	1.0
San Antonio	57,654	7.3	421,774	53.7
Phoenix.............	37,682	4.9	115,572	15.1
Indianapolis	152,626	21.8	6,145	0.9
San Francisco........	86,414	12.7	83,373	12.3
Memphis	307,702	47.6	5,225	0.8
Washington, D.C.	448,229	70.3	17,652	2.8
San Jose	29,157	4.6	140,574	22.1
Milwaukee	146,940	23.1	26,111	4.1
Cleveland	251,347	43.8	17,772	3.1
Columbus, Ohio	124,880	22.1	4,651	0.8
Boston..............	126,229	22.4	36,068	6.4
New Orleans	308,136	55.3	19,219	3.4
Jacksonville	137,324	25.4	9,775	1.8
Seattle..............	46,755	9.5	12,646	2.6
Denver	59,252	12.1	91,937	18.7
Nashville............	105,942	23.3	3,627	0.8
St. Louis............	206,386	45.6	5,531	1.2
Kansas City, Mo.......	122,699	27.4	14,703	3.3
El Paso	13,466	3.2	265,819	62.5
Atlanta	282,912	66.6	5,842	1.4
Pittsburgh...........	101,813	24.0	3,196	0.8

Source: Reprinted from "U.S. News and World Report," May 4, 1981. Copyright 1981, U.S. News and World Report, Inc.

gained ground. At the very least, the northern states, which did not allow slavery, wanted to stop the spread of the institution from the South into the newly developing regions of the West. The tension built and was brought to fever pitch by the Supreme Court's *Dred Scott* decision in 1857, in which Chief Justice Roger Taney declared that a slave had no constitutional rights because he was not a citizen under the Constitution.

The South seceded over the slavery issue. The Civil War was fought primarily over the determination of Lincoln and the North to restore the Union. But when it was over, the issue that had precipitated the war had to be dealt with. The South was for slavery, and the South lost. The Thirteenth Amendment abolished slavery in 1865; the Fourteenth Amendment in 1868 reversed the *Dred Scott* decision, made citizens of the former slaves, and included the stern instruction so much quoted in later court decisions that "no State shall . . . deny to any person within its jurisdiction the equal protection of the laws." In 1870 the Fifteenth

Amendment gave black males the right to vote, and it was followed in 1875 by the Civil Rights Act, which provided for equal public accommodations for blacks.

RECONSTRUCTION AND REACTION

These legal guarantees for black people were issued during the period of Reconstruction, which was interpreted by the South as a vengeful effort by northerners to destroy their way of life. They awaited their opportunity to strike back, and they took as their signal a decision by the United States Supreme Court in 1883 declaring the 1875 Civil Rights Act unconstitutional. The southern states passed "Jim Crow" laws to make segregation of the races official, and blacks who challenged the laws in any way were intimidated, sometimes terrorized, and sometimes even lynched. (In the 1880s and 1890s there were over one hundred lynchings a year.)

In defiance of the Fourteenth and Fifteenth Amendments, blacks were kept from the polls by discriminatory registration requirements, by a "poll tax" that most blacks were too poor to pay, and by physical threats. One-party dominance by the Democrats also served to keep black people from access to political power by preventing the possibility of an alternative party bidding for their votes. Thus the only real competition took place in the primaries, which were private affairs for whites only. Increasingly blacks moved away from the South, only to encounter discrimination and poverty in the northern cities.

Not until the 1930s did the federal government do much for them. Then in the New Deal they began to share in some of the benefits the government provided. World War II brought them jobs, and the nation sought their help as fighting men—in segregated units. When the war was over, steps were taken to reduce discrimination in the armed services, federal employment, and government-backed mortgages. But there was still no momentum behind the efforts to obtain equal rights for black people.

THE CIVIL RIGHTS BREAKTHROUGH

Gradually, however, that momentum developed, and it moved on several fronts. First there were the courts. From the late 1930s black leaders had begun to file suits in which they challenged the "separate but equal" doctrine, which had been established by the Supreme Court in *Plessy* v. *Ferguson* (1896). In 1950 the Supreme Court made two decisions[4] reducing the obstacles to blacks' getting into graduate schools. Then in 1954 came the momentous decision in *Brown* v. *Topeka Board of Education* that separation solely on grounds of race inherently denied the constitutional guarantee of equal protection of the laws. The Court went on in subsequent years to uphold congressional statutes banning segregation in public accommodations, public facilities, juries, and other fields in which state government action resulted in discrimination.

Concurrently with the help they were getting from the courts, black people took direct action to seek redress of their grievances. In December 1955, in Montgomery, Alabama, a black working woman, Rosa Parks, refused to follow the rule that black passengers give up their seats in the front of the bus to whites and move to the back. She was arrested and fined, but blacks conducted a year-long boycott of the Montgomery buses led by an extraordinary Baptist minister, Martin Luther King, Jr. King's home was bombed, and he went to jail. But in November 1956, a federal court injunction put an end to bus segregation in Montgomery.

On the basis of this experience King built an organization, the Southern Christian Leadership Conference (SCLC), and developed the strategy of nonviolent civil disobedience. Sit-ins and demonstrations spread throughout the South, and "freedom rides" brought white and black civil rights activists from the North. Then came the events in Birmingham, Alabama, in the spring of 1963. "Bull" Connor, the Birmingham police chief, set police dogs on a crowd of civil rights demonstrators. Television covered the event, and a shock wave swept the nation. Demonstrations and protests, in some cases riots, followed in cities throughout the country. The mood of outrage was turned to dedication by a great march on Washington, where King told more than 200,000 people of his dream of an America free from prejudice and discrimination.

The impetus was established for federal legislation. After an intensive lobbying campaign by civil rights forces, the Civil Rights Act of 1964 passed. The act expanded the federal protection of voting rights; gave the attorney general authority to bring civil suits against discrimination or segregation in public facilities and such public accommodations as restaurants, lunch counters, gas stations, theaters, stadiums, hotels, or lodging houses (except for owner-occupied units with five rooms or less); empowered the attorney general to file suit for the desegregation of public schools; authorized the U.S. Office of Education to report on desegregation progress and give technical and financial assistance, on request, to school systems embarked on desegregation; extended the life and expanded the jurisdiction of the Civil Rights Commission; created an Equal Employment Opportunities Commission charged with the task of promoting and enforcing equal job opportunities in businesses or unions with twenty-five or more workers; and created a Community Relations Service to work in local communities. One other significant provision was set forth in Title VI of the bill: "No person in the United States shall, on the ground of race, color, or national origin, be excluded from participation in, be denied the benefit of, or be subjected to discrimination under any program or activity receiving federal financial assistance."

Congress, spurred by demonstrations for black voting rights in Selma, Alabama, and other southern communities, followed the 1964 act with the Voting Rights Act of 1965. This act banned the use of literacy or other tests to qualify voters; authorized the appointment of federal voting examiners empowered to order the registration of minorities in districts where there was an obvious pattern of discrimination; and required preclearance by the Justice Department of all changes in election laws of any state covered by the act. Nine states came under the provisions of the Voting Rights Act: Alabama, Alaska, Arizona, Georgia, Louisiana, Mississippi, South Carolina, Texas, and Virginia, along with counties in thirteen other states. The effects of the law were dramatic, especially in the South. In 1964 black registration in eight of the southern states was about 1.5 million. By 1980 it was more than 3.3 million.

Thus the Civil Rights Act of 1964 finally spelled out in specific terms the provisions of the Fourteenth Amendment of 1868. And the Fifteenth Amendment's promise of the right to vote, made in 1870, was given the full weight of governmental power by the act of 1965. It had taken almost a hundred years, but at last it seemed that the courts, the executive and legislative branches of government, and the civil rights movement had succeeded in ending the barriers against the full enjoyment of their constitutional rights by black people.

VIOLENCE IN THE CITIES

Euphoria was not to last. In the summer of 1964, the year of the great Civil Rights Act, riots broke out in the black neighborhoods of seven cities, including New York, Chicago, and Philadelphia. In the summer of 1965, the year of Voting Rights, there was an eruption of violence in the Los Angeles black ghetto of Watts that far surpassed previous outbreaks elsewhere. It lasted six days, achieving a

Paul Conrad, © 1965 *Los Angeles Times*. Reprinted with permission.

"We're to blame for the riots?! . . . Why, I've never been in a ghetto in my life!"

scale that led some commentators to use words like "revolt" or "rebellion" rather than riot. The National Guard was finally called in to restore order. The violence in Watts left thirty-four dead and over one thousand injured. Property damage was estimated at about $40 million, and there were almost four thousand arrests.

In 1966 there were outbreaks in several other cities, smaller in scale than Watts but enough to destroy the assumption of whites in the communities in which they occurred that they were free from serious racial tensions. Then came the summer of 1967, the most violent the nation had experienced since the Civil War. There were forty-one serious disorders, eight of which assumed major proportions. Eighty-three people were killed, most of them in Detroit and Newark and most of them blacks. Local police were unable to contain the major uprisings, and peace was restored only when the National Guard had taken over the affected areas.

The repeated experience of the total breakdown of order in whole sections of major cities, murderous exchanges of gunfire, city blocks set to the torch, and uncontrolled looting—all carried live on television—led to the appointment by President Johnson of a commission under Governor Otto Kerner of Illinois to study the riots and make recommendations to prevent their recurrence. In March 1968, the National Advisory Commission on Civil Disorders submitted its report.[5] Its basic conclusion was: "Our nation is moving toward two societies, one black, one white—separate and unequal." Further, the report asserted that massive corrective measures must be undertaken to offset the "white racism" that was at the heart of the problems. Programs must be launched to improve conditions in the inner cities, and the trend toward segregation must be reversed. Otherwise, said the commission, "Large-scale and continuing violence could result, followed by white retaliation, and ultimately, the separation of the two communities in a garrison state."

By 1982 the catastrophe foreseen by the commission had not occurred. There had been no other outbreaks on the scale of Watts in 1965 and Detroit in 1968. Still, riots erupted in Miami in 1980. Moreover, white violence against blacks showed itself in the assassination of Martin Luther King by a deranged racist in 1968, and a nearly fatal shooting of another black leader, Urban League president Vernon Jordan in 1980.

CONTINUING BLACK-WHITE DISPARITIES

Clearly tensions, resentments, and counterresentments persist. At the root of the problem are differences in the quality of life between the majority of whites and the majority of blacks. In important respects most of these differences have narrowed. But they have not been eliminated, and they remain sources of discontent for the nearly 12 percent of the population who are black.

Income.   The median black family income in 1980 was $12,600, up from $4,000 in 1965, and the proportion of blacks with incomes in the middle ranges has gone up faster than among whites. Still, white family income in 1980 was over $21,000, so the black family median income in 1980 was only about 60 percent of the white median. (See table 13-3.)

TABLE 13-3 Black median family income as proportion of white median family income

Year	Percentage
1965	54
1970	60
1975	61
1980	60

Source: U.S., Department of Commerce, Bureau of the Census.

Occupation.   The proportion of blacks in white-collar jobs has almost tripled in the past twenty years to about 36 percent. However, some 52 percent of whites are in white-collar occupations. The unemployment rate among blacks is almost double the rate for whites,[6] and usually at least a third of black teenagers—over 60 percent in some central cities—are out of work.

Education.   In years of education completed, the gap between blacks and whites has narrowed dramatically since 1960. (See figure 13-1.)

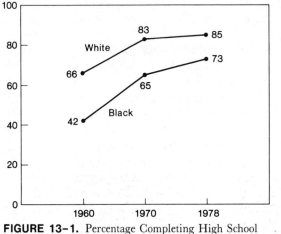

FIGURE 13-1. Percentage Completing High School
Source: U.S., Departments of Commerce and Labor.

The same trend has been at work with respect to college education. In 1965 only 10 percent of blacks aged 18 to 24 were enrolled in college as compared with 26 percent of whites. In 1978 the figure for whites was essentially unchanged, but 20 percent of young blacks were enrolled in college.

On the other hand, the quality of primary and secondary education received by black children is generally below that available to whites, and a smaller proportion of blacks than whites graduate from college. Moreover, much of their early education is in segregated schools. Although 90 percent of black children in the South attended integrated schools by 1973, in a number of big city schools in the North and West blacks continue to constitute a majority of the students and sometimes the entire student body.

Health.   Black Americans tend to have more problems with their health than whites as a result of lower incomes, poorer housing, and the lower than average availability of medical facilities and health care personnel in the black ghettoes.

Life expectancy.   On the average whites live about five years longer than blacks. The life expectancy of black males at birth is about 65, of white males 70; of black females 73, of white females nearly 78. Although the black infant mortality rate (the proportion dying before the age of 1) has gone down significantly in recent years, it is still almost twice the rate for whites.

Family structure.   Black family structure has weakened even more than among whites. In 1980 almost one out of five American families with children still at home included only one parent, an increase of almost 80 percent from 1970. But the problem was still greater among black families, of which over half are now one-parent families.[7]

Political power.   Black political power has been increasing, with a surge of black voters enfranchised by the 1965 Voting Rights Act and the election of blacks as mayors of some big northern and southern cities, as well as to other high state posts.[8] However, with no black members in the United States Senate in 1981, sixteen in the House of Representatives, one Supreme Court justice, and less than 1 percent of all the state and local elected officials in the country, it is clear that blacks are still very much underrepresented in the political system.

Consequently, as black people see it, white America pays lip service to the highest moral principles but has not lived up to these principles in its treatment of blacks. This problem, said the Swedish sociologist Gunnar Myrdal in his great study of black people in America in 1944, was an American dilemma,[9] and most blacks in America do not believe that dilemma has yet been resolved.

HISPANICS: A NEW ASSERTIVENESS

People of Spanish origin came very early to America, living in the Southwest long before there was a California, a Texas, or a New Mexico. Today, as we saw in tables 13-1 and 13-2, they are a rapidly increasing proportion of the total population: at least 6.4 percent by 1980. They constitute more than a third of the people of New Mexico and about a fifth of the populations of Texas and California; they are a majority in El Paso and San Antonio and close to a majority of the school children of the Los Angeles school district.

About half of them derive from Mexico, and the largest number of these *Chicanos* live in California, Texas, and Arizona. Some two million are of Puerto Rican background, and they are found predominately in New York, Chicago, and other northern cities. There are more than a million Cuban-Americans, heavily concentrated in Miami and other parts of Florida. Another two million or so come from various Central and South American countries.

The problems facing these groups vary considerably, partly because of the very different Chicano, Cuban-American, and Puerto Rican cultures, partly because their occupational status and living conditions are dissimilar. A high proportion of the Cuban-Americans are middle-class refugees from Castro's Cuba and have established themselves in the United States as professionals and businesspeople,[10] whereas the bulk of the Mexican-Americans and Puerto Ricans came from rural areas or urban poverty districts.

However, the main Latino organizations commonly stress three kinds of grievances: socioeconomic disadvantages, the language question, and the illegal status of many Latinos.

SOCIOECONOMIC DISADVANTAGES

The median family income of Latinos, $14,700 in 1980, although slightly higher than the median income of the blacks, is much lower than the median income of the majority. Indeed, some of the worst living conditions of any group of Americans are found among Mexican-American farm workers in the Southwest and among Latinos who work in the sweatshop conditions of the garment trade in New York and Los Angeles. And unemployment levels are high, especially among teenagers in the barrios.

Educationally, Mexican-Americans have been making important gains: high school graduation rates among Mexican-American males went up from 34 percent in 1960 to 64 percent in 1976, among females from 35 percent to 58 percent. But these figures were still below the rates for blacks, and, like the blacks, large numbers of Hispanic children go to segregated schools.

Politically Hispanics are becoming an important factor in some states. Their leaders are taking on a new assertiveness, and San Antonio in 1980 became the first major city to elect a Latino as mayor. However, only six Hispanics served in Congress in 1981, all in the House of Representatives, and the number of Hispanic elected officials nationally is even smaller proportionately than among blacks.

THE LANGUAGE QUESTION

Latinos have pressed for bilingual education for their children for three reasons. First, they argue that because many of the children come to school speaking only Spanish, they are subjected to a grave learning disadvantage unless teachers take account of this drawback in the classroom. Second, many Latinos have a strong attachment to their native heritage and want to keep their language and culture alive. Third, they argue that because there will soon be more Latinos than any other group in several cities and even in a few states, their native language should be given equal status with English in those areas.

THE ILLEGAL STATUS OF MANY LATINOS

Probably somewhere between 1.5 and 3 million Latinos live and work in the United States without the resident visas required by our immigration laws. Mostly they have come across the border from Mexico. Some arrive to do seasonal work on farms or in factories and then go home after a few months. But many have settled here for several years, paid taxes, and sent their children to the local schools.

Because they are in the country illegally, they accept low wages and poor conditions. It is time, say Latino leaders, to recognize that it is impossible to keep out of this rich country people from an adjoining country that has a high rate of unemployment and a common border nearly two thousand miles long. The United States should therefore legitimize the status of those people who have settled in this country, increase the immigration quota from Hispanic countries, and make it much easier for people who want to come here for short periods to do so legally, thereby freeing them from the exploitation of employers and landlords.

OTHER DISADVANTAGED MINORITIES

According to the 1980 census there are now well over a million American Indians, or native Americans; about half of them live in or near a reservation and are members of one of the tribes that are recognized as separate peoples with the authority to govern their internal affairs under general supervision by Congress.

The tribes are accorded certain privileges under the law, and their members are granted some special benefits. Yet they are American citizens in the full sense, with the right to vote. Moreover, some tribes own land, the value of which has appreciated enormously, and mineral rights that bring in substantial income; and in recent years Congress and the courts have acted to compensate the tribes for wrongs inflicted on them in the past.

Nonetheless, the experience of being driven from their lands by white settlers, of the unkept promises and broken treaties, and of the long history of neglect has left a legacy of deprivation and poverty for the majority of American Indians; and on some of their reservations there are still seriously inadequate housing, health, and educational facilities.

The 3.5 million Asian-Americans can also point to histories of discrimination. In the nineteenth century large numbers of Chinese were brought to this country to work under harsh conditions in building the railroads. And in the aftermath of the Japanese attack on Pearl Harbor that brought the United States into World War II, all the Japanese-Americans on the West Coast, including some whose families had lived in this country for generations, were rounded up and held in internment camps.

Despite these earlier problems, Americans of Asian origin have now established themselves among the most upwardly mobile groups, occupationally and educationally, of any segment of American society.

However, in the past few years other groups of new arrivals from Asia (168,000 by State Department estimates in 1978) encountered special problems. These people came here as refugees from the terrible upheavals experienced in Indochina. Because many fled in panic as "boat people," arriving without belongings in a strange culture, there will be at least an interim period in which they will inevitably make claims for support and assistance from the society at large.

WOMEN AND THE ERA

Obviously it is even more difficult to generalize about the socioeconomic condition of women than about the other groups we have discussed in this chapter. Certainly we cannot classify women as such as an economically disadvantaged group, because they are distributed among all segments of the population, and a high proportion of the wealth of the country is held by women.

However, several women's organizations have argued that women in America do not enjoy equality of rights or opportunity with men. Although the disparity in undergraduate college enrollment between the sexes is not great, a wide gap appears at the graduate level. Furthermore, women earn about 59 percent as much as men do, mostly because they work in such low-paid fields as teaching, nursing, secretarial, and food services, but also because they tend not to be promoted as readily as men or to be given equal pay for equal work. In politics, women are being elected in rapidly increasing numbers: in 1981, women state legislators constituted 12 percent of the total. But their representation, especially at the national level, still fell far short of their numbers in the population.

So women pressed for the Equal Rights Amendment to the Constitution, the complete wording of which is: "Equality of rights under the law shall not be denied or abridged by the United States or by any State on account of sex." However, in 1982, despite a congressional extension of time, the amendment fell short of the number of states needed for ratification. Then, as we saw in our discussion of the Supreme Court in chapter 10, women have argued that, given the fact that large numbers of women are concentrated in low-paid fields in which few men are employed, equal pay for equal work is no longer enough. We must move on to a theory of "comparable worth," according to which salaries should be based not just on supply and demand pressures but on considerations of the relative contribution to society of different occupations. Thus nurses might be regarded as more valuable than lawyers and teachers as more valuable than auto mechanics, and the rewards adjusted accordingly.

DISADVANTAGED GROUPS AND THE POLICY-MAKING PROCESS

All of the elements of our political system come into play in the context of the policy issues of this chapter. Here we shall focus on public opinion, interest groups, the presidency, Congress, the federal bureaucracies, and the Supreme Court.

PUBLIC OPINION

In the past three decades the climate of majority opinion has been moving toward increasing tolerance. Sympathy for the plight of native Americans has grown, and movies and television programs about the frontier days are now more likely to depict the Indians as noble victims than as bloodthirsty savages. Newspapers no longer carry cartoons picturing Chicanos as slow-moving, amiable incompetents.

World War II hostility toward Japanese-Americans persisted for a while after the war in some communities, but it has greatly diminished since then.

The most dramatic shift of all has occurred in the attitudes of whites towards blacks. A 1980 poll showed that 81 percent of whites favored integration of the races in schools, compared with only 51 percent in 1956.[11] The idea of a black as a neighbor was regarded as moderately or very upsetting by 53 percent of whites in 1963, but only by 30 percent in 1978.[12] By 1981 four-fifths of whites declared themselves ready to vote for a properly qualified black candidate for president, as against only two-fifths in 1958. And there has been a major reduction of white stereotypes about blacks, as shown in table 13-4.

Yet it would be a considerable overstatement to suggest that prejudice among whites toward blacks and other minorities has all but disappeared. Large numbers of whites persist in holding certain stereotypes about blacks. Thus in 1978 49 percent of whites believed that "blacks tend to have less ambition than whites"; 36 percent held the view that "blacks want to live off handouts"; and 29 percent agreed with the statement: "Blacks breed crime."[13]

There is also strong, in some cases overwhelming, white opposition to such government-backed programs as busing, which was designed to achieve racial balance in the schools, "affirmative action" programs designed to favor blacks over whites because of past discrimination, and "fair housing" laws denying homeowners the right to refuse to sell their houses to blacks.

On two of these latter issues blacks see things very differently from whites (table 13-5), and blacks also believe that discrimination is much more widespread than whites believe (table 13-6).

The contrast between black and white attitudes received its clearest expression in the late 1960s in the emergence of the idea of "black power." Exponents of this concept argued that from the time of slavery, whites had systematically and calculatedly stripped black people of their cultural heritage and their identity.

TABLE 13-4 White perceptions of blacks (percent)

	1963	1978
"Blacks are inferior to white people."	31	15
"Blacks have less native intelligence than whites."	39	25
"Blacks care less for their families than whites."	31	18

Source: *Public Opinion*, April–May 1981, p. 33.

TABLE 13-5 White/black attitudes toward antidiscrimination programs, 1981 (percent)

	Whites		Blacks	
	Support	Oppose	Support	Oppose
School busing	18	82	67	33
Fair housing	45	55	74	26
Affirmative action	27	73	46	54

Source: *Public Opinion*, April–May 1981, p. 33.

TABLE 13-6 White/black attitudes on the extent of discrimination, 1981 (percent alleging discrimination)

	Whites	Blacks
"Getting a quality education"	6	28
"Getting decent housing"	17	44
"Getting skilled labor jobs"	21	61
"The wages that are paid in most jobs"	13	57

Source: *Public Opinion,* April–May 1981, p. 33.

With no picture of themselves except that which the white man had foisted on them—that of a docile, subservient group equipped for only a subordinate role in society—black people had been deprived of the character traits that could bring them out of their bondage.

For this reason, blacks should abandon the idea of integration (which was a phantom idea anyway, because despite the lip service of white liberals, America was becoming increasingly segregated) and turn the reality of segregation to their advantage. The ghettoes could provide a power base for producing black political leaders, for gaining community control of schools and other public institutions, for building economic power by compelling white owners to appoint local black managers and by promoting black ownership of businesses, and for enabling black people to rebuild their sense of identity and self-confidence.

By the mid-1970s the black power movement was no longer a significant force. Indeed, its call for separatism had never commanded much support among blacks, the great majority of whom have consistently favored integrated schools, neighborhoods, and workplaces. However, the proposal to build black people's pride in their racial identity caught the imagination of most blacks. And, as table 13-6 makes clear, the deep sense of frustration and resentment that fueled the black power doctrine is still widely shared in the black communities.

Nor are the differences in attitudes and expectations limited to the differences between whites and blacks. Latinos in the Southwest, we noted, feel that people here from Mexico and other Latin American countries without legal status contribute significantly to the well-being of the community, yet they are shamefully exploited and their rights are denied. Among the majority community, however, there is widespread resentment against the influx of large numbers of illegal immigrants, who are perceived by many as an unwelcome burden on the communities and states in which they settle.

INTEREST GROUPS

A considerable number of organizations speak for the various groups we are discussing.

The leading organizations of blacks are the National Association for the Advancement of Colored People (NAACP) and the NAACP Legal Defense Fund, which is particularly active in bringing court suits to enforce integration; the National Urban League, which works in the fields of jobs and other economic issues; and the group founded by Martin Luther King, the Southern Christian Leadership Conference (SCLC). The Reverend Jesse Jackson has attracted a good deal of national attention for his efforts to extend the work of his organization PUSH to public school districts around the country. And in Washington the Congressional Black Caucus provides a focal point for black organizations' legislative programs.

Black interest groups have generally been most effective in coalition with other groups, such as the AFL–CIO, the Americans for Democratic Action, and civic and church social action groups. One such coalition, calling itself the Leadership Conference for Civil Rights, mounted the massive pressure operation that was instrumental in passing the 1964 Civil Rights Act, the Voting Rights Act of 1965, and the Fair Housing Act of 1968.

Latino organizations reflect the diversity of national and cultural backgrounds they represent: the Mexican-American Political Association and the Mexican-American Legal Defense and Education Fund; the Puerto Rican Legal Defense and Education Fund; and the La Raza Unida Party of Texas. In Cesar Chavez, leader of the mostly Mexican-American United Farm Workers, the Latinos have a spokesman who has achieved national stature. Efforts to coordinate the work of these various organizations are made through the United Latin American Citizens (ULAC) and through the Hispanic-American Democrats, founded for political action purposes in 1979.

Several organizations, as well, speak for the concerns of native Americans and for the several Asian-American nationality groups.[14]

There is, of course, conflict within each of the minority populations. The Southern Christian Leadership Conference leaders are critical of the Urban League for being too eager to work with business leaders; and both of them disagree very strongly with the viewpoints put forward by a very conservative group of black academic, professional, and business people including economists Thomas Sowell of UCLA and Walter Williams of Temple University. However, the most publicized disagreement within groups is between such pro-ERA organizations as the National Organization for Women (NOW) and an opposition group, Stop ERA, whose best-known spokesperson is Phyllis Schlafly. NOW and its allies were extraordinarily effective in securing the passage of the Equal Rights Amendment through both houses of Congress and thirty-five state legislatures, and then getting Congress to approve an extension of time for ratification of the amendment. However, the anti-ERA groups were ultimately even more effective, because they applied so much pressure to the remaining legislatures that the ratification drive stalled at thirty-five states.

THE PRESIDENCY

Minorities have looked to Democratic rather than Republican presidents to attend to their interests ever since Franklin Roosevelt moved the black vote away from its historical allegiance to the Republican party established by Lincoln and secured it firmly to the Democratic cause.

Yet Roosevelt, concerned about holding the support of southerners in Congress, introduced no civil rights legislation, so his appeal to blacks and other minorities was based on his general economic and welfare measures that helped the poor as a class. Harry Truman addressed the needs of minorities more directly by using his executive powers to create a Commission on Human Rights, abolish segregation in the military, and issue orders against discrimination in government and in federally aided housing programs. But although he proposed civil rights legislation, Congress refused to act on it. No civil rights proposals came out of the Kennedy White House, although President Kennedy had given orders for a bill to be prepared just before his assassination. Jimmy Carter appointed considerable numbers of minorities and women to key positions, but he had nothing of significance to offer them in the form of new legislation.

So of all the Democratic presidents the only one who achieved dramatic breakthroughs on behalf of minorities was Lyndon Johnson. He picked up the plan for civil rights legislation prepared by the Kennedy staff, and it became the Civil Rights Act of 1964. The voting rights bill of 1965 became his personal crusade, and it passed after he made an impassioned plea to Congress. The whole thrust of Johnson's War on Poverty was of special significance to underprivileged minorities. It was also Lyndon Johnson who signed two executive orders in 1965 and 1967 that instructed the recipients of government contracts that they must provide "equal employment opportunity," and that this order required more than nondiscrimination. Positive "affirmative action" to prevent the perpetuation of the inequalities caused by past discrimination was now mandated.

Republican presidents have not depended on the votes of black people for their election, have been less inclined to seek legislation or issue executive orders on their behalf, and have appointed somewhat fewer minority members to high places in their administrations than have Democrats. Blacks were strongly critical of the Nixon administration's plea to the Supreme Court in 1969 to allow the South more time to carry out the desegregation mandate of *Brown* v. *Board of Education*, and of an unsuccessful effort to dilute the Voting Rights Act when it came up for renewal. Blacks took much the same view of the Ford administration.

During the Reagan administration blacks were joined by other minorities in protesting that much of the progress of the past twenty years was being jettisoned. The sharp cuts in the federal budget hit hardest at the inner-city areas. The head of the Justice Department's civil rights division declared his dislike of mandatory busing. Although the Justice Department under Carter had submitted legal briefs to the Supreme Court supporting busing, the briefs written by Reagan's Justice Department opposed proposals for busing.

There were complaints, too, that Reagan was slow to appoint minorities to high positions, and that those individuals he did appoint were not true representatives of their groups. When Reagan proposed an immigration bill that would legalize the status of many undocumented aliens and admit up to fifty thousand "guest workers" a year, Latino leaders charged that the bill was grossly inadequate and demeaning to the immigrants and that the guest worker provision merely regularized the exploitation of Mexican labor.[15] Latinos were unhappy, too, at the cuts in federal funding for bilingual education. And there was criticism from pro-ERA women's groups, objecting to Reagan's opposition to their cause.

However, Republican presidents have not been totally oblivious to the concerns of the disadvantaged minorities. Eisenhower, albeit with great reluctance, sent federal paratroops to Little Rock in 1957 to enforce the Supreme Court's order to integrate the high school. Nixon appointed a number of blacks to White House staff and subcabinet positions, ambassadorships, and other significant posts. He also increased funds for civil rights enforcement and for black colleges and businesses.

Although Reagan's initial proposals on the Voting Rights Act disappointed civil rights leaders, he nonetheless favored a ten-year extension of the law, and he gave his support to a Senate compromise on the issue that was passed into law.[16] Then, Reagan balanced his opposition to the ERA by appointing the first woman to the Supreme Court.

CONGRESS

When presidents dragged their feet on civil rights legislation, Congress rarely took the initiative. In fact, it was southern power in the Congress, exercised through control of committees and use of the filibuster, that long made Congress an almost insurmountable barrier to legislation designed to help black people.

Although the leadership that passed the civil rights bills of 1957 and 1960 came from Congress, those bills were weak measures. Only when the White House moved into action in 1964 and 1965 did Congress respond impressively, breaking southern filibusters to pass the Civil Rights and Voting Rights Acts, and following these bills with a strong "open housing" law in 1968 that prohibited discrimination in the sale and rental of about 80 percent of all the housing in the country.

After that, however, Congress was generally not disposed to push forward with new civil rights legislation under either Democratic or Republican administrations. In fact, on the busing issue Congress passed a bill in 1972 requiring the postponement of mandatory busing until all court appeals had been exhausted; and year after year one house or the other, sometimes both, passed bills designed to limit or even halt the use of busing as a tool of desegregation. The Republican Congress of 1981–1982 was particularly vigorous in its efforts to halt busing programs. On the other hand, the Judiciary Committee of that Senate, chaired by a long-standing nemesis of civil rights causes, Strom Thurmond of South Carolina, produced a compromise extension of the Voting Rights Act that was acceptable to liberals as well as conservatives.

THE BUREAUCRACIES

A large number of federal agencies are involved in implementing laws and dispersing funds for programs of particular importance to minorities. Notable among these agencies have been units within the Department of Health, Education, and Welfare (now Health and Human Services), the Department of Housing and Urban Development, and the Justice Department. Some of these agencies have reflected the wishes of constituencies opposed to integration. Thus, until 1947 the

Federal Housing Authority's official manual warned federal officials not to insure property unless it was protected from "adverse influences" such as "inharmonious racial groups." A firm order from President Truman finally expunged this policy of reinforcing housing segregation in the communities.

Still, there have been other groups within the bureaucracy who saw as their first responsibility the advancement of the cause of minorities. Clearly this responsibility has been the mandate of the Equal Employment Opportunity Commission and of the United States Civil Rights Commission, which has issued a series of reports over the years calling for stepping up the pace of integration and for more rigorous application of the Fourteenth Amendment to the rights of minorities and women.[17] Within several other federal departments there are units, usually with minorities and women in responsible positions, charged with the task of monitoring the implementation of federal civil rights laws and regulations.

In some areas a great deal of discretion is delegated to these officials. Thus the affirmative action regulations require contractors with the federal government to submit written plans that must be approved by the appropriate government agency. The plans must be based on surveys of the work force in the fields in which hiring is to take place to determine the extent of "underutilization" of blacks, people with Spanish surnames, people of Oriental ancestry, American Indians, and women. Goals must be established, with timetables for hiring people in the underutilized categories. The goals are not to take the form of quotas— that is, hard and fast targets that must be achieved by a given date. Thus, if the employer proves not to have achieved the goals, an extension of time may be given if the employer can show he or she has acted in good faith and has made a strong effort to comply.

Clearly each of these requirements and guidelines—reviewing reports, determining underutilization for each group, setting goals, and judging what constitutes good faith—leaves a great deal to the discretion of the federal officials. Some have used their authority to the full, pressing repeatedly for compliance, demanding to inspect the personnel files of companies and universities to determine whether or not there has been a pattern of discrimination. This pressure has provoked strong protests from the affected contractors and demands that the administration lessen the zeal of the investigators.

The extent to which these protests are attended to has varied with the administration. Generally speaking, civil rights enforcement was more vigorous during the Johnson and Carter administrations than during the Nixon and Ford years (although the Nixon Justice Department filed suits to enforce a large number of court orders to desegregate school districts). The Reagan administration's passionate commitment to the elimination or softening of federal regulations led to a considerable reduction of affirmative action and other civil rights rules as compared to the trend under Jimmy Carter.

THE COURTS

As we have noted, the key Supreme Court decisions in the nineteenth century went against the blacks. The *Dred Scott* decision came down on the side of slavery, and in 1883 the Civil Rights Act of 1875 was struck down. With *Plessy* v. *Ferguson* in 1896, the Court put the seal of approval on the South's "Jim Crow" laws by declaring that separate public facilities could be provided as long as they were of equal quality.

From the 1930s, however, Supreme Court decisions started to favor black people. And under the leadership of Earl Warren the court began the process of moving into the civil rights vacuum left by the president and Congress.

In *Brown* v. *Board of Education* in 1954, the Court reviewed the refusal of the Topeka, Kansas, Board of Education to allow a black girl to enroll in a nearby all-white school, requiring her instead to be bused some distance away to an all-black school. This action, said the chief justice speaking for a unanimous court, was a denial of the Fourteenth Amendment's guarantee of the equal protection of the laws. In public education, "the doctrine of 'separate but equal' has no place. Separate educational facilities are inherently unequal."

A follow-up decision in 1955 required the South to move toward school deseg-regation "with all deliberate speed." But the South's school districts moved with more deliberation than speed, so the Burger Court had to tell the South in 1969 to get the job done "at once," and keep it done "now and hereafter."[18] The South complied to such an extent that within a few years only a small proportion of black children in the southern states still went to all-black schools.

Now the school problem shifted to the northern and western cities, which had large numbers of schools in which all or most of the children were blacks or Latinos. This situation did not result from state and local laws actually requiring segregation, as had been the case in the South, but the result was the same: the segregation of minorities. And in *Brown* v. *Board of Education* the Supreme Court had said that "separate educational facilities are inherently unequal."

Moreover, the separation of the races in the schools was sometimes created, or at least reinforced, by actions of governmental bodies, such as the drawing of school boundary lines or the selection of sites for new schools. In such situations segregation of the races in school might be seen not merely as *de facto* (the result "in fact" of neighborhood racial patterns), but as *de jure* (imposed by law).

The Burger Court has addressed this question in a number of cases since 1971 and has sometimes upheld mandatory desegregation, including busing, sometimes not. The distinction the Court has made appears to be based on whether or not racial separation has clearly resulted from actions of governmental bodies, espe-cially where intent to achieve segregation is apparent. By this test the Court found in favor of lower court judgements requiring desegregation in both the North (Denver,[19] Boston, and Wilmington, Delaware,[20] among others) as well as in the South (notably Charlotte, N.C.).[21]

But there were other cases in which the Court did not find sufficient evidence of government-created segregation to justify mandatory busing. Burger, in par-ticular, was extremely reluctant to support desegregation plans across school dis-trict lines. In the Wilmington, Delaware, case the Court had upheld a city-suburb busing plan because the connivance of governmental bodies was patently clear: a 1968 Delaware law had required small districts to merge with each other, yet had forbidden predominantly black Wilmington to expand its boundaries to take in a neighboring white district. But lacking such gross violations of the Constitution, said Burger, "the notion that school district lines may be casually ignored or created as a mere administrative convenience is contrary to the history of public education in our country."[22] Consequently a proposal to require integration of the schools of Detroit and fifty-three surrounding suburban schools was rejected by the Court. The mere existence of segregation was not enough, said Burger. Unless the school district lines had been deliberately drawn to create racial segregation, or each of the districts involved had been found to practice racial discrimination, busing across the boundary lines could not be required.[23]

Apart from its decisions regarding the schools, the Supreme Court had been an important factor in a number of other areas affecting the rights of minorities. *Brown* v. *Board of Education* was followed in the 1950s and 1960s by a number of other decisions that forbade segregation in all kinds of public facilities and outlawed discrimination in the sale of private housing.[24]

However, under Chief Justice Burger the picture has become increasingly ambiguous in the fields of housing, education, and employment. Although the Court ruled that government-subsidized housing for low-income people in the suburbs is an appropriate means of attacking housing segregation, it drew the line at forcing a predominately white suburb to change its zoning laws to permit housing for low-income minorities because the Court was not convinced that the zoning laws had been deliberately contrived to keep blacks out.[25]

The Court has walked an even finer line in affirmative action cases. In *The University of California* v. *Bakke* (1968) the Court rejected an admissions program of the medical school at the university's Davis campus that set aside a certain number of places for blacks and other minorities. Yet the Court was split five to four. Each of the judges had his own special approach to the problem, and the majority opinion delivered by Justice Powell[26] declared that affirmative action programs as such were not necessarily unconstitutional. Rigid quotas must be avoided, but a plan that took race and ethnicity into account as a means of ensuring a diversified student body might be entirely acceptable.[27]

Subsequently the Supreme Court upheld a training program of a private company in which a specific quota of places was set aside for blacks,[28] and accepted a provision of the 1977 Public Works Act that required that no less than 10 percent of federal funds awarded to local public works projects be contracted to business enterprises owned by "citizens who are Negroes, Spanish-speaking, Orientals, Indians, Eskimos, and Aleuts."[29]

As we saw when we discussed the Supreme Court in chapter 10, the rights of women have also been variously and ambiguously interpreted by the Burger Court. The wording of the Fourteenth Amendment and other applicable sections of the Constitution may seem clear enough. But the demands for equality of treatment by various groups in America today are the subject of intense conflict within public opinion and within each of our political institutions. It is unlikely that the courts will be able to arrive at clear, consistent resolutions of these conflicts, except in situations where the grievances of the affected groups are as clear and irrefutable as they were in the segregation cases in the 1950s and 1960s.

Courtesy Scripps-Howard Newspapers
"The Winner!"

FIVE PERSPECTIVES ON MINORITY RIGHTS

THE CENTRISTS: NOT THE MILLENIUM, BUT REAL PROGRESS

To centrists America still has a considerable distance to go in providing blacks and other minorities with the full benefits of our system. However, they believe that great progress has been made and will continue to be made if we act with intelligence and restraint.

The seriousness of the problem is revealed in the harsh statistics on income, welfare, quality of schooling, and residential and school segregation. The continuing gap between the minority of blacks and Hispanics on the one hand and the majority of whites on the other is morally wrong. It is also bad for our political system, because it creates tensions and hostilities that make it difficult for political leaders to work out those reasonable compromises on which a democratic society depends for its progress.

Yet, say the centrists, we must set the problem in perspective. The fundamental point to bear in mind is that the condition of blacks and other minorities has improved enormously in the past three decades. The depiction of black people as a great, poverty-stricken, deprived mass is a gross distortion, because large numbers of them have moved up into the middle stratum of society. In fact, says one centrist analyst, "the emergence of such substantial numbers of blacks into the American middle class is nothing less than a revolutionary development."[30] This revolutionary development is not immediately apparent when we look at the figures for all blacks, because the average is pulled down by two factors: first, slightly over half of all blacks still live in the poorest part of the country, the South, and second, a substantial proportion of black families have only one parent, usually the mother. But if we focus on young, husband-and-wife families outside the South, we find there is now little or no difference in earnings between blacks and whites. There have also been dramatic increases in the number of blacks working in white-collar and skilled craft jobs, in the proportion attending college, and in home ownership by blacks. Infant mortality among blacks has declined substantially over the past twenty years, and the difference in life expectancies of blacks and whites has narrowed considerably.

Even in fields where the gap is not closing, the situation is not quite as disastrous as it appears, say the centrists. The increased numbers of blacks on welfare does not mean that more blacks have sunk into poverty, but that welfare is easier to get than it used to be. Actually, as we saw in the last chapter, the proportion of blacks living below the poverty line has declined sharply since 1960. As for the high rate of black teenage unemployment, much of this statistic is accounted for by young people who are going to school and are looking for part-time work.

Moreover, segregation and discrimination have been dramatically reduced in the South in a few short years. The extent of segregation in northern cities is deplorable, but much of it is due to the preference of blacks, like any other ethnic group, to live among people of their own background. Nor should we overlook the fact that more and more blacks are moving out of the inner cities into the suburbs. Chicago, Detroit, Milwaukee, St. Louis, Washington, D.C., Newark, and Los Angeles are all experiencing "black flight" into the suburban areas, an indication that large numbers of blacks are achieving middle-class status and, like the white middle class, want to move into better neighborhoods. As this trend continues, it will help blur the confrontation between white suburbs and black cities predicted by the Kerner Commission. And white stereotypes of blacks will continue to change as more blacks rise into the middle class, become media celebrities, and establish themselves as successful, moderate political leaders.

In politics, blacks, Latinos, and other minority groups have a long way to go to achieve full representation, but every election brings increases in the number of elected minority officials. And as minorities win offices in the lower ranks of politics, they gain footholds from which they will move rapidly up the ladder.

There is every reason to believe that the progress achieved thus far can be sustained if we proceed intelligently. But full economic parity and total integration cannot be accomplished overnight. The prospect of future gains will be gravely jeopardized if we raise expectations that cannot possibly be fulfilled and if we undertake measures that arouse the antipathy of the majority of the population.

There is every reason to believe that the progress achieved thus far can be sustained if we proceed intelligently. But full economic parity and total integration cannot be accomplished overnight. The prospect of future gains will be gravely jeopardized if we raise expectations that cannot possibly be fulfilled and if we undertake measures that arouse the antipathy of the majority of the population.

The right way to improve the education of minority children is (1) to provide funding at substantial but not lavish levels for programs that improve basic learning skills; and (2) to encourage integration by voluntary busing programs, redrawing those boundary lines that were aimed at separating the races and developing "magnet" schools that are made so attractive that white parents *and* minorities will want to send their children to them because of their academic superiority. The wrong way is large-scale mandatory busing. Busing is wrong for four reasons. First, it undermines the enormously popular principle of the neighborhood school. Second, busing is detested by the great majority of whites who do not want their children bused to inner-city schools where performance levels are low and violence is frequent. Although racist hostilities are undoubtedly provoked by forced busing, it is unfair to describe as racism a reluctance to have one's children bused many miles to get an inferior education and to be exposed to abuse and physical danger. In any case, many black parents, too, have no enthusiasm for having their children bused out of their communities, and there is even more reluctance among Hispanic parents, whose strong family and community feeling is offended by having their children bused to a distant part of town. Third, forced busing does not work. It does not improve the quality of education for either black or white children because time is wasted by the process of transportation and the tensions resulting from forced integration inhibit effective learning. Fourth, busing does not achieve integration, for court-ordered mandatory busing simply provokes white parents to move away from the communities affected by busing, or to put their children into private schools, leaving the public schools even more segregated than before.[31]

Then, too, the right way to promote increases in the number of minorities and women on university faculties and in the professions is to provide funds for special training programs that enable talented people from the disadvantaged groups to overcome the disadvantages associated with their background. The wrong way is to establish affirmative action programs, which are essentially programs of reverse discrimination. As we saw in table 13-5, affirmative action does not even receive approval from a majority among blacks. They perceive it as a slur on their ability to succeed without preferential treatment, and they recognize that inevitably it will stir up resentment among whites.

To sum up, centrists admit that much more needs to be done to help minorities achieve their places in the sun. Yet centrists are pleased with the gains that have been made, are hopeful about the future, and are concerned that further progress may be endangered on the one hand by the liberals' rigid and ill-conceived efforts to force the pace of change, and on the other hand by the extent to which the conservatives are proceeding to slash programs that are of great importance to the well-being of minorities.

THE CONSERVATIVES: IT'S UP TO THE MINORITIES, NOT THE GOVERNMENT

Until the 1960s the conservative position on civil rights was closely identified with the cause of the southern segregationists. Northern conservatives might not agree with the southerners that blacks were inherently inferior to whites or that at best they would take generations to be capable of full participation in the system. But the national debate revolved around the problem of the South, and conservatives in all parts of the country sided with the southerners in their plea for states' rights, particularly the right to maintain white dominance in the South.

Today, however, the South does not provide the most effective conservative arguments on race. In large measure the old South has been beaten on the issue, and the emphasis has shifted to a more sophisticated level of debate, with national rather than only southern implications.

Thus the conservatives' position today on blacks and other minorities is that they should be given every opportunity to assume their full human rights and that the federal courts have an important role in striking down *de jure* segregation of the kind established by statute in the South.

However, conservatives insist that ending segregation must take time. They do not believe that segregation that has not clearly and deliberately been created by law calls for court interference, they are strongly opposed to mandatory busing, and they find affirmative action programs abhorrent.

In these repects the arguments put forward by conservatives echo those we have identified with the centrists. There are, however, differences in both tone and substance between conservatives and centrists on these issues.

Centrists view busing as a foolish idea that we have been pushed into by well-meaning but misguided idealists. To conservatives there is more to it than that. The government is being used by the "social engineers"—sociologists and educators who have determined that the root of the problem facing blacks and other low-income minorities is the environment in which their children grow up. Therefore everything possible must be done to reduce the influence of the culturally deprived home and the slum environment. Busing serves this purpose nicely because it takes the minority children to distant schools removed from the influence of their parents.

Affirmative action programs provide another example of manipulative social engineering. They set out to solve an alleged injustice by an even greater injustice, and in the process expand the sway of government bureaucrats.

Further, conservatives do not accept the centrists' willingness to spend a good deal of federal money on improving the living and educational standards of minorities. They believe that the minorities, like all Americans, are much better served if government lets private enterprise get on with the job. Minority incomes have risen not because of the muddled efforts of the federal government, but because the economy has been expanding under the impetus of private businesses. If government will stop trying to help minorities by paternalism and social engineering, business will create plenty of opportunities for jobs and rising incomes. As the conservatives see it, this great hope for minorities is generated by the Reagan administration's program of cuts in federal spending, taxes, and regulation.

The rest is up to the individual. Those people who want to take advantage of the opportunities created by the business system will do well. Those people who do not, whatever their color, national origin, or sex, should not expect favored treatment from the government or society.

It is true, say the conservatives, that blacks have been discriminated against and that on the whole they still do not live as well as the whites. But the legal barriers have been removed. It is time to stop dwelling on the past. Other groups, such as the Irish, Jews, Poles, and Italians, came to this country with nothing and suffered discrimination. But in time they made it to full participation in the American system. In recent years Asian-Americans have been moving up the income and occupational ladder with remarkable speed. Black people have their chance to do the same.

The Latinos also have this opportunity, say the conservatives. To the argument that Latino children face a language barrier, conservatives answer that the same was true of the children of the immigrants from Eastern and Southern Europe. But in their case demands were not made through the political system for large amounts of money to be spent on bilingual education or for the printing of ballots and election material in their separate languages. Conservatives value tradition and the preservation of cultures, but this responsibility belongs to individuals and groups, not to government.

As for the demands to legitimize the increase in immigration from Latin American countries, conservatives are of two minds. On the one hand those conservatives who subscribe to the pure principles of free enterprise cannot support artificial barriers to the free flow of commodities or of people across national boundaries. Moreover, there is little opposition among conservatives to the migration to this country of the kind of business and professional people who fled Castro's Cuba and quickly established themselves as solid and substantial contributors to our society.

On the other hand, most conservatives are not at all pleased with the idea of our having to absorb very large numbers of poor, unskilled people, whom they see as a drain on our resources, a burden on our taxpayers, and a source of trouble and instability. This description would apply, in their view, to the majority of those immigrants coming from Mexico and from Haiti, as well as from Cuba in 1980, when Castro, accepting the demands for emigration of some political dissidents, also sent to our shores a number of hardened criminals.

Our system, say the conservatives, already has more than enough sources of discontent and tension. We should take more care in our immigration policies to accept only people who see this country as one that provides unparalleled opportunities for people who are willing to make the effort, rather than people who come here to make strident demands for special treatment.

Finally, say the conservatives, we must resist the frequently heard argument that, unless we spend more money in the inner cities and give more preferential treatment to minorities, crime will increase and the kind of riots we experienced in the 1960s will be repeated. Crime and riots cannot be dealt with by buying off and rewarding the criminals and rioters. Minorities, like everyone else, must be made to understand that lawbreakers will be dealt with firmly by law-enforcement agencies and the courts.

Equal protection of the laws, no more and no less, must be the standard. And the fact is that today members of minority groups are the least likely to receive the protection that is their due, not because of white exploitation and oppression, but because they are the most frequent victims of the high rates of crime and violence found in many ghetto and barrio communities. Thus firm enforcement of the law is the most important gift that the government can give to its minority citizens.

THE RADICAL RIGHT: CIVIL RIGHTS AND THE COMMUNIST CONSPIRACY

A central theme—sometimes the central theme—in the history of radical rights movements in America has been racial purity. The Ku Klux Klan came into existence to express fear of black demands for equality, then added warnings against Jews, Catholics, and almost everyone except fundamentalist Protestant whites. Today a major preoccupation of the Klan and other far right organizations is the expanded immigration of people from Mexico, Cuba, Haiti, and Southeast Asia. In opposing this immigration they have struck some responsive chords. For example, in a district in southern California in 1980 the Grand Dragon of the Klan for San Diego County narrowly won the Democratic nomination for Congress. He was thoroughly beaten by his Republican opponent in November, but his success in the primary was interpreted as a protest by a sizable bloc of voters against the presence in the area of a large number of people from across the border in Mexico, many of them there illegally.

However, except for the Klan, the American Nazi Party, and some small groups that circulate angry pamphlets and mimeographed sheets, overt antiblack and antiminority sentiments are rarely expressed in public by radical right groups today.

Leaders of the John Birch Society, in fact, protest that they are not racist or prejudiced. Their bitter attacks on the civil rights movement, they insist, are attacks not on minorities as such but on the Communists. The Civil Rights Act of 1964 was "part of the pattern for the Communist takeover of America. . . . The whole racial agitation was designed and is directed by the international Communist conspiracy."[32]

Minorities, in the view of the Birch Society, are better off and have made greater gains in this country than anywhere else in the world. Unfortunately they have become the target of communist propaganda and infiltration, and some are allowing themselves to become dupes of the Communists.[33]

Moreover, says the radical right, with the expanding flow of immigrants from non-European countries, we are bringing to our shores more and more people whose purpose is to undermine our institutions or to provide eager audiences for those subversives who advocate the transformation of America into an anticapitalist, anti-Christian country.

THE LIBERALS: SOME PROGRESS, BUT NOT NEARLY ENOUGH

Liberals have found repeatedly that achievements in the field of civil rights quickly turned to disappointment. They had hoped that the legislation of 1964 and 1965 would usher in a new era of racial harmony and progress. But on the heels of their greatest triumphs, Watts exploded in violence, its example soon to be followed by other major cities. Then came a reaction against those events—a white "blacklash"—which was refueled in the controversies over busing and affirmative action.

Liberals express further disappointment over what they see as an inadequate response to the Kerner Commission's recommendations for large-scale and dramatic action to deal with the plight of blacks. Only just enough was done, they suggest, to prevent the continuation of the urban riots, and not nearly enough to remove the underlying causes of these riots: poverty, unemployment, bad housing, poor public services, segregation, and so on.

Liberals do not deny that there have been some long-term improvements in the condition of blacks in America. But whereas the centrists focus on the gains, liberals concentrate on the gap that remains between the conditions of blacks and whites. Centrists draw our attention to the advances in income of young, black, married couples in the North and West, but liberals respond that these couples constitute a minority of blacks because more than half of all blacks live in the South and more than half of all black families include only one parent. Even though the black middle class has increased considerably, left behind in the inner-city ghettoes is a large group of people who have had a poor education, lack the kind of skills needed in a technological society, and consequently are becoming a kind of permanent "underclass"—a group of people who, in effect, are told by society that it has no need for them. With half to two-thirds of black teenagers in some inner cities out of work (a much higher proportion than among whites), the prospect is that this underclass will grow larger, more hopeless, less likely to see any future within the normal opportunities provided by society.

Liberals were particularly worried by the cutbacks in government services being forced through by the Reagan administration. Inadequate as the previous programs were, they at least opened up some opportunities for talented blacks to move out of their conditions of hopelessness and provided a minimum standard of living for all the poor in the cities. But the Reagan proposals, said the liberals, were eroding that minimum and then falling back on the classical conservative response to the rising crime levels that their policies produced: harsh measures of "law and order."

As for the political gains that blacks have been making, these gains are only minor inroads in the system of power in America. The most dramatic advances are in the cities, but blacks are becoming mayors of cities that are in serious economic decline and that represent harrowing problems rather than political opportunities. The very fact that blacks have been winning office in the cities is a consequence of the most insidious aspect of the race problem today: the desertion of the cities by whites, their occupation by blacks and other minorities, and the resulting separation of the races. Although many blacks have also been leaving the poverty ghettoes, few of them move into predominately white communities. They occupy other areas that whites leave. The ghetto remains a ghetto; it simply expands.

Moreover, say the liberals, these problems are not limited to blacks. Among Mexican-Americans, Puerto Ricans, and native Americans there is a high incidence of poverty and unemployment, their housing conditions are well below the national average, and they suffer from poor schooling and inadequate career skills. Progress in the barrios and on the reservations, say the liberals, is as painfully slow as in the ghettoes, and no less calculated to produce feelings of resentment toward the larger society. If we are to avoid the splitting of our society into warring groups divided by race and national origin, we must launch, say the liberals, an all-out attack on substandard living conditions and segregation.

On the economic front we should proceed with the kind of programs proposed in the previous two chapters to abolish poverty and urban blight. Liberals recognize that government programs designed to help minorities may be taken by the white majority as a threat to their own rights and opportunities. But, if these programs can be presented as part of a general governmental attack on a whole range of deficiencies in our society, the danger of conflict can be greatly reduced. After all, great numbers of whites are not so securely above the poverty line that an illness, injury, or loss of a job could not result in economic calamity for them and their families. They need programs in such fields as health insurance, employment, and job training, which are as important to the majority as to the poor.

Conflict arises out of the economics of scarcity. When there are not enough jobs to go around, when incomes are not keeping up with prices, hostilities grow as people jostle each other for the limited supplies available. In an economy of abundance, stimulated by well-conceived federal programs, there will be less reason for conflict, and people—white, black, and brown—will discover their shared interests rather than their differences.

In fact, say the liberals, in a properly functioning economy there would be no need for hostility to increased immigration from Mexico and other countries, because there would be a scarcity rather than a surplus of labor. This statement does not mean that liberals support the Reagan administration's immigration proposals, which they see as efforts to supply employers with an increased supply of cheap nonunion labor. The precondition for higher rates of immigration is the revitalization of the American economy along the lines suggested by liberals. Without this revitalization, they argue, bringing in considerable numbers of people equipped to work only at unskilled jobs is bound to arouse the hostility of American working people.

Liberals are, in general, favorably disposed toward affirmative action programs. No doubt they do represent a kind of discrimination in reverse, but for a time they will be necessary. In the case of blacks, the most profound and persistent discrimination has been practiced against them throughout our history as a nation. So equality cannot be obtained merely by ending the discrimination; it will have to be reversed to give blacks a chance to catch up and overcome the unfair advantage that society has given whites over blacks for centuries. To say that other ethnic groups have risen out of poverty without reverse discrimination, and that blacks should do the same, misses the point. Poles, Italians, Irish, and Jews may have come to this country in poverty, but not in chains. They did not live here as slaves, suffer the deliberate smashing of their family structure by the slaveowners, then live for a century after slavery under legally imposed segregation, discrimination, and humiliation.

The story is somewhat different with respect to the other groups protected by affirmative action. However, the wrongs inflicted on American Indians need hardly be detailed. Hispanics, too, have experienced prejudice and discrimination. And without the pressures applied by affirmative ac-

tion, women would continue to be denied opportunities for career advancement.

Yet liberals are not happy about the fact that affirmative action is needed. They have always argued for color-blind laws, so they are uncomfortable about the fact that, in order to put affirmative action into effect, statistics have to be compiled listing employees or students by race and sex, and schedules have to be established for reaching agreed-on goals for minorities and women. Liberals support affirmative action as a temporary expedient and as only a small part of the answer. The larger part of the answer is not to argue over who should get the limited number of positions, but to increase the total number of opportunities.

Liberals call for rapid advances toward an integrated society. They respect the demand of minorities for a reaffirmation of their respective cultures. Black studies programs are needed to restore the pride of black people in their heritage. Bilingual education for Hispanic children is appropriate as a means of overcoming educational disadvantages, and as a recognition of a language that was the dominant tongue in the Southwest before English was spoken there.

But acceptance of cultural diversity must never obscure the fact that we are one nation, and within one nation the segregation of particular groups is unacceptable. Separate cannot be equal, particularly in the field of education. Integration can be accomplished by a variety of devices, such as redrawing boundary lines between school districts and attendance areas and establishing "magnet schools." But a certain amount of busing will be required in some communities. This busing has caused some white families to leave, but civil rights spokespersons insist that the decline in the number of white children in city schools has less to do with busing than with falling birth rates and the general shift of population away from the cities. Moreover, although the examples of violent resistance to busing have captured the headlines, some major cities have been peacefully integrating their schools using many methods, including busing. In Dallas and Milwaukee, for example, community leaders and white and black parents worked together in a successful effort to create a climate of acceptance.

In any case, say the liberals, busing and other such policies are merely partial correctives to the underlying problem—segregation resulting from residential patterns. As long as minorities live in separate communities (and zoning laws, federal housing policies, and discrimination by realtors have helped bring this separation about, so there is no such thing as purely *de facto* segregation), school integration can be accomplished only by artificial means. What is needed is an enormous increase in the opportunities for blacks and other minorities to move from the ghettoes and the barrios into integrated neighborhoods.

Only by these means, say the liberals, will it be possible to overcome the minorities' sense of isolation and injustice and afford them the rights and the equal protection of the laws that the Constitution guarantees to every individual.

THE RADICAL LEFT: CAPITALISM BREEDS RACISM

In the eyes of the left, the analyses of the other four perspectives are at best a thin veneer to protect established privileges, and at worst masks for repression.

The reality of repression is a daily experience in the minority communities. Harassment at the hands of local police forces is commonplace. Petty burglaries carried out by blacks or Latinos are dealt with much more harshly than large-scale embezzlements by middle-class whites. Prison populations are made up largely of minority group members; and as a result we tolerate prison conditions—overcrowded, brutal, destructive of any possibility of rehabilitation—that are the shame of an allegedly civilized country. The repressive character of our system was further revealed in the persistent efforts of the FBI under its late director, J. Edgar Hoover, to smash black organizations by illegal wiretaps, by searches and arrests without warrants, and by infiltration designed to stir up rivalries among black organizations.

The evidence cited by defenders of the system to prove that minorities have made progress misses the point. It is true that there has been much desegregation in the South. But if this fact is a defeat for the old-line southern conservatives, it is quite acceptable to the southern industrial interests who prefer to get away from the crudities of the past. However, like their northern counterparts, they continue to exploit their black workers even more than the whites.

As for the liberals, the shortcomings of their analysis are revealed with particular clarity in the context of race. The Kerner Commission produced an essentially liberal manifesto. Accurately, it declared that "white racism" was largely responsible for the existence of the black ghettos and for the abominable conditions therein. But the report's recommendations—integration and more money—were the standard liberal answers, which fail to come to grips with the root causes of racism. The root problems are the division of America into profoundly unequal classes; the need of the dominant class to perpetuate an underclass that provides cheap manufacturing and domestic labor; and the deliberate playing on race prejudice to sow division among the masses.

Then, too, labor, a key element in the liberal civil rights coalition, is a prime practitioner of racism, by establishing apprenticeship programs and other barriers to entry into craft jobs that discriminate against blacks. Finally, liberals covertly resist the claims of minorities through "institutional racism." Liberals support affirmative action programs that increase the number of minorities hired in police and fire departments and other such jobs, but in universities, where liberals hold many of the administrative and faculty jobs, their support of affirmative action is less enthusiastic. They say they are eager to see more blacks appointed, but few black people can meet the qualifications that the institutions require.

Consequently, says the left, there is no hope for minorities in their traditional alliance with liberals. Instead, minorities should join with other alienated elements to force a radical reconstruction of American society.[34] Beyond the national context one should look to the entire Third World, where the poor people, whether or not they are nominally independent of colonial rule, are still subject to neocolonial, imperialist oppression, including the oppression that emanates from the United States. The Third World consists predominantly of nonwhites, and the nonwhite population of the world far outnumbers the whites. Blacks and other minorities in the United States should therefore identify with people everywhere in the world who are fighting against American imperialism.

CONCLUSION

Each of our five perspectives can point to certain trends developing in America since the 1960s that bolster their view of the proper treatment of minority groups in America.

Centrists take comfort in the signs of increasing tolerance and the decline of hostile racial and ethnic stereotypes.

Observers left of center can take note of the fact that it is no longer just the blacks who must carry the brunt of the struggle to overcome minority disadvantages, because their example has inspired Latinos, Asian-Americans, native Americans, and women to undertake similar efforts to gain long-denied rights and opportunities.

Right of center there is reason to believe that, at least for the time being, their approach has gained wide support. Until the mid-1960s the issues were focused on the South, and the broad body of opinion in the country sided with the liberals in their opposition to southern segregation. Now the problem has moved to the North and West; busing, affirmative action, welfare costs, and rising crime rates have made the white majority more conservative; and the centrist analysis in this chapter has more in common with the conservatives' position than with the liberals'.

Whatever the perspective, it is apparent that as a nation we have a long way to go on this issue. The heady optimism of 1964 is no longer tenable, as even centrists agree. It is an incredibly difficult task to accommodate diverse cultures within a single society and to provide each group with full access to the benefits created by that society.

It has also become clear that this problem is not only an American dilemma. Few if any societies are entirely free from racial and ethnic prejudice and discrimination, and very few have prevented the emergence of wide gaps in income, status, and power among different racial and ethnic groups.

Wherever those gaps appear they are a prime source of tension and instability, which is still very much the case in the United States. Although it is helpful to know that we are far from being the only country to face the problem, there is little reassurance in that fact.

NOTES AND REFERENCES

1. See, for example, Michael Novak, *The Rise of the Unmeltable Ethnics* (New York: Macmillan, 1971).

2. There is no consensus on a generic name for all those people whose ultimate origin is Spanish. Currently the main contenders are *Hispanic* and *Latino*.

3. Robert William Fogel and Stanley L. Engerman, *Time on the Cross: The Economics of American Negro Slavery* (Boston: Little, Brown, 1974).

4. *Sweatt* v. *Painter* (1950); *McLaurin* v. *Oklahoma* (1950).

5. National Advisory Commission on Civil Disorders, *Report* (Washington, D.C.: Government Printing Office, March 1, 1968).

6. Black unemployment reached 18.4 percent in April 1982.

7. In 1979 55 percent of all black children were born out of wedlock. For whites the figure was about 10 percent.

8. Black elected officials in the eleven southern states increased from 72 in 1965 to almost 2,500 in 1980.

9. Gunnar Myrdal, *An American Dilemma: The Negro Problem and Modern Democracy,* Twentieth Anniversary ed. (New York: Harper & Row, 1962).

10. A second wave of refugees in 1980 included many more working-class and low-income people.

11. *Public Opinion,* April–May 1981, p. 33. Another poll indicated that only 5 percent of white parents in 1980 objected to sending their children to a school in which a few of the other children were black, and only 22 percent would object if half the children were black.

12. Ibid., p. 34.

13. Ibid.

14. Asian-American associations include the Chinese-American Citizens Alliance, the Friends of Free China, the Associated Japan-America Societies in the U.S., the Japanese American Citizens League, the Asian-American Legal Defense and Education Fund, and the Asian-American Women's Political Caucus.

15. Reagan's proposed immigration bill provided for: (a) legalization of undocumented aliens living in the United States since before January 1, 1980 by allowing them to apply for temporary resident permits until, after 10 years, they could request permanent status; (b) a pilot program admitting up to 50,000 workers a year as "guest workers"; (c) issuance of 100,000 extra visas a year for all countries, and permission for Mexico to borrow from the Canadian quota; (d) three-year renewable visas for Cuban and Haitian refugees living here since January 1, 1981, with permanent resident status possible after five years; and (e) fines for employers who "knowingly" hire four or more illegal workers.

16. Reagan, after initially indicating he would accept a tough measure passed by the House, modified his position under pressure from Attorney General William French Smith. Reagan wanted to make it less difficult for the states covered by the act to "bail out" of its provision by establishing an improved record on minority voting. The House bill would outlaw any voting practice that had a discriminatory *effect*. Reagan preferred existing language prohibiting a biased *intent* (which civil rights leaders contended was extremely difficult to prove). The compromise worked out by the Senate Judiciary Committee, and endorsed by President Reagan, would allow election results to be used as an indicator of discriminatory effects but contained no requirement to use racial quotas as a remedy for discrimination.

17. President Reagan ousted Arthur Flemming from the chairmanship of the U.S. Civil Rights Commission. Flemming, who had been appointed to the position by Nixon, was an outspoken advocate of vigorous enforcement of civil rights laws and had criticized Reagan for backing away from affirmative action, busing, and other programs favored by minorities. Reagan's choice to succeed Flemming was Clarence Pendeleton, president of the San Diego Urban League. Although he was black, Pendeleton was considered more conservative than Flemming.

18. *Alexander* v. *Holmes County Board of Education* (1969).

19. *Keyes* v. *Denver School District* (1973).

20. *Buchanan* v. *Evans* (1975).
21. *Swann* v. *Charlotte-Mecklenburg* (1971).
22. *Milliken* v. *Bradley* (1974).
23. The biggest of all desegregation battles was fought over the Los Angeles schools. There the California Supreme Court upheld a lower court judgement that school segregation in Los Angeles violated the *state* constitution's provision for equal protection of the laws. A busing program over long distances was put into effect. But then in a statewide election California voters approved an amendment to the California constitution that restricted California courts to the same school desegregation criteria as the criteria established by the federal courts. The California Supreme Court then found that, by these criteria, the Los Angeles busing plan went too far, and mandatory busing ended in Los Angeles. The U.S. Supreme Court rejected an appeal against this decision in July 1982. On the same day, however, the Court found a Washington antibusing initiative unconstitutional, for it prohibited local school districts from imposing busing if they wished to (in contrast to the California initiative, which restricted the courts' powers to impose busing on school districts).
24. *Jones* v. *Mayer* (1968). In this decision the Court cited the Thirteenth Amendment abolishing slavery, and the 1866 Civil Rights Act giving blacks as well as whites the right to buy, sell, and hold property.
25. *Arlington Heights* v. *Metropolitan Housing Corporation* (1977).
26. Powell sided with four justices who held that the Davis plan was unconstitutional, but with the other four justices in their view that the right kind of affirmative action could well be constitutional.
27. Powell cited Harvard College's undergraduate admissions plan, which, in the quest for a diverse student body, included race among several nonacademic factors in its admissions criteria.
28. *Steelworkers* v. *Weber* (1979).
29. *Fullilove* v. *Klutnick* (1980).
30. Ben J. Wattenberg, *The Real America: A Surprising Examination of the State of the Union* (New York: Capricorn Books, 1976), p. 124.
31. See "Integration Yes; Busing No," interview with James S. Coleman, *New York Times Magazine,* 24 August 1975, pp. 10–11.
32. Quoted by William F. Buckley, "The John Birch Society," *National Review,* 19 October 1965, pp. 916–918.
33. See Robert Welch, "To the Negroes of America," reprinted in Gilbert Abcarian, *American Political Radicalism* (Waltham, Mass.: Xerox College Publishing, 1971), pp. 94–100.
34. See, for example, Carl Wittman and Thomas Hayden, "An Interracial Movement of the Poor," in Mitchell Cohen and Dennis Hale, eds., *The New Student Left* (Boston: Beacon Press, 1967), pp. 182–211.

chapter fourteen

ENERGY AND THE ENVIRONMENT

The issues we examined in chapters 12 and 13—the distribution of wealth and the relations among the races—have been prime sources of contention throughout our history. But the problems considered in this chapter—the deterioration of our natural environment and the dwindling of our sources of energy—did not become central concerns of most politicians until recently. Actually, the problems had been there all along, but we had not done much about them. Then a few dramatic events suddenly projected them into our national consciousness as full-blown crises. After a brief period in which everyone feared that each of these crises would overwhelm us, the panic receded and the crises were renamed "problems." Nonetheless, these two interwoven issues, the protection of the environment and the quest for energy sources, continue to be recognized as important matters demanding attention from the American political system. Their political salience—the extent to which they must be taken seriously by politicians—rises and falls as circumstances change. But they will never again be relegated to the status of questions of minor importance, of interest only to a few groups and a few regions.

HOW THE ISSUES EVOLVED

There are two main strands to the issues under review here. On the one hand there is the depletion of natural resources, such as land, minerals, fossil fuels, timber, and water, the supply of which (at least in easily accessible form) is limited and will eventually run out, thus leading to the importance of conservation. On the other hand there is the problem of pollution: the damage inflicted on the environment by human effluents, or waste products. At first, little attention was paid to either of these problems. Although writers have cried out against the "rape of the earth" since the beginnings of industrialization, their voices were not heeded in America during the long period in which the land was seen as a great cornucopia, its riches available to anyone who wanted to seize them. Government, far from providing checks against private exploitation, sold off or even gave away the public domain to encourage the settlement of the land.

Then, in the latter part of the nineteenth century, as the era of the expanding frontier ended, attitudes on the use of natural resources began to change. Pressure for conservation built as whole forests disappeared; more people wanted to enjoy outdoor recreation and scenic beauty; industry needed assurance of a long-term supply of natural resources; and new scientific knowledge was gained of how to replenish the forests and husband other resources. The federal government began to enter the picture, especially from Theodore Roosevelt's time, by establishing national parks and forests, reclaiming arid lands through irrigation projects, constructing dams, preserving wildlife, and regulating the production of oil and other mineral resources. Then Franklin Roosevelt's New Deal, bringing a spate of government regulations and seeking ways of putting people to work, undertook a huge expansion of programs in all of these fields. Still, as America became increasingly urbanized, only a minority of the population were directly interested in the conservation issue: farmers; mining, logging, and oil companies; and campers, mountain climbers, and others with a special love of open spaces and wildlife.

Gradually the concern of a few groups widened into a general concern not only about conservation but also about pollution, and at the end of the 1960s the two strands merged into the issue of the environment. A number of writers, organizations, and political leaders helped bring this issue to the public's attention, as we shall see later in the chapter. But the context in which they worked was shaped by two primary factors: population and technology.

At the time of the American Revolution the population of the American colonies numbered about 3 million. By 1982 it had passed 230 million. So, although the land area of the United States has increased in the last 200 years, its resources today have to sustain far more people per acre. This limitation in itself is not the problem. The land could easily sustain the needs of 230 million people—living in the style of the eighteenth century. But we are now a technological society. Technology, particularly in the forms favored in recent years, has brought immense increases in the Gross National Product. It has also required enormous inputs of energy and resources and spewed forth many millions of tons of waste. Both its voracious appetite and its massive wastes impose intense pressures on the environment.

THE DAMAGE BECOMES CLEAR

By the 1960s the damage was painfully apparent. The air, the inland waters, and the oceans were being polluted. The danger to health from the smog in Los Angeles was notorious, but smog affected many other cities, including communities throughout the western states that had long boasted about the purity of their air. Noise pollution achieved ruinous levels in neighborhoods bordering on jet airports. Effluents from industry and homes poured into the rivers and the lakes. Dumps filled with noxious chemical wastes from industry became a threat to the health of nearby communities. And the disposal of solid wastes became an ever more complicated problem for municipalities as garbage sites were filled and as industry made increasing use of plastics and other nonbiodegradable materials, which are not broken down through natural biological processes.

Not only were we polluting our environment; we were also engaged in a relentless exploitation of its resources. Millions of acres of prime agricultural land were lost each year through soil erosion and urban and highway expansion. The inexorable march of the land developers cut deeply into the supply of accessible open space and debased the natural splendors of coastal areas. The demand for fresh water for industrial, agricultural, and household use was taking considerably more out of the country's underground sources than was going back into them, thus creating the long-term prospect of serious shortages in the Southwest and the East.

Moreover, human efforts to eliminate anything in our environment that threatened our health or convenience produced some unpleasant surprises. For example, pesticides, especially DDT, wiped out mosquitos and protected crops from blight but also killed fish, birds, and beneficial insects and had harmful effects on humans, who stored up pesticide residues in their body tissues.

Nor was the consequence of these problems limited to the United States. For one thing, the United States, with about 5 percent of the world's population, devoured over 40 percent of the world's scarce or nonreplaceable resources. And due to the population explosion, world population reached almost 4.5 billion by 1981, nearly three times the number at the beginning of the century and almost 2 billion more than the total in 1950. If current trends continue world population could exceed 6 billion by the end of the century, with most of the increase occurring in the poorest regions of the world. (See table 14-1.)

TABLE 14–1 Population projections by region (based on present trends)

	1981 (millions)	2000 (millions)	Annual rate of increase (percent)
World	4,492	6,095	1.7
Africa	486	833	2.9
Latin America	366	562	2.3
Asia	2,608	3,564	1.8
Oceania	23	30	1.3
North America	254	286	0.7
Europe	486	511	0.4

Source: United Nations Studies.

Moreover, technology proceeded apace in many parts of the globe, and the pressures of people and technology on the environment played havoc universally, polluting the air and rivers and devouring limited resources.

According to some ecologists—students of the relationships among animals (including humans), plants, and their environments—the aggregation of these local problems would lead to disasters on an unprecedented scale. Famine, they said, would strike down vast populations. In the eighteenth century British economist Thomas Malthus argued that periodic plagues and famines were nature's way of reacting when population growth outstripped the available food supply. The Malthusian nightmare, said the ecologists, would become a terrible reality before the end of the twentieth century, and their prediction was supported by a number of computerized studies, including one by U.S. government agencies, *Global 2000*.[1] This report put forward a number of terrifying prospects: "Serious deterioration of agricultural soils will occur due to erosion, loss of organic matter, desertification, salinization, alkalinization and waterlogging." "Acid rain from increased combustion of fossil fuels (especially coal) threatens damage to lakes, soils, and crops." "Perhaps as many as 20 percent of all species on earth will be irretrievably lost as their habitats vanish." "A carbon dioxide–induced temperature rise is expected to be three or four times greater at the poles than in the middle latitudes. An increase of 5–10 degrees Centigrade could eventually lead to the melting of the Greenland and Antarctic ice caps and a gradual rise in sea level, forcing abandonment of many coastal cities."

Each of the reports predicting impending doom was quickly challenged by other studies claiming that the dangers had been vastly exaggerated, and insisting that with careful, selective growth we need not outstrip the earth's resources or make our environment uninhabitable.[2] However, by the late 1960s the fears of the ecologists, given passionate voice in some widely read books and articles,[3] had made a strong impact on the public consciousness.

Then came a series of developments that dramatically brought home the dangers that faced us from the damage to the environment and the depletion of resources.

On January 28, 1969, the pollution problem was brought into focus by an incident off the coast of Santa Barbara, California. A leak developed in an offshore well of the Union Oil Company, and hundreds of thousands of gallons of oil spilled into the ocean, spreading a slick extending over hundreds of square miles, fouling beaches and harbors, and killing large numbers of birds and fish.

The event provided dramatic television material. There was color coverage of magnificent beaches soiled by filthy oil; birds unable to fly because their wings were soaked with oil; and a handful of protesters in rowboats hampering the efforts of a great corporation to install a new oil rig. Newspapers and magazines were full of the story. For the media, the Santa Barbara affair was a perfect catalyst for a growing uneasiness throughout the country about the despoiling of the environment by industry and technology.

College students played their part in keeping the issue before the public. They proclaimed April 22, 1970 "Earth Day," and on campuses all over the country they held teach-ins and demonstrations, wore gas masks, buried auto engines, strewed mounds of garbage and then meticulously collected them.

By then politicians at all levels, local, state, and federal, were galvanized into action. President Nixon in his 1970 State of the Union address declared that, next to world peace, the major concern of the next decade might well be the quality of the environment. Federal, state, and local laws were passed to protect the air and the water. Environmental impact statements had to be prepared and approved before new construction could be undertaken on any project involving substantial federal funding.

The environment was a major factor in the decision not to build the Supersonic

Transport (SST) in 1971. Intense pressures from Boeing and other corporations, labor, the House leadership, and the White House failed to overcome the environmentalists' arguments about sonic boom, intolerable levels of noise around airports, extremely high fuel consumption, and a possible increase in skin cancers caused by the depletion by the plane's exhaust of the ozone barrier protecting the earth from the sun's rays.

Clearly the early predictions by skeptics that the environmental issue was a passing fad destined to disappear as soon as television and students moved on to their next temporary enthusiasm were proven wrong. The problem continued to command the attention of the public and the politicians. And the consequence of all this attention was some improvement in the quality of the natural environment, or at least a slowing down of its deterioration.

However, the problem was far from solved. The air, the waters, and the land all continued to suffer damage inflicted by technological civilization. And the cost of reducing that damage was high. According to an Environmental Protection Agency report in 1981 the total bill for pollution control between 1970 and 1987 would be close to $500 billion, about half of which was to protect air quality.

Inevitably there would be resistances to some of the existing and proposed methods for improving the environment; and the consensus that had emerged in the 1970s that something had to be done about the problem would not free it in the 1980s from political conflict.

THE GREAT OIL SHOCKS OF 1973 AND 1979

The other dimension of our relationship to our environment, our dependence on natural resources, leaped into the headlines in 1973. Abundant, cheap energy had always been taken for granted by the American people with only occasional portents of the possibility of breakdowns, as in power shortages in New York and a few other cities. But now there were warnings that power shortages could happen all over the country, because the construction of new electric power plants had not kept up with the accelerating demand resulting from economic growth and rising standards of living, and the accompanying demand for air conditioners and sophisticated appliances of all kinds in homes and offices.

By 1973 gasoline shortages began to appear. Prices rose. Some gas stations went out of business for lack of supplies. Others closed early or limited the number of gallons per customer. Cities and counties that had previously chosen among several competing bids for their gasoline needs suddenly found only one oil company bidding for their business at much higher prices. And sometimes there were no bids at all. This situation would not improve, said the oil companies. Demand was outstripping supply.

Then the supply shrank further. In October 1973, the Middle East erupted in war. The United States helped replace the severe losses in weapons that the Israelis sustained, and Saudi Arabia and other Arab states retaliated by cutting off all oil supplies to the United States. Although the United States was less dependent than Japan or several Western European countries on Arab oil, the embargo intensified alarmingly an already serious, long-term problem—the gradual diminution of our domestic supplies of oil.

A number of measures were put into effect immediately. Cutbacks were imposed on home heating oil and airplane fuel. Speed limits on the highways were reduced nationally to 55 mph. The price of gas and heating oil went up sharply. Limited allocations of gasoline were made for each region of the country. In many areas long lines formed at the gas pumps, and motorists were permitted to buy gas only every other day. Nothing could have shocked the American people into an awareness of the resource problem more than being forced to wait in line for gasoline. The automobile has become a projection of our personality, and to be denied easy, instantaneous access to gas was a profoundly disorienting experience.

Moreover, the media were full of grim news about the rising cost of oil imports. In 1970 our oil imports cost us less than $3 billion a year. By 1973 the figure was up to about $8 billion and, by 1975, to $24 billion. The figure had reached more than $35 billion by 1976 and was still rising sharply. These increases reflected two developments: the steep price rises imposed by the oil-producing nations and the United States' growing reliance on oil imports as domestic production fell. By the end of 1976 we were importing over 40 percent of our oil.

Now the search began in earnest for alternative sources of power—coal, oil shale, nuclear, synthetic fuels, hydroelectric, solar, and geothermal (steam generated by the earth's internal heat). But here, too, costs were high. We have plenty of coal, but converting it to gas is expensive. Nuclear energy costs are rising at an alarming rate. Solar energy can make a significant contribution to our total energy needs only after very large developmental costs. Still, the oil embargo generated a national determination to launch a frontal attack on the energy problem. By all accounts, energy was the newest top national priority.

However, as happens with so many crises, as soon as the immediate urgency passes, the media, the public, and the politicians find it difficult to sustain their commitment to the problem. Soon after the embargo ended, gasoline became abundantly available again. Its price had gone up steeply and continued to creep upward, but this increase did not break the dependence of most people on the automobile, and long summer vacations at the wheel of a car became commonplace again.

Another sharp blow at complacency was struck early in 1977, this time not by foreign countries but by nature. An especially harsh winter froze the Midwest, the East, and much of the South. The supply of natural gas, the clean, efficient fuel used by much of industry and a high proportion of homes, ran short as production declined. More than a million workers were laid off as industrial plants and many other kinds of businesses ground to a halt for lack of fuel. Emergency measures were undertaken to divert gas supplies from the West; and, as the worst of the cold subsided, business gradually resumed, and workers were able to get back to their jobs.

Natural gas shortages did not recur, but oil shortages did, because in 1979 a revolution in Iran led to a decline in oil production. Although the amount lost was only about 5 percent of the world's exports, it caused a panic among buyers in an already tight oil market and led to serious shortages in the oil-importing countries, including the United States. Again there were long lines at the gas pumps; again gasoline and heating oil prices rose sharply; again there was renewed determination that urgent measures must be taken through the governmental-political system to reduce our dependence on a foreign cartel—the Organization of Petroleum Exporting Countries (OPEC)—for the lifeblood of our economy. (See figure 14-1.)

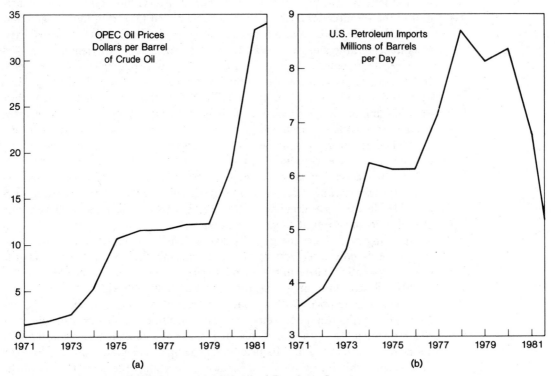

FIGURE 14-1. Oil Prices and Petroleum Imports
Source: U.S., Department of Energy.

Legislation that had been stalled in congressional committees began to move. State and local governments and industry followed the federal lead in trying to reduce energy use. And individual consumers, faced with huge increases in gas prices, drove less, switched to more fuel-efficient cars, and brought consumption—and thus the need for imports—down.

In 1981 the decline in demand, which was a worldwide, not merely an American phenomenon, had at last produced a weakening in the position of OPEC, and the rise in oil prices slowed almost to a halt. Predictions were heard on all sides that prices would be likely to rise only modestly for the rest of the century, as compared with the 24 percent annual rise (after inflation) from 1973 to 1981, mainly because increases in oil consumption had slowed to a fraction of their earlier pace.[4]

Yet world demand for oil in the early 1980s was held down partly by depressed economic conditions. A recovery could bring another surge of demand. Moreover, in 1981 over two-thirds of the $70 billion spent by the United States on oil imports went to the OPEC countries, and there had to be serious concern about so much dependence on these nations, many of which were politically unstable.

As for the prospect of cutting down on our use of oil, table 14-2 suggests that there are some prospects of achieving this goal, but that at least until the end of the decade we shall continue to consume large quantities of oil, and thus spend huge amounts of money on our import bill.

TABLE 14–2 Energy supply projections (quadrillion British thermal units)

Sources of supply[a]	1978	1985 (projected[b])	1990 (projected[b])
Oil	37.8	30.8	31.3
Gas	20.4	19.0	19.5
Coal	14.1	22.8	26.6
Nuclear	3.0	5.6	8.2
Other	3.0	3.4	3.7
Total	78.3	81.6	89.3

[a] Export/import net.
[b] Projections are middle estimates selected from low, middle, and high estimates.
Source: U.S., Department of Energy, Energy Information Administration.

THE CLASH OF ISSUES: ENVIRONMENTALISM VERSUS ENERGY

In a sense, the two issues we have been considering are different sides of the same coin. Environmentalists are concerned, we have noted, about pollution on the one hand and the depletion of resources on the other. As long as the energy problem is dealt with by conservation programs, environmentalists can only applaud. Conserving energy by reducing the amount of gasoline used by automobiles lessens the smog-producing emissions. Recycling waste products is an increasingly important means of economizing on energy.

Yet there are other respects in which the goals of protecting the environment and dealing with the energy shortage can come into conflict. Antipollution devices on automobiles may cut gasoline mileage. Offshore drilling to exploit coastal oil reserves runs the risk of producing more oil spills. Coal and oil with a high sulfur content are cheaper and more abundant than the low-sulfur supplies, but they cause more air pollution.

The dangers presented by nuclear power plants were brought home dramatically to the public by an accident at the Three Mile Island nuclear power plant near Harrisburg, Pa., on March 28, 1979. A pump in the water-cooling system failed, setting in motion a chain of failures in the system that stopped just short of a cataclysmic meltdown of the reactor, which would have released heavy doses of radioactivity into the surrounding, densely populated region.

The catastrophe did not occur and only minor amounts of radioactivity escaped, and remedial measures were ordered in similar plants around the country.[5] However, clearing the Three Mile Island plant of radioactivity remained a massively costly and lengthy process. Wherever nuclear plants were operating, under construction, or being considered, there was acute anxiety in the nearby communities.

Finally, antipollution and energy problems competed for federal funds. Both called for enormous outlays by government. Even in the more free-spending Jimmy Carter era, hard choices had to be made. In the Reagan budget-cutting age the conflict between the two objectives, both highly desirable, became especially acute.

ENERGY AND THE ENVIRONMENT: THE POLICY-MAKING PROCESS

The shaping of public policy on the issues of energy and the environment has involved, in various degrees, all of our governmental institutions. Most significant in this context have been the presidency and Congress, the bureaucracies, state and local governments, public opinion, and the interest groups on each side.

PRESIDENT AND CONGRESS

The conflict between president and Congress, and within different power bases in Congress, has been particularly visible in the arguments over the environment and energy.

On the environment the conflicts were relatively subdued, at least until the Reagan administration. During the 1960s, despite jurisdictional conflicts among various congressional committees, Congress was able to work effectively with the White House in passing legislation dealing with air and water pollution, and research and development on solid-waste disposal.

The tensions became more severe after the 1969 Santa Barbara oil spill. The stakes now were higher, and a Republican president faced a Democratic Congress. Nixon proposed a broad-ranging program dealing with water and air pollution and recreational land. Congress outbid him, passing the Clean Air Act of 1970,[6] which required federal and state governments to set air quality standards for all major pollutants. Then came the 1972 Water Pollution Act Amendments,[7] which called for the expenditure of almost $25 billion to clean up the nation's waters by 1985, starting with $5 billion in 1973 and $6 billion in 1974.[8]

Carter favored the environmental laws, and in 1977 he signed with enthusiasm the first federal strip-mining regulations. Reagan, on the other hand, had strong reservations about these efforts. He insisted that he was committed to preserving the environment, and his administration took steps to clean up the worst of the nation's toxic waste-disposal sites.[9] Nonetheless, Reagan placed more emphasis on growth than on conservation. He also felt that the environmental programs cost the federal government too much and inhibited energy production. Further, he detested the proliferation of bureaucratic regulations that gushed from environmental legislation.

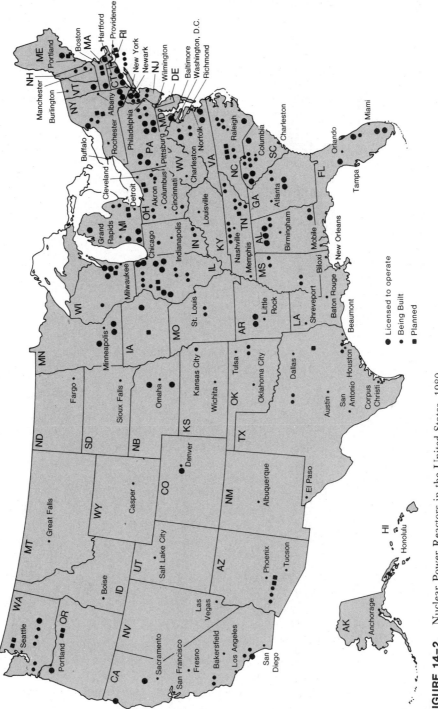

FIGURE 14-2. Nuclear Power Reactors in the United States, 1980
Source: Atomic Industrial Forum, Inc.

Consequently the Reagan administration moved to bring about a sharp reduction in the number of environmental regulations and to make many of the regulations that remained less stringent. Thus the administration proposed to relax controls on acid-forming sulfur-dioxide emissions from coal-fired plants and on nitrogen oxides from automobiles, as well as to weaken the strip-mining regulations. These proposals were not received enthusiastically by Congress, and even some rather conservative Republicans expressed unhappiness about the extent to which the environmental programs were being diluted.

Even more intense than the divergencies on the pollution front have been the struggles that have surrounded the passage of laws on energy sources since 1973. Proposals to deal with the problem first by Nixon, then by Ford, were strongly attacked by the Democratic majorities in Congress, who particularly disliked the presidential proposals to encourage conservation of energy by allowing prices to rise. Eventually Congress managed to pull together the proposals emanating from four committees in the House (Commerce, Armed Services, Ways and Means, and Banking) and nine in the Senate (Commerce, Armed Services, Interior, Public Works, Government Operations, Finance, Banking, Labor, and Judiciary) and write a bill that President Ford reluctantly signed. The main features of the bill were gradual decontrol of oil prices and a mandate to the auto industry to produce cars averaging 27.5 miles to the gallon by 1985.

In addition Congress and president reached agreement, after long delays, on the construction of an oil pipeline from new fields in Alaska, the almost complete repeal of the "oil depletion allowance"[10] (a special tax break for the oil industry dating from 1926), and the provision of funds for research and development for energy sources, especially nuclear.

Taken together these measures still fell well short of a comprehensive energy program, and incoming President Carter took it as his responsibility to focus the efforts of the American people on the energy problem, which he saw as "the moral equivalent of war." He proposed a number of actions to cut the use of energy on the one hand and step up production of alternatives to oil on the other.

Congress and the president were now of the same party. Both houses of Congress managed to avoid the duplication and jurisdictional conflict that had prevented fast action in this field in previous years,[11] and Congress approved Carter's request to create a Department of Energy. Even so, it took Congress eighteen months from the time Carter put forward his energy proposals to complete passage of a general energy bill.

Moreover, when the second oil crisis came in 1979 it was clear that the measure passed by Congress the previous year was inadequate, and further struggles between president and Congress took place before new legislation was agreed to.[12]

The resulting national energy program featured conservation through the following means:

- price increases resulting from the end of price controls on gasoline (by 1981) and natural gas (by 1985);
- mandatory improvements in automobile fuel efficiency and a heavy tax on new cars with high fuel consumption;

- tax credits to homeowners who install insulation and solar energy devices and to industry to encourage a shift from oil and gas to coal;
- the banning of oil and gas to generate electricity by 1990 (except where coal or other fuels would produce a serious pollution problem);
- a freeze on the level of oil imports, which must never exceed the 1978 level of 8.2 million barrels a day;
- a standby gasoline rationing plan in case of a national energy emergency (such as a serious reduction in oil supply from abroad);
- establishment of a strategic petroleum reserve to store a substantial quantity as insurance against interruptions in supply.

The program also featured increased production through the following means:

- incentives resulting from the increased profits generated by the end of price controls (however, a portion of these profits was to be paid by the oil companies to the federal government as a "windfall profits tax");
- establishment of a federal synthetic fuels corporation to use up to $17 billion in subsidizing the development of processes to extract crude oil from tar sands, oil shale, and coal;
- subsidies for solar, nuclear, and other alternative energy sources.

In his 1980 election campaign Ronald Reagan made it clear that much of this new program was not to his taste. He preferred market forces to government intervention; he wanted the emphasis to be on increasing production rather than on conservation; he disliked the 55 mph speed limit, the windfall profits tax, and the synthetic fuels corporation; and he was more favorably disposed toward nuclear energy than was Carter.[13]

With Reagan as president these attitudes produced some changes in federal energy policies. Price controls on oil were lifted six months before the September 1981 deadline set by Congress. The automobile companies were given more leeway on emission controls in order to encourage greater fuel efficiency. The president accepted new tax advantages given oil producers by Congress as part of the 1981 tax bills.

However, the 55 mph speed limit was not immediately abandoned; his massive tax reduction program made him reluctant to abandon the windfall profits tax on oil because the oil tax would be a useful means of limiting the deficit in the federal budget; and after a struggle within the Reagan administration, the president in 1981 approved federal loan guarantees of over $3.5 billion for three coal gasification and oil shale projects.

THE FEDERAL BUREAUCRACIES

Efforts to develop coherent, integrated policies in the environmental and energy fields have been greatly complicated by the existence in each area of a number of federal agencies, each assigned its separate functions.

In recent years the principal institutions charged with looking after the environment have been the Environmental Protection Agency, established by President

Nixon to coordinate governmental antipollution efforts; the Council on Environmental Quality, also created by Nixon, to provide policy advice directly to the president; the Department of the Interior, whose functions include the development and conservation of the nation's natural resources; the Army Corps of Engineers, which undertakes flood-control projects; and the Nuclear Regulatory Commission, which is responsible for monitoring nuclear plants.

In the energy field there was a still greater proliferation of agencies, until in 1977 Jimmy Carter established the Department of Energy, which took over the Federal Energy Administration, the Federal Power Commission, and the Energy Research and Development Administration (which had already absorbed the Atomic Energy Commission), as well as the energy-related functions of a number of other federal agencies.[14]

Inevitably, within both the environmental and energy fields, conflicts have arisen among different agencies, or among different units of a single agency. For example, the Army Corps of Engineers, backed by members of Congress who want flood-control projects in their districts, has often been at cross-purposes with environmental agencies who see dam construction as a threat to recreational areas and wildlife.

But for reasons we have already discussed there are far more sources of conflict between agencies charged with protecting the environment and those agencies responsible for increasing energy output. In the case of the Santa Barbara oil spill conflict was internalized in the Department of the Interior because that department is charged with both development and protection of natural resources. Secretary Stewart Udall, although deeply concerned about aesthetic and pollution considerations, accepted the advice of experts in his department who claimed that without the offshore oil the West Coast would soon face severe shortages.[15]

In the Reagan administration a strong effort has been made to minimize energy versus environment conflicts among the bureaucracies by appointing like-minded people to run the various agencies. Reagan's administrator of the Environmental Protection Agency, Ann Gorsuch, argued that the cost of pollution control laws was getting to be so great that the laws might have to be modified,[16] a view that would be most acceptable to Energy Secretary James Edwards. This stand was also the position of James Watt, the secretary of the interior. Watt viewed his responsibility for development of the resources of the land as no less important than his function of protecting it. He preferred to open up wilderness areas by providing easier access and more facilities rather than leaving them untouched. He also moved to reduce the restrictions on the development of the nation's energy resources. Among these restrictions were rules that made strip mining (surface mining of coal) more expensive by requiring restoration of the land after mining is completed. Watt was also eager to push ahead with offshore oil development and to increase substantially the leasing of federal lands for the development of their oil, gas, and mineral resources.[17] To accomplish these changes from his predecessor's policies Watt ordered the rewriting and reduction of his department's rules and regulations, cut the federal regulatory staffs in the Office of Surface Mining and other units, replaced upper-level officials wherever possible with more development-minded people, and made it clear to the rest of the staff that it was a new era.

As a further step toward the integration of his environmental and energy policies, the president established the Council on Natural Resources and Environment as a subcommittee of his cabinet. Watt was named chair of the council, which included the energy secretary and the EPA administrator.

Yet the possibility of conflict remained. The various operating departments might be of one mind, but all needed money, and Office of Management and Budget Director David Stockman was not always ready to support their spending plans. Reagan's approval of the synfuels loan guarantees in 1981 came after fierce infighting between Stockman, who opposed the proposal, and James Edwards, who was able to prevail largely because he had the support of key Republican Senate chairs. (However, Edwards' victory proved to be far from complete, for declining oil prices and rising costs forced the cancellation of some of the more ambitious corporate synfuel projects.)

STATE AND LOCAL GOVERNMENTS

The issues considered in this chapter highlight both the strengths and the weaknesses of the federal system. On the positive side, several of the states assumed strong leadership in the fight against pollution. For example, the state of California and the county of Los Angeles passed regulations to ban the burning of trash in backyard incinerators, control industrial effluents, and force the car manufacturers to move toward the reduction of harmful auto emissions. Oregon banned the use of "no-return" bottles for soft drinks and other nonbiodegradable containers.

Still, the fact remained that many of our forests, mountains, and rivers are not conveniently contained within state boundaries. And the profusion of subfederal government agencies, "each jealously guarding its prerogatives and each diligently ignoring and working at cross-purposes with its neighboring governments,"[18] was a serious barrier to antipollution programs. Although there were a number of interstate compact agencies concerned with such problems as the control of wastes discharged into rivers crossing several states, their effectiveness was limited.

The energy crisis intensified the problems of intergovernmental relations. State interests clashed with federal interests. States that produced oil and natural gas resented federal price controls. Coastal states fought the federal government over who controlled offshore oil and gas beds.

There was also conflict among states. Western states such as Montana, Colorado, New Mexico, and Wyoming, which contained great quantities of coal, feared that wide-scale strip mining or gasification projects would destroy the scenic beauty of their land. And almost everyone preferred to have nuclear power plants in adjoining states rather than in their own. On the other hand, some of the western governors gave support to the "sagebrush rebellion," a movement of ranchers and others to force the federal government to give them access to some of its vast land holdings in their states.

PUBLIC OPINION

From the mid-1960s surveys registered significant increases in public concern about pollution. By 1970, when a Gallup poll asked people to name the three topics they thought should receive the most governmental attention, air and water pollution were mentioned by 53 percent, second only to crime.

There is still strong public support for governmental measures to combat pollution. However, the 1981 Gallup poll presented in table 14-3 makes it clear that

TABLE 14-3 Public opinion on the environment and energy, 1981

Do you agree or disagree with the following statements about the environment?	Agree (percent)	Disagree (percent)	Do you favor or oppose the following proposals that are now being considered by the Federal government?	Favor (percent)	Oppose (percent)
Government regulations and requirements to protect the environment are worth the extra costs added to the products and services the average person buys	58	36	Easing restrictions on strip-mining to provide more coal	48	39
			Reducing auto-exhaust regulations that add to the price of new cars	42	53
In order to help solve our energy problems, we should slow down the rate at which we are working to improve the environment	36	55	Increasing oil exploration and other commercial uses of Federal lands (not including national parks)	76	19
It is possible to maintain strong economic growth in the United States and still maintain high environmental standards	75	17	Spending money to improve the condition of the national parks rather than expanding the national-park system	73	20
			Relaxing clean-air requirements to permit industry to burn more coal rather than imported oil	55	36
			Enlarging the area of offshore oil drilling on the East and West coasts	70	22
			Forcing the oil companies to pay coastal communities if offshore oil drilling damages their local environment	85	9

Don't knows have been omitted.

Source: The Gallup Organization, *Newsweek,* 29 June 1981, p. 29.

substantial majorities are supportive of several of the Reagan administration's proposals to modify pollution-control laws. There was majority resistance only to softening of auto-exhaust regulations, and the majority in that instance was narrow. Evidently, wherever there is a possible trade-off between environmental protection and securing sufficient energy, a substantial proportion of the electorate opts for energy.[19]

INTEREST GROUPS

Public policy on environmental and energy matters has been powerfully affected by intense pressures applied by a large number of interest groups on all sides of every issue.

Business. Business corporations have, of course, been deeply involved in environmental and energy matters. Although industrial executives as individuals have tended to approve antipollution measures, there are inevitable limits to industry's enthusiasm for the fight against pollution. Oil companies with an investment of over $100 million in the Alaskan pipeline could hardly be expected to applaud the delays that environmentalists forced on them before approval for the construction was finally given. Automobile manufacturers fought hard for postponement of the deadlines for pollution-free emissions set by antismog laws and managed to secure a series of extensions of time. Throughout industry, concern spread about the burden of cost increases imposed by the installation of environmental-protection devices and about the projects delayed or abandoned because elaborate studies would have to be undertaken and reviewed by governmental agencies to prove that the projects did not have an adverse effect on the environment.

Pressures by business groups did not reach their peak, however, until the struggle over energy legislation after the 1973 oil crisis. The oil industry is the most influential of the business groups in the energy field for a number of reasons. The major oil companies are among the biggest business corporations in America, and they have engaged in "vertical integration"—that is, controlling the oil industry all the way down the line from the initial exploration and production, through refining, and then selling their products. Some have also invested profits in what is known as "horizontal integration"—reaching out to acquire holdings in coal and other energy fields. And some oil companies have become conglomerates, venturing into fields totally unrelated to energy.

The oil companies spend a great deal of time and money promoting their legislative interests. They are represented in Washington by the American Petroleum Institute, which works closely with the members of Congress from oil-producing states. The industry has contributed heavily to political campaigns, and Mobil, Exxon, and other major oil corporations have spent large amounts of money to get their case before the public by taking full-page ads in newspapers and magazines.

All of the other businesses involved in the energy industry—coal, natural gas, electric utilities, nuclear, and others—are also well represented by lobbyists in Washington. Altogether during the congressional struggles over energy policy in the late 1970s the energy industries were represented in Washington by 37 organizations and 337 individuals. They have not always agreed with each other. The smaller, independent oil companies have fought against legislation that they felt was designed to help the majors put them out of business. On the broad issues, however, the various energy companies have been on the same side more often than not.

Environmental lobbies. Frequently arrayed against business have been the environmental lobbies. Traditionally, the protection of the natural environment was the domain of such associations as the Sierra Club, the Friends of the Earth, and the National Audubon Society, whose members have a deep commitment to the preservation of the land, waters, and wildlife of America. When the environmental and energy issues came to the fore in the 1970s, new conservationist groups proliferated, notably the Environmental Defense Fund, a coalition of scientists, lawyers, and others that brought cases before the courts and government agencies; Ralph Nader's Critical Mass Energy Project; and antinuclear organizations like the Alliance for Survival, the Union of Concerned Scientists, and the Campaign for Economic Democracy, headed by Tom Hayden and Jane Fonda. These groups were supported by public interest organizations like Common Cause and received some industrial backing from industry groups in such fields as insulation and solar energy.

The environmental organizations lobbied hard in Washington and engaged extensively in mass mailings to spread their message and appeal for funds. Their effectiveness was demonstrated in the defeat of the supersonic transport in 1971, the main pressure in that case being applied by Common Cause, the Friends of the Earth, and the tiny Citizens League against the Sonic Boom. And the repeal of the oil depletion allowance in 1975 was at least partly attributable to the work of the environmentalist lobbies.

They might have been more effective still had it not been for the fact that labor, usually a potent element on the liberal side of domestic issues, was ambivalent on environmental and energy questions. On the one hand, labor was active in some aspects of the environmental cause. The AFL–CIO and the United Auto Workers joined a number of other groups to form the Citizens Crusade for Clean Water, which led Congress in 1969 to vote considerably more funds to fight water pollution than President Nixon had asked for. The AFL–CIO came out in favor of strip-mining controls and called for antitrust legislation to force the major oil companies to divest themselves of their marketing operations and their holdings in coal, natural gas, and uranium, as well as to treat them as public utilities subject to strict federal regulation.

However, labor organizations could not ignore the possible threat to jobs represented by antipollution and energy conservation laws. Some companies, unable or unwilling to pay for the installation of required antipollution equipment, closed their doors and threw their employees out of work. Another of the traditional components in the liberal coalition, the low-income minorities, could not be counted on when it came to environmental protection. Poor blacks living in squalid tenements are not likely to be especially horrified by an oil slick off Santa Barbara.

They are more inclined to be interested in the extermination of rats and roaches in urban slum areas than in the survival of salmon and sea gulls. To most blacks, in fact, the environmental issue has been a diversion from efforts to deal with the urban crisis.

TWO PERSPECTIVES ON ENERGY AND THE ENVIRONMENT

Because this is the last of our chapters on domestic policy, and some of the main elements in the debates being considered have already been set forth in previous chapters, we shall limit ourselves here to an examination of the liberal and conservative perspectives. It is not that the other positions are unimportant. There is an enormous amount of writing on these subjects by people who fall within our centrist band of opinion, and radical left analysts are militant supporters of environmentalism and see the oil companies as supreme examples of all that is wrong with the capitalist system.

Just the same, at this stage the reader should have little difficulty in constructing a centrist analysis in the middle ground between liberals and conservatives, and in projecting the radical left and right as more extreme versions of the liberal and conservative interpretations respectively.

THE LIBERALS: DON'T LEAVE IT TO BUSINESS

Liberals agree with the basic teaching of the ecologists—that we cannot go on heedlessly despoiling the earth of its limited supply of fossil fuels and other natural resources and polluting our environment in the process. They believe that we must move as soon as possible to a lower resource-consuming economy.

The fact that we have not paid sufficient heed to this message is primarily the fault, say the liberals, of business corporations. The greed of industrial enterprises for profit, no matter what the cost to the public interest, is incompatible with the effort to sustain a reasonable relationship with the natural environment.

It is the same with the energy problem. Long before the oil embargo the corporations were engaged in practices that were bound to produce a shortage eventually. For decades business aggres-

sively pushed the sale of energy. The consumer was bombarded with messages from electricity companies identifying "the good life" with electric gadgets. The automobile and oil lobbies combined to make the private automobile the principal means of transportation, with the result that public transportation, which is far more economical in its use of energy, suffered gross neglect.

Then, too, the oil industry has been concerned more with keeping prices up than with increasing the supply. So it persuaded Congress and the administration to shelter it behind import quotas that limited the use of foreign crude oil and drained domestic reserves. American companies, aided by favorable tax laws that they helped write, invested heavily in Middle Eastern oil production and refining. They owned much of the oil until the Arab countries confiscated it or bought them out, and even then they continued to work closely with the Arabs in providing technical assistance and equipment. These measures were undertaken by a small number of huge corporations whose relationships, said the liberals, were characterized not by competition but by collusion.

To deal with the environmental-energy problems liberals propose the continuation of environmental controls, shifting to qualitative growth, and an energy program.

Continuation of environmental controls. Clean air, pure water, and open land are even more important to the quality of our lives than an ample supply of consumer goods. They must be protected from the ravages of industry and technology, and only government can ensure this protection. It is true that the controls result in some workers' losing their jobs; but antipollution programs, and the introduction of new, nonpolluting energy sources, create new jobs. Government can ease the transition by compensating workers who lose their positions because of environmental controls and by retraining them for the new jobs.

Shifting to qualitative growth.   The argument of some ecologists for a much slower rate of economic growth as a means of lessening the strain on the environment and conserving the earth's natural resources worries liberals, because they believe that without continued expansion of the Gross National Product they will not be able to overcome resistance to social welfare and other desirable programs. They propose to resolve this dilemma by replacing the reckless, uncontrolled growth of the past, which was measured primarily in terms of increased material goods, by careful, planned growth that emphasizes educational, recreational, health, and other services that do little damage to the environment.

An energy program.   Liberals urge an energy program that emphasizes the following features:

1. Conservation. Conservation is easily the quickest and most effective way of reducing dependence on oil imports. Since 1972 more efficient uses of energy in industry and the home have already delivered the equivalent of millions of barrels of oil a day. Yet we are still extravagant in our uses of energy. Japan, France, and Sweden all use much less energy per capita than we do, yet their standards of living are close to our own. Major investments in methods of recycling heat, insulation, more efficient lighting, auto fuel economy, and other such techniques would produce a much greater return than the vast amounts of money going into synthetic fuels, which are massively polluting and require huge amounts of water in already water-scarce regions. A well-conceived conservation program, in fact, could cut our total demand for energy by as much as 30 to 40 percent by the year 2000.[20]

2. Alternative, low-pollution energy sources. Solar energy in particular could become much more practicable and less expensive than it is now with enough research and development and the creation of a mass market.

3. Taxing the oil companies' "windfall profits." These taxes could be used for federal research programs into conservation and alternative energy sources and for energy subsidies to low-income families.

4. Splitting up the giant oil corporations. Splitting them up would take away their ability to corner the market by producing, refining, and selling their products.

5. Rationing gasoline and heating oil in another acute shortage. Prices have already gone up so much that it would be unconscionable to allow further large price increases should there be another drastic interruption of supplies. If prices went up further, the rich would be able to get all they want, but the poor and the lower-middle-income people would be unable to drive or to heat their homes.

In all these respects, say the liberals, the Reagan administration is pursuing precisely the wrong remedies. First it is neglecting conservation. Then it is putting its faith in the oil companies' using their bloated profits to increase energy output. Yet the oil corporations already have great sums of money that they have been investing in fields totally unrelated to energy. For example, Exxon bought J.C. Penney, and Mobil took over Montgomery Ward. Other oil companies have invested heavily in land development and copper mining.

Also, despite Three Mile Island, despite the fact that no safe way has yet been discovered for disposing of nuclear wastes, and despite escalating costs in the nuclear industry, the Reagan administration is persisting with the nuclear option and even proceeding with the breeder reactor, thus signaling other nations that we no longer care about the spread of nuclear weapons or the danger of nuclear terrorism.

Finally, there is the dismaying retreat being conducted by Interior Secretary James Watt from the century-long national commitment to the preservation of the natural beauty of the American landscape. Before his cabinet appointment, Watt had been president of the Mountain States Legal

Foundation, in which capacity he had taken the federal government to court repeatedly to try to open public lands to recreational power boats, to cattle grazing, and to mining, oil, and timber exploitation. Now, with the president's enthusiastic support, he was placed, like the fox among the chickens, to carry on his anticonservation goals from a position of high public authority. Of all the reversals of previous policy embarked on by the Reagan administration, none offended the liberals more than the course embarked on by Secretary Watt. Not surprisingly liberals organized petitions for his dismissal, and not surprisingly the president rejected them out of hand.

THE CONSERVATIVES: LEAVE IT TO BUSINESS

The conservatives' faith in the private enterprise system provides them with an explanation of and a solution to the energy problem, and also (although with some qualifications) to the environmental issue.

On the energy question the conservative analysis is clear and unequivocal: government interference caused us to be so vulnerable to the OPEC countries, and we can solve our problem by getting rid of government interference. Government price controls on oil and gas kept prices down artificially, which provided energy at rates so cheap that it was squandered. If prices had been allowed to find their natural level, we would have been forced into conservation much earlier. The solution is to allow the market to take over and to remove all government controls on prices. This action would take care of the conservation question without the need for the elaborate array of heavily subsidized conservation programs that provide more jobs for bureaucrats and more cost to the taxpayer.

The other advantage of higher prices would be to provide business with more money to invest in exploration and production of the needed additional resources. To the liberals' claim that oil corporations would simply take their increased profits and invest them in nonenergy fields, conservatives reply that, although this result has oc-

curred in some cases, there has in fact been a large increase in domestic exploration and production since prices and profits moved up; and there would be still more once the oil companies can be sure that further government interference will not undermine the profitability of the energy field.

The other respect in which government intervention has damaged the ability to provide for our energy needs is in environmental controls. In this area conservatives do not call for the complete removal of controls. Conservationist organizations like the Sierra Club include members of strong conservative leanings; and we have noted that pressure from California Republicans, who tend to be strongly conservative politically, helped discourage the granting of offshore oil leases in 1981.

Moreover, conservative economists recognize that in this area the market system does not perform perfectly. Milton Friedman has observed: "The preservation of the environment and the avoidance of undue pollution are real problems . . . concerning which the government has an important role to play."[21] The reason is that typically pollution is caused by several individuals or companies and affects many individuals so that it is too complicated to determine who should pay how much to whom by voluntary transactions, and so some degree of government regulation is called for.

Unfortunately, say the conservatives, government is itself a very crude mechanism for accomplishing anything, and the environmental issue provides a painful example of the tendency of government bureaucracies to engage in overkill. They have taken a necessary but limited function and carried it to absurd extremes. The bureaucrats, backed by ecological fanatics to whom environmental protection is the only value to be considered, behave as though the slightest impurity in our surroundings is intolerable. Yet there is no such thing as a 100 percent pollution-free environment. In fact, many of the hazards that we blame on humankind are also found in the state of nature; carcinogens (cancer-causing agents) exist, at least in small quantities, in a number of plants in their pure organic state.

Nonetheless, the ecologists persist in their determination to ban anything that might cause the slightest risk to human, animal, or vegetable health. They have sharply curtailed the use of the insecticide DDT in the United States, and they have carried their crusade to the United Nations, trying to secure a worldwide ban. But the World Health Organization and the Food and Agriculture Organization pointed out that without DDT about half of the poor nations' cotton production would be destroyed; India's plans for increased agricultural output could never be realized; and tens, perhaps hundreds, of thousands of people would die of malaria. Although the World Health Organization was testing alternative pesticides, none had appeared that was effective enough and cheap enough to replace DDT. Yet the liberals, the great champions of the poor, were fighting to inflict this terrible damage on the poor countries.

The environmentalists were also asking the United Nations to organize an international crusade against pollution in order to head off the threat to the environment caused by the industrialization of the newly developing countries. But antipollution equipment is expensive. Suppose, said the representatives of the poorer nations, the advanced industrial countries had been forced to accept severe pollution controls during their earlier industrial history. How far advanced would they be today? And why should the poor nations deny themselves an opportunity to pull themselves out of their poverty?

The cost of these excessive efforts to have government protect us from all possible dangers is enormous. A large part of the cumbersome and vastly expensive structure of regulations and paperwork that we detailed in our discussion of the bureaucracies in chapter 9 is attributable to the environmental field. A substantial portion of the cost of new capital construction goes into antipollution equipment.

Perhaps the most serious cost of all is in the obstacles placed in the way of our solving the energy problem by environmental extremism. Liberals fought the construction of the Alaskan pipeline. They forced delays that increased our import bill by perhaps $2 billion a year, and, if they had had their way, we should never have gotten any oil from Alaska. More billions of dollars in imports resulted from the closing down of the Santa Barbara oil fields and from the cost of removing lead from gasoline and other forms of emission controls. In fact, no matter what proposals are made, the liberals find them unacceptable: offshore oil, strip mining, and oil shale are all intolerable to them.

Liberals preserve their most passionate attacks for nuclear energy, claiming that it is much too dangerous and should be banned completely. Yet no one was killed at Three Mile Island. In fact, it could be said in 1980: "No member of the general public has been killed from nuclear power anywhere in the world. No U.S. atomic power plant worker has been killed due to an accident in a nuclear power plant."[22] Even if there were a major nuclear accident with a release of radioactivity, far fewer people would be killed than die each year from accidents or health hazards related to almost any other form of energy.[23]

The liberals dote on solar energy, although this source cannot handle more than a small fraction of our needs for decades to come. (It is more polluting than liberals recognize, because the solar cells and other necessary equipment cannot be manufactured without affecting the environment.) Even hydroelectric development has been hindered by the absurdities of liberal-sponsored environmental legislation. In 1976, a $600 million hydroelectric project in New England was held up because botanists found some specimens of the furbish lousewort in a remote area of northern Maine. Nobody claims that the furbish lousewort, a fernlike wild snapdragon, is beautiful or even pretty, and it has no commercial value. But it is rare; in fact, it had been assumed to be extinct before its discovery in Maine. And the Endangered Species Act of 1973 bars federal projects from destroying rare and endangered species of plants and animals. So the entire project stopped until the lousewort was found in another area.[24]

PAUL CONRAD, © 1974, LOS ANGELES TIMES. REPRINTED WITH PERMISSION.

"And on the seventh day he was still waiting for the environmental impact report."

To sum up, conservatives believe we can handle our energy problem successfully if we accept the following principles:

1. Adopt a reasonable approach to environmental controls. To begin with, reject the charge that pollution is caused solely or primarily by business. Consumers demand the material goods and power sources that inflict damage on the environment. Most of us drive automobiles. All of us, inevitably, are polluters. We all share in the problem and must all pay part of the cost of its solution.

We must also recognize that improving the environment requires resources that could be used for other desirable purposes. Thus we must measure the benefits obtained for any environmental gain against the cost, and ask in each instance whether we are prepared to pay that cost.

A reasonable environmental policy allows an important role for government. But it must be a limited role, rejecting the excesses that the ecologists, the liberals, and the bureaucrats have forced on us. And even there, methods involving the market pricing system could be used in place of detailed government controls.[25]

2. Reject a no-growth policy. There is no need to accept the end of economic growth in America because of energy shortages. There is plenty of energy in this country, including a 47-year supply of oil and oil shale; at least a 27-year supply of natural gas; and a more than 300-year supply of coal.

3. Give private enterprise its head. The free market can generate all the energy we need if we allow prices to rise to world levels, thus forcing conservation on individuals and businesses and providing industry with the profits and incentives to develop our abundant resources.

In assessing the Reagan administration's early performance against these principles, conservatives expressed some reservations. They disapproved of the delay in getting rid of price controls on natural gas and the failure to repeal the windfall profits tax on oil. (What was the point, they asked, in giving the oil companies greater incentives through increased prices, then taxing the incentives away?) Nor were they pleased with the decision to provide billions of dollars in loan guarantees for the development of synfuels. Business was better equipped than government to decide whether or not synthetics represented a profitable future market, and, if the decision was affirmative, energy corporations and financial institutions should be able to provide the investment capital without turning to government to remove the risk.

On the whole, however, conservatives had to applaud the Reagan administration's insistence that the solutions to the energy problems must come primarily through private enterprise. They also liked Secretary Watt's approach to environmental controls, believing that it retained adequate protection for our natural resources while recognizing the need for easier access to those resources and for limited exploration and development of mineral and oil sources.

CONCLUSION

Some of the issues in the debates over the environment and energy of the 1970s are not heard from very much now, either because consensus has replaced conflict or because one side in the debate has clearly won public opinion over to its side. The liberals fought hard against the removal of price controls, contending that high prices were unfair to the poor and would not be effective in cutting down the demand for oil and natural gas. But, even if higher prices hurt the poor, there was no preventing steep increases in the long run in the face of OPEC's actions; and those increases obviously have been instrumental in cutting consumption, forcing the shift to smaller automobiles, and increasing the supply of natural gas. On their side, conservatives are now somewhat more ready than they used to be to concede that pollution cannot be controlled without some degree of government intervention.

Nonetheless, sharp differences remain on energy and the environment between protagonists on the left and the right of center. The ideological bases of these differences have been set forth in this chapter, and that cleavage is even wider when we move to the radical positions on our spectrum.

But the problem of arriving at acceptable solutions is further compounded by the difficulty of getting at the facts. Experts with impeccable credentials are found on either side of every question we have been discussing. For example, we do not know how serious a threat to our future is posed by pollution. Is it really possible that we could cause the polar ice caps to melt? Was economist Robert Heilbroner right when he told us we could not avoid great disasters from "large-scale fatal urban temperature inversions, massive crop failures, resource shortages,"[26] and that these disasters would lead eventually to the end of democratic freedoms, because only authoritarian regimes could act decisively enough to prevent total extinction? Or shall we be guided by the cheerful scenarios of Herman Kahn, who tells us we are heading toward a future of abundance? What world population shall we plan for when expert predictions for the end of the century differ by a billion or more? What do we do about specific pollutants when a leading environmental scientist, René Dubos, warns us that "even if we had limitless resources we could not formulate really effective control programs because we know so little about the origin, nature, and effects of most air pollutants,"[27] and even less about chemical pollutants in water supplies?

Experts also disagree bitterly on the extent of the danger of a nuclear explosion, some suggesting that if we keep building new plants a disaster is inevitable sooner or later, others insisting that the risk is minuscule.

In the energy field we do not know with any precision the extent of world reserves of fossil fuels. We have estimates of the time left before the United States runs out of oil (excluding oil shale) and natural gas that range from less than twenty-five years to more than sixty years.

Confronted by such uncertainties, the ordinary citizen may well be inclined to feel bewildered and turn away from the subject in despair. However, out of the welter of conflicting facts and opinions it is possible to suggest the following conclusion: It would be folly to ignore the warnings that the future is full of dangers from the pollution of the environment and the depletion of resources. We are not compelled to accept the most gloomy of the predictions; in fact, they are being treated with skepticism by a growing body of expert opinion. But the pessimists include a large number of scientists and other specialists of considerable reputation. The stakes are so high, the consequences if they are even partially correct are so serious, that a prudent society will assume that a finite risk exists, and that it should take out insurance against that risk. We dare not go back to the lack of concern about pollution and energy that existed before the 1970s. We would also be well advised to commit much greater resources to trying to get more authoritative data than we have today so that we can propose solutions to our problems with more assurance.

NOTES AND REFERENCES

1. U.S. Council on Environmental Quality and the Department of State, *The Global 2000 Report to the President,* 3 vols. (Washington, D.C.: Government Printing Office, 1980–1981).
2. See Herman Kahn, William Brown, and Leon Martel, *The Next 200 Years: A Scenario for America and the World* (New York: Morrow, 1976).
3. See, for example, Rachel Carson, *Silent Spring* (Boston: Houghton Mifflin, 1962).
4. Major oil discoveries in Mexico and the North Sea also contributed to a diminished dependence on OPEC production.
5. A similar incident occurred in March 1980 at the Crystal River plant of the Florida Power Corporation, but the application of the lessons learned from Three Mile Island resulted in a safe shutdown of the plant.
6. This act was actually a series of amendments to air quality legislation passed in 1955, 1963, 1966, and 1967.
7. These amended laws passed in 1948, 1956, and 1965.
8. Nixon vetoed the Water Pollution amendments as inflationary, but Congress overrode his veto. Nixon "impounded" some of the funds—that is, he refused to spend them—and Congress took him to court. Impounding was found to be unconstitutional, and the funds were released.
9. A first list of over one hundred sites was released in October 1981, and a total of four hundred sites were eligible for cleanup with the help of a $1.6 billion federal fund.
10. In 1969 the allowance was reduced from 27.5 to 22 percent, and its virtual abolition for the big corporations in 1975 came in the wake of their enormous profits resulting from the sudden jump in prices.
11. The Senate created a Committee on Energy and Natural Resources, the House an Ad Hoc Select Committee on Energy.
12. One source of disagreement was a Carter proposal for a fee on oil imports that would have led to an increase of ten cents a gallon in the price of gasoline. Congress repealed the fee, Carter vetoed the repeal, and Congress overrode the veto.
13. Reagan supported the development of the "breeder" reactor, which produced more fuel (plutonium) than it used. Carter had opposed the breeder reactor to discourage the worldwide availability of plutonium, with which atom bombs can be made more easily than with uranium.
14. The Nuclear Regulatory Commission, which had been split off from the Atomic Energy Commission (AEC) in 1975 to protect it from the AEC's pressure for more production, remained outside the Department of Energy.

15. Udall was also pressured to proceed by the Budget Bureau, which wanted the $602 million from the oil leases to help pay for the Vietnam War.

16. Gorsuch reduced substantially the number of environmental regulations and the size of her staff. However, she resisted, with some success, proposals of the Office of Management and Budget to impose further drastic cuts in her agency's 1983 budget.

17. In 1981 Watt dropped a plan to issue oil exploration leases off the northern California coast at least until 1983 after an adverse court ruling and objections from California Republicans. Even so, in March 1982 Watt announced his intention to press ahead with a plan to offer 1 billion acres of offshore oil and gas leases for sale over the next 5 years.

18. J. Clarence Davies III, *The Politics of Pollution* (Indianapolis, Ind.: Pegasus, 1970), p. 130.

19. See also Robert Cameron Mitchell, "Silent Spring/Solid Majorities," *Public Opinion,* August/September 1979, vol. 2, pp. 16–20, 55.

20. See Daniel Yergin and Robert Stobaugh, eds., *Energy Future: Report of the Energy Project of the Harvard Business School* (New York: Random House, 1979).

21. Milton Friedman and Rose Friedman, *Free to Choose* (New York: Harcourt Brace Jovanovich, 1979), p. 204.

22. Thomas Gale Moore, "Energy Options," in *The United States in the 1980s* (Stanford, Calif.: Hoover Institution, 1980), p. 240.

23. Ibid., p. 241.

24. Similarly, in 1977 construction of the Tellico Dam in Tennessee was delayed by the threat to a tiny fish, the snail darter, until President Carter signed a bill in September 1979 exempting Tellico from the federal restrictions. The controversy abated when another habitat was discovered in which the darters could survive.

25. Government could determine how much pollutant was tolerable in a given area; the rights to generate this pollution would be sold on the open market; companies would bid against each other for these rights; and the price would eventually reach a point at which companies would rather clean up the remaining pollutants than pay more for the right to pollute. See Allen V. Kneese, "Environmental Policy," in *The United States in the 1980s;* and William Tucker, "Marketing Pollution," *Harper's,* May 1981, pp. 31–38. A version of this idea was proposed by the Environmental Protection Agency in late 1981.

26. Robert Heilbroner, *An Inquiry into the Human Prospect* (New York: Norton, 1974), pp. 132–33, 136.

27. Rene

chapter fifteen

FOREIGN POLICY: A NEW ERA?

As we turn our attention to foreign policy, we find ourselves in a very different setting than prevails in domestic politics. At home regular procedures have been devised for creating domestic policy and for dealing with conflicts over that policy. These procedures include a system of courts and a machinery of law enforcement to carry out the decisions of the courts.

International politics is much more fluid. The participants are nations or nation-states; each of them is sovereign, in the sense that each nation controls its own affairs through its recognized government; and each pursues its foreign policy, or its relations with other nation-states, largely on the basis of what it determines to be its own national interest.

It would be too much to say that nations live with each other in a state of pure anarchy. A body of international law has grown up out of a combination of custom and treaties among these nation-states. In addition, the United Nations (created at the close of World War II) and the International Court of Justice, or World Court, were both established with the objective of encouraging cooperation among the nations. There are also alliances into which groups of nations form themselves from time to time to ensure mutual economic or military cooperation. And in the midst of all these arrangements there is a constant process of bargaining and compromise among nations that constitutes the greater part of international, as it does of domestic, politics.

Yet when negotiations break down, nations tend to assert their separate and sovereign interests, even if it means defying international law. The United Nations can try to bring them to account, but it may not be able to do so unless the major powers agree to take concerted action. The International Court can intervene only where its jurisdiction has been accepted by all the parties concerned. Given the weakness of these constraints on the actions of individual nations, conflicts sometimes lead to confrontations and—periodically—to war.

In this chapter we shall examine the foreign policy that the United States has evolved to find its way through the semianarchy of world politics. We shall devote the larger part of our discussion to American policy—mostly an adversary policy—in relation to the Soviet Union and other communist nations since the end of World War II, paying particular attention to the nuclear arms race and to the lessons of the Vietnam War. After looking at the precepts of American foreign policy we shall discuss the policy makers. Although the preeminent role of the president in making foreign policy will quickly become apparent, we shall also consider the roles of Congress, the foreign-policy and military bureaucracies, interest groups, and public opinion. Then we shall turn to our five perspectives for contrasting views of the merits and the flaws of American foreign policy.

U.S. FOREIGN POLICY: THE BACKGROUND

A generally *isolationist* mood prevailed at the beginning of our history as a nation, a mood that was captured in George Washington's warning against involvement in any "permanent alliance." The Monroe Doctrine in 1823 told the European powers to stay out of our territory—the Western Hemisphere—and promised that we would not meddle in European affairs. Of course, we could not do entirely without a foreign policy, because we were embroiled in wars with Britain (in 1812); with Mexico (in 1846), which led to our annexation of Texas; and with Spain (in 1898), which led to our acquisition of the Philippines, Puerto Rico, and Guam. Moreover, our trade and overseas investments led us into various kinds of international economic involvements.

Still, with so much land to settle in our early days, we did not need to follow the European example of building empires at great distances from our shores, and the prevailing attitudes remained introverted. When at last we did intervene on a massive scale in European affairs by entering World War I in 1917–1918, the aftermath was a powerful desire to untangle ourselves from the Old World and its troubles. Thus Woodrow Wilson's desperate attempt to persuade the country to join the fledgling League of Nations, which its supporters hoped would put an end to war for all time, was rejected by the Senate, and the United States stayed out of the league, drawing back into its former state of isolationism.

We continued to stay out of the turmoil that engulfed Europe in the 1930s. We did nothing when Spain went fascist after a bitter civil war; when fascist Italy invaded and bombed an African state, Abyssinia; and when Nazi Germany took over Austria and part of Czechoslovakia. Even after World War II had broken out, the Germans had overrun Poland, France, Belgium, Holland, Denmark, and Norway and had invaded the Soviet Union, and Britain stood in grave danger, the dominant sentiment in this country was to send supplies to the British but to stay out of the war. At last the Japanese attack on Pearl Harbor in 1941 led to our joining Britain, the Soviet Union, and the nations occupied by the Germans in a war against Japan, Germany, and Italy.

The war in Europe ended with Germany's capitulation in April 1945. In August the Japanese surrendered after the first—and only—two nuclear bombs ever to be used in war destroyed Hiroshima and Nagasaki. The U.S. role in the war—especially the production of vast quantities of weapons and the possession and deployment of nuclear weapons—established this country as a military power of unparalleled might.

From this time on isolationism was to give way to *internationalism*. The selection of New York as the headquarters for the United Nations symbolized the leading part that the United States would henceforth play in world politics. A great many elements have gone into shaping the foreign policy that grew out of this leadership role. Paramount among them has been the concern over the rival power represented by communist countries, especially the Soviet Union.

When World War II ended, communist governments backed by great numbers of Russian troops were in control of most of Eastern Europe, including East Germany and East Berlin. Only Czechoslovakia retained a degree of independence, and it was swallowed up in a communist coup in 1948. To our top policy makers the extension of Soviet power represented a direct military threat to our Western European allies and thus to our national security. Because communism is a system that abolishes the private ownership of the means of production and distribution and that takes the form of a one-party dictatorship, it has no use for capitalist democracy. And the diagnosis of communist intentions by the U.S. government was that the Russians and their allies planned to spread their ideology and power throughout the world.

CONTAINING SOVIET POWER

The problem of resisting the expansion of communist influence had to be approached carefully. Soviet troops could not be dislodged from Eastern Europe without an all-out war, but after the end of World War II most American troops were quickly withdrawn from Europe. So the doctrine of *containment* was adopted. If communism could not be rolled back, at least it could be prevented from spreading. Greece received American military help to forestall a communist takeover, and military aid was granted Turkey to discourage any Soviet ambitions there. Berlin became a crisis point. It was a partitioned city: the eastern part was Soviet territory, and the western part of the city, although surrounded by East German territory, was incorporated into West Germany and thus independent of communist rule. The Soviets tried to break the connection between West Berlin and West Germany in 1948 by imposing a blockade, cutting off all land routes from West Germany to Berlin. The United States airlifted food and supplies into the western part of the city and eventually broke the blockade.

These actions were the forerunners of a long-term strategy to contain communism, a strategy that incorporated five main components: (1) creating a series of alliances; (2) building stockpiles of nuclear weapons, known as "mutual deterrence" or "Mutual Assured Destruction" (MAD); (3) engaging in "conventional," or nonnuclear, war; (4) giving economic and military aid to foreign countries; and (5) carrying on clandestine activities, notably by the Central Intelligence Agency.

ALLIANCES

Since the end of World War II, the United States has taken the initiative in setting up a network of alliances with other countries that share our determination to resist the expansion of communism. These alliances are based on collective security treaties, formal agreements under which each of the member nations is expected to come to the aid of any ally attacked by a communist power.

The most important of these alliances is the North Atlantic Treaty Organization (NATO), founded in 1949. Initially, NATO consisted of the United States, Canada, the United Kingdom, France, Italy, Luxembourg, the Netherlands, Belgium, Denmark, Norway, Iceland, and Portugal, which were later joined by West Germany, Greece, and Turkey. Other alliances of the United States include the Organization of American States (OAS), formed in 1948 and encompassing twenty Latin American countries along with the United States. (Cuba was suspended from the OAS in 1962 because of allegations of Castro's aggressive intentions against some of the organization's members.) Through such alliances U.S. troops have been stationed at bases around the world for the purpose of preventing communist expansion.[1]

MUTUAL DETERRENCE: THE BALANCE OF TERROR

Far transcending in importance any other method of containing communism has been our building of a huge armory of atom and hydrogen bombs and missiles. The Soviet Union has engaged in a similar buildup of nuclear and thermonuclear weapons. (*Nuclear* refers to the atom bomb; *thermonuclear*, to the hydrogen bomb.) The existence of these awesome stockpiles has changed the nature of world politics. The scale of destructive capacity they represent is of a different order than anything that came before. The atom bomb that was dropped on Hiroshima exploded with the force of about 20 kilotons—the equivalent of 20,000 tons of TNT—and gave off deadly radiation as well as a huge fireball. The official number of civilian casualties was 306,000, including 78,000 killed. Only three buildings were left standing in the city. The hydrogen bomb multiplied even this destructive force by a factor of a thousand, and now the calculations were in megatons (millions of tons).

Brooding over foreign policy since the early 1950s had been the dread of an ultimate, thermonuclear holocaust. And the possession of these weapons has acted as a restraining factor, because each side has known that the other possessed these fearsome weapons and was able to deliver them to the other's territory. Each has also recognized the reality behind the concept of Mutual Assured Destruction —that it could not by unleashing a surprise attack wipe out the other side's ability to hit back.

In the case of the United States, the ability to retaliate if the Soviets struck first depended on the dispersion of bombers on bases in several parts of the globe. Then we moved into the age of missiles. These weapons included intercontinental ballistic missiles (ICBMs), maintained on our own territory, kept underground in silos "hardened" by deep layers of concrete, and vulnerable only to an almost direct thermonuclear hit. There were also thermonuclear weapons on Polaris missiles carried by nuclear submarines moving around the depths of the ocean on random courses and capable of firing their weapons without having to surface. These three systems—the bombers, the land-based ICBMs, and the Polaris submarines—have constituted the "triad" of U.S. defense policy.

The Russians, too, had bombers, hardened ICBMs, and missile-carrying nuclear submarines. The number of warheads available to them was considerably less than the number in the American armory. Still, it was more than could possibly be knocked out by us; and, even it they hit only a few of our cities, the consequences would be catastrophic, for many of their warheads had bigger megatonnage than ours.

Consequently, both sides could suffer a "first strike" by the other and still retain an "assured destruction capability" sufficient to inflict "unacceptable damage" on the other side. Opinions might vary as to what was "unacceptable." But by the late 1960s Defense Department estimates of the havoc that a U.S. retaliatory strike would wreak on the Soviet Union ranged from a minimum of 37 million killed and 59 percent of industrial capacity destroyed up to almost 120 million deaths and 77 percent of industry wiped out. Calculations of potential damage to the even more urbanized and industrialized United States were of a similar order. (See figure 15-1.) Some experts insisted that, however terrible the idea of thermonuclear war, a clear possibility remained that, if such a war occurred, either or both protagonists could survive and even recover.[2] But in the minds of most political leaders the deaths of a minimum of 37 million of their own people could not be considered an "acceptable" hazard.

Thus emerged the state of "mutual deterrence," both sides being deterred from attacking the other because of the inevitability of a shattering counterattack. In Winston Churchill's graphic phrase, there existed a "balance of terror . . . in which by a process of sublime irony, survival is the twin brother of destruction." Peace was preserved through fear. It was an abominable condition—but at least the peace was preserved. Moreover, one of the tenets of communist ideology had been changed. Stalin had proclaimed that, as long as there was large-scale capitalism, there would be large-scale war, leaving communism to take over as the final stage of social evolution. But by the early 1960s the thermonuclear stockpiles drove Khrushchev to the conclusion that total war was too dangerous for communism as well as for capitalism. Wars between great powers were no longer inevitable or tolerable, he said, so that even the Soviet Union and the United States must seek the paths to "peaceful coexistence."

A precarious balance. This balance of terror between the United States and the Soviet Union prevented direct confrontation between the two countries. Yet these nations did not enjoy genuine security. As long as the stockpiles existed, the possibility of holocaust could not be overlooked. One side might misread the other's intentions, pushing hard in the belief that the opponent would back down, then discovering it was mistaken at the point at which both sides were committed too deeply to withdraw. Or each side might back a different country in a local war; then find themselves getting more deeply embroiled; then become direct protagonists. If this situation occurred, and if one party appeared to face defeat, the

FIGURE 15–1. Prime Strategic Targets in U.S.
Source: U.S., Department of Defense.

temptation might increase to move on from "conventional" to nuclear weapons. These weapons need not be H-bombs or even devices on the Hiroshima scale. "Tactical" nuclear weapons that could be used by infantry against battlefield targets were available to provide a new range of military options. But, if the introduction of such weapons turned the tide of battle, the pressure would be great for the losing side to introduce similar devices. The steps from there to an all-out thermonuclear exchange, if not inevitable, would be very easy to imagine.

Then, too, with so much explosive potential around, the possibility of a war breaking out through an electronic malfunction or human error could not be completely ruled out. Although the most elaborate "fail-safe" precautions were taken by the United States against this danger, no humanly devised system can be infallible. Nor could we be sure that the safety requirements of other countries with hydrogen bombs were as rigorous as our own. Although the precautions might be adequate in normal periods, the danger of accidents increases in times of crisis.

The dreadful danger implicit in the balance of terror was vividly revealed in the Cuban missile crisis in 1962. Photographs taken by U.S. reconnaissance planes revealed that the Soviet Union was constructing missile bases in Cuba, capable of delivering an initial salvo of forty thermonuclear warheads on U.S. targets east of the Mississippi and killing up to eighty million Americans.

It was a calculated attempt to change the balance of power, because at the time the United States had a clear advantage in the number of thermonuclear missiles that could reach Soviet territory. Apparently, Khrushchev assumed that President Kennedy would not risk a thermonuclear confrontation over the matter. It was a miscalculation. Kennedy presented Khrushchev with an ultimatum to stop shipping missiles and to withdraw those missiles already in Cuba. At the same time he let Khrushchev know that, if the missiles were withdrawn, there would be no American attempt to oust Castro. This promise gave Khrushchev a chance to save face, because he had installed the missiles after Castro had appealed to the Soviet Union for protection against the United States. Kennedy's assurance that he would leave Castro alone would allow Khrushchev to say he had achieved his purpose and could therefore withdraw the missiles. However, by this stage of the confrontation Soviet credibility and prestige were deeply involved, and for several tense days it was not clear whether Kennedy had calculated correctly. Finally, Khrushchev withdrew the missiles. But for a time the leaders on both sides had looked into the abyss.

After the Cuban missile crisis, the two powers began to take tentative steps away from the brink. Kennedy spoke of the need to "reexamine our attitude toward the cold war." In 1963 a treaty was signed between the two powers, forbidding further testing of nuclear weapons in the atmosphere. Other treaties were entered into later, banning the use (although not the placement) of nuclear weapons in outer space and discouraging nuclear proliferation to other countries.

These agreements did not prevent the continuation of the arms race. The two nations continued to build more weapons and work on new systems, such as the antiballistic missile (ABM), designed to shoot down attacking missiles before they hit their targets. This competition raised fears on both sides that the other was forging ahead in the arms race and might even achieve a breakthrough that would put the opponent at its mercy. Thus the situation was acutely unstable, and the prospects of war by miscalculation or accident remained high. It was also enormously expensive, placing severe burdens on the two economies.

At last, negotiations were begun in an effort to slow down the arms race and eventually reduce the stockpiles. The end of the first stage of the Strategic Arms Limitations Talks (SALT) came in May 1972, when President Nixon and the Soviet Union's leader Leonid Brezhnev signed agreements that stabilized the levels of strategic offensive missiles for five years and limited ABM systems to two sites for each country—one for the purpose of defending a major city and the other to defend an offensive-missile base.

Still the arms race went on. The Russians had been engaged in an intensive effort to catch up with the Americans. By the early 1970s the Soviets had succeeded in narrowing the gap sharply and had almost as many ICBMs and SLBMs (submarine-launched ballistic missiles) as the United States had. By 1980 the Soviets had actually forged ahead in the number of strategic missiles. Moreover, the Soviets now had more megatonnage in their arsenal than we had, because their biggest missiles carried much larger warheads than our ICBMs. And they were spending even more on armaments than was the United States.

But this fact does not mean that the United States was falling hopelessly behind in the arms race. In 1980 we still had more long-range strategic bombers. And although we had done very little to build our strategic missile strength toward the allowable SALT limit we had not been idle. Rather than increase the number of missiles, we had been increasing the number of warheads by transforming some of the missiles into MIRVs—multiple, individually targeted reentry vehicles. The MIRV is a kind of space bus carrying several warheads that it can direct to a number of separate targets either individually or in clusters. Through "MIRV-ing," despite our having fewer strategic missiles than the Soviets, we had more deliverable warheads. In addition we were developing the cruise missile, a slow, low-flying robot aircraft that can be carried by a bomber or a submarine and guided to its target by its carrier. Its special advantages are that it can fly below radar and is much less expensive than other nuclear weapons.

The United States also started the process of replacing the Poseidon nuclear-firing submarine (which had already replaced the Polaris) with the longer-range Trident. Further, it was considering plans for a new generation of nuclear-armed, manned bombers to replace the aging B-52s; for the neutron bomb, designed to kill troops primarily through bursts of short-lived radiation, with relatively little damage to buildings and terrain; and for the MX (Missile Experimental), a supermissile to be shuttled, in a gigantic shell game, between underground silos, or moved around on trucks, barges, planes, or submarines.

In the meantime the Soviets pressed ahead with a series of new weapons systems. They, too, launched a MIRVing program, and by 1981 they were closing in on the United States' lead in strategic warheads. The Soviets deployed improved versions of their ICBMs; in Europe they supplemented their medium-range SS-4 and SS-5 missiles with SS-20s, each with three warheads that could reach capital cities in Western Europe, China, and Japan; they built a medium-range bomber, the Backfire; and they expanded their submarine fleet, successfully testing an SLBM with a range of six thousand miles.

Further efforts were made by the two antagonists to bring this accelerating arms race under control. In 1974 they had reached an agreement in principle to set a limit of 2,400 strategic missiles, of which 1,320 could be MIRVed. Then negotiations moved on toward another set of limitations—SALT II. In June 1979 President Carter signed a treaty with the Soviets that confirmed the limits agreed on in principle in 1974 (limits that the Soviets had already exceeded) and reduced the limit to 2,250 by the end of 1981. Negotiations toward much more substantial reductions were to be undertaken as SALT III.

However, SALT II represented only a slight slowing down in the arms race. Its terms allowed each side to develop one new missile system and, within certain restrictions, to modernize its existing weapons. In any case, resistance in the U.S. Senate by members who believed the treaty favored the Soviets prevented the issue from coming to a vote; President Carter held up his ratification efforts when the Soviet Union invaded Afghanistan in December 1979; and the election of Ronald

Reagan as president meant that SALT II in the form negotiated by the Carter administration was dead.

The new president, in fact, believed that the Soviet Union was now forging into the lead in the thermonuclear race, that within a few years our ICBM system might be vulnerable to a Soviet first strike, and that we must move rapidly to prevent our falling into a position of strategic inferiority. This conclusion meant that we would engage in a big buildup of our weaponry, which would include more MIRVing of our missiles, and basing intermediate-range missiles (the Pershing II) and cruise missiles in Western Europe to counterbalance the Soviet SS-20s, SS-4s, and SS-5s. The Reagan administration also declared its intention of reviving two projects vetoed by Carter, the neutron bomb and a new manned bomber, the B-1.[3] Though Reagan rejected the mobile MX system proposed by Carter, he pressed ahead with plans to install the MX missile under one or another of various fixed-base versions.

That the Soviets might respond with an increased readiness to come to the bargaining table when confronted by this buildup was the declared hope of the Reagan administration. It sent a negotiating team to Geneva to discuss with the Soviets proposals for reductions in nuclear armaments in Europe;[4] and in May 1982 Reagan proposed Strategic Arms Reduction Talks (START), in the first stage of which each side would dismantle one-third of its long-range ballistic missile warheads. It was possible, however, that the Soviets would respond to the acceleration in U.S. defense spending with a further buildup of their own.

There was still another complication in the way of reaching an agreement to halt and then reverse the arms race. The weaponry that both sides had been developing was not only more and more powerful; it was also increasingly accurate and sophisticated. This evolution made possible the development from the early 1970s of new strategic alternatives. Instead of relying exclusively on Mutual Assured Destruction, which is a total war concept based on the threat of wiping out cities and their civilian populations, military planners could envision scenarios in which the superpowers could engage in limited thermonuclear wars. These could involve pinpointed attacks on military bases and industrial plants, accompanied by a threat of all-out destruction of cities if the country under attack retaliated.[5]

Whether or not this scenario is realistic, the fact that it was considered plausible by civilian and military leaders made it more difficult than ever to devise arms control agreements that would satisfy the fears of both sides that the other side was within reach of attaining a decisive strategic advantage.

Nuclear proliferation.   So far we have discussed the dangers inherent in the nuclear race between the two superpowers. But four other countries—Britain, France, China, and India—have joined the nuclear arms club; several more, including West Germany, Japan, Pakistan, South Africa, Israel, Canada, and Sweden, have the technological capacity to build nuclear weapons; and many other countries could develop that capacity within the next decade.

Clearly the multiplication of nuclear powers would considerably increase the dangers of a nuclear war breaking out sometime, somewhere, which would be difficult to limit to the nations involved at the outset.

"CONVENTIONAL" WAR: KOREA AND VIETNAM

A peace preserved by a nuclear balance of terror is far from being a condition of tranquility. It still assumes hostile attitudes between the superpowers. The prevailing situation of restrained belligerency came to be known as a "cold war"— a state of belligerency in which the conflicting parties refrained from attacking each other's territory.

However, the nuclear standoff did not cover all eventualities. For one thing, there could be many localized situations in which the use of atomic bombs would be totally out of proportion to the scale of the problem. In fact, nobody would believe that we would wipe out a country over some minor dispute—especially because that might invite massive retaliation on us by the Soviet Union. And even at major confrontation points, like West Germany, our leaders felt that we should be able to mount the kind of "conventional," or nonnuclear, military force that would discourage a Soviet invasion and thus provide at least a temporary alternative to nuclear war.

As part of our NATO agreements of 1949 we have maintained over 250,000 troops in Western Europe. Although we have not had to use these troops in battle, we have used military force elsewhere—for example, in Lebanon in 1958 and the Dominican Republic in 1965. And, faced with the takeover of China by Communists in 1949, the United States extended the containment principle from Europe to Asia and engaged our troops in two wars—Korea and Vietnam.

The Korean War began in June 1950, when the post–World War II division of Korea into two nations was challenged by an invasion of South Korea from the communist North. The United Nations Security Council (in the absence of the Soviet Union, which was boycotting the council) declared North Korea an aggressor, and the United States sent troops to lead the United Nations forces to repel the invasion. The tide of battle swung back and forth, first driving the North Koreans almost to the Chinese border, then driving the U.N. forces deep into South Korean territory as Chinese troops entered the war, then moving up again as the U.N. army counterattacked. After prolonged truce talks during which the fighting went on, the war came to an end in July 1953, with an agreement to divide Korea again along the 38th parallel.

A still larger and more devastating war was to come in Vietnam. France had been the colonial ruler of Indochina, but its defeat at Dien Bien Phu at the hands of communist forces in 1954 ended French power in Vietnam. Here again there was a partition into the communist North and the noncommunist South. The government of South Vietnam was threatened by armed insurrection, which, said the South Vietnamese, was controlled by the communist North. Under Eisenhower (who had refused to help the French at Dien Bien Phu), a limited amount of economic and military aid was sent to the South Vietnamese government. President Kennedy expanded this aid considerably, dispatching sixteen thousand "advisers" to train the South Vietnamese army and back them up militarily. This assistance was not sufficient to halt the communist forces, and in 1965 Lyndon Johnson decided that South Vietnam must not be allowed to fall. So Johnson launched a full-scale war against the National Liberation Front, or Viet Cong, and their supporters in North Vietnam. More men and more bombings were called for by the generals and military advisers. Escalation followed escalation, but as more U.S. troops were sent and more bombs dropped, the other side also stepped up its efforts. At last, in March 1968, Johnson rejected another request from the Joint Chiefs of Staff for more troops and began the process of scaling down our involvement in the war.

As president, Richard Nixon continued that process, pursuing a policy of "Vietnamization" of the war—turning it over to the South Vietnamese, while still giving them strong backing with bombers, supplies, and a diminishing number of American troops. The process lasted through Nixon's entire first term; and along the way U.S. forces invaded neighboring Cambodia and Laos (which provided sources of refuge for communist troops), intensified their bombing attacks, which came to include the North Vietnamese capital, Hanoi, and mined Haiphong harbor. At last an agreement was reached early in 1973 that resulted in the withdrawal of all U.S. troops from Vietnam. However, the hope that this agreement would lead to the survival of a noncommunist government in Saigon was soon to be dashed. Fighting resumed among the Vietnamese, resulting in the total collapse of the regime we had been supporting and the takeover of South Vietnam by the National Liberation Front in April of 1975.

DETENTE—AND AFTER

Armed confrontation with communist powers had had mixed results, at best. But, even while the Vietnam war raged, other approaches to dealing with communism were being developed. The United States was coming to the conclusion that it was no longer dealing with a completely united communist bloc headquartered in Moscow. Now the communist world was becoming polycentric—split into several centers of power. The most significant feature of polycentrism was the growing rivalry between the Soviet Union and the People's Republic of China, which had rejected Moscow's leadership and proposed its own version of communism, *Maoism* (named after Chinese Communist Party Chairman Mao Tse-tung). Consequently, the Chinese decided to unsettle the Russians by making an overture to communist China's great enemy, the United States. The Chinese let it be known that they would welcome a visit from President Nixon. In 1972 Nixon met the Chinese leaders in Peking, and from there he went on to Moscow to consult with Brezhnev and the other Soviet leaders.

The era of détente—of defusing the tensions and seeking areas of agreement—had begun and was pursued in a series of informal discussions conducted by Henry Kissinger with communist leaders. Among the products of détente was an increase in trade, including a massive sale of U.S. grain to the Soviet Union. Another outcome was a conference on Europe in Helsinki in 1975 at which the

West gave up its opposition to Soviet dominance in Eastern Europe in exchange for Soviet promises to ease its restrictions on foreign journalists and visitors, encourage more cultural exchanges, and loosen its restraints on emigration from the Soviet Union.

It must be emphasized, however, that détente never meant the end of conflict between the superpowers. The Soviet Union still insisted that communism must eventually supersede capitalism. And the United States remained committed to the containment of communism. Thus, when the Cambodian regime seized an American merchant ship, the *Mayaguez*, in 1975 (they said the ship was in their territorial waters, and we claimed it was in international waters), President Ford ordered a gunboat into Cambodia. The crew of the *Mayaguez* was rescued after an exchange of gunfire in which more U.S. marines were killed than the number of crew members rescued. In the Middle East, when the Soviet Union took the side of the Arab states in the 1973 Arab-Israeli war, the United States warned the Soviets to stay out, alerted U.S. forces around the world, and replaced the weapons the Israelis had lost in the war.

So détente meant not the end of tensions between the United States and the communist nations or even the abandonment of military confrontations, but rather an effort to reduce the tensions and confrontations that might lead to large-scale war.

Even that pallid version of détente did not last long. In December 1979 the Soviet Union, faced with spreading turbulence in a country it considered to be within its sphere of influence, invaded Afghanistan. Jimmy Carter responded with a ban on grain exports to the Soviet Union and the establishment of new restrictions on the sale to the Soviets of trucks, computers, and other products that could be put to military uses. Carter also called on U.S. and other athletes to boycott the 1980 Olympic games in Moscow.

The Reagan administration ended the grain boycott, but in other respects it took an even harder line toward the Soviet Union than did Jimmy Carter in his last year as president. It was Reagan's view that in all parts of the globe Soviet power was being used to undermine the security of this country and its allies, and that it was able to pursue its aggressive designs because everywhere the Soviets had achieved military superiority. We have already noted the Reagan administration's belief that the Soviets were gaining a clear advantage in nuclear weaponry; but in the ability to fight conventional wars the Soviets had a still larger lead, with more than double the United States' two million service personnel.

The same was true in particular areas of the world where vital U.S. interests were at stake, as in Europe, where the Warsaw Pact nations had considerably more troops, tanks, and other conventional weapons than the NATO countries (the latter having an advantage only with respect to tactical nuclear weapons).

Given its assessment of a deepening U.S. military inferiority, the Reagan administration pushed for an increase in defense outlays considerably beyond the substantial increases that Carter had called for. This increase would pay for the expansion of the strategic nuclear forces mentioned above, as well as more fighter planes, tanks, and ships, a buildup of our rapid deployment forces,[6] and military pay and benefit increases. (See figure 15-2.)

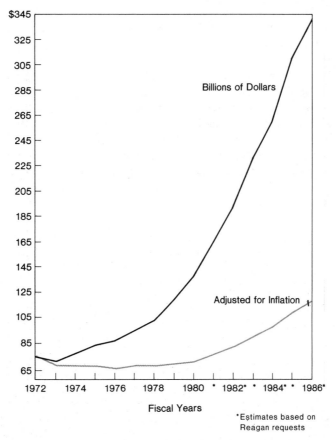

FIGURE 15–2.   United States Defense Spending
Source: U.S., Office of Management and Budget.

As a further indication of his concern with the Soviet challenge, Reagan changed his earlier opposition to the system of draft registration introduced by Carter and decided that registration would cut the time needed to introduce a draft should it become necessary.

FOREIGN AID

Another instrument used to hold back the advance of Soviet communism is foreign aid, which has taken two forms. First there is economic aid in the form of grants, loans, and technical assistance. Some of this assistance is sent for purely human-itarian purposes to relieve desperate conditions resulting from earthquakes, floods, famines, and other natural catastrophes. But in large measure economic aid is provided to build other nations' economies, thereby preventing their turning to the Soviets for support and relieving the social and political tensions on which communism thrives.

This intention was the driving force behind the Marshall Plan, proposed by Truman's Secretary of State George Marshall, which brought billions of dollars to the European economies that had been ravaged by World War II. Subsequently large amounts of economic aid were made available to many of the poor, or "developing," nations of the world.

The other kind of foreign aid is direct military assistance—supplying arms and training military forces, again with the objective of bolstering the will and the ability to resist communism.

From the end of World War II through 1980, the United States contributed close to $200 billion in economic and military aid, almost two-thirds falling in the economic assistance category (although the dividing line between economic and military aid is often hazy). Countries receiving the largest amounts in 1981 are shown in table 15-1.

TABLE 15–1 U.S. foreign aid, 1981

Recipients of most economic aid (in millions of dollars)		Recipients of most military aid (in millions of dollars)	
1. Egypt	$1,189	Israel	$1,400
2. Israel	785	Egypt	551
3. India	244	Turkey	252
4. Turkey	200	Greece	177
5. Bangladesh	155	Korea	161
6. Indonesia	128	Spain	126
7. Sudan	105	Philippines	76
8. Nicaragua	95	Portugal	53
9. Philippines	92	Thailand	51
10. Peru	81	Jordan	43

Source: World Bank, U.S. Agency for Economic Development.

Also of great economic significance to the developing nations are U.S. trade and foreign investment. In 1980 the United States imported $113 billion worth of imports from developing nations and exported to them goods worth $81 billion. In the same year U.S. direct investments in the developing nations amounted to almost $53 billion—about a quarter of all our direct investment overseas.

CLANDESTINE ACTIVITIES

Through the Central Intelligence Agency (CIA) and other intelligence-gathering units the United States has sought to find out the strength of the Soviet's military forces and its strategic and political plans. In addition the CIA has undertaken "covert" operations through the use of secret agents and the provision of money and arms to foreign groups in an effort to undermine or overthrow governments we believed to be sympathetic to Soviet communism or unable to provide the leadership necessary to resist communism.

Thus the CIA helped overthrow governments in Iran in 1953 and Guatemala in 1954. The Bay of Pigs in 1961 was an abortive CIA-directed plan to bring about the end of the Castro regime in Cuba. Between 1963 and 1973 the CIA subsidized political parties and newspapers, first to prevent the election of Salvador Allende in Chile, then to contribute to his overthrow. The CIA also participated in efforts to get rid of Rafael Trujillo in the Dominican Republic and Ngo Dinh Diem in South Vietnam in the early 1960s.

Other CIA tactics have included attempts to assassinate foreign leaders deemed sympathetic to the Soviets. Special toxins were prepared for Congolese leader Patrice Lumumba in 1960 to be put on "anything he could get to his mouth, whether it was food or a toothbrush."[7] There were also plans to kill Cuban president Fidel Castro, including exploding seashells, poisoned cigars, and a poisoned diving suit.[8]

OTHER DIMENSIONS OF U.S. FOREIGN POLICY

The containment of Soviet communism, we have seen, has been the most important element in U.S. foreign policy since World War II. In considerable measure this policy has been driven by ideology. Yet there has been a growing rapprochement between the United States and the People's Republic of China (CPR), which is quite clearly a communist country yet is deeply hostile to the Soviet Union. The Reagan administration has been more reluctant than its predecessors to weaken U.S. ties with the anticommunist Chinese regime on Taiwan, and the Peking government was greatly irritated by the continued sale of U.S. military equipment to Taiwan. However, Reagan's decision in January 1982 not to provide Taiwan with an advanced fighter plane, although it did not mollify the CPR, was an indication of his desire to sustain the Nixon-initiated link with the CPR.

Thus it has become increasingly clear that the main threat perceived by U.S. policy makers is the power of the Soviet Union and its allies.

But if the Soviet challenge has been at the center of U.S. foreign policy concerns, other considerations have also been of considerable importance.

Relations with other affluent, industrialized countries. These relations, with countries such as Britain, Germany, France, Japan, and Canada, include the development of anti-Soviet alliances, but they also involve large-scale trade, which is sometimes the cause of tension and conflict (as with Japanese automobile imports). Moreover, many of the major U.S. corporations are multinationals that have extensive holdings in industrialized countries abroad (that sometimes return the favor with large investments in the United States).

Relations with the developing nations. The developing nations of Latin America, Asia, and Africa (the "Third World") are of interest to us for more reasons than their potential for being taken over by Soviet communism. The conditions of life in many of the developing nations stand in stark contrast to conditions in the industrialized world, as shown in table 15-2. The poverty among the poorest of the developing nations brings with it the danger of periodic famines and pestilence and is therefore a source of international instability. Although most of these countries are now freed from the colonial status that was common before World War II, they still complain that the rich countries are exploiting them and

TABLE 15–2 Living conditions in selected developing and industrialized nations, 1981

	Gross national product (dollars per capita)	Life expectation at birth (years)
Developing Nations		
Bangladesh	90	49
India	190	52
Nigeria	670	56
Philippines	600	62
Tanzania	260	52
Industrialized Nations		
West Germany	11,730	73
Japan	8,810	76
Sweden	11,930	76
United Kingdom	6,320	73
United States	10,630	74

Source: World Bank.

buying their raw materials too cheaply. This resentment must be a cause of concern to us, because their raw materials are important to our economy, and some of our multinational corporations have large investments in developing nations, particularly in Latin America.

Relations with the newly rich, nonindustrialized countries. The affluence of these countries results from their ownership of large supplies of a scarce resource. The obvious examples here are the Arab states, which are the core members of the Organization of Petroleum Exporting Countries. Although the United States is concerned about Soviet infiltration in the Middle East, a more vital concern for our economy, and thus for our foreign policy, is to ensure the continued flow of oil.

Control of terrorism and other violations of international law. The outbreak in the 1970s of a large number of incidents of terrorist violence in various parts of the world has been a source of considerable concern to U.S. foreign-policy makers. Many, but by no means all, of these acts have been driven by political ideology.

In fact, that particularly outrageous violation of international law—the seizure by a group of Iranians, backed by their government, of the U.S. embassy in Teheran and the holding of a number of Americans as hostages from November 1979 until January 1981—was an act of revolutionaries who were mostly inspired by nationalistic, anti-American fervor rather than communist sympathies.

Protecting human rights. Particularly during the Carter presidency the defense of individual rights against governmental torture, arbitrary execution or imprisonment, or denial of free expression has been a declared theme of U.S. foreign policy. The Soviet Union's persecution of dissenters, intellectuals, and Jews was a prime target of Carter's human rights campaign. But the United States also tried to intercede on behalf of individuals whose rights were denied by right-wing governments in Latin America.

With the Reagan administration, however, public protests to foreign governments have been reserved mostly for communist rather than right-wing regimes.

The development of international organizations.   Having turned away from isolationism to internationalism, the United States has looked for ways of replacing international conflict with cooperation. To this end we helped found the United Nations in 1945, and the United States is one of the five permanent members of the Security Council, the executive committee of the United Nations. (The other permanent members of the Security Council are the USSR, the People's Republic of China, Britain, and France, and there are nineteen others chosen for two-year terms).

However, the United States has been disappointed in its hopes that a spirit of amity and cooperation would prevail in the United Nations. Conflicts have repeatedly broken out in the world organization, and both the United States and the Soviet Union have resorted to the use of the veto (to which permanent members of the Security Council are entitled) over U.N. decisions. In the General Assembly of the United Nations, no country has such veto power; and, because every nation, however large or small, has one vote in the assembly, the United States and the affluent nations are often outvoted by Third World countries. Similarly, in some of the specialized agencies and councils that deal with economic, social, and cultural matters, positions are sometimes adopted that the United States strongly opposes. American opposition has been particularly strong with respect to actions taken by a combination of Third World, Arab, and communist nations against Israel, a close ally of the United States. Even so, the United States continues to support the United Nations as an important forum for discussion and negotiation.

To sum up, U.S. foreign policy consists of many networks of relationships. Of all the themes that sustain these networks the containment of communism has been the most significant and the most persistent since the Second World War. But we cannot fully understand American foreign policy without taking into account some of the other elements mentioned here.

FOREIGN AFFAIRS AND THE POLICY-MAKING PROCESS

THE PRESIDENCY

As we saw in chapter 7, as chief diplomat and commander-in-chief of the armed forces, the president has the prime responsibility for making and carrying out foreign policy. Only Congress has the constitutional authority to declare war. Yet, without clear authority from Congress, Truman intervened in Korea and stationed seven U.S. divisions in Germany; Eisenhower sent troops to Lebanon; Kennedy approved the Bay of Pigs invasion; Johnson took military action in the Dominican Republic and Vietnam; and Nixon attacked Cambodia and Laos. Each executive could point to many precedents.

Jefferson, who is often quoted by senators who want to limit the president's power, made the Louisiana Purchase and told the Senate about it later. Polk got into a war with Mexico in 1846, then secured Congress's declaration of war. Wilson sent troops to Siberia to fight the Bolsheviks in 1918, although the United

States was not at war with Russia. Roosevelt provided protection for British convoys in 1940–1941 and sent them some old U.S. destroyers before we entered World War II and before getting Congress' sanction. Not one of these actions was challenged by the Supreme Court.

The Senate, says the Constitution, must review all treaties and may nullify them, and the larger numbers of all U.S. agreements with other countries are acted on by Congress as "statutory agreements."[9] However, presidents, using the power they say is implied in the constitutional roles of principal foreign policy spokesperson, commander-in-chief, and chief executive, have also made "executive agreements" with foreign countries that do not require the approval of the Senate. Every year there are considerably more executive agreements made than treaties. Most of them are on routine technical matters. (Eisenhower's secretary of state, John Foster Dulles, once said that "every time we open a new privy, we have to have an executive agreement.") But some agreements, to establish military bases abroad, for example, can have great importance and consequences.

In exercising their great authority in foreign affairs, presidents have been eager to demonstrate their determination to contain communism. This determination inspired Kennedy's refusal to accept the emplacement of missiles in Cuba in 1962 and his refusal to agree immediately to a Soviet demand to pull U.S. bases out of Turkey in exchange for the withdrawal of missiles from Cuba. (Kennedy had actually given the order for dismantling the Turkish bases some time before and was appalled to discover it had not yet been done. But he decided that to do it publicly, under pressure, would be read as a sign of weakness.) The determination to contain communism underlay Nixon's explanation after invading Cambodia in 1971 that the United States must not act "like a pitiful helpless giant." It was also the reason for Carter's boycott of the Moscow Olympics.

But the insistence of American presidents on resisting communism has been paralleled by their preoccupation with the danger of thermonuclear war. This concern led to Eisenhower's doing nothing when Soviet troops marched into Hungary in a brutal suppression of an uprising in 1956; to Kennedy's allowing Khrushchev to save face as he withdrew the Cuban missiles by giving him a guarantee that Castro would remain (and that the Turkish bases would be dismantled quietly after a decent interval had elapsed); and to Johnson's finally rejecting the generals' demand for two hundred thousand more troops for Vietnam. Fear of thermonuclear war also led to détente and to SALT.

Both of these concerns powerfully affected decision making by presidents as they thought about the verdict of history on their administrations. On the one hand, they did not want to be blamed in history books for presiding over a defeat in war or the decline of American power in the world. On the other hand, if their recklessness or misjudgment should plunge the world into thermonuclear war, there might not be any history books to discuss the record of their administration.

CONGRESS

Between the end of World War II and the late 1960s Congress rarely challenged the dominance of the executive branch in foreign policy. When the president called for the support of Congress, he usually obtained it. Only in the field of economic aid were the administration foreign policy budgetary proposals regularly cut by Congress.

With Vietnam, however, the Senate Foreign Relations Committee began to challenge presidential power, and in 1969 the Senate approved the National Commitments Resolution, which put presidents on notice that they must make no more military commitments abroad without involving Congress. Subsequently, Congress repealed the Tonkin Gulf resolution, which had given Lyndon Johnson a free hand in Vietnam; and in 1973 Congress passed, over Nixon's veto, the War Powers Act, which set a limit of ninety days to the president's authority to send U.S. troops into a combat area without specific congressional approval.

Gerald Ford had his foreign policy difficulties with Congress, which cut off military aid to Turkey while Secretary of State Kissinger was trying to settle a conflict between Turkey and Greece over Cyprus. Jimmy Carter secured the two-thirds Senate vote needed to ratify his negotiation of the Panama Canal Treaty only after long debate and by the narrowest of margins, and he never came close to the necessary two-thirds of the Senate for the SALT II treaty he had signed with the Soviets.

Ronald Reagan won his battle for congressional approval of his plan to sell an Airborne Warning and Combat System (AWACS) to Saudi Arabia in 1981, but this victory, too, was achieved by a narrow margin in the Senate and despite rejection in the House by a large margin.[10]

Nonetheless, the president still retains a great deal of autonomy in his conduct of foreign affairs. Where the safety of American troops is threatened, the president can claim that he will be derelict in his responsibilities as commander-in-chief if he does not do everything in his power to protect them. If the troops have all been withdrawn, he can still argue that he must do everything necessary to protect an ally or preserve the integrity of a treaty or an executive agreement in accordance with his constitutional responsibility to maintain peace and the national security. And giving the president authority to commit troops to combat for ninety days may leave Congress with little opportunity to cancel the commitment once it is made.

THE FEDERAL BUREAUCRACIES

We noted in earlier chapters that, in making their decisions, presidents have not relied only on the traditional structures of government. They have built their own staffs in the Executive Office and turned to people they trusted for advice wherever they were located. This arrangement has been especially true in foreign policy, where the need for speed and confidentiality in the decision-making process leads presidents to seek as much flexibility and informality as possible.

Still, foreign policy cannot be formed or carried out by a few people operating in a free-wheeling, impromptu fashion. There have to be elaborate sources of information and analysis and large numbers of people to carry out the myriad details of policy. In other words, there have to be institutions.

The National Security Council. The National Security Council (NSC) is located in the Executive Office and directed by the president's adviser for national security. It was established in 1947 as the principal instrument for pulling together all the various sources of advice and information a president needs to integrate "domestic, foreign, and military policies relating to the national security." The president chairs the NSC, and its members include the vice-president and the secretaries of state and defense. The chairperson of the Joint Chiefs of Staff and the director of the CIA are advisers to the council, and other officials, such as the secretary of the treasury and the director of the U.S. Information Agency, attend at the president's invitation.

The State Department. The impatience of some presidents with the NSC has been far exceeded by their frustration with the State Department. In some cases this frustration has resulted from dissatisfaction with the performance of the State Department's head, the secretary of state. As the State Department sees it, the secretary of state is the president's principal adviser in the formulation of foreign policy and the conduct of foreign relations. This belief was true enough of Eisenhower's secretary of state, John Foster Dulles, and, of course, Henry Kissinger. But, as we have seen, it was far from true of Dean Rusk under Kennedy or William Rogers under Nixon, both of whom had less influence than the White House national security assistant.

However, even the more powerful secretaries of state have rarely been able to provide the kind of speedy response, initiative, and coherent planning that presidents sorely need. The problem is that the State Department is a sprawling, poorly coordinated agency. As figure 15-3 indicates, the State Department encompasses an enormous range of agencies and activities, including a policy planning staff; geographical bureaus headed by assistant secretaries; a variety of bureaus concerned with specific functional areas, such as international organizations, congressional relations, intelligence gathering, economic and business affairs, and protocol; the group of professional diplomats who constitute the U.S. Foreign Service; and about 275 overseas consulates and embassies.

Other Foreign Affairs Units. The Agency for International Development (AID) operates as a semiautonomous arm of the State Department. Its job is to administer programs of financial and technical assistance to developing nations.

The Peace Corps, created by President Kennedy in 1961, sends Americans (mostly, although not exclusively, young) to provide various kinds of organizational and technical help to poorer nations. Under President Nixon the Peace Corps became part of ACTION, which administers a variety of domestic and overseas volunteer programs.

The United States Information Agency (USIA) is the overseas information and propaganda arm of the U.S. government. It operates libraries and information centers abroad and produces and distributes films and magazines. The USIA also operates the Voice of America, a worldwide shortwave radio network broadcasting in thirty-nine languages.

The Department of Defense. With a budget moving upward from $200 billion a year, the Department of Defense (DOD) is clearly a force to be reckoned with

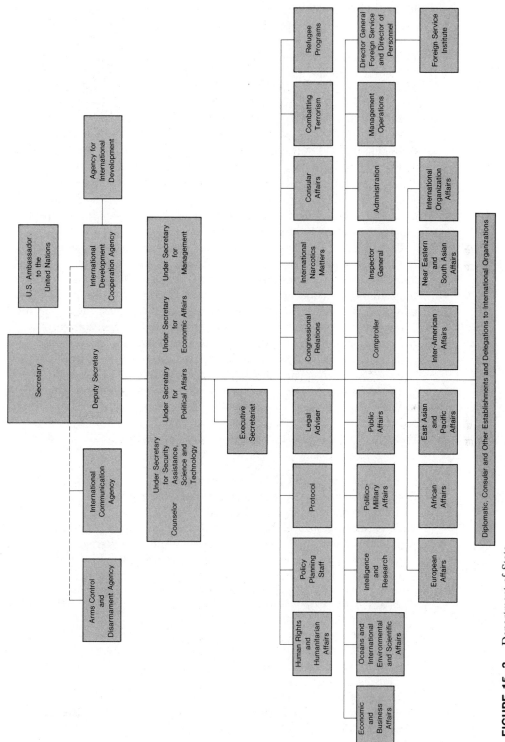

FIGURE 15–3. Department of State
Source: *U.S. Government Manual 1981–1982.*

in the field of foreign policy. Although DOD is concerned with building military strength, the American political tradition requires that the military be subject to civilian control. Thus the president is commander-in-chief of the armed services. Heading the Department of Defense is the secretary of defense, to whom report the deputy secretary, several assistant secretaries, and the secretaries of the Army, Navy, and Air Force (who head up the three armed forces departments). Working for DOD, in the Pentagon in Washington and in other U.S. and foreign locations, are over a million civilian employees.

Despite the ultimate civilian control of the DOD, the military has a major voice in shaping foreign and national security policy. The armed services include close to two million members. They are led by the chiefs of the Army and the Air Force, the chief of naval operations, and the commandant of the Marine Corps. Each reports to the secretary for the Army, Navy, or Air Force. But each is also a member of the Joint Chiefs of Staff (JCS), and, through its chairperson, each reports directly to the secretary of defense.

Periodically, there have been sharp conflicts between civilian and military leaders in the shaping of defense policies. The military's role was particularly threatened when the thermonuclear era arrived, because military officers were trained for battles between armies, navies, and air forces, not for planning the mutual annihilation of whole countries with a few missiles. Consequently, in the early 1960s President Kennedy's secretary of defense, Robert McNamara, brought into the Pentagon a group of brilliant young civilian systems analysts—the so-called "whiz kids"—who seized the initiative from the resentful generals in designing and coordinating new military strategies. Civilians continue to be involved at the upper levels of Pentagon strategic planning; but today there is a new breed of military officers, trained in the latest tools of strategic analysis and exposed in a ten-month program at the National War College to a sophisticated curriculum that explores the social, economic, political, and even ethical context of military policy.

The Arms Control and Disarmament Agency.   An independent agency established by Congress at the request of President Kennedy in 1961, the Arms Control and Disarmament Agency (ACDA) advises the president and the State Department on disarmament and arms control questions, manages the conduct of negotiations in those fields, and carries out programs of long-range research. It has played a major role in the various treaties, including the 1963 nuclear test ban, the Nuclear Nonproliferation Treaty, and the SALT negotiations.

The Intelligence Agencies.   Conducting foreign policy in a world of separate, sometimes mutually hostile, nation-states involves a constant effort to discover the extent of the strength, resources, and intentions of other nations. Some of the data are openly available, but some are not. The United States maintains a number of agencies that spend billions of dollars a year gathering and analyzing information from abroad. The principal ones are the Central Intelligence Agency (CIA); the Pentagon's Defense Intelligence Agency (DIA) and its National Security Agency (which makes and breaks codes); and the State Department's Bureau of Intelligence and Research (INR).

The CIA has been assigned the key leadership role among these agencies, because the director of the CIA also has broad responsibility for all foreign intelligence activities. The CIA has two main divisions. One collects and analyzes data from a variety of sources: published material, photographs taken by orbiting satellites and high-flying U-2 planes, and espionage. The other engages in covert or clandestine activities.

Espionage often involves methods that break the laws of other countries and arouse criticism at home. Much more controversial, however, are the CIA's covert activities, which have included not only the efforts to overthrow or assassinate foreign leaders mentioned earlier, but also subsidies to the National Student Association from 1952 to 1967 to help American students compete with the Soviet Union in the world student movement[11] and confidential research grants to a number of professors in U.S. universities.[12]

As revelations about these activities came to light through congressional and media investigations, a public outcry led to changes in the top leadership of the CIA and the structure of the intelligence services. Executive orders by Presidents Ford and Carter, as well as new congressional legislation,[13] sought to prevent further abuses and reduce covert activities. In turn these reforms led to countercharges that our intelligence services were being hobbled and that we were falling behind in the task of discovering the plans of the Soviet Union, terrorist organizations, and other enemies of our national security. Under the Reagan administration there was less enthusiasm in the White House for tight restrictions on the work of the CIA, and an executive order was issued giving the CIA more leeway in its activities within the United States.[14] Even so, the CIA's more fanciful exploits of the past were less likely to be undertaken in the future.

Although the CIA has devoted a major part of its energies to opposing Soviet power, it has not always agreed with the military's assessment of the extent of that power. During Vietnam the CIA was more critical of the wisdom of escalation and much less inclined than the Pentagon to underestimate the strength and will of the Vietcong and the North Vietnamese. The CIA has also generally been less pessimistic than the military about the extent to which the Soviets have gained the advantage in the nuclear arms race.[15]

INTEREST GROUPS

Foreign policy attracts pressures from a wide array of interest groups. Those groups engaged in exporting and importing usually favor free trade, and business study groups such as the Committee for Economic Development advocate a policy of removing all artificial barriers to the flow of commerce between nations. On the other side, business and farm groups, sometimes backed by labor, that feel threatened by foreign competition press for Congress and the administration to impose tariffs or quotas on imports.

On defense issues, industries that manufacture weapons lobby long and hard for federal contracts. Very large sums of money (over $40 billion in 1982) are spent on procurement of weapons and equipment by the armed services each year. About two-thirds of the contracts for major weapons systems go to major corporations such as Lockheed, General Dynamics, and Boeing. These companies work closely with the Department of Defense and with the senators and representatives whose constituencies stand to benefit from the contracts for weapons production, as well as from military installations. Thus the California, Texas, and New York delegations engage in bitter battles to keep contracts in their states or to attract them away from the others. The committees of Congress concerned with the military, the Armed Services and Appropriations Committees, have generally been highly receptive to the views of the military, and their chairpersons have been especially receptive. Mendel Rivers, Democratic chair of the House Armed Services Committee for many years, used the campaign slogan, "Rivers Delivers," and he was instrumental in delivering to Charleston, South Carolina, a military payroll of $200 million a year from a variety of installations, including two Polaris missile facilities, a shipyard, and Army, Navy, and Marine centers.

Moreover, the defense contractors support the efforts of the Pentagon to use arms sales as a means of tying other countries to U.S. policies. In 1980 over $600 billion worth of American arms were sold abroad, about 23 percent of the total world arms trade.

In 1980, fifty-eight companies did more than $200 million worth of business with the Department of Defense. The top ten are shown in table 15-3.

TABLE 15–3 Top ten U.S. corporations doing business with the Department of Defense, 1980 (in thousands of dollars)

1.	General Dynamics	$3,517,906
2.	McDonnell Douglas	3,246,557
3.	United Technologies	3,108,901
4.	Boeing	2,385,459
5.	General Electric	2,202,042
6.	Lockheed	2,037,044
7.	Hughes Aircraft	1,819,058
8.	Raytheon	1,745,107
9.	Tenneco	1,524,414
10.	Grumman	1,322,023

Source: U.S., Department of Defense.

Defense contractors have been among the leading contributors to public campaigns for higher defense spending, for specific weapons systems like the antiballistic missile, and for organizations dedicated to these causes, like the American Security Council and the Committee on the Present Danger. The latter, which was formed in late 1976 to persuade the public and the incoming Carter administration to take a stronger stand against the Soviets, included former members of the Johnson administration like Paul Nitze and Eugene Rostow,[16] the secretary-treasurer of the AFL–CIO, and academics like Dr. Albert Wohlstetter, a nuclear war strategist from the University of Chicago.

Although there are no specific economic interest groups fighting against higher defense spending, substantial campaigns of opposition have been mounted by a variety of liberal and antiwar groups. These groups have included the National Committee for a Sane Nuclear Policy (SANE); the Council for a Liveable World; the Center for Defense Information (headed by a retired rear admiral, Gene LaRocque); the Center for the Study of National Security; and such labor organizations as the United Auto Workers and the Machinists Union. A new coordinating group emerged late in 1981 to organize the Nuclear Weapons Freeze Campaign, an effort, backed by several members of the Senate and the House, to pressure the administration to negotiate with the Soviets a freeze on the testing and production of nuclear weaponry.

Another kind of interest group is heard from as we consider American policy toward countries or regions. Ethnic groups and immigrants, or the descendants of immigrants, voice their concerns over the fate of the country from which they or their forebears came. Pressure from Greek-Americans was at least partly responsible for Congress's cutting off arms aid to Turkey in the Turkish-Greek conflict over Cyprus. Black leaders push for action against white-supremacist South Africa and Rhodesia. Refugees from Castro's Cuba resist proposals for détente with Castro.

In the case of the Middle East the cause of Israel has been effectively argued by such organizations as the American Israel Public Affairs Committee, the Anti-Defamation League of B'nai B'rith, and the American Jewish Committee. These organizations have constituencies of considerable political effectiveness, because Jews tend to be politically active; they have included some of the most effective campaign fundraisers for key members of Congress; they are well represented among journalists, academics, and lawyers; and their votes are concentrated in northern and western states such as New York and California, which are particularly important in presidential election strategies.

Historically, the Arab side has not been nearly as well represented in American politics as the Israeli cause, because there are fewer than 2 million Americans of Arab heritage as compared with almost 6 million Jewish Americans. Still, there are increasingly effective organizations of Arab-Americans, including the National Association of Arab-Americans, the Arab-American University Graduates, and the Palestine Congress of North America. The League of Arab States finances Arab Information Centers in American cities. More important, the oil money of the Arab states has become a factor to be reckoned with domestically. Great sums of that money have been invested in American bonds, banks, businesses, and land developments and have paid for the lobbying and legal services of former cabinet officers like Clark Clifford, Richard Kleindienst, William Rogers, and John Connally, former Kennedy aide and liberal activist Fred Dutton, and former chairman of the Senate Foreign Relations Committee J. W. Fulbright. Moreover, those major oil corporations that have heavy investments in the Middle East have generally offered advice in Washington favorable to the Arab side,[17] as have big construction companies like Bechtel (of which Caspar Weinberger and George Shultz were top executives before becoming Reagan's secretary of defense and secretary of state, respectively).

PUBLIC OPINION

The policy leadership of the executive branches of government and of interest groups always has to be set within a context of mass public opinion. Thus the effectiveness of the pro-Israel lobby results from the support of Israel revealed by opinion polls as well as from the budget of the American Israel Public Affairs Committee.

But what factors shape public opinion on foreign policy? To a considerable extent it is the leadership exercised by the president. Until recently almost every major presidential initiative since World War II, whether toward war or peace, has been followed by a surge of public support. Thus the majority supported both the Marshall Plan to rebuild Europe's war-shattered economy during the Truman administration and the Bay of Pigs invasion approved by President Kennedy. Majority opinion also approved all of Johnson's escalations during the Vietnam War, including the mining of North Vietnam's harbors, and Nixon's visit to Peking.

However, there are limits to how far the majority will follow the president. Before the end of the Korean War there was little support left among the electorate for continuing our involvement. In Vietnam there was growing sentiment for getting out as time went on. Students and other antiwar activists launched furious demonstrations; and, although a majority of the public were critical of the demonstrators and their tactics, the air of tension and passionate protest that was generated created a pervasive sense that the war was controversial and politically unpalatable. This attitude was intensified as the media, particularly television newscasters and commentators, turned away from their earlier neutrality or support for the war and became openly critical. Johnson's standing in the opinion polls plummeted.

After Vietnam the trend of opinion in the country was toward reducing our overseas involvements, cutting our defense spending, and avoiding sending our troops to help allies if they were attacked. A 1975 Harris poll indicated that the only country a majority of Americans would want to protect with our troops in the event of an invasion was Canada.

By 1978 there were majorities in favor of sending troops if Panama closed the canal to the United States and if the Soviets invaded Western Europe, but not to deal with any other threats. Thus only 21 percent would support the sending of troops to defend South Korea against an attack by North Korea, although we had fought a long and bloody war with exactly that provocation in 1950. (See table 15-4.)

On the other hand, the post-Vietnam support for reduced defense spending gradually weakened, according to a Gallup poll, and by 1981 had given way to a 64 to 29 percent margin in favor of the Reagan administration's plans for a major increase in the defense budget.[18] The same poll indicated that 54 percent believed we should aim for more military power than the Soviet Union as against 37 percent who thought that parity would be enough; and there was a 49 to 43 percent margin in favor of returning to the military draft.

Yet the public had not given up on the idea of an arms control agreement. By

TABLE 15-4 Attitudes toward sending U.S. troops, 1978

Question: There has been some discussion about the circumstances that might justify using U.S. troops in other parts of the world. I'd like to ask your opinion about several situations. First, would you favor or oppose the use of U.S. troops if: (read list)

	Percent in favor
Panama closes Canal to U.S.	58
Soviets invade Western Europe	54
Soviets take West Berlin	48
Arabs cut off oil to U.S.	36
Arabs invade Israel	22
North Korea invades South Korea	21
China invades Taiwan	20
Israel invades Arab states	11

Source: John E. Reilly (ed.), *American Public Opinion and U.S. Foreign Policy, 1979* (Chicago: The Chicago Council on Foreign Relations, 1979), p. 26. Survey was conducted by the Gallup Organization for the Council.

59 to 31 percent there was support for "signing another arms agreement with the Soviet Union to limit some nuclear weapons on both sides"; and members of Congress and pollsters reported in 1982 that the proposal for a mutual freeze on nuclear weaponry was gaining wide support among the public. Moreover, the huge federal budget deficits had again eroded the public's enthusiasm for higher defense spending by the fall of 1982.

FIVE PERSPECTIVES ON FOREIGN POLICY

THE LIBERALS: TOO MUCH NATIONALISM, TOO MUCH ANTICOMMUNISM

To the liberals there have been two great flaws in American foreign policy since World War II— an obsession with the danger of international communism and a persistent attachment to an outmoded nationalism. With respect to communism, liberals have been among its harshest critics. They were bitterly opposed to many of the policies of the Soviet Union during the Stalin era. They are deeply critical of the continued persecution of Russian writers, scientists, and other intellectuals in the 1970s. They do not believe that all the troubles of the world have been caused by the United States, or that in an age of nuclear weapons, when the Soviets have vast stockpiles, we can unilaterally dispense with our entire nuclear armory.

What they do believe is that the cold war is the result of actions, some planned, some blundered into, by both sides and that we and the Russians

must both bear some of the blame. Our part of the blame lies in our having adopted a rigidly ideological hostility to the Soviet Union; in refusing to see until many years had passed that Moscow was losing its control over communist parties in other parts of the world; and in pursuing a policy dedicated primarily to the preservation of the privileges of the "have" nations of the world against the "have-nots" and of corrupt dictators against the aspirations of the masses of the people.

The second defect in our policy, as the liberals see it, is the obstinate reluctance to depart in any significant degree from the belief that the solutions to world problems can be found through the pursuit of our separate national interest rather than focusing on the needs that all people have in common. The world may not be ready, liberals recognize, to abandon the nation-state. But our problems now are global, and the greatest nation in the world should be helping all the others to see that simply national solutions are irrelevant and obsolete. Instead, our foreign policy has clung fearfully to the symbols of nationalism and super-patriotism.

There have been three damaging consequences of this combination of anticommunism and nationalism. First, we have engaged in a buildup of nuclear and thermonuclear weapons far exceeding the needs of our national security. Second, we have allowed ourselves to take on a series of military involvements, some on a very large scale. Third, we have interfered in other countries' politics through particularly vicious and degrading activities.

The arms race. We have been spending ruinous amounts of money on our stockpiles of thermonuclear weapons. All we require is "minimum deterrence"—the least amount needed to guarantee that the Soviets would not unleash an attack on us because to do so would mean their destruction as well as ours. Instead we have gone on to build "overkill"—the capacity to destroy any potential enemy's population several times over.

But now the military and their conservative supporters are claiming that we need more nuclear missiles, bigger and more accurate missiles, smaller missiles for battlefield use, mobile missiles to fool the Soviets, space missiles for satellite warfare, and civil defense programs in an impossible attempt to save the population and industry in case of a thermonuclear attack. So rapid is the Soviet buildup, say our military leaders, that unless we give them everything they are asking for we run a high risk that by the mid- or late 1980s the Soviets could wipe out our entire ICBM force with one sudden strike.

The liberals recognize that the Soviets have indeed been engaged in a huge expansion of their arsenal of nuclear weapons. But liberals believe that the fears of the U.S. military are absurdly exaggerated. First, in assessing the relative power of the two sides, the military fail to mention that a considerable part of the Soviet nuclear armory is targeted not on the United States and its allies but on China, whereas we suffer from no such preoccupation with a two-front nuclear war.

Next, the military's scenarios assume much too great a level of accuracy by Soviet (or U.S.) missiles. Nuclear missiles, fortunately, have never been tested in a real war situation, and the Soviets cannot believe that they would be able to prevent a considerable number of our ICBMs from being fired at the Soviet Union in retaliation. Furthermore, even if *all* our ICBMs were knocked out, there would still be our bomber fleet, our nuclear weapons in Europe, and our fleet of nuclear-armed submarines, each with enough destructive power to wipe out several Soviet cities. Only a completely mad, utterly suicidal Soviet leadership would be willing to bring down the certainty of such destruction on its people.

Why, then, do we have so much pressure for a huge increase in nuclear arms spending? The first reason is our leaders' nationalist and ideological obsessions, which force us to aim for superiority rather than acceptance of enough to provide for our national security.

Then there are the internal political pressures from what President Eisenhower in his farewell address called "the military-industrial complex." This complex includes the various branches of the military themselves, each presenting its own shopping list every year to protect its own position not only from the Soviets but also from each other. The Air Force wants more MIRVing, new bombers, fighters, helicopters, and radar systems. The Navy insists on more and better nuclear submarines and nuclear-powered aircraft carriers. The Army asks for more and smaller tactical nuclear weapons, tanks, guns, troops, and a great deal of almost everything else usable in war.

Working hand in hand with the military are the defense industries that profit from the production of these weapons systems. They hire retired senior military officers to present the case for *their* company to the Pentagon. They take out lavish advertisements in magazines (charged to the taxpayer as a business expense), making the case for a new missile or plane. They work on Congress both indirectly, through the Pentagon, and in direct discussions with the legislators from the districts in which their plants are located.

Thus Congress, too, becomes part of the military-industrial complex.

And, of course, our presidents have been highly responsive to the pressures of this military-industrial complex. Kennedy ordered a vast increase in nuclear weapons, which continued until Secretary of Defense Robert McNamara decided we had enough by 1967–1968. Under Nixon we moved ahead with MIRVing. Carter, after promising defense reductions and rejecting the B-1 bomber and the neutron bomb, proceeded to endorse the most expensive weapons system ever, the MX. And Reagan launched a spending program that could lead to an outlay of a third of a trillion dollars in 1986.

This spending, say the liberals, would be ut-

RANAN LURIE, 1970.

terly ruinous. As was suggested in our discussion of the economy in chapter 12, spending of such proportions would generate the same kind of long-term inflationary pressure inflicted on us by Vietnam, and it would be the cause of even more savage cuts in social programs than the Reagan administration has already embarked on. It would have an acutely damaging effect on our industrial system, because it would divert from the development of the new products on which our economic survival depended a large proportion of our scarce supply of scientists and engineers. Indeed, our heavy investments in armaments may well be a significant factor in our growing competitive disadvantage with Japan. U.S. defense spending was moving up from 5.5 percent of our Gross National Product in 1982, while the Japanese (under intense pressure from the United States to increase their outlays) were spending a little under 1 percent of their GNP.

Most dangerous of all, the U.S. buildup would surely be matched by the Soviets, and the escalation of the arms race would nullify any hopes of slowing the proliferation of nuclear weapons to more and more countries. All these developments would multiply many times over the threat pointed to by British historian A.J.P. Taylor: "If weapons exist they will one day be used. The deterrent will work ninety-nine times out of a hundred. At the hundredth time it will not. One side will judge that it can win or, even worse, that without immediate action it will lose. Such is the lesson of history. . . ."[19]

Overextending our military commitments. Just as liberals accept the case for building a certain level of thermonuclear force, they argue for maintaining conventional military forces to defend our vital national interests, which include the survival of democratic societies in areas such as Western Europe, Israel, and Japan.

But, liberals contend, since the end of World War II we have extended our responsibilities far beyond these basic requirements of foreign policy and allowed our obsession with the threat of communism to force us into the role of policeman to the world. Although this action has not so far led us into any nuclear confrontations, we have used conventional weapons, and, in Korea and Vietnam, on a very large and bloody scale.

In the case of Korea there was at least the rationale that an army had launched an invasion across an established frontier, and the United Nations condemned the attack and joined the efforts to stop it militarily. This rationale did not exist in Vietnam. We got into and expanded the war in Vietnam, according to the liberals, for two principal reasons. Fear of communism was the point of departure. Any regime, no matter how corrupt and reactionary, was to be preferred to communism, which had taken over in China, North Korea, and Cuba and must not be allowed to advance further. In Asia, Vietnam was seen as the vital test, the domino that must not fall.

To this underlying motivation was added a second factor—nationalistic arrogance. To Lyndon Johnson, Secretary of Defense McNamara, and the other key members of the administration, it seemed inconceivable that the enormous might of America would not be able to overwhelm a small agrarian country. To McNamara in particular, Vietnam represented a problem that, like all problems, could be dealt with by the new technologies and modes of analysis that he and his aides had brought with them into the Pentagon.

As the years went by and the carnage increased, the obstinate self-delusion of some of these men broke down. McNamara and White House National Security Advisor McGeorge Bundy left the administration. Lyndon Johnson, surrounded now only by true believers in a lost cause, persisted until the new Secretary of Defense Clark Clifford and elder statesmen like Dean Acheson (Harry Truman's secretary of state) advised him not to accept the generals' request for another 206,000 troops. Johnson at last started the process of scaling down the war.

Richard Nixon continued the process of winding down the war, but the pace was agonizingly slow. Gradually, he and Kissinger played out the game of Vietnamization, launching periodic savage strikes and spreading the carnage to Cambodia and Laos.

Our credibility was at stake, said Nixon. We had made commitments as a nation. No one would believe our word in the future if we defected on our commitments to stand by South Vietnam. The fact that the commitments should never have been made in the first place and were impossible to fulfill made no impression on Nixon.

The cease-fire, when at last it came, was hailed as a masterpiece of patient negotiation and as the achievement of "peace with honor." But there was no honor, the liberals charged, in the use of our overwhelming military might to inflict devastation on a tiny, mostly agrarian country; in the defoliation of its forests; in the use of napalm on women and children; and in the brutal massacre of civilians at My Lai.

Moreover, Vietnam had inflicted devastation on our own political system. The misuse of presidential power was demonstrated in its most arrogant form. Instead of open government we had insulated, secret decision making. The president brazenly lied to Congress and the people about the prolonged bombing of Cambodia. And the passion for secrecy, the obsession with security that the Vietnam War spawned, led to the insidious growth of a grave threat to democratic institutions. When Daniel Ellsberg released a copy of the Pentagon papers and when antiwar activists engaged in acts of civil disobedience, the Nixon administration formed a group charged with illegal domestic spying and thereby started on the road to Watergate.

The final irony was that it was all for nought. The Vietnam cease-fire held up only briefly. Saigon was overrun and became Ho Chi Minh City. Our commitments had not prevailed, and fifty thousand Americans had died in vain.

Looking back on it all, some policy makers admitted they had blundered. Henry Kissinger said in 1975, "We probably made a mistake in . . . turning Vietnam into a test case for our policy. . . . We should have seen the Vietnam problem in Vietnamese terms, rather than as the outward thrust of a global conspiracy."[20] We and the Vietnamese, said the liberals, had paid a terrible price so that our leaders could learn such a transparently obvious lesson.

As the Reagan foreign policy unfolded, liberals wondered how well the lesson of Vietnam had been learned. In particular, they worried that Reagan's determination to counter left-wing forces in El Salvador and other Central American countries could embroil us, step by step, in another brutal, long, drawn-out war.

Illegal interventions in other countries' internal affairs. A third basic defect of U.S. foreign policy since World War II, say the liberals, has been the use of grossly illegal and immoral methods to undermine governments abroad suspected of being sympathetic or vulnerable to communism. Liberals do not deny that in a world of nation-states it is necessary for each nation to get the best information it can about possible threats to its security. But they are outraged by the way the CIA has overthrown foreign governments, debased other countries' systems by putting politicians on their payroll, planned (however ineptly) the assassinations of foreign leaders, and raised, paid, and led small armies—all in the name of preserving democracy and liberty. Liberals were also disturbed by President Reagan's 1981 executive order authorizing the CIA to conduct certain covert activities within the United States, doubting that the safeguards included in the order were sufficient to prevent serious intrusions into our civil liberties.

On the other hand liberals were supportive of the kind of public, official pressure mounted by Jimmy Carter as part of his human rights policy and directed at regimes of the right as well as of the left. Correspondingly they criticized the Reagan administration's reluctance to apply pressure to right-wing governments.

What should be done? The liberals' foreign policy proposals flow naturally from the critique we have just presented:

1. Avoid the obsession with communism. The Soviet brand of communism is obnoxious, but it is not the only, or even the prime, source of problems in the world today. Moreover, developments in Yugoslavia and in Poland indicate that communism can change toward greater openness, and this kind of evolution can be nurtured by the relaxation of world tensions.

2. Hold down the nuclear arms budget. We can hold the line on nuclear spending, and even reduce it significantly, yet still provide the minimum deterrence needed to prevent the Soviet Union from launching a strike against us. This approach would create the climate needed for arms reduction agreements with the Soviets, discourage other nations from joining the nuclear club, and start the process of reducing world outlays on armaments, which had reached $500 billion a year by 1980.

But there can be no hope of moving in this direction unless we abandon strategies based on the notion of limited nuclear or thermonuclear war. It is ludicrous to believe that once nuclear weapons, even neutron bombs, have been used, it will be possible to prevent escalation into a war of total mutual destruction.

3. Reduce the number of American troops abroad. We do not need over three hundred thousand troops in Western Europe. The notion that the Russians will risk a nuclear war by sending an invading army across the borders of our allies is pure fantasy.

4. Intervene militarily in other parts of the globe only where our clear national interest is directly involved, such as a flagrant attack on our own, legitimately stationed forces or an invasion of the territory of a country bound to us by clearly established mutual interests and a similarity of institutions and values.

5. Stop the indiscriminate sale of American armaments. We should not be the munitions maker to the world.

6. Help reduce the gross inequalities between the rich and the poor nations. Although our economic aid to developing nations increased from $4 billion in 1965 to $7.1 billion in 1980, it actually declined as a proportion of our Gross National Product over the period from 0.58 percent

to 0.26 percent, a much smaller proportion of our GNP than is provided to the developing nations by several other industrialized countries.

In allocating our economic aid we should support the aspirations of the developing nations without demanding anticommunist allegiance, and we should side with black people against white supremacists in southern Africa.

We should also place our emphasis on economic and humanitarian assistance and cut our military aid to right-wing dictators.

7. Encourage international cooperation instead of national conflict by strengthening the United Nations and channeling more of our economic aid through the U.N.

8. Speak out for human rights wherever these rights are denied, whether by governments of the left or of the right.

THE RADICAL LEFT: IMPERIALIST AMERICA

The left agrees with much of the liberals' critique of American foreign policy, but leftists go further. They also refuse to absolve the liberals from some share of the blame for what has gone wrong.

Radical left critics declare that the cold war is largely the creation of the United States. With the end of World War II we proceeded to encircle the Soviet Union with military bases. In answer to this encirclement and to our possession of the new weapons of terror, the Soviet Union constructed its own nuclear weapons, and, again following us, it developed the hydrogen bomb. It was natural then that the People's Republic of China, faced with active enmity, should create its own weaponry.

What is the driving force of American foreign policy? To some extent it is a straightforward expression of private business interests. At home, military spending is the essential underpinning of the economy, the principal device for preventing another Great Depression. Abroad, our foreign policy is a form of economic imperialism, protecting the overseas investments of American corporations, especially the multinationals. One example of this policy occurred in 1970, when

ITT twice approached agencies of the U.S. government, including the CIA, with an offer of $1 million to be used in Chile to prevent the election of a man of the moderate left, Salvador Allende, as president. Under Allende, ITT's large holdings in Chile's telephone system were likely to be taken over by the Chilean government with very little compensation to the corporation.

However, more fundamental than direct financial exploitation is the ideology of corporate capitalism. At the heart of this ideology is the fear of revolution, particularly communist revolution. This fear has permeated American domestic as well as foreign policy and has poisoned our political atmosphere, leading to McCarthyism, Watergate, and all the other manifestations of repression of dissent. And the liberals, who now criticize our foreign policy makers for being obsessed with anticommunism, were themselves among the prime contributors to the obsession in the early years of the cold war because, fearful that they might be accused of being soft on communism, liberal organizations such as the Americans for Democratic Action stridently attacked the Soviet Union as the principal source of world tensions.

What these liberals failed to recognize was that, in subscribing to the ideology of anticommunism, they were supporting a doctrine that would not only undermine their policies at home but also create a profound threat to world peace. This threat, in fact, was much more pervasive than the threat presented by the mere advancement of American financial interests abroad. For example, we would not have plunged into Vietnam merely to support the rather limited investments of U.S. companies in Indochina. It was the more general fear of communist gains that pulled our leaders further and further into that shameful war.

The danger inherent in the anticommunist paranoia reached its most acute form at the time of the Cuban missile confrontation. In that crisis, Kennedy was prepared to unleash thermonuclear annihilation to compel the Soviet Union to withdraw some missiles that did not really threaten our security, because whether missiles were based in Cuba or the Soviet Union made little difference to the balance of terror.

Yet Kennedy was ready to risk the annihilation of vast populations. Nothing could justify such a decision. Although most American leftists today do not admire the Soviet Union, they do not believe that life under communism (whose undesirable features would be no more difficult to change than would the undesirable features of corporate capitalism) would be worse than the horrors of all-out thermonuclear war.

As the left sees it, anticommunism is absurd as the basis of foreign policy. Although some variants of communism, including the version which has developed in the Soviet Union, have themselves become repressive, communist powers have generally favored the aspirations for social justice and a decent standard of living of the dispossessed peoples of the world and have supported the revolutions that are the indispensable condition for achieving those aspirations. Our foreign policy should adopt at least benevolent neutrality toward those revolutions and preferably should actively support them.

The policies we have followed worldwide are the natural product of the ruling elite that runs this country. At every one of the major decision points, the men the president called on for advice shared power-elite values; and the elder statesmen of the power elite—John McCloy, Clark Clifford, and Dean Acheson—were called in at times of crisis. Usually the decisions on which these men were consulted involved imperialist aggressions, and most of the time they were on the belligerent side of the issues. It is true that, on Vietnam, Acheson and Clifford, who had favored the earlier escalations, told Johnson in 1968 to reverse the process. They changed their minds not because they had suddenly become peace lovers. They simply realized that their policy had failed. It was affecting the balance of payments, and the dollar was threatened. Economics had become more important than ideology, as it ultimately must be for the power elite when the two come into conflict.

Economics was also an important component in the decision to seek a lowering of tensions with the Chinese People's Republic. China represents an enormous potential market, and capitalism, Lenin showed, must eventually collapse without foreign markets to exploit. In addition, there is the strategic factor: by making mischief between China and the Soviet Union, we improve our situation in the global struggle with the Soviets.

Consequently Reagan, although long a defender of the anticommunist government on Taiwan, did little to change the China policy of Nixon, Ford, and Carter. This policy is one more example of the continuity of the ruling elite's foreign policies. Reagan talks tougher than Carter, and he may be more eager to provoke confrontations in specific situations than was Carter. But the main lines of American postwar foreign policy were laid down in the 1940s by the Truman Doctrine, which promised support to anticommunist governments; and that doctrine has been used by every president since then to justify support for right-wing military dictators and the suppression of even moderate movements and governments that we have judged to be insufficiently zealous in their anticommunism.

Jimmy Carter's pious utterances about human rights changed this picture only in a minor degree; and his decision to increase military spending and to proceed with the most monstrously expensive and provocative weapons system ever devised, the mobile MX, revealed the true nature of his presidency. On the whole, most people on the left believe we may be better off with a Reagan than a Carter, because with Reagan there are no ambiguities and inconsistencies. The true feelings of the ruling elite about armament spending, weapons sales, the suppression of popular movements, and the support of military juntas in Latin America and white racist governments in South Africa are made transparently clear, and the American people will at last be able to see how dangerous and cruel those policies are.

THE CONSERVATIVES: NATIONALISM AND ANTICOMMUNISM

Two principal strands of thought go into the conservatives' approach to foreign policy. The first is nationalism. Whereas liberals see nationalism as an outmoded, increasingly dangerous concept, conservatives cherish it as a means of maintaining diversity in the world and as an expression of pride in our own system and its accomplishments. Conservatives are hostile to any proposal that might undermine our national sovereignty, our right to run our own affairs without interference from abroad.

The second element in conservative foreign policy is a passionate anticommunism. To the conservatives the arguments of the left that the United States started the cold war and of the liberals that both sides started it are arrant nonsense. It was started by the Soviet Union. It has been sustained by the Soviet Union and aggravated by communist China and other communist countries.

Since the 1960s our leaders have been increasingly impressed by the argument that communism has changed since Stalin passed from the scene and now seeks genuine accommodations with the West. From time to time communist tactics change, and Lenin, the master communist theoretician of this century, laid down the principle that a communist country might, whenever the circumstances were unfavorable, pull back from direct confrontations with capitalist powers. But the strategy must remain the same. Capitalism must be overthrown. Time is on the side of communism. Patience is necessary sometimes, and major concessions might have to be made, but the long-range purposes must remain implacable. When the Soviet Union was faced with massive thermonuclear power, a change in tactics was decided on. But Stalin's successors have not changed their central intent, which is world domination.

In dealing with this great threat to American interests and survival, we have shown weakness and vacillation. We have hoped for the best. We have put faith in the word of communist leaders when their practice and their Marxist-Leninist theory have presented us with undeniable evidence that their word is not to be trusted, that truth or lies are equally available as weapons to achieve their purposes. Our central preoccupation has been peace. Certainly we all want it. But we

have not understood that the Communists' prime objective has not been peace but victory. The consequences of this failure of understanding have been demonstrated in every major area of foreign policy.

Nuclear armaments. Consider, in the first place, the relative nuclear strength of the two sides. For a time we were the only nuclear power. Then, as we entered the thermonuclear age, we possessed an overwhelming lead. Now that lead is gone, and the Soviet Union is forging ahead.

They have more strategic weapons than we do. They are rapidly overcoming the huge lead we had until quite recently in the number of warheads. The total amount of megatonnage on their side is much greater than ours. They are building submarines much faster than we are. They have an ABM system around Moscow, whereas we have none around Washington.

So vast is the Soviet buildup that it is entirely conceivable that well before the end of the 1980s they will have the capacity to hit every one of our ICBM bases in this country and knock them out.

Of course, we also have our nuclear-powered, nuclear-armed submarines and bombers. But tracking systems are now being developed that could make even these submarines vulnerable to a concerted sudden attack. Moreover, with the kind of breakdown of communications that a thermonuclear attack could cause, our submarines might not know when or whether to unleash their armory. As for our B-52 bombers, they would have great difficulty getting through today's sophisticated antiaircraft defenses.

It is true that the Soviets would still be running a very great risk that enough of our nuclear weaponry would survive their first strike to inflict terrible damage on their cities. But Soviet strategic plans have for some time included the possibility of limited thermonuclear war mentioned earlier. They might strike a few of our missile bases or defense plants, then send an ultimatum that we give in to their demands or suffer the destruction of our cities. Even though we could still launch some of our missiles, would we do so, knowing what the consequences would be for our people—and knowing that they had amassed much greater nuclear force than we had?

We must remember, too, say the conservatives, that communism is a fanatical doctrine. Individual human life is less important than the ultimate triumph of communism. The leaders of this doctrine—if not today's leaders, then tomorrow's—might well decide that a few cities, a few million people, are a necessary sacrifice to ensure the victory of communism throughout the world.

But even if we leave aside the possibility of a Soviet first strike, at least for the next few years, another danger in the Soviet megatonnage lead cannot be denied: the threat of "nuclear blackmail." Given the advantage we have allowed them to accumulate, they can now press us hard in any area of the world and know that our resistance will be shadowed by fear that we will provoke them into a nuclear attack. The fact that the Soviets withdrew their missiles from Cuba in 1962 was the result of our lead in nuclear armament. That lead is gone. If anything like the Cuban missile crisis were to occur today, it is extremely unlikely that the Soviets would back down.

Even in 1962, conservatives point out, we did not press our advantage home. We could have seized the opportunity to get rid of Castro and make amends for our pathetic showing at the Bay of Pigs. But we were afraid of running the small risk involved. Today, given the Soviet buildup, the risk would be much greater and we would lack the will to prevent the Soviets from having their way.

It is not the conservatives' contention that we should provoke a thermonuclear war. But they argue against a policy of peace at any price. Peace is not the only value. Freedom, the avoidance of the slavery that is communism, must not be jettisoned out of fear. In any case, the best way to preserve the peace is to counter communist power with even greater power. The only language they understand is strength; to allow ourselves to become weak is the surest path to war.

The decline of the West. Finally, the Communists have left a vital escape clause in their doctrine of "peaceful coexistence." They would prefer for the time being not to have a direct thermonuclear confrontation with the free world. But they have left themselves free to support "wars of liberation," especially guerrilla wars conducted against "colonialist" powers. This kind of war is almost risk-free for the Soviet Union. They need not commit their own troops but merely send military and technical assistance, or fight through surrogates, like the Cuban troops who fought in Angola and elsewhere. The Soviets can compel us to commit our forces all over the world on terrain unsuited to conventional military tactics. They can harass and embarrass us, knowing that we will not commit nuclear weapons to small-scale hostilities. The objective will be to take over one small area at a time by the use of what has been called "salami tactics"—taking one thin slice, then another, then another, until the whole salami is gone.

Faced with this danger, we have repeatedly made inept half-decisions. At the Bay of Pigs we supported an invasion by Cubans but withheld the air power that was an indispensable component of the original plan. Again in 1962 during the Cuban missile crisis we compromised. In Vietnam we sent in great numbers of troops but constrained them within a "no-win" policy. Over and over again military leaders told us what we had to do to win, including such steps as closing the port of Haiphong, destroying railroads and the irrigation system, and cutting off the supply trails through Laos and Cambodia. Ironically, some of these measures were finally adopted but at a stage of the war when our purpose was merely to cover our withdrawal and force the enemy to negotiate the terms of our withdrawal.

The outcome of our weakness has been a grave deterioration in our international position. At the end of World War II we were easily the world's dominant power. But we did not use our strength to protect our interests. At the Yalta Conference between Roosevelt, Churchill, and Stalin in 1945, Roosevelt gave away Eastern Europe to the Communists. Then we evolved the doctrine of containment, which resulted in our standing by helplessly while the Russians took over Czechoslovakia, built the monstrous Berlin wall, then brutally suppressed the efforts of the people of Hungary to loosen their subjection to Soviet imperialism. Subsequently, the Soviet Union and its Eastern European allies (the members of the Warsaw Pact) have built up much greater military strength than the NATO allies.

Only in the number of tactical nuclear weapons is the West ahead, and there is grave doubt that these devices would be used for fear of setting off a total thermonuclear war. The Communists have more troops (and could mobilize their forces much more quickly than the West), more aircraft, and far more tanks than the West. This superiority offers a very strong temptation to the Soviet Union to press home their military advantage. At the very least, it increases the Soviets' ability to encourage internal communist takeovers in Western Europe countries or to neutralize the region by encouraging its rapidly growing pacifist and anti-American movements. So even in Europe, where the doctrine of containment began, its maintenance is increasingly in jeopardy.

As for other regions of the world, containment has failed dismally. Almost a quarter of the entire population of the earth fell under communism in China. North Korea, North Vietnam, and finally South Vietnam went communist. Close to our own shores we allowed Cuba to become a communist country, a Soviet protectorate, and a base for subversion in Latin America and Africa; and then we gave away our long-established rights to the Panama Canal. Elsewhere we condoned, even encouraged, neutralist doctrines that leaned toward communism and lavished foreign aid on unstable regimes that repaid us by abusing us and voting against us in the United Nations. We have treated shabbily any nation accused of colonialism or racism, although these countries have been bulwarks against communism. We have meekly accepted charges of immorality and brutality in Vietnam despite the massive corruption and brutality that characterize the regimes of many Third World countries.

We have pinned too many hopes on a United Nations that is heavily influenced by the communist countries and that represents a threat to our sovereignty as a nation. And for the political advantage of presidents and the doubtful gains from some trade deals, we have negotiated with the Russians and the communist Chinese in the foolish belief that the Communists will stick to their agreements and that being nice to them can lessen their dedication to destroying us.

The result of all this, say the conservatives, is a disastrous decline in American power and prestige in the world. A particularly humiliating illustration of this decline came in the seizing of the American embassy in Teheran in 1979 and in the holding of U.S. nationals as hostages for almost fourteen months by a band of terrorists with the full backing of the Iranian government. This situation was an ordeal not only for the hostages but also for America, as, month after month, television cameras recorded the screaming mobs hurling insults at the United States. And our response was to plead with them to show mercy, until the damage to Carter's reputation became too great and we engaged in an abortive rescue attempt that revealed all too clearly the sad condition into which we had allowed our military strength to fall.

These events are the fruits, say the conservatives, of our being ruled by a liberal establishment. Democratic and Republican regimes have succeeded each other, but essentially the same men, all members of the Council on Foreign Relations, all favored by Wall Street and eastern industrialists, have set the basic policies in foreign affairs. In doing so they have pushed aside the military leaders, the professionals whose job it is to study the intentions of their counterparts abroad, and have replaced their advice with a reading of communist intentions that persistently puts them in the most favorable light possible.

What should be done? Conservatives hoped that the election of Ronald Reagan would at last produce a change from the liberal consensus of the past. The principles they wanted to see adopted are as follows:

1. A major increase in nuclear and nonnuclear spending. In the face of the most obvious indications that the Russians were catching up with us, and then moving ahead, liberals continued to lobby against our committing the resources necessary to protect our national security. Consequently, as figure 12-2 showed, for several years our spending on defense hardly increased at all, and actually declined as a proportion of our Gross National Product. So much for the vaunted power of the military-industrial complex!

At last the Reagan administration embarked on the necessary increases. Liberals complain that we cannot afford such increases. But we dare not give anything less than the highest priority to our survival as a free nation. Moreover, as was suggested in our discussion of economic policy in chapter 12, we will not suffer adverse economic effects if we pursue policies that regenerate the American economy and provide for a faster rate of growth than in the past. Admittedly, say the conservatives, there is a good deal of waste in defense programs, as there is in any government-sponsored field, and we must ensure that we get full value for our money from the military and the defense industries.

Nevertheless, conservatives do not doubt the need for large increases in defense spending, and they applauded Reagan's plan for enlarging and updating the strategic nuclear stockpile, the development of the neutron bomb and of new generations of bombers, the proposals for a serious effort at civil defense,[21] and the improvement of our capacity to fight conventional wars. In fact, if conservatives had a criticism of Reagan in this area, it was that he was not ready to spend enough, as was indicated by his postponement, perhaps abandonment, of the mobile MX in favor of simply placing the MX in existing silos. This decision, said some conservative analysts, could leave us dangerously vulnerable to a surprise Soviet attack in the middle or late 1980s.[22]

2. Reasserting our standing in the world. It is time to make it clear to the Soviets that they cannot expect to expand their power any further, either directly or indirectly through surrogates; to Castro

and other Soviet allies that their foreign adventures will no longer be tolerated; and to all other nations that we will not be afraid to use our power to defend our interests.

We will use our military power with restraint, but without apology, wherever necessary. We must also make the full use of our intelligence agencies. Liberals have almost nullified the effectiveness of the CIA. Yet the Russians have their secret police (KGB), their spies, and their clandestine activities agencies. The British, the French, and many other countries have organizations that conduct espionage and undertake "dirty tricks" abroad. Ours is the only country in the world that has exposed the workings of its foreign intelligence agency in day-after-day screaming headlines. This publicity has caused great damage to our national security, and it has seriously reduced our ability to counter international terrorist organizations that have been trained and financed by the Soviet Union. Although some of the CIA's undertakings in the past have undoubtedly been handled ineptly, it is essential that we restore the agency's ability to function with less public surveillance and fewer restrictions.

3. Standing by our friends—and the enemies of our enemies. We must let our allies know that they can count on our support in their efforts to resist Soviet aggression. These allies should include Canada, most Western European countries, Japan, South Korea, the Philippines, Taiwan, South Africa, anticommunist nations in Latin America, Israel, and the nonradical Arab countries. Not all of these countries are democracies, and some may run their internal affairs with methods that seem to us harsh and arbitrary. But we should not write them off as long as they side with us in world politics and are "authoritarian" rather than "totalitarian." (The important difference, as conservatives define it, is that a totalitarian system, particularly communism, controls all aspects of a nation's life and is able to prevent any real internal challenge to its continuation. An authoritarian regime, on the other hand, uses repression in some areas, but leaves other aspects of the

society alone; this system provides the potential, which has sometimes been realized, for change toward a more democratic structure.)

However, conservatives insist that alliances must be reciprocal relationships. They resent the reluctance of Japan and others to increase their defense outlays, and the resistance in Western Europe to provide the United States with air bases and with locations for deploying the neutron bomb.

4. Helping poor nations to help themselves. Far too much American money has been squandered on poorly conceived foreign aid programs that are generally unproductive and riddled with corruption and that make the recipient countries more and more dependent on outside aid.

Our assistance should be provided only to nations that show they are accepting it not as a handout, but as a means of developing their economic independence. Moreover, we should be most sympathetic to the requests of countries who rely on what President Reagan called "the magic of the marketplace." As he observed: "We cannot have prosperity and economic development without economic freedom."[23]

The conservatives also argue that we should cease all aid to countries that take our money, then abuse us and side with the Soviets in the United Nations and other forums. It is essential that we make clear to the world that the era of the decline and humiliation of the United States has come to an end.

THE RADICAL RIGHT: THE BETRAYAL OF AMERICA

As we have noted, the radical right sees international communism as predatory, amoral, criminal, and atheistic. Clearly it would be immoral to bargain with this inherently evil force.

In this respect, the radical right analysis is a somewhat more extreme version of the conservatives' analysis of communism and of the defects of American foreign policy. The radical right, however, goes much further than the conservatives in its assessment of how far communism has already succeeded in accomplishing its purposes. To the far right, Communists have already taken over a large part of the world; the United Nations is totally a communist agency; and, because our own country is being rapidly infiltrated by Communists and their sympathizers, they are on the verge of taking us over, too.

This situation has come about because our leaders have either been blind to the realities of communism or have actively connived in advancing the communist cause. Vietnam was a perfect illustration. We could easily have won that war if we had wanted to do so. But our leaders set up a phony anticommunist war that they had no intention of winning in order to establish controls over the lives of the people that would culminate in the establishment of a police state. Otherwise, a war against communism in Vietnam would have been highly desirable, and we should have sought and obtained a rapid victory. In the absence of a will to win, however, we should never have gotten into such a war.

Why are our leaders, the Rockefellers and the rest of the eastern internationalist bankers and industrialists, so ready to play the Communists' game? Because they have been working out deals with the Communists to carve up world markets between them. Now they are getting together to exploit each other's markets, and the distinction between Soviet communism and American welfare-state socialism becomes even murkier.

The Council on Foreign Relations is the most important American institution for producing these policies. Another is the United World Federalists, "whose membership is heavily interlocked with that of the Council on Foreign Relations. The UWF advocate turning the U.N. into a full-fledged world government which would include the Communist nations." Richard Nixon was working in precisely this direction. He was "far too clever to actually join the UWF, but he has supported their legislative program since his early days in Congress."[24]

More recently we had the Trilateral Commission, through which David Rockefeller advanced the interests of his family and the Chase Manhattan Bank and had the entire Carter administration at his service. Henry Kissinger, Nelson Rockefeller's agent, had left the White House and the State Department; but Zbigniew Brzezinski, David Rockefeller's man, had taken over at the president's elbow. The "insiders" changed chairs for a while. Even under Reagan the Trilateral Commission's influence lived on: Vice-President George Bush was once a member.

It is almost, but not quite, too late to stop the complete takeover of America by communism. We must get out of the United Nations—and get the United Nations out of this country. We must fight against the deals with communist China, which are the culmination of the initial betrayal of China to communism by our leaders. We must stop trading and negotiating with the Soviet Union. We must end the giveaway programs to the alleged neutralists, who hardly bother to conceal their affection for communism. Our foreign policy must be based on friendship only for those nations—and there are very few left in the world—that are dedicated to holding out against a world communist government.

THE CENTRISTS: STRENGTH AND RESTRAINT

Given the broad range that the centrist band of opinion encompasses, it is obvious that there would be sharp disagreements among centrists over a field as important and as multifaceted as foreign policy. However, American foreign policy, as we defined it at the beginning of this chapter, is essentially the work of centrists, most of whom persist in defending the general lines they have taken against the attacks of the critics from both sides.

Thus they have argued that we have followed a prudent middle course between strength and restraint. On the whole the conservatives' diagnosis of Soviet intentions was regarded by centrists as more accurate than the liberals'. On the other hand, the liberals' warnings that military power must be held in check and that military leaders must not be given all they ask for have been heeded.

Our posture in crisis after crisis shows that,

although we would not allow Soviet and Chinese communism to take over the world, neither would we plunge into thermonuclear war. A war would probably have started if we had tried to knock down the Berlin wall. But when the Russians tried to cut off supplies to the people of West Berlin, we took the reasonable risk of supplying them by an airlift. Our handling of the Cuban missile crisis in 1962 was a masterpiece of firm but restrained decision making. We forced the Russians to pull their missiles out, yet we avoided war by refraining from pushing Khrushchev beyond the point at which he would have no alternative but to fight.

With respect to the arms race, we have had no alternative but to build our strength as long as the Soviets were increasing theirs. But we have also demonstrated our eagerness to negotiate arms control agreements.

Centrists are now ready to concede that Vietnam was a mistake. But hindsight, they argue, is remarkably clear; and projecting ourselves back into the climate of the time, the Vietnam War can be explained as an understandable error of reasonable men doing their best to cope with an extraordinarily difficult situation. Communist forces in South Vietnam were gaining ground. If they took power without any U.S. opposition, it could very well encourage Communists everywhere to believe they could act with impunity. So, a step at a time, and without realizing at each step how costly the effort would be, we became heavily committed. Then it became harder to retrace our steps, because a great power cannot easily withdraw from such a situation without doing grave damage to the credibility of its foreign policy.

Moreover, the liberals' charge that our Vietnam policy was one of unrestrained militarism was untrue. The Joint Chiefs of Staff were always given less than they asked for. Vietnam, in fact, was a strategy carefully balanced between the application of strength and the avoidance of direct confrontation with the Soviet Union and the People's Republic of China. Thus we did not accept the demands of the right wing in America to invade North Vietnam.

The loss of Vietnam should not be taken as an indictment of American foreign policy as a whole. Since World War II, in fact, the record had been reasonably good.

Much of the world, it is true, has fallen under communist domination. But the communist advance has slowed. There is deep dissension in the communist world, particularly between the Soviet Union and the People's Republic of China. Within the Soviet sphere there is intense dissatisfaction, as indicated by the events in Poland from 1981. Outside that sphere the Soviet model is no longer as attractive as it once appeared to the developing nations; and communist parties in the advanced industrial countries (the countries that, according to Marx, should have been the natural breeding grounds for communism) are in a state of decline.

On our side, despite the reverses we have suffered, we are still a vital and enormously powerful country. Although we have become dependent on other countries for some of our oil, we are still the granary of the world. In 1980 45 percent of all the world's wheat exports, 70 percent of the exports of corn, 60 percent of the soybeans, and 24 percent of the rice came from the United States. Inevitably our resources of food, technological skill, and military power will sustain our position as one of enormous importance on the international scene.

Our power should give us the self-confidence to continue our prudent, balanced approach to the problems that face us in the world today. So we must undertake a further buildup of our armed strength yet keep the way open for mutually agreed-on reductions of nuclear forces. We must continue to seek to relax tensions with the Soviet Union and the People's Republic of China, but not lose sight of their hostility to capitalism or their oppression of basic freedoms. We must work for closer cooperation with the noncommunist advanced industrialized countries but not ignore the needs of the poverty-stricken nations of the world. And we must support the United Nations as an international forum and symbol of world order, but also protect our own national interest and the interests of our friends in the world.

CONCLUSION

In foreign as in economic policy the election of Ronald Reagan shifted the debate over the issues in the direction of the conservatives. Previously there were changes in approach from administration to administration (more, perhaps, than either left or right concede), but the changes usually fell within a broad consensual framework. With the Reagan administration, however, we find a tendency to rely on much of the analysis and language presented in this chapter under the conservative perspective.

That perspective is built around the assumption that the principal problems we face in the world today stem from the aggressive designs of the Soviet Union and its allies. To a considerable extent this argument will make a good deal of sense to the American public. The vast Soviet weapons buildup, the invasion of Afghanistan, the Cuban adventures in Africa, the brutal treatment of dissenters in the Soviet Union and other communist countries, and the poor economic performance of communist systems generally make Soviet-style communism appear enormously unattractive to most people in this country. And the frustration caused by the Iranian hostage episode created a climate that would support enthusiastically a tougher line toward our adversaries abroad.

Nonetheless there are limits to how far any administration can go in applying the conservative foreign policy prescription. First, there is the sheer fact of Soviet military power. It may be immoral to bargain with wicked, unscrupulous leaders; but when they have at their disposal the kind of thermonuclear stockpiles accumulated by the Soviet Union, the Reagan administration will necessarily tread warily and, on some issues at least, will enter into open or tacit accommodations.

Second, no American foreign policy can be built purely on resistance to communism because, as we noted earlier, there are many sources of international conflict other than communism. Some terrorists may well be underwritten by the Soviets or their allies, but others are driven by religious or nationalistic fervor rather than ideology. Some of the most dangerous rivalries in the world today have little or nothing to do with communism. Both Saudi Arabia and Israel are hostile to the Soviet Union; but the Reagan administration's efforts to recruit both of them in a Middle Eastern anti-Soviet alliance are unlikely to succeed in the face of their mutual hostility. Racial antipathies in southern Africa, nationalist-religious differences between India and Pakistan may attract big-power interest, but they are not primarily related to the communist versus anticommunist issue.

Other sources of tension are the widening gap between the rich and poor nations, the enormous increase in population in the poorest nations, the struggle over the earth's dwindling natural resources, and the worldwide spread of pollution of the land, the waters, and the atmosphere. These problems would exist if the October 1917 revolution had never occurred in the Soviet Union. And, despite the fact that we have slipped somewhat from being the most efficient and affluent nation on earth, ours is still easily the most abundant of all economies, with resources of grain and other products that make large portions of the world heavily dependent on us.

So although the Reagan administration's foreign policy will be a constant target of criticism from liberals and the left, it is likely that at least some of the actions of the administration in world affairs will cause disappointment and resentment among conservatives.

NOTES AND REFERENCES

1. The Southeast Asia Treaty Organization (SEATO), set up in 1954 and comprising Thailand, the Philippines, Pakistan, Australia, New Zealand, France, and Britain, was dissolved in 1977. CENTO, the Central Treaty Organization, formed in 1955, and the Mutual Defense Treaty with Taiwan, signed in 1954, have also been dissolved. Still surviving are the Japan, Philippine, Anzus, and South Korea Mutual Defense Treaties and the Rio Treaty (Inter-American Treaty of Reciprocal Assistance).
2. See, for example, Herman Kahn, *On Thermo-Nuclear War* (Princeton, N.J.: Princeton University Press, 1960).
3. In addition, the Reagan administration planned to move forward with the development of another Carter administration proposal—the Stealth bomber, which would succeed the B-1. The Stealth plane would be constructed and equipped to penetrate air defenses by deceiving an enemy's radar.
4. The United States offered to cancel its plans to deploy the Pershing IIs and cruise missiles in Europe if the Soviet Union would withdraw the SS-20s, SS-4s, and SS-5s targeted on Western Europe.

5. This kind of doctrine was first given currency in the United States by the Department of Defense in 1973 and was confirmed by Presidential Directive 59 issued by Jimmy Carter in 1980.

6. Rapid deployment forces are air, sea, and land forces that can be deployed quickly in localized crisis situations, such as those disputes that might erupt over the Middle East oil fields.

7. See U.S. Congress, Senate Select Committee to Study Governmental Operations with Respect to Intelligence Activities, *Final Report* (1976). The committee was chaired by Senator Frank Church.

8. The CIA also involved U.S. organized crime figures in trying to get the job done.

9. See Johnson, Loch, and James M. McCormick, "The Making of International Agreements: A Reappraisal of Congressional Involvement," *The Journal of Politics* 40 (1978).

10. Under the terms of a congressional statute covering this kind of executive action, the president's decision could only be vetoed by majority vote of *both* houses of Congress.

11. Payments were also made to individual students attending international youth festivals in return for reports on Soviet security practices and Soviet and Third World personalities.

12. The 1947 National Security Act establishing the CIA limited its role to foreign affairs, but the CIA has interpreted its responsibilities broadly, claiming that its support of student organizations, professors, and others in America has had a clear relationship to foreign policy.

13. Congress took the initiative in passing the 1978 Wiretap Law and the 1980 Intelligence Oversight Act.

14. President Reagan's executive order, issued on December 4, 1981, changed the guidelines issued by President Carter by giving the CIA authority to conduct covert activities within the United States as long as they do not affect U.S. domestic policies, politics, or news media. The CIA was also allowed, under safeguards approved by the attorney general, to infiltrate U.S. organizations that were believed to be acting in behalf of a foreign power. The CIA's authority to shadow U.S. citizens abroad for foreign intelligence was also expanded. The executive order established a White House Intelligence Oversight Board to guard against unlawful intelligence activities.

15. In 1976 a CIA draft of an intelligence report on Soviet strategic strength was rejected by the Ford administration as an underestimate, and the administration called in a group of outside experts headed by Harvard professor Richard Pipes to work with the CIA in producing a revised estimate upward.

16. In 1981 Nitze and Rostow were appointed by President Reagan to his three-man team to head up the arms control negotiations with the Soviets. The third, Lt-Gen. Edwin Rownes, had retired from the army in 1979 to campaign against SALT II.

17. In one of a series of ads in leading newspapers in 1981, the Mobil Corporation declared: "Even without Aramco and the largest U.S. oil companies, American business now holds well in excess of $35 billion in contracts for work with Saudi Arabia. . . . The U.S. business relationship with Saudi Arabia has resulted in jobs here for hundreds of thousands of men and women. . . . Saudi Arabia is far more than oil— it means trade for America, jobs for Americans, and strength for the dollar."

18. *Newsweek*, 8 June 1981, p. 31.

19. A.J.P. Taylor, "Rational Wars?" *New York Review of Books*, 4 November 1971, p. 37.

20. Henry Kissinger with Barbara Walters on NBC's "Today" program, May 6, 1975.

21. Reagan administration officials, in supporting proposals for an enlarged civil defense program, insisted that a combination of shelters, evacuation plans from major cities, and protection measures for industry could enable the bulk of the American population to survive a thermonuclear attack and make possible the restoration of the American economy within a few years of such an attack.

22. The mobile MX had been seen as a means of closing what Reagan himself had earlier called a "window of vulnerability"—a period in the middle or late 1980s when the Soviet lead in thermonuclear weaponry could become so wide as to make us extremely vulnerable to attack.

23. Address to the 36th annual meeting of the World Bank and the International Monetary Fund, Washington, D.C., September 29, 1981.

24. Gary Allen, *None Dare Call It Conspiracy* (Rossmoor, Calif.: Concord Press, 1971), p. 122.

chapter sixteen

POWER AND POLITICS: A REVIEW OF THE FIVE PERSPECTIVES

We have now spent fifteen chapters examining the electoral and political processes, the institutions, and the policies of the American system of government and politics. We have considered masses of data on each of the topics into which our subject has been divided. But we have done much more than present a compilation of facts. We have been dealing with highly charged information that lends itself to widely divergent and passionately argued interpretations. From the almost limitless number of possible analyses, we have selected five ideological groupings, and each of these perspectives has been represented in relation to most of the subjects we have discussed (although for reasons given in the preface, some of the perspectives have been given more attention than others).

Now the time has come to sum up. Let us begin by reviewing the attitudes and postures of each perspective, using the framework of the political spectrum that we established in chapter 1. We open our discussion of each perspective by reminding ourselves of its basic values or ideals. Then we ask how each ideological grouping sees the reality of power in America today. Next we examine how much change is required to bring the reality close to the ideal. And finally we shall assess the prospects for achieving those changes.

THE LIBERALS

The America that liberals would like to see is a country in which there are no enormous disparities of income, wealth, power, and status; in which government expresses the needs of the many, not just the few; and in which individual expression and personal freedom flourish. The liberals' ideal America would also act as a beacon to the world, seeking to replace competing nationalisms with a cooperative effort to bring social justice and individual liberty to people everywhere.

The America that liberals see is quite different from this ideal. They see some people enjoying vast amounts of money and possessions while millions are condemned to abysmal poverty. They believe that the wealthy maintain their privileges by the disproportionate influence they exert on government. Business and monied interests are excessively represented in elections as a result of their campaign contributions, and in the decision-making process as a result of their lobbying.

Liberals also believe that government has all too often ridden roughshod over the rights of individuals. The fragility of our First Amendment freedoms was vividly demonstrated by the Nixon administration's abuses of power, which might not have been curbed but for a series of lucky accidents. These domestic shortcomings have all been reflected in American foreign policy, which has repeatedly put us on the side of corrupt dictators and privileged classes and squandered resources on the military in an absurd and recklessly dangerous effort to assert our superiority over the exaggerated power of communism.

To change this situation is a difficult task in view of the obstacles imposed by the nature of our governmental and political system. This system provides abundant opportunities for vested interests to resist reforms. The constitutional separation of powers fragments decision making so that stalemate and inertia take the place of action. Generations had to pass before we were able to put through very modest improvements like Medicare and federal aid to education, and it required the exceptional circumstances of the period following the assassination of President Kennedy to get those very limited measures passed into law.

The election of 1980 took away from liberals their prospects for even the most incremental advances. In fact, many of the gains they had made since the 1930s—inadequate though they believed them to be—were now subjected to severe cutbacks or elimination. In the Reagan administration liberals saw the full-blown, blatant expression of most of the aspects of American life they objected to: the glorification of private wealth, the disdainful neglect of the poor and minorities, the lack of concern with the public interest, the despoiling of the environment, and the aggressive assertion of chauvinistic pride.

However, liberals have not conceded that the future belongs to the kind of conservatism represented by the Reaganites. The latter came to power, the liberals believe, through the frustration of the American people with the inadequate performance of a succession of governments, and on the basis of a number of promises that could not possibly be fulfilled. With the passage of time, say the liberals, the emptiness of those promises will become increasingly evident, and the pendulum will swing back.

In fact, it is the liberals' hope that this time the pendulum may swing farther toward liberalism than ever before, because now is the first time since the 1920s that the people have been subjected to the application of conservative ideas in relatively undiluted form. They will come to realize that those ideas are on the one hand morally bankrupt, being based on a code of dog-eat-dog, and on the other hand economically unworkable. Once this realization strikes home the people will look for alternatives. Since they turned to Reaganism because they were disenchanted with the muddled centrism of his predecessors, liberals argue that at last the people may turn to the kind of policies that the liberals have been offering for many years, and which, liberals contend, have never been tried except in the form of weak half-measures.

Liberals do not expect that their policies will be accepted intact. They recognize the need for compromise, and they are not seeking the polarization of American politics. But they contend that, unless the electorate accepts a considerable part of the liberal program, we shall be unable to cope with the many dangers we have talked about in this book: economic decline, racial tensions, ecological deterioration, and thermonuclear confrontation.

In the liberals' view, significant change in the direction they propose must not be long delayed, because they fear that the time available to us to deal with our problems is fast running out.

THE RADICAL LEFT

The goal of the left is to establish a socialist society. Such a society is based on the principle of equality. It is a society in which distinctions based on income, class, and race have disappeared. Property, except for a few personal possessions, is communally owned. Cooperation is the principal mode of human relations, and everyone participates in the decision-making process. To this end institutions are decentralized and reduced to human scale.

Nor is the leftist ideal limited to the United States. The radical left envisions a world made up of socialist communities, so the objective of our foreign policy should be to support those forces in other countries that are pressing for socialism.

As the members of the radical left look at the United States, they see a system totally antithetical to their ideal. From their perspective, America is a living symbol of corporate capitalism. The dominant values of corporate capitalism are gross inequality, class discrimination, racism, exploitation of workers, ruthless competition, and obsession with material accumulation. These values are maintained by a small ruling elite. Although the masses of the people are given the illusion of participation by the sham of elections and the empty game of party politics, they are shut out of all the important decisions.

Although the ruling elite works through the enormously overgrown institutions of the presidency and the federal bureaucracies, the ultimate power centers are the corporate boardrooms. The intimate relationships between economic and political power are well illustrated throughout this book: ITT's successful effort to hold on to Hartford Insurance; the great oil companies' dominance over energy policy; the huge corporations' contributions to Nixon's reelection campaign; Reagan's tax cuts for corporations and the rich; and on and on.

Abroad, U.S. foreign policy serves the interests of American capitalism in general and the multinational corporations in particular. It is a policy of imperialism, driven by a near-paranoiac hostility toward communist countries and bent on subjugating the economies of poor nations to our own. Foreign policy has led to brutally immoral wars, such as Korea and Vietnam; has taken us to the brink of thermonuclear annihilation, particularly during the Cuban missile crisis; and, through the vehicle of the CIA, has encouraged methods that reveal the complete moral bankruptcy of the American political system.

In challenging the ruling elite's power, the liberals' method of reform within the system is pathetically inadequate. Even where it achieves minor improvements in the conditions of the people (and these reforms typically take decades to bring about), reformism does nothing to alter the fundamental injustice of the system. In fact, by throwing a sop to the masses, these improvements lower the prospect of fundamental change, because they reduce the level of dissatisfaction just enough to impede the potential for radical or revolutionary change.

The activists of the left are fully aware of the obstacles to radical change. The ruling elite controls the military and the police. Through the rulers' power over the media and the educational system, the people are manipulated into believing that they are free. With the end of the Vietnam War, there seem to be no sharp issues to galvanize students and other potential sympathizers into action against the system. So the number who have developed a revolutionary consciousness is small.

Just the same, the radicals of the left are convinced that the obstacles are not insurmountable. They point to the evidence of declining trust in institutions—not just governmental institutions but business, too—and the polarization of opinion among the electorate. The traditional forms of politics, they argue, are worn out, discredited. Corporate capitalism is less and less able to cope with the problems of unemployment, inflation, and declining energy and other resources. Once the people, especially the disenchanted young, are shown that real alternatives exist, they will turn to them.

What methods are needed to provide these alternatives? Militant confrontations are one tactic. Violence is not as attractive to most radicals as it was in the sixties, because the force available to the ruling class is overwhelming, and the masses are alienated and antagonized when innocent bystanders are hurt. But demonstrations, marches, occupations of buildings, picketing, and other shows of strength and forms of civil disobedience are useful means of attracting the media's attention. In fact, very few important changes have ever come about in America without the use of abrasive and disruptive tactics.[1]

Radical groups have created new grass-roots institutions to involve people in the effort to change conditions in their communities. We saw in our discussion of state and local politics that the radical left has sometimes engaged in electoral politics, but in most cases this involvement has been outside the existing two-party structure and designed to show people that political action does not have to be undertaken under the meaningless labels of Democrat and Republican.

Finally, the establishment of small communities, either in rural areas or in urban neighborhoods, gives the left the opportunity to demonstrate the possibilities of cooperation rather than competition, common ownership rather than private property, and a sufficiency for all rather than riches for some and poverty for others.

Through these methods, the left radicals believe that—slowly at first and then with gathering momentum—a revolution of power and styles of living will overtake America. And in many other countries where corporate capitalism is less powerfully entrenched, the revolution may proceed faster. The old communist left still looks to the Soviet Union to act as the vanguard for the worldwide socialist revolution. The new left regards the Soviet Union as too heavily bureaucratic and centralized to serve as a proper model for socialism. But all factions on the left share the belief that the days of the capitalist systems everywhere are numbered and destined to give way to a different and superior form of social organization.

THE CONSERVATIVES

The conservative vision of America is a land in which individuals are encouraged to improve themselves by hard work, initiative, and imagination; and, if they do so, they are rewarded by the right to acquire property, use it with a minimum of interference, and pass it along to their children. The conservatives' ideal America is a country where power is exercised primarily at the state and local levels. It is also a society that prizes traditional beliefs and customs, a culture firmly rooted in family, religion, and neighborhood. Finally, America, to conservatives, should be a leader among nations, proud of its own history and traditions, respecting the integrity of other nations, and ready to take a firm stand against those nations, like the communist countries, that threaten the rights of others to live in freedom.

America was once like this model, the conservatives believe, but America has been corrupted beyond recognition. At first gradually, and then with breakneck speed from the 1930s, America became a welfare state, leveling everyone to a condition of drab uniformity. Incentives to advance oneself were destroyed. The rights of property owners and businesspeople were impinged on by punitive rules and regulations and confiscatory tax rates. Rewards were provided not for enterprise and effort but for laziness and incompetence. There was a general debasement of moral standards. All other sources of authority—family, church, state, and community—were undermined by the power of the central government, which standardized and regimented our lives. Patriotism, too, became a declining force. As we lost respect for ourselves and our traditions, the world lost respect for us, and our international position deteriorated in inverse proportion to the surging power of communism.

This debasement of our freedoms at home and our strength abroad was the direct consequence of the power of an elite of intellectuals, the liberal establishment. These people had no respect for the values and moral standards on which the greatness of this country was founded. Through the New Deal, the Great Society, and then through the programs of the Carter administration, they built so much power into the presidency and the federal bureaucracy (aided and abetted by the Supreme Court, particularly during the Warren era) that the separation of powers and the federal division of powers became almost meaningless.

The liberal establishment proceeded almost unchecked in its "social engineering," its experiments in centralized, national planning, producing bureaucratic monstrosities like the War on Poverty, school busing, affirmative action, and so on, all of which served only to create antagonisms between classes and races. Problems such as the energy shortage were in large part created by governmental bungling. And the obvious solutions, so readily available through the free-market system and the efforts of private business, were ignored in favor of the cumbersome administrative schemes of the planners.

This same liberal establishment persistently refused to face the true meaning of communist aggression, responding only when the danger became particularly menacing and then—as in Korea, the Cuban missile crisis, and Vietnam—with pallid half-measures instead of the decisive actions needed for victory. Now we are in a situation in which even these half-measures could not succeed because they were based on our superiority in nuclear weaponry, which no longer exists because of our leaders' refusal to provide the military with the resources it needs.

The election of Ronald Reagan and a Republican Senate in 1980 was an unmistakable signal that the American people had had enough of the policies of the liberal establishment. They had become disenchanted with the tax burdens of the welfare state, oppressive not only to the wealthy but also to the vast middle class; with the reverse discrimination of affirmative action and busing; with the explosion of violent crime and the erosion of traditional values; and with the decline of America's reputation and strength in the world.

The victory of conservative Republicans in 1980 represented not only a repudiation of the past but an opportunity to bring about a permanent change in the purposes of government in America. In many respects the Reagan administration showed that it intended to take advantage of this opportunity. The danger, say the conservatives, is that the administration will falter in the face of short-term political considerations and the unrelenting opposition of the liberal elite, still strongly entrenched in the bureaucracies, in the media, and in the universities. The task of conservatives is to apply constant pressure on the administration and on Congress and to elect to public office still more of the kind of right-minded leaders who understand and will fight to restore the original intent of the Founding Fathers: to establish *limited* government.

THE RADICAL RIGHT

We noted in our opening chapter that it is difficult to distill a single set of values out of the two differing strands of thought on the radical right. On the one hand, there is the more elitist position, typified by the John Birch Society, which believes in an America of competitive individualism and unrestricted business enterprise. Government in their ideal society would be delegated to those individuals best qualified to rule by their ability and their economic success. As these rightists see it, the Founding Fathers established the perfect model to achieve this goal. But on the other hand, the populist rightists seek a much broader base for their ideal system, in which large numbers participate in shaping policy.

Nonetheless, there are certain values to which both of these strands of thought subscribe. Their values have already been suggested in our statement of the conservative perspective, but the values of the radical right are expressed in more extreme form. All groups on the radical right work toward an America in which pride in their country; and patriotism, or Americanism, is the most intense and frequently articulated of their values.

This belief is the key to their international as well as their domestic aspirations. All on the radical right call for a foreign policy that asserts the strength and prestige of America, looks for allies only among those countries that support similar ideals to our own, and displays undying hostility to atheistic, imperialistic communism.

There is little disagreement among the various factions on the radical right about their perceptions of the reality of America today. All insist that we are heading pell-mell for socialism and/or communism. They believe that through civil rights and antipoverty legislation we have created a new privileged class, in which the poor, blacks, and other minorities are rewarded for sloth, irresponsibility, and hostile behavior. They see the total degradation of traditional values and institutions and warn that, just as the Roman Empire wallowed in corruption and debauchery before it fell, so our intellectuals and our counterculturists are pushing America toward its decline by attacking the Bible, the family and traditional male-female roles, and by urging permissiveness toward drugs, pornography, sexual licentiousness, crime, civil disruptions, and treason.

Power, say the radicals of the right, is almost completely in the hands of a small, affluent elite who are either Communists or "insiders" working hand in hand with the Communists. They work their will through the White House, the bureaucracies, the Supreme Court, the Congress, the media, the intellectuals, organized labor, and other special interest groups. The left-wing elite manipulate public opinion by stirring up exaggerated fears of damage to the environment and the depletion of energy and other natural resources, all the while insisting that the problems can be resolved only by placing even more power in their hands.

Nor is the present situation the result, as the conservatives seem to suggest, of the efforts of misguided although probably well-meaning people. It is all part of a malign plan, a conspiracy of power by the Rockefellers and their fellow insiders. And the conspiracy is worldwide. Insiders in the United States are working with their counterparts in the Soviet Union, China, and the other communist powers to divide the world into mutually profitable spheres of control.

Somehow the mass of the people must be roused out of their apathy to take a stand against the totalitarians who rule them. Perhaps it is already too late. The damage done to the cause of Americanism by the Communists and their allies may be irreversible. But the growing distrust of governmental institutions is a signal that at last the people are tiring of the corruption and moral delinquency of our rulers and their policies of favoring the poor against the middle class, blacks against whites, patriots against draft dodgers, communist and Third World nations against our few friends abroad.

The leadership needed to capture these resentments cannot be found in the ranks of the conservatives. Despite their attacks on the establishment, most conservatives are too busy playing the old political games to be trustworthy. For the moment, the radicals of the right cannot point to a standard-bearer of the caliber needed to help America recapture her former glory. But they have no doubt that, when the opportunity arrives, the leaders will be there. In the meantime there is work to be done educating the people through speeches and publications, entering the electoral arena whenever the right candidates and issues present themselves, and enlisting in organizations all those individuals who understand the extent of the present danger.

THE CENTRISTS

Centrists aspire to a land of moderation and reasonableness. They want a country of diversity and multiple interests. Conflict, therefore, is inevitable. But conflict should be handled by negotiation and resolved by compromise. Thus the centrists' values fall between the opposing ideals to their left and right. They believe in equality of opportunity but allow substantial variations in income and property. They respect property rights but would subject them to social controls. They support freedom of expression but not moral anarchy or the disruption of law. This careful balancing of values they apply to the international scene, too, arguing that foreign policy should be a judicious mixture of firmness and restraint. And the governmental system through which these values are put into effect should be pluralistic, with power checked and restrained and diffused among many centers.

Centrists do not claim that we have attained this ideal condition in America today. They recognize that, especially since the early 1960s, we have suffered some significant failures both at home and abroad. They concede that for a time the system became unbalanced, and too much power gravitated toward the presidency. And they are somewhat concerned about the decline of trust in government.

But centrists do not agree with the sweeping criticisms of the system by liberals and conservatives, let alone the total condemnation by the radicals of left and right. If the system has not performed perfectly, this fact does not startle the centrists; the world to them is an imperfect place and the ideal is never fully realizable. Nor are the failures nearly as serious as the critics contend. The American system, after all, has produced unequaled benefits for large numbers of people, including a high standard of living, abundant opportunities for higher education, and an expanding array of public services. And progress continues to be made: in the last twenty years poverty has declined, the middle class has expanded, and the condition of black people and other minorities has improved in every respect.

Clearly the shrill warnings heard from left and right have been proved wrong. We have not been turned into a garrison state by racial war, as the liberals predicted, or brought to the edge of collapse by leftist terrorism, as the conservatives seemed to suggest. Although we face serious problems in the fields of energy and inflation, our difficulties in these areas are less acute than the problems of many other industrialized countries.

Similarly, in foreign policy, events have not borne out the dire prophecies of the critics. Liberals and the radical left repeatedly charged that the world was about to blow up because of the arms race, the pressure of the military-industrial complex, and so on. Yet World War III has not broken out, the danger of thermonuclear confrontations seems to have receded, and we will not have any more Vietnams. At the same time we still possess enormous military power, despite the charges from conservatives and the radical right that we have allowed our strength to decline disastrously.

As for our governmental institutions, they have survived all the challenges of recent years. The perpetrators of Watergate were brought down because of the checks and balances of the system. Although these checks and balances can be thrown out of kilter temporarily, eventually they reassert themselves. And in the aftermath of Watergate the necessary corrective measures have been taken. America is still a country firmly committed to self-government, to free elections, and to providing people with moderate choices of leaders and policies.

This view does not rule out the need for change. Step-by-step change is an integral part of the system. And gradualist change is exactly what the people want. It would be a mistake to read into the 1980 election results a mandate for a complete reversal of the policies of the past. The election recorded dissatisfaction with the last administration's performance, together with weariness with government's taking on too many tasks at too high a cost with too little attention to the wishes of the majority.

So the 1980 election should be interpreted in the same light as the 1952 and 1968 elections: an indication that the electorate wanted a slowing down of the pace of change and a limitation of overly ambitious designs by governmental leaders. Unfortunately the Reagan administration seized on the accession to power to bring about too drastic a change of direction.

Centrists hoped that political realities would quickly intrude on the plans of the administration and result in a less adventurous set of policies. If not, the centrists predicted, the basic procedure provided by the political system—the process of elections—would reestablish the checks and balances of the system and replace the excesses of ideological fervor with the basic political virtues of good sense, moderation, and willingness to compromise.

WHY BOTHER WITH POLITICS?

However wide the differences between our five perspectives, they all agree on one point: the importance of political activity. This message is not universally understood. Some people say: "I don't care much about politics, so I guess that makes me a centrist." But this conclusion is a misreading of centrist views. Although centrists see less need for the expansion of political participation than, say, the liberals, they are devout believers in the practice of politics. Others may present a pseudoradical rationale for not being involved: "The whole system is run by a small clique; there is nothing we can do, so why try?" But radicals of both left and right are attacking politics *as it is now practiced* and are pleading with people to become deeply committed to *their* kinds of politics.

It is unquestionably clear that a considerable, and perhaps increasing, number of people have turned away from politics. This fact comes as no surprise in the light of the material we have reviewed in this book. We have seen examples of tawdry and venal behavior, of betrayals of the public trust, and of gross abuses of power. We have examined vast institutions that seem to have become too big and cumbersome to serve individual human purposes. We have talked about policy issues of bewildering complexity, in which the search for solutions is made even more difficult by the inadequacy of the methods available to analyze the problem and the simple inability to determine the basic facts. Finally, we have demonstrated that every topic, every issue, is the subject of bitter disagreement, with ideological squabbling pushing aside the possibility of effective problem solving.

But if these arguments against politics seem compelling, we must still ask: What is the alternative to politics? Shall we turn policy making over to a small group of wise, dispassionate people who will make the decisions for us? But even if this choice were desirable, who are these people? Do any of us know even one person of such exalted qualities? Should we, then, try to eliminate the element of human self-interest entirely by developing the ultimate computer, programmed to solve all our problems? But we know that no technological device can make decisions for human beings on what kind of world they want to live in or how they should choose among alternative ways of reaching their goals. There are always choices to be made, and we cannot escape the responsibility for choice.

And that, in the last analysis, is what politics is about—the making of choices among competing purposes and values. We have set forth in this book five alternative sets of purposes. They do not exhaust the list of possibilities. You may prefer some variation or combination of them, or even an entirely different solution to the problem. But for anyone who cares in the least about the survival of the human race and about the need to prevent the degradation and debasement of life, some kind of commitment—fraught though it may be with the perils of corruption, inconsistency, and frustration—is indispensable.

NOTES AND REFERENCES

1. See Jerome Skolnick, *The Politics of Protest* (New York: Ballantine, 1969); and William A. Gamson, "Violence and Political Power," *Psychology Today*, July 1974, pp. 35–41.

THE CONSTITUTION OF THE UNITED STATES OF AMERICA

 e the People of the United States, in Order to form a more perfect Union, establish Justice, insure domestic Tranquility, provide for the common defence, promote the general Welfare, and secure the Blessings of Liberty to ourselves and our Posterity, do ordain and establish this Constitution for the United States of America.

ARTICLE I

Section 1. All legislative Powers herein granted shall be vested in a Congress of the United States, which shall consist of a Senate and House of Representatives.

Section 2. The House of Representatives shall be composed of Members chosen every second Year by the People of the several States, and the Electors in each State shall have the Qualifications requisite for Electors of the most numerous Branch of the State Legislature.

No Person shall be a Representative who shall not have attained to the age of twenty five Years, and been seven Years a Citizen of the United States, and who shall not, when elected, be an Inhabitant of that State in which he shall be chosen.

Representatives and direct Taxes shall be apportioned among the several States which may be included within this Union, according to their respective Numbers, which shall be determined by adding to the whole Number of free Persons, including those bound to Service for a Term of Years, and excluding Indians not taxed, three fifths of all other persons. The actual Enumeration shall be made within three Years after the first Meeting of the Congress of the United States, and within every subsequent Term of ten Years, in such Manner as they shall by Law direct. The Number of Representatives shall not exceed one for every thirty Thousand, but each State shall have at Least one Representative; and until such enumeration shall be made, the State of New Hampshire shall be entitled to chuse three, Massachusetts eight, Rhode-Island and Providence Plantations one, Connecticut five, New-York six, New Jersey four, Pennsylvania eight, Delaware one, Maryland six, Virginia ten, North Carolina five, South Carolina five, and Georgia three.

When vacancies happen in the Representation from any State, the Executive Authority thereof shall issue Writs of Election to fill such Vacancies.

The House of Representatives shall chuse their Speaker and other Officers; and shall have the sole Power of Impeachment.

Section 3.   The Senate of the United States shall be composed of two Senators from each State, chosen by the Legislature thereof, for six Years; and each Senator shall have one Vote.

Immediately after they shall be assembled in Consequence of the first Election, they shall be divided as equally as may be into three Classes. The Seats of the Senators of the first Class shall be vacated at the Expiration of the second Year, of the second Class at the Expiration of the fourth Year, and of the third Class at the Expiration of the sixth Year, so that one third may be chosen every second Year; and if Vacancies happen by Resignation, or otherwise! during the Recess of the Legislature of any State, the Executive thereof may make temporary Appointments until the next Meeting of the Legislature, which shall then fill such Vacancies.

No Person shall be a Senator who shall not have attained to the Age of thirty Years, and been nine Years a Citizen of the United States, and who shall not, when elected, be an Inhabitant of the State for which he shall be chosen.

The Vice President of the United States shall be President of the Senate, but shall have no Vote, unless they be equally divided.

The Senate shall chuse their other Officers, and also a President pro tempore, in the Absence of the Vice President, or when he shall exercise the Office of the President of the United States.

The Senate shall have the sole Power to try all Impeachments. When sitting for that Purpose, they shall be on Oath or Affirmation. When the President of the United States is tried, the Chief Justice shall preside: And no Person shall be convicted without the Concurrence of two thirds of the Members present.

Judgment in Cases of Impeachment shall not extend further than to removal from Office, and disqualification to hold and enjoy any Office of honor, Trust or Profit under the United States: but the Party convicted shall nevertheless be liable and subject to Indictment, Trial, Judgment and Punishment, according to Law.

Section 4.   The Times, Places and Manner of holding Elections for Senators and Representatives, shall be prescribed in each State by the Legislature thereof; but the Congress may at any time by Law make or alter such Regulations, except as to the Places of chusing Senators.

The Congress shall assemble at least once in every Year, and such Meeting shall be on the first Monday in December, unless they shall by Law appoint a different Day.

Section 5.   Each House shall be the Judge of the Elections, Returns and Qualifications of its own Members, and a Majority of each shall constitute a Quorum to do Business: but a smaller Number may adjourn from day to day, and may be authorized to compel the Attendance of absent Members, in such Manner, and under such Penalties as each House may provide.

Each House may determine the Rules of its Proceedings, punish its Members for disorderly Behaviour, and, with the Concurrence of two thirds, expel a Member.

Each House shall keep a Journal of its Proceedings, and from time to time publish the same, excepting such Parts as may in their Judgment require Secrecy; and the Yeas and

Nays of the Members of either House on any question shall, at the Desire of one fifth of those Present, be entered on the Journal.

Neither House, during the Session of Congress, shall, without the Consent of the other, adjourn for more than three days, nor to any other Place than that in which the two Houses shall be sitting.

Section 6. The Senators and Representatives shall receive a Compensation for their Services, to be ascertained by Law, and paid out of the Treasury of the United States. They shall be in all Cases, except Treason, Felony and Breach of the Peace, be privileged from Arrest during their Attendance at the Session of their respective Houses, and in going to and returning from the same; and for any Speech or Debate in either House, they shall not be questioned in any other Place.

No Senator or Representative shall, during the Time for which he was elected, be appointed to any civil Office under the Authority of the United States, which shall have been created, or the Emoluments whereof shall have been encreased during such time; and no Person holding any Office under the United States, shall be a Member of either House during his Continuance in Office.

Section 7. All Bills for raising Revenue shall originate in the House of Representatives; but the Senate may propose or concur with Amendments as on other Bills.

Every Bill which shall have passed the House of Representatives and the Senate, shall, before it become a Law, be presented to the President of the United States; if he approve he shall sign it, but if not he shall return it, with his Objections to that House in which it shall have originated, who shall enter the Objections at large on their Journal, and proceed to reconsider it. If after such Reconsideration two thirds of that House shall agree to pass the Bill, it shall be sent, together with the Objections, to the other House, by which it shall likewise be reconsidered, and if approved by two thirds of that House, it shall become a Law. But in all such Cases the Votes of both Houses shall be determined by Yeas and Nays, and the Names of the Persons voting for and against the Bill shall be entered on the Journal of each House respectively. If any Bill shall not be returned by the President within ten Days (Sundays excepted) after it shall have been presented to him, the Same shall be a Law, in like Manner as if he had signed it, unless the Congress by their Adjournment prevent its Return, in which Case it shall not be a Law.

Every Order, Resolution, or Vote to which the Concurrence of the Senate and House of Representatives may be necessary (except on a question of Adjournment) shall be presented to the President of the United States; and before the Same shall take Effect, shall be approved by him, or being disapproved by him, shall be repassed by two thirds of the Senate and House of Representatives, according to the Rules and Limitations prescribed in the Case of a Bill.

Section 8. The Congress shall have Power to lay and collect Taxes, Duties, Imposts and Excises, to pay the Debts and provide for the common Defence and general Welfare of the United States; but all Duties, Imposts and Excises shall be uniform throughout the United States;

To borrow Money on the credit of the United States;

To regulate Commerce with foreign Nations, and among the several States, and with the Indian Tribes;

To establish a uniform Rule of Naturalization, and uniform Laws on the subject of Bankruptcies, throughout the United States;

To coin Money, regulate the Value thereof, and of foreign Coin, and fix the Standard of Weights and Measures;

To provide for the Punishment of counterfeiting the Securities and current Coin of the United States;

To establish Post Offices and post Roads;

To promote the Progress of Science and useful Arts, by securing for limited Times to Authors and Inventors the exclusive Right to their respective Writings and Discoveries;

To constitute Tribunals inferior to the Supreme Court;

To define and punish Piracies and Felonies committed on the high Seas, and Offences against the Law of Nations;

To declare War, grant Letters of Marque and Reprisal, and make Rules concerning Captures on Land and Water;

To raise and support Armies, but no Appropriation of Money to that Use shall be for a longer Term than two Years;

To provide and maintain a Navy;

To make Rules for the Government and Regulation of the land and naval Forces;

To provide for calling forth the Militia to execute the Laws of the Union, suppress Insurrections and repel Invasions;

To provide for organizing, arming, and disciplining the Militia, and for governing such Part of them as may be employed in the Service of the United States, reserving to the states respectively, the Appointment of the Officers, and the Authority of training the Militia according to the discipline prescribed by Congress;

To exercise exclusive Legislation in all Cases whatsoever, over such District (not exceeding ten miles square) as may, by Cession of particular States, and the Acceptance of Congress, become the Seat of the Government of the United States, and to exercise like Authority over all Places purchased by the Consent of the Legislature of the State in which the Same shall be, for the Erection of Forts, Magazines, Arsenals, dock-Yards, and other needful Buildings;—And

To make all Laws which shall be necessary and proper for carrying into Execution the foregoing Powers, and all other Powers vested by this Constitution in the Government of the United States, or in any Department or Office thereof.

Section 9. The Migration or Importation of such Persons as any of the States now existing shall think proper to admit, shall not be prohibited by the Congress prior to the Year one thousand eight hundred and eight, but a Tax or duty may be imposed on such Importation, not exceeding ten dollars for each Person.

The Privilege of the Writ of Habeas Corpus shall not be suspended, unless when in Cases of Rebellion or Invasion the public Safety may require it.

No Bill of Attainder of ex post facto Law shall be passed.

No Capitation, or other direct, Tax shall be laid, unless in Proportion to the Census or Enumeration herein before directed to be taken.

No Tax or Duty shall be laid on Articles exported from any State.

No Preference shall be given by any Regulation of Commerce or Revenue to the Ports of one State over those of another: nor shall Vessels bound to, or from, one State, be obliged to enter, clear, or pay Duties in another.

No Money shall be drawn from the Treasury, but in Consequence of Appropriations made by Law; and a regular Statement and Account of the Receipts and Expenditures of all public Money shall be published from time to time.

No title of Nobility shall be granted by the United States: And no Person holding any

Office of Profit or Trust under them, shall, without the Consent of the Congress, accept of any present, Emolument, Office, or Title, of any kind whatever, from any King, Prince, or foreign State.

Section 10. No State shall enter into any Treaty, Alliance, or Confederation; grant Letters of Marque and Reprisal; coin Money; emit Bills of Credit; make any Thing but gold and silver Coin a Tender in Payment of Debts; pass any Bill of Attainder, ex post facto Law, or Law impairing the Obligation of Contracts, or Grant any Title of Nobility.

No State shall, without the Consent of the Congress, lay any Imposts or Duties on Imports or Exports, except what may be absolutely necessary for executing its inspection Laws: and the net Produce of all Duties and Imposts, laid by any State on Imports or Exports, shall be for the Use of the Treasury of the United States; and all such Laws shall be subject to the Revision and Control of the Congress.

No State shall, without the Consent of Congress, lay any Duty of Tonnage, keep Troops, or Ships of War in time of Peace, enter into any Agreement or Compact with another State, or with a foreign Power, or engage in War, unless actually invaded, or in such imminent Danger as will not admit of delay.

ARTICLE II

Section 1. The executive Power shall be vested in a President of the United States of America. He shall hold his Office during the Term of four Years, and, together with the Vice President, chosen for the same Term be elected as follows:

Each State shall appoint, in such Manner as the Legislature thereof may direct, a Number of Electors, equal to the whole Number of Senators and Representatives to which the State may be entitled in the Congress but no Senator or Representative, or Person holding an Office of Trust or Profit under the United States, shall be appointed an Elector.

The Electors shall meet in their respective States, and vote by Ballot for two Persons, of whom one at least shall not be an Inhabitant of the same State with themselves. And they shall make a List of all the Persons voted for, and of the Number of Votes, for each; which List they shall sign and certify, and transmit sealed to the Seat of the Government of the United States, directed to the President of the Senate. The President of the Senate shall, in the Presence of the Senate and House of Representatives, open all the Certificates, and the Votes shall then be counted. The Person having the greatest Number of Votes shall be the President, if such Number be a Majority of the whole Number of Electors appointed; and if there be more than one who have such Majority, and have an equal Number of Votes, then the House of Representatives shall immediately chuse by Ballot one of them for President; and if no Person have a Majority, then from the five highest on the List the said House shall in like Manner chuse the President. But in chusing the President, the Votes shall be taken by States, the Representation from each State having one Vote; A quorum for this purpose shall consist of a Member or Members from two thirds of the States, and a Majority of all the States shall be necessary to a Choice. In every Case, after the Choice of the President, the Person having the greatest Number of Votes of the Electors shall be the Vice President. But if there should remain two or more who have equal Votes, the Senate shall chuse from them by Ballot the Vice President.

The Congress may determine the Time of chusing the Electors, and the Day on which they shall give their Votes; which Day shall be the same throughout the United States.

No Person except a natural born Citizen, or a Citizen of the United States, at the time of the Adoption of this Constitution, shall be eligible to the Office of President; neither shall any Person be eligible to that Office who shall not have attained to the Age of thirty five Years, and been fourteen Years a Resident within the United States.

In case of the Removal of the President from Office, or his Death, Resignation, or Inability to discharge the Powers and duties of the said Office, the Same shall devolve on the Vice President, and the Congress may by Law provide for the Case of Removal, Death, Resignation or Inability, both of the President and Vice President, declaring what Officer shall then act as President, and such Officer shall act accordingly, until the Disability be removed, or a President shall be elected.

The President shall, at stated Times, receive for his Services, a Compensation which shall neither be encreased nor diminished during the Period for which he shall have been elected, and he shall not receive within that Period any other Emolument from the United States, or any of them.

Before he enter on the Execution of his Office, he shall take the following Oath or Affirmation:—"I do solemnly swear (or affirm) that I will faithfully execute the Office of President of the United States, and will to the best of my Ability, preserve, protect and defend the Constitution of the United States."

Section 2. The President shall be Commander in Chief of the Army and Navy of the United States, and of the Militia of the several States, when called into the actual service of the United States; he may require the Opinion, in writing, of the principal Officer in each of the executive Departments, upon any Subject relating to the Duties of their respective Offices, and he shall have Power to grant Reprieves and Pardons for Offences against the United States, except in Cases of Impeachment.

He shall have Power, by and with the Advice and Consent of the Senate, to make Treaties, provided two thirds of the Senators present concur; and he shall nominate, and by and with the Advice and Consent of the Senate, shall appoint Ambassadors, and other public Ministers and Consuls, Judges of the Supreme Court, and all other Officers of the United States, whose Appointments are not herein otherwise provided for, and which shall be established by Law: but the Congress may by Law vest the Appointment of such inferior Officers, as they think proper, in the President alone, in the Courts of Law, or in the heads of Departments.

The President shall have Power to fill up all Vacancies that may happen during the Recess of the Senate, by granting Commissions which shall expire at the End of their next Session.

Section 3. He shall from time to time give to the Congress Information of the State of the Union, and recommend to their Consideration such Measures as he shall judge necessary and expedient; he may, on extraordinary Occasions, convene both Houses, or either of them, and in Case of Disagreement between them, with Respect to the Time of Adjournment, he may adjourn them to such time as he shall think proper; he shall receive ambassadors and other public Ministers, he shall take Care that the Laws be faithfully executed, and shall Commission all the Officers of the United States.

Section 4. The President, Vice President, and all civil Officers of the United States, shall be removed from Office on Impeachment for; and Conviction of Treason, Bribery, or other high Crimes and Misdemeanors.

ARTICLE III

Section 1. The judicial Power of the United States, shall be vested in one supreme Court and in such inferior Courts as the Congress may from time to time ordain and establish. The Judges, both of the supreme and inferior Courts, shall hold their Offices during good Behavior, and shall, at stated Times, receive for their Services, a Compensation which shall not be diminished during their Continuance in Office.

Section 2. The judicial Power shall extend to all Cases, in Law and Equity, arising under this Constitution, the Laws of the United States, and Treaties made, or which shall be made, under their Authority;—to all Cases affecting Ambassadors, other public Ministers and Consuls;—to all Cases of admiralty and maritime Jurisdiction;—to Controversies to which the United States shall be a Party—to Controversies between two or more States;—between a State and Citizens of another State;—between Citizens of different states; between Citizens of the same State claiming Lands under Grants of different States, and between a State or the Citizens thereof, and foreign States, Citizens, or Subjects.

In all cases affecting Ambassadors, other public Ministers and Consuls, and those in which a State shall be Party, the supreme Court shall have original Jurisdiction. In all the other Cases before mentioned, the supreme Court shall have appellate Jurisdiction, both as to Law and Fact, with such Exceptions, and under such Regulations as the Congress shall make.

The Trial of all Crimes, except in Cases of Impeachment, shall be by Jury; and such Trial shall be held in the State where the said Crimes shall have been committed; but when not committed within any State, the Trial shall be at such Place or Places as the Congress may by Law have directed.

Section 3. Treason against the United States, shall consist only in levying War against them, or in adhering to their Enemies, giving them Aid and Comfort. No Person shall be convicted of Treason unless on the Testimony of two Witnesses to the same overt Act, or on Confession in open Court.

The Congress shall have Power to declare the Punishment of Treason, but no Attainder of Treason shall work Corruption of Blood, or Forfeiture except during the Life of the Person attained.

ARTICLE IV

Section 1. Full Faith and Credit shall be given in each State to the public Acts, Records, and judicial Proceedings of every other State. And the Congress may by general Laws prescribe the Manner in which such Acts, Records, and Proceedings shall be proved, and the Effect thereof.

Section 2. The Citizens of each State shall be entitled to all Privileges and immunities of Citizens in the several States.

A Person charged in any State with Treason, Felony, or other Crime, who shall flee from Justice, and be found in another State, shall on Demand of the executive Authority of the State from which he fled, be delivered up, to be removed to the State having Jurisdiction of the Crime.

No person held to Service or Labour in one State, under the Laws thereof, escaping into another, shall in Consequence of any Law or Regulation therein be discharged from such

Service or Labour but shall be delivered upon claim of the Party to whom such Service or Labour may be due.

Section 3.   New States may be admitted by the Congress into this Union; but no new State shall be formed or erected within the Jurisdiction of any other State; nor any State be formed by the Junction of two or more States, or Parts of States, without the Consent of the Legislatures of the States concerned as well as of the Congress.

The Congress shall have Power to dispose of and make all needful Rules and Regulations respecting the Territory or other Property belonging to the United States; and nothing in this Constitution shall be so construed as to Prejudice any claims of the United States, or of any particular State.

Section 4.   The United States shall guarantee to every State in this Union a Republican Form of Government, and shall protect each of them against Invasion; and on Application of the Legislature, or of the Executive (when the Legislature cannot be convened) against domestic violence.

ARTICLE V

The Congress, whenever two thirds of both Houses shall deem it necessary, shall propose Amendments to this Constitution, or, on the Application of the Legislatures of two thirds of the several States, shall call a Convention for proposing Amendments, which, in either Case, shall be valid to all Intents and Purposes, as Part of this Constitution, when ratified by the Legislatures of three fourths of the several States, or by Conventions in three fourths thereof, as the one or the other Mode of Ratification may be proposed by the Congress; Provided that no Amendment which may be made prior to the Year One thousand eight hundred and eight shall in any Manner affect the first and fourth Clauses in the Ninth Section of the first Article; and that no State, without its Consent, shall be deprived of its equal Suffrage in the Senate.

ARTICLE VI

All Debts contracted and Engagements entered into, before the Adoption of this Constitution, shall be as valid against the United States under this Constitution, as under the Confederation.

This Constitution, and the Laws of the United States which shall be made in Pursuance thereof; and all Treaties made, or which shall be made, under the Authority of the United States, shall be the supreme Law of the Land; and the Judges in every State shall be bound thereby, any Thing in the Constitution of Laws of any State to the Contrary notwithstanding.

The Senators and Representatives before mentioned, and the Members of the several State Legislatures, and all executive and judicial Officers, both of the United States and of the several States, shall be bound by Oath or Affirmation to support this Constitution; but no religious Test shall ever be required as a Qualification to any Office or public Trust under the United States.

ARTICLE VII

The Ratification of the Conventions of nine States, shall be sufficient for the Establishment of this Constitution between the States so ratifying the Same.

Done in Convention by the Unanimous Consent of the States present the Seventeenth Day of September in the Year of our Lord one thousand seven hundred and eighty seven and of the Independence of the United States of America the twelfth. In witness whereof We have hereunto subscribed our Names.

Articles in addition to, and amendment of, the Constitution of the United States of America, proposed by Congress, and ratified by the several states, pursuant to the Fifth Article of the Original Constitution:

AMENDMENT I

Congress shall make no law respecting an establishment of religion, or prohibiting the free exercise thereof; or abridging the freedom of speech, or of the press; or the right of the people peaceably to assemble, and to petition the Government for a redress of grievances.

AMENDMENT II

A well regulated Militia, being necessary to the security of a free State, the right of the people to keep and bear Arms, shall not be infringed.

AMENDMENT III

No Soldier shall, in time of peace be quartered in any house, without the consent of the Owner, nor in time of war, but in a manner to be prescribed by law.

AMENDMENT IV

The right of the people to be secure in their persons, houses, papers, and effects, against unreasonable searches and seizures, shall not be violated, and no Warrants shall issue, but upon probable cause, supported by Oath or affirmation, and particularly describing the place to be searched, and the persons or things to be seized.

AMENDMENT V

No person shall be held to answer for a capital, or other infamous crime, unless on a presentment or indictment of a Grand Jury, except in cases arising in the land or naval forces, or in the Militia, when in actual service in time of War or public danger; nor shall any person be subject for the same offence to be twice put in jeopardy of life or limb; nor shall be compelled in any criminal case to be a witness against himself, nor be deprived of life, liberty, or property without due process of law; nor shall private property be taken for public use, without just compensation.

AMENDMENT VI

In all criminal prosecutions, the accused shall enjoy the right to a speedy and public trial, by an impartial jury of the State and district wherein the crime shall have been committed, which district shall have been previously ascertained in law, and to be informed of the nature and cause of the accusation; to be confronted with the witness against him; to have compulsory process of obtaining witness in his favor, and to have the Assistance of Counsel for his defense.

AMENDMENT VII

In Suits at common law, where the value in controversy shall exceed twenty dollars, the right of trial by jury shall be preserved, and no fact tried by a jury, shall be otherwise reexamined in any Court of the United States, than according to the rules of the common law.

AMENDMENT VIII

Excessive bail shall not be required, nor excessive fines imposed, nor cruel and unusual punishments inflicted.

AMENDMENT IX

The enumeration in the Constitution, of certain rights, shall not be construed to deny or disparage others retained by the people.

AMENDMENT X

The powers not delegated to the United States by the Constitution, nor prohibited by it to the States, are reserved to the States respectively, or to the people.

AMENDMENT XI [JANUARY 8, 1798]

The Judicial power of the United States shall not be construed to extend to any suit in law or equity, commenced or prosecuted against one of the United States by Citizens of another State, or by Citizens or Subjects of any Foreign State.

AMENDMENT XII [SEPTEMBER 25, 1804]

The Electors shall meet in their respective states and vote by ballot for President and Vice President, one of whom, at least, shall not be an inhabitant of the same state with themselves; they shall name in their ballots the person voted for as President, and in distinct ballots the person voted for as Vice President, and they shall make distinct lists of all persons voted for as President and of all persons voted for as Vice President, and of the number of votes for each, which lists they shall sign and certify, and transmit sealed to the seat of the government of the United States, directed to the President of the Senate;—The President of the Senate shall, in the presence of Senate and House of Representatives, open all the certificates and the votes shall then be counted;—The person having the greatest number of votes for President, shall be the President, if such number be a majority of the whole number of Electors appointed; and if no person have such majority, then from the persons having the highest numbers not exceeding three on the list of those voted for as President, the House of Representatives shall choose immediately, by ballot, the President. But in choosing the President, the votes shall be taken by states, the representation from each state having one vote; a quorum for this purpose shall consist of a member or members from two-thirds of the states, and a majority of all the states shall be necessary to a choice.

And if the House of Representatives shall not choose a President whenever the right of choice shall devolve upon them, before the fourth day of March next following, then the Vice President shall act as President, as in the case of the death or other constitutional disability of the President.—The person having the greatest number of votes as Vice President shall be the Vice President, if such number be a majority of the whole number of Electors appointed, and if no person have a majority, then from the two highest numbers on the list, the Senate shall choose the Vice President; a quorum for the purpose shall consist of two-thirds of the whole number of Senators, and a majority of the whole number shall be necessary to a choice, but no person constitutionally ineligible to the office of President shall be eligible to that of Vice President of the United States.

AMENDMENT XIII [DECEMBER 18, 1865]

Section 1. Neither slavery nor involuntary servitude, except as a punishment for crime whereof the party shall have been duly convicted, shall exist within the United States, or any place subject to their jurisdiction.

Section 2. Congress shall have power to enforce this article by appropriate legislation.

AMENDMENT XIV [JULY 28, 1869]

Section 1. All persons born or naturalized in the United States, and subject to the jurisdiction thereof, are citizens of the United States and of the State wherein they reside. No State shall make or enforce any law which shall abridge the privileges or immunities of citizens of the United States; nor shall any State deprive any person of life, liberty, or property without due process of law; nor deny to any person within its jurisdiction the equal protection of the laws.

Section 2. Representatives shall be apportioned among the several States according to their respective numbers, counting the whole number of persons in each State, excluding Indians not taxed. But when the right to vote at any election for the choice of electors for President and Vice President of the United States, Representatives in Congress, the Executive and Judicial officers of a State, or the members of the Legislature thereof, is denied to any of the male inhabitants of such State, being twenty-one years of age, and citizens of the United States, or in any way abridged, except for participation in rebellion, or other crime, the basis of representation therein shall be reduced in the proportion which the number of such male citizens shall bear to the whole number of male citizens twenty-one years of age in such State.

Section 3. No person shall be a Senator or Representative in Congress, or elector of President and Vice President, or hold any office, civil or military, under the United States, or under any State, who, having previously taken an oath, as a member of Congress, or as an officer of the United States, or as a member of any State legislature, or as an executive or judicial officer of any State, to support the Constitution of the United States, shall have engaged in insurrection or rebellion against the same, or given aid or comfort to the enemies thereof. But Congress may by a vote of two thirds of each House, remove such disability.

Section 4. The validity of the public debt of the United States, authorized by law, including debts incurred for payment of pensions and bounties for services in suppressing insurrection or rebellion, shall not be questioned. But neither the United States nor any State shall assume or pay any debt or obligation incurred in aid of insurrection or rebellion against the United States, or any claim for the loss or emancipation of any slave; but all such debts, obligations, and claims shall be held illegal and void.

Section 5. The Congress shall have power to enforce, by appropriate legislation, the provisions of this article.

AMENDMENT XV [MARCH 30, 1870]

Section 1. The right of citizens of the United States to vote shall not be denied or abridged by the United States or by any State on account of race, color, or previous condition of servitude.

Section 2. The Congress shall have power to enforce this article by appropriate legislation.

AMENDMENT XVI [FEBRUARY 25, 1913]

The Congress shall have power to lay and collect taxes on income, from whatever source derived, without apportionment among the several States, and without regard to any census or enumeration.

AMENDMENT XVII [MAY 31, 1913]

The Senate of the United States shall be composed of two Senators from each State, elected by the people thereof, for six years; and each Senator shall have one vote. The electors in each State shall have the qualifications requisite for electors of the most numerous branch of the State legislature.

When vacancies happen in the representation of any State in the Senate, the executive authority of such State shall issue writs of election to fill such vacancies: Provided, That the legislature of any State may empower the executive thereof to make temporary appointments until the people fill the vacancies by election as the legislature may direct.

This amendment shall not be so construed as to affect the election or term of any Senator chosen before it becomes valid as part of the Constitution.

AMENDMENT XVIII [JANUARY 29, 1919]

Section 1. After one year from the ratification of this article the manufacture, sale, or transportation of intoxicating liquors within, the importation thereof into, or the exportation thereof from the United States and all territory subject to the jurisdiction thereof for beverage purposes is hereby prohibited.

Section 2. The Congress and the several states shall have concurrent power to enforce this article by appropriate legislation.

Section 3. This article shall be inoperative unless it shall have been ratified as an amendment to the Constitution by the legislatures of the several States, as provided in the

Constitution, within seven years from the date of the submission hereof to the States by the Congress.

AMENDMENT XIX [AUGUST 26, 1920]

The right of citizens of the United States to vote shall not be denied or abridged by the United States or by any State on account of sex.

Congress shall have power to enforce this article by appropriate legislation.

AMENDMENT XX [FEBRUARY 6, 1933]

Section 1. The terms of the President and Vice President shall end at noon on the 20th day of January, and the terms of Senators and Representatives at noon on the 3rd day of January, of the years in which such terms would have ended if this article had not been ratified; and the terms of their successors shall then begin.

Section 2. The Congress shall assemble at least once in every year, and such meeting shall begin at noon on the 3rd day of January, unless they shall by law appoint a different day.

Section 3. If, at the time fixed for the beginning of the term of the President, the President elect shall have died, the Vice President elect shall become President. If a President shall not have been chosen before the time fixed for the beginning of his term, or if the President elect shall have failed to qualify, then the Vice President elect shall act as President until a President shall have qualified; and the Congress may by law provide for the case wherein neither a President elect nor a Vice President elect shall have qualified, declaring who shall then act as President, or the manner in which one who is to act shall be selected, and such person shall act accordingly until a President or Vice President shall have qualified.

Section 4. The Congress may by law provide for the case of the death of any of the persons from whom the House of Representatives may choose a President whenever the right of choice shall have devolved upon them, and for the case of the death of any of the persons from whom the Senate may choose a Vice President whenever the right of choice shall have devolved upon them.

Section 5. Sections 1 and 2 shall take effect on the 15th day of October following the ratification of this article.

Section 6. This article shall be inoperative unless it shall have been ratified as an amendment to the Constitution by the legislatures of three-fourths of the several States within seven years from the date of its submission.

AMENDMENT XXI [DECEMBER 5, 1933]

Section 1. The eighteenth article of amendment to the Constitution of the United States is hereby repealed.

Section 2. The transportation or importation into any State, Territory, or possession of the United States for delivery or use therein of intoxicating liquors, in violation of the laws thereof, is hereby prohibited.

Section 3.   This article shall be inoperative unless it shall have been ratified as an amendment to the Constitution by conventions in the several States, as provided in the Constitution, within seven years of the date of the submission hereof to the States by the Congress.

AMENDMENT XXII [FEBRUARY 26, 1951]

Section 1.   No person shall be elected to the office of the President more than twice, and no person who has held the office of President, or acted as President, for more than two years of a term to which some other person was elected President shall be elected to the office of President more than once. But this Article shall not apply to any person holding the office of President when this Article was proposed by the Congress, and shall not prevent any person who may be holding the office of President, or acting as President, during the term within which this Article becomes operative from holding the office of President or acting as President during the remainder of such term.

Section 2.   This article shall be inoperative unless it shall have been ratified as an amendment to the Constitution by the legislatures of three-fourths of the several States within seven years from the date of its submission to the States by the Congress.

AMENDMENT XXIII [MARCH 29, 1961]

Section 1.   The District constituting the seat of Government of the United States shall appoint in such manner as the Congress may direct:

A number of electors of President and Vice President equal to the whole number of Senators and Representatives in Congress to which the District would be entitled if it were a State, but in no event more than the least populous State; they shall be in addition to those appointed by the States, but they shall be considered, for the purposes of the election of President and Vice President, to be electors appointed by a State; and they shall meet in the District and perform such duties as provided by the twelfth article of amendment.

Section 2.   The Congress shall have power to enforce this article by appropriate legislation.

AMENDMENT XXIV [JANUARY 23, 1964]

Section 1.   The right of citizens of the United States to vote in any primary or other election for President or Vice President, for electors for President or Vice President, or for Senator or Representative in Congress, shall not be denied or abridged by the United States or any state by reason of failure to pay any tax.

Section 2.   The Congress shall have the power to enforce this article by appropriate legislation.

AMENDMENT XXV [FEBRUARY 10, 1967]

Section 1.   In case of the removal of the President from office or of his death or resignation, the Vice President shall become President.

Section 2.   Whenever there is a vacancy in the office of the Vice President, the President shall nominate a Vice President who shall take office upon confirmation by a majority vote of both Houses of Congress.

Section 3. Whenever the President transmits to the President pro tempore of the Senate and the Speaker of the House of Representatives his written declaration that he is unable to discharge the powers and duties of his office, and until he transmits to them a written declaration to the contrary, such powers and duties shall be discharged by the Vice President as Acting President.

Section 4.   Whenever the Vice President and a majority of either the principal officers of the executive departments or of such other body as Congress may by law provide, transmit to the President pro tempore of the Senate and the Speaker of the House of Representatives their written declaration that the President is unable to discharge the powers and duties of his office, the Vice President shall immediately assume the powers and duties of the office as Acting President.

Thereafter, when the President transmits to the President pro tempore of the Senate and the Speaker of the House of Representatives his written declaration that no inability exists, he shall resume the powers and duties of his office unless the Vice President and a majority of either the principal officers of the executive departments or of such other body as Congress may by law provide, transmit within four days to the President pro tempore of the Senate and the Speaker of the House of Representatives their written declaration that the President is unable to discharge the powers and duties of his office. Thereupon Congress shall decide the issue, assembling within forty-eight hours for that purpose if not in session. If the Congress, within twenty-one days after receipt of the latter written declaration, or, if Congress is not in session, within twenty-one days after Congress is required to assemble, determines by two-thirds vote of both Houses that the President is unable to discharge the powers and duties of his office, the Vice President shall continue to discharge the same as Acting President; otherwise, the President shall resume the powers and duties of his office.

AMENDMENT XXVI [JULY 5, 1971]

Section 1.   The right of citizens of the United States, who are eighteen years of age or older, to vote shall not be denied or abridged by the United States or by any State on account of age.

Section 2.   The Congress shall have power to enforce this article by appropriate legislation.

PRESIDENTS OF THE UNITED STATES

	President	Term	Party
1.	George Washington	1789–97	Federalist
2.	John Adams	1797–1801	Federalist
3.	Thomas Jefferson	1801–09	Democratic-Republican
4.	James Madison	1809–17	Democratic-Republican
5.	James Monroe	1817–25	Democratic-Republican
6.	John Quincy Adams	1825–29	Democratic-Republican
7.	Andrew Jackson	1829–37	Democratic
8.	Martin Van Buren	1837–41	Democratic
9.	William Harrison	1841	Whig
10.	John Tyler	1841–45	Whig
11.	James K. Polk	1845–49	Democratic
12.	Zachary Taylor	1849–50	Whig
13.	Millard Fillmore	1850–53	Whig
14.	Franklin Pierce	1853–57	Democratic
15.	James Buchanan	1857–61	Democratic
16.	Abraham Lincoln	1861–65	Republican
17.	Andrew Johnson	1865–69	Union
18.	U. S. Grant	1869–77	Republican
19.	Rutherford Hayes	1877–81	Republican
20.	James Garfield	1881	Republican
21.	Chester Arthur	1881–85	Republican
22.	Grover Cleveland	1885–89	Democratic
23.	Benjamin Harrison	1889–93	Republican
24.	Grover Cleveland	1893–97	Democratic
25.	William McKinley	1897–1901	Republican
26.	Theodore Roosevelt	1901–09	Republican
27.	William Taft	1909–13	Republican
28.	Woodrow Wilson	1913–21	Democratic
29.	Warren Harding	1921–23	Republican
30.	Calvin Coolidge	1923–29	Republican
31.	Herbert Hoover	1929–33	Republican
32.	Franklin Roosevelt	1933–45	Democratic
33.	Harry Truman	1945–53	Democratic
34.	Dwight Eisenhower	1953–61	Republican
35.	John Kennedy	1961–63	Democratic
36.	Lyndon Johnson	1963–69	Democratic
37.	Richard Nixon	1969–74	Republican
38.	Gerald Ford	1974–77	Republican
39.	Jimmy Carter	1977–81	Democratic
40.	Ronald Reagan	1981–	Republican

selected bibliography

**CHAPTER 1 FIVE PERSPECTIVES
ON THE AMERICAN POLITICAL SYSTEM**

*Allen, Gary. *None Dare Call It Conspiracy.* Rossmoor, Calif.: Concord Press, 1971. A radical right statement by a freelance journalist arguing that a wealthy elite in America is in collusion with the Soviet Union to control domestic and world decisions.

*Bell, Daniel, ed. *The Radical Right.* Garden City, N.Y.: Doubleday, 1963. Critical commentaries on the radical right by centrist, liberal, and conservative scholars, including Daniel Bell, Richard Hofstadter, David Riesman, Nathan Glazer, Peter Viereck, Talcott Parsons, and Alan F. Westin.

*Burns, James MacGregor. *The Deadlock of Democracy.* 2nd ed. Englewood Cliffs, N.J.: Prentice-Hall, 1966.

*Burns, James MacGregor. *Uncommon Sense.* New York: Harper & Row, 1972.

*de Toledano, Ralph, and Hess, Karl, eds. *The Conservative Papers.* Garden City, N.Y.: Doubleday/Anchor, 1964.

*Dolbeare, Kenneth M., and Dolbeare, Patricia. *American Ideologies: The Competing Political Beliefs of the 1970s.* 3rd ed. Chicago: Rand McNally, 1976. An examination of the role of various contemporary ideologies in America, with categories that are slightly different from the categories in *Power and Politics in America.*

*Domhoff, G. William. *The Higher Circles.* New York: Random House, 1970.

*Domhoff, G. William. *Who Rules America?* Englewood Cliffs, N.J.: Prentice-Hall, 1967.

*Dye, Thomas, and Zeigler, L. Harmon. *The Irony of Democracy.* 3rd ed. North Scituate, Mass.: Duxbury Press, 1975. An analysis of the American system by two political scientists, one of the left, the other conservative, based on the propostion that "elites, not masses, govern America."

Dye, Thomas R. *Who's Running America?* 2nd ed. Englewood Cliffs, N.J.: Prentice-Hall, 1979.

*Etzkowitz, Henry, and Schwab, Peter, eds. *Is America Necessary?* St. Paul, Minn.: West, 1976. A reader presenting conservative, liberal, and socialist perspectives on American political institutions.

*Evans, M. Stanton. *Clear and Present Dangers: A Conservative View of America's Government.* New York: Harcourt Brace Jovanovich, 1975.

*Friedman, Milton. *Capitalism and Freedom.* Chicago: University of Chicago Press, 1962. An economist's argument that capitalism is an indispensable condition for the free society.

*Friedman, Milton, and Friedman, Rose. *Free to Choose.* New York: Harcourt Brace Jovanovich, 1980.

*Goldwater, Barry. *Conscience of a Conservative.* New York: Macfadden-Bartell, 1964.

Kendall, Willmoore. *The Conservative Affirmation.* Chicago: Henry Regnery, 1963. A critique of liberal ideology from the perspective of a conservative political scientist.

*Mills, C. Wright. *The Power Elite.* New York: Oxford Univerity Press, 1956.

*Oglesby, Carl, ed. *The New Left Reader.* New York: Grove Press, 1969. Selections from some of the central figures of the new left, including C. Wright Mills, Herbert Marcuse, Mark Rudd, Frantz Fanon, Huey Newton, Rudi Dutschke, and Daniel Cohn-Bendit.

*Parenti, Michael. *Democracy for the Few.* New York: St. Martin's Press, 1980. American government text from left perspective.

*Available in paperback.

*Rose, Arnold M. *The Power Structure*. New York: Oxford University Press, 1967. A sociologist's analysis of American politics as a pluralist system. Rejects Mills' power-elite analysis as "a caricature of American society."

*Rosenstone, Robert A., ed. *Protest from the Right*. Encino, Calif.: Glencoe Press, 1968. Articles by and about the extreme right.

*Schoenberger, Robert A., ed. *The American Right Wing: Readings in Political Behavior*. New York: Holt, Rinehart & Winston, 1969.

*Steinfels, Peter. *The Neo Conservatives*. New York: Simon & Schuster, 1979.

Viguerie, Richard A. *The New Right: We're Ready to Lead*. Aurora, Ill.: Caroline House, 1981.

CHAPTER 2 CONSTITUTIONAL FRAMEWORK

Beard, Charles A. *An Economic Interpretation of the Constitution of the United States*. New York: Macmillan, 1913.

*Becker, Carl L. *The Declaration of Independence*. New York: Knopf, 1942. An examination of the Declaration and its historical context.

*Corwin, Edward S. *The Constitution and What It Means Today*. Revised by Harold W. Case and Craig R. Ducat. Princeton, N.J.: Princeton University Press, 1974. A detailed review of the Constitution by one of its leading scholars.

*de Tocqueville, Alexis. *Democracy in America*. New York: Knopf, 1945. (Originally published, 1835.)

*Holcombe, Arthur N. *The Constitutional System*. Glenview, Ill.: Scott, Foresman, 1964. A centrist scholar's explanation of the principles embodied in the Constitution.

*Madison, James; Hamilton, Alexander; and Jay, John. *The Federalist*. Available in various editions. The basic exposition of the principles embodied in the U.S. Constitution by some of the men who shaped it.

*Peltason, J.W. *Corwin and Peltason's Understanding the Constitution*. 8th ed. New York: Holt, Rinehart & Winston, 1979.

CHAPTER 3 PUBLIC OPINION: WHO CARES ABOUT POLITICS?

*Almond, Gabriel A., and Verba, Sidney. *The Civic Culture*. Princeton, N.J.: Princeton University Press, 1963. Comparative study of political attitudes in the United States, Mexico, Great Britain, Germany, and Italy.

Buchanan, Patrick. *The New Majority*. Philadelphia: Girard Bank, 1973.

*Campbell, Angus; Converse, Philip E.; Miller, Warren E.; and Stokes, Donald E. *The American Voter*. New York: Wiley, 1960.

Greenstein, Fred I. *Children and Politics*. Rev. ed. New Haven, Conn.: Yale University Press, 1970. The formation of political attitudes in young children.

*Hennessy, Bernard C. *Public Opinion*. 4th ed. Monterey, Calif.: Brooks/Cole, 1981.

Key, V.O., Jr. *Public Opinion and American Democracy*. New York: Knopf, 1961. Standard work in this field.

*Key, V.O., Jr. *The Responsible Electorate*. Cambridge, Mass.: Belknap Press of Harvard University Press, 1966.

*Lane, Robert E., and Sears, David O. *Public Opinion*. Englewood Cliffs, N.J.: Prentice-Hall, 1964. Impact on political opinions of family, groups, and other societal influences.

*Lazarsfeld, Paul; Berelson, Bernard; and Gaudet, Hazel. *The People's Choice: How the Voter Makes Up His Mind in a Presidential Campaign*. 3rd ed. New York: Columbia University Press, 1968.

Miller, Warren E., and Levitin, Teresa E. *Leadership and Change: The New Politics and the American Electorate*. Cambridge, Mass.: Winthrop, 1976. Voting behavior and attitudes from 1948 to 1974.

*Nie, Norman H.; Verba, Sidney; and Petrocik, John R. *The Changing American Voter*. Cambridge, Mass.: Harvard University Press, 1979.

Schattschneider, Elmer Eric. *The Semisovereign People: A Realist's View of Democracy in America.* Hinsdale, Ill.: Dryden Press, 1975. An analysis of the role of the people at large in contemporary democracy.

*Wolfinger,Raymond E., and Rosenstone, Steven J. *Who Votes?* New Haven, Conn.: Yale University Press, 1980.

CHAPTER 4 POLITICAL PARTIES:
DO WE NEED THEM?

*Broder, David S. *The Party's Over: The Failure of Politics in America.* New York: Harper & Row, 1972.

*Clem, Alan L. *American Electoral Politics.* New York: D. Van Nostrand, 1981.

*Goldwin, Robert E., ed. *Political Parties in the Eighties.* Washington, D.C.: American Enterprise Institute, 1980. Essays by leading political scientists on political change and party reforms.

*Greenstein, Fred I. *The American Party System and the American People.* 2nd ed. Englewood Cliffs, N.J.: Prentice-Hall, 1970. Synthesis of research on parties "in terms of their contribution to democracy, stability, and 'effective policy-making.'"

*Herring, Edward Pendleton. *The Politics of Democracy.* New York: Norton, 1965.

Hess, Stephen. *The Washington Reporters.* Washington, D.C.: Brookings Institution, 1981.

Key, V. O., Jr. *Politics, Parties and Pressure Groups.* 5th ed. New York: Thomas Y. Crowell, 1964.

*Key, V. O., Jr. *Southern Politics in State and Nation.* New York: Knopf, 1949.

*Ladd, Everett Carl, Jr. *Where Have All the Voters Gone?* New York, Norton, 1978. The undermining of the political system resulting from reforms in the presidential election process.

Ranney, Austin. *Curing the Mischiefs of Faction: Party Reform in America.* Berkeley, Calif.: University of California Press, 1975. Study of three periods of major reforms in the party system.

*Rusher, William A. *The Making of the New Majority Party.* New York: Sheed and Ward, 1975.

*Scammon, Richard M., and Wattenberg, Ben J. *The Real Majority.* New York: Coward McCann & Geoghegan, 1970.

Schattschneider, Elmer Eric. *Party Government.* New York: Farrar and Rinehart, 1942.

*Sundquist, James L. *Dynamics of the Party System: Alignment and Realignment of Political Parties in the United States.* Washington, D.C.: The Brookings Institution, 1973. Historical survey of the relative strength of political parties.

CHAPTER 5 ELECTIONS:
MAJORITIES, MEDIA, AND MONEY

Alexander, Herbert E. *Financing Politics.* 2nd ed. Washington, D.C.: Congressional Quarterly Press, 1980.

*DeVries, Walter, and Tarrance, V. Lance. *The Ticket-Splitter: A New Force in American Politics.* Grand Rapids, Mich.: William B. Eerdmans, 1971. Analysis of the increase in ticket-splitting as party ties weaken.

Keech, William R., and Matthews, Donald R. *The Party's Choice.* Washington, D.C.: The Brookings Institution, 1976. How presidential candidates were nominated from 1936 to 1972.

*Kelley, Stanley, Jr. *Professional Public Relations and Political Power.* Baltimore, Md.: Johns Hopkins University Press, 1966. The role of public relations firms in elections.

*McGinniss, Joe. *The Selling of the President, 1968.* New York: Trident Press, 1969.

*Mailer, Norman. *Miami and the Siege of Chicago.* New York: World, 1968. Brilliantly written study of the 1968 Republican and Democratic conventions.

*Mailer, Norman. *St. George and the Godfather*. New York: American Library, 1972. Equally well-written study of the 1972 Republican and Democratic conventions.

*Nimmo, Dan. *The Political Persuaders*. Englewood Cliffs, N.J.: Prentice-Hall, 1970. Techniques of modern election campaigns. Includes discussion of television, the role of campaign consultants, and the implication of the new communications technologies for democratic politics.

*Polsby, Nelson W., and Wildavsky, Aaron B. *Presidential Elections*. 5th ed. New York: Scribner's, 1980. Analysis of alternative strategies for winning nomination and election.

*Pomper, Gerald M., with Lederman, Susan S. *Elections in America*. 2nd ed. New York: Dodd, Longman, 1980. Study of our electoral processes at federal and state levels.

*Pomper, Gerald M.; Baker, Ross K.; Frankovic, Kathleen A.; Jacob, Charles E.; McWilliams, Wilson Carey; and Plotkin, Henry A. *The Election of 1980: Reports and Interpretations*. Chatham, N.J.: Chatham House, 1981.

Ranney, Austin, ed. *The American Elections of 1980*. Washington, D.C.: American Enterprise Institute, 1981.

*White, Theodore H. *The Making of the President, 1960*. New York: Atheneum, 1961.

*White, Theodore H. *The Making of the President, 1964*. New York: Atheneum, 1965.

*White, Theodore H. *The Making of the President, 1968*. New York: Atheneum, 1969.

*White, Theodore H. *The Making of the President, 1972*. New York: Atheneum, 1973. The 1960 study is the best of the four White books, but all are interesting, blow-by-blow accounts of the elections and their context of political and social forces.

CHAPTER 6 INTEREST
GROUPS AND THE PUBLIC INTEREST

*Congressional Quarterly. *The Washington Lobby*. 2nd ed. Washington, D.C.: Congressional Quarterly Press, 1974.

Engler, Robert. *The Brotherhood of Oil*. Chicago: University of Chicago Press, 1977. Study of the impact of the oil industry on the legislative and political process.

*Galbraith, John Kenneth. *The New Industrial State*. 2nd rev. ed. Boston: Houghton Mifflin, 1971.

*Greenwald, Carol S. *Group Power*. New York: Praeger, 1977. Analysis of interest groups that argues that they are an important and legitimate part of the making of public policy.

Holtzman, Abraham. *Interest Groups and Lobbying*. New York: Macmillan, 1966.

*Kolko, Gabriel. *Wealth and Power in America*. New York: Praeger, 1962.

*Lowi, Theodore J. *The End of Liberalism: Ideology, Policy, and the Crisis of Public Authority*. New York: Norton, 1969. Critical analysis of the interest group process and its consequences for the making of public policy.

Milbrath, Lester W. *The Washington Lobbyists*. Chicago: Rand McNally, 1963.

Nader, Ralph; Green, Mark; and Seligman, Joel. *Taming the Giant Corporation*. New York: Norton, 1976.

Ornstein, Norman J., and Elder, Shirley. *Interest Groups, Lobbying and Policy Making*. Washington, D.C.: Congressional Quarterly Press, 1978. Analyses of interest group process, with examples of grass-roots lobbying.

Truman, David B. *The Governmental Process*. 2nd ed. New York: Knopf, 1971. Government and politics in America as an expression of the group process.

CHAPTER 7 THE PRESIDENCY:
A NEW DESPOTISM?

*Barber, James David. *The Presidential Character: Predicting Performance in the White House*. 2nd ed. Englewood Cliffs, N.J.: Prentice-Hall, 1977.

Corwin, Edward S. *The President: Office and Powers*. New York: New York University Press, 1980.

*Cronin, Thomas E. *The State of the Presidency*. 2nd ed. Boston: Little, Brown, 1980. The modern presidency, with particular reference to the personality cult that surrounds the chief executive.

*Hargrove, Erwin C. *The Power of the Modern Presidency*. Philadelphia: Temple University Press, 1974.

Hess, Stephen. *Organizing the Presidency*. Washington, D.C.: The Brookings Institution, 1976. Proposals for reorganizing the president's office.

*Koenig, Louis W. *The Chief Executive*. 4th ed. New York: Harcourt Brace Jovanovich, 1981.

*Neustadt, Richard. *Presidential Power*. Rev. ed. New York: Wiley, 1980.

Reedy, George E. *The Twilight of the Presidency*. New York: World, 1970.

*Rossiter, Clinton. *The American Presidency*. New York: Harcourt, Brace & World, 1960. The historical development of the several roles of the president.

*Schlesinger, Arthur M., Jr. *A Thousand Days*. Boston: Houghton Mifflin, 1965. The Kennedy presidency described by a liberal historian who worked in the White House during the Kennedy era.

*Schlesinger, Arthur M., Jr. *The Imperial Presidency*. Boston: Houghton Mifflin, 1973. A reassessment of the presidency, in which Schlesinger expresses his concerns about the trends toward a monarchical presidency.

CHAPTER 8 THE CONGRESS: HOW MUCH HAS IT CHANGED?

*Dodd, Lawrence C., and Oppenheimer, Bruce I., eds. *Congress Reconsidered*. 2nd ed. Washington, D.C.: Congressional Quarterly Press, 1981. Readings on Congress in change.

*Fenno, Richard F., Jr. *Home Style: House Members in Their Districts*. Boston: Little, Brown, 1978.

Foley, Michael. *The New Senate*. New Haven, Conn.: Yale University Press, 1980.

*Green, Mark J.; Fallows, James M.; and Zwick, David R. *Who Runs Congress?* Rev. ed. New York: Bantam Books, 1975.

*Manley, John F. *The Politics of Finance: The House Committee on Ways and Means*. Boston: Little, Brown, 1970.

Matthews, Donald R. *U.S. Senators and Their World*. New York: Random House, 1960.

Olesezek, Walter. *Congressional Procedure and the Policy Process*. Washington, D.C.: Congressional Quarterly Press, 1978.

*Orfield, Gary. *Congressional Power: Congress and Social Change*. New York: Harcourt Brace Jovanovich, 1975. Study of Congress in the making of policy. Argues that Congress is more important and less conservative than is generally believed.

*Polsby, Nelson W. *Congress and the Presidency*. 3rd ed. Englewood Cliffs, N.J.: Prentice-Hall, 1976.

*Truman, David B., ed. *The Congress and America's Future*. 2nd ed. Englewood Cliffs, N.J.: Prentice-Hall, 1973. Essays by Truman, Samuel P. Huntington, Richard F. Fenno, Ralph K. Huitt, Richard E. Neustadt on prospective roles of the Congress.

CHAPTER 9 THE FEDERAL BUREAUCRACY: A FOURTH BRANCH

*Dodd, Lawrence, and Schott, Richard. *Congress and The Administrative State*. New York: Wiley, 1979.

*Downs, Anthony. *Inside Bureaucracy*. Boston: Little, Brown, 1967. An attempt to build a theory of bureaucratic decision making, starting from the premise that "bureaucratic officials, like all other agents in society, are significantly—though not solely—motivated by their own self-interests."

Drucker, Peter F. *The Age of Discontinuity*. New York: Harper & Row, 1969.

*Fellmeth, Robert. *The Interstate Commerce Commission*. New York: Grossman, 1970. One of the Ralph Nader study reports on the ICC and the Food and Drug Administration.

Galbraith, John Kenneth. *Economics and the Public Purpose*. Boston: Houghton Mifflin,

1973. Galbraith pulls together and revises many of the ideas he expressed earlier in *The Affluent Society* and *The New Industrial State* and makes some proposals for a limited kind of socialism.

*Kaufman, Herbert. *Are Government Organizations Immortal?* Washington, D.C.: The Brookings Institution, 1976. Examines the self-perpetuating tendencies of federal agencies.

*McConnell, Grant. *Private Power and American Democracy.* New York: Knopf, 1966.

*Schumacher, E. F. *Small is Beautiful: Economics As If People Mattered.* New York: Harper & Row, 1973. A British economist's argument for smallness of scale in human organization.

*Turner, James S. *The Chemical Feast.* New York: Grossman, 1970. One of the Ralph Nader study reports on the ICC and the Food and Drug Administration.

*Wildavsky, Aaron. *Politics of the Budgetary Process.* 2nd ed. Boston: Little, Brown, 1974. The shaping of the federal budget viewed as a prime function of the bureaucracy and a key to the political process.

*Woll, Peter. *American Bureaucracy.* 2nd ed. New York: Norton, 1977.

CHAPTER 10 THE SUPREME
COURT AND CONSTITUTIONAL RIGHTS

*Abraham, Henry J. *The Judicial Process.* 4th ed. New York: Oxford University Press, 1980.

*Berman, Daniel S. *It Is So Ordered.* New York: Norton, 1966. An introduction to the judicial process by an examination of the steps leading to *Brown* v. *Board of Education.*

Bickel, Alexander M. *The Supreme Court and the Idea of Progress.* New York: Harper & Row, 1970. A centrist scholar's view that suggests some reservations about the activism of the Warren Court.

*Cox, Archibald. *The Role of the Supreme Court in American Government.* New York: Oxford University Press, 1976. Lectures on the Supreme Court by the law professor who, as Watergate special prosecutor, was fired in the "Saturday night massacre."

*Cushman, Robert F. *Leading Constitutional Decisions.* 15th ed. Englewood Cliffs, N.J.: Prentice-Hall, 1976. Excerpts from key decisions of the Supreme Court.

*Lewis, Anthony. *Gideon's Trumpet.* New York: Random House, 1964.

*McCloskey, Robert G. *The Modern Supreme Court.* Cambridge, Mass.: Harvard University Press, 1972.

*Woodward, Bob, and Armstrong, Scott. *The Brethren: Inside the Supreme Court.* New York: Simon & Schuster, 1980.

CHAPTER 11 FEDERALISM:
STATES AND CITIES

Anderson, Martin. *The Federal Bulldozer: A Critical Analysis of Urban Renewal.* Cambridge, Mass.: The MIT Press, 1964.

*Banfield, Edward C. *The Unheavenly City.* Boston: Little, Brown, 1970.

*Banfield, Edward C. *The Unheavenly City Revisited.* Boston: Little, Brown, 1974.

*Banfield, Edward C., and Wilson, James Q. *City Politics.* Cambridge, Mass.: Harvard University Press, 1963. Systematic exposition of the nature of city politics, its structures and styles, and the political roles of various groups and classes. Posits a shift from the "immigrant ethos" to the "middle-class ideal."

*Dahl, Robert A. *Who Governs?* New Haven, Conn.: Yale University Press, 1961. Study of New Haven leading to pluralist conclusions.

*Elazar, Daniel J. *American Federalism: A View from the States.* 2nd ed. New York: Thomas Y. Crowell, 1972.

*Goldwin, Robert A., ed. *A Nation of States.* 2nd ed. Chicago: Rand McNally, 1974. Contrasting perspectives on federalism in America.

Grodzins, Morton. *The American System*. Chicago: Rand McNally, 1966.

Hale, George E., and Palley, Marian L. *Politics and Federal Grants*. Washington, D.C.: Congressional Quarterly Press, 1981.

Hunter, Floyd. *Community Power Structure*. Chapel Hill, N.C.: University of North Carolina Press, 1953. Study of the concentrated power structure of Atlanta.

Pritchett, C. Herman. *The Federal System in Constitutional Law*. Englewood Cliffs, N.J.: Prentice-Hall, 1978.

CHAPTER 12 ECONOMIC POLICY: SHARING THE WEALTH

Cloward, Richard A., and Piven, Frances Fox. *The Politics of Turmoil: Essays on Poverty, Race, and the Urban Crisis*. New York: Pantheon, 1974.

Duignan, Peter, and Rabushka, Alvin. *The United States in the 1980's*. Palo Alto, Calif.: The Hoover Institution, 1980. Essays on economic, social, and foreign policy by several conservative scholars.

*Friedman, Milton, and Friedman, Rose. *Free to Choose*. New York: Harcourt Brace Jovanovich, 1980.

*Galbraith, John Kenneth. *The Affluent Society*. 3rd rev. ed. Boston: Houghton Mifflin, 1976.

*Gildes, George. *Wealth and Poverty*. New York: Basic Books, 1981. An argument for capitalism in ethical as well as economic terms.

*Harrington, Michael. *The Other America*. Rev. ed. New York: Macmillan, 1969.

Lewis, Oscar. *La Vida*. New York: Random House, 1966.

Moynihan, Daniel P. *Maximum Feasible Misunderstanding*. New York: The Free Press, 1969.

Moynihan, Daniel P. *The Politics of a Guaranteed Income*. New York: Random House, 1973.

*Pechman, Joseph, ed. *Setting National Priorities: Agenda for the 1980's*. Washington, D.C.: The Brookings Institution, 1980.

*Wattenberg, Ben J. *The Real America: A Surprising Examination of the State of the Union*. New York: G. P. Putnam's Sons, 1976.

Wildavsky, Aaron. *How to Limit Government Spending*. Berkeley, Calif.: University of California Press, 1980. Case for a constitutional amendment limiting increases in federal budget to increases in GNP.

CHAPTER 13 EQUAL PROTECTION? RACE, ETHNICITY, GENDER

*Brown, Dee. *Bury My Heart at Wounded Knee*. New York: Holt, Rinehart & Winston, 1970.

*Carmichael, Stokely, and Hamilton, Charles V. *Black Power*. New York: Random House, 1967.

*Freeman, Jo. *The Politics of Women's Liberation*. New York: David McKay, 1975.

*Franklin, John Hope. *From Slavery to Freedom*. 4th ed. New York: Knopf, 1974. History of blacks in America.

*Grier, William H., and Cobbs, Price M. *Black Rage*. New York: Basic Books, 1968.

*King, Martin Luther, Jr. *Why We Can't Wait*. New York: Harper & Row, 1964. A compilation of essays, including the "Letter from a Birmingham Jail."

*Little, Malcolm. *The Autobiography of Malcolm X*. New York: Grove Press, 1965.

*Myrdal, Gunnar. *An American Dilemma: The Negro Problem and Modern Democracy*. 20th ed. New York: Harper & Row, 1962.

*Novak, Michael. *The Rise of the Unmeltable Ethnics*. New York: Macmillan, 1972. A plea for recognition of the aspirations of ethnic white groups—Poles, Italians, Greeks, and Slavs.

Rendon, Armando. *Chicano Manifesto*. New York: Collier Books, 1972.

Report of the National Advisory Commission on Civil Disorders. Washington, D.C.:

Government Printing Office, 1968.

*Sindler, Allan P. *Bakke, De Funis, and Minority Admissions*. New York: Longman, 1978.

*Woodward, C. Vann. *The Strange Career of Jim Crow*. 3rd rev. ed. New York: Oxford University Press, 1974. Post–Civil War segregation in the South.

CHAPTER 14 ENERGY AND THE ENVIRONMENT

*Carson, Rachel. *Silent Spring*. Boston: Houghton Mifflin, 1962.

*Davis, David Howard. *Energy Politics*. New York: St. Martin's Press, 1974.

Ehrlich, Paul R., and Ehrlich, Anne H. *Population, Resources, Environment: Issues in Human Ecology*. 2nd ed. San Francisco: W.H. Freeman, 1972.

*Esposito, John C. *Vanishing Air*. New York: Grossman, 1970. The report of the Nader study group on air pollution.

*Meadows, Donnella H.; Meadows, Dennis L.; Randers, Jorgen; and Behrens, William W., III. *The Limits to Growth*. 2nd ed. New York: New American Library, 1974. The "Club of Rome." Study warning of the prospect of global environmental catastrophe.

*Mesarovic, Mihajlo, and Pestel, Eduard. *Mankind at the Turning Point*. New York: New American Library, 1974. A second report to the Club of Rome proposing some ways of avoiding environmental disaster.

Sawhill, John C., ed. *Energy: Conservation and Public Policy*. New York: Spectrum, 1979.

*Stobaugh, Robert, and Yergin, Daniel. *Energy Future*. New York: Random House, 1979.

CHAPTER 15 FOREIGN POLICY: A NEW ERA?

*Allison, Graham. *Essence of Decision: Explaining the Cuban Missile Crisis*. Boston: Little, Brown, 1971.

*Alperovitz, Gar, ed. *Cold War Essays*. Cambridge, Mass.: Schenkman, 1970.

Ambrose, Stephen E. *Rise to Globalism: American Foreign Policy, 1938–1980*. 2nd ed. New York: Penguin, 1980.

*Barnet, Richard J., and Müller, Ronald E. *Global Reach: The Power of the Multinational Corporations*. New York: Simon & Schuster, 1974.

*Halberstam, David. *The Best and the Brightest*. New York: Random House, 1972.

Hilsman, Roger. *To Move a Nation*. Garden City, N.Y.: Doubleday, 1967. The politics of foreign policy during the Kennedy administration.

*Hoopes, Townsend. *The Limits of Intervention*. New York: David McKay, 1969.

*Huntington, Samuel P. *The Soldier and the State: The Theory and Politics of Civil-Military Relations*. Cambridge, Mass.: Harvard University Press, 1959.

Kahn, Herman. *On Thermonuclear War*. Princeton, N.J.: Princeton University Press, 1961.

Kennan, George. *The Cloud of Danger*. Boston: Atlantic–Little, Brown, 1977.

*Kennedy, Robert F. *Thirteen Days*. New York: Norton, 1969. Memoir of the Cuban missile crisis.

*Kissinger, Henry A. *Nuclear Weapons and Foreign Policy*. New York: Harper for the Council on Foreign Relations, 1957. An influential analysis of the consequences of nuclear weaponry for foreign policy.

Kissinger, Henry A. *White House Years*. Boston: Little, Brown, 1979.

Korb, Lawrence J. *The Fall and Rise of the Pentagon: American Defense Politics in the 1970's*. Westport, Conn.: Greenwood Press, 1979.

Melman, Seymour. *Pentagon Capitalism*. New York: McGraw-Hill, 1970.

*New York Times. *The Pentagon Papers*. New York: Bantam Books, 1971.

Schell, Jonathan. *The Fate of the Earth*. Knopf, 1982. Detailed horrifying analysis of available technical data concluding that a nuclear war might lead to the extinction of the human species.

Spanier, John. *American Foreign Policy Since World War II*. 8th ed. New York: Holt, Rinehart & Winston, 1980.

Thompson, W. Scott, ed. *National Security in the 1980's: From Weakness to Strength*. San Francisco: Institute for Contemporary Studies, 1980.

*Williams, William Appleman. *The Tragedy of American Diplomacy*. 2nd ed., revised. New York: Dell, 1972.

*Wise, David. *The Invisible Government*. New York: Random House, 1964.

Yergin, Daniel. *Shattered Peace: The Origins of the Cold War and the National Security State*. Boston: Houghton Mifflin, 1977.

CHAPTER 16 POWER AND POLITICS:
A REVIEW OF THE FIVE PERSPECTIVES

*Graham, Hugh Davis, and Gurr, Ted Robert. *Violence in America: Historical and Comparative Perspectives*. New York: Bantam Books, 1970.

*Roszak, Theodore. *The Making of a Counter Culture*. Garden City, N.Y.: Doubleday, 1969.

*Roszak, Theodore. *Where the Wasteland Ends*. Garden City, N.Y.: Doubleday, 1972.

Skolnick, Jerome H. *The Politics of Protest*. Washington, D.C.: Government Printing Office, 1969.

INDEX

Abington Township School District v.
    Schempp (1963), 260
Abortion, 77, 263–264
Abplanalp, Robert 190
Abscam affair, 203
Accused, rights of, 260–261, 266–268
Acheson, Dean, 432, 435
Adams, Sherman, 167
Adjudication, by federal agencies,
    233–234
Administrative agencies, 230
Administrative oversight, by Congress,
    197
Affirmative action, 359–360, 362, 364,
    366, 368, 369, 373
Afghanistan, Soviet invasion of, 414
Age:
    political implications of, 50, 60–61,
        62, 78, 87–88
    population distribution by, 47–48
    poverty and, 315, 330
Agee, Philip, 265
Agency for International Development
    (AID), 422
Agnew, Spiro, 109, 147, 175, 290
Agriculture, 45, 140, 442
Aid to Families With Dependent
    Children (AFDC), 322, 323–324,
    325, 333
Ailes, Roger, 118, 128, 132–133
Airborne Warning and Control System
    (AWACS), 182, 421
Air traffic controllers, 182
Akey, Denise S., 142
Allen, James B., 80
Allende, Salvador, 417, 434
Alliance for Survival, 394
Amendments, constitutional, 8, 12, 27,
    30, 31, 464–470 (*see also* Bill of
    Rights):
    Thirteenth, 349, 466
    Fourteenth, 261, 266, 286, 349, 352,
        364, 366, 466–467
    Fifteenth, 53–54, 349–350, 352, 467
    Sixteenth, 39, 467
    Nineteenth, 54, 468
    Twenty-second, 185, 469
    Twenty-sixth, 54, 60–61, 470
    proposed Equal Rights, 40 n. 3, 77,
        141, 358, 361
    proposed Liberty, 39
American Association of University
    Women, 150
American Civil Liberties Union
    (ACLU), 153, 268
American Conservative Union, 5, 141
American Enterprise Institute, 52, 67,
    68, 92

American Farm Bureau Federation,
    140
American Federation of Labor-
    Congress of Industrial Relations
    (AFL-CIO), 124, 139, 151, 394
American Independent Party, 93, 99
    n. 14
American Indians, *see* Minorities; Race
American Israel Public Affairs
    Committee, 427, 428
American Jewish Committee, 427
American Legion, 152
American Medical Association, 140,
    147, 224
American National Cattlemen's
    Association, 140
American Security Council, 426
Americans for Constitutional Action, 76
Americans for Democratic Action
    (ADA), 5, 76, 141, 434
Anderson, John, 55, 74, 78, 79, 90,
    113–114, 115, 118, 121
Anderson, Martin, 328
Antiballistic missile (ABM), 409, 426,
    436
Anti-Defamation League of B'nai
    B'rith, 427
Antifederalists, 27, 32, 73
Antitrust laws, 139
Appropriations, congressional, 215
Arab-Israeli conflicts, 414, 427, 428
Armed services, *see* Military, the
Arms Control and Disarmament
    Agency (ACDA), 424
Arms race, 406–412, 430–431 (*see also*
    Nuclear power)
Armstrong, Scott, 269, 270
Army Corps of Engineers, 390
Articles of Confederation, 25, 27
Asians, *see* Minorities; Race
Astin, Alexander, 83
Astin, J. Paul, 190
Atom bomb, 406 (*see also* Hiroshima;
    Nagasaki; Nuclear power)
Audubon Society, 394
Authoritarian systems, 439–440
Authority, 22 n. 2, 450
Authorizations, congressional, 215

Baker, Bobby, 202
Baker, James, 181, 189
Baker v. *Carr* (1962), 261
Baldridge, Malcolm, 328
Banfield, Edward C., 304
Barber, James, 185, 187
Barnet, Richard, 6
Bay of Pigs, 168, 416, 419, 428

Beard, Charles, 33
Bernstein, Carl, 173
Betts v. *Brady* (1942), 276
Bilingual education, 356
Bill of Rights, 8, 12, 27, 30, 31,
    464–465
    Supreme Court and, 258–261,
        264–265, 266–268, 275, 276
Birth rates, 47, 48
Black, Hugo, 259, 260, 262, 263
Black Caucus, congressional, 361
Black Liberation Army, 22 n. 11
Blackmun, Harry, 263, 273
Black power movement, 359, 360
Blacks, *see* Minorities; Race
Blumenthal, Michael, 191
Bolling, Richard, 209
Boll weevils, the, 207–208
Brennan, William, 262, 281 n. 9
Brezhnev, Leonid, 409, 413
Broder, David, 51
Brogan, D. W., 163
Brookings Institution, 52, 68
Brown, Jerry, 123
Brown v. *Board of Education of
    Topeka, Kansas* (1954), 261, 276,
    350, 362, 365
Broyles, J. Allen, 22 n. 15
Bryan, William Jennings, 79
Brzezinski, Zbigniew, 191, 441
Buchanan, Patrick, 67
Buckley, James, 123, 126
Buckley, William, 5, 14
Budget, federal, 318–319, 324–326, 332
    defense spending in, 415, 425–427,
        428, 430–431, 433, 439
Bundy, McGeorge, 161, 190, 432
Bureaucracies, federal:
    autonomy of, 235–237
    disadvantaged groups, policy issues,
        and, 363–364
    economic issues and, 327–329
    environmental and energy issues and,
        389–391
    foreign policy and, 421–425
    as fourth branch, 228–253
    perspectives on, 238–251
    presidency and, 161, 234–235, 237
    range of functions of, 231–234
Burger, Warren, 262–269, 272, 273,
    275, 277, 365–366
Burnham, James, 225
Burns, Arthur, 329
Burns, James MacGregor, 4, 35, 246,
    277
Bush, George, 55, 102, 109, 117–118,
    160, 189, 441
Business, (*see also* Capitalism):

Business, (*continued*)
  Constitution on commerce and, 27, 37
  corporate elite of, 66–67, 448
  environmental and energy issues and, 393–394, 395–399
  foreign policy issues and, 425–427, 434
  government regulation of, 230, 240, 242, 247–249, 450
  interest groups for, 139, 145–146, 329–330
  the public interest and, 151–152
Business Council, 14
Business Roundtable, 139

Cabinet, *see* Presidency, the
Campaign for Economic Democracy, 18, 141, 394
Campaigns:
  financing, 118–120, 123–134
  participation in, 54, 58–61
  tactics of, 116–123
Candidates, 55, 101–111, 118–120, 185
Capitalism, 9, 10, 11, 14, 22 n. 6, 374–375, 407, 434, 436
  (*see also* Business)
Carter, Jimmy, 56, 58, 74, 78, 79, 81
  foreign policy of, 410, 418, 433, 435
  in 1976 election, 90, 111–112, 113, 117, 118, 119, 133, 136 n. 11
  in 1980 election, 88, 95–96, 112–114, 119–120, 121–122, 128, 133, 135 n. 2
  nomination of, 102, 103, 104–105, 106, 107, 108–109
  presidency of, 163, 176–180, 185, 187, 190, 191, 218, 245, 324, 362, 386, 388, 390
Carter, Rosalynn, 162
Castro, Fidel, 168, 188, 406, 416, 417
Center for Defense Information, 427
Center for Policy Studies, 6
Center for the Study of National Security, 427
Central Intelligence Agency (CIA), 188, 405, 416–417, 424–425, 433, 439
Central Treaty Organization (CENTO), 443 n. 1
Centrists, 3–4, 11–13, 15–16, 19, 453–454
  Congress and, 221–225
  Constitution and, 33–34
  economy, poverty and, 341–342
  elections and, 132–134
  federal bureaucracies and, 245–246
  federalism and, 305–306
  foreign policy and, 441–442
  interest groups and, 152–154
  minority rights and, 367–369
  political parties and, 94–96
  presidency and, 191–193
  public opinion and, 64–65
  Supreme Court and, 279
Chamber of Commerce of the United States, 139

Change, perspectives on, *see* Spectrum, political
Changing American Voter, The (Nie, Verba, Petrocik), 56–57, 58, 84
Chapin, Dwight, 175
Chavez, Cesar, 140, 361
Checks and balances, Constitution's, 12, 29–30, 32–33, 34, 35, 74, 86, 157, 197, 274, 454
Chicanos, *see* Hispanics; Minorities
China, People's Republic of (PRC), 413, 417, 428, 430, 435, 438, 442
Christian Crusade, 6
Chrysler Corporation, 249
Church, Frank, 220
Churchill, Winston, 407
Cities, 289, 295–299, 300, 303–305, 315, 330, 349, 352–353
Citizens Crusade for Clean Water, 394
Citizens League against the Sonic Boom, 394
Civil liberties, perspectives on, 8, 11, 12, 19, 49–50, 76
Civil Rights Act (1875), 364
Civil Rights Act (1964), 214, 264, 350, 351–352, 361, 362
Civil Rights Commission, U.S., 364
Civil rights programs, 76, 81, 350–352, 361–363, 371
Civil Service, 236
Civil War, 16, 81, 349
Clark, Ed, 22 n. 12
Clark, Tom, 262
Clean Air Act (1970), 386
Clements, Bill, 123
Cleveland, Grover, 115
Clifford, Clark, 427, 432, 435
Cloture, 214
Coexistence (U.S.–Soviet), 407
Cold war, 412, 429
Colson, Charles, 172, 175
Commager, Henry Steele, 135
Committee for Economic Development, 14, 52, 69, 139, 425
Committee for the Reelection of the President (CRP/CREEP), 125–126, 132, 133, 172–173
Committee on the Present Danger, 426
Committees, congressional, 208–210, 211, 214, 216, 220, 426
Common Cause, 141, 145, 148, 151, 153, 394
Communism, 10, 15, 50, 69, 381, 407, 413, 451 (*see also* Soviet Union):
  containment of, 405–406, 412, 414, 420, 429, 431–432, 433, 434–435, 436, 438, 440, 441–442
Communist Action Organization, 22 n. 11
Communist Party, USA, 5, 9, 22 n. 3, 93, 259
Community Action Program (CAP), 329, 341, 344 n. 12
Competition:
  loss of U.S. edge in, 311–312
  values, and perspectives on, 10, 11, 145, 149

Comprehensive Employment and Training Act (CETA), 321, 325
Compromise, 16, 17, 26–27, 34, 453
Condition, equality of, 11
Conflicts of interest, 204, 220, 221, 290–291
Congress:
  campaigns for, 58, 130, 134
  committees in, 208–210, 211, 214, 216, 220, 426
  constituencies of, 58, 198–204
  Constitution on, 28, 29, 30
  economic issues and, 326–327, 361, 363
  environmental and energy issues and, 386–389
  federal bureaucracies and, 232, 235, 237
  foreign policy and, 420–421
  functions of, 196–197, 212–214
  members of, 197–198
  perspectives on, 215–226
  political parties and, 86, 205–208
  power in, 204–212
  president and, 32, 160, 162, 196, 421
  procedures of, 196, 212–215, 216
  reforms of, 204, 219–221, 224–225
Connally, John, 55, 133, 427
Connecticut Compromise, 27
Conservation, *see* Environmental issues
Conservative Caucus, 5
Conservative coalition, 207
Conservative Democratic Forum, 207–208
Conservatives, 3–5, 7–8, 10–11, 14–15, 17, 19, 22 n. 6, 75–76, 450–451
  Congress and, 225–226
  Constitution and, 37–38
  economy, poverty and, 334–336
  elections and, 130–132
  environmental and energy issues and, 397–399
  federal bureaucracies and, 238–244
  federalism and, 302–305
  foreign policy and, 181, 435–440
  interest groups and, 149–152
  minority rights and, 369–371
  political parties and, 90–92
  presidency and, 187–189
  public opinion and, 67–68
  Supreme Court and, 273–275
Constituencies:
  power of, 143–144
  of Congress, 198–204
  of federal bureaucracies, 237
Constitution, the, 12, 24–41, 456–470 (*see also* Amendments; Bill of Rights):
  checks and balances in, 12, 29–30, 32–33, 34, 35, 74, 86, 157, 197, 274, 454
  Supreme Court and, 29, 30, 31–33, 38, 254–282
  on war, treaties, and foreign policy, 419, 420
Constitutional Convention, 25–27, 29, 37–38

Consumer Product Safety Commission, 248

Consumers, interest groups for, 140, 151

Containment, doctrine of, *see under* Communism

Conventions, national, *see under* Political parties

Coolidge, Calvin, 180

Corporate power, *see* Business

Corruption:
in federal agencies, 241–242
of public officials, 290–291

Corrupt Practices Act (1925), 125

Council for a Liveable World, 427

Council of Economic Advisers, 161

Council on Environmental Quality, 390

Council on Foreign Relations, 14, 52, 67, 68, 69, 438, 440

County of Washington v. *Gunther* (1981), 281 n. 14

Court system (*see also* Supreme Court):
at state level, 285
structure of U.S., 162, 254–255

Cox, Archibald, 174

Cranston, Alan, 220, 222–223

Crime rates, 296, 370–371

Critical Mass Energy Project, 394

Cronin, Thomas, 193

Cuban missile crisis, 168, 408–409, 420, 434–435, 437

Daughtery, Harry, 103–104

Davis, John, 104

Davis–Bacon Act (1931), 156 n. 7

Dean, John, 173–174, 175

Death penalty, Supreme Court on, 267

Death rates, 47, 355

Deaver, Michael, 181

Debs, Eugene V., 99 n. 12

Decentralization (of federal bureaucracy), 243, 245

Declaration of Independence, 24, 30

Defense, Department of (DOD), 422, 424

Defense Intelligence Agency (DIA), 424

Defense spending, 415, 425–427, 428, 430–431, 433, 439

Delaney Amendment, 233, 235

Dellums, Ronald, 5, 81

Democracy, 28, 36, 44, 74–75
Campaign for Economic, 18, 141, 394

Democratic centralism, Soviet Union's, 39, 41 n. 14

Democratic National Committee (DNC), 172

Democratic Party, *see* Political parties

Democratic Socialist Organizing Committee, 18

Democratic Study Group, 207, 211

Dennis v. *United States,* 259

Desegregation, *see under* Schools

Détente, policy of, 171, 413–415

Developing countries, U.S. relations with, 415–416, 417–418, 433–434, 439

Dewey, Thomas, 80, 90

Diem, Ngo Dinh, 417

Direct democracy, 28

Dirkson, Everett, 262

Disarmament, 424

Disclosure (by members of Congress), 204, 220

Discrimination, *see* Minorities; Prejudice; Race, Sexism

Divorce rates, 48, 49

Dodd, Thomas, 203

Dole, Robert, 55, 105, 133

Domestic affairs, president's role in, 160, 169–170 (*see also specific issues, e.g.,* Economy; Energy; Housing)

Domhoff, G. William, 93, 94, 341

Douglas, William O., 259, 262, 263

Dred Scott decision (1857), 349, 364

Drucker, Peter, 241

Dubos, René, 400

Dulles, John Foster, 167, 190, 420, 422

Dutton, Fred, 427

Eagleton, Thomas, 136 n. 10

Eastland, James, 278

Ecology, *see* Environmental issues

Economic aid (to developing nations), 416, 417–418, 433–434, 439

Economic individualism, 10

Economic interests, groups concerned with, 139

Economic liberty, perspectives on, 8, 11–12, 19

Economy, the:
government intervention in, 76, 150, 316–322
perspectives on, 8, 76, 334–342
policy issues about, 77, 310–345
services and goods in, 45
state and local finances, and, 294–295

Education, 45, 67 (*see also* Schools):
federal aid to, 218–219, 321–322
lobbyists for, 140, 150, 153, 330
political implications of level of, 49, 50, 57, 59–60, 61, 78–79, 87–88

Edwards, James, 390, 391

Ehrlichman, John, 161, 171, 173, 174, 175

Eisenhower, Dwight, 15, 80, 104, 107, 117, 118, 430
presidency of, 90, 163, 167–168, 185, 259, 273, 363, 419

Elections, 57, 58, 75 (*see also* Campaigns; Voting):
majorities, media, money, and, 51, 100–137
in parliamentary systems, 35–36
perspectives on, 128–134
strategies for general, 111–116
at state and local levels, 285–286, 288–289

Electoral college, 28, 29, 32, 111, 114–116, 129, 130–131

Elites, power of, 12, 13, 14, 66–67, 189–190, 448–449, 450, 452

Ellsberg, Daniel, 173, 188, 265, 432

Employment, 45, 48, 60, 78–79, 354
equal opportunity for, 362, 364
on farms, 45, 140
in federal bureaucracies, 228–229, 247
levels of, 312, 313, 325, 340
by local governments, 283

Employment Act (1946), 161

Endangered Species Act (1973), 398

Energy issues, 77, 378–402

Enforcement function, federal agencies', 234

Engel v. *Vitale,* 260

Environmental Defense Fund, 394

Environmental issues, 378–402

Environmental Protection Agency, 382, 389–390

Equality:
perspectives on, 7–12, 19, 49
realities of, 346–377

Equal Employment Opportunity Commission, 364

Equal Rights Amendment (ERA), 40 n. 3, 77, 141, 358, 361

Ervin, Sam, 173

Escobedo v. *Illinois* (1964), 260, 276

Espionage, 425, 439

Ethics, Congressional, 202–204

Ethnicity (*see also* Minorities; Race):
Carter's remarks on, 110
foreign policy and, 427
population distribution by, 46

Evans, M. Stanton, 38, 130

Everson v. *Board of Education* (1947), 281 n. 10

Executive agencies, 230 (*see also* Bureaucracies, federal)

Executive branch, *see* Presidency, the

Executive Office, 161, 229

Exner, Judith, 188

Fair Deal, 167

Fair Housing Act (1968), 361

Fair housing issue, 359–360, 363–364

Falwell, Jerry, 19

Family Assistance Plan, 172, 323, 327, 331

Family structure, 48–49, 355

Federal Communications Commission (FCC), 230, 232

Federal Election Campaign Act (1971), 124, 129

Federal Election Campaign Act (1974), 125–128, 129, 130, 134

Federal Election Commission, 126

Federalism, 29, 162, 283–308

Federalists, 27, 32, 33, 73, 254

Federal Regulation of Lobbying Act (1946), 144, 146

Federal Reserve Board (FRB), 329

Federal Trade Commission (FTC), 232–233, 235, 248

Filibusters, 214, 220, 222–223
Fiscal policy, federal government's, 317–319 (*see also* Budget; Money)
Flacks, Richard, 5
Flemming, Arthur, 376 n. 17
Food and Drug Administration (FDA), 233, 235, 238–240, 248
Food stamps, 322, 323
Ford, Gerald, 4, 55, 81, 102–109 *passim,* 128, 158
  in 1976 election, 112, 113, 117, 119, 122, 133
  presidency of, 90, 163, 175–176, 185, 187, 189, 191, 304, 388, 421
Ford Foundation, 14, 53, 69
Foreign aid, 415–416, 417–418, 433–434, 439
Foreign policy, 76, 403–445, 448–449
  background of, 404–405
  Congress and, 420–421
  interest groups and, 425–427
  president's role in, 159, 161, 177, 181, 419–420, 428
  public opinion and, 428–429
Foreign Policy Association, 69
Fortas, Abe, 262, 263
Foundations, 14, 53, 69
Frankfurter, Felix, 276
Franklin, Benjamin, 25
Freedom, 11, 12, 238–240 (*see also* Liberty)
Freedom of Information Act (1966, 1974), 246
Free speech, *see* Bill of Rights
Friedman, Milton, 5,149,304,335, 397
Friends of the Earth, 394
Fulbright, J. W., 427
Fundamentalist religious groups, 11, 19

Galbraith, John Kenneth, 4, 18
Gallup polls, 54, 55–56, 120–122
Garn, Jake, 220
Gender:
  population data by, 48
  political implications of, 61, 78, 88
Geneen, Harold, 147, 156 n. 3
General Services Administration (GSA), 242
Gerrymandering, 200
Gideon v. *Wainwright* (1963), 260, 276
Ginzburg v. *United States* (1966), 281 n. 9
Gitlin, Todd, 6
Glazer, Nathan, 18
Global 2000, 381
Goldberg, Arthur, 262
Goldwater, Barry, 5, 17, 80, 90, 95, 101–102, 106, 107, 109
Goods, producers of, 45
GOP ("Grand Old Party"), 75
Gorsuch, Ann, 390
Government, 3, 7-12, 33, 157 (*see also* Bureaucracies; Congress; Local government; Presidency; State government; Supreme Court):
  aid to education by, 218–219, 321–322

Government,(*continued*)
  distrust (and fear) of, 33, 62–63, 67, 69
  economic policies of, 76, 150, 316–322
  individual freedom and, 238–240
  interest groups for, 141
  political parties and, 73–74, 85–86
  principle of limited, 37, 38, 451
  principle of shared (national and state), 37–38
  Reagan's concept of, 180–181
Government corporations, 230
Gradualism, 16–17
Graft, *see* Corruption
Great Depression, 16, 84, 140, 166, 179, 312
Great Society, 170
Greer, Scott, 306
Gross National Product, 247, 310–311, 431, 433–434, 439
Group balance, 12, 152–153 (*see also* Interest groups)
Gun control, 219

Haig, Alexander, 189, 190
Haldeman, H. R., 161–162, 171, 173, 174, 175, 189–190
Hamilton, Alexander, 25, 27, 33, 254
Harding, Warren, 159
Hargis, Billy James, 6, 278
Harlan, John Marshall, 262, 263, 276
Harrington, Michael, 18
Harriss case (1954), 144
Harris (Louis) polls, 54, 120–122
Hart, Gary, 146
Hatch, Orrin, 5, 220
Hatch Act (1939), 125
Hatfield, Mark, 223
Hayden, Tom, 18, 394
Hays, Wayne, 212
Health:
  party platforms on, 77
  race and, 355
Health insurance, national, 218, 223–224
Heilbroner, Robert, 400
Heinz, John, III, 123
Heller, Walter, 308 n. 5
Helms, Jesse, 80, 123, 124, 220
Henry, Patrick, 27
Heritage Foundation, 67, 92
Hiroshima, 159, 167, 405
Hispanics, 355–357, 361 (*see also* Minorities; Race)
Holmes, Oliver Wendall, Jr., 259
Homosexuals, 50, 264
Hoover, Herbert, 166
Hoover, J. Edgar, 188
Hoover Institution, 52, 67, 68, 92
Hopkins, Harry, 162
House, Colonel E. M., 162, 191
House of Representatives, *see* Congress
Housing:
  public, 219, 321
  race and, 359–360, 363–364
Hudson Institute, 67

Hughes, Charles Evans, 257, 258
Human rights, U.S. on protecting, 418–419, 433, 434, 435
Humphrey, Hubert, 102, 107, 109, 115, 118, 122, 126
Hunt, E. Howard, 172, 173
Hunter, Floyd, 302
Huston, Tom, 194 n. 6

Ideology, 19–20, 79–80, 82–83
Illuminati, the, 15
Immigration, 47, 49
  illegal, 356–357, 370
Impeachment, Nixon's resignation to avoid, 174–175
Income (U.S. family), 45, 49–50, 60, 78–79, 88, 311, 314
  guaranteed annual, 339
  race and, 353–354, 356
Income taxes:
  federal, 319–320
  state, 301
Incumbency advantage (in Congress), 130, 134
Independent agencies, 230
Independents, 74, 84, 85
Individualism, economic, 10
Individual rights, 28, 30, 35, 238–240, 254–282 (*see also* Bill of Rights; Civil liberties)
Individuals, financial contributions from, 124–128
Inflation, 313–314, 332, 340
Institute for Policy Studies, 52, 67
Intellectuals, 52, 450, 451 (*see also* Universities and colleges)
Intelligence agencies, 424–425, 439 (*see also* Central Intelligence Agency)
Intercontinental ballistic missiles (ICBMs), 406–407, 409–410, 430, 436
Interest groups (*see also* Political parties):
  Congress and, 202
  economic issues and, 329–331
  on environmental and energy issues, 393–395
  financial contributions from, 123–124
  foreign policy and, 425–427
  for minority populations, 360–361
  perspectives on, 145–154
  for the professions, 140
  the public interest and, 138–156
International Court of Justice, 403
Internationalism, 405, 419, 434
International Telephone and Telegraph (ITT), 147, 153, 156 n. 3, 9, 434
Iran, CIA and (1953), 416
Iranian hostage crisis, 177, 418, 438
Isolationism, 404–405
Israeli–Arab conflicts, 414, 427, 428
Issues (*see also* Ideology; *and specific issues, e.g.,* Economy; Foreign policy):
  candidates' blurring of, 129
  of energy and the environment, 386–395

Issues (*continued*)
  political parties and, 77, 83, 84–85
  in public policy, 2, 309
  public's knowledge of, and interest
    in, 55–57, 66

Jackson, Andrew, 115, 164
Jackson, Jesse, 361
Jackson, Robert H., 271
Javits, Jacob, 80
Jaworski, Leon, 174
Jay, John, 27
Jefferson, Thomas, 33, 73, 75, 164,
  419
Jillson, Calvin, C., 40 n. 6
Jim Crow laws, 350, 365
John Birch Society, 6, 11, 15, 18, 20,
  68, 69, 94, 152, 191, 278, 371
Johnson, Lyndon, 95, 103, 107, 109,
  122, 126, 132, 163, 185
  foreign policy of, 170, 186, 413, 419,
    428, 432, 435
  presidency of, 169–170, 179, 188,
    218, 321, 329, 362
Jordan, Hamilton, 161, 178, 180
Jordan, Vernon, 353
Judicial branch, *see* Supreme Court
Judicial restraint, 272, 274–275
Judicial review, Supreme Court and,
  255–257
Jurisdictional conflicts, 289–290

Kahn, Herman, 400
Kefauver, Estes, 136 n. 4
Kemp, Jack, 55
Kendall, Donald, 190
Kendall, Willmoore, 225
Kennedy, Edward, 102, 104–105,
  108–109, 110, 124, 135 n. 2, 220
Kennedy, John F., 101, 106, 107, 114,
  117, 118, 124, 132, 136 n. 4
  assassination of, 158, 159
  foreign policy of, 168, 408–409, 419,
    420, 424, 431, 434–435
  presidency of, 163, 168–169, 185,
    188, 362, 409, 412
Kennedy, Robert, 102, 117, 124, 169
Kennedy family, 124, 169
Kerner, Otto, 353, 371
Kerr, Robert, 218
Keynes, John Maynard, 191, 317, 325,
  342–343
Khrushchev, Nikita, 168, 407, 409, 441
Kilpatrick, James, 242, 248
King, Martin Luther, Jr., 188, 351,
  353, 361
Kissinger, Henry, 104, 117, 161, 171,
  176, 190, 191, 413, 421, 422, 432,
  441
Kleindienst, Richard, 156 n. 3, 173,
  427
Korean War, 167, 412, 419, 428, 432
Kraft, Joseph, 51
Kristol, Irving, 18
Ku Klux Klan, 6–7, 11, 22 n. 5, 371

Labor unions:
  conservatives on, 156 n. 7

Labor Unions: (*continued*)
  financial contributions by, 124
  as interest groups, 139–140, 153, 330
  membership of, 78–79, 139–140
  as monopolies, 149–150
Ladd, Everett C., 99 n. 8
Lance, Bert, 180
Landrum–Griffin Act (1959), 140, 153
LaRocque, Gene, 427
Latham, Earl, 154
Latinos, *see* Hispanics; Minorities
Leaders/leadership, 50–51, 62–63, 77,
  135, 217–219, 222–224 (*see also*
  Presidency)
Leadership Conference for Civil Rights,
  361
League of Nations, 404
League of Women Voters, 141, 150
Left, radical, *see* Radical left; Socialism
Legislation, *see* Congress
Legislatures:
  in parliamentary systems, 35
  reapportionment of, 261, 263
  state, 284
Lenin, Vladimir Ilich, 5, 22 n. 3
Liberals, 3, 4–5, 8, 13, 16, 19, 67–68,
  75–76, 446–448
  Congress and, 215, 217–221
  Constitution and, 34–36
  economy and poverty and, 337–341
  elections and, 128–130
  environmental and energy issues and,
    395–397
  federal bureaucracies and, 246–251
  federalism and, 299–301
  foreign policy and, 429–434
  interest groups and, 145–148, 151
  minority rights and, 371–374
  political parties and, 88–90
  presidency and, 185–187
  public opinion and, 65–66
  Supreme Court and, 275–278
Libertarian Party, 20
Liberty, 7–12, 19, 246–247
Liberty Amendment, 39
Liddy, G. Gordon, 173
Life expectancy, *see* Death rates
Lincoln, Abraham, 79, 164
Lippmann, Walter, 22 n. 6
Lobbyists, *see* Political pressure
Local governments, 283, 285, 288–299,
  300–307, 391
Localism, of Congress, 201–202, 217,
  222
Long, Huey, 214
Long, Russell, 327
Los Angeles, California, 352–353,
  377 n. 23
Louisiana Purchase, 419
Lumumba, Patrice, 417

MacArthur, Douglas, 167
Machinists Union, 427
Madison, James, 25, 27, 31
Magazines, public opinion and, 52, 66
Magruder, Jeb, 172, 175
Majority rule, 100–137, 277

Mallory v. *United States* (1957), 260
Malthus, Thomas, 380–381
Maoism, 413
Mao Tse-tung, 5, 22 n. 3, 413
Marbury v. *Madison* (1803), 31, 256
Marcuse, Herbert, 5
Marriage rates, 48, 49
Marshall, George, 416
Marshall, John, 32, 256, 272, 276
Marshall, Thurgood, 262, 277
Marshall Plan, 167, 416, 428
Marx, Karl, 5, 9
Mass media, 32, 51–52, 66–67, 108,
  110, 116–120, 123–128, 265 (*see
  also* Television)
Mathias, Charles, 223
Mayaguez (ship), 414
McCarthy, Eugene, 90, 117, 124, 126
McCarthy, Joseph, 168, 220, 259
McCloy, John J., 190, 435
McCollum v. *Board of Education*
  (1948), 260
McCord, James, 172
McGovern, George, 4–5, 95, 102, 103,
  107, 114, 117, 119, 124, 128,
  132–133, 136 n. 10
McNamara, Robert, 189, 424, 431, 432
Medicaid, 322, 323
Medicare, 218, 224, 249, 321, 322
Meese, Edwin, 181
Memoirs v. *Masssachusetts,* 260
Metropolitan areas, 289, 295–299, 300,
  303–305, 315, 330, 349, 352–353
Metzenbaum, Howard, 124
Michels, Robert, 154
Middle class, *see* Centrists
Middle East, 414, 427
Military, the, 424, 426, 430–433
Military-industrial complex, 430–431
Miller, William, 109
Miller v. *California* (1973), 265
Mills, C. Wright, 13, 302
Mills, Wilbur, 212, 218, 223
Minorities, 315, 346–377 (*see also*
  Race)
Miranda v. *Arizona* (1966), 260–261,
  266–267, 276
MIRVs (multiple, individually targeted
  reentry vehicles), 410–411,
  430–431
Missiles, age of, 406–412
Mitchell, John, 172, 175
Moderates, 83
Mondale, Walter, 4, 105, 109,
  110–111, 112, 160, 191
Monetary policy, federal government's,
  316, 329
Money:
  actions of Congress to raise, 196,
    215, 220
  elections, mass media, majority rule,
    and, 118–120, 123–134
  from federal to state and local levels,
    286–288, 293–294
  to finance federal bureaucracies, 238
  spent by federal government
    (1901–1980), 229

Money (*continued*)
for state and local governments, 292–295, 297–298
as type of political pressure, 143
Monroe Doctrine, 404
Montgomery, Sonny, 82
Moral Majority, 19, 92, 141, 152
Morris, Gouverneur, 25
Morse, Wayne, 214
Mott, Stewart, 124
Moyers, Bill, 161
Mudd, Roger, 109, 110
Muskie, Edmund, 110
Mutual Assured Destruction (MAD), 405, 406, 411
Mutual deterrence, policy of, 406–412
MX (Missile Experimental), 410, 411, 431, 435, 439
Myers, Michael, 203
My Lai, 432
Myrdal, Gunnar, 355

Nader, Ralph, 4, 140, 145, 146, 148, 151, 249, 394
Nagasaki, 167, 405
National Aeronautics and Space Administration (NASA), 230
National Association for the Advancement of Colored People (NAACP), 360
National Association of Manufacturers (NAM), 139
National Committee for a Sane Nuclear Policy (SANE), 427
National Conservative Political Action Committee, 5, 92
National Education Association, 140, 330
National Farmers Organization, 140
National Farmers Union, 140
National Grange, 140
Nationalism, U.S.'s, 429–430
National Labor Relations Board, 230, 233–234
National Organization for Women (NOW), 361
National Rifle Association (NRA), 147, 153–154, 219
National Security Agency, 424
National Security Council (NSC), 161, 167, 169, 422
National Student Association, 425
National Urban League, 360–361
National War College, 424
National Welfare Rights Organization (NWRO), 331
Nazis, 6–7, 20, 22 n. 4, 93, 371
Negative income tax, 345 n. 17
Neoconservatives, 18–19, 92
Neustadt, Richard, 166
New Deal, 5, 14, 68, 79, 81, 84, 91, 166, 257–258, 321
New federalism, 293–294, 301, 303
New Frontier, 168
New Jersey Plan, 27, 32
News, coverage of, 51–52

Newspapers, 51, 66, 265
New York City, 297–298, 304–305
Nitze, Paul, 426
Nixon, Richard, 90, 95, 107, 109, 114–128 *passim*, 132–133
foreign policy of, 413, 419, 431, 432
presidency of, 161–162, 163, 171–175, 185, 186, 188–189, 190, 191, 303, 323, 362, 390
Nominations, presidential candidates, 101–111
North Atlantic Treaty Organization (NATO), 406, 412, 414
Nuclear Nonproliferation Treaty, 424
Nuclear power, 385–386, 387, 396, 398 (*see also* Hiroshima):
U.S. foreign policy and, 406–412, 429–431, 436–437, 439
Nuclear Weapons Freeze Campaign, 427

O'Brien, Lawrence, 172
Obscenity, Supreme Court on, 259–260, 265–266
Occupation, 45, 48, 60, 78–79, 354 (*see also* Employment)
Occupational Safety and Health Administration (OSHA), 249
O'Connor, Sandra Day, 268, 274
Office of Economic Opportunity (OEO), 329
Office of Management and Budget (OMB), 161
Oil-related issues, 177, 381, 382–385, 390, 393, 418
Oligarchy, 154
Olympic games, U.S. boycott of 1980 Moscow, 414, 420
O'Neill, "Tip," 203
Opinions (*see also* Public opinion):
observation and, 21
influences on one's, 44–53
Opportunity, equality of, 11
Organization of American States (OAS), 406
Organization of Petroleum Exporting Countries (OPEC), 177, 384–385, 418
Organizations, 54, 79, 142 (*see also* Interest groups)
Ottinger, Richard, 123

Palevsky, Max, 124
Panama Canal Treaty, 421
Parenti, Michael, 36, 302, 341
Park, Tongsun, 203
Parks, Rosa, 350–351
Parliamentary model, 35–36, 183–184, 187
Participation (in political process), 58–61
Peace and Freedom Party, 93
Peace Corps, 422
Pell, Claiborne, 220
Pendeleton, Clarence, 376 n. 17
Pentagon, the, 424, 430
Percy, Charles, 80, 124, 223

Personal characteristics, 20–21
presidential candidates', 106–107, 110–111, 118–120, 185
Pertinent data, 21
Platforms, political party, 76, 77, 104
Plessy v. *Ferguson* (1896), 261, 276, 350, 365
Pluralism, 13
Plurality (of votes), 75
Pocket veto, 214
Podhoretz, Norman, 18
Polaris submarines, 406–407
Policy-making, *see* Domestic affairs; Foreign policy; Issues; Political system
Political Action Committees (PACs), 124, 128, 130, 134, 143, 146
Political participation, 3, 44, 49–50, 54–63, 70–71 n. 13, 83, 129, 288–289, 454–455 (*see also* Elections; Interest groups)
Political parties:
evolution of, 29, 32, 74–90, 96–97
functions of, 72–74
future of, 97–98
lack of loyalty to, 83–85
leaders of, 77
membership in, and organization of, 82–83
national conventions of, 103–106
need for, 72–100
nomination process and, 101–106, 109, 137 n. 22
in parliamentary systems, 35–36
perspectives on, 66, 80, 86–96
platforms of, 76, 77, 104
presidency and, 77–80, 160
role in Congress, of, 205–208, 220
socioeconomic factors and, 77–79
at state and local levels, 286
Political pressure, 141–144, 146–147, 151–152, 153, 394–395 (*see also* Interest groups)
Political spectrum, *see* Spectrum, political
Political system:
policy-making process and, 358–367
Supreme Court as instrument of, 257–269
Polk, James K., 419
Poll tax, 350
Polls, political, *see* Public opinion
Pollution, *see* Environmental issues
Poor people, 49, 63, 66, 314–316, 321–324, 330–334, 362
perspectives on, 334–342
Population, environmental and energy issues and, 379, 380–381
Population patterns, 45–50, 78, 91, 296–297, 299, 346–349
Populism, right wing, 11, 69
Pornography, Supreme Court on, 259–260, 265–266
Poseidon nuclear-firing submarines, 410
Postal Service, 230, 232, 247

Poverty, culture of, 316 (*see also* Poor people)
Powell, Lewis, 263, 273, 366
Power (political), 2–3, 7, 12–15, 19, 22 n. 2, 66–67, 355, 446–455
  checks and balances (or, separation) of, 12, 32–33, 34, 35, 74, 86, 157, 197, 274, 454
  in Congress, 204–212
  of elites, 12, 13, 14, 66–67, 189–190, 448–449, 450, 452
  government's economic, 76, 150, 316–322
  judiciary's, 254
  of presidency, 158–195
  at state and local levels, 284, 286–288
Prayer in public schools, 260
Precedent, 272, 275, 276
Prejudice, 359–360 (*see also* Minorities; Race)
Presidency, the, 28, 29, 30, 31, 35, 58, 59, 85, 471 (*see also names of Presidents, e.g.,* Eisenhower; Kennedy; Truman):
  Cabinet of, 229–230, 231
  Congress and, 32, 160, 162, 196, 421
  economic issues and, 322–326
  environmental and energy issues and, 386–389
  federal bureaucracies, and, 161, 234–235, 237
  foreign policy and, 159, 161, 177, 181, 419–420, 428
  growth of, 38, 159–162
  minority groups, policy issues, and, 361–363
  perspectives on, 185–193
  power of, 158–195
President Pro Tempore (of the Senate), 205, 206
Pressure politics, *see* Interest groups; Political pressure
Primary elections, 101–103
Proletariat, dictatorship of, 9
Property rights, 10, 11, 14, 33, 36–37, 39, 76, 302–303, 450
Property taxes, local, 292
Proportional representation, 98 n. 2, 136 n. 2
Proxmire, William, 241
Public Citizen, Inc., 140
Public interest, the, interest groups and, 138–156
Public opinion, 44–71
  on disadvantaged groups, and policy issues, 358–360
  on economic issues, 331–334
  on environmental and energy issues, 391–393
  foreign policy and, 428–429
  leaders of, 50–51, 160
  mass media and, 51–52, 56–57, 66, 67, 136 n. 15
  perspectives on, 64–69, 92
  political participation and, 54–63
  polls of, 54, 120–123, 136 n. 15, 163

Public Opinion (*continued*)
  socioeconomic context of, 45–50
Public policy, *see* Domestic affairs; Foreign policy; Issues; Political system
Public Works Act (1977), 366

Race (*see also* Minorities):
  education and, 168, 261–262, 264, 351, 354, 356, 359, 362, 363, 365–369, 377 n. 23
  political implication of, 78, 81, 87, 358–375
  population distribution by, 46, 346–349, 352–353
  poverty and, 315, 333
Radical left, 3, 5–6, 8–9, 13–14, 16–17, 19, 448–450 (*see also* Socialism):
  Constitution and, 36–37
  economy, poverty and, 341
  federal bureaucracies and, 244–245
  federalism and, 301–302
  foreign policy and, 434–435, 448–449
  interest groups and, 148–149
  minority rights and, 374–375
  political parties and, 92–94
  presidency and, 189–191
  public opinion and, 66–67
  Supreme Court and, 278–279
Radical right, 3, 6–7, 11, 15, 17–18, 19, 451–453
  Constitution and, 38–39
  economy, poverty and, 336–337
  federal bureaucracies and, 244
  federalism and, 305
  foreign policy and, 440–441, 452
  interest groups and, 152
  minority rights and, 371
  political parties and, 92–94
  presidency and, 191
  public opinion and, 68–69
  Supreme Court and, 278
Radio, public opinion and, 51
Rand Corporation, 52, 67
Raskin, Marcus, 6
Ratification, 27
Reagan, Ronald, 19, 55, 90–91, 94, 158, 176
  foreign policy of, 411–421 *passim,* 431–440 *passim*
  1980 election of, 17, 58, 78, 79, 81, 88, 92, 95–96, 112–114, 117–121 *passim,* 127, 128, 133, 451, 454
  nomination of, 102, 103, 104, 106, 107, 122
  presidency of, 91, 180–183, 185, 187, 189, 190, 293–294, 301, 303, 305, 324–329, 362–363, 386–391 *passim,* 396–397, 399
  Supreme Court and, 268–269
Reapportionment, Supreme Court and, 261, 263
Rebozo, Bebe, 190
Reconstruction era, 81, 350
Reeves, Rosser, 117

Reform proposals:
  for campaign finance, 125–126
  for Congress, 204, 219–221, 224–225
  for elections, 128–130
  for electoral college, 114–116
  for federal bureaucracies, 242–244, 250–251
  by liberals, 66, 128–130
  for lobbying, 144
  for nominating procedure, 103
  for political parties, 66
  for the presidency, 183–185
  radical left on, 449
Regan, Donald, 328–329
Registration (for voting), 58–59, 66, 68
Regulatory agencies, 230, 240, 247–249, 320
Rehnquist, William, 263, 266
Religion, 11, 19, 39, 46–47, 49, 78, 260
Representation, by Congress, 196
Representative democracy, 28
Republic, U.S. as, 39
Republican Party, *see* Political parties
Reputational index, 108
Research centers, public opinion and, 52
Revenue Act (1971), 124
Revenue sharing, 301, 303
Revolutionary War, 24
Reynolds v. *Sims* (1964), 261
Richardson, Eliot, 55
Right, radical, *see* Radical right
Rivers, Mendel, 426
Roberts, Owen, 257, 258
Rockefeller, David, 68, 191, 440–441
Rockefeller, Jay, 124
Rockefeller, Nelson, 124, 133, 176, 189, 191, 441
Rockefeller, Winthrop, 124
Rockefeller family, 15, 124, 440
Rockefeller Foundation, 14, 53, 69
Roe v. *Wade,* 263–264, 273
Rogers, Will, 82
Rogers, William, 190, 422, 427
Romney, George, 110
Roosevelt, Franklin Delano, 79, 81, 163, 165–166, 179, 185, 258, 362, 419
Roosevelt, Theodore, 74, 79, 84, 164–165, 181, 185
Roper polls, 120–122
Rosenstone, Steven J., 60, 61
Rosenthal, Benjamin, 81
Rossiter, Clinton, 22 n. 6
Rostow, Eugene, 426
Rostow, W. W., 161, 190
Ruling class, 13
Rusher, William, 5
Rusk, Dean, 422
Russian Revolution (1917), 15

Sampling method, 54
Santa Barbara, California, 381, 390
Schlafly, Phyllis, 361
Schlesinger, Arthur, Jr., 170
Schmitz, John, 99 n. 14

Schools (*see also* Education):
  prayers in, 260
  minorities, race, and, 168, 261–262,
    264, 351, 354, 356, 359, 362, 363,
    365–369, 377 n. 23
Schultz, George, 190
Schweicker, Richard, 91
Secretaries of state, 422
Segregation, *see* Minorities; Race;
  Schools
Segretti, Donald, 126, 173
Senate, *see* Congress
Seniority, in Congress, 211–212, 220,
  223
Separation of powers, Constitution's,
  29–30, 32–33, 34, 35, 74, 86, 157,
  197, 274, 454
Services, providers of, 45
Sex, *see* Gender
Sexism:
  in employment, 48
  in voting rights, 53
  Supreme Court on, 264–265,
    281 n. 14
Shapp, Milton, 124
Shays's Rebellion, 25, 33, 36
Shultz, George, 427
Sierra Club, 394, 397
Simon, William, 55
Sirica, John, 173, 174, 186
Slaves/slavery, 27, 31, 40n, 349
Smith, Adam, 152
Smith, Howard, 213
Smith, William French, 282 n. 19,
  376 n. 16
Smith Act (1940), 259
Smoot, Dan, 38–39, 69, 278
Socialism, 9, 17, 247, 336–337, 448
Socialist Workers Party, 22 n. 3, 93,
  99 n. 12
Socialization, 50
Social Security, 249, 321, 323, 324
Social welfare programs, 76, 141,
  320–322, 329–331, 332
Socioeconomic factors:
  political parties and, 77–79
  public opinion and, 45–50
Sorenson, Theodore, 161, 169
Southeast Asia Treaty Organization
  (SEATO), 443 n. 1
Southern Christian Leadership
  Conference (SCLC), 351, 361
Soviet Union, 9, 22 n. 3, 39, 41 n. 14,
  167–168, 259, 450
  U.S. foreign policy and, 404,
    405–417, 429–431, 434–435,
    436–438, 441, 442
Sowell, Thomas, 361
Speaker of the House, 205
Spectrum, political, 3–7, 15–21,
  23 n. 17, 80, 83 (*see also* Centrists;
  Conservatives; Liberals; Radical
  Left; Radical Right)
Spoils system, 236
Staffs:
  of members of Congress, 210–211
  White House, 161–162, 171, 184,

Staffs (*continued*)
  327, 328
Stagflation, 314
Stalin, Joseph, 5, 22 n. 3, 407, 429
Standard of living, American, 10
State Department, the, 422, 423, 424
State governments, 284–285
  contemporary problems of, 288–295,
    300–307
  employees and units of, 283
  environmental and energy issues and,
    391
  federalism and, 283–308
States' rights, 29, 38
Statute (congressional), Constitution
  and, 31
Stealth bomber, 443 n. 2
Stevens, John Paul, 263
Stevenson, Adlai, 105, 117, 190
Stewart, Potter, 262, 267, 268
Stockman, David, 136 n. 13, 182, 328,
  338–339, 391
Stone, W. Clement, 124, 125, 129
Strategic Arms Limitations Talks
  (SALT), 177, 409–411, 421, 424
Strategic Arms Reduction Talks
  (START), 411
Strategic targets, U.S., 408
Student movements, CIA and, 425
Students for a Democratic Society
  (SDS), 5, 18, 265
Submarine-launched ballistic missiles
  (SLBMs), 409, 410
Suffrage, *see* Voting
Sunshine Act (1976), 251
Supersonic Transport (SST), 381–382
Supplemental Security Income, 322,
  323
Supply-side economics, 344 n. 10, n. 14
Supreme Court (U.S.):
  appointments to, 91
  in the Constitution, 29, 30
  Constitutional interpretations by,
    31–33, 38, 254–282
  disadvantaged groups, policy issues,
    and, 364–367
  on Federal Election Commission, 126
  as instrument of political system,
    257–269
  as judicial body, 269–273
  on lobbying, 144
  perspectives on, 273–279
  president's power and, 162
  on school desegregation, 168,
    261–262, 264
  on slave rights, 349, 364
Sweezy, Paul, 5

Taft, Roger, 80, 90, 104
Taft, William Howard, 164
Taft-Hartley Act (1947), 139–140,
  146, 151
Talmadge, Herman, 203
Taney, Roger, 349
Tax revenues, 247, 292, 301, 319–320,
  325–326, 337–339
Taylor, A. J. P., 431

Teamsters Union, 139
Television:
  as campaigns' focal point, 116–118,
    120, 128–129
  party meetings versus appearances
    on, 82
  public opinion and, 51, 56, 57, 66,
    67, 136 n. 15
Tennessee Valley Authority, 230, 232
Terror, balance of (nuclear), 406–412
Terrorism, 17, 418
Thermonuclear weapons, 406–409,
  430, 436, 437
Thomas, Norman, 99 n. 12
Thompson, James, 123
Three Mile Island, Pennsylvania,
  385–386
Thurmond, Strom, 5, 214, 220
Tilden, Samuel, 115
Tonkin Gulf resolution, 170, 186, 421
Totalitarian systems, 439
Tower, John, 123, 220
Towns (townships), 307–308 n. 1
Towster, Julian, 41 n. 14
Treaties, 420, 443 n. 1 (*see also*
  Foreign policy)
Trident submarines, 410
Trilateral Commission, 14, 68, 191,
  440–441
Trotsky, Leon, 5, 22 n. 3
Trujillo, Rafael, 417
Truman, Harry, 163, 185
  election of, 84, 107, 109, 115, 116
  foreign policy of, 90, 419, 435
  presidency of, 166–167, 218–219,
    362
  Supreme Court and, 162

Udall, Stewart, 390
Un-American Activities Committee,
  259 (*see also* McCarthy, Joseph)
Unemployment, 312, 313
Union of Concerned Scientists, 394
Unions, *see* Labor unions
United Auto Workers, 394, 427
United Electrical Workers, 139
United Farm Workers Union, 140
United Latin American Citizens
  (ULAC), 361
United Mineworkers, 139
United Nations, 15, 398, 403, 405, 412,
  419, 438, 440, 442
United States v. *Curtis-Wright Export
  Corp.*, 194 n. 3
United States v. *Nixon* (1974), 273
United States Information Agency
  (USIA), 422
United World Federalists (UWF), 440
Universities and colleges, 52, 67, 68,
  69, 425
University of California, The v. *Bakke*
  (1968), 366
Urban areas, 289, 295–299, 300,
  303–305, 315, 330, 349, 352–353
Urban League, 360–361

Values, questions about, 7–12 (*see also*
  Spectrum, political)

Veterans Administration, 230, 232
Veto:
    president's, 214
    in United Nations, 419
Vice-presidency, 105, 108, 160
Viereck, Peter, 22 n. 6
Vietnam War, 170, 412–413, 425, 434,
    437, 441–442
    Johnson and, 170, 186, 419, 428,
    432, 435
    Nixon and, 171–172, 188, 432–433
    president's power and, 193, 421
Viguerie, Richard, 92, 124
Vinson, Fred, 259
Villages, 308 n. 1
Violence, 17–18, 418
Virginia Plan, 26–27, 29, 32
Volcker, Paul, 328, 329
Voting, 31, 53–54, 58–61, 62, 129 (*see
    also* Elections; Electoral college):
    registration (and qualifications) for,
    28, 58–59, 66, 68, 350
    turnouts for, 58–61, 62, 129,
    288–289
Voting Rights Act (1965), 53–54, 59,
    129, 214, 351, 361, 362, 363

Wagner Labor Relations Act (1935),
    139, 257
Wallace, George, 69, 74, 93–94,
    99 n. 13, 115, 116, 124, 126
Wallace, Henry, 90, 99 n. 12

Wallace v. *Ohio* (1968), 272
Wall Street, 14
War (*see also* Korean War; Vietnam
    War):
    Congress and, 419–421
    conventional, 412–413
    potential of nuclear, 406–412
    World, 404–405
War on Poverty, 321–322, 329, 362
War Powers Act (1973), 421
Warren, Earl, 91, 257, 258–262, 274,
    277, 278, 365
Warsaw-Pact, 438
Washington, George, 25, 72, 404
Waskow, Arthur, 6
Watergate, 51, 56, 90, 162, 193
    campaign financing and, 125–126,
    133–134
    Nixon's presidency and, 172–175,
    186, 188
Water Pollution Act Amendments
    (1972), 386
Watt, James, 390, 391, 396–397
Wattenberg, Ben J., 341
Weather Underground, 17, 22 n. 11
Weicker, Lowell, 80
Weidenbaum, Murray, 328
Weinberger, Caspar, 190, 427
Welch, Robert, 6, 15, 68, 191, 278
Welfare, *see* Social welfare programs
Wesberry v. *Sanders,* 200
Whips, party, 205

White, Byron, 262, 267
White, Theodore, 101, 193
White House staff, 161–162, 171, 184,
    327, 328
Whitten, Jamie, 82
Wilkie, Wendell, 90
Williams, Harrison, 204
Williams, Walter, 361
Wilson, Charles, 189
Wilson, Woodrow, 74, 79, 191, 404,
    419
Wirtz, Willard, 241
Wohlstetter, Albert, 426
Wolfinger, Raymond E., 60, 61
Women (*see also* Abortion; Sexism):
    Democratic party and, 88
    Equal Rights Amendment for, 40
    n. 3, 77, 141, 358, 361, 366
    political participation of, 61, 70–71
    n. 13
    poverty and, 315
    voting rights for, 54
    in work force, 45, 48
Woodward, Robert, 173, 269, 270
Work force, *see* Employment
Works Projects Administration (WPA),
    321
World Health Organization, 398
World War I, 404
World War II, 404–405

Yalta Conference, 437